LIGHTING FOR FILM AND ELECTRONIC CINEMATOGRAPHY

LIGHTING

for Film and Electronic Cinematography

Dave Viera

With the collaboration of Maria Viera

CALIFORNIA STATE UNIVERSITY, LONG BEACH
UNIVERSITY OF NORTH CAROLINA, CHAPEL HILL

Wadsworth Publishing Company
BELMONT, CALIFORNIA
A DIVISION OF WADSWORTH, INC.

Publisher: Rebecca Hayden
Development editor: John Bergez
Editorial assistant: Katherine Hartlove
Production editor: Sandra Craig
Managing designer: Andrew H. Ogus
Print buyer: Randy Hurst
Art editor: Kelly Murphy
Permissions editor: Robert Kauser
Copy editor: Margaret Moore
Signing representative: JoAnn Ludovici
Cover: Seventeenth Street Studios
Design, illustration, and composition: Seventeenth Street Studios
Prepress services: Color Tech
Printing and binding: Courier, Kendallville, Indiana

CREDITS

Cover Photo: From the motion picture *Guardian Angel,* directed by Goran Paskaljevic; director of photography: Milan Spasic. Official Selection Cannes International Festival. Quainzaine des Realisateurs, Cannes 1987.

Text Photos: Robin Hood Dial II: Chapter Opening 3; Figure 2.14b. **Gerald Lang:** Chapter Openings 12, 14; Figure 7.4d. **The Museum of Modern Art Film/Stills Archive:** Figures 1.5c, 1.7, 2.4a–b, 2.5a–b, 2.8d, 2.9a, 2.14a, 2.15a, 2.16c, 2.17, 2.19b, 2.20d, 2.21a–b, 2.22a–b, 2.23a–b, 2.24, 2.25c, 7.7g, 7.10d, 9.1a–h, 9.2, 9.4a–b, 9.6, 9.7b, 10.3a–c, 10.5a, 10.6, 10.7a–c, 11.1a–c, 11.2, 11.4, 11.5, 11.6, 11.7a–c. **Steven Rosenberg:** Chapter Opening 11. **Mike Rubin:** Color Plates 10, 12. **Lee Scott:** Color Plate 14. **Elizabeth Lear Sher:** Chapter Opening 8; Figure 7.6. **Joyce Shöffner:** Figure 2.14c. **Nikola Stanjevich:** Color Plates 9, 11. **Jennifer A. Tucker:** Chapter Openings 9, 10; Figures 7.4c, 9.3c. **Warner Bros. Inc:** Figure 2.17, © 1982 The Blade Runner Partnership; all rights reserved.

Graphs: Figure 5.9a, p. 72, reprinted by permission of Agfa-Gevaert N.V. Figure 5.9b, p. 73, reprinted by permission of Fuji Photo Film USA, Inc. Figure 5.9c, pp. 74–75, reprinted courtesy of Eastman Kodak Company.

Printed in the United States of America

3 4 5 6 7 8 9 10—97

Library of Congress Cataloging-in-Publication Data
Viera, John David.
Lighting for film and electronic cinematography / Dave Viera : assisted by Maria Viera.
p. cm.
Includes bibliographical references and index.
ISBN 0-534-12810-6
1. Cinematography—Lighting. I. Viera, Maria. II. Title.
TR891.V54 1993
778.5'343—dc20 92-14321

To Maria, my collaborator in all the best senses

CONTENTS

7 COMMON EXPOSURE SITUATIONS 86

PART III
LIGHTING APPLICATIONS 107

8 LIGHTING CONTRAST RATIOS 108

9 LIGHTING SETUPS 122

PREFACE

CINEMATOGRAPHERS are responsible for creating interesting film and video images, but they must have the support and collaboration of directors to sustain images of great aesthetic value. This is why we often speak of director/cinematographer teams—Ingmar Bergman/Sven Nykvist, D. W. Griffith/Billy Bitzer, Sergei Eisenstein/Eduard Tisse, Orson Welles/Gregg Toland, Francis Coppola/Vittorio Storaro, and Woody Allen/Gordon Willis, for example. Ultimately, the contents of this book derive from the wonderful images these and other cinematographers have put on the screen.

Lighting is an art that requires awareness of the visual properties of images, technical knowledge about how to achieve visual effects, and the ability to respond to unforeseen and unforeseeable production factors. One way to advance aesthetic awareness and technique is to analyze the work of other cinematographers. This book thus concentrates on improving your ability to "read" the screen. It provides the vocabulary and a set of principles and concepts, including a lighting system—key, fill, rim, background, and facial and subject/background ratios—to serve as analytical tools. The conceptual approach used integrates technical and aesthetic concerns and emphasizes that the best "text" for learning lighting is the study of film examples. This book will help make that "text" accessible.

Special Features

PHOTOGRAPHIC EXAMPLES A wide variety of photographic examples illustrate various lighting points. Examples are taken from films as well as photography and exemplify a number of lighting styles.

LIGHTING ANALYSES To facilitate the understanding of the all-important photographic illustrations, Part V provides lighting diagrams and detailed analyses for a representative sample of photographs. Photos in Parts I–IV that are analyzed in Part V are identified with this symbol: ◣.

ZONE SYSTEM The zone system developed by photographers such as Ansel Adams has been modified and applied to both film and video lighting.

APPENDIXES Ten appendixes cover advanced topics that go beyond the scope of the text or provide "refresher" information.

GLOSSARY A glossary provides definitions of central terms and concepts. Glossary entries are boldface where they first appear in the text.

Premises

A fundamental premise of this book is that exposure theory and sensitometry provide the scientific basis for understanding the possibilities and techniques of lighting. Without exposure theory, cinematographers cannot dissect and analyze such techniques as keytone placement or lighting ratio. The exposure sections examine the function of the incident meter and how it relates subject luminance range to an emulsion's characteristic curve. They also illustrate how to determine the straight line and overall useful range for any emulsion.

To analyze a film's lighting requires a vocabulary. To that end the zone system has been adapted to film and video so that it allows for a precise relation of visual values in the subject to screen values and the film emulsion. The zone system thus functions as a language for exposure. In addition, lighting terminology based on the work of Walter Nurnberg is used for referring to light placements and lighting ratios. This second language is more functional and can serve as a guide for exploring lighting both as a technique and as an aesthetic dimension in the final film.

Readers are assumed to be familiar with at least the basic filmmaking books, such as *Filmmaker's Handbook* by Edward Pincus and Steven Ascher; *Primer for Filmmaking* by Kenneth H. Roberts and Win Sharples, Jr.; *Cinematography* by Kris Malkiewicz; and *Independent Filmmaking* by Lenny Lipton. In addition, certain chapters presuppose a basic working knowledge of fundamentals; readers can refer to the appropriate appendix as necessary. For instance, Chapter 1 assumes a working knowledge of the information in Appendix A, "Lighting and Grip Gear." Chapter 2 presupposes a working knowledge of light meters, as provided in Appendix B.

Lighting can be studied through intensive analysis of videotape copies of films and also through analyses of paintings, theater productions, and photographs. Aspiring cinematographers can choose a body of work to analyze based on their particular goals. Those who aspire to a Hollywood career might study Oscar nominees and winners for best cinematography and films singled out by the American Society of Cinematographers. Others might prefer to learn from foreign or independent cinematographers, and still others might select documentary or experimental works to study.

Structure

The book is divided into five parts: Part I reviews fundamental lighting concepts and basic light placements; Part II covers exposure theory, including the zone system; Part III explores the applications of lighting theory, including the creation of lighting setups, lighting ratios, interiors and exteriors, lighting analyses, examples, and exercises; Part IV applies film techniques to video; and Part V provides detailed analyses of lighting examples. The integrating theme throughout the book is that lighting is a combination of the art of seeing and the science of exposure.

Terminology

Two terms—"feel" and "look"—are used extensively and require some explanation. Like the jazz term "soul," these terms are inherently vague, perhaps because they are used to describe visual qualities that are difficult, if not impossible, to verbalize. As used here, **feel** means all the emotional, subjective nuances of a shot—its rhythms, textures, colors, and tonal values. These subtle distinctions are what cause viewers to say that a shot has the feel of emptiness or richness, of boredom or vitality. Feel goes to the depth of an image, to its connotative, meaning level. In contrast, **look** refers to the surface properties and visual style of images. Adjectives such as *slick, hard, soft, bright,* or *dark* are used to describe a film's look. You can also talk about the look of a particular cinematographer's work—such as Nestor Almendros's work in *Days of Heaven*—or the look of a certain type of film—such as a music video or television commercial. Feel is the emotional experience of the image; look is the more sensory experience.

In general the term "cinematographer" is used rather than "director of photography" or "lighting cameraman" (as in England). Director of photography (DP) conjures up images of large-scale, feature film practices. Even if your goal is the Hollywood-scale shoot, in the beginning you will face different sorts of problems and may find methods other than standardized Hollywood techniques useful. Through use of the term "cinematographer," this book seeks to reference types of filmmaking besides features: documentaries, poetic and experimental films, student and amateur films. Such films may have small crews or even one person handling the cinematography.

Acknowledgments

Many people have aided in the realization of this book. First, let me thank all those photographers who allowed me to use their work in this book: Jennifer A. Tucker, Gerald Lang, Elizabeth Lear Sher, Steven Rosenberg, Robin H. Dial II, Joyce Shöffner, Lee Scott, Michael Rubin, and Nikola Stanjevich. Thanks to those who helped me set up and illustrate key lighting points: photographers Kelly Kiebala and Robin H. Dial II, Paul Durazzo, Harriet Rosenberg, Barb Ward, Dave Fortino, and Judi Kriss. Thanks to Dave Walton for the Macintosh work and to Terry Geesken at the Museum of Modern Art for all the help with the archive stills.

Thanks to the Eastman Kodak Company, Fuji Photo Film U.S.A., Inc., and the Agfa Corporation for allowing me to reproduce their characteristic curves. Thanks to Kevin O'Brien for helping me locate artwork for those curves.

Thanks to California State University, Long Beach for the sabbatical that launched this project and to the University Research Council at the University of North Carolina for two production grants that helped with the costs of the photographs. Thanks to the production faculty at the University of Southern California and the London International Film School, who taught me so much.

In addition, I would like to thank all the models who posed for long hours to illustrate lighting points: Kenneth Bizzell, Paul Durazzo, Michele Ebaugh, Robert J. Gwyn, Temple Hemric, Nancy Tulloch Hoch, George P. Jobes II, Wendy John, Jason Jou, Susan Kim, Donald Klees, Paul Kocela, James S. Lee, Michelle J. Lyn, Susan Moore, Nina Meledandri, Kelly Peters, Sandra Price, Juana Richard, Teresa Y. Roberson, Harriet Rosenberg, Lee Scott, Melissa Stone, Loui A. Terriér, Barb Ward, Stan Ward, and Patricia M. Willert.

Thanks also to all the reviewers who painstakingly fought their way through my manuscript and gave me many suggestions: Warren Bass, Temple University; Lilly Ann Boruszkowski, Southern Illinois University at Carbondale; Tim Cassidy, Jersey City State College; Michael Cohn, University of Texas, Austin; Ian Conner, Loyola Marymount University; William Lawson, Boston University; Julius Rascheff, University of Illinois, Urbana; Peter Reader, Seton Hall University; and Donald Zirpola, Loyola Marymount University.

Last, but not least, I would like to thank the following for their help and inspiration: Jorge Guerra; Phil Mottram; Marcia Hesselroth; Eddie, Renata, Suzie, and Kent in Vienna; George and Kelly at Cafe Gourmet; copy editors Susan Schwartz and Margaret Moore; indexer Anne Morey; designer Randall Goodall at Seventeenth Street Studios; the staff at Wadsworth—Sandra Craig, production editor; Kelly Murphy, art editor; Andrew Ogus, managing designer; and publisher Becky Hayden, my guiding light—and, of course, Maria, my traveling companion.

—Dave Viera

FUNDAMENTALS OF LIGHTING

There is only one way of learning how to build up photographic lighting—by learning to "see." There is also only one way of learning how to apply this photographic lighting—by learning to feel sensitively and to think intelligently.

—Walter Nurnberg
Lighting for Photography

BASIC LIGHTING CONCEPTS

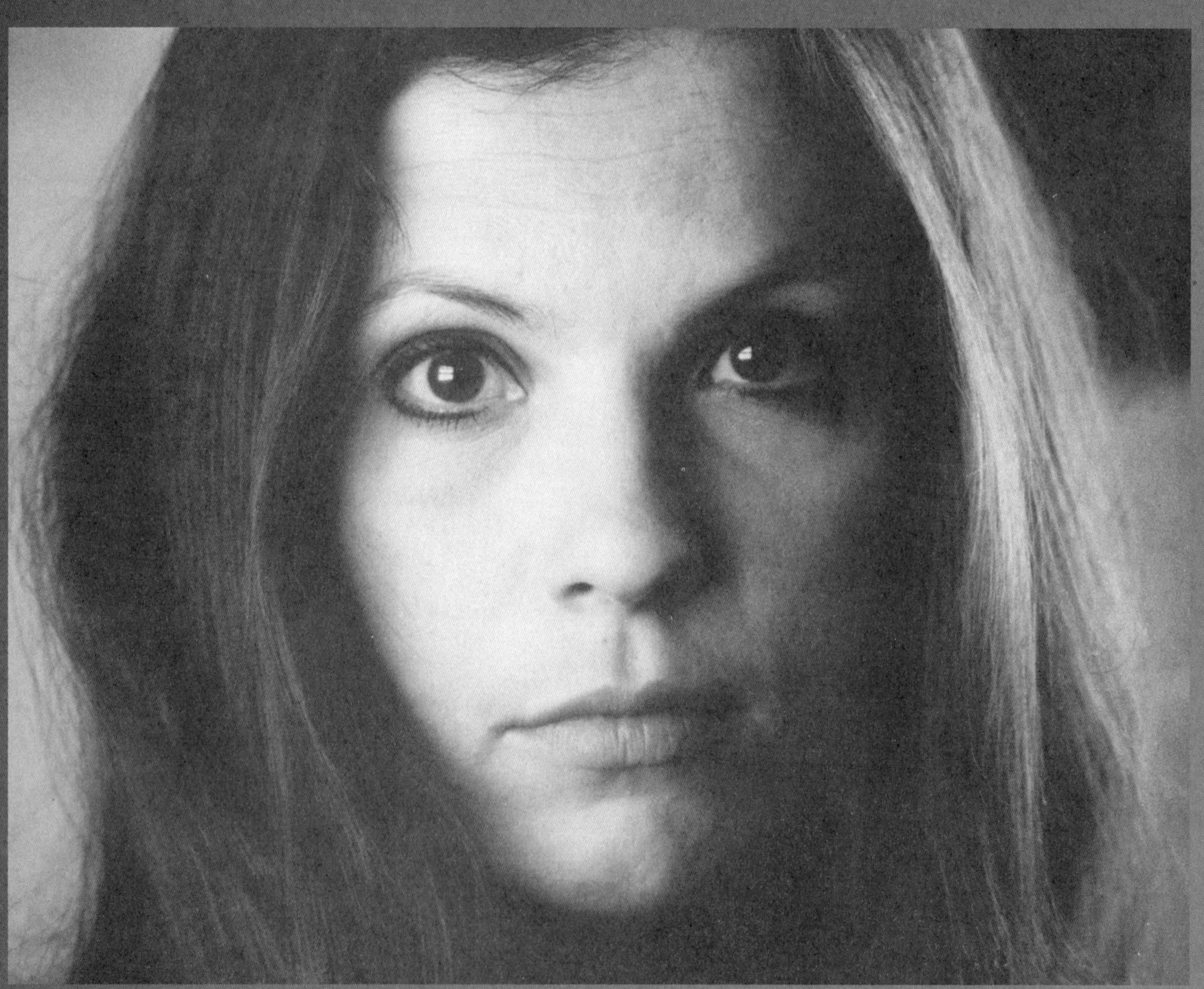

"soft light"

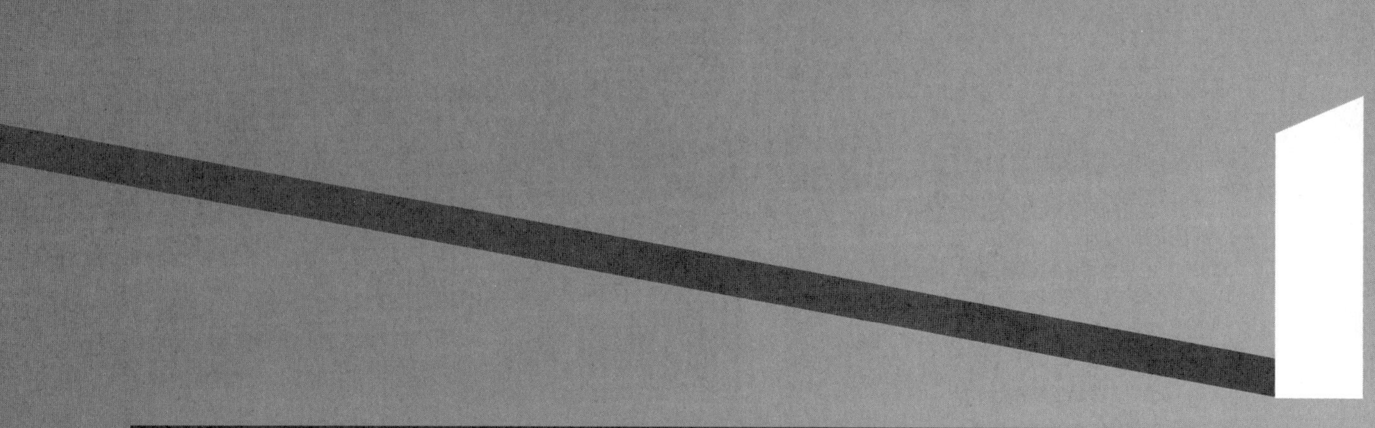

Three basic features of light are crucial to the cinematographer: the photographic quality of the light, the directionality of the light, and the resulting pattern of light and shadow. In this chapter, we explore these three concepts. In the next chapter, we shall discuss ways of working with these concepts to create lighting setups. Before continuing, you may wish to review the materials in Appendix A, "Lighting and Grip Gear."

IN CONTEMPORARY cinematography, almost any light source can be used for filming: household bulbs, neon lights, kerosene lamps, torches, flashlights, candles, street lights, and, of course, naturally available daylight. Fast lenses and improved emulsion speeds allow for a wide range of possibilities. But whether the cinematographer uses 12,000-watt lights or 25-watt household bulbs, the essential lighting challenge remains: to create images with mood and significance, images that generate interesting film spaces.

There is a tendency for beginners to become fascinated by all the grip and lighting gear used in cinematography. An experienced cinematographer, however, concentrates on the "look" of the images. Lighting and grip gear are the tools the cinematographer uses to create the desired image look. Certain lighting tools are essential for certain lighting styles, and the cinematographer must be aware of this.

In *Professional Cinematography,* noted Hollywood cinematographer Charles Clarke states that all lighting is premised on humanity's years of experience with the sun, the basic light source. For example, the fact that the sun is high above most of the time makes lighting from above seem natural. The variety of atmospheric conditions we encounter render us sensitive to the differences between **hard light**—direct, high-contrast sunlight—and **soft light**—indirect, low-contrast twilight or the gray light on an overcast day. These extremes of light quality produce a variety of moods that cinematographers learn to exploit in their images.

LIGHT QUALITY

An important lighting decision centers around what kind of light to apply to a scene. This is true whether we are using artificial illumination or **available light**—light naturally present at the location, for example, the daylight coming into a room from a window or the neon signs and street lights on a big city street.

Light is "hard" when its shadows are sharply defined. Hard light is inherently high in contrast and thus gives us very black shadows. It is also highly directional (focused, like with a spotlight) and emanates from

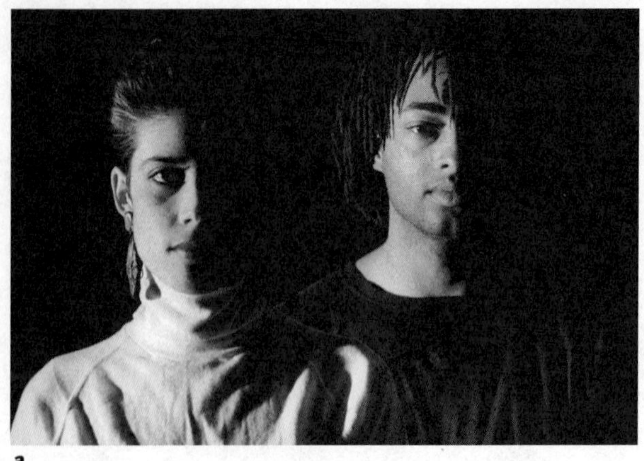
a

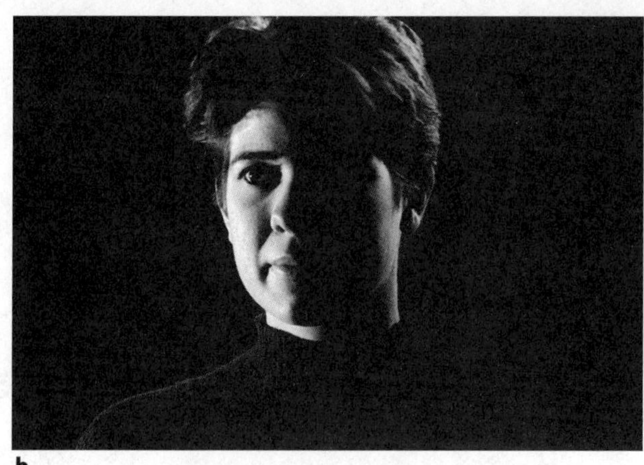
b

Figure 1.1 Hard and Soft Light
Faces lit with hard light (a and b) and soft light (c and d) reveal dramatically different shadows and moods.

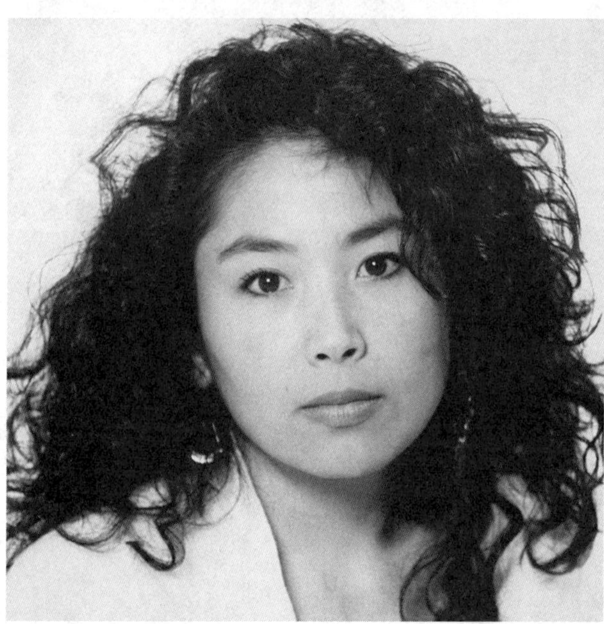
c

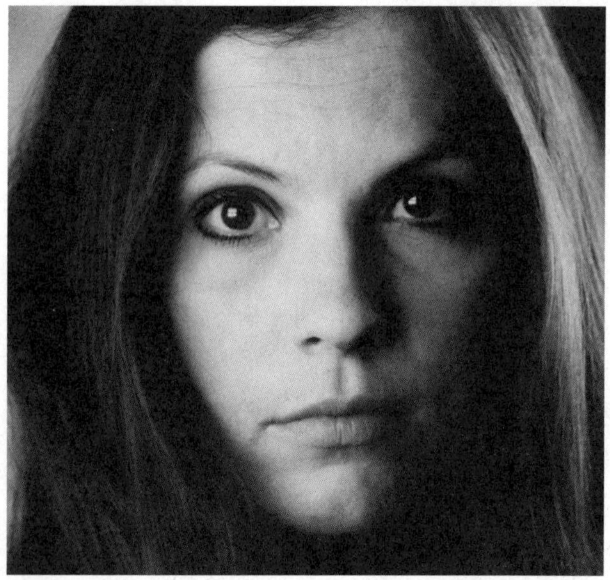
d

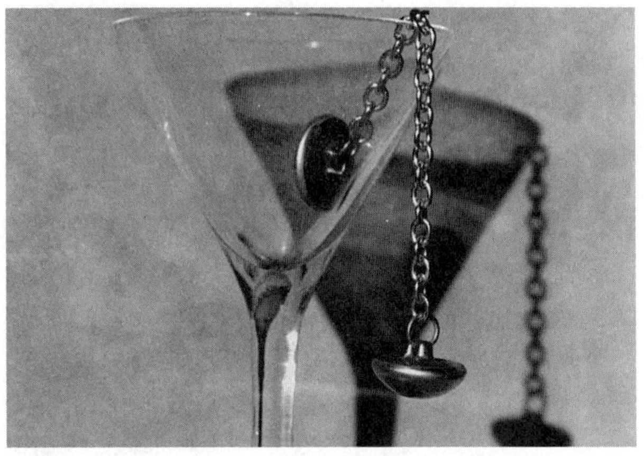

a

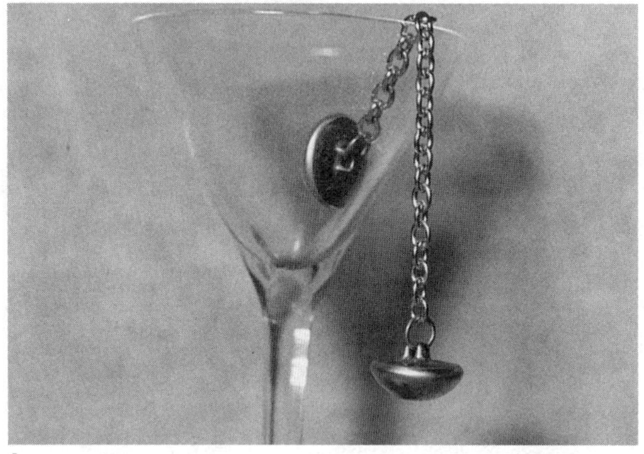

b

Figure 1.2 Shadows *A glass and a button lit with hard light (a) and soft light (b) illustrate the different shadow properties resulting from the quality of the light.*

small point sources. Direct sunlight, arc lights, and Fresneled spots are good hard-light sources (see Figure 1.1 and Appendix A).

Light is "soft" when its shadows are formed gradually with indistinct edges. Soft light is lower in contrast than hard light and consequently has lighter, more gray shadows. It is less directional than hard light and is often called omnidirectional or "directionless." Large light sources that are heavily diffused, bounced, reflected, or filtered yield light which is soft in quality. Examples include the painter's north light—reflected sky light such as in a Vermeer interior—the shadows under a tree, a gray overcast sky, softlights, and bounced lights (see Figure 1.2 and Appendix A).

The current range of possibilities from hardest sunlight to softest twilight is as follows:

- Direct sunlight
- Carbon arcs
- Elipsoidal spotlights
- Fresneled lights—HMIs and Quartz
- PAR bulbs
- Open-face lamps of all kinds, mainly Quartz types: Broads, Floods, Scoops, Lowell DPs, and the like
- The above lights diffused—usually open–face lights but sometimes Fresnels, with diffusion positioned between lamp and subject, either mounted on the lamp or as self-standing frames. Diffusion is accomplished with gels such as Tough Frost or Tough Silk, or materials such as tracing paper, muslin, silk, and other fabrics.
- Fluorescents, photofloods, and frosted household bulbs
- Softlights
- Bounced light—Fresnels or open-face lamps bounced off foam-core, white walls, and the like

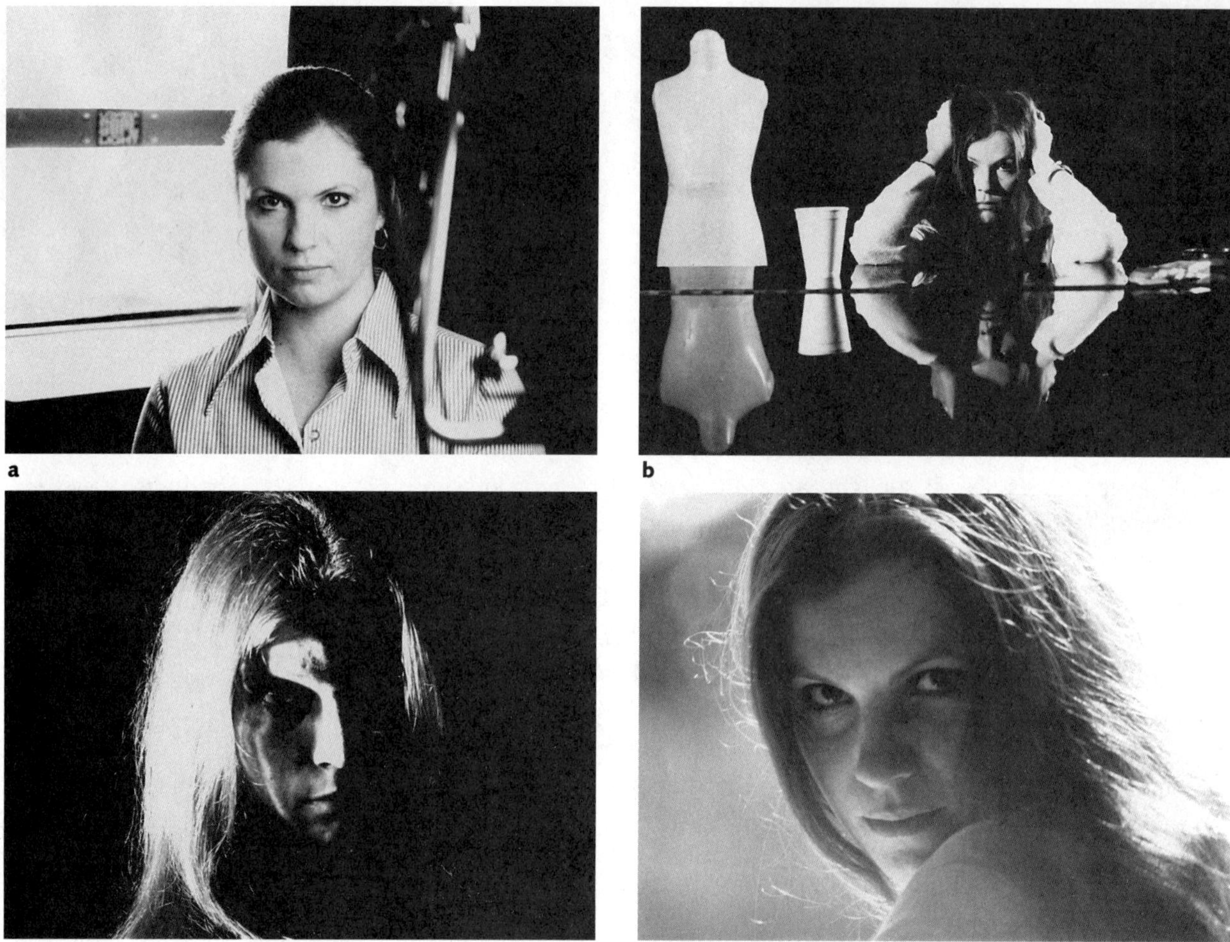

Figure 1.3 Light Source Directionality Determines Shadow Formation *Shadows become more and more dominant as the angle of light-incidence increases. Light comes from the front (a), the three-quarter front (b), the side (c), and the back (d). Comparing a–d shows that light quality and the relative proportions of light and shadow determine image mood.*

- Gray overcast skies, fog
- Twilight and deep-shade situations such as in a forest or cave entrance

Another way of comparing hard and soft light is by describing a light unit's spread or beam pattern. Beam patterns range from direct (focused, beamed) to indirect (directionless, shadowless). Fresneled spotlights provide small, concentrated beams, whereas softlights have no apparent beam at all since they are designed to be directionless. Beam spread and size can be controlled by the design of the lamp housing and the amount of focusing resulting from its lens. For example, PAR sealed beam bulbs are available with beam spreads from narrow to wide (see Appendix A).

LIGHT SOURCE DIRECTIONALITY

Light may come from various positions relative to the subject: front (zero degrees), side (90 degrees), back (180 degrees), or anywhere in between. **Light source directionality** (also called the **angle of light-incidence**) refers to the direction the lighting in a particular setup

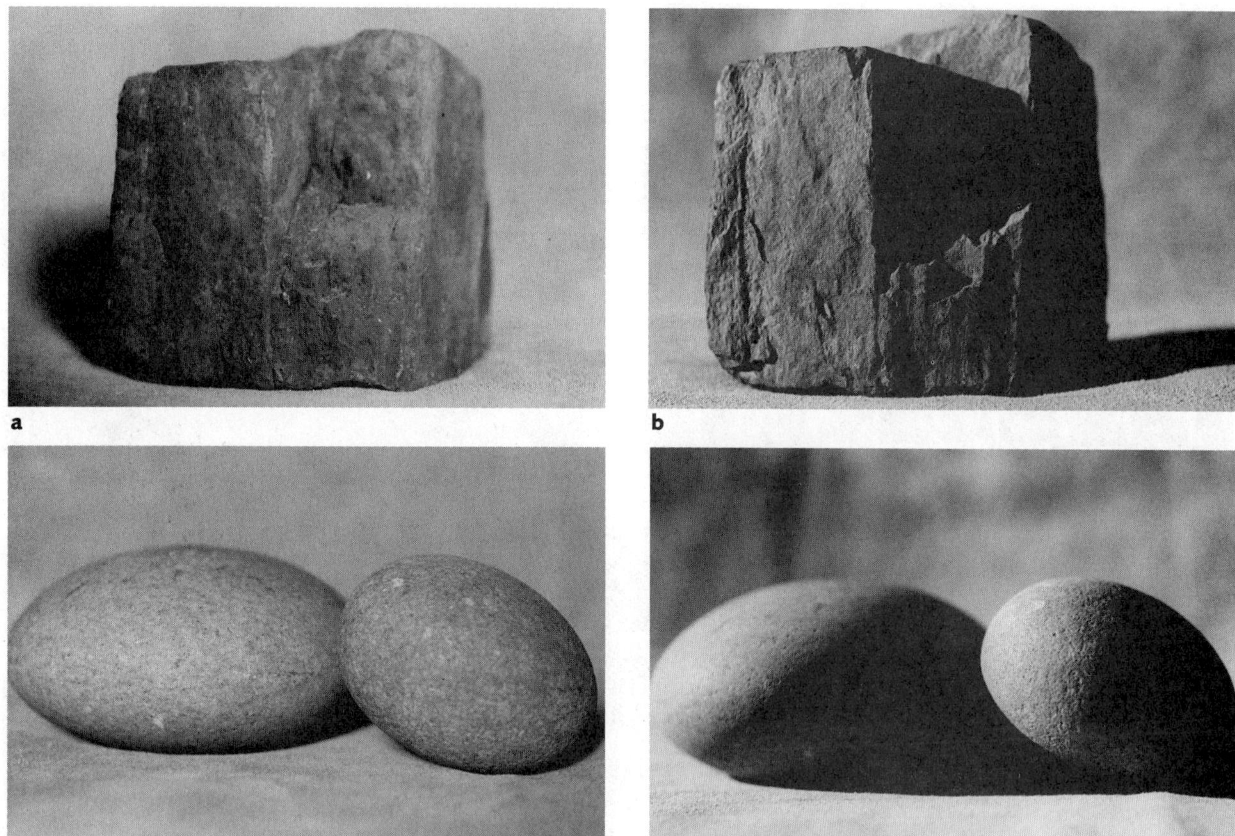

Figure 1.4 Light Source Directionality Influences How an Object Appears *Rocks lit frontally with soft light (a and c) and from the side with hard light (b and d) reveal the importance of the direction of the light in defining an object's shape.*

comes from as referenced to the camera/subject axis. Actual light placements will be examined in Chapter 2.

Light source directionality has an important influence on the amount of shadow area in the frame. Shadows become more and more dominant as the angle of light-incidence increases—as the lighting moves from front to back positions. This in turn affects the overall mood of the image (see Figures 1.1 and 1.3).

The directionality of the principal light source, the **key light**, can strongly influence the appearance of the photographic subject, particularly for unfamiliar objects (see Figure 1.4). Frontal light minimizes shadows and texture and tends to flatten and hide an object's true shape. Side light creates shadow and texture patterns that reveal the object's three-dimensional shape.

To establish the illusion of reality and give a naturalistic logic to the lighting, cinematographers utilize "motivated" lighting schemes. **Motivated lighting** means the illumination appears to come from a particular light source such as a window, table lamp, or ceiling light. This light source is either in-shot or has been identified previously. Once established, the logic of this source directionality is usually maintained throughout the scene. Where there is no in-shot light source to motivate the lighting, the cinematographer often invents one so the lighting looks as if it comes from an out-of-frame source (see Figure 1.5).

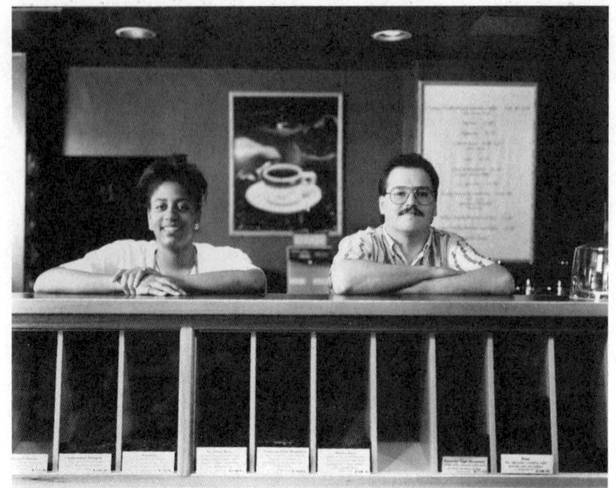

a

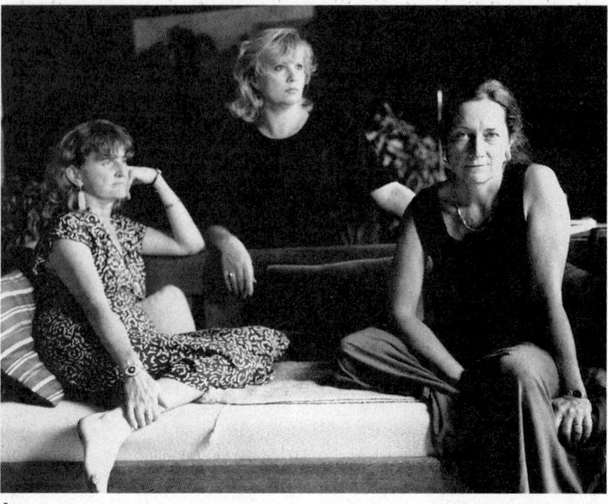

b

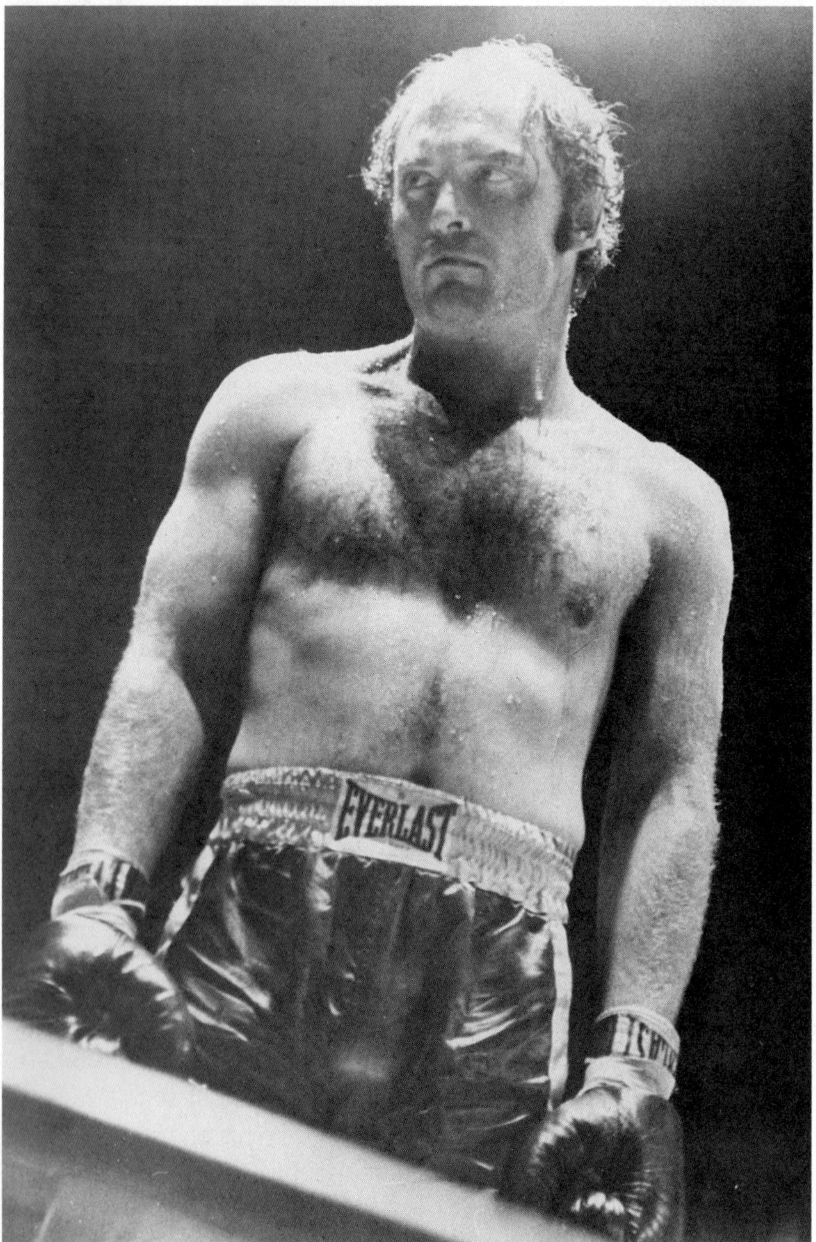

c

Figure 1.5 Motivated Lighting *Though not visible in the shot, windows frame left and right provide "motivation" for the lighting in shots (a) and (b), respectively. The motivation in shot (c) depends on our knowing that boxing rings are lit from above* (Fat City, *Columbia Pictures, 1972*).

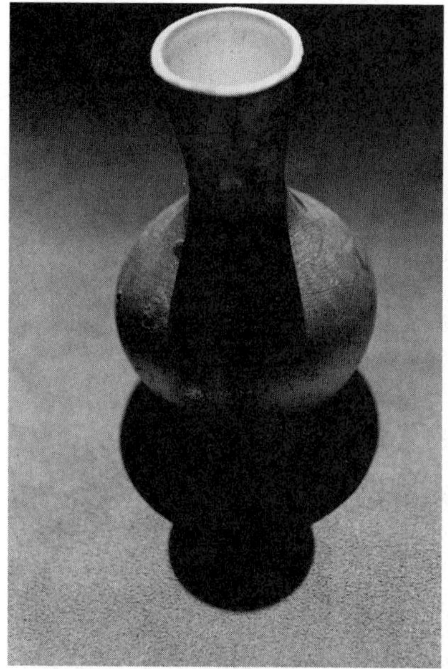

a

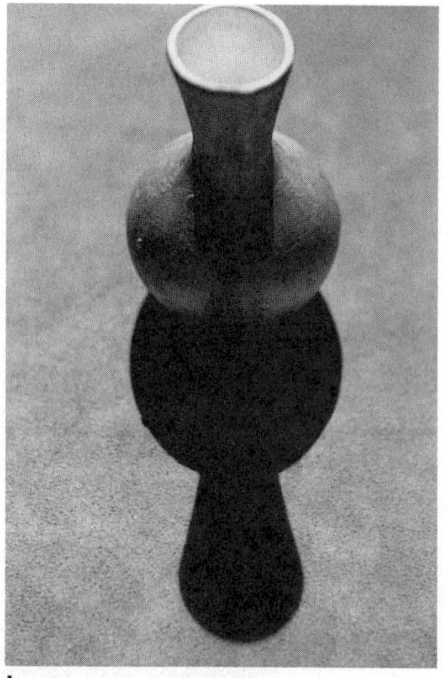

b

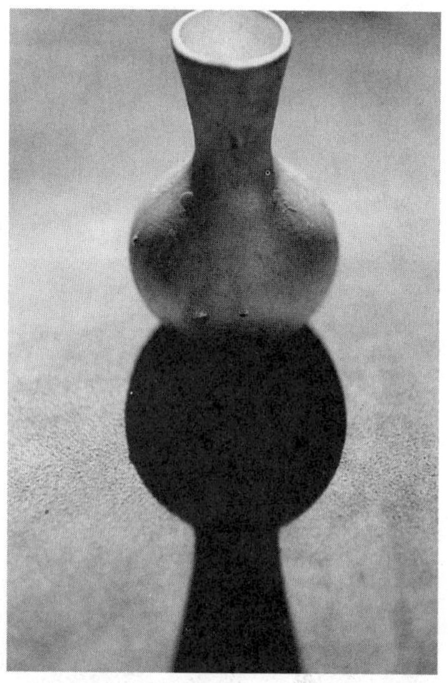

c

Figure 1.6 Effects of Light Source Elevation on Shadow Size *This vase is lit from behind by a hard light from a 70-degree elevation (a), from a 45-degree elevation (b), and from a 20-degree elevation (c). The effects on the object's shadow are quite dramatic. At 45 degrees, the length of the shadow is equal to the height of the vase.*

Light source directionality also has important effects on color saturation. Fullest saturation is obtained with frontal lighting. Desaturation results from back lighting. Tracing the color change in the blue of the sky, the green of the shrubs, or the red of the bricks in Color Plate 1 reveals the effect light angle has on color saturation.

SHADOWS

Some cinematographers say the most important thing in lighting is what you don't light. They are referring to the relative effects of light and shadow. There are two basic types of shadows: cast and bogus. A **cast shadow** is where the object forms its shadow by shutting out light. A **bogus shadow** is an unlit area of the frame. The bogus shadow does not result from an object blocking light. Rather, it is a matter of tonal gradation. Both types of shadows are involved in creating atmosphere and moods.

The elevation of the illumination influences the shape of the shadow. This can be seen in Figure 1.6. Controlling the degree of blackness in the shadows requires adding light to illuminate the shadow areas. This light is called a **fill light** (see Figure 1.7).

Shadows play an important role in rendering texture. To maximize texture, we use side (cross) lighting. Side lighting creates long shadows that interact with the lit parts of the subject to yield good texture patterns (see Figure 1.8). To minimize texture, we use frontal light since it is "shadowless" (see Figure 1.4).

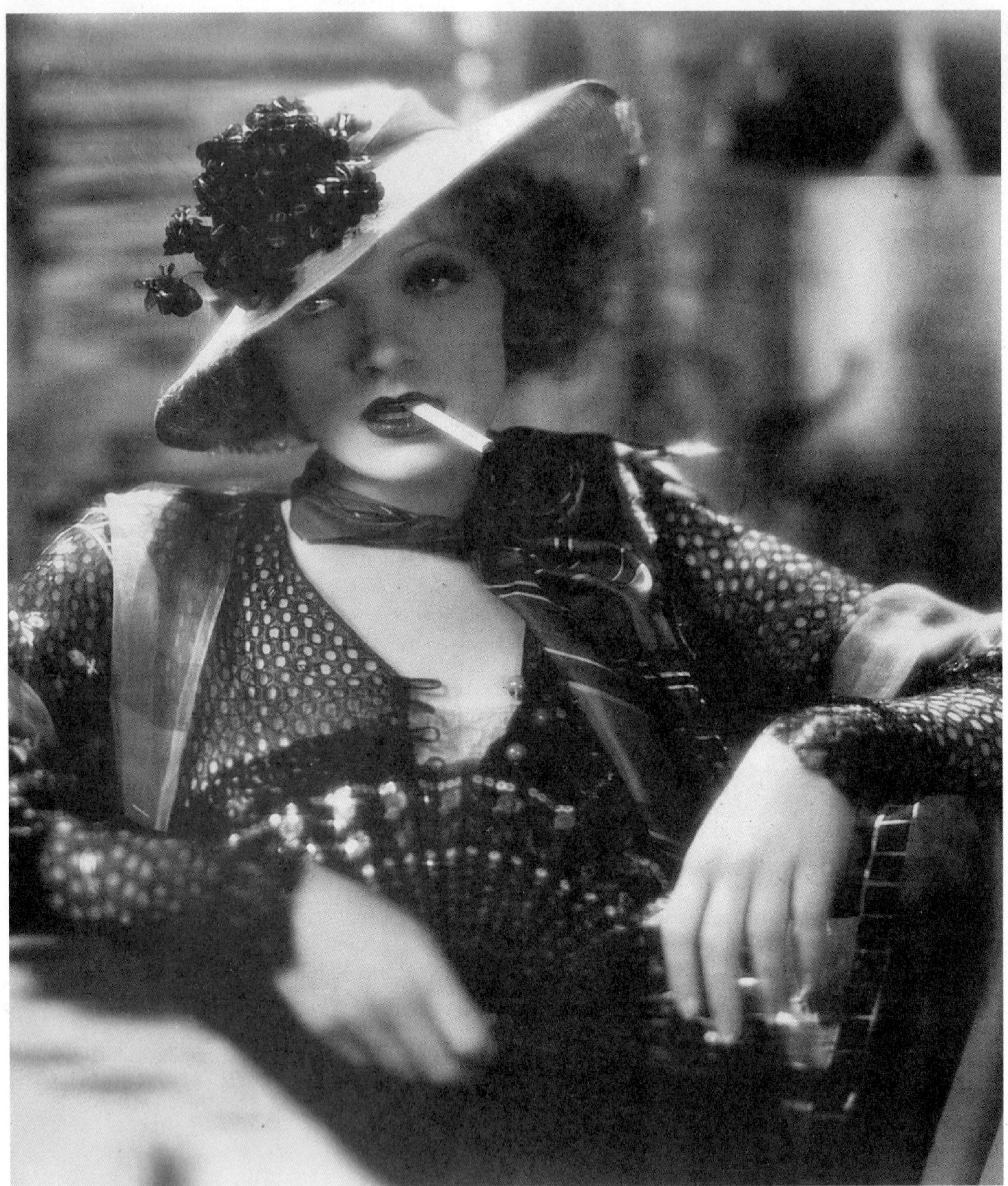

Figure 1.7 Fill Light *The shadow area under the hat has been illuminated with soft light from the front. This fill light creates reflections in the eyes ("eyelights") that bring life to the face* (Blonde Venus, *Paramount, 1932).*

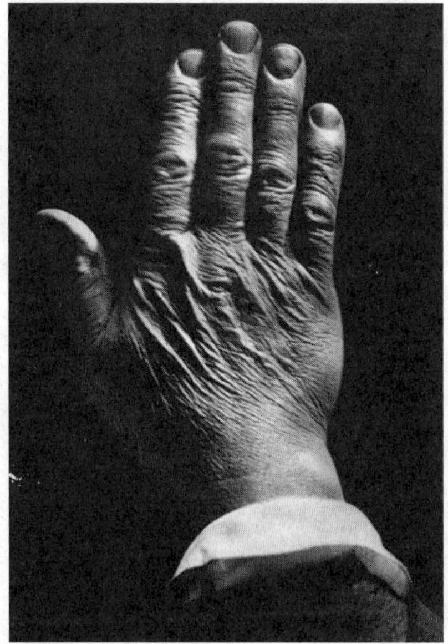

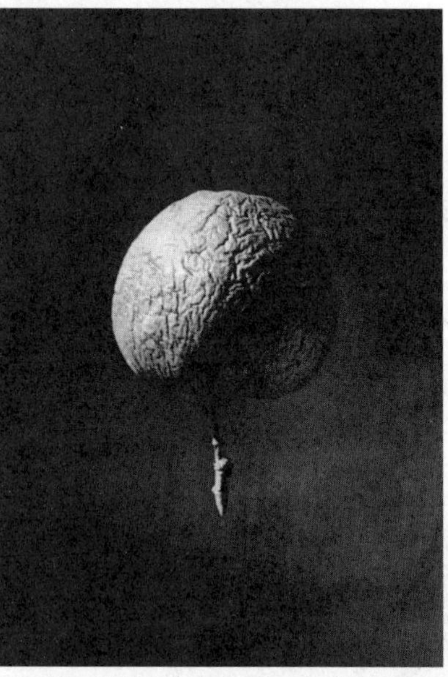

Figure 1.8 Side Light
Side lighting reveals an object's texture (photos by James Naysmith, 1874).

SUMMARY

- A central challenge to the cinematographer is to create images with mood and significance. When lighting, cinematographers work with three basics of illumination: quality, directionality, and shadow configuration. Together, these three create a field of light and shadow and color hues with gradations from white to gray and black.
- Quality, directionality, and shadow are intertwined; changing one alters the other. Changing light quality alters the "feel" of shadows. Changing source directionality allows control over shape and the location of shadows.

LIGHTING SETUPS: BASIC LIGHT PLACEMENTS

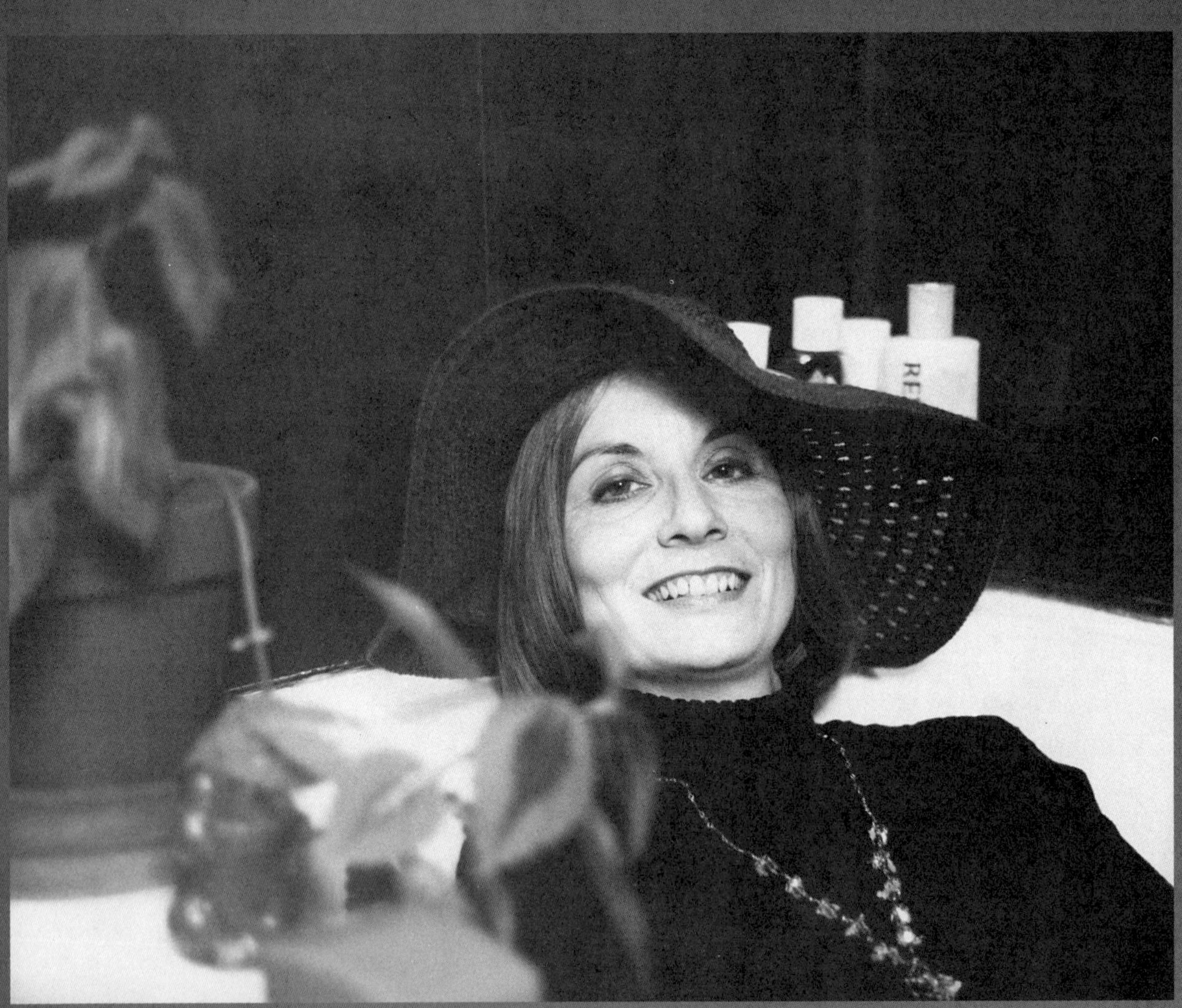

"frontal light"

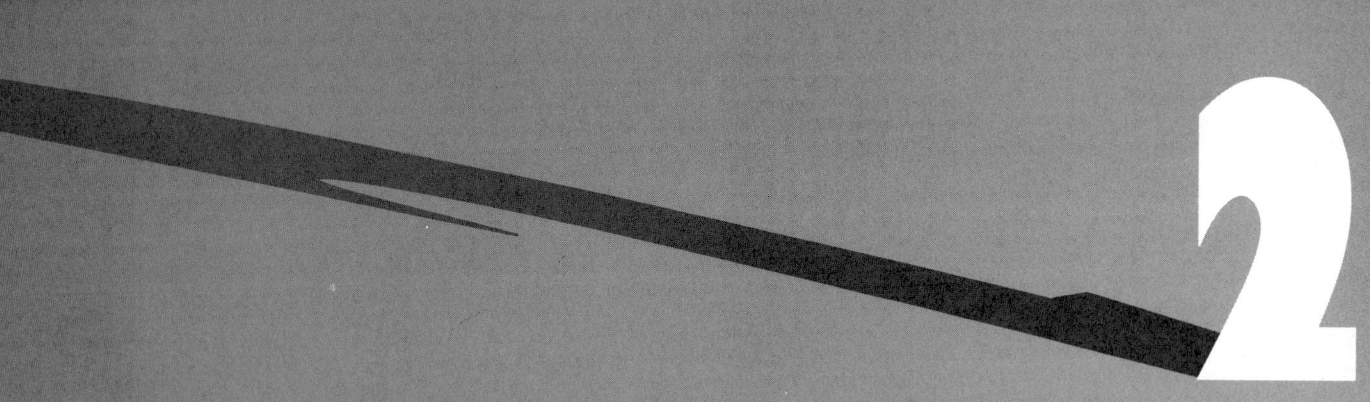

Establishing a lighting setup may be divided into five central concerns: choosing a source directionality and placing key lights based on the logic of that directionality; adding fill light to control shadow renditions; adding rim and back light to model actors and create subject/background separations; placing set and background lights to complete the realistic illusion; and positioning specialized lights to add depth and emphasis to characters and objects. This chapter assumes a working knowledge of light meters. You may want to consult Chapter 6 "Basic Exposure Theory: Light Meter and Keytone Method," and Appendix B, "Light Meters," to refresh your memory as needed.

LIKE ALL artistic skills, lighting can be mastered only through personal experience and analysis of acknowledged works of excellence. Analysis requires a language for conceptualizing and critiquing. This chapter lays out the basic light placements for creating and analyzing lighting setups. Lighting can be broken down into these basic functions:

- *Key light* is the main subject light that establishes source directionality, the logic for the lighting scheme, mood, and shape.
- *Fill light* supplements key lights by lightening shadow densities, principally on faces.
- *Back and rim light* supplements key and fill lights. It models, accentuates, and separates actors and objects from backgrounds.
- *Background and set light* illuminates backgrounds relative to key light intensities.
- *Specialized lights* include eyelights and hair lights used to fine-tune the setup.

KEY LIGHT

As its name implies, the **key light**, or **key**, is the most important light source affecting the shot. It establishes the directionality and source motivation for the lighting and determines the placement of facial shadows. A number of lights may be used to establish the key light source, particularly where there is a lot of actor movement to cover. These lights are usually arranged so as to appear to come from a single direction in order to maintain the overall motivated lighting scheme.

Because the subject moves in film and video, we have to design lighting combinations to cover ordinary changes such as a head turn. Sometimes, a lighting setup is so restrictive that an actor must stay on a certain mark in order to be in the light. At other times the lighting is "looser" and allows for freer actor movement.

Figure 2.1 Key Light Positions

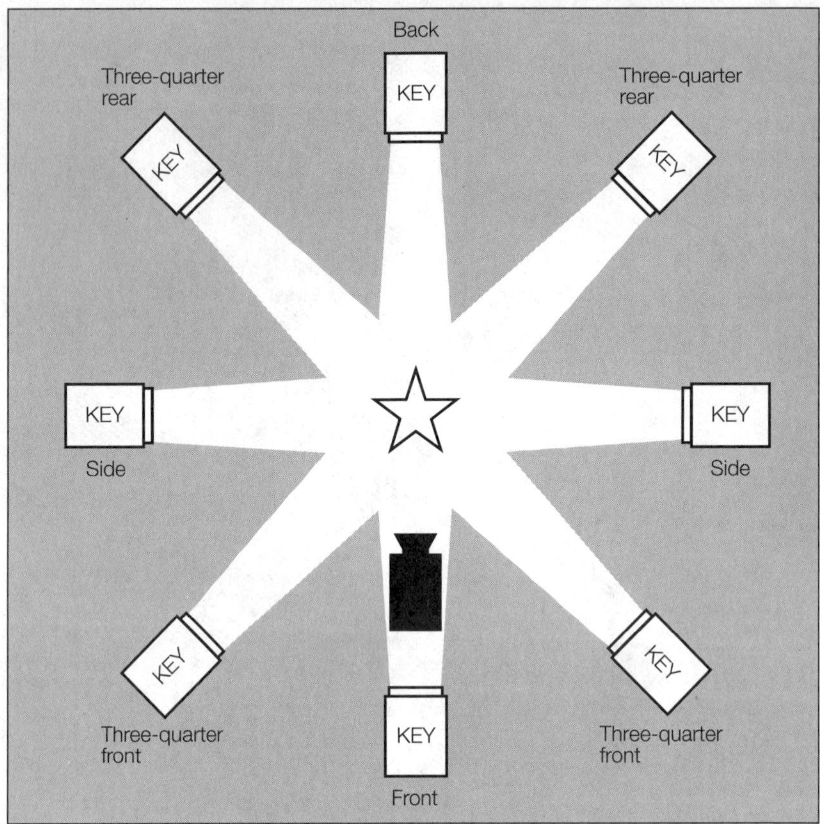

As we saw in Chapter 1, front, side, and back are the principal directions used for lighting a subject. Figure 2.1 elaborates this further and presents a working vocabulary for referring to key light placements. In the horizontal plane, we can identify five important positions: front, three-quarter front, side, three-quarter rear, and back. These designations result from a simple 45-degree scale and are referenced to the camera/subject axis.

These five placements for the key are for our convenience in talking about lighting and are not to be construed as "rules" for key light placement. An actual key light is usually positioned by eye with reference to its effects on the particular subject. These descriptions are thus only approximations made for our verbal convenience.

In the vertical plane, keys may be positioned at a variety of elevations. Four placement positions are adequate for description: below (low angle), camera level, above (30 to 60 degrees but commonly about 45 degrees), and high (typically 60 to 90 degrees, the latter being called "top" lighting). Most key lights come from elevations around 45 degrees above the subject. The higher positions are used mostly for hair and back lighting. Camera-level placements are used for fill lighting and frontal or side key effects. Because of distortions, we tend to avoid low-angle placements except for special effect.

Besides these source positionings, we have to factor in the quality/shadow differences of soft and hard light. Add to that the fact that actors are in constant movement and the complexities of lighting may seem insurmountable.

Let us start our investigation of this complex art by illustrating these major key light placements more fully. We will take the simplest possible situation—a portrait of an actor. Two truisms concerning lighting, which are particularly important when lighting actors' faces, should be stressed:

- The effect of a particular key on a particular subject is variable; that is, different faces demand different light positionings. Thus we often have to test lighting combinations on faces to ascertain their photogenic effects.
- Lighting is basically done by eye. This means the cinematographer must be sensitive to the particular subject and how light affects it.

Frontal Keys

Light from a low-angle, frontal position creates that familiar horror film/vampire picture look that we duplicated as kids by putting a flashlight under our chins. Sunlight and most interior lighting come from overhead. Lighting from below seems strange because it is so unusual (see Figure 2.2a and d).

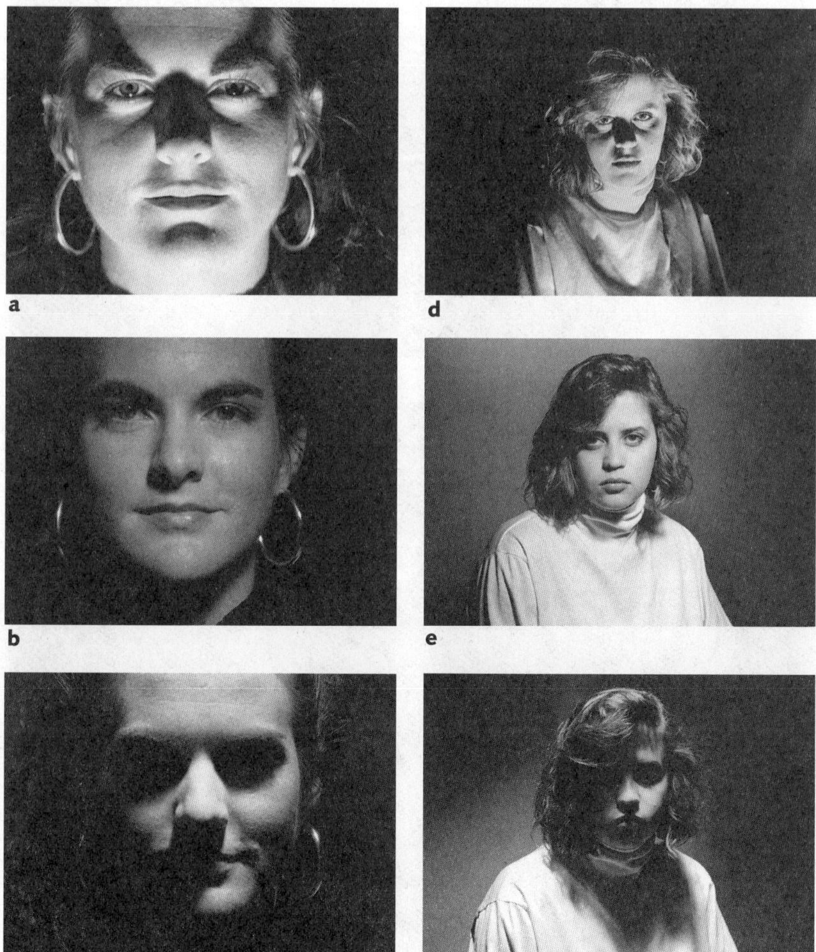

Figure 2.2 Frontal Key Elevations *Different elevations for a key light produce differing facial shadows and facial effects. In these shots, the key light positions are from below (a and d), from slightly above camera level (b and e), and from a high angle (c and f). Though rather unflattering, the higher elevations, such as in (c) and (f) can be useful—see the lighting on Marlon Brando in* The Godfather *and the pastiche opening of* The Freshman.

Figure 2.3 Frontal Keys at Camera Level

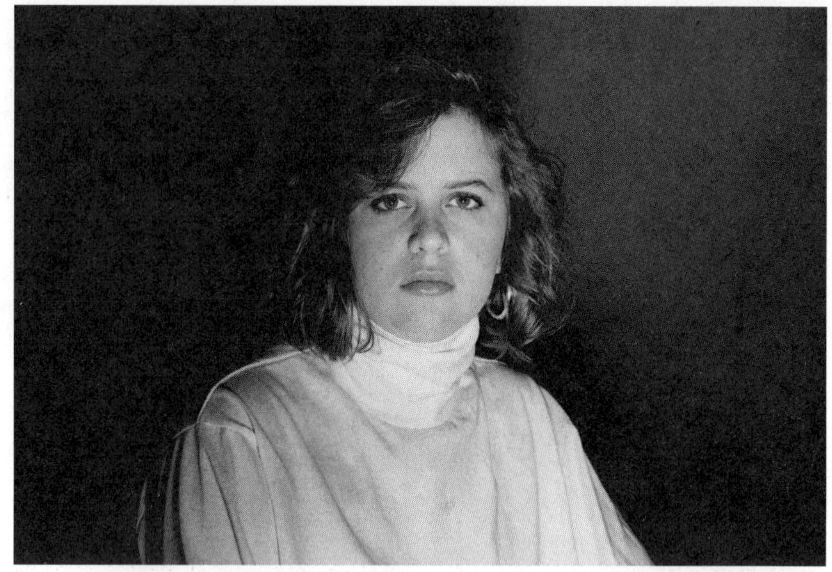

a

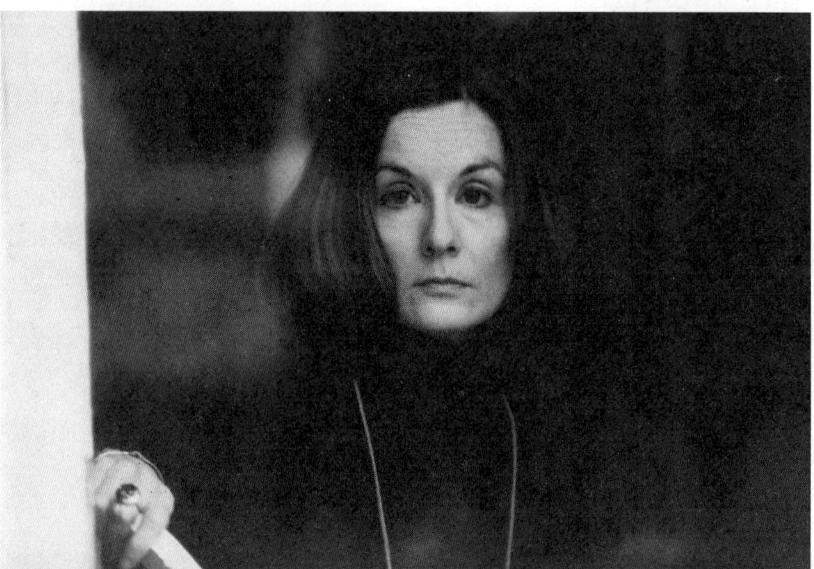

b

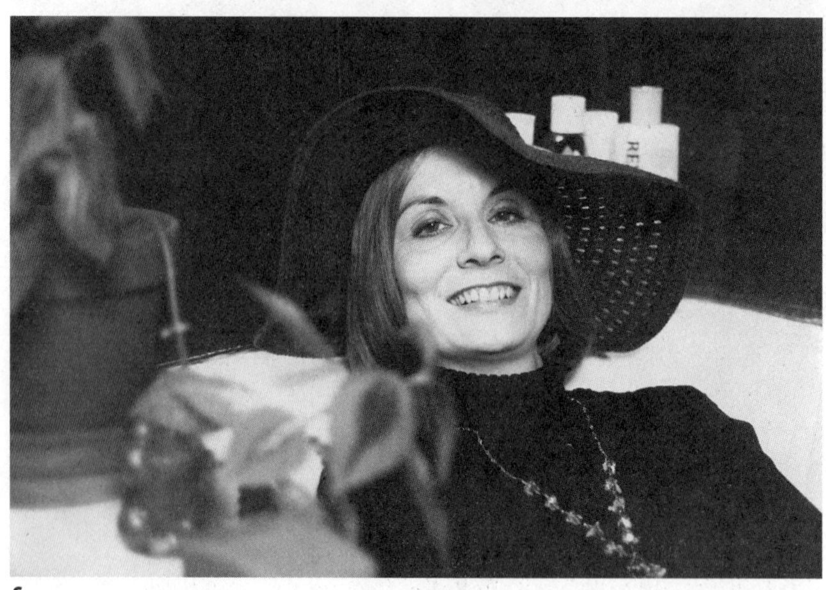

c

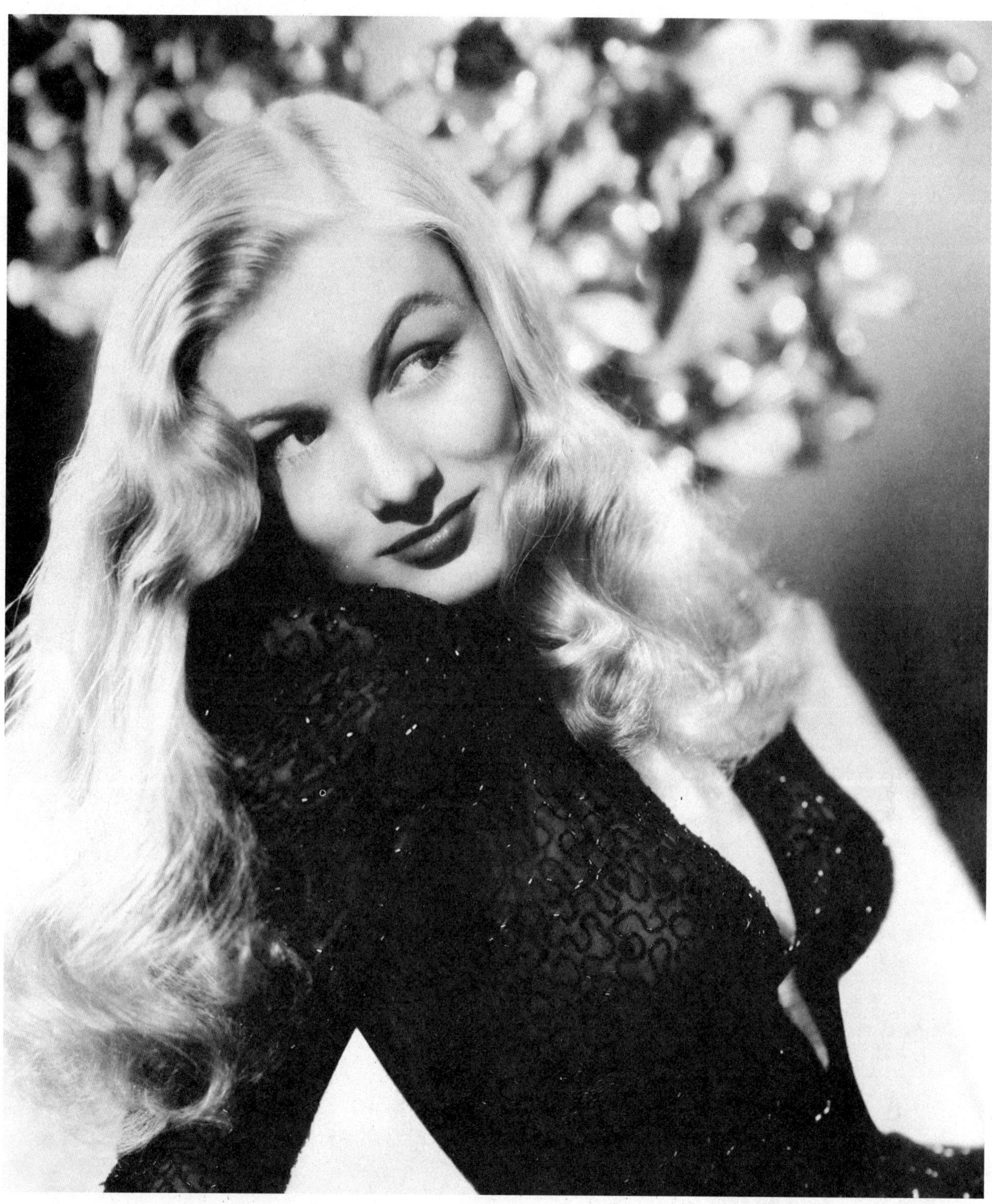

Figure 2.4 Hollywood Star Lighting Style
(Paramount Pictures publicity photo of Veronica Lake)

When placed at camera level or slightly above, a frontal key produces a flat, straight-on illumination that de-emphasizes depth and creates a feeling of two-dimensionality. Such frontal lighting minimizes the effects of wrinkles, lines, and other marks on the face (see Figure 2.3).

As we elevate the key above camera level, we obtain positions that can be very flattering to certain faces. This is because cheek bones and noses cast pleasing shadows (see Figure 2.4). The frontal key, from

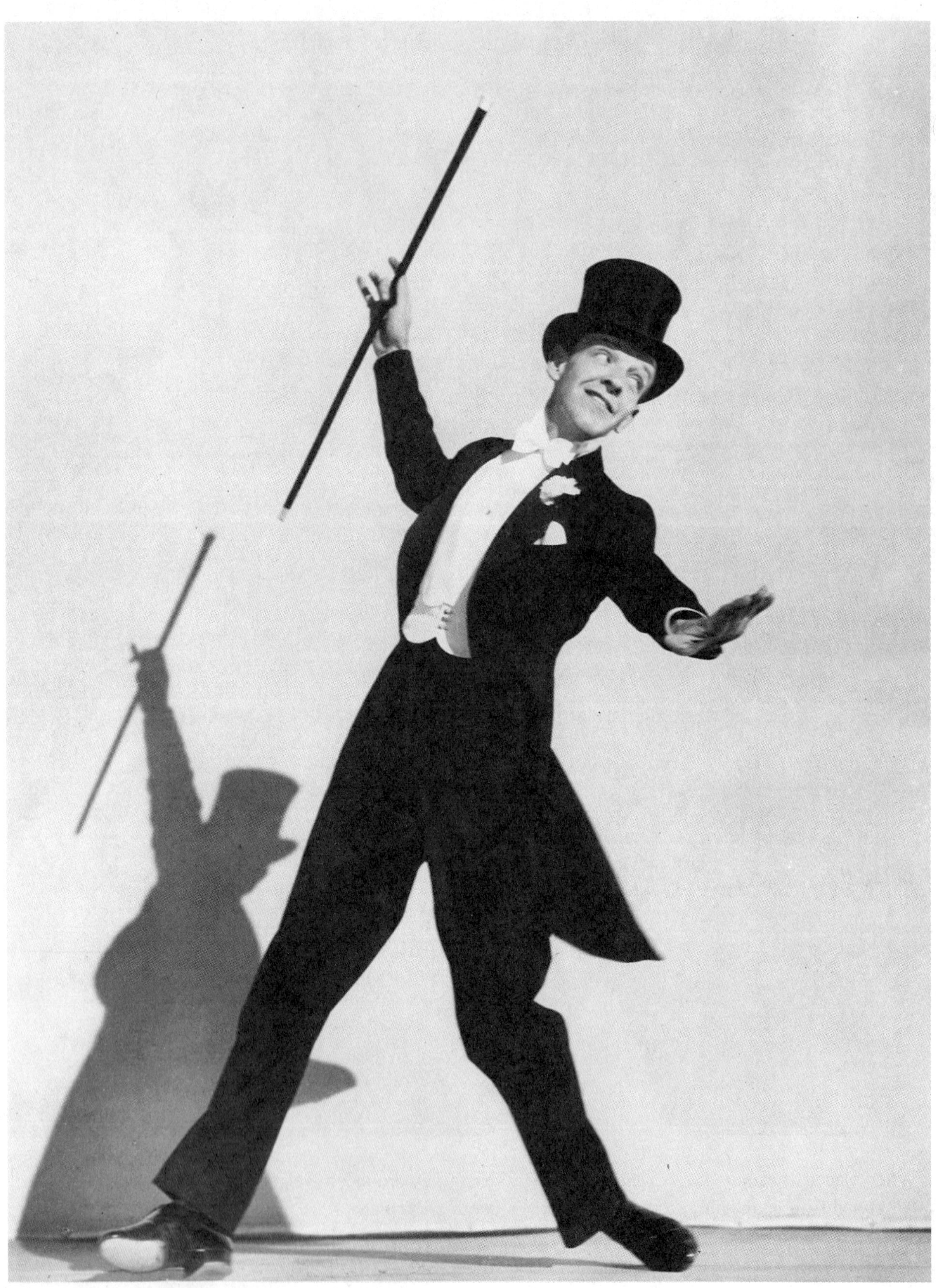

Figure 2.4 (continued)
(Top Hat, *RKO Radio Pictures, 1935)*

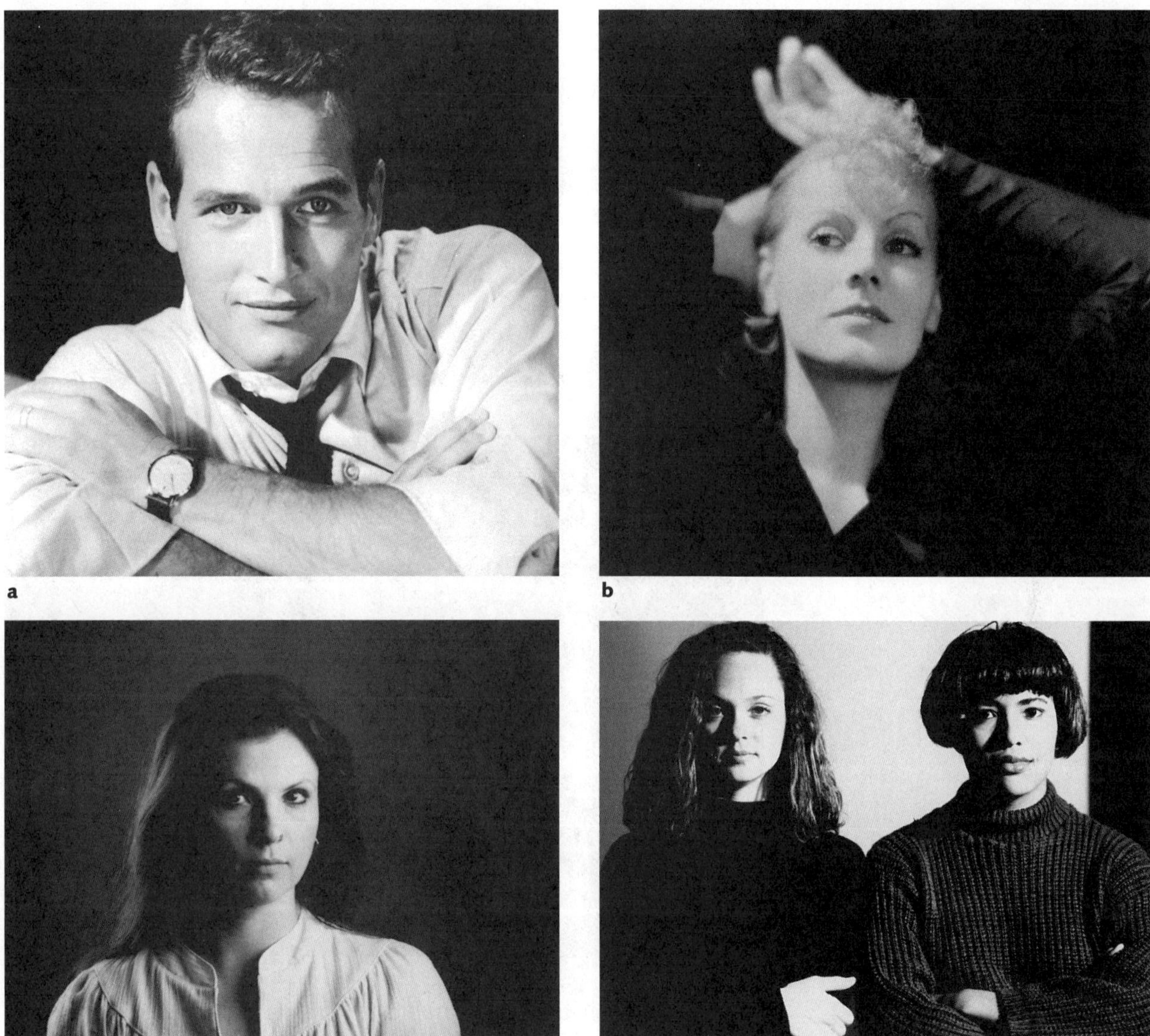

Figure 2.5 Three-Quarter Front Keys *This is a very popular key light position. Sometimes the shadow side eye is in the patch of light (c and d), and other times it is left dark (a and b, publicity photos of Paul Newman and Greta Garbo, Museum of Modern Art).*

about 30 to 45 degrees above, is often used on film stars. It gives a bit of modeling to the face but still softens facial features and minimizes skin textures. Used in combination with diffusion, it is a very popular, Hollywood star lighting style (see Figure 2.4).

As the higher positions are reached, we lose the glamour effect. Texture appears, eye sockets become dark and black, and elongated shadows appear under the lips and nose. Instead of glamour we now have an unflattering effect, an effect all too common under ordinary fluorescent ceiling lighting (see Figure 2.2c and f).

Three-Quarter Front Keys

The **three-quarter front key** is the favored position for the key in classic Hollywood-style lighting (see Figure 2.5). It comes from above at about a 45-degree angle and creates the familiar triangle-shaped patch

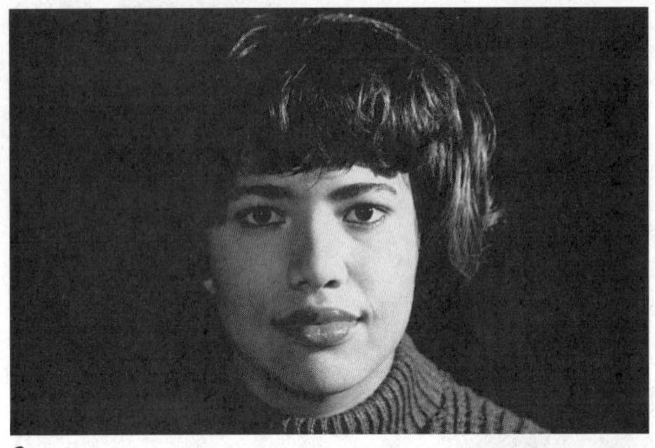

a

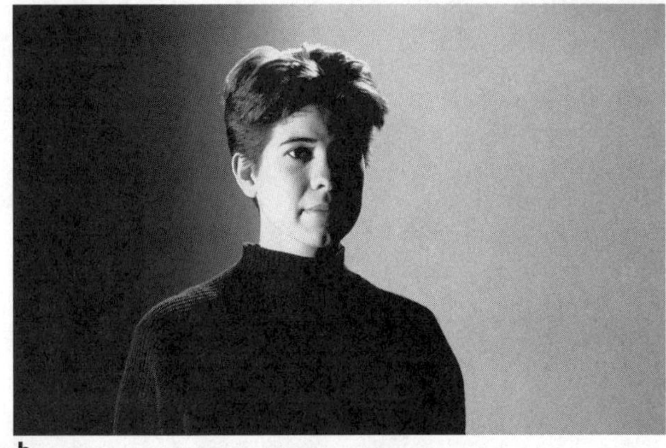

b

Figure 2.6 Side Keys at Camera Level

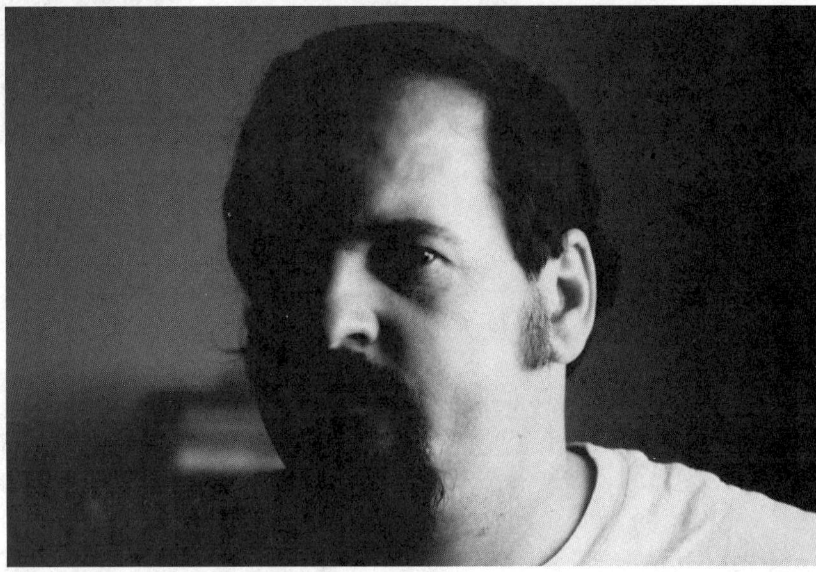

c

of light on the shadow side of the face. This key was so prevalent during the 1940s and 1950s that for many people "key" meant three-quarter front. Today, cinematographers are more free with their key placements, though three-quarter front is still considered a highly useful position.

A reminder: How high a three-quarter front key should be positioned and the exact angle to be utilized depend on the aesthetic intent of the shot and the particular actor's face—whether it is oval or angular, for example.

Side Keys

Certain key light positions work best with soft light; the **side key** is an example. A camera-level side key on a frontal face is a classic lighting setup. The lighting divides the face in half with a vertical shadow (see Figure 2.6).

The side key provides a great deal of visual variety to hold our attention. Interesting effects are obtained with this key as the subject turns from front to three-quarter to profile position (see Figure 2.7).

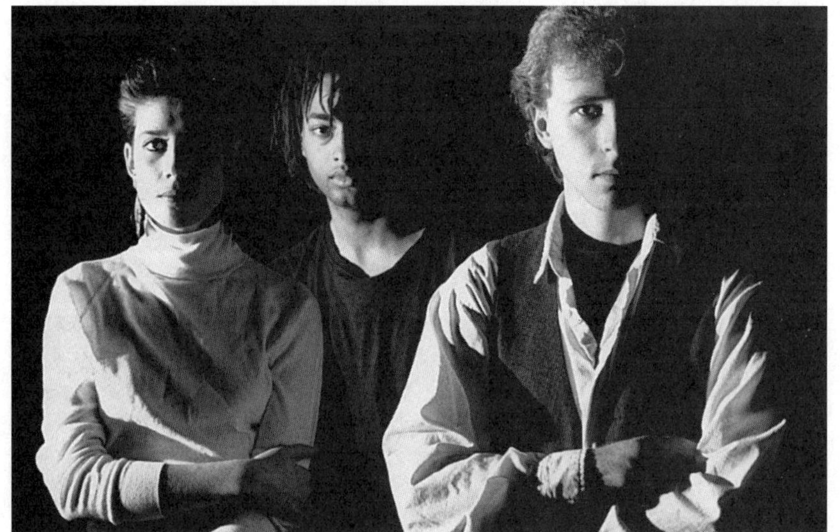

a

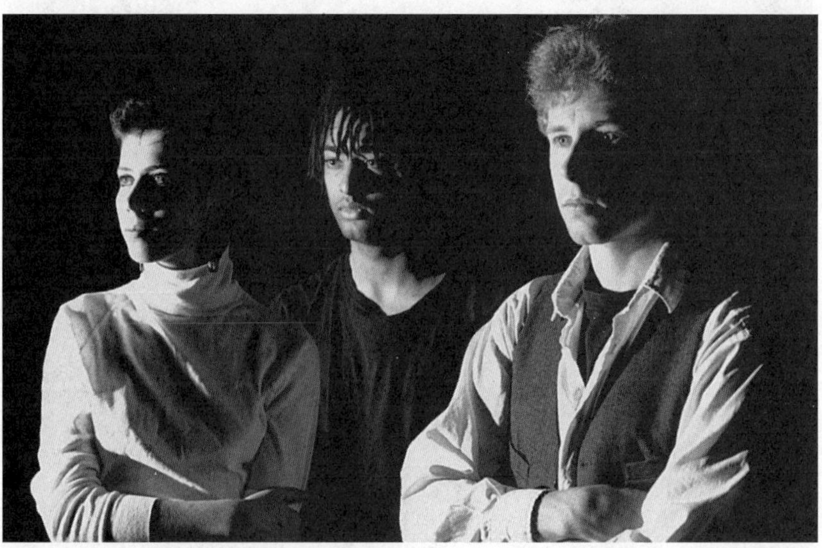

b

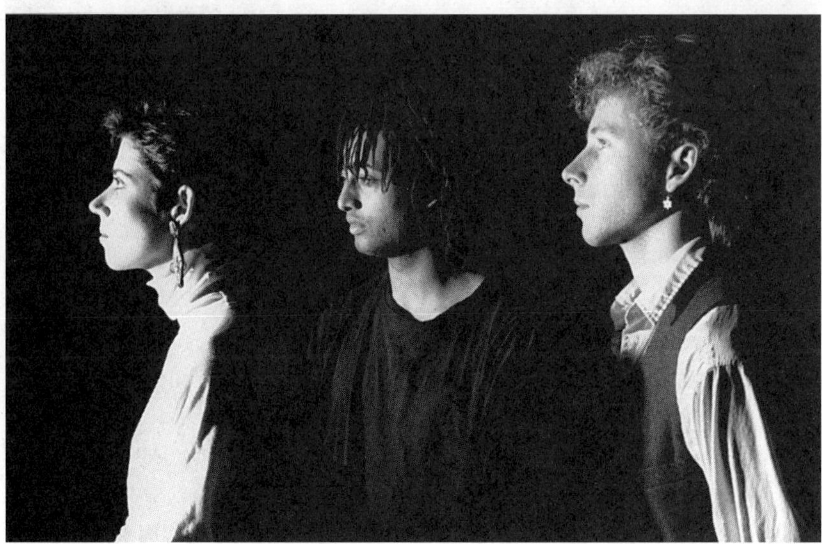

c

Figure 2.7 Effects of Side Keys on Actor Movement *A common situation is where the key light starts as a side key (a), turns into a three-quarter front effect as the actors turn their head (b), and ends as a full face effect as the actors reach profile (c).*

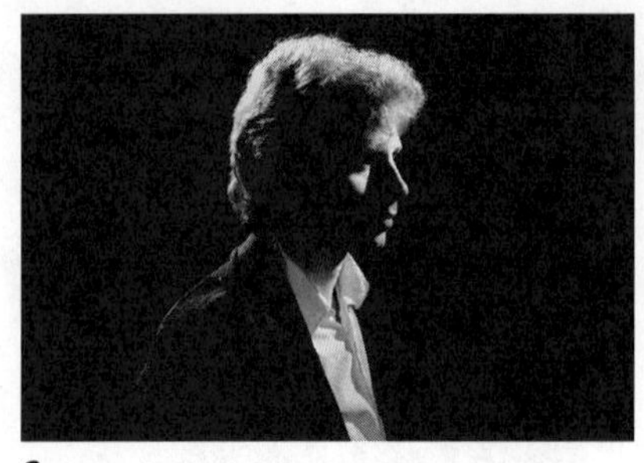

a

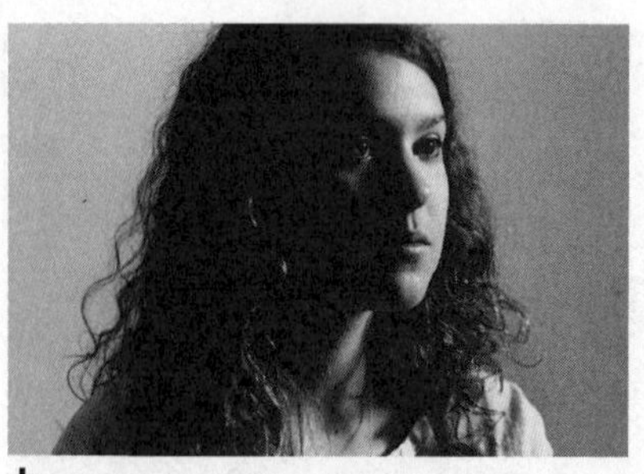

b

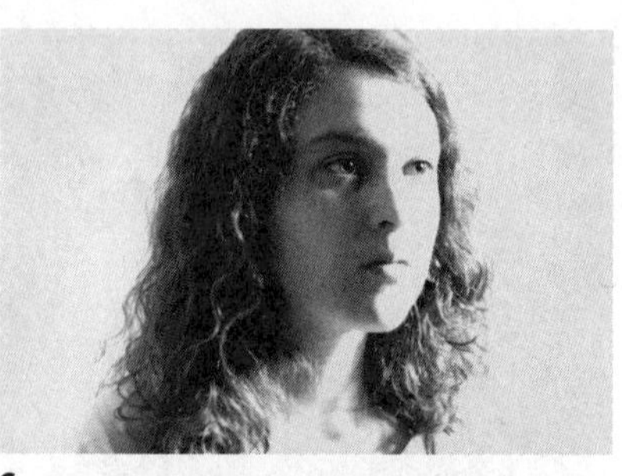

c

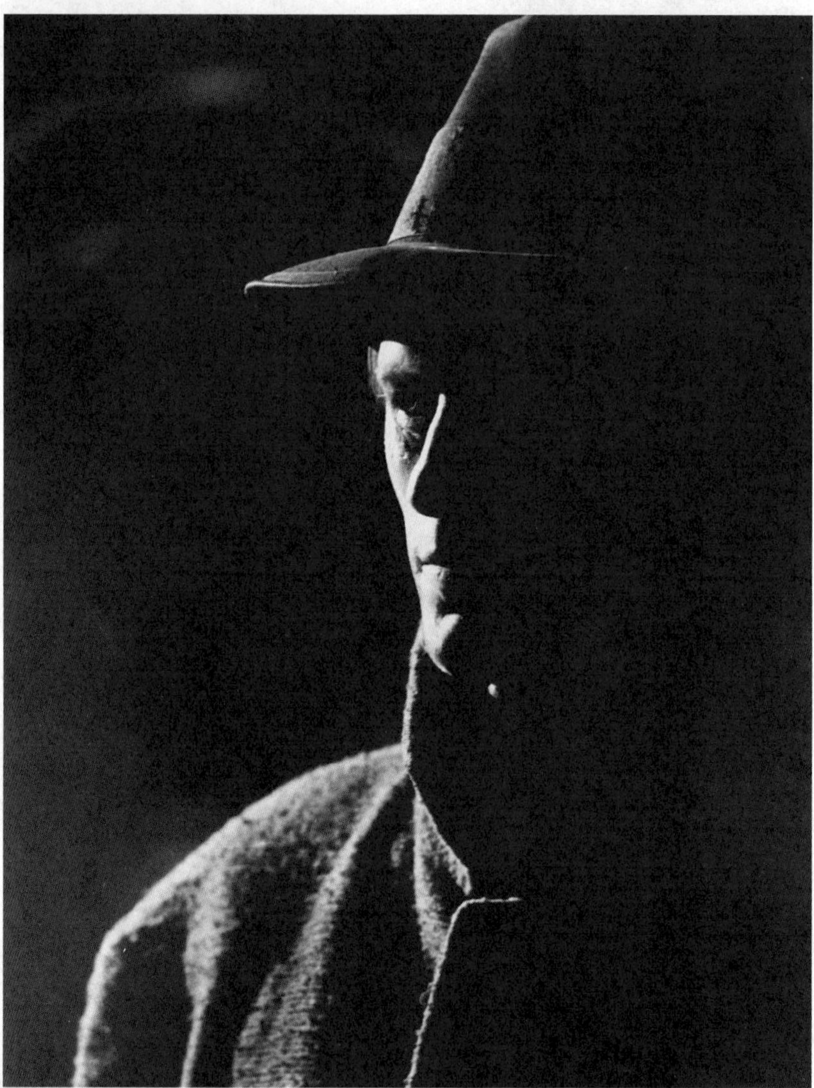

d

Figure 2.8 Three-Quarter Rear Keys *Various effects of keys from the three-quarter rear position are illustrated. Note the different mood obtained in (c) by exposing for the shadow side of the face as compared to (b), which is exposed for the lit side of the face. This effect is often used to simulate the effects of window light. The publicity still in (d) is from* Raggedy Man, *Universal City Studios, 1981.*

Three-Quarter Rear Keys

The **three-quarter rear key** is the backside version of the three-quarter front key. It is is a very dramatic, moody key that is often used for night exteriors. The three-quarter rear key works best using a hard light source with a "film noir" or melodrama lighting scheme (see Figure 2.8).

A "raw" facial-lighting effect can be obtained by using two three-quarter rear keys, one from each side of the figure (see Figure 2.9).

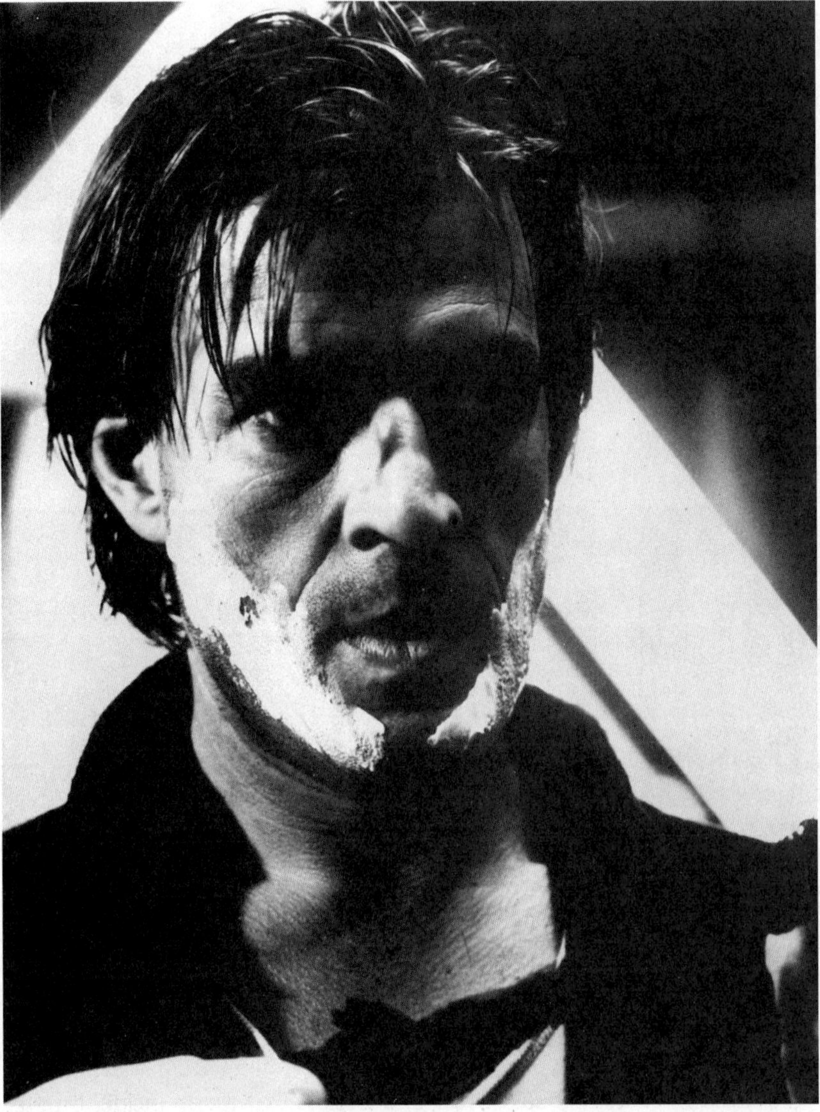

a

b

c

d

Figure 2.9 Double Three-Quarter Rear Keys *Use of two three-quarter rear keys produces a distinct lighting style (a) in which a shadow area is left on the center of the face (*The 4th Man, *International Spectrafilm Distribution, 1984). The effects of this lighting setup on actor movement are shown in (b) and (c). In two-shot situations, one actor's key is the other actor's rim (d).*

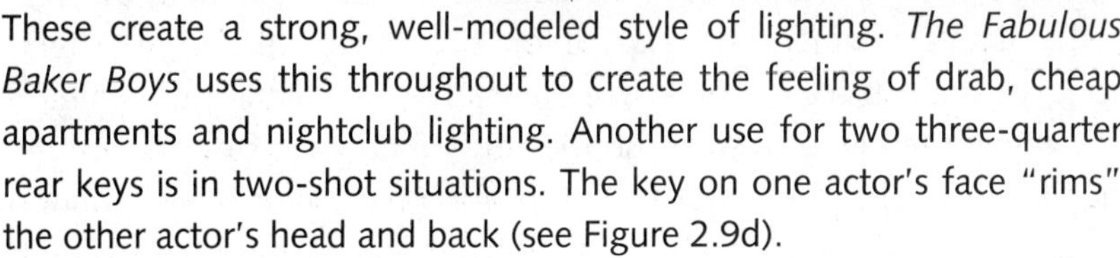

These create a strong, well-modeled style of lighting. *The Fabulous Baker Boys* uses this throughout to create the feeling of drab, cheap apartments and nightclub lighting. Another use for two three-quarter rear keys is in two-shot situations. The key on one actor's face "rims" the other actor's head and back (see Figure 2.9d).

Back Key Positions

A light from the rear is the key when it is the dominant light on the figure. Applying a back key to a person automatically creates a dark, moody effect useful for night interiors and exteriors (see Figure 2.10). Where the actor is in profile, back light can create very interesting images. We see little detail but obtain mystery and darkness.

Like the three-quarter rear key, back light positions are often used for supplemental modeling light. This function will be discussed shortly.

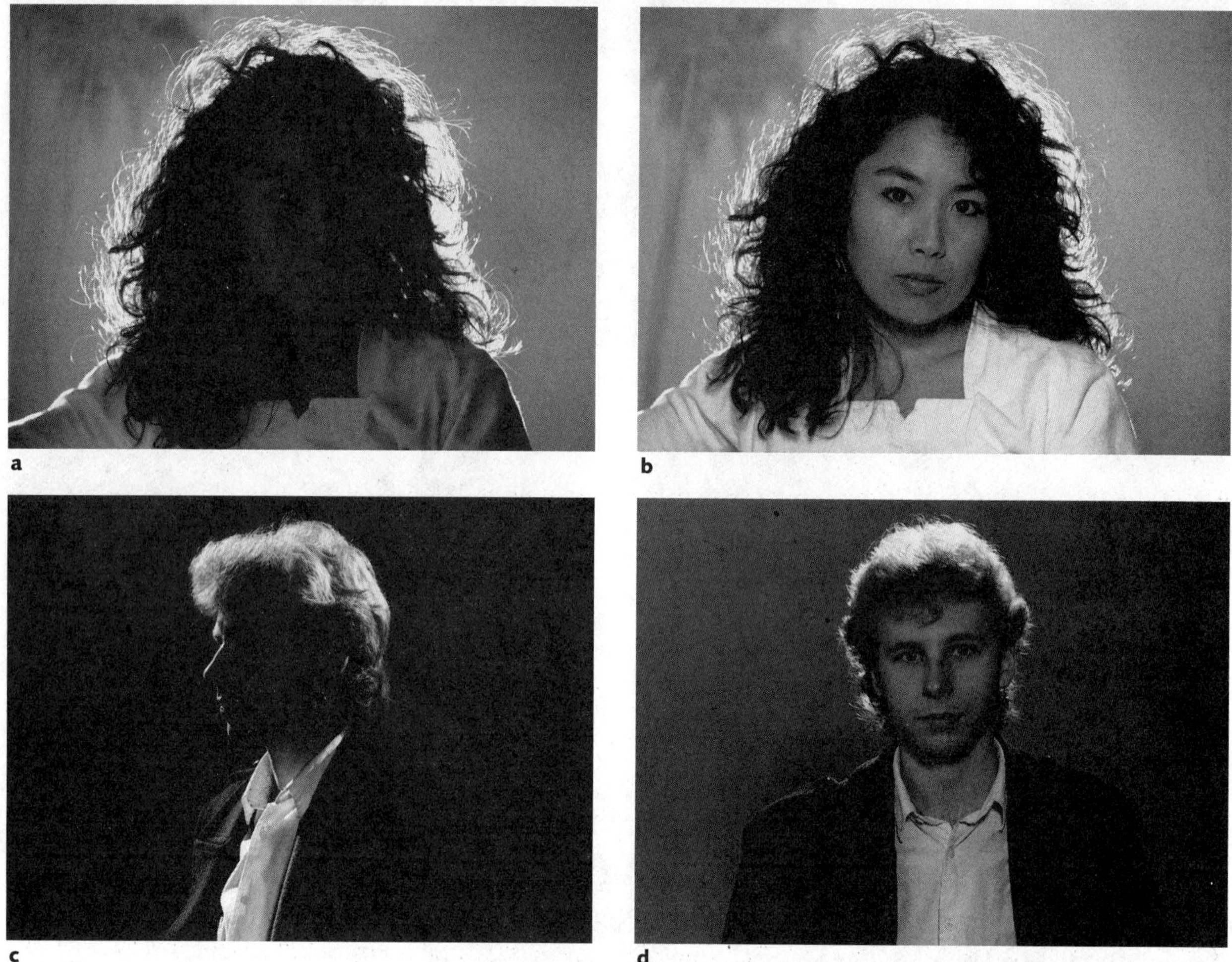

Figure 2.10 Back Key Positions
A back key light comes from behind the actor and emphasizes the hair and outline of the head. Frontal fill light has been added in (b) and (d).

Exposure for Three-Quarter Rear and Back Key Positions

Exposing for three-quarter rear and back keys with an incident meter can be tricky. One technique is to point the incident meter at the light, rather than the camera, and expose for the indicated reading. This tends to leave the subject too dark (see Figure 2.11c). Pointing the meter at the camera tends to overexpose the lighting about a stop for a three-quarter rear light to three or four stops for a back light. The amount of overexposure depends on how intense the rear or back light is compared with the frontal lighting, if any, on the subject.

Some cinematographers would expose halfway between these two readings, a compromise exposure. With a three-quarter rear key, you will arrive at the same effect by pointing the meter at the camera in the usual way and then intentionally underexposing one-half to one stop (see Figure 2.11b).

The addition of fill light complicates the exposure determination. At a certain point the fill becomes functionally more important than the back light and the rim or back light becomes supplemental. In this case, exposure is taken for the frontal "fill" light in the normal way.

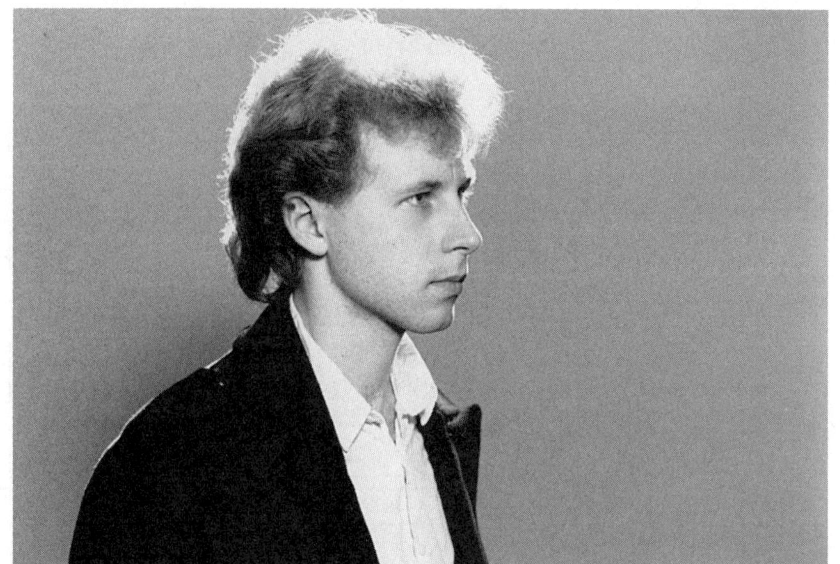

a

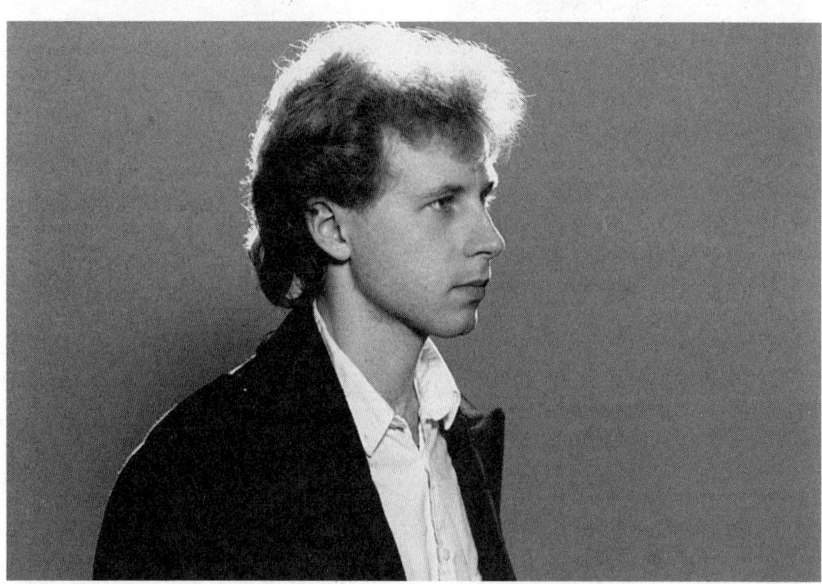

b

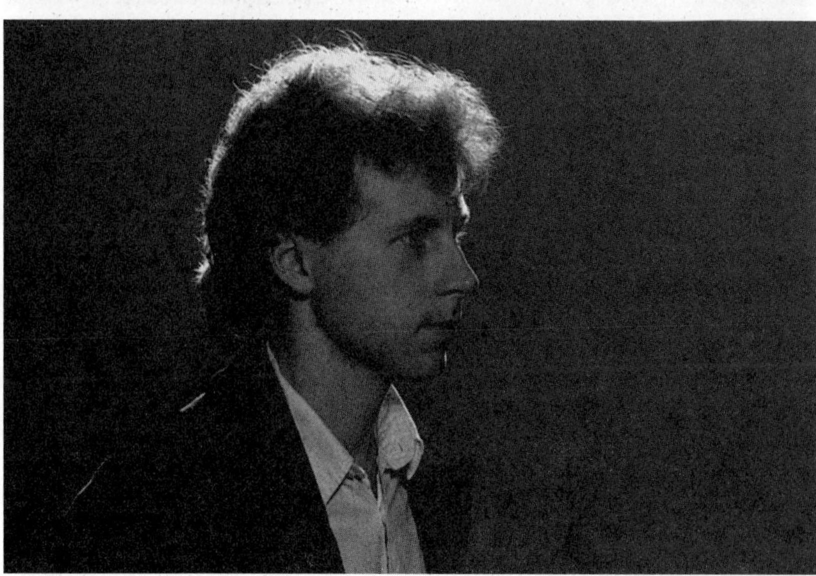

c

Figure 2.11 Exposing for Three-Quarter Rear and Back Key Positions *In this example, three exposure possibilities are shown: (a) exposure for face, (b) exposure in between (compromise exposure), and (c) exposure for back light. Note the various effects the different exposures have on the background.*

Figure 2.12 Fill Light Positions
Three common positions for the fill are (1) frontal from slightly above the camera, (2) slightly off-axis on the key side of the subject, and (3) slightly off-axis on the shadow side of the subject.

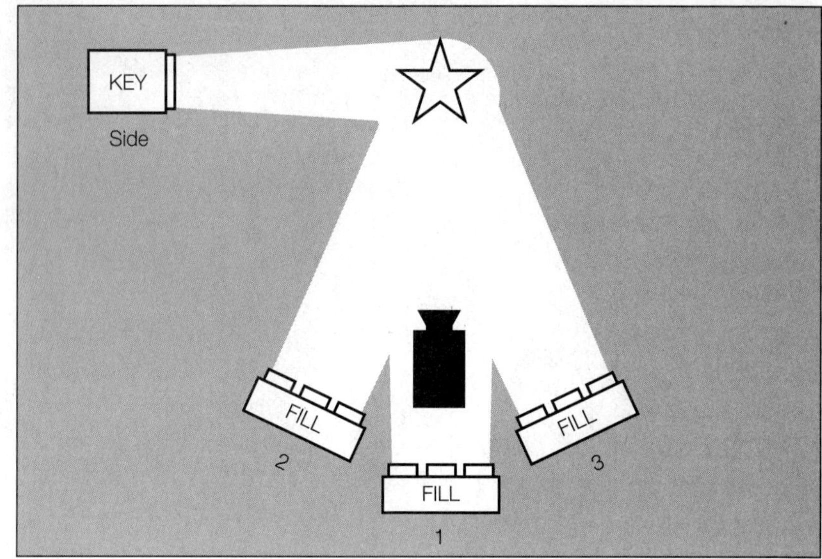

FILL LIGHT

The key light determines shadow placement. The **fill light** is used to lighten (fill in) those shadows while avoiding the formation of new shadows. Fill lights are almost always soft, even when keys are hard. This is because the slow fall-off of soft light provides a more natural "fill," almost invisible in its effects.

Fills tend to be placed in one of four positions. The first and most common is from a frontal position along the camera/subject axis slightly above the camera. This position is preferred because it creates no new shadows of its own (see Figure 2.12). A second position for the fill is from the key side of the camera/subject axis. This position allows for a more modeled effect than does the camera/subject axis position. Another possibility is to fill from the off-key side of the face, taking great care not to create a new set of shadows, particularly on the nose. This position also allows for a modeled effect but because of actor movement can easily lead to shadow problems.

Some texts define the fill light as light coming from the side of the face opposite the key at what amounts to a three-quarter front position. With closeups this is not a recommended position for the fill since it yields unflattering, double nose shadows and, if the subject is near the background, a double shadow on the wall (see Figure 2.13). With such a fill position, you also risk destroying the mood effects of the key unless you keep the fill at very low levels. A frontal key without fill is generally preferable.

For long shots, the effects of this double frontal 45-degree position are not so devastating. In fact, two three-quarter keys can be used to create a broad area of overall illumination, flat but useful, particularly for television news coverage of, for example, a board meeting.[1]

A last fill position is from high above, a technique used by Swedish cinematographer Sven Nykvist. Its main advantage is that it lessens the risk of casting multiple shadows on the walls behind a moving subject.[2]

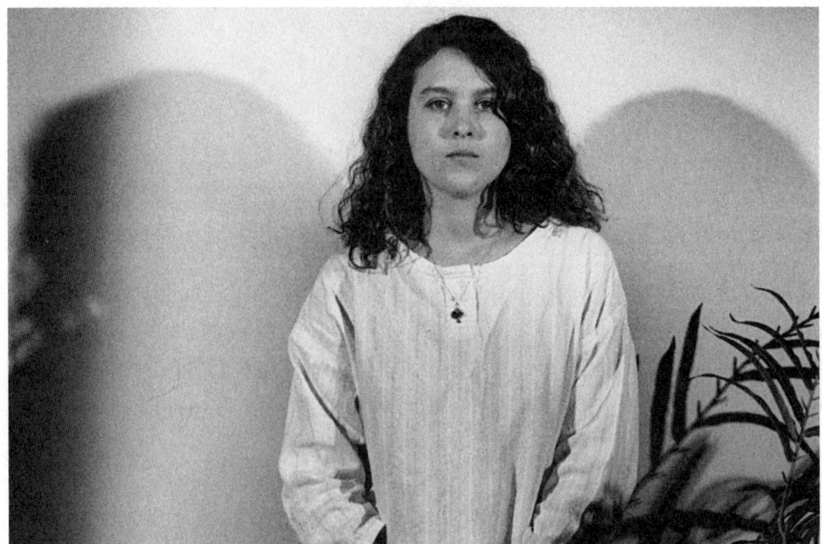

Figure 2.13 Double Three-Quarter Front Setup *Both key and fill come from three-quarter front positions and create distracting double nose shadows as well as double wall shadows in cases where the actor is close to the wall.*

Shadows cast by lighting from above tend to fall onto the floor. The higher the light, the closer the shadow is cast to the actor's feet. This fact is useful for key light placement as well. A possible disadvantage is the lack of fill in eye sockets and other facial indentations due to the high angle of incidence.

A variation on the frontal fill is the **roving fill** used with tracking and dollying shots. The light is either mounted on the camera or dolly, or carried by a grip. The idea is that wherever the camera goes, the fill will follow. For example, the camera follows two dancers in a large ballroom scene. As they turn and revolve, they will be filled in by the camera-mounted light. The moving fill, or even moving key, is very useful and has a large number of applications.

The intensity of the fill light has important effects on image mood. These are sometimes referred to as "high-key" and "low-key." In **high-key**—light, bright, cheery moods and effects—the fill light, if any, will be nearly as bright as the key light (see Figure 2.14a). With **low-key** effects and their accompanying mysterious, morose, dark moods, the fill will be of low intensity relative to the key light. Sometimes no fill is used at all (see Figure 2.14b and c; also Figures 2.8d and 2.9).

The usage of "key" to indicate the overall mood of the lighting should be distinguished from the concept of key light discussed earlier. The two have little to do with one another and are an unfortunate terminological overlap.

The exact position of the fill in a particular shot will be determined by moving shadow considerations and the overall modeling effect required.

BACK, RIM, AND KICKER LIGHT

In most general terms, light from the rear of the subject is called *back lighting*. Back lighting may be further differentiated, depending on the angle it comes from and its effect on the subject (see Figure 2.15).

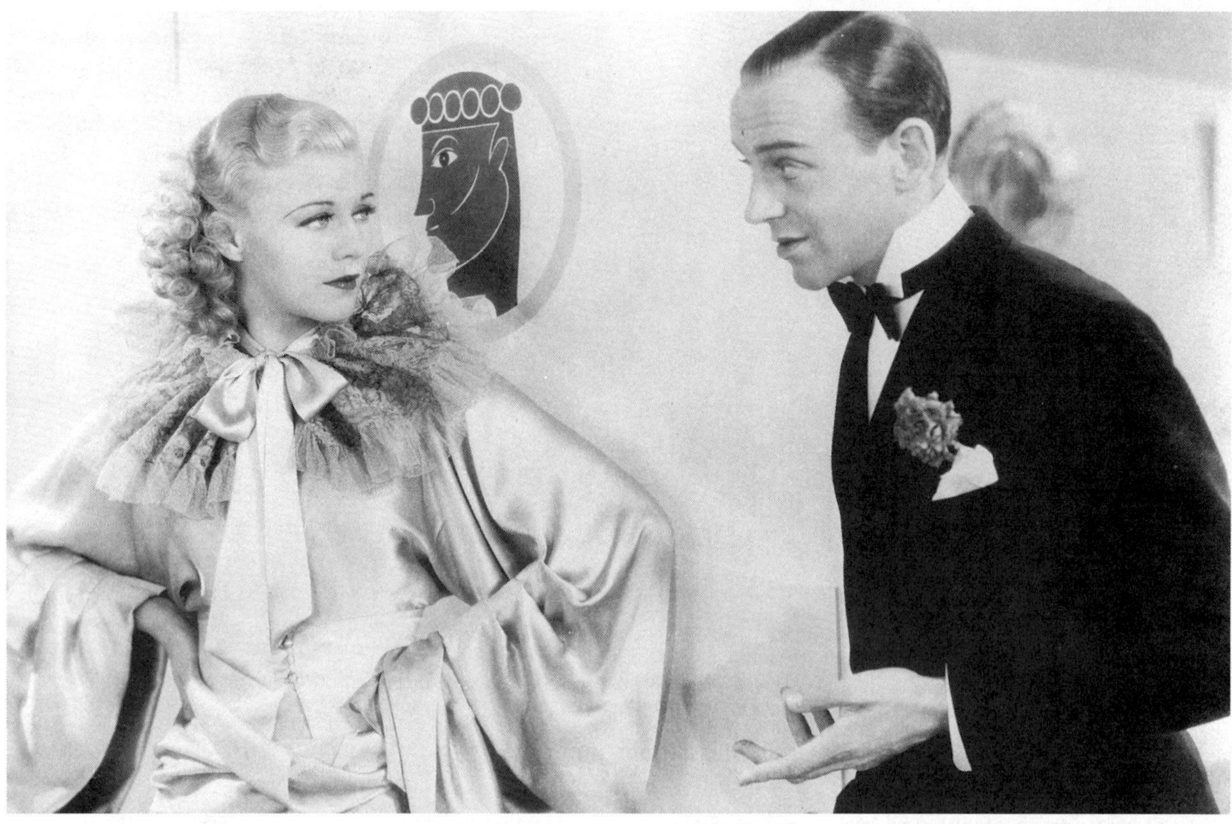

a

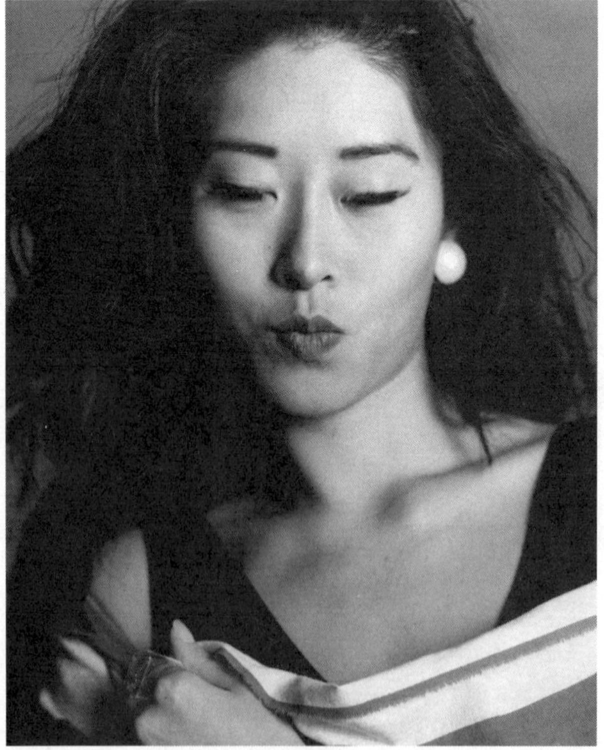

b

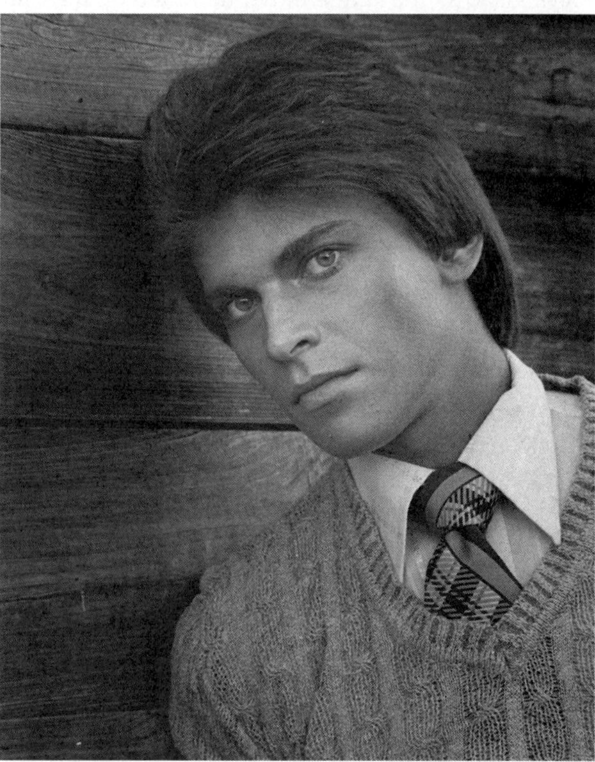

c

Figure 2.14 Examples of High- and Low-Key Lighting *The intensity of the fill light, where present, is a factor in creating either a high-key mood (a) or a low-key effect (b and c). Frontal keys as in (a) of course require no fill (*Top Hat, RKO Radio Pictures, 1935*). Photo (b) by Robin Hood Dial II. Photo (c) by Joyce Shöffner.*

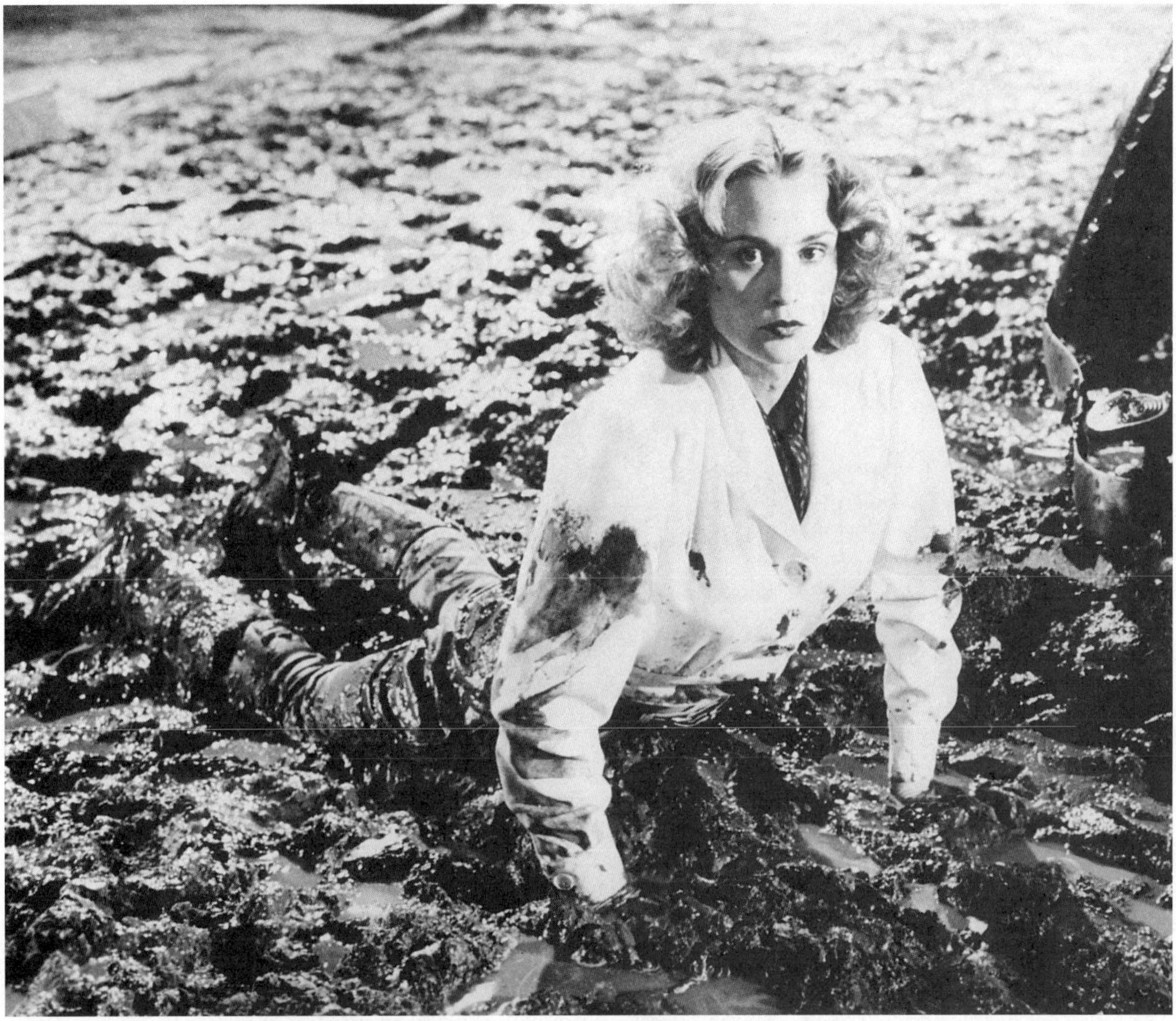

a

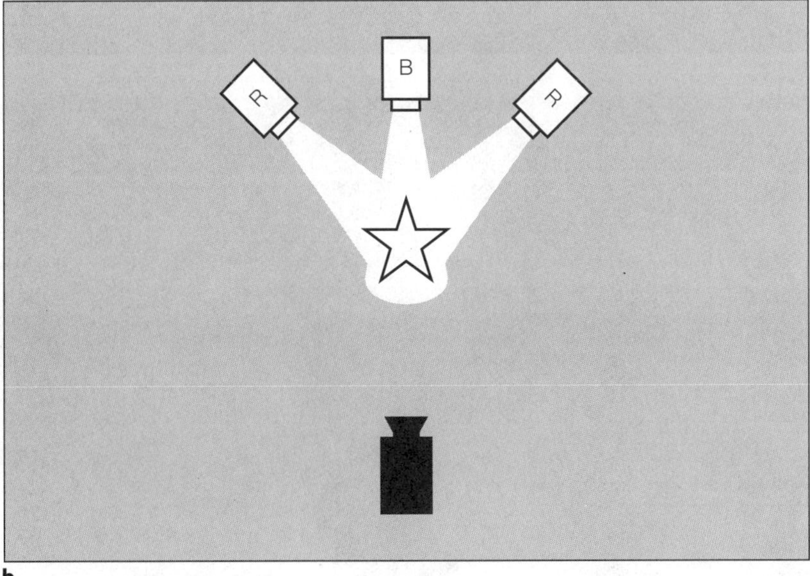

b

Figure 2.15a Back Lighting *Here the cinematographer has raked the mud with strong back light to emphasize the texture, creating the sensation of mud (*Frances, *Universal City Studios, 1982).*

Figure 2.15b Back Lighting Defined *The diagram shows how this book distinguishes between back light and rim light. If the rim in either of the three-quarter rear key positions were accompanied by a three-quarter front key, the rim would be labeled a "kicker."*

Figure 2.16 Rim and Back Light
Rim and back lights are generally from high elevations and are capable of a variety of effects, from the facial effects in (a), to the hair accent in (b), and the full-figure rim effect in (c), which is from 8 1/2 (Embassy Pictures, 1963).

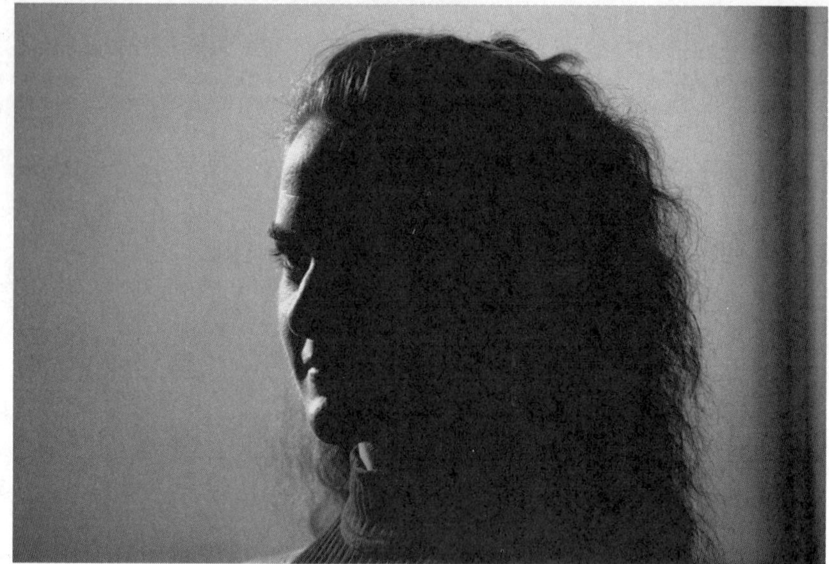

a

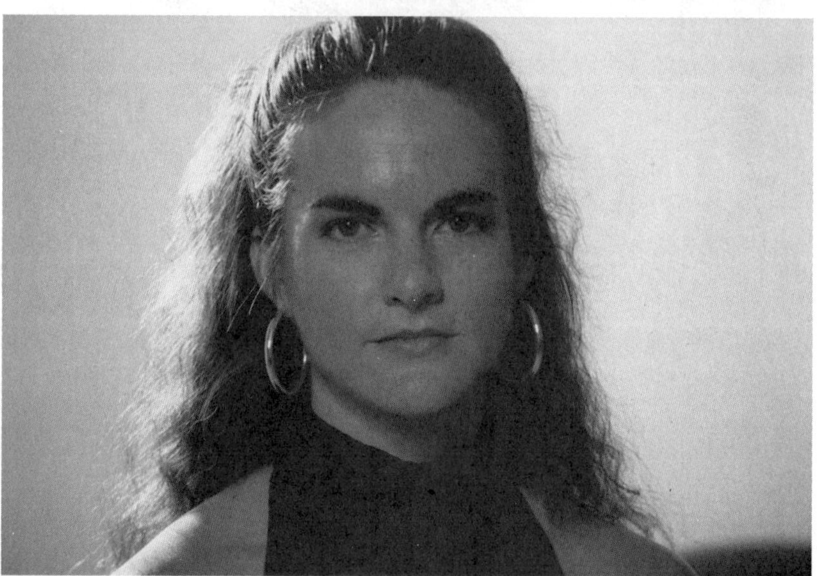

b

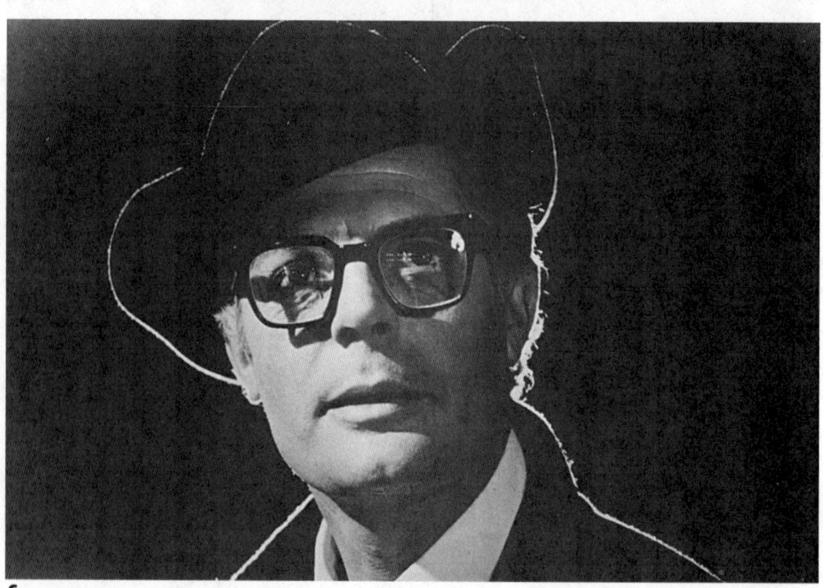

c

We shall use three terms to describe the different types of back lighting: *back light, rim light,* and *kicker light*. These are defined as follows.

Light coming from directly behind the subject and usually from above we shall term **back light**. Back light is used to highlight hair and separate the subject from the background. Angled light from the rear that "rims" or outlines all or part of the subject we shall call **rim light**. Rims are also used to create the highlights on hair and edges of cheeks to which we have become accustomed. Some authors use the term *kicker* for this light. Still others call it a back light, but we shall use the term **rim**, which emphasizes the effect and allows for more than one of these lights in a particular setup (see Figure 2.16).

Kicker shall be used in this book to stand for a particular type of rim light—light from a three-quarter rear position used in conjunction with a three-quarter front key (see Figure 2.18c). In the 1940s when the three-quarter front key was the favored key position, the "kick light" came from the three-quarter rear directly across the subject from the key.[3]

Kicker is also used to mean a light that selectively highlights a certain portion of the shot, say a bottle of perfume in a commercial. This type of kicker would not necessarily come from a rear position.

The distinctions used here derive from English photographer Walter Nurnberg, who developed a very precise system for analyzing lighting.[4] We use a simplified version of Nurnberg's system throughout this book to label and identify light placements. Because lighting terminology derives from a mixture of concepts and terms from physics, photography, theater, and film, it is not yet standardized and its vocabulary remains loose. You should also remember that terms vary from geographic region to geographic region as well as from country to country. For example, a "cross" light in England is a three-quarter front light, whereas in the United States it would be a "side" light.

The main functions of back, rim, and kicker lights are to create depth, to model the subject, and to separate the subject from the background. Referenced to keys, rim lights go best with three-quarter front and side keys; back lighting works best with frontal keys.

Rim and back lights are often used for window effects. For example, assume a sunny early morning interior with a subject sitting at a kitchen table. We can use a rim light from outside the window to create the effect of daylight streaming in. A side key is also usable for this effect.

Hard light sources are commonly used for rim and back lighting because they minimize the danger of lens flare and unwanted light spilling onto areas of the set. With rim and back light, it is often necessary to flag the lens as matte boxes and lens shades often aren't enough to prevent flare.

Exposure for Rim and Back Lights

Rim and back lights used for modeling effects do not affect exposure. Exposure is a function of key plus fill. You generally set key and fill,

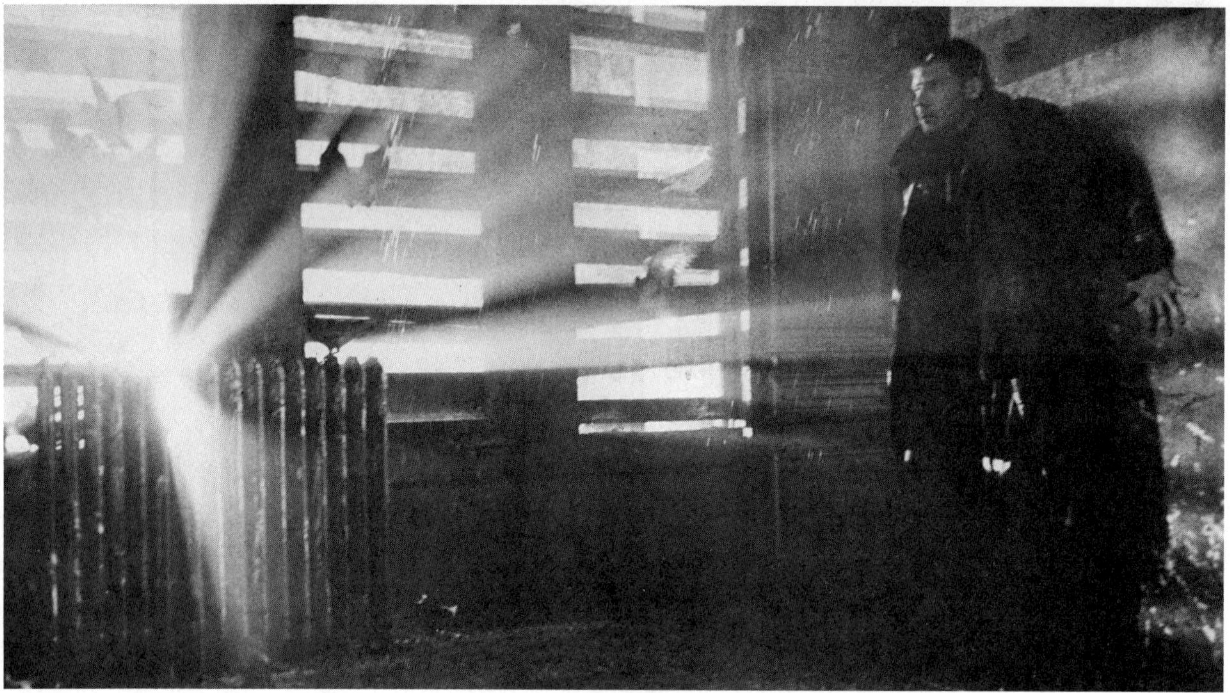

Figure 2.17 Smoke Used to Enhance a Back Light Effect (Blade Runner, *The Ladd Company, 1982)*

determine an exposure reading, and then position the rim light. When taking an exposure reading with the incident meter, you turn off the rim and back light or shield the meter from them.

Generally, rim and back lights are "hotter" (higher in intensity) than the key, from one to three stops brighter depending on the mood intended. For subtle modeling effects, rim and back lights will be set to the same intensity as the key. We need to know the intensity of the key in footcandles (fc) in order to set the intensity of the various back lights. For example, let's say the key is 100 fc and we desire to overexpose a rim or back light by two stops. We would set that rim or back light for 400 fc to accomplish this. This measurement can be determined simply: With the photodisk in place, point the meter directly at each light for its reading.

Not only are rim and back lights overexposed, they are often colored as well. A current technique is to overexpose the rims about two stops while using a bluish gel. This, coupled with warmer keys, is used to create night interior/exterior looks.

Atmospheric Effects

Back light is essential in order to show fog or smoke and is used to establish atmosphere in locations such as smoke-filled bars. Without quite a bit of back light, the effect would be invisible to the camera. Likewise, artificial smoke is put into the air so that a beam of light can be seen—a favorite effect in music videos that was developed earlier in feature films such as *Blade Runner* (see Figure 2.17). Back light also reveals rain and other translucent atmospheric effects—situations in which intentional underexposure may be desirable.

Three-Point Lighting Style

The triple combination of three-quarter front key, fill, and kicker (three-quarter rim) forms a **three-point lighting** style (see Figure 2.18). Based on the **Rembrandt effect** and its familiar triangle-shaped patch of light on the shadow side of the face, the three-point technique was the standard way to light actors in the classic Hollywood film style, as in Figure 2.5a and b, and is still common today, both for indoor and outdoor effects (see Figure 2.15a). Though perhaps overused, the technique offers a good starting point for face and figure lighting in cinematography.

BACKGROUND AND SET LIGHTING

Lighting is generally conceptualized in terms of subject, background, and foreground planes. Where actors are staged in depth we have more than one subject plane. When possible we light backgrounds and foregrounds separately from subject areas (see Figure 2.19a). Our choice of the principal plane determines the overall T-stop used. The other planes are lit at levels referenced to that T-stop. Standard practice is to illuminate backgrounds with the same source directionality as the key light, which preserves the illusion of reality (see Figure 2.19b).

Some cinematographers like to light the background first, creating interesting visual patterns there and then working up to subject areas.[5] Others begin with the subject and work their way to the background. In either case, while director and actors are rehearsing or shooting on one set, preliminary lighting (prelighting) can be set up on another.

Through the 1970s, cinematographers often applied an overall base-level fill light ("filler") to the set, which ensured that all objects within the frame would be at a minimum acceptable level. This technique is generally not used much today except in television, as the improved quality (greater straight lines) of current film emulsions allows for more shadow detail without our having to light for those shadow values.

Day interiors and night interiors are often shot on the same set but appear different because of how the backgrounds are lit, night being represented by darker levels than day. As a rule, backgrounds and foregrounds are kept roughly one stop darker than the subject (see Figure 2.20).

Backgrounds lit to levels about the same as the subject plane are a feature of high-key lighting. These backgrounds are generally light-toned and brightly colored as well (see Figure 2.21a). Low-key styles require differentiations greater than one stop between background or foreground and subject (see Figure 2.21b). This can be accomplished by set design as well as background lighting.

To create the illusion of reality and to avoid visual boredom, it is best not to light a background evenly. Instead, cinematographers strive to establish the tonal variations found in real-life situations. This is done by

Figure 2.18 The Rembrandt Effect *The three-point lighting style consists of a three-quarter front key (a), to which is added a fill (b) and a kicker (c). The term is also used to refer to any combination of key, fill, and back light.*

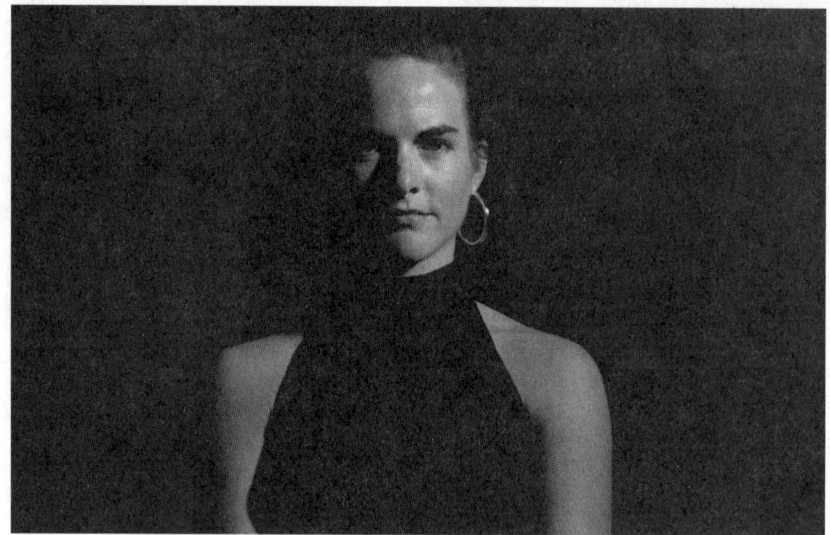

a

b

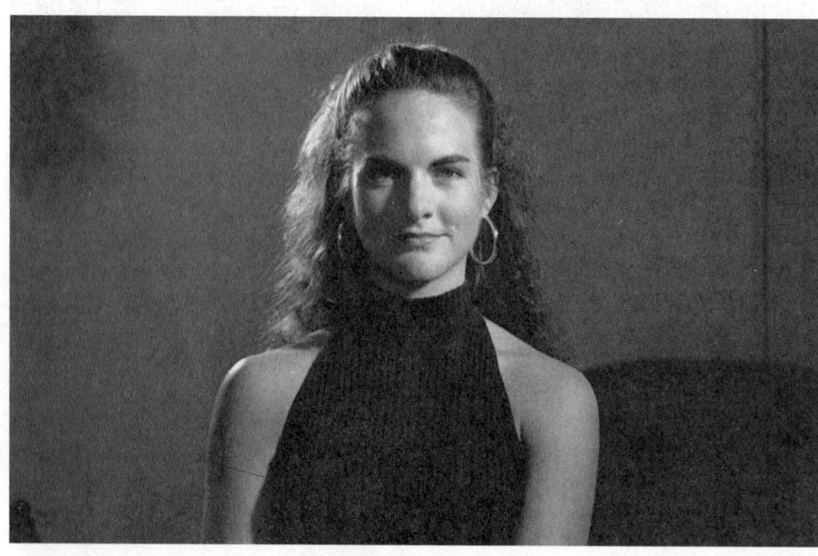

c

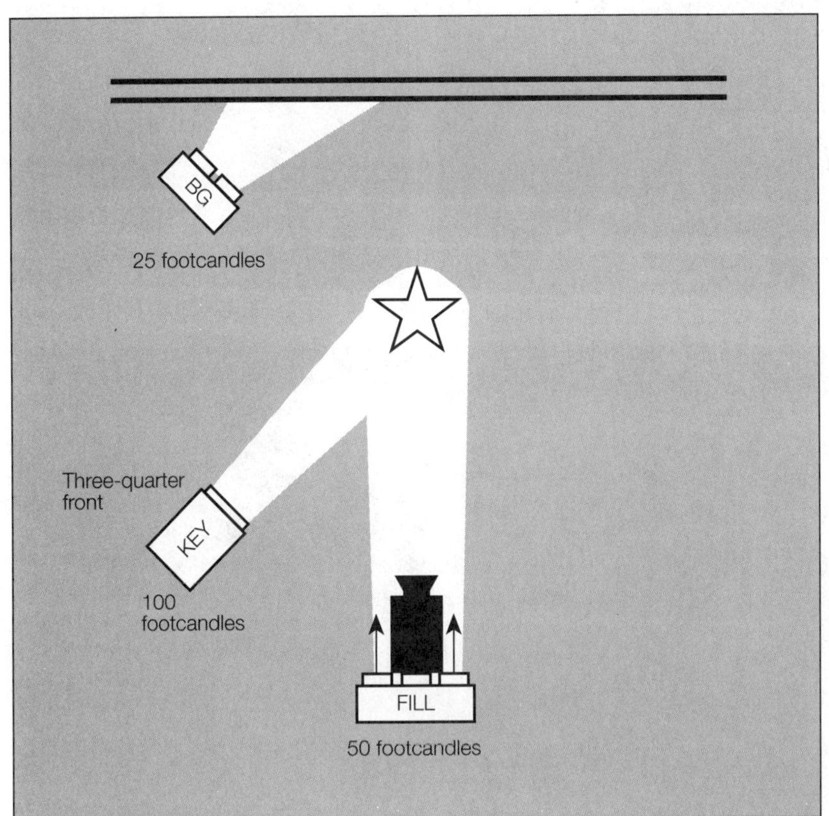

a

Figure 2.19a A Typical Background Light

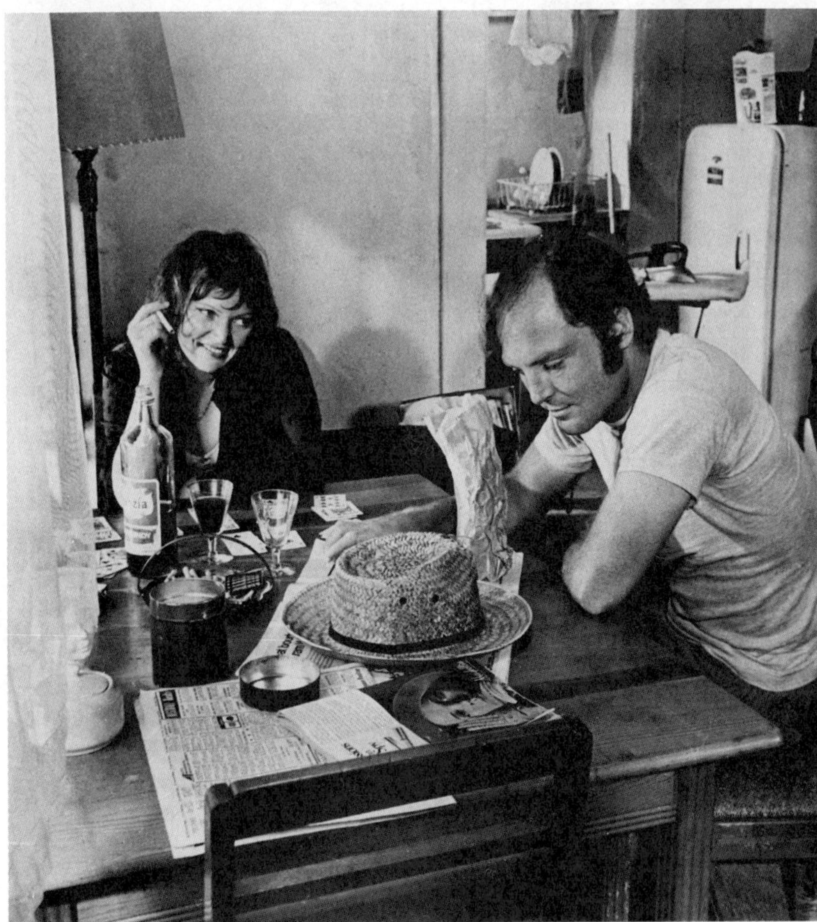

b

Figure 2.19b Background Lighting *The kitchen in the background appears to be lit with a source coming from the same direction as the foreground light on the actors at the table* (Fat City, *Columbia Pictures, 1972).*

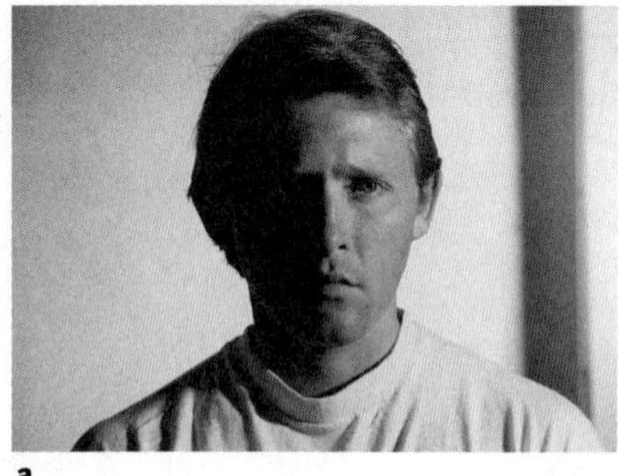

a

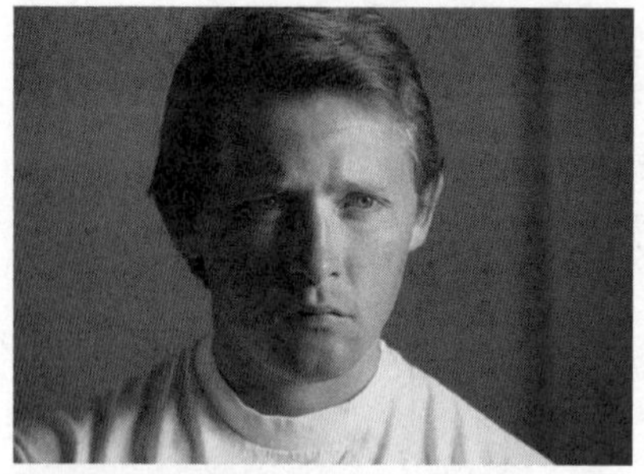

b

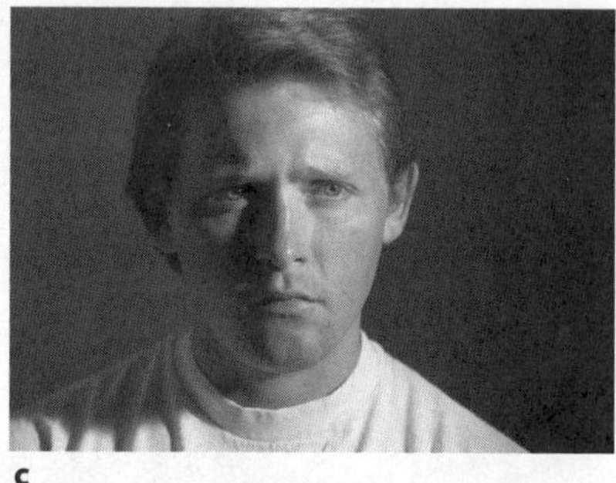

c

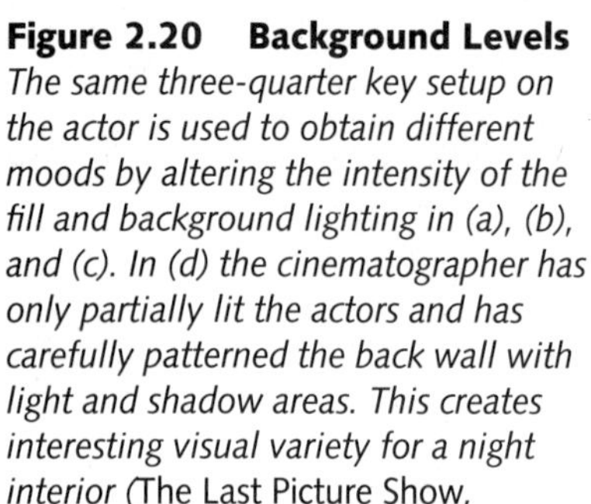

Figure 2.20 Background Levels *The same three-quarter key setup on the actor is used to obtain different moods by altering the intensity of the fill and background lighting in (a), (b), and (c). In (d) the cinematographer has only partially lit the actors and has carefully patterned the back wall with light and shadow areas. This creates interesting visual variety for a night interior (*The Last Picture Show*, Columbia Pictures, 1973).*

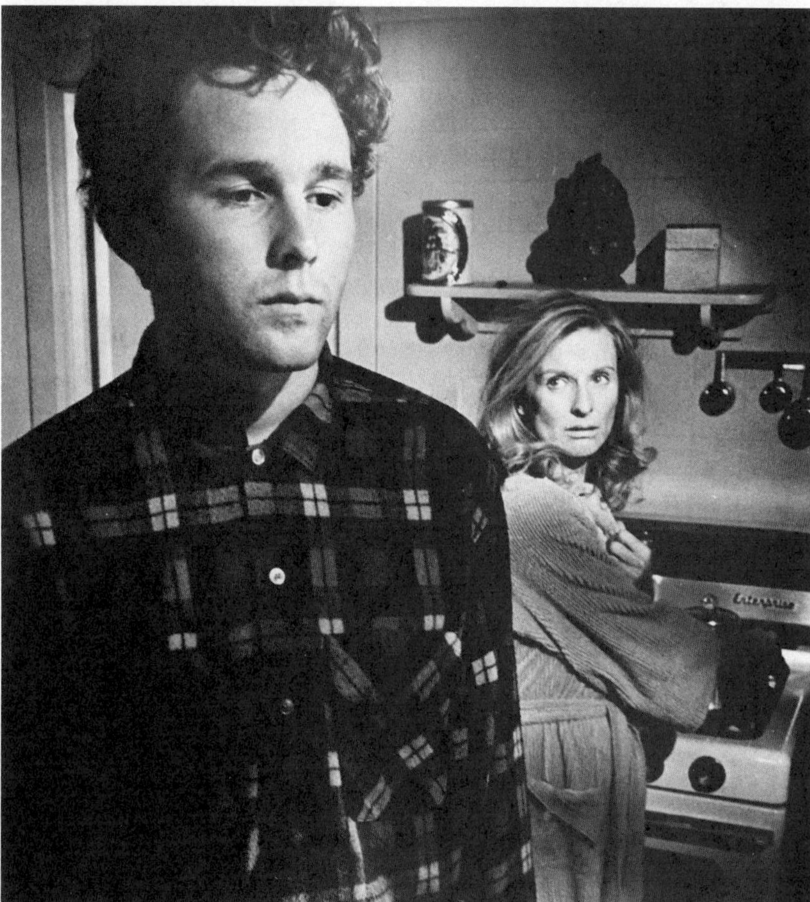

d

flagging (cutting out light), scrimming (cutting back on intensity), and utilizing natural light fall-off (see Figures 2.20d and 2.22).

It is sometimes useful to add background or foreground accents for compositional reasons. For example, we might light a selected portion of the background so as to create a visual balance within the frame (see Figure 2.23).

In TV commercials and music videos, backgrounds are sometimes kept intentionally nondescript, putting the subject in a visual limbo. The background is made just one color, without shadow or depth, so that the image space becomes flat and indefinite. This is particularly effective with product commercials, where the goal is to get the audience to watch only the product and not the background.

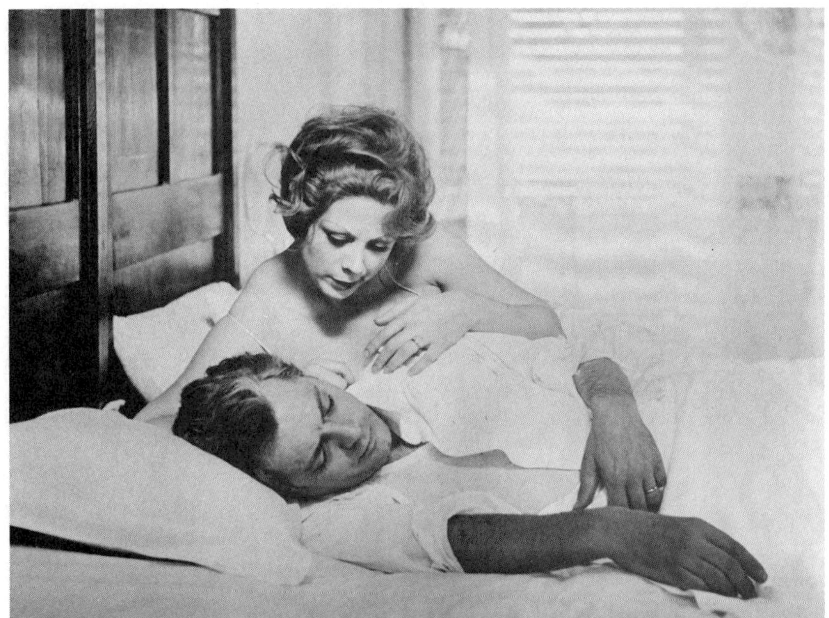

a

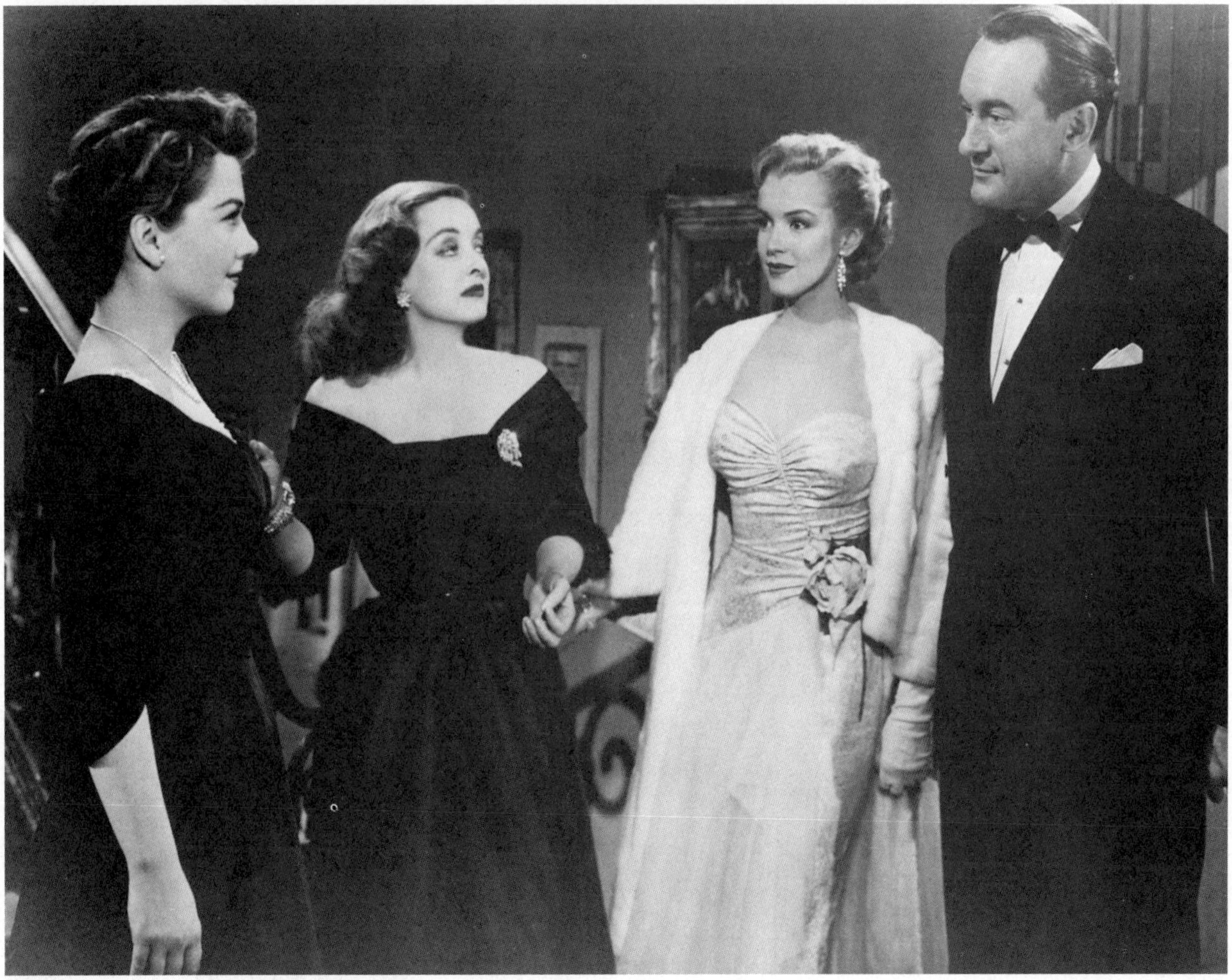

Figure 2.21 High-Key and Low-Key Backgrounds *A high-key effect is created by the cinematographer in (a) through use of the window, blinds, and curtain effect as background (*8 1/2*, Embassy Pictures, 1963). By ensuring the window brightness, we know it is day. In (b) the darkness of the background reinforces the night interior effect (*All About Eve*, Twentieth Century Fox, 1950).*

b

Figure 2.22 Background Lighting Used to Create Visual Variety *In (a) the cinematographer has lit a glow on the wall behind the subject and allowed the light to fall off unevenly to dark gray at the edge of frame (Paramount Pictures publicity photo of Marlene Dietrich). In (b) the background has been divided into a black and white field that functions to separate the two characters and create an interesting pattern of light and shadow (*The Third Man*, Twentieth Century Fox, 1949).*

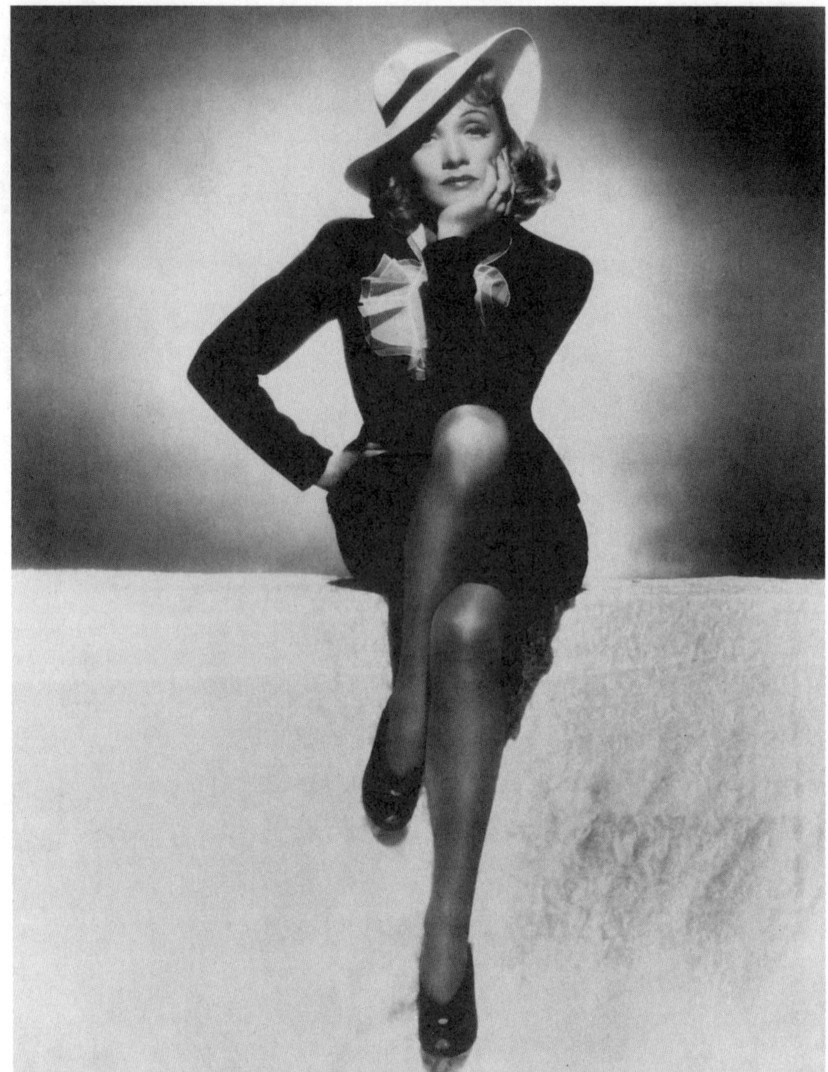

a

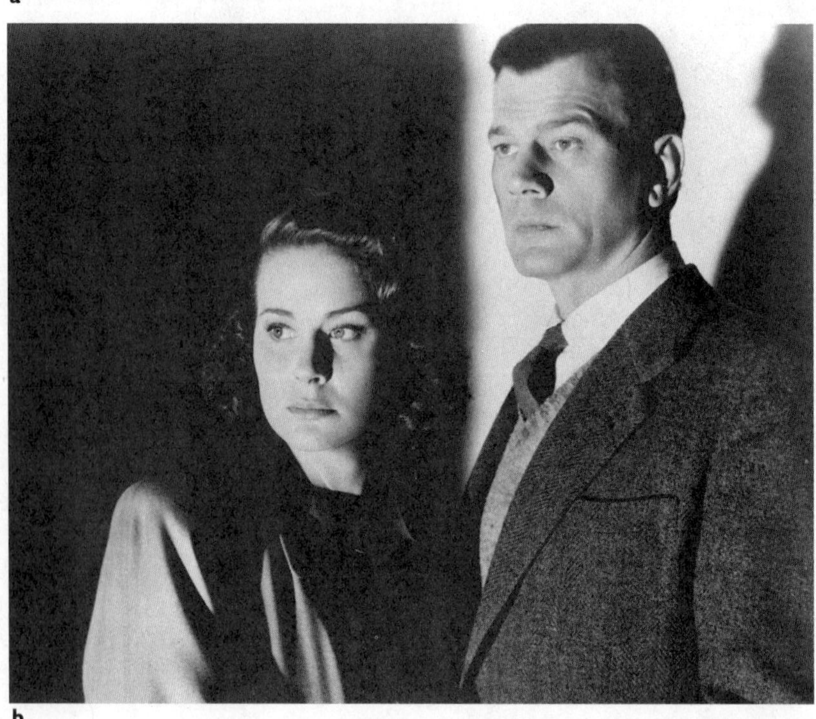

b

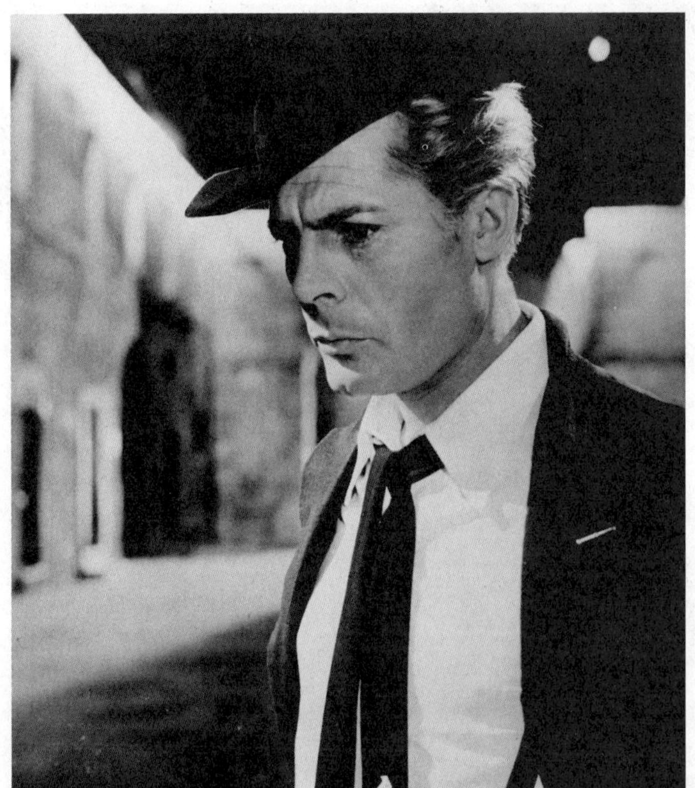

a

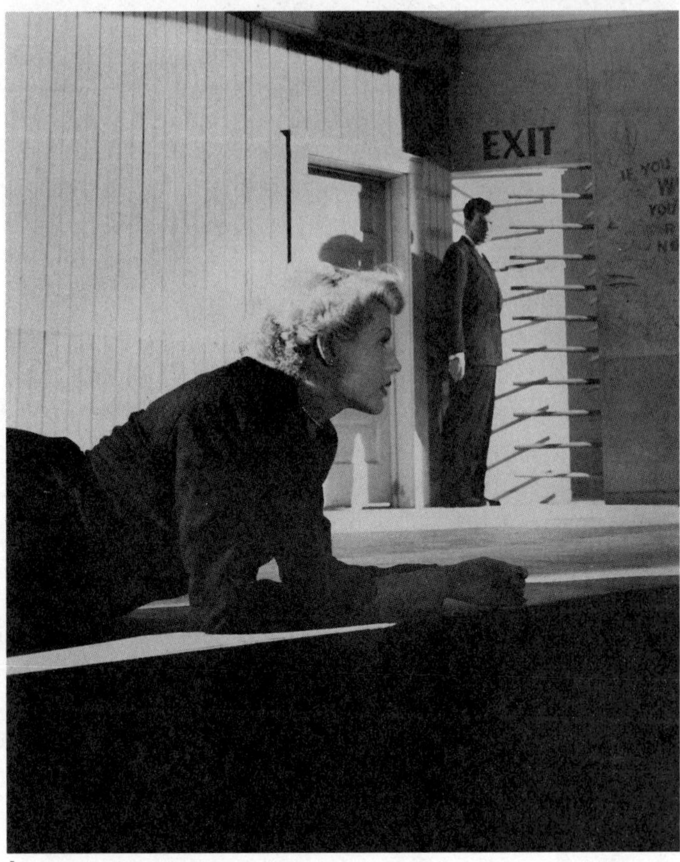

b

Figure 2.23 Background Light Used to Create Compositional Balance *Note how in (a) the lighting of the building and piazza pavement has been composed so as to create diagonals frame left that lead our eyes to the face (*8 1/2, *Embassy Pictures, 1963). Much the same effect is present in (b) as the actors are balanced vertically between the black foreground and the white background (*The Lady from Shanghai, *Columbia Pictures, 1947).*

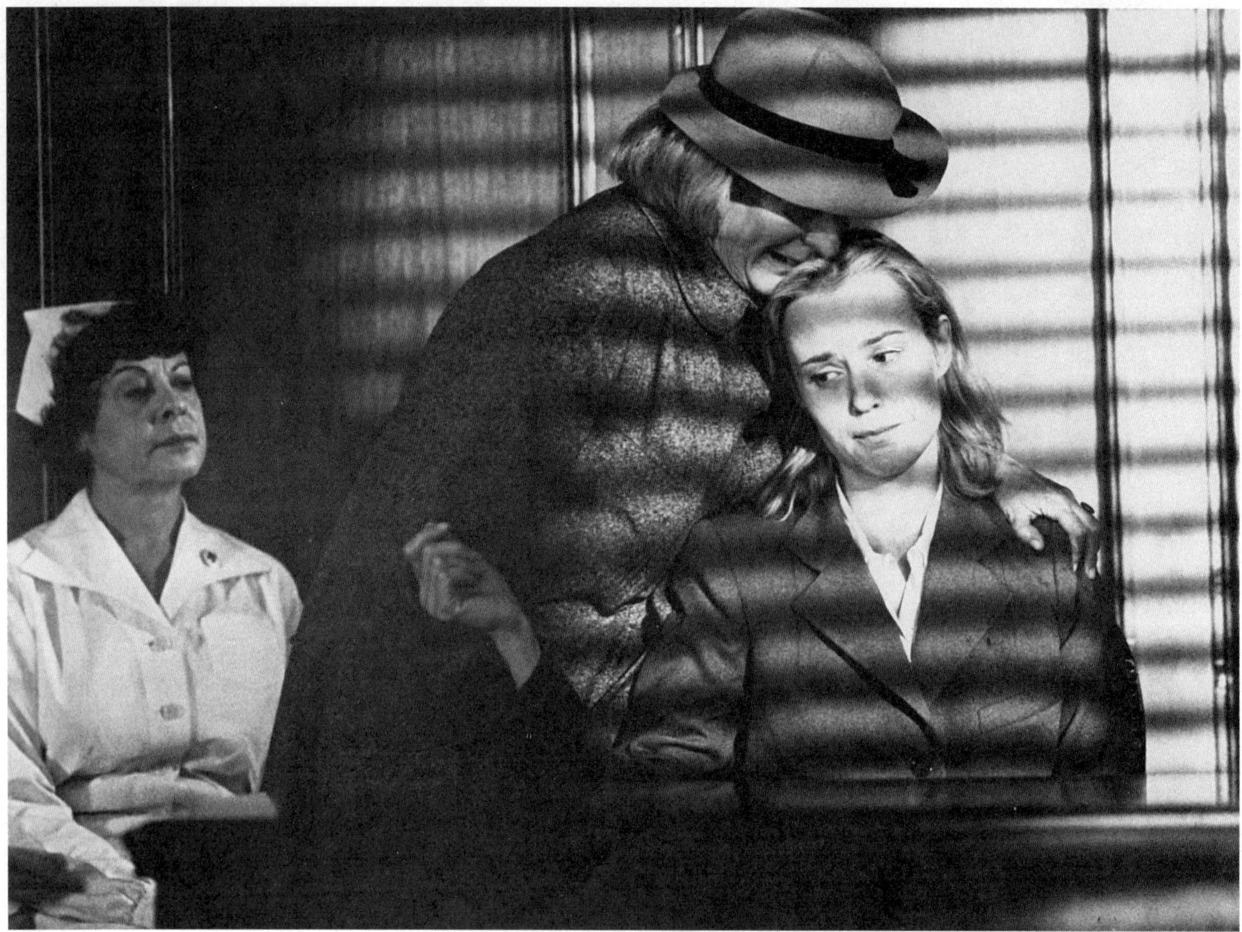

Figure 2.24 Venetian-Blind Shadow Projected on Background
The shadow pattern is also used effectively on the actors in this example (Frances, *Universal City Studios, 1982).*

By using separate lighting for subjects and backgrounds, we are able to avoid shadow problems on the background. In small, documentary-style, TV news situations, wall shadows are often a problem because the key light illuminates the background as well as the subject. There is no aesthetic advantage to using the same light for both subject and background, just less expense and faster setups.

In the classic B & W style of lighting, it was very popular to project shadows onto background walls. Think of the horror films with their shadow of the monster appearing on the wall; or the film noir style where the venetian blinds are shadowed on the background. This effect is also common in "color noir" films such as *The Two Jakes, Blade Runner,* and *Body Heat.* In general, background projections are associated with stylized lighting such as noir.

To create a shadow on a background, we can place a **cucaloris** ("cookie") between the wall and the set light or we can use a **shadow projection device**. The latter is a special spotlight designed to project a variety of patterns onto walls (see Figure 2.24).

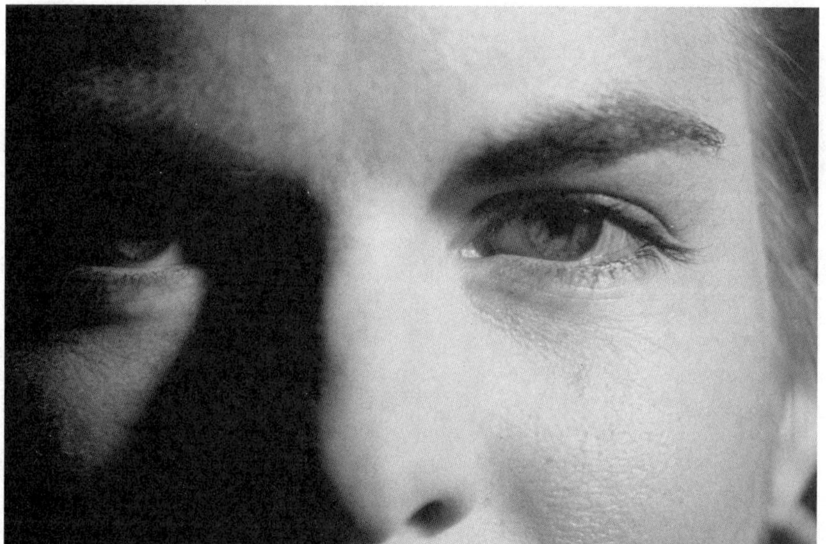

a

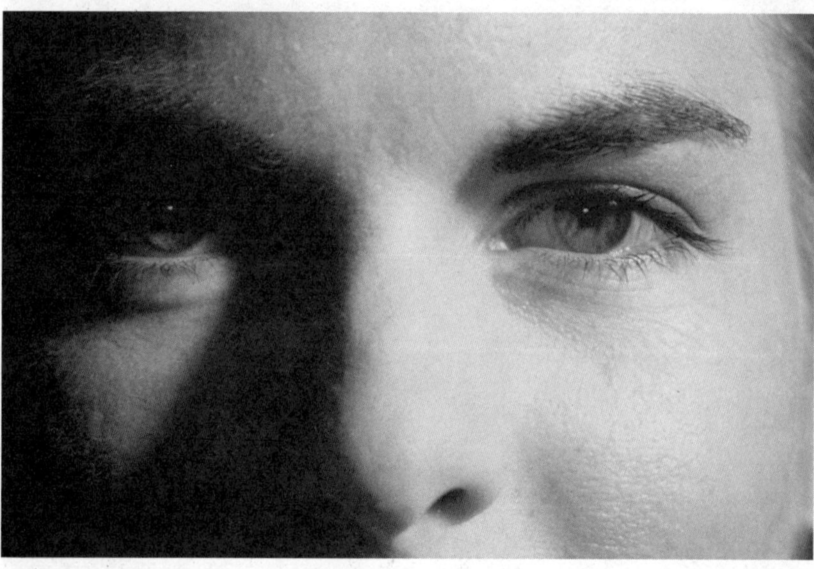

b

Figure 2.25 Eyelights *The small eyelights coming from the fill light in (b) bring the actor's eyes alive in comparison to (a), which lacks an eyelight.*

SPECIALIZED LIGHT PLACEMENTS

Once we have completed lighting the subject and set, we sometimes need to fine-tune our lighting setup. To do this we use a variety of specialized lights.

Eyelights

The **eyelight** is a very important light. It is used not to illuminate in the exposure sense but to create a reflection and give a sense of aliveness to the eyes (see Figure 2.25). Eyelights are also used for special effects. For example, eyelights with odd shapes or colors are used to create a feeling of strangeness or an alien nature—a technique used in the film *Cat People*.

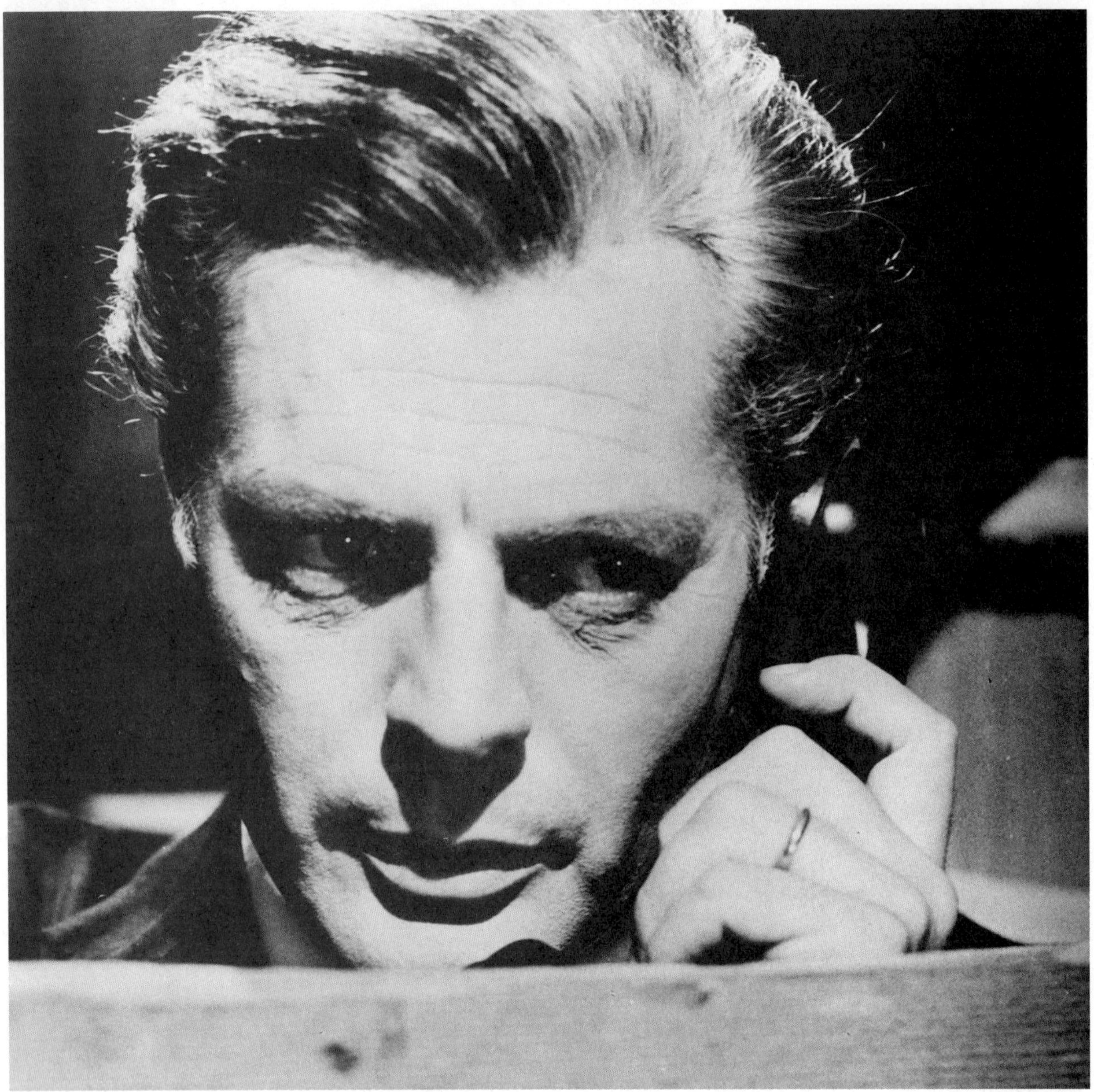

c

Figure 2.25 (continued) *The eyelight in (c) gives a very interesting look to the eyes (8 1/2, Embassy Pictures, 1963). Without this eyelight, the eyes would have been lost in pools of shadow. Many of the photos in this book have interesting eyelights. See, for example, Figure 1.1b, c, d, and Figure 1.7.*

Eyelights are easy to arrange. A fill light positioned on the camera/subject axis will simultaneously function as an eyelight. Where there is no such fill, we can mount a small light above the camera, as with a roving fill light. Wherever the camera is pointed, there is a light that reflects in the eye. Another technique is to use a hand-held light close to the subject on the camera/subject axis. During the shot it can be moved as necessary. The eyelight does not have to illuminate the subject, just reflect off the eyes. Eyelights are generally of low intensity; any open filament bulb will suffice. Some cinematographers even use flashlights to create eyelights.

Set lights can cause multiple reflections in the eyes. Usually more than two is disturbing, unrealistic, and undesirable. A good rule of thumb when lighting actors is to check the eyes, both for the deadness caused by a lack of eyelight and for the opposite problem of too many reflections.

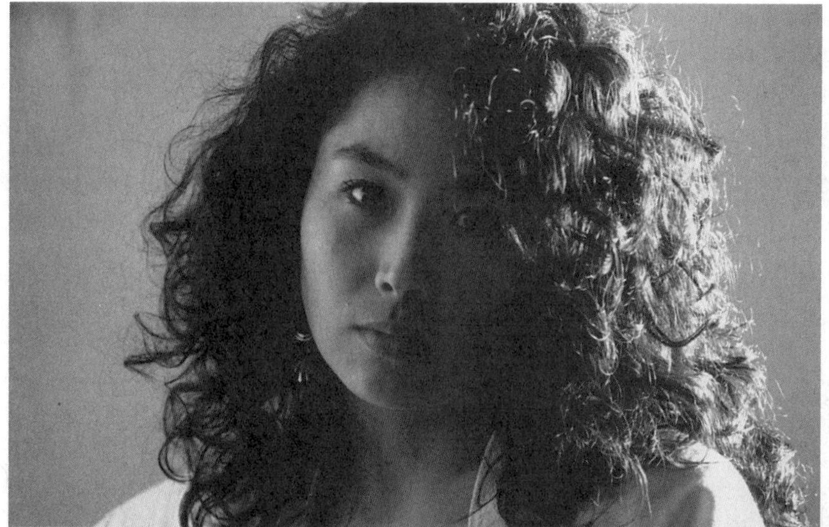

a

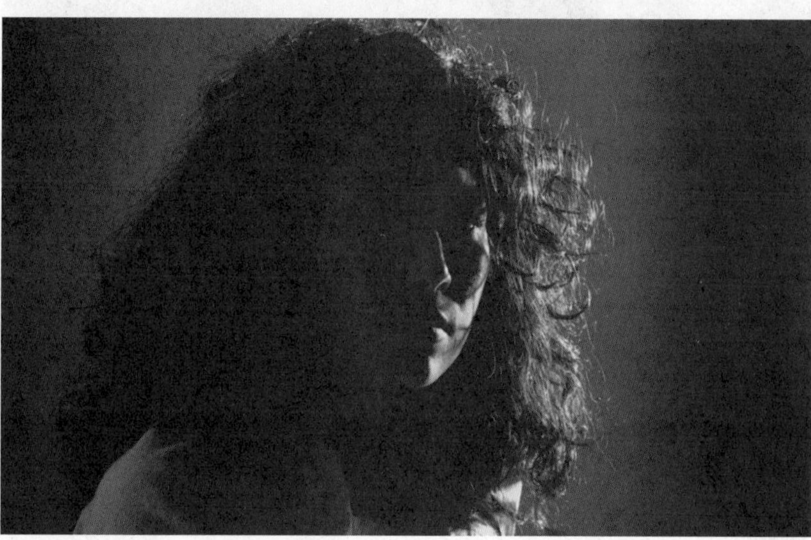

b

Figure 2.26 Hair Lights *Both hairlights in (a) and (b) are from the side. Note the different moods created by the amount of darkness in the facial shadows. See also the examples in Figure 2.10.*

Hair Lights

In shampoo commercials and glamour cinematography, hair light plays an important role. There are several types of **hair lights**: from directly overhead (see Figure 2.25c), from more oblique angles that can be used for dramatic effects (see Figure 2.26), and from behind the subject giving a kind of halo effect (see Figure 2.10).

Other Specialized Placements

It is often necessary to light a specific object such as an iron railing or a leafy fern or a significant prop. These objects often provide compositional balance or require thematic emphasis. Details like this add to the image's sophistication. Object lights are common in product commercials where they are applied to food, beverages, and other products to be sold. Sometimes the objects can be lit by lights present in the shot (**practicals**), such as a table lamp or a candle.

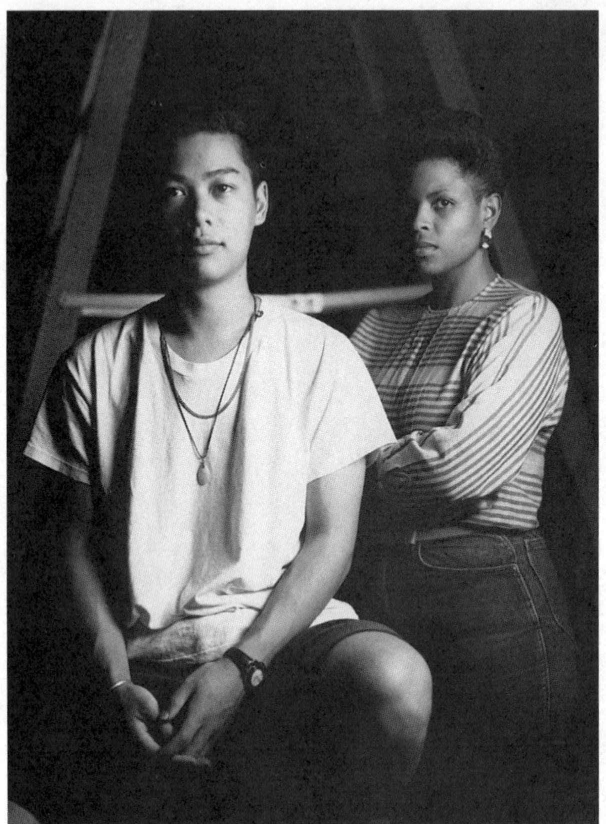

a

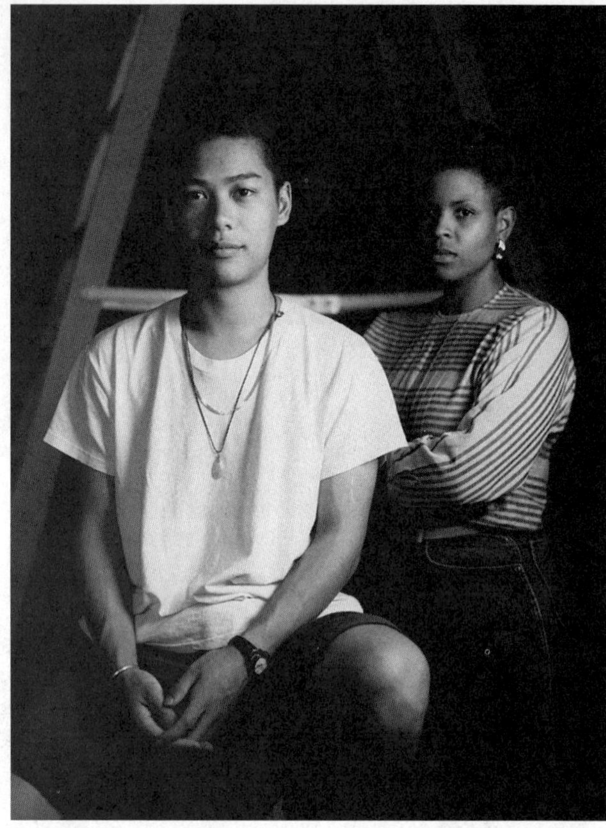

b

Figure 2.27 Basic Lighting Scheme Using Four Lights
Building a lighting scheme using (a) key only, (b) key and fill, (c) key, fill, and hair light, and (d) key, fill, hair, and background light.

Clothing is often isolated from the key/fill applied to the face and given its own treatment with a clothes light. Many times side lighting is used to emphasize texture.

SUMMARY

We have identified five basic light placements in this chapter: key, fill, rim/back, background/set, and a variety of specialized lights. These five lighting concepts provide the cinematographer a starting point for establishing a lighting scheme (see Figure 2.27).[6]

It must be emphasized that the concepts presented in this chapter do not depend on the use of artificial light sources. Many of the effects described can be accomplished with the selective use of available light. In the final analysis, lighting is a series of visual choices, not the automatic turning on of light units.

NOTES

1. Advocacy of this position for the fill light seems to derive from television lighting texts. I can find no film lighting book that recommends this fill placement. The notion of a 45-degree fill probably derives from earlier theater techniques and found its way into film around 1912 with Vitagraph Studio films (see Barry Salt, *Film Style and Technology: History and Analysis*

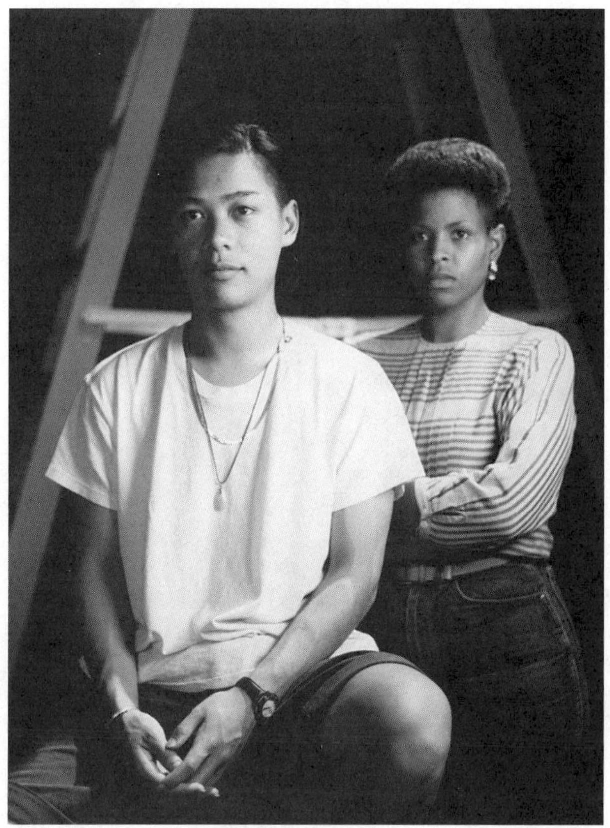

c

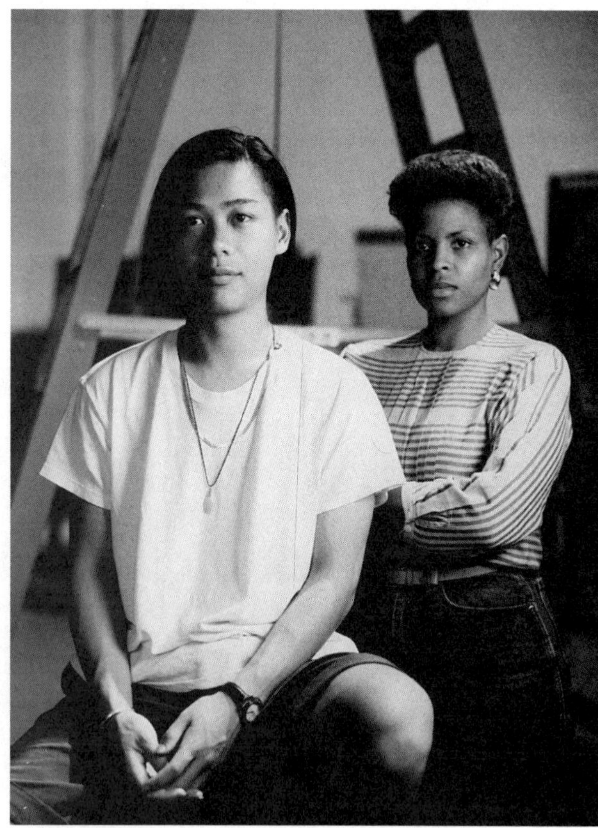

d

[London: Starword, 1983], pp. 98, 139, 141). In a personal correspondence, Warren Bass pointed out that "double 45-degree lighting was codified into classic lighting theory [for theater] by Stanley McCandless in the 1930s." Bass noted that since early television lighting designers tended to come from theater and not film, the position became institutionalized in television—hence the use of a 45-degree fill position in television texts.

2. See Kris Malkiewicz, assisted by Barbara J. Gryboski, *Film Lighting* (New York: Prentice-Hall, 1986), pp. 118–19.

3. See Charles G. Clarke, *Professional Cinematography*, 2nd ed. (Hollywood: American Society of Cinematographers, 1968), pp. 97, 104, 106.

4. See Walter Nurnberg, *Lighting for Photography*, 16th rev. ed. (Philadelphia: Chilton, 1968), and *Lighting for Portraiture*, 7th ed. (Philadelphia: Chilton, 1969).

5. See Charles G. Clarke, *Professional Cinematography*, pp. 101–2.

6. Lighting as we know it developed in Hollywood throughout the studio era. Cinematographers used an Eight Light Technique (sometimes seven depending on who was doing the counting). Charles G. Clarke lists the seven basic lights he utilized as: key, fill, back, set, kick, eye, and clothes light. This system amounts to the triangle technique of key, fill, and back/kick with the addition of set and supplemental lights. (See Charles G. Clarke, *Professional Cinematography*, pp. 97–109.)

John Alton lists the following eight lights as the Hollywood style: fill light, keylight, filler light (this is the additional eighth light—overall set illumination), clothes light, back light, kicker light, eyelight, and background light. (See John Alton, *Painting with Light* [New York: Macmillan, 1949], p. 99.)

FUNDAMENTALS OF EXPOSURE

II

The proper use of light can embellish and dramatize every object—and that carries us into the province of the artist. . . . We cannot see without light, and we cannot photograph without it. Therefore the knowledge of what light means and how it affects what it strikes is the first step in the direction of what photography means.

—*Josef von Sternberg*
Fun in a Chinese Laundry

BASIC EXPOSURE CONCEPTS

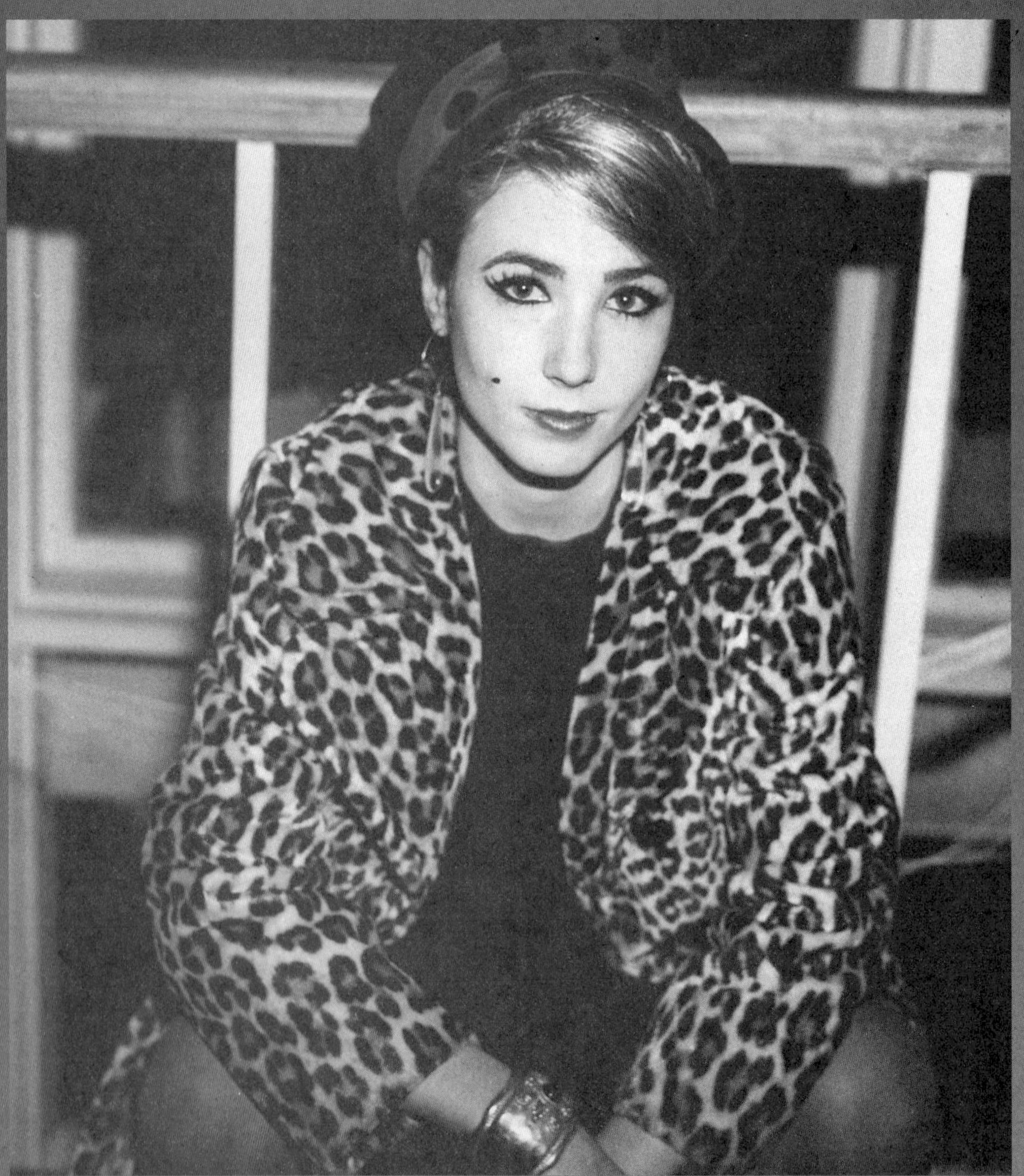

Photo by Robin Hood Dial II *"subject luminance range"*

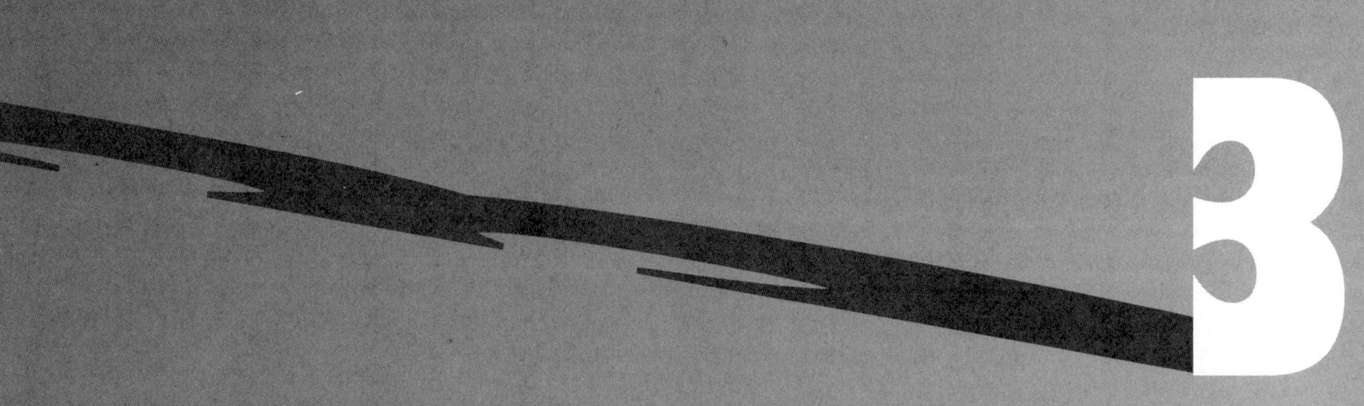

3

Exposure is an important technical basis for the art of lighting. The cinematographer must understand concepts such as reflectance, luminance value, and the relationship between the two. Above all the cinematographer must be able to control subject luminance range as this is fundamental to both exposure and lighting.

LIGHTING AND exposure techniques are inseparable and interdependent. As we shall see, **lighting** is the creation of a *subject luminance range*. **Exposure** is the placing of that range onto the characteristic curve of the negative in a controlled manner. In more technical terms, exposure is the scientific way to relate *log E values* (subject luminance range) to negative density values and, ultimately, print values. This will be made clear in Chapter 5.[1]

For many cinematographers, exposure is as creative as lighting. To master exposure technique and to control the look of images requires a knowledge of light and an awareness of the subject's visual properties. Chapters 3 through 6 provide a basic vocabulary for discussing the relationship between subject luminance values and screen values. Incident and reflected light meters are standardized to certain exposure assumptions. These are made explicit and integrated into an overall exposure theory in Chapter 6. Chapter 7 examines certain common, recurring exposure situations.

INCIDENT AND REFLECTED LIGHT

Incident light is the light that illuminates objects. It may come directly from a light source—the sun, the sky, or a light bulb—or it may be reflected onto an object from other objects. For example, the moon reflects light to the earth; a white wall reflects light around a room.

Incident light meters measure the intensity of incident light in units called **footcandles**. An important point: Since the incident meter measures the intensity of the light falling onto the scene, it is unaffected by the actual content of the scene—that is, whether the scene is high or low contrast, or contains lots of whites or blacks or grays.

Objects can absorb, transmit, or reflect incident light. **Reflected light** allows us to perceive objects as well as photograph them. The light reflected by an object is measured by a reflected light meter in units called **footlamberts**.[2]

Figure 3.1 Specular and Diffuse Reflection

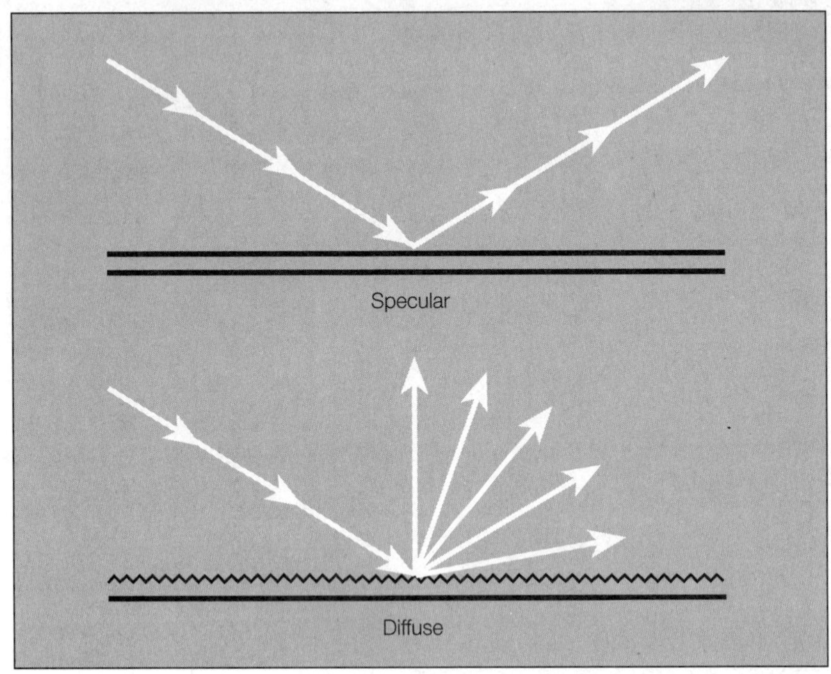

The surface texture of an object determines the way it will reflect light. Most objects have textured surfaces and scatter the light falling on them in various directions. This is called diffuse reflection and is the most common type of reflection (see Figure 3.1). Smooth, shiny objects such as mirrors, metals, and liquids are specular reflectors. They reflect light in only a single direction. When they reflect the image of the light source itself, we call it a "hot spot" as it often distracts from the lighting on our main subject. Since most objects absorb some of the light falling onto them, reflected light is less than incident light except for instances of specular reflection as with a mirror. Many objects exhibit a mixture of both types of reflection.

REFLECTANCE (REFLECTION FACTOR)

Most objects reflect only a percentage of the light falling onto them. This property of the object is termed its **diffuse reflectance** or **reflection factor**. The reflection factor is the ratio of reflected light to incident light and is expressed as a percentage.

For example, a white object reflects most of the light falling onto it, 90% or more, and is said to have a high reflection factor. A black object absorbs most of the incident light and reflects small amounts; consequently it has a low reflection factor, around 2%–4%. If we shine 100 footcandles of light onto white chalk, it reflects 96% of the footcandles, expressed as 96 footlamberts. Similarly, black velvet reflects 2%, or 2 footlamberts.

The typical range of diffuse reflectances commonly found in a group of objects with whites and blacks is about 96% to 2%, usually expressed as the ratio 48:1. (See Table 3.1.) Photographic pioneers Hurter and Driffield found that the average of all diffuse reflectances in nature is about 18%, a calculation of importance to exposure theory as will be explained shortly.

LUMINANCE

Reflected and incident light are related as follows: footlamberts = footcandles x reflectance (%). **Luminance** refers to the actual quantitative measurement in footlamberts. Thus, a white surface with a reflection factor of 96% subjected to 100 footcandles of incident light will, by definition, reflect 96 footlamberts to the camera. Under this lighting setup, the white surface is said to have a luminance value of 96 footlamberts. Likewise, if 100 footcandles of light are incident upon a Caucasian face (reflection factor 36%), then that face will have a luminance value of 36 footlamberts.

The term *luminance* was adopted by photographers to replace the older term *brightness*. The reason is that brightness is relative to context whereas luminance is an objective, quantitative measurement. A reflected light meter can measure the range of luminances in the subject. This range is called *subject luminance range* (overall luminance range) or sometimes *brightness range*.

Material	Reflection factor
White chalk	**96%**
Off-whites	**80%**
Light grays	**70%**
Caucasian face	**36%**
Midgray	**18%**
Brown face	**16%**
Green leaves	**14%**
Black face	**10%**
Black velvet	**2%**

Table 3.1 Typical Reflection Factors (Diffuse Reflectances)

THE RELATIONSHIP BETWEEN REFLECTANCE AND LUMINANCE

Reflectance and luminance are to be sharply distinguished. Reflectance is a consistent property of the object. Midgray is always an 18% reflectance, no matter what the lighting. An object's actual luminance value, however, will vary with the illumination as follows:

- *Intensity of the illumination*. The stronger the lighting in footcandles, the higher the luminance value in footlamberts.
- *Light source directionality*. For a given light source, frontal illumination provides the highest luminance values.

As an example, take a Caucasian face (reflection factor = 36%) lit with 100 footcandles at an angle. Only the lit side of the face will reflect 36 footlamberts. The shadow side of the face will have a lower luminance value, say 2.25 footlamberts. But note that both lit and shadow side have the same reflectance, 36% (see Figure 3.2). Another way to describe this lighting situation is to say that the two sides of the subject's face have a luminance range of 16:1 (36 divided by 2.25); that is, the lit side is 16 times brighter than the shadow side.

An additional example may make this clearer. Assume a white cube with 96% reflectance is lit at an angle so that side A is in the light while side B is in the shadow. Assume the light source measures 100 footcan-

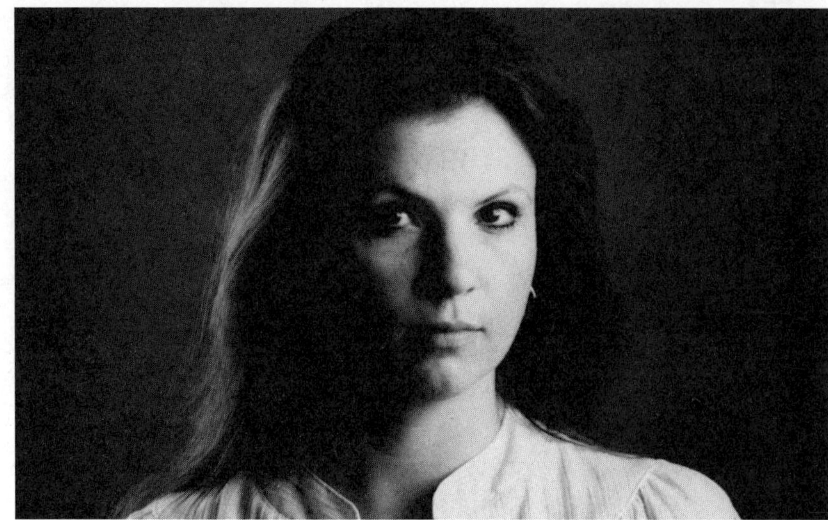

Figure 3.2 The Relationship Between Reflectance and Luminance Referenced to a Face *Both sides of this Caucasian face are the same 36% reflectance, but their luminance value differs greatly due to the lighting, which leaves a dark shadow on the frame-left side of the subject.*

dles at the surface of the cube with the incident meter pointed toward the camera. Side A will have a luminance of 96 footlamberts since it reflects 96% of the light falling onto it (see Figure 3.3).

But what about side B in the shadow? It still has a 96% reflectance but obviously reflects less light to the eye than side A. Side B is illuminated only by bounce light—light reflected onto it by, and from, its surroundings. If we assume the luminance value for side B is 12 footlamberts, we set up the following ratio:

$$\frac{\text{side A} = 96 \text{ footlamberts}}{\text{side B} = 12 \text{ footlamberts}} = \text{an 8:1 ratio}$$

Side B has the same reflectance as side A but provides a lower luminance value. We say the cube, as lit, sends off luminances from its two sides with an 8:1 ratio.

SUBJECT LUMINANCE RANGE

The typical range of natural reflectances, from white chalk to black velvet, is 48:1, but luminance ranges are usually higher than that figure due to the effects of source directionality. As with the white cube example in Figure 3.3, any angle to the illumination automatically results in a secondary, shadow range of luminances. This shadow range still has a 48:1 range, but it is at a different intensity level than the lit side. The **overall luminance range** of the subject thus commonly extends to 500:1 or more (see Figure 3.4).

For each distinct angle of light-incidence, there is a corresponding luminance range. These luminance ranges overlap and intermesh to create the total overall luminance range, the **subject luminance range**, which is the ratio of highest significant luminance to lowest. For example, imagine a sunny-day exterior scene with a deep forest on the left

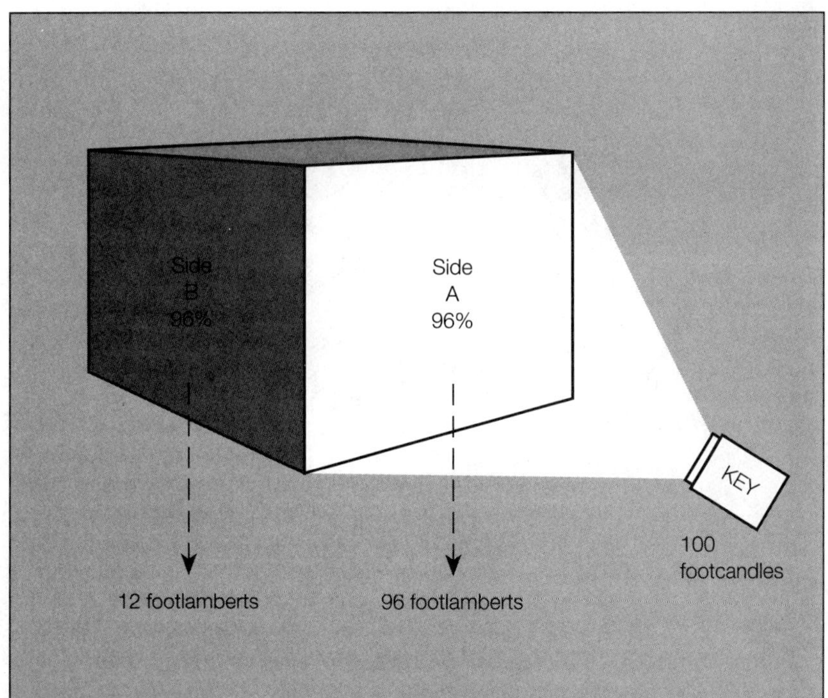

Figure 3.3 Luminance Range Created by Angled Lighting on a White Cube

and a meadow on the right. Other than sunlit areas there are shadows and degrees of shadows, depending on how much reflected sky-light reaches them—which would be very little in the forest.

The ratio of the highest luminance in the sunlit meadow to the lowest luminance in the shadow of the dark forest would determine the subject luminance range. If we were to measure these luminances, we might find that a white sunlit object measures 10,000 footlamberts whereas a black object in the shadows measures 5 footlamberts. The result is a ratio of 2000:1 (about 11 T-stops). This extreme subject luminance range is caused by wide variations in illumination levels.

Another example would be the interior of a room with daylight pouring through a window onto a white cat. An electric light is on in one shadowy corner. A black cat lies half hidden under a coat in the darkest part of the room. The white cat might measure around 4000 footlamberts and the black cat around 4 footlamberts, a total luminance range of 1000:1.

According to Hollywood cinematographer Joseph Mascelli, normal subject luminance ranges outdoors go from 30:1 to 800:1 with 160:1 a good average. A flat foggy scene may be only 10:1. A sunny, harsh contrast subject may reach 1000:1. Many cinematographers keep the overall luminance range—ratio of brightest significant object to darkest significant object—at 256:1 (eight stops) for Eastman Color Negative. When filming for color TV release, this ratio is reduced to 50:1, and even 30:1 when using a television camera. According to light meter inventor J. F. Dunn, the assumed average subject luminance range is 128:1. When the effect of lens and camera flare are taken into account, the ratio is reduced to the range of 64:1 or 32:1.[3]

Figure 3.4 Subject Luminance Range *Where a subject already has a luminance range from white to black of 48:1 as in (a), the addition of light from an angle will create a second, shadow-side range of 48:1 (b). The ratio between the luminance values of the white strip on the lit side of the cube and the dark strip on the shadow side constitutes the subject luminance range, in this case about 96:1. The white strip lit by 100 footcandles reflects 96 footlamberts. The black strip lit by 50 footcandles of ambient bounced light reflects 1 footlambert (50 fc x .02 = 1 footlambert). This gives us a ratio of 96:1.*

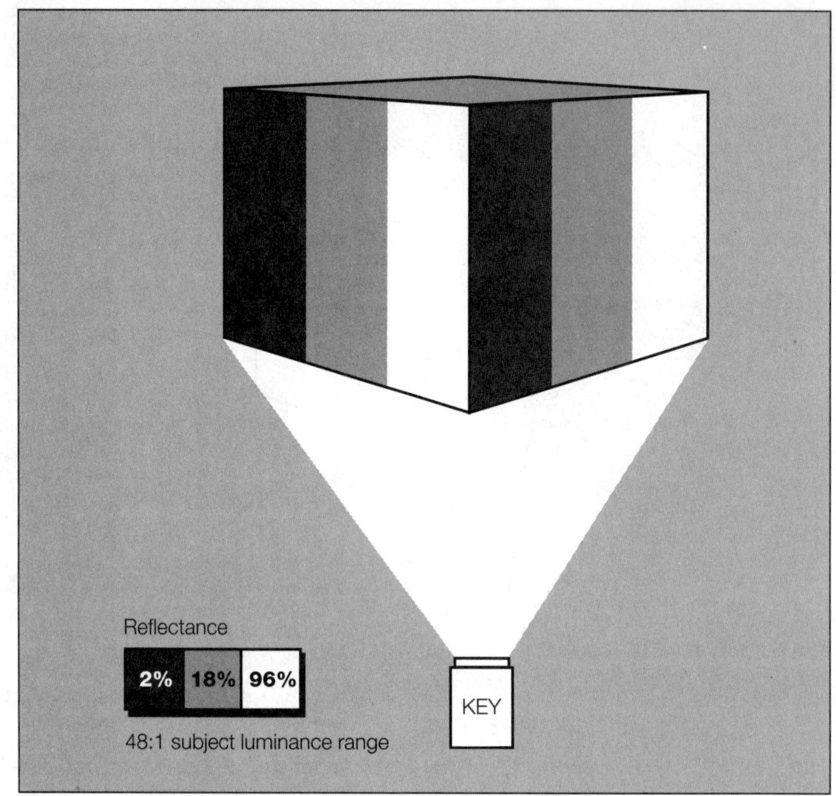

a

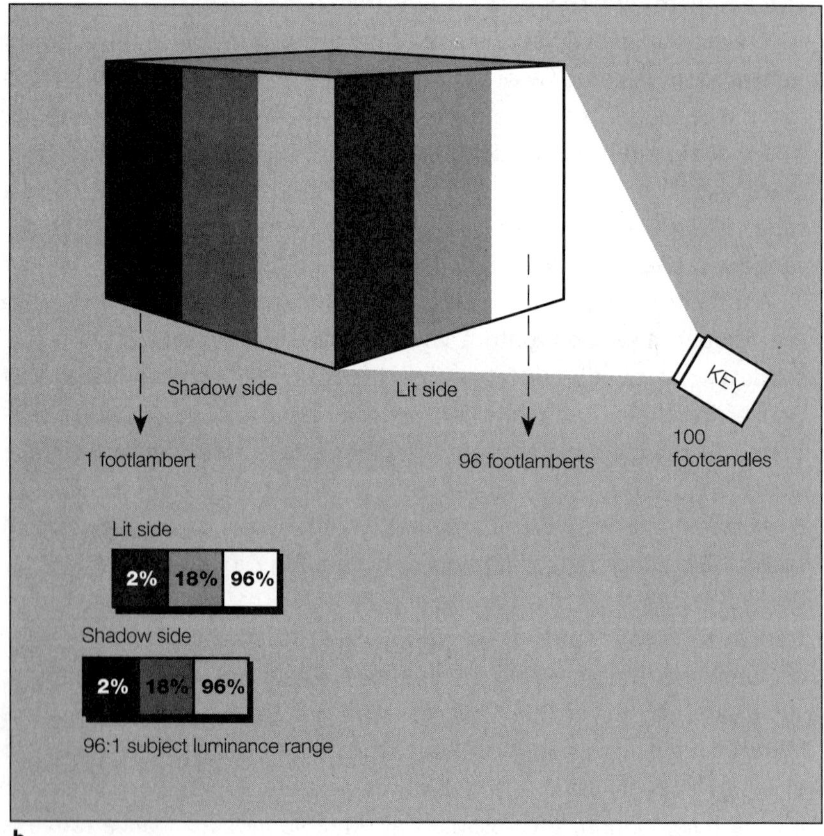

b

What's important to realize here is that a cinematographer often faces a wide range of interwoven luminances in the subject to be filmed. Since a film stock can handle only a limited range of subject luminances, the cinematographer must choose what to expose for as well as how to light the scene.

SUMMARY

We have defined five key exposure concepts in this chapter:

- *Incident light*—the light that illuminates objects measured in footcandles.
- *Reflected Light*—the light we see and use to expose film.
- *Reflectance (reflection factor)*—the percentage of light an object reflects.
- *Luminance*—the amount of reflected light measured in footlamberts.
- *Subject luminance range*—the ratio of the highest to the lowest significant luminance value in the subject.

These concepts allow us to see that exposure is not just a mechanical act. Rather, exposure is a creative choice—a choice selected from a number of possibilities.

NOTES

1. In sensitometric science, exposure is defined as the product of the light intensity (I), which is controlled by the T-stop setting on the lens, and the shutter speed (T) of the camera. This is called the law of reciprocity, $E = I \times T$.

   In cinematography the shutter speed is based on a 24 f.p.s. rate and is invariably around 1/50–1/60th of a second. Unlike photography, altering a film camera's shutter speed is uncommon. In film, nonstandard shutter speeds can adversely affect the illusion of motion. Therefore, exposure is normally controlled by changing the T-stop setting on the lens.

2. Reflected light is also measured in candles/sq ft. The two units are related as per the following formula: candles/sq ft = footlamberts divided by pi. Different spot meters may utilize differing scales to measure reflected light. Metric equivalents to these terms are listed in Appendix E, "Some Basic Units of Illumination."

3. See Jack F. Dunn and George L. Wakefield, *Exposure Manual*, 3rd ed. (Kings Langley, England: Fountain Press, 1974), pp. 18–21.

ZONE SYSTEM BASICS

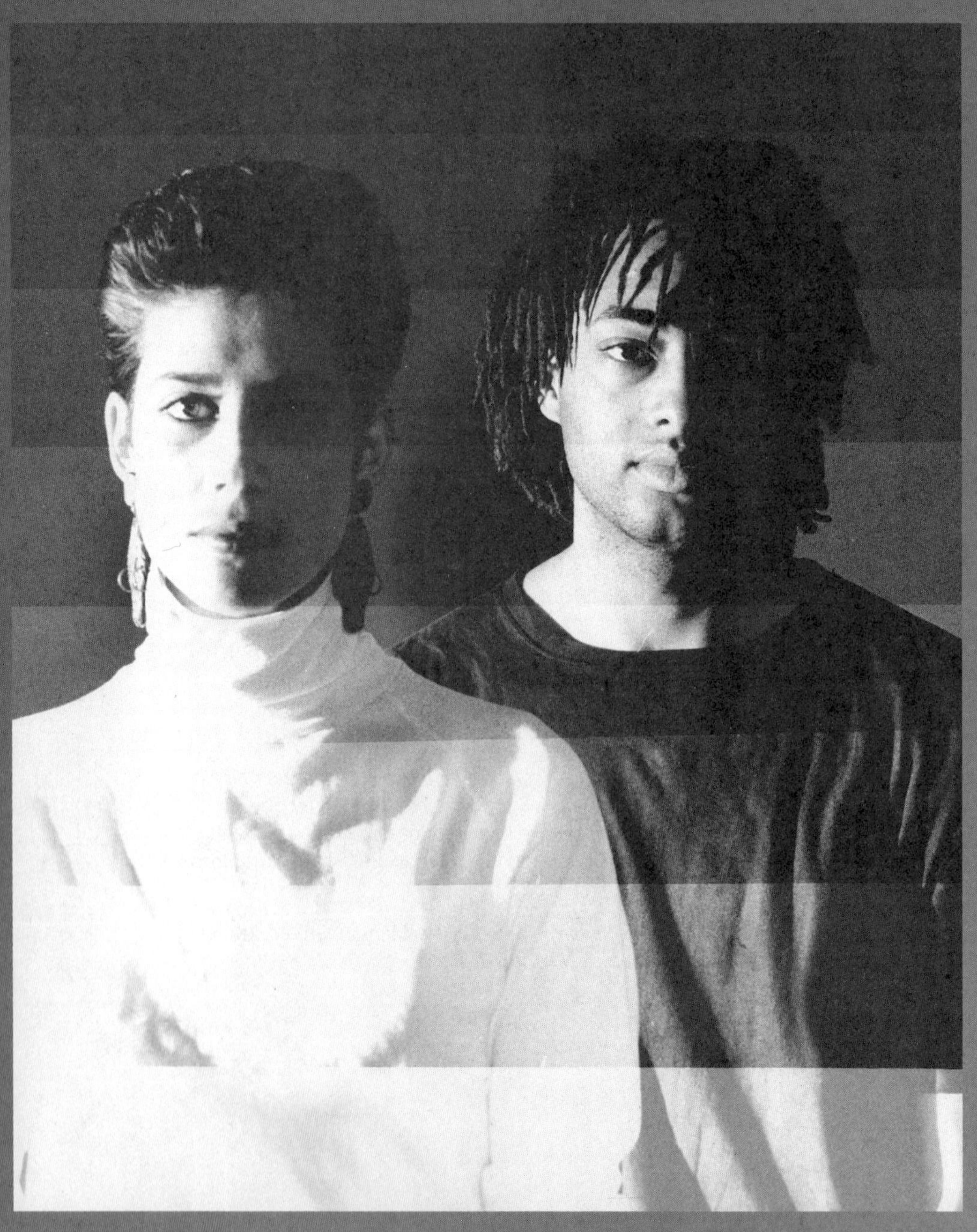

"the zone system"

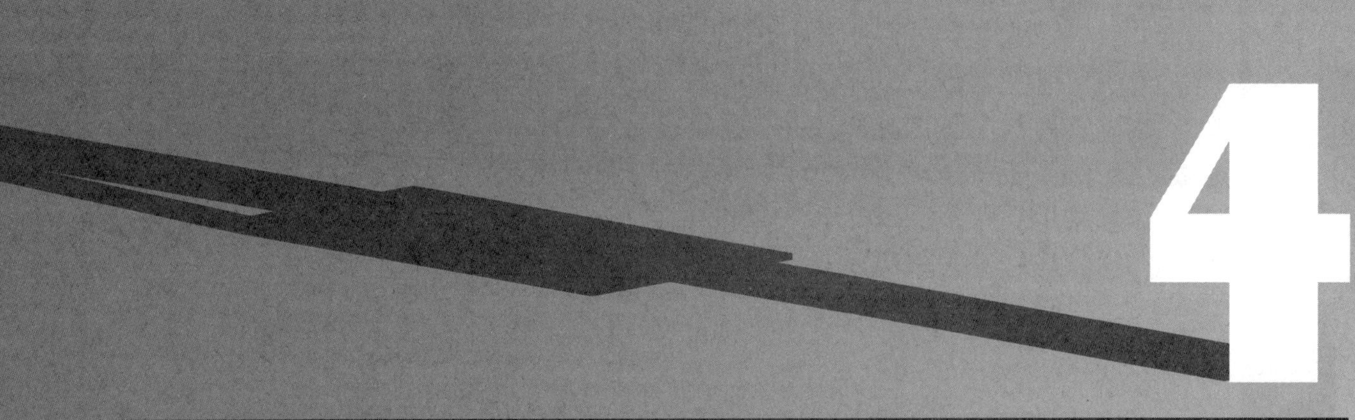

4

The zone system is a "language" which allows us to be verbally precise about visual values. Learning the zone system leads to the ability to previsualize lighting effects and gives us a way to analyze, understand, and discuss filmic images in terms of their luminance placements.

IN THE PREVIOUS chapter, we encountered technical terms such as luminance and luminance range—terms that have no fixed visual meaning. For instance, try to imagine a luminance value of 200 footlamberts and you'll see the difficulty. What is needed is a language we can use to discuss visual values and their link to characteristic curves and images on the screen. This language, long used in photography, is the zone system.

THE GRAY SCALE

The eleven steps or zones of the gray scale form the basis for the **zone system** as devised by photographer Ansel Adams.[1] The gray scale, which can be applied to both subject luminances and density values on the negative, is ultimately viewed as screen values. Figure 4.1 describes the typical contents of each zone.

By far the most useful zones in film are 4, 5, 6, and 7 since most facetones and other important subject values fall within this range. The next most important zones are the highlight zones, 8 and 9. Our eyes go to bright areas of the screen after scanning the image for faces.

Adams based his system on how the human eye perceives brightnesses. The zones of the gray scale make a geometric progression and represent equal spacings for the eye. As we ascend the scale, each zone is twice as bright as the one before; for example, zone 4 is twice as bright as zone 3, zone 5 is twice as bright as zone 4, and so forth.

An important similarity exists between the zone scale and T-stops. Both are based on a logarithmic progression of 2x; that is, from one zone to the next is equivalent to a multiple of two, and from one T-stop to the next is equivalent to a doubling or halving of exposure depending on whether the iris is opening or closing.

Since both zones and T-stops represent a doubling of values, they are often used synonymously. For example, we say we intentionally overexposed the facetones two stops, or we moved the facetones up two

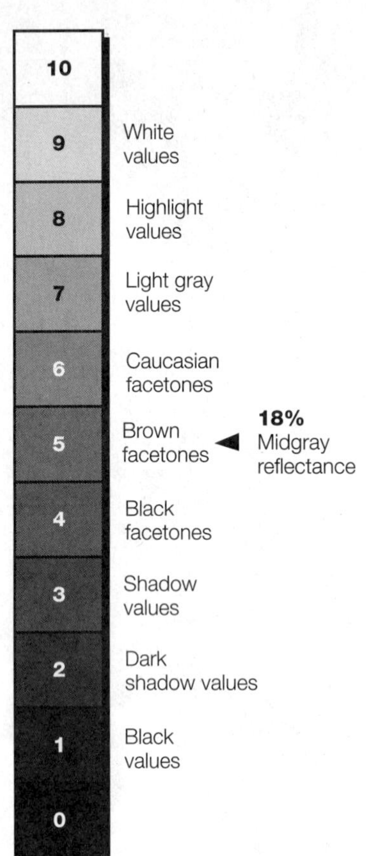

Figure 4.1 The Zone System Scale

zones. Opening up a stop is equivalent to moving a value up one zone, opening up two stops will move a value up two zones, and so on.

Both zones and T-stops relate simply to the **log E** axis of the characteristic curve where an increment of .3, the log of 2, is equivalent to a doubling of the subject luminance value. Moving from zone 6 to 7 represents an increase of .3 on the log E scale.[2] Table 4.1 makes this clear.

COLORS CONCEIVED AS ZONES

Moving a color up or down the zone scale is equivalent to changing its tint or shade. For example, if a red object is progressively overexposed, it becomes lighter and desaturated, culminating in white, total overexposure. Likewise, if a red object is underexposed and moved down the gray scale, it becomes a darker shade of red. Since the object moves up or down in zonal increments, with practice it is possible to visualize these changes. This is particularly important in lighting where we often want to balance a background for a certain subject. The technique is used to visualize what will happen to the background colors if, for example, they are lit two zones darker than the subject.

RELATIVITY OF THE ZONES

The zone system is totally relative because a zone represents no fixed luminance value. With the aid of a light meter, we can place any luminance value on any specific zone as desired. For example, a cinematographer may place a black object at its normal zone 1 value or, through manipulation of lighting and exposure controls, render it at any other zone. An object such as a background wall can be made dark gray, gray, light gray, or even white through controlled overexposure (see Figure 2.20).

2x scale	1	2	4	8	16	32	64	128	256	512	1024
zones	0	1	2	3	4	5	6	7	8	9	10
log E	0	.3	.6	.9	1.2	1.5	1.8	2.1	2.4	2.7	3.0
T-stops	1	1.4	2	2.8	4	5.6	8	11	16	22	32

Table 4.1 Relation of Zones and T-Stops to Log E Axis

AUTOMATIC LUMINANCE PLACEMENT

Once a certain luminance is placed on a certain zone, all other luminances automatically fall into place on their respective zones. For example, if we expose so that a human face with a luminance value of 200 footlamberts is placed on zone 6, then other subject luminances, if present, will fall onto zones 0–10 automatically, as shown in Table 4.2. This is very important. The cinematographer gets a choice, but only one. Once the key value is exposed for, the others shift inevitably into their respective zones. There is an advantage here, however: Selecting the key element in the shot, or creating the desired key element through lighting, allows the cinematographer to know what will happen with all other luminance values.

For most exposure purposes, we rely on a **zone 5 exposure** technique. This will be discussed in Chapter 6, but here we can say that the incident light meter assumes in its reading that we want to place a midgray subject value at zone 5. This means, for example, that if zone 5 is correlated with a value of 250 footlamberts, the scale of relationships in Table 4.3 would be established.

As we shall see in the next chapter, our best film stocks can reproduce only nine zones of subject luminance range, and then only six or seven will fall on the straight line. A subject luminance range greater than nine zones (512:1) makes it impossible to retain details in all values of the subject. The cinematographer has to choose whether to alter the subject luminance range through lighting or to render only part of the subject faithfully, letting other parts go to shadow or burned-out values. This

Table 4.2

Zone	Value in Footlamberts*
10	*3200*
9	*1600*
8	*800*
7	*400*
6	*200*
5	*100*
4	*50*
3	*25*
2	*12*
1	*6*
0	*3*

* Rounded off to whole numbers.

Table 4.3

Zone	Value in Footlamberts*
10	*8000*
9	*4000*
8	*2000*
7	*1000*
6	*500*
5	*250*
4	*125*
3	*63*
2	*32*
1	*16*
0	*8*

* Rounded off to whole numbers.

common situation and how to deal with it will be discussed in Part III, "Lighting Applications."

In cinematography, middle zone values 4, 5, and 6, where faces fall, and high zone values 7, 8, and 9, which represent the light gray and white parts of the subject, so dominate perception that invariably the cinematographer sacrifices lower zone shadow values and concentrates on consistent placement of facetones and control of highlight values.

SUMMARY

The zone system requires the cinematographer to explore a subject's visual values and relationships. This facilitates the creative use of exposure technique. With practice, the zone system will allow an accurate previsualization of exposure and lighting setups. The cinematographer will be in control of the medium and able to see as the film stock "sees."

NOTES

1. I cannot overestimate the value of a complete understanding of Chapters 1 and 4 of Ansel Adams's book *The Negative* (Boston: Little, Brown, 1981). In his 1981 revision of *The Negative,* Adams added zone 10 to his earlier system—which consisted of ten zones, 0–9—in order to make zone 5 the geometric middle zone (p.xi). The zone system was designed for B & W still photography and relies on a reflected light technique with shadow value placements. Cinematographers concentrate on facetones and highlights and utilize an incident technique; they are unable to vary development as photographers do. But we can use the zone system as a language to help us analyze and discuss visual values.

   Because we use only a part of Adams's total system, I have simplified the terminology as follows: (1) I forgo the roman numerals, and (2) I refer to all values—luminance, exposure, negative, and screen—by a zone designation, unlike Adams who distinguishes Zone V exposure value from subject Value V and print Value V. (See Adams, *The Negative*, p. 48). These two adjustments make it simpler to use the system for cinematography.

2. See Appendix C, "Film Stocks and Characteristic Curves," for an explanation of log E.

LUMINANCE RANGE AND CHARACTERISTIC CURVES

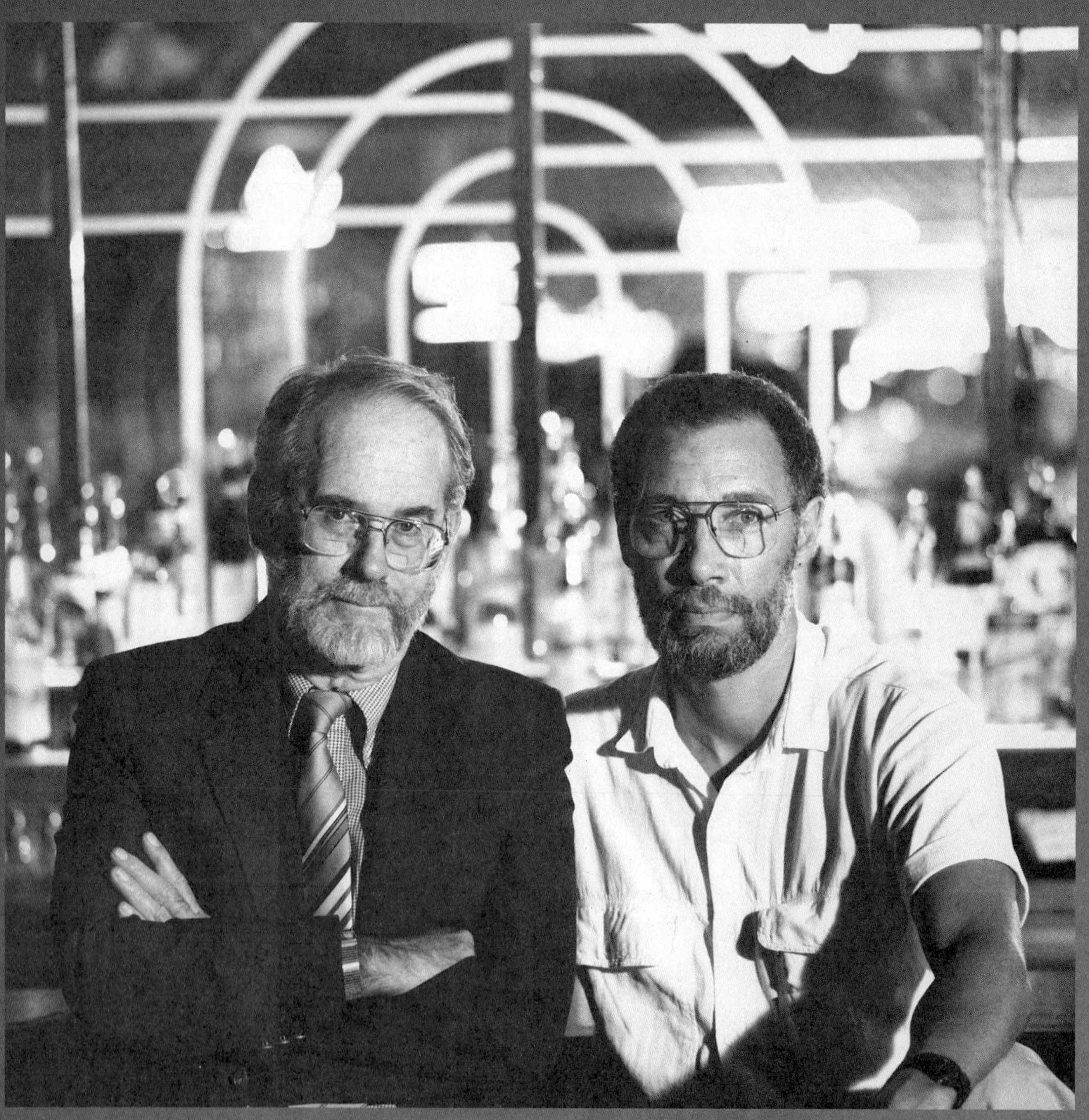

"exposing subject luminance range"

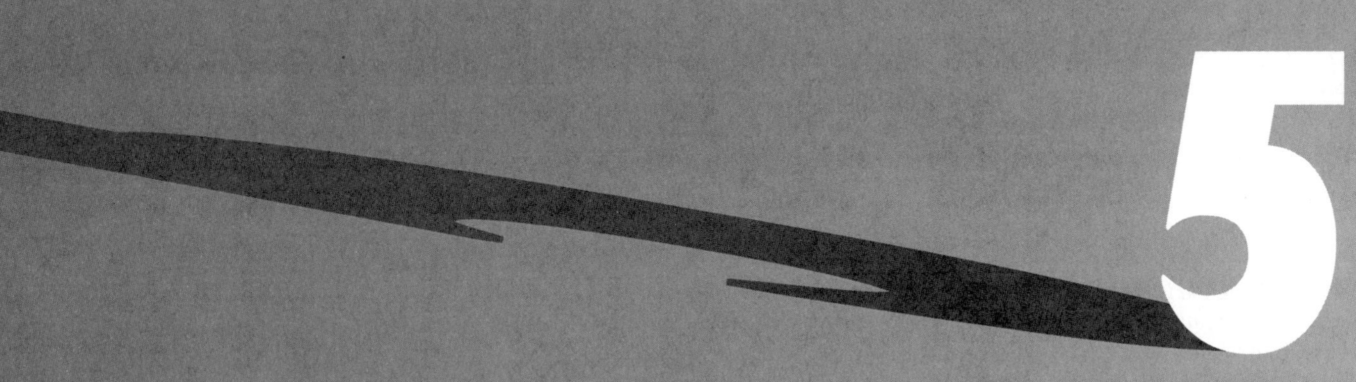

In this chapter, we carefully examine the characteristic curve and its components: straight line, toe, shoulder, and density and log E axes. We pay particular attention to calculating the length of the straight line and determining the overall useful range for a particular emulsion. Concepts such as gamma, overall gamma, and printing and projection contrast are explored to further our understanding of log E range—the sensitometric equivalent to subject luminance range. The ultimate aim is to be able to read the sensitometric data published by the film stock manufacturers and to link that data back to the zone system concepts we developed in the previous chapter and the incident light meter, which will be discussed in Chapter 6.

(You may wish to consult Appendix C, "Film Stocks and Characteristic Curves," and Appendix D, "Logarithms," for a refresher course in the basics.)

CONTRAST IS fundamental to images. To control contrast involves a delicate blend of exposure and lighting techniques. To understand and control these techniques involves working with the findings of sensitometry—the science of exposure. Exposure involves a variety of technical concepts such as gamma and the complication of overall gamma. For exposure and lighting purposes we are interested in the range of subject luminances we can place onto the characteristic curve of a particular film emulsion through exposure. The characteristic curve allows us to understand the placement of subject luminances and is the basis for understanding exposure theory.

THE CHARACTERISTIC CURVE

A cinematographer places the subject luminance range onto the **characteristic curve** when exposing; in effect this recreates the luminances as a corresponding range of density values, first in the negative, then in the print (see Figure 5.1). Luminances placed on (pegged to) the **straight line** will be represented by **proportional density differences** on the negative and subsequent prints. This means their original relationships will be reproduced in the negative and on the screen when projected (see Figure 5.2).

The **toe** and **shoulder** of the characteristic curve are also useful for rendering luminance range. However, density values for the toe and shoulder are not proportional to log E values. This means the toe and shoulder distort visual relationships in the subject, but there is enough differentiation to enhance the image. For example, in Figure 5.2 the .3 log E range from 2.4 to 2.7 is translated by the curve into approximately a .2 density difference rather than the .3 given to values falling on the straight line.

By projecting the straight line portion of the curve onto the log E axis, we can calculate the amount of luminance range in log E values that the emulsion can handle accurately. This we will refer to as the **log E range of the straight line (latitude)** or the **length of the straight line**.[1]

Figure 5.1 Placement of Subject Luminance Range: Idealized Negative with a Gamma of 1.0 *A film stock is able to reproduce a certain luminance range in the final print so that higher luminance values reproduce as whites, middle values as grays, and lower values as blacks. On a negative, as here, high values have high densities and are black. This is, of course, reversed on the final print. In this figure, the toe is the curved region to the left of point A. The shoulder is to the right of point B, and the straight line is from A to B.*

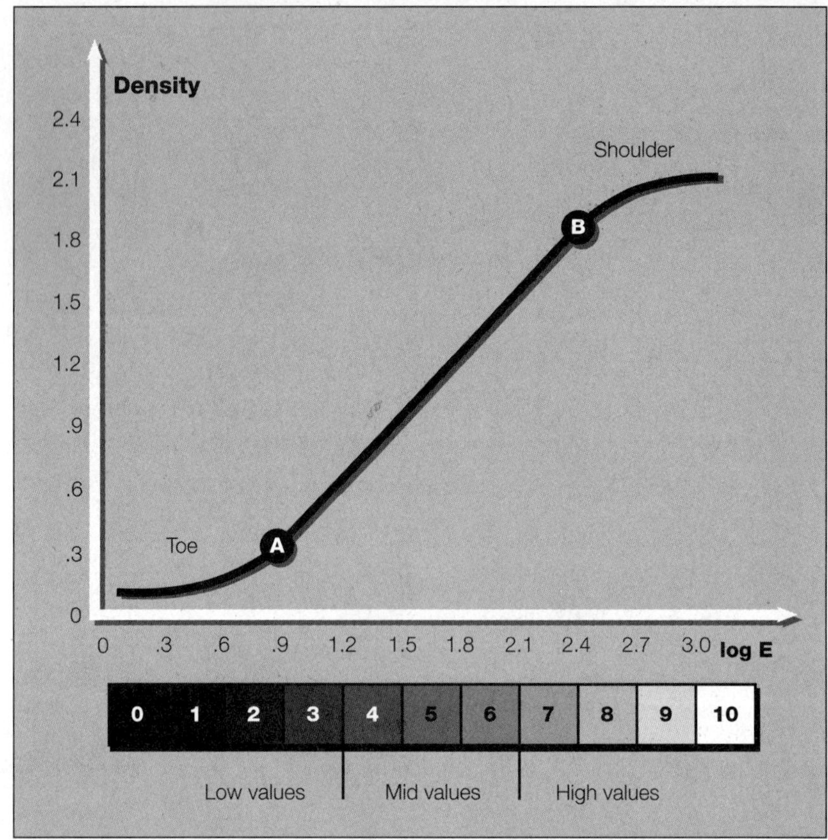

Figure 5.2 Translating Log E Values into Density Differences: Idealized Negative with a Gamma of 1.0 *Log E values with a .3 difference—for example, the .3 range from 1.5 to 1.8—are translated into .3 density increments—in this case, from .9 to 1.2—by the straight line on an idealized negative with gamma of 1.0.*

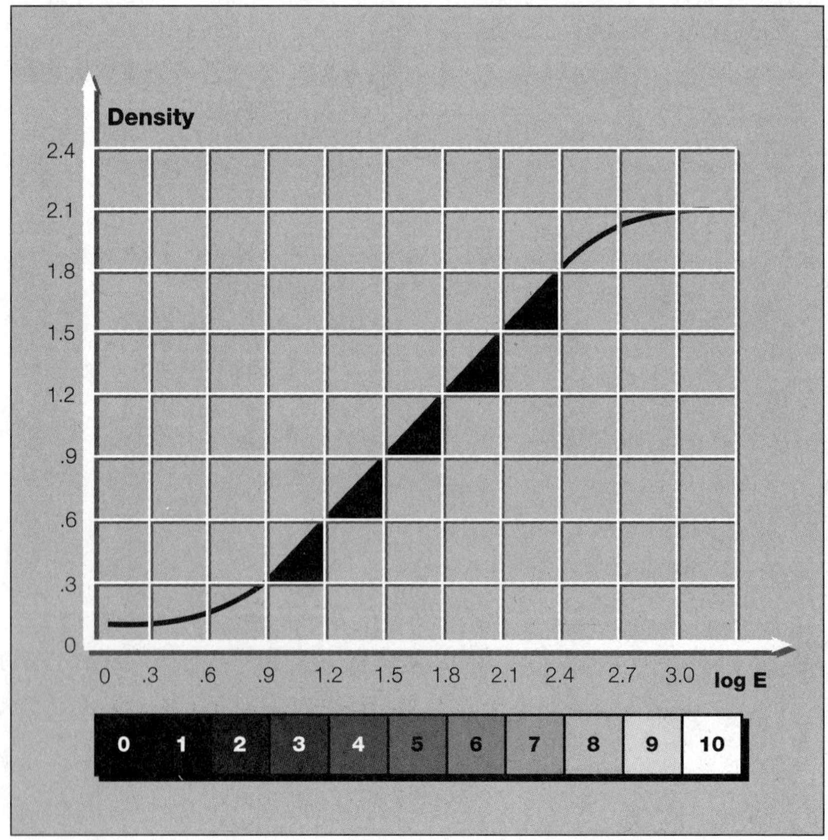

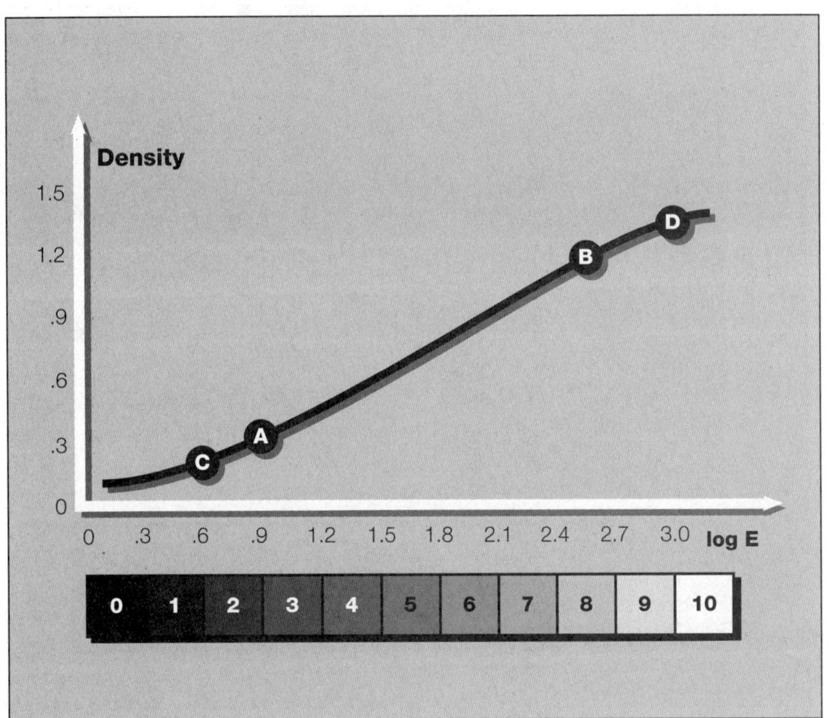

Figure 5.3 Straight Line Length and Overall Useful Range on a Typical Color Negative (Red Curve Only) with a Gamma of .65 *If we project the straight line portion (A–B) of this emulsion onto the log E axis, we see that it can translate a range of 1.65 log E into density differences. Adding in the toe and shoulder (C–D) increases the range to about 2.4 log E.*

Straight line (A–B) = 1.65 log E range (2.55 - 0.9 = 1.65). This equals 5 1/2 zones (50:1).

Overall useful range (C–D) = 2.40 log E range (3.0 - 0.6 = 2.4). This equals 8 zones (256:1).

The combination of straight line plus toe and shoulder we will call the **overall useful range** of the film stock. The longer the straight line and overall useful range, the larger the subject luminance range that can be translated and reproduced, and the more subtle the visual rendition possible (see Figure 5.3).

Current color negative emulsions provide straight lines capable of handling luminance ranges from 32:1 to over 128:1. The same emulsions can handle overall luminance ranges (using the straight line plus toe and shoulder) on the order of 256:1 (log E range of 2.4) to 512:1 (log E range of 2.7).

RELATING ZONES TO CHARACTERISTIC CURVES

Since each zone of the gray scale represents a .3 log E, it is simple to correlate zones to the characteristic curve. The 11 zones are represented on the negative as indicated in Figures 5.1 to 5.3.

To obtain the **zone range of the straight line**, divide the log E range by .3. For example, if a color negative has a straight line of 1.5 log E, it has a five-zone range (1.5 divided by .3 = 5). If a color negative has an overall range of 2.4 log E, this is equivalent to an eight-zone overall range, though in this case lower and upper subject zones will be compressed relative to the all-important middle ones that fall on the straight line (see Figures 5.3 and 5.4).

Figure 5.4 Relating Zones to Characteristic Curves: Typical B & W Negative with a Gamma of .8 *Straight line (A–B) = 1.5 log E (2.4 - 0.9). This equals 5 zones (32:1).*

Overall useful range (C–D) = 2.4 log E (2.8 - 0.4). This equals 8 zones (256:1).

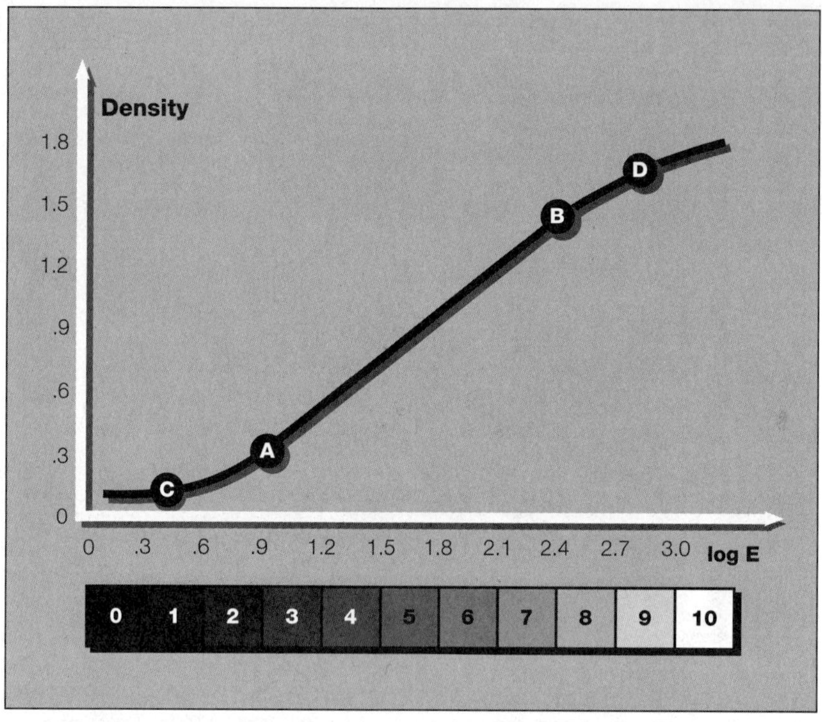

Figure 5.5 Defining Gamma: Idealized Negative with a Gamma of 1.0 *Gamma = X_D divided by X_E*
Where $X_D = X_E$ gamma = 1.0
Where $X_D < X_E$ gamma is less than 1.0
Where $X_D > X_E$ gamma is greater than 1.0

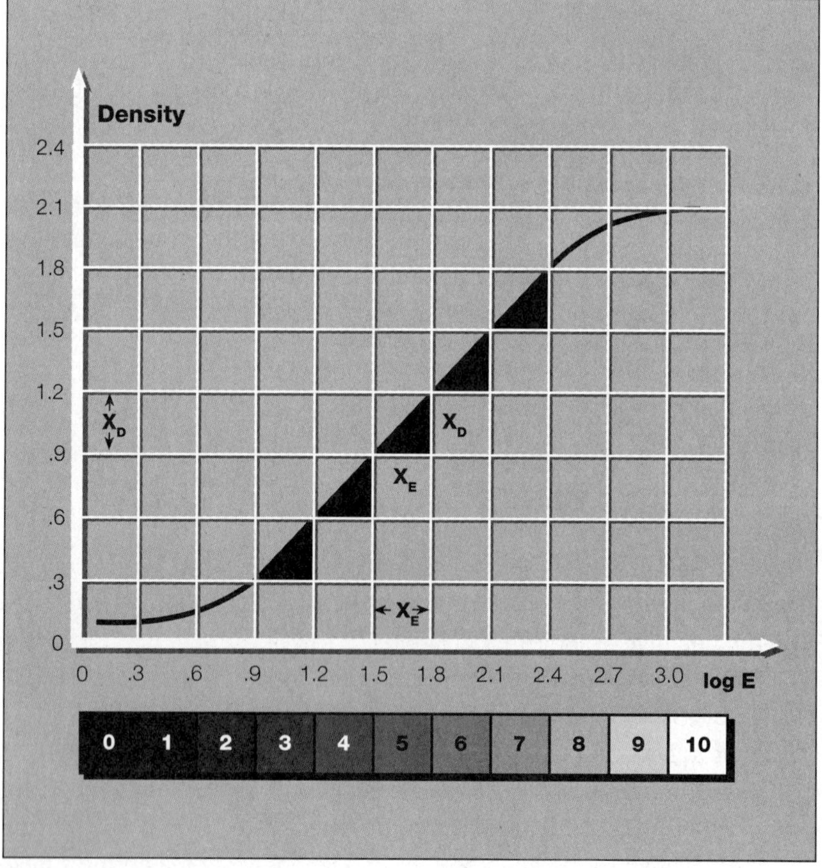

GAMMA AND OVERALL GAMMA

The concept of gamma is important to our understanding of how different film stocks translate luminance range into a range of densities. Gamma also involves the workings of the processing department in the film lab, which uses it for standardization techniques.[2] Figure 5.5 defines and illustrates **gamma**. A gamma of 1.0 means the film stock faithfully reproduces the subject's luminance range, or at least the important part of it, by providing a corresponding density range such that increments of X_D and increments of X_E are equal (see Figure 5.5). Though what's on the screen "looks like" the original subject, this is a visual translation, not an exact reproduction.

Theoretically, a gamma of 1.0 would be the ideal overall gamma to strive for on the screen. In practice, however, other factors are involved, such as projector lens flare and screen reflectance. A camera original is but one link in a complete system involving print stock, internegative, processing specifications, and so on. **Overall gamma** is the term for linking these disparate elements together. Overall gamma equals the product of the gammas of the individual components in the total imaging system. In *Photographic Theory for the Motion Picture Cameraman*, Russell Campbell gives the following example of overall gamma, which should be studied carefully.[3]

Original Scene		Lens Flare		Neg Gamma		Printer Gamma		Print		Projector + Cinema		Overall
1.0	x	.9	x	.65	x	.95	x	2.6	x	.9	=	1.3

According to Campbell, research has shown that audiences prefer a screen image slightly more contrasty than in reality. Currently, the ideal overall gamma is equal to about 1.4 depending on intended use.[4] This means that increments of X_D are greater than increments of X_E. The screen image exhibits a greater contrast than the original subject (see Figure 5.6).

Gamma can be discussed only in terms of the straight line since the toe and shoulder are curved and have no consistent proportional response. Gamma is a function of development; consequently, force developing a film stock yields an increase in gamma. Visually speaking, an increase in gamma means an increase in contrast (see Figure 5.7).

PRINTING AND PROJECTION CONTRAST

For color negatives, such as Eastman Color Negative EXR 7248 or Fuji F-125, the best prints are obtainable when the negative gamma is around .6–.7. An emulsion with a gamma in this range is said to have **printing contrast** since it is designed for printing rather than project-

Figure 5.6 Comparing Overall Gammas of 1.0 and 1.4 *Using a negative characteristic curve with a gamma of 1.4 will result in on-screen images with greater contrast than a negative with a gamma of 1.0. This is because with gammas greater than 1.0 increments of density (X_D) are greater than increments of log E (X_E).*

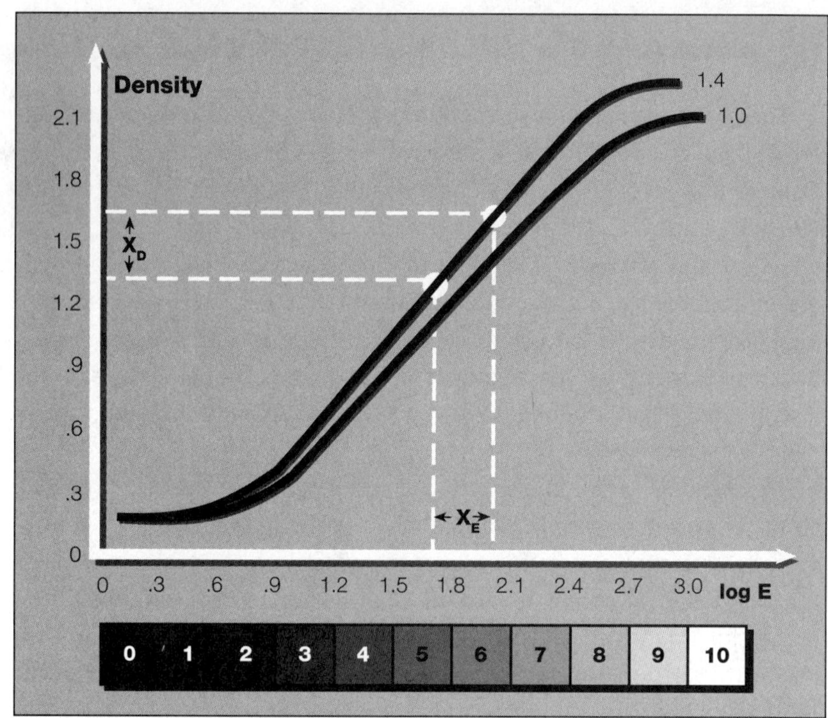

Figure 5.7 Pushing increases Gamma

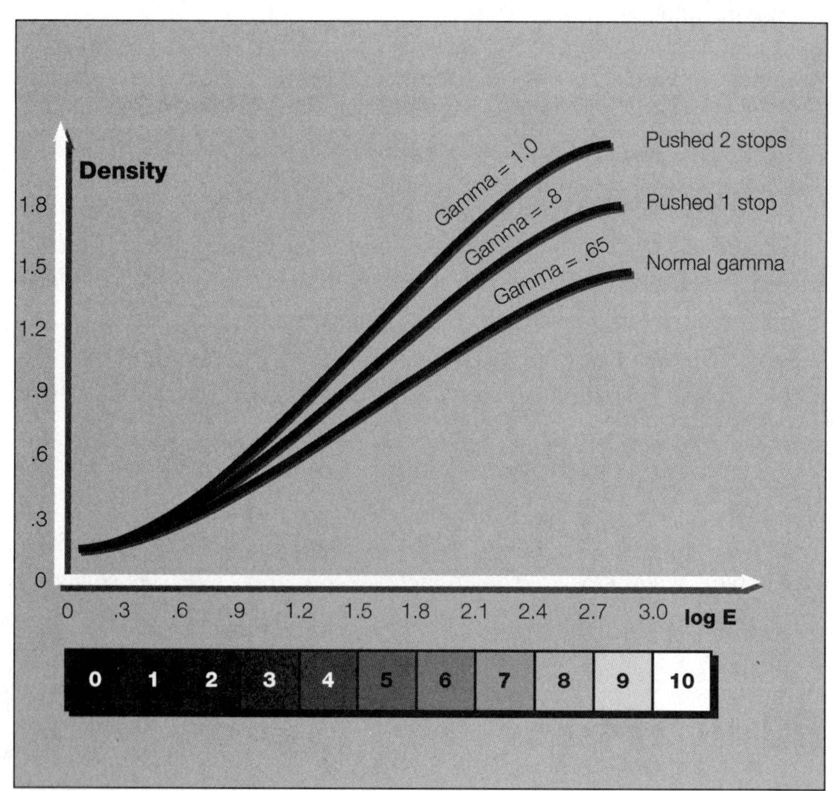

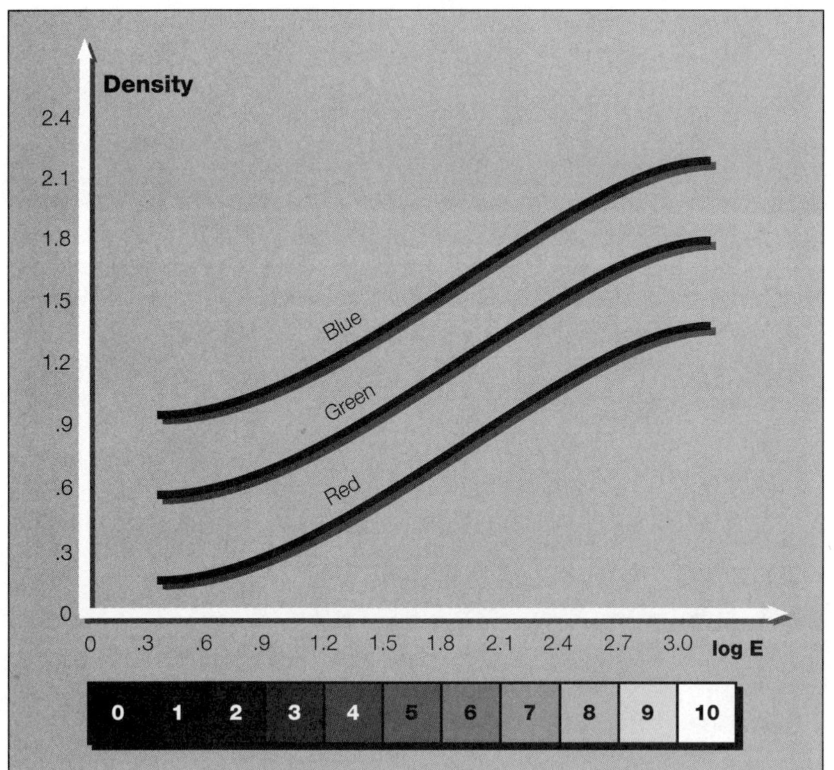

a

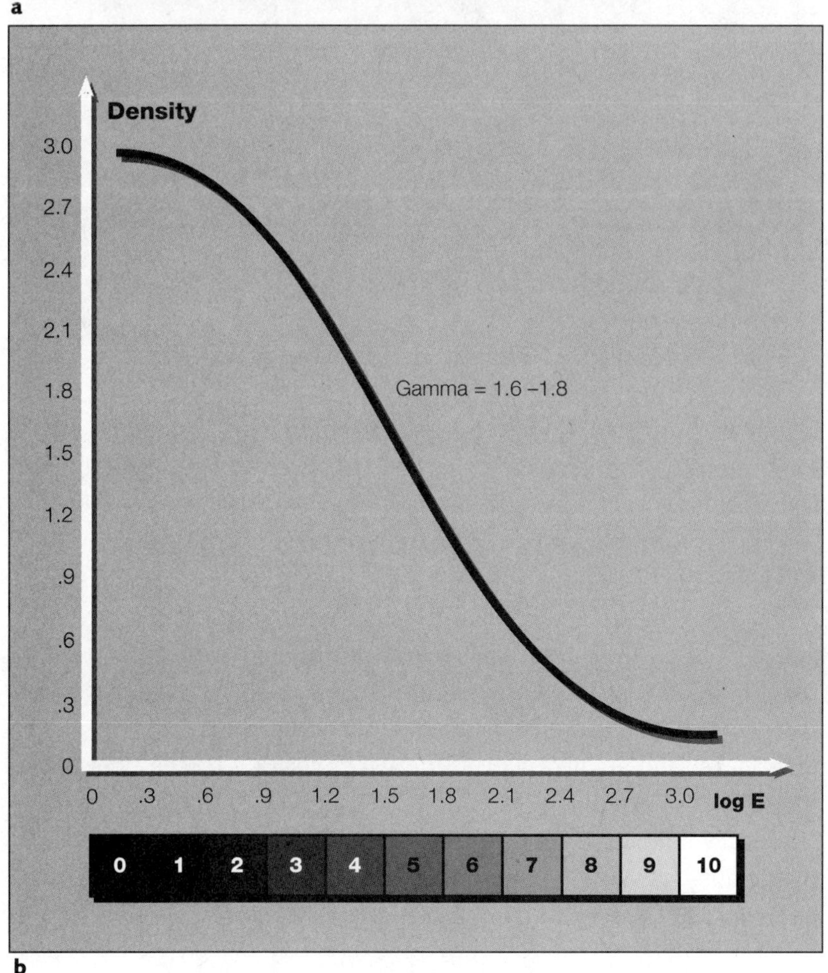

b

Figure 5.8 Typical Color Negative and Print Gammas
In (a) a typical color negative with a gamma of .65–.70; in (b) a typical release print with a gamma of 1.6–1.8; in (c) (page 70) a typical color print stock with a gamma of 2.6–2.8. The combination of a color negative with a gamma of .65 and a color print stock with a gamma of 2.6 results in a release print with a gamma of 1.7 (.65 x 2.6 = 1.7).

Figure 5.8 (continued)

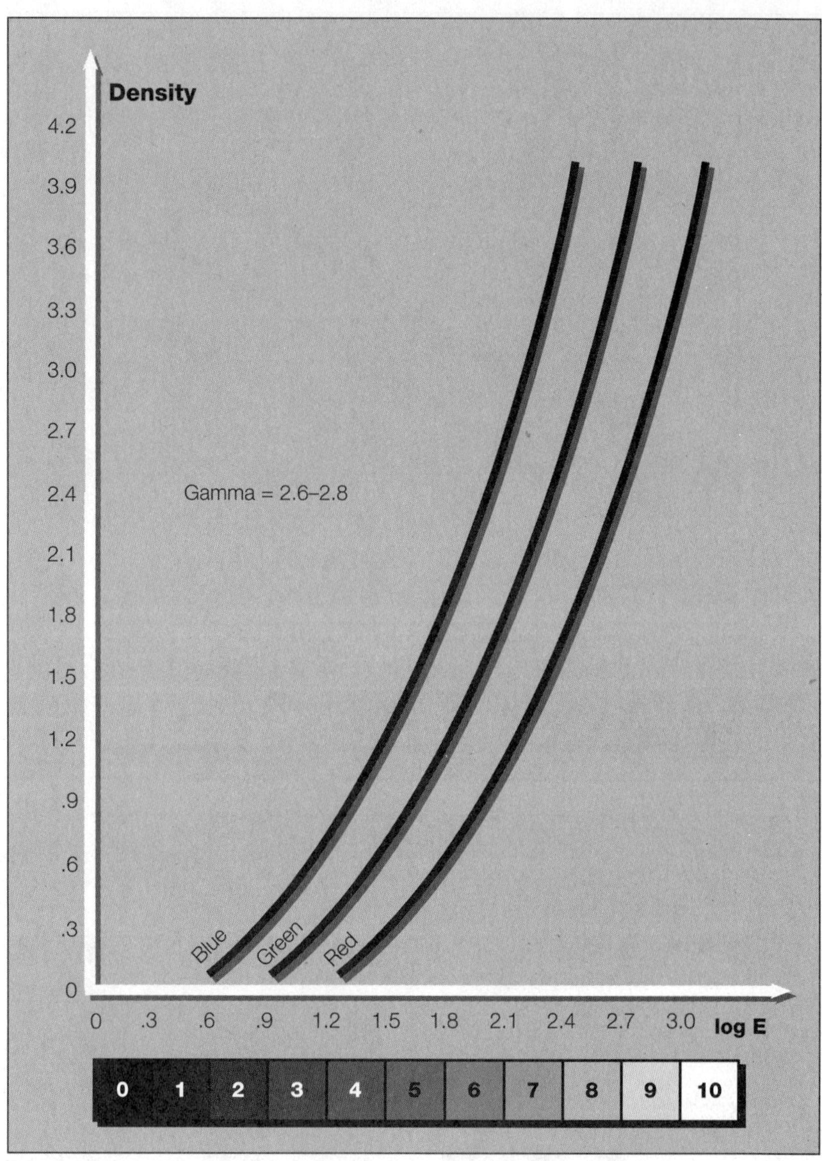

c

ing. These stocks are low contrast since their density increments X_D are less than their plotted X_E values. When negatives are coupled with their corresponding print stocks, which have gammas around 2.6–2.8, they yield prints with the standard projection contrast of 1.6–1.8 (.65 x 2.6 = 1.7; see Figure 5.8).

Camera originals are designed to yield the best possible prints for projection. To this end, it has been found that the most acceptable images come from prints with gammas in the range 1.6–1.8. Known as **projection** contrast, this gamma range is reduced by projector flare, screen reflectance, and ambient light to near the ideal 1.4 by the time it's on the screen.

Negatives are used almost exclusively in 35mm and 16mm color cinematography. B & W reversals are used in 16mm. Reversal stocks are designed with projection contrast and have gammas around 1.6–1.8.

Such gammas cause reversal stocks to have too much contrast when printed on normal print stocks.

Negatives are much favored because of the subtlety of their visual renditions. This is due to their long straight lines, a direct result of their low gamma values. Because of these straight lines, negatives are able to translate larger ranges of log E values into density differences compared to reversal originals.

ACTUAL CHARACTERISTIC CURVES AND HOW TO READ THEM

Figure 5.9a, b, c illustrates actual characteristic curves for color negatives as published by Agfa (page 72), Fuji (page 73), and Eastman Kodak (pages 74 and 75). Our goal is to understand the manufacturers' scalings for these curves. It may be necessary to review the basic log theory in Appendix D.

With density, the scale usually starts at 0.0 and progresses in logarithmic increments of .2 (Agfa), .5 (Fuji), or 1.0 (Kodak), up to 2.4–4.0, depending on the manufacturer. Note that density ranges for the color negatives are around 2.0–2.2, as measured from the low density of the red curve to the high density of the blue (see Figure 5.9).

The log E axis is the most important for cinematography. Again, logarithmic scales are used: Fuji uses a .5 scale, Kodak uses a 1.0 scale, and Agfa uses both. Fuji and Kodak label their exposure axes in log E values based on lux-seconds. Agfa labels its exposure axis "log Hv," which is the international standard for log E and means the same thing (see Figure 5.9a).

Unfortunately, the scalings are in negative logs, moving from $\bar{3}.5$ up to 0.0 and then to positive values. A negative log is the log for a fraction. For example, $\bar{3}.0$ is the log for .001 lux-second, $\bar{2}.0$ for .01 lux-second, and $\bar{1}.0$ for .1 lux-second.

Negative logs can be very confusing, but luckily we do not need to be concerned with actual values. What interests us is the range of log E values. For example, it makes no difference to us if the log E moves from $\bar{3}.0$ to 0.0 or from 0.0 to 3.0 because a range of 3.0 is still 3.0.

What we have to learn to do is take an actual curve and calculate the log E range for the straight line and for the overall useful range. Here are two examples.

FUJI F-125 EXAMPLE Using the red curve in Figure 5.10, measure the straight line as best you can with a ruler. You should arrive at points A and B, which project onto the log E axis at $\bar{1}.5$ (halfway between $\bar{2}.0$ and $\bar{1}.0$) and 0.0 respectively. Earlier we saw that we can convert log E range into zones by dividing by .3 log E. The trick with these actual curves is in being able to determine the log E range to start with since the negative log scales are not as easy to work with as our idealized example in Figure 5.3 (page 65).

Figure 5.9a Agfa 16mm Color Negative and Print Stock Characteristic Curves *(Reprinted courtesy of Agfa Corporation)*

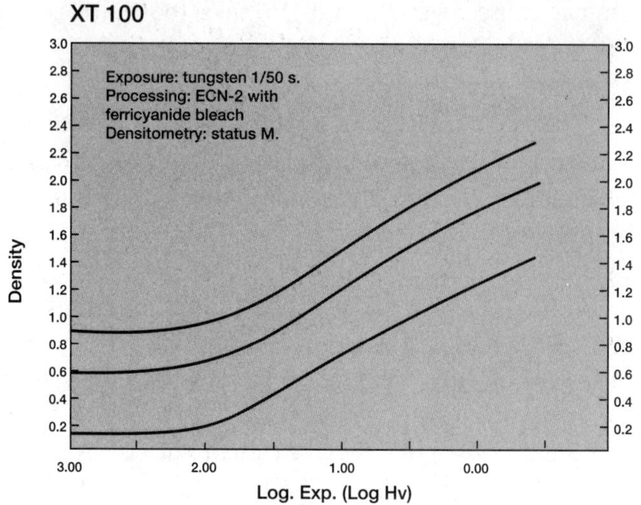

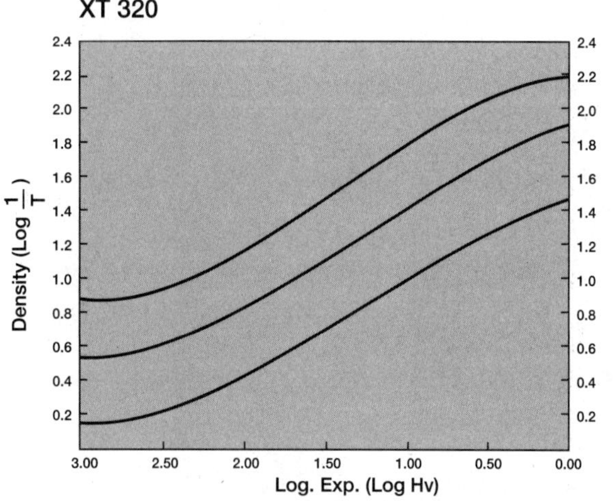

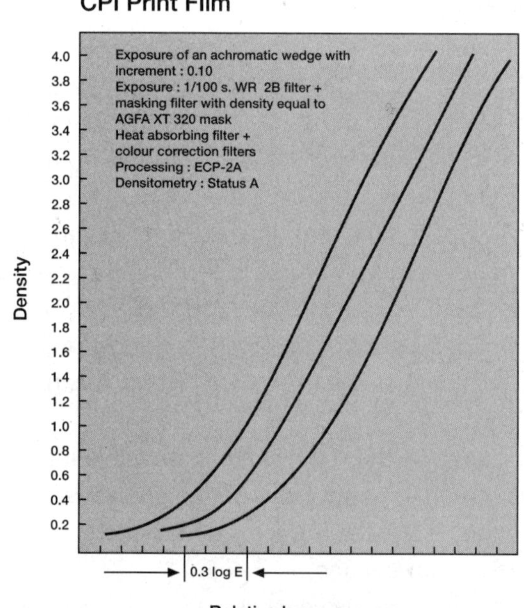

Figure 5.9b Fujicolor 16mm Color Negative and Print Stock Characteristic Curves *(Reprinted courtesy of Fuji Photo Film U.S.A., Inc.)*

F-64
(3200K, 1/50 sec)
Density
Log exposure

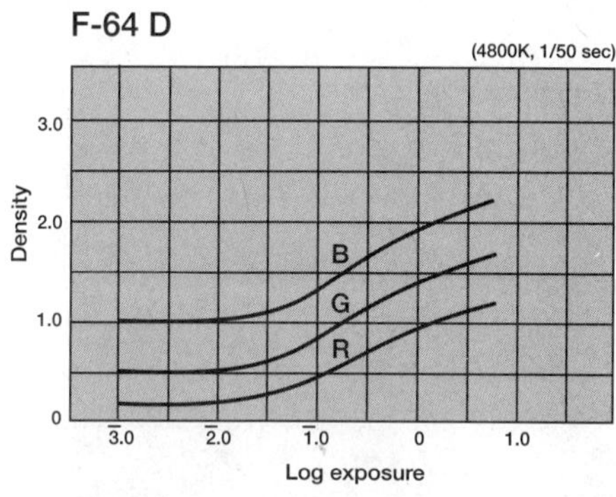

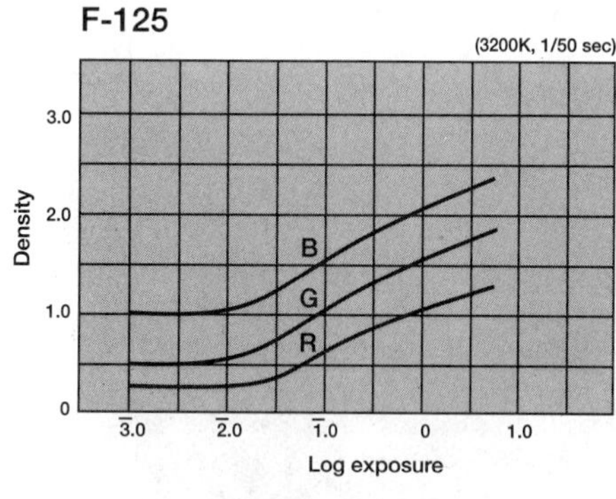

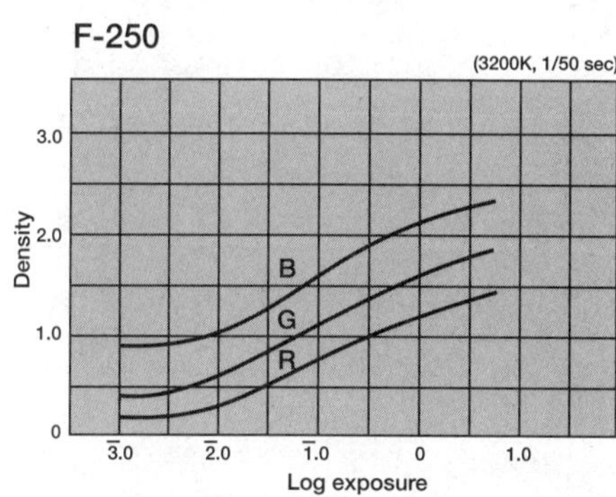

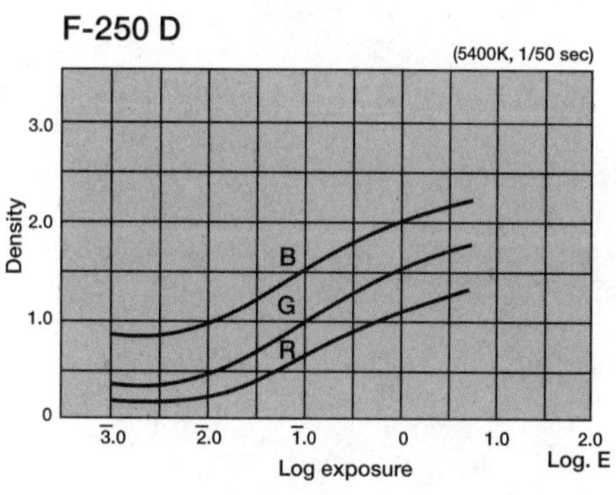

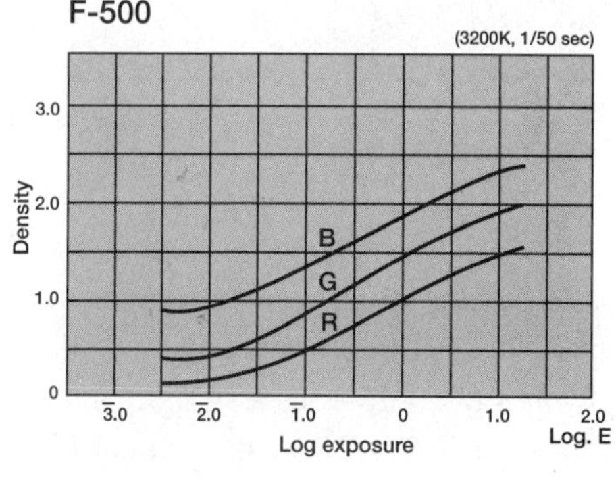

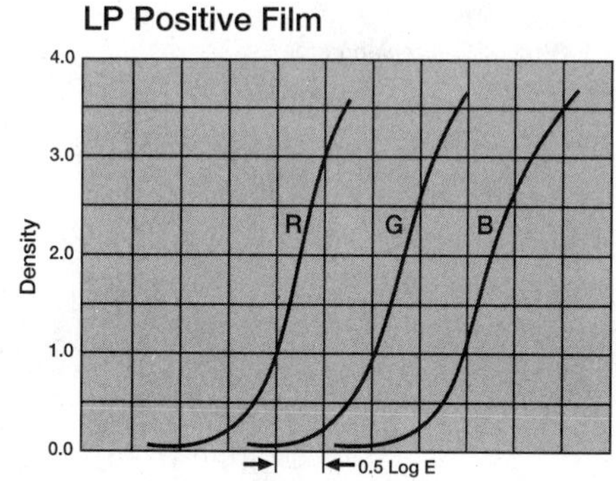

Figure 5.9c Eastman 16mm Color Negative and Print Stock Characteristic Curves (continued on facing page) *(Reprinted courtesy of Eastman Kodak Company)*

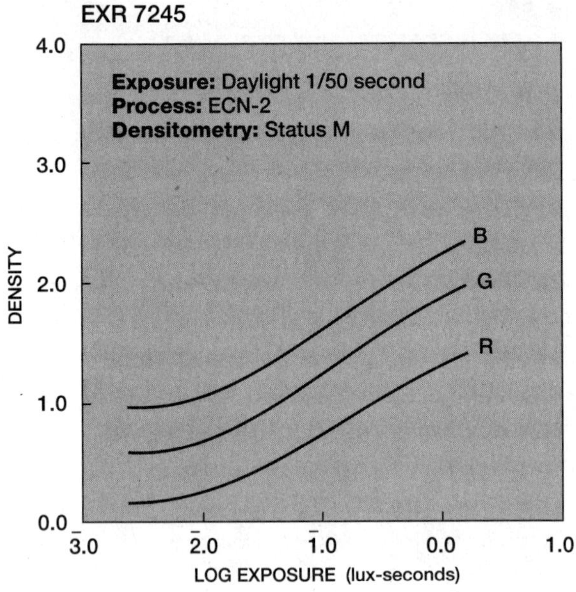

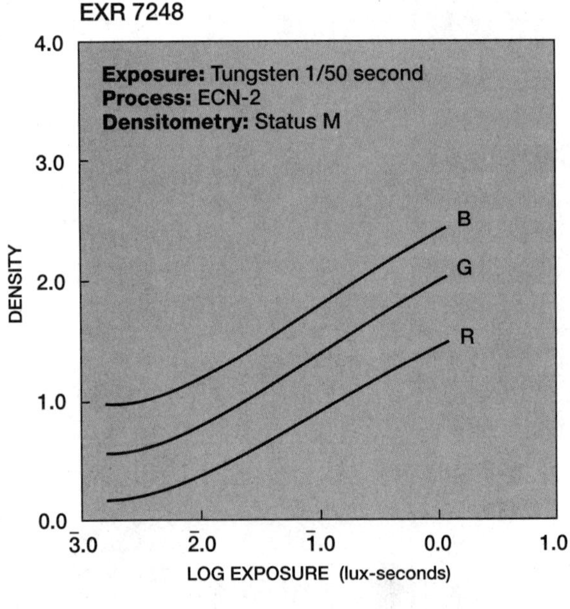

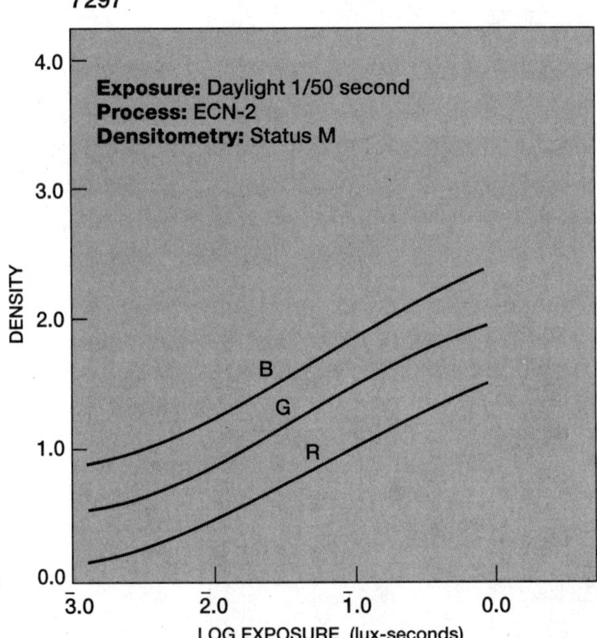

In Figure 5.10, the distance from A ($\bar{1}.5$, or halfway between $\bar{2}.0$ and $\bar{1}.0$) to B (0.0) is 1.5 log E units. As you can see, if we count by units of .5 log E as per Fuji's scaling, from A to B is three units long, with each unit representing .5 log E. Multiplying 3 by .5 gives us a straight line log E range (A–B) of 1.5 log E units. Dividing 1.5 by .3 gives a straight line length of five zones (32:1) for Fuji F-125.

To determine the useful range, try to locate where the toe and shoulder flatten out, or where the density differentiations are tiny. Mark these

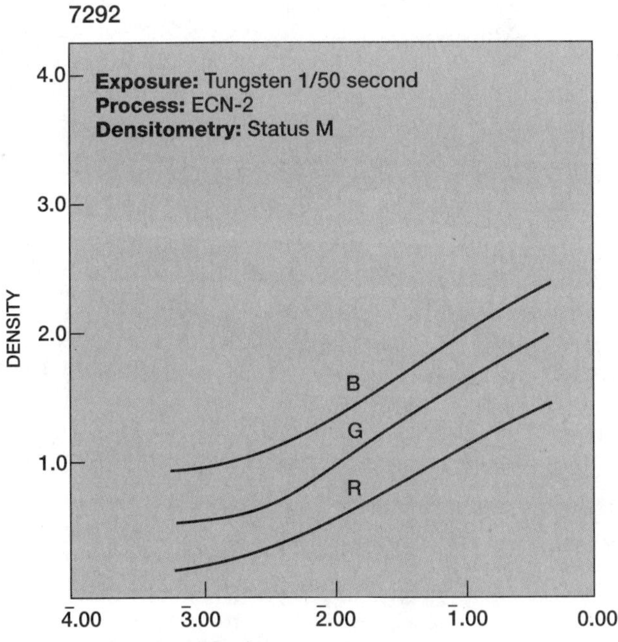

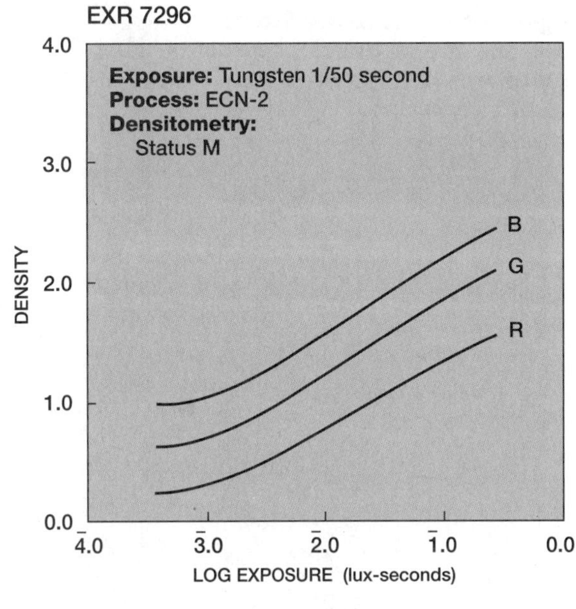

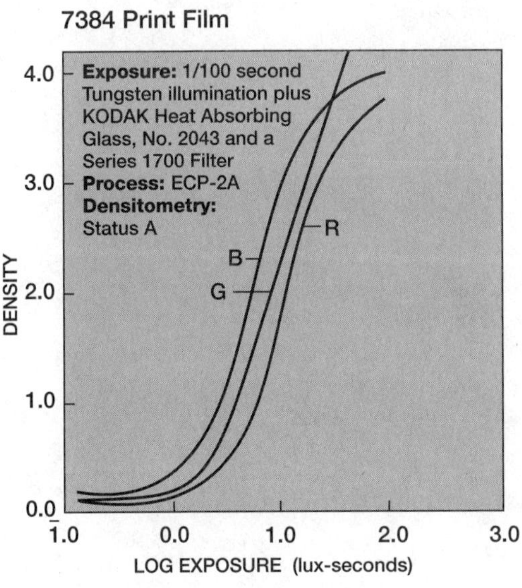

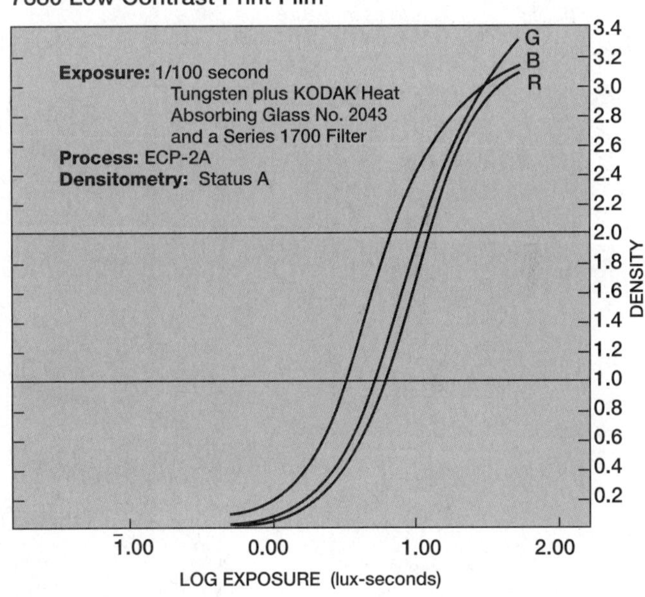

as points C and D (see Figure 5.10). Point C is slightly lower than point A. Call it $\bar{1}$.6, which is .1 log E left of the scaled $\bar{1}$.5. Point D is about 0.8, three units to the right of 0.5. From C to D thus represents two units of 1.0 log E (2.0 log E units) plus the .1 log E for C and the .3 log E for D. This gives us a useful range of 2.4 log E, which is eight zones (256:1). This is quite good, but remember the toe and shoulder distort subject luminance relationships.

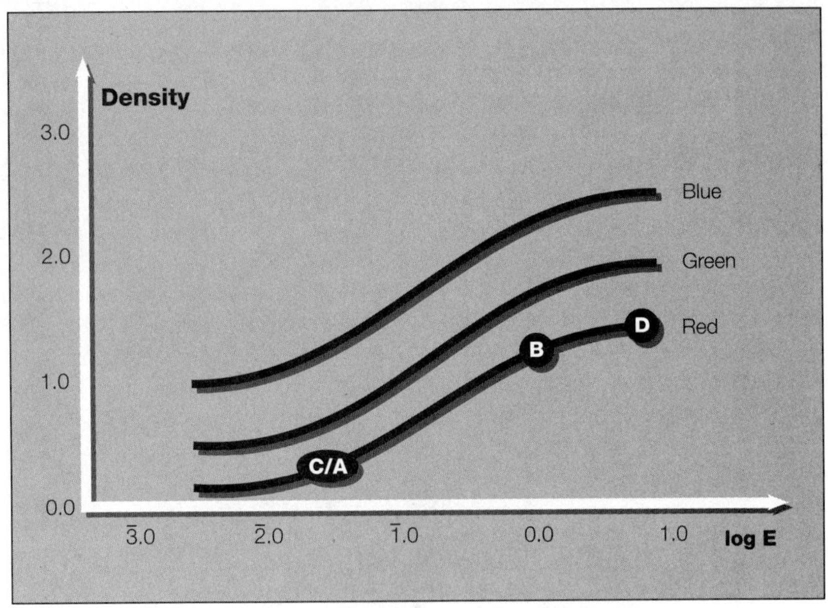

Figure 5.10 Measuring Straight Line and Overall Useful Range on Fujicolor F-125 *Approximation scaled as per published Fuji curves in Figure 5.9b.*

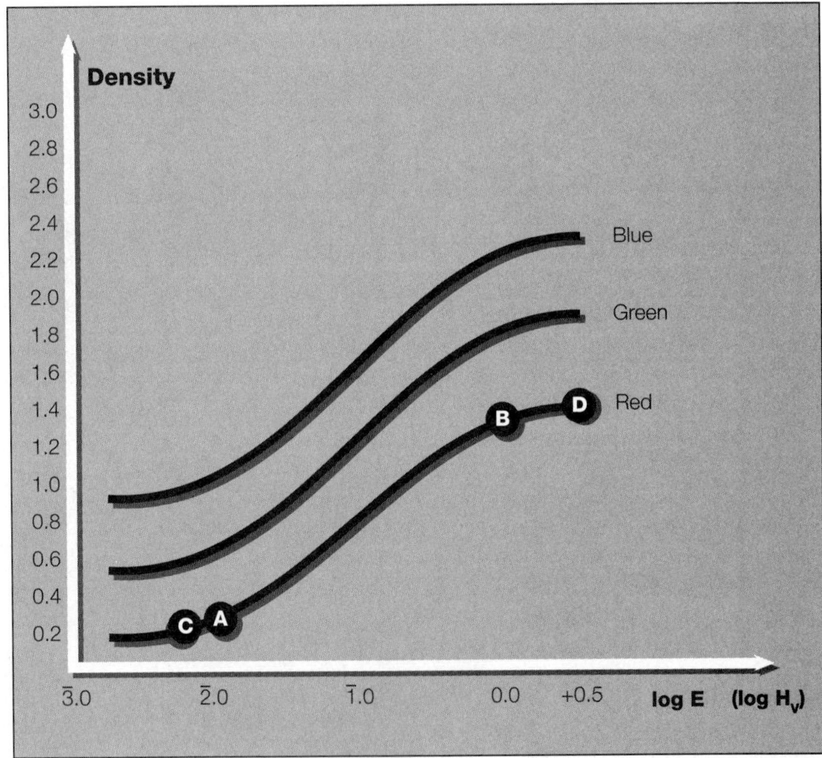

Figure 5.11 Measuring Straight Line and Overall Useful Range on Agfa XT 100 *Approximation scaled as per published Agfa curves in Figure 5.9a.*

AGFA XT 100 EXAMPLE Following the procedures just outlined, we obtain for the straight line: point A approximately 2.0 and point B at 0.0. This represents two units of 1.0 log E, or a 2.0 log E range. Dividing 2.0 by .3 gives us $6^2/_3$ zones, or slightly less than 128:1 (see Figure 5.11). For the overall useful range, we obtain point C at 2.2 and point D at +0.5. This gives us two units of 1.0 log E plus .2 log E for C and .5 log E for D. This equals a log E range of 2.7. Dividing 2.7 by .3 gives us nine zones (512:1).

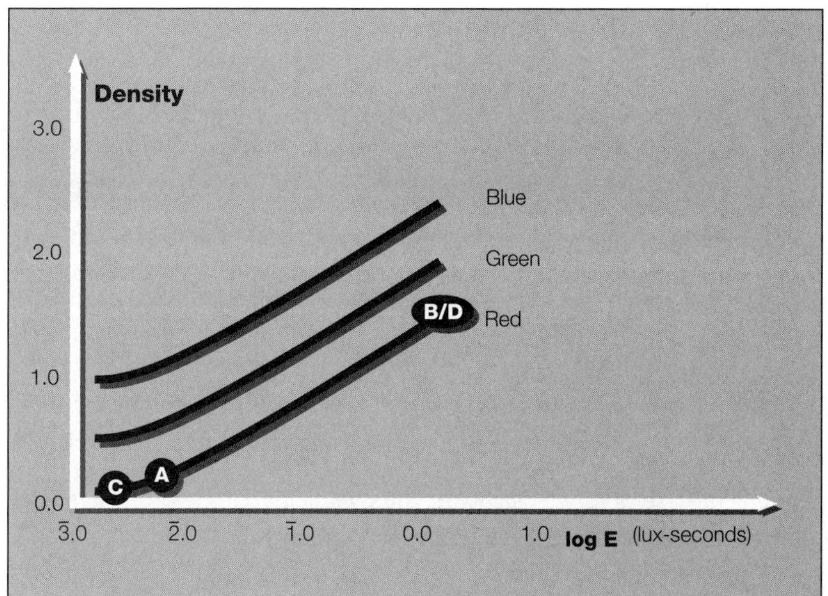

Figure 5.12 Measuring Straight Line and Overall Useful Range on Eastman EXR 7248 *Approximation scaled as per published Eastman curves in Figure 5.9c.*

Straight line (A–B) = 2.3 log E units ($\bar{2}.2 + 0.1 = 2.3$). This equals $7\frac{2}{3}$ zones.

Overall useful range (C–D) = 2.8 log E units (2.7 + 0.1 = 2.8). This equals $9\frac{1}{3}$ zones.

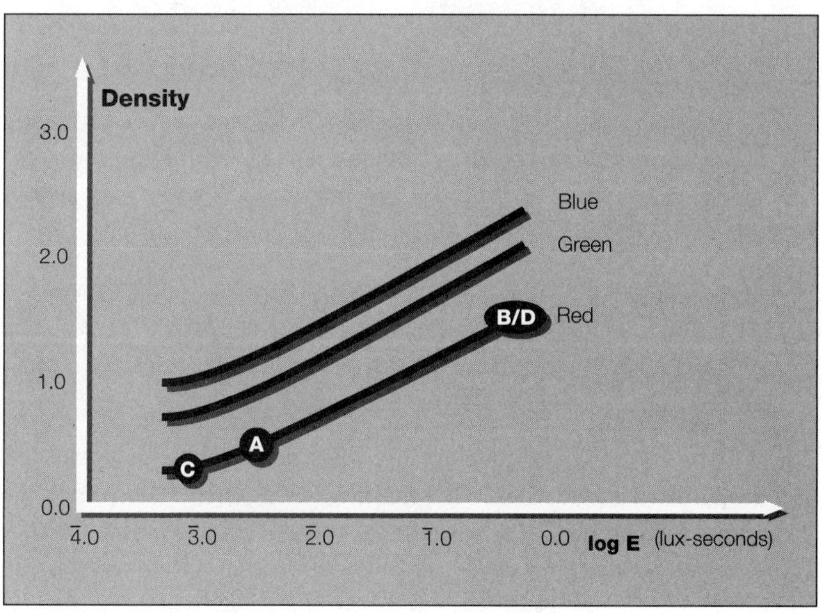

Figure 5.13 Measuring Straight Line and Overall Useful Range on Eastman EXR 7296 *Approximation scaled as per published Eastman curves in Figure 5.9c.*

Straight line (A–B) = 2.1 log E units ($\bar{2}.5 - 0.4 = 2.1$). This equals 7 zones.

Overall useful range (C–D) = 2.8 log E units ($\bar{3}.2 - 0.4 = 2.8$). This equals $9\frac{1}{3}$ zones.

KODAK EXR 7248 AND 7296 EXAMPLES Two curves from Kodak's extended range stocks are marked in Figures 5.12 and 5.13 and are provided for comparison purposes. Historically speaking, these are very long straight lines and useful ranges for color motion picture stocks.[5]

The cinematographer can utilize characteristic curves to test an emulsion's processing and printing specifications and to coordinate lighting with image quality and image look. For example, curves can be used to test an emulsion's capacity for under- and overdevelopment and to determine how far the cinematographer can go with under- and overexposure and still generate acceptable images with corrections at the printing stage.[6]

SUMMARY

In this chapter, we have seen that exposure relates the subject's luminance range to the emulsion's characteristic curve in controllable ways. The following concepts were examined in detail:

- *Characteristic curves* graphically illustrate how an emulsion reacts to light. On the straight line, the reaction is proportional—increments of exposure (log E) are given proportional increments of density. This relationship is distorted on the toe and shoulder of the curve.
- *Log E range of the straight line* is the length of the straight line in log E units determined by projecting the straight line onto the log E axis.
- *Overall useful range* calculates the overall log E range for the negative by adding the log E range of the toe and shoulder to the log E range of the straight line.
- *Relating zones to the characteristic curve.* Both straight line and overall useful ranges can be scaled in zone values. This is done by dividing their log E ranges by .3 log E (remember, .3 = the log of 2).
- *Gamma* refers to the angle the straight line makes relative to the log E axis. Gamma measures how the emulsion allocates density values to log E increments. In theory, a gamma of 1.0 represents an accurate reproduction of the range of luminances in the original.
- *Overall gamma* factors in all the components of the imaging system—from the negative gamma to the gamma of the cinema screen—in determining the contrast properties of the system. The current standard overall gamma is around 1.45.
- *Printing contrast.* Negatives designed for printing have low-contrast properties with gammas in the range of .6 to .7. These low-contrast gammas allow the negative to translate long log E ranges (subject luminance ranges).
- *Projection contrast.* Prints and reversal camera originals are designed for projection and exhibit relatively high gammas—in the 1.6 to 1.8 range. Projection contrast makes it difficult to arrive at high-quality prints from the original.
- *Reading actual characteristic curves.* Detailed examples of how to do this were discussed.

Again, we see that exposure allows for many creative possibilities and that exposure choice works hand in hand with lighting to determine an image's final look.

NOTES

1. This log E range is traditionally called latitude, an unfortunate term since it implies there is room for error in exposure, which there isn't except with very low contrast subjects. Latitude has little to do with "permissible error," but rather with the length of the straight line projection onto the log E axis. We shall avoid the term and use *straight line* and *log E range of the straight line* in its place.

2. For a good exploration of gamma see Leslie Wheeler, *Principles of Cinematography* (London: Fountain Press, 1965), pp. 188–191. Also useful is the Kodak publication *Basic Photographic Sensitometry Workbook*, 2nd ed., Kodak Publication No. Z-22-ED (Rochester, N.Y.: Eastman Kodak, 1971).

   Many photographers have replaced the term *gamma* with *contrast index*, a term more useful for their purposes since stocks with similar gammas, that is, parallel straight lines, can have differing contrast effects in their final prints. Another system involves *mean gradient* ($\bar{G}$), a term that attempts to account for emulsions with much curve and little straight line. For our purposes, the somewhat hypothetical *straight line* and the term *gamma* will suffice since we do not require the precision postulated by the new terms for photography. See Ansel Adams, *The Negative* (Boston: Little, Brown,1981), p. 89, for his views on this.

3. Russell Campbell (ed.), *Photographic Theory for the Motion Picture Cameraman* (New York: A. S. Barnes, 1981), p. 104.

4. In his article "Film to Tape Mysteries Unraveled," Frank Reinking lists the ideal overall as 1.45 for cinema projection (1.6 for final print gamma x .9 for the projection = 1.44) and recommends a careful control over gamma when transferring film to video. Gamma for such transfers depends on whether the Rank Cintel transfer is from a negative, CRI, or print which may be standard or low contrast. Frank Reinking, "Film to Tape Mysteries Unraveled," *American Cinematographer* (September 1989): 73–80.

5. Table 7.1 lists the straight line and overall useful ranges for most color negatives. We shall discuss this topic further in Chapter 7.

6. See Appendix J, "Suggested Exposure and Lighting Exercises." Also see Kris Malkiewicz, *Cinematography*, 2nd ed. (New York: Prentice-Hall, 1989), p. 87, for a good discussion of emulsion tests.

BASIC EXPOSURE THEORY: LIGHT METER AND KEYTONE METHOD

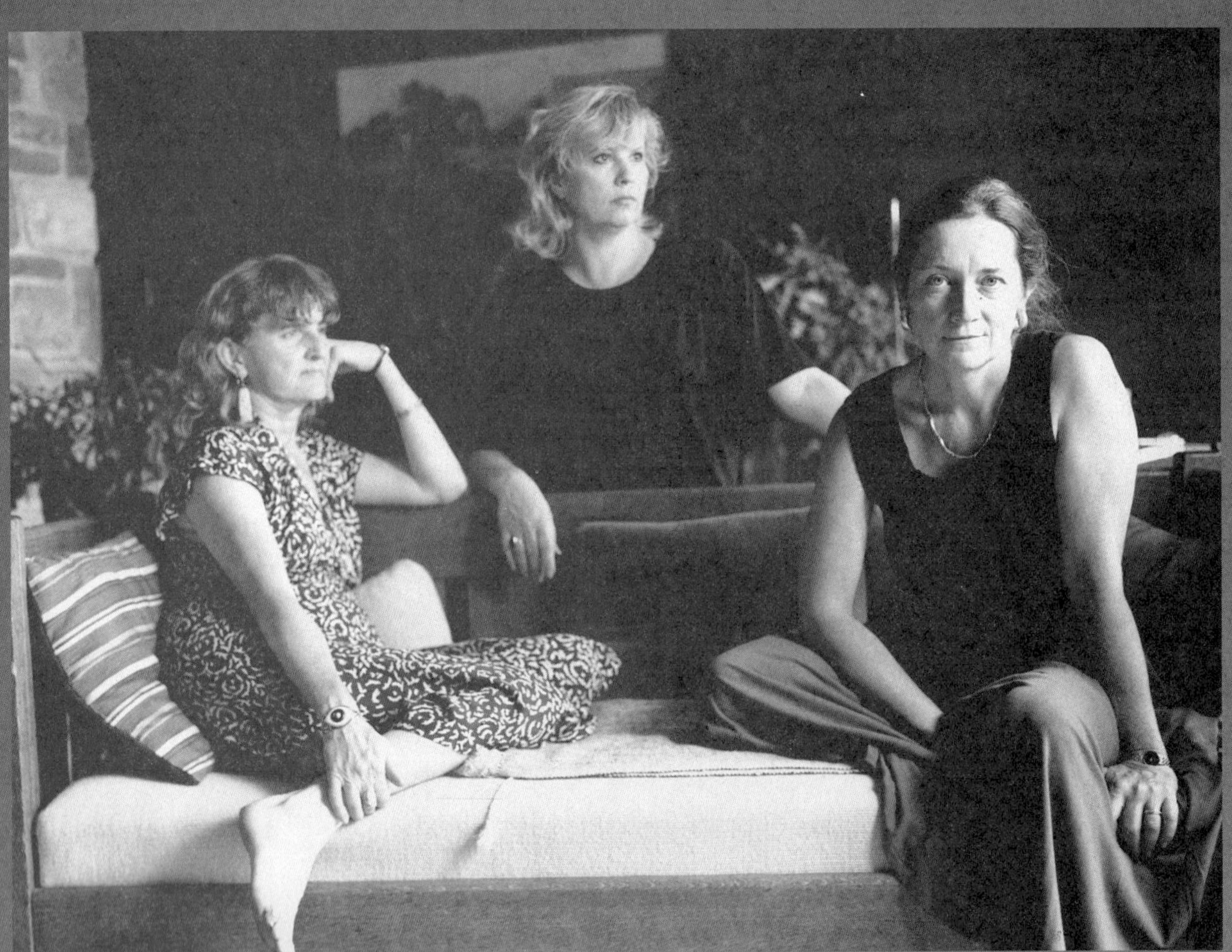

"zone 5 exposure"

There are two methods for taking an exposure reading: incident and reflected. This chapter examines the roles of the incident and reflected meters in exposure and explains their central assumption: that a zone 5, midgray, 18% subject reflectance should be rendered at the mid-density point on the characteristic curve.

PLACEMENT OF zone 5 is the basis for cinematographic exposure theory and is called the keytone method. Using the keytone method we place zone 5 at a predetermined point on the characteristic curve. The remaining zones fall into place automatically.

APPROACHES TO EXPOSURE

There are two main approaches to exposure:

- The *incident (highlight or keytone)* method, which arrives at an exposure by measuring the light incident upon the subject.
- The *reflected method*, which measures the light reflected from the subject to the camera and the subject's luminance range.

These two exposure methods place different emphases on the two key concerns addressed by any exposure method:

1. The intensity of the light falling on the subject.
2. The specific luminance values present in the subject (subject luminance range), all of which must be accounted for in terms of the characteristic curve.

The **incident method** emphasizes concern number one—the intensity of the light incident upon the subject. The **reflected method** emphasizes number two—the actual subject luminance values present. For precise control of exposure, the incident and reflected methods must take into account both of these key concerns.

Although cinematography relies heavily on the incident method, certain situations require a reflected reading for exposure determination. Others require a reflected reading that is then integrated into the lighting design and the overall incident exposure determination. Thus, cinematographers use both methods—represented respectively by the incident and reflected light meters.

BASIC PROPERTIES OF THE INCIDENT LIGHT METER

The incident method (keytone or **highlight method**) emphasizes consistency of tonal rendition. It assumes that **midgray** in the subject should always be reproduced as a midgray on the emulsion. Further, this method ensures constant densities for certain **keytones** (zones 4–7) independent of their context. For example, faces, which vary from zone 4 to zone 6½ depending on skin color, will be rendered consistently no matter what the content of the rest of the shot. The incident method is ideal for cinematography because consistency of skin tone from shot to shot is very important.

The incident method is sometimes called the highlight method since it is concerned with the straight line and shoulder of the characteristic curve at the expense of the toe. Note that this is perfect for cinema, since the viewer first watches faces, if present, and then bright, highlight areas.

The overriding rule with incident meters is this: To duplicate what you see, place the light meter in the light falling on the subject, point the photosphere at the camera, and expose with the indicated reading. In cinematography, the problem of where to place particular subject luminances is simplified by the assumption that the middle zones are of primary importance.

Zone 5 Exposure

The incident meter is designed to reproduce zone 5, midgray, 18% reflectances at the **mid-density point** on the characteristic curve. This is called a **zone 5 exposure**. Exposing for (pegging) zone 5 places the other two middle zones, 4 and 6, highlight zones 7 and 8, and lower values 2 and 3, at their respective density points (see Figure 6.1).

It does not matter for exposure purposes that a zone 5 value is not always present in the shot. What counts is that all zones present are automatically pegged to their optimum density points for cinematographic purposes. Pegging ensures good highlight renditions and safe exposures for the all-important middle zones.

Incident meters ensure precise consistency because they calculate exposure for all lighting setups from the same object—the meter's photosphere (lumisphere), which is equivalent to an inbuilt **gray card.** The only variables—the intensity and angle of the illumination—are accounted for through T-stop adjustments to the exposure given. The result is that within a scene, a particular actor's face is rendered with a consistent density and the illusion of reality is maintained.

Exposure index (EI) measures the relative speed by which an emulsion reacts to light. By setting the ASA/ISO scale on the light meter we are in effect calibrating the meter to that particular film stock.[1] Over a number of scenes, as the illumination varies, the meter will indicate a

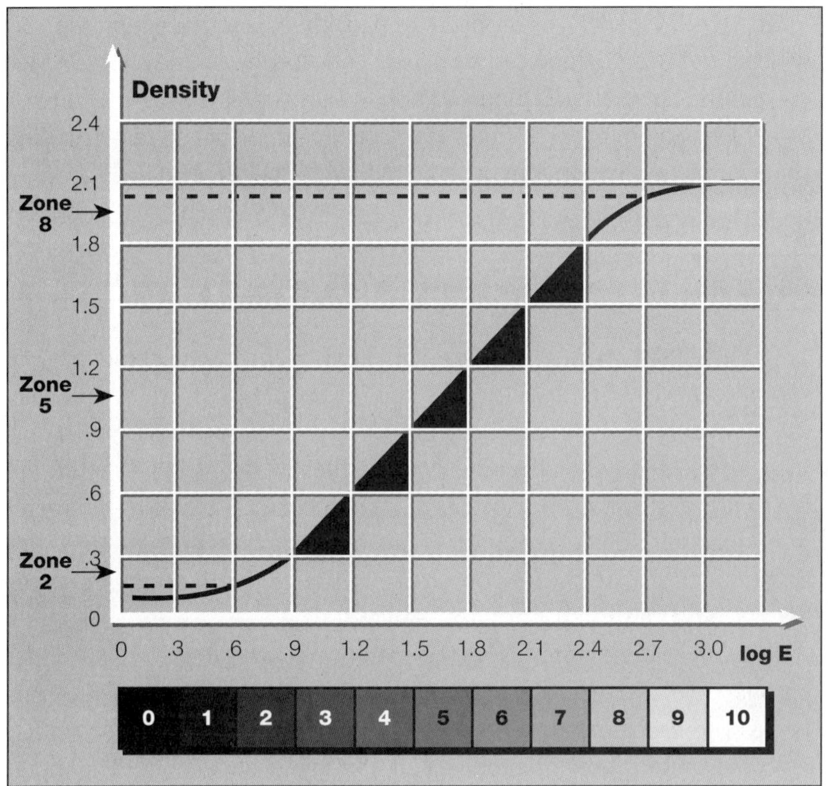

Figure 6.1 Zone 5 Exposure
A zone 5 exposure is the normal exposure *in film and faithfully reproduces key middle zones by placing the zone 5 subject luminance at the mid-density point on the characteristic curve. The rest of the zones then progress outward from that key point. Zones which fall outside the straight line onto the shoulder and toe will be compressed as are zones 2 and 8 in this example. Luminance values outside those for zones 2 and 8 will be represented as a black and a white respectively.*

To place zone 5 at the mid-density point still leaves one very important variable: which subject luminance to place at zone 5. The incident meter answers this automatically: an 18% reflectance. The reflected meter requires a decision by the cinematographer.

variety of exposure combinations. On the emulsion, however, all zone 5 values will have the same density and, hence, will look the same when projected onto the screen.

THE KEYTONE METHOD

As we have seen, incident light meters assure the cinematographer of consistent densities for facetones independent of context and lighting variations. The cinematographer measures the intensity of the light falling on the subject, usually a face, and calculates an exposure setting that automatically pegs an 18% reflectance, if present, to a mid-density point on the characteristic curve, resulting in a zone 5 value on the screen. Zone 6 Caucasian facetones, zone 4 black facetones, and other zones fall into place naturally. Since the photosphere is pointed at the camera lens, the angle of the incident light is accounted for as well as its intensity. The white globe effectively represents the insertion of a standardized three-dimensional object into the lighting setup. The advantage for the cinematographer is that the meter does all of this automatically.

The incident method is also referred to as the **keytone method** since we concentrate on placing certain "key" tones—faces and 18% mid-grays—on the characteristic curve and ignore actual subject luminance values, though we take these into account in our lighting and our choice of exactly what to expose for, as we shall see in Chapters 7 and 10.

The basic "theory" of exposure in film, then, is to have a method by which a defined keytone can be placed consistently on the characteristic curve. The incident keytone method ensures this through a zone 5 placement for midgray. This is particularly important when matching shots within a scene that may be filmed over a period of days.

REFLECTED LIGHT READINGS IN FILM

Reflected light readings are used in film under certain conditions. The spot meter is the best tool for reflected readings though we occasionally use an averaging-type meter such as the Gossen Luna Pro, or a Sekonic with a reflected light attachment. With the averaging-type meter, we try to use a gray card or closeup reading technique to make the meter more precise. Inbuilt, through-the-lens meters are reflected meters, not as precise as spot meters but more selective than averaging types because you can zoom in to take readings.

Like an incident meter, reflected meters are calibrated so as to render a zone 5 subject value at the mid-density point on the characteristic curve. The problem is that the reading from a spot meter, or any other reflected meter, must be modified by the user's experience. The meter itself always assumes that it's being pointed at an 18% gray card. When pointed at a particular luminance—no matter whether white, black, or gray—a spot meter gives a reading which will render that luminance value as a zone 5 midgray. The situation is worsened by use of an averaging-type meter since it's difficult to even know which luminances it's reading.

Though not impossible to work with in cinematography, spot meters leave room for human error when determining T-stop because of the need to adjust the given reading for the particular luminance value being read. This can be improved upon by using a standardized reflectance to determine T-stop—say, always reading off a gray card held in the light illuminating the subject. But this is what an incident meter already does—and more simply.

In cinematography, we rely mainly on the incident method since our main concern is with the zonal renditions of facial and highlight portions of the frame. However, there are special circumstances that require a reflected reading for exposure determination. A good example is where **luminous objects** are present—a situation that will be discussed thoroughly in Chapter 7.

We also use reflected meters to determine T-stop when it's impossible or impractical to take an incident meter reading. An example: You are in a jet and need an exposure through the window. This kind of reflected reading is usually of the overall averaging variety and is done on an emergency basis. Some cinematographers just use their experience and "guess" the exposure.

The last common use for reflected readings, in this case a spot meter, is to check subject luminance range and lighting ratios. Incident meters can also be used for this purpose, as we'll see in Chapter 7. Once major highlights and facetones are arranged, most film stocks can easily handle all but extraordinary luminance ranges. Television and video, however, cannot handle the same ranges as film: Consequently, television lighting directors use spot meters and **waveform monitors** (electronic means for measuring video signals) regularly to ensure subject luminance ranges are within acceptable tolerances. We will discuss this topic more thoroughly in Part IV, "Electronic Cinematography."

SUMMARY

Through exposure and lighting, the cinematographer has complete control over two key variables affecting the photographic quality of the image. The first is *keytone placement*: Through exposure we place (peg) the keytone (zone 5) at a predetermined point on the characteristic curve; the remaining zones then fall into place automatically. The second variable is *overall subject luminance range*: Through lighting we alter or create the range of luminances we desire, either expanding or contracting the given range.

Once the main subject is "visualized," the cinematographer decides where to put the light meter for a reading. The meter pegs the important middle and high zones into place on the characteristic curve, taking into account the brightness of the illumination by indicating a set of T-stop/shutter speed combinations.

Any zone 5 value in the main subject lighting will be rendered at a mid-density point on the characteristic curve for that emulsion, and all other zones will fall into place proportionally. With the incident meter any given object will have the same look under varying illuminations because it will be reproduced with the same density value on the negative. Not only that, all other reflectances will maintain their uniformity as well. This gives the cinematographer a fixed point from which to work.

NOTE

1. ASA stands for American Standards Association, now known as ANSI, American National Standards Institute. ISO stands for International Standards Organization. Motion picture film stocks have exposure indices to calibrate with light meters' ASA/ISO scales. We say that fast Fuji negative has an exposure index of 500, not that it has a speed of 500 ASA, though it amounts to the same thing on the light meter. For a good discussion of this, see Daan M. Zwick, "The Technical Basis of Photographic Speed Determination, or What Is a Normal Exposure?" *SMPTE Journal* (August 1979), pp. 533–37.

COMMON EXPOSURE SITUATIONS

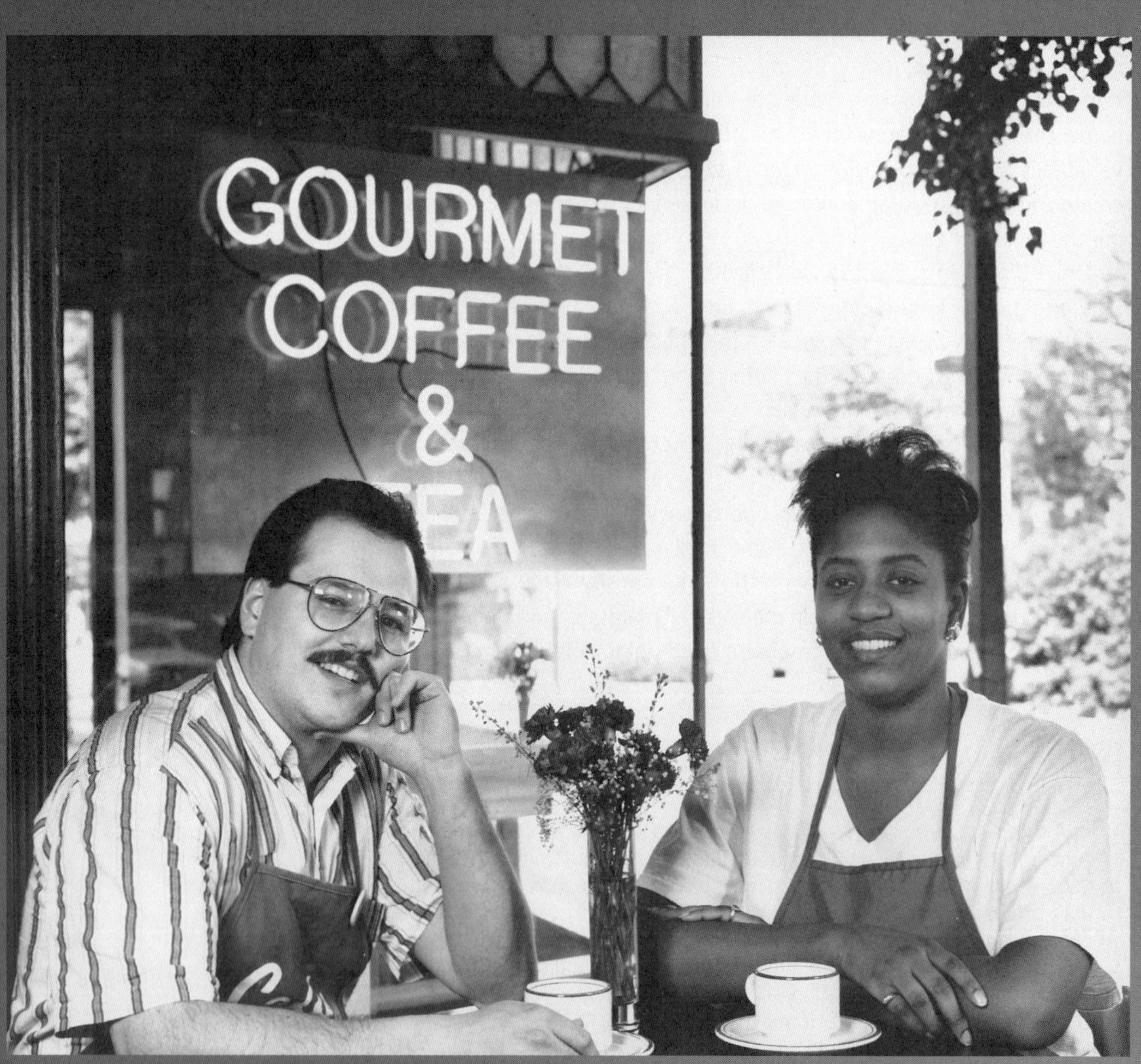

"interior/exterior"

7

Since exposure has creative possibilities, the cinematographer has choices when selecting what to expose for. This problem is highlighted in the handling of overall subject luminance range, which we shall look at in this chapter. In addition, there are a number of recurring exposure situations that we shall investigate for their creative possibilities as well as their problems. These include the handling of luminous objects, compromise exposure, use of under- and overexposure, the handling of all-dark and all-light subjects, and pulling T-stop.

AS WE HAVE seen, the incident meter reliably pegs keytones and handles the problem of light intensity (brightness), but the problem of overall luminance range remains the cinematographer's. Lighting technique allows control over the luminance range, which may be previsualized using the zone system or measured with a spot meter. The characteristic curve reveals sensitometric data, but to coordinate all of this requires more than just measurement and data. It requires visualization and artistry. The cinematographer must rely on mind and eye as much as on the light meter.

LUMINANCE RANGE CONSIDERATIONS

The zone system tells us what happens to objects not in the same lighting intensity as the main subject. Take for example a two-person interior setup with a window effect at frame right. Obviously the person nearer the window will be brighter than the person to frame left (see Figure 7.1). Now suppose there is a two-stop difference in lighting intensity between the two figures. Exposure for the person frame right will correctly render that person and underexpose the person frame left by two stops; that is, she will be rendered at zone 4 rather than zone 6 (see Figure 7.1a). Likewise, exposure for the person frame left will render her correctly at zone 6 but overexpose the person at frame right by two zones (see Figure 7.1d).

Of course, it is possible to expose somewhere in between the two extremes and arrive at acceptable placements (see Figure 7.1b and c). The point is that by taking an incident reading for each person, we can determine the difference in lighting intensity, previsualize how each will render in terms of zones, and make an exposure choice based on that previsualization.

Likewise for the cat in the window in Figure 7.2. Exposure for outside the window (Figure 7.2a) and the shadow side of the cat (Figure 7.2c) gives us two extremes, both of which we can previsualize based on the difference between the actual T-stop readings, which in this case is

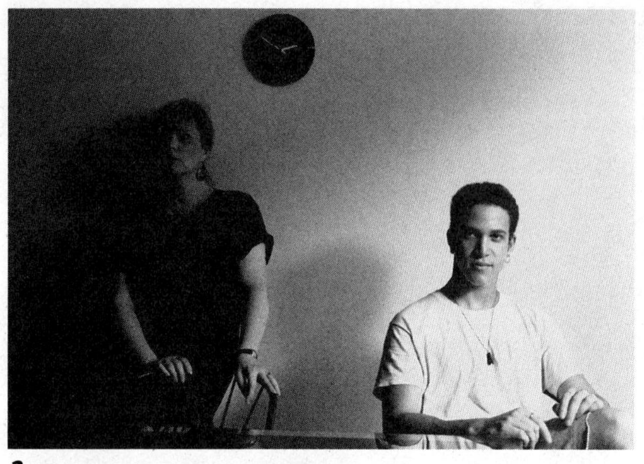
a

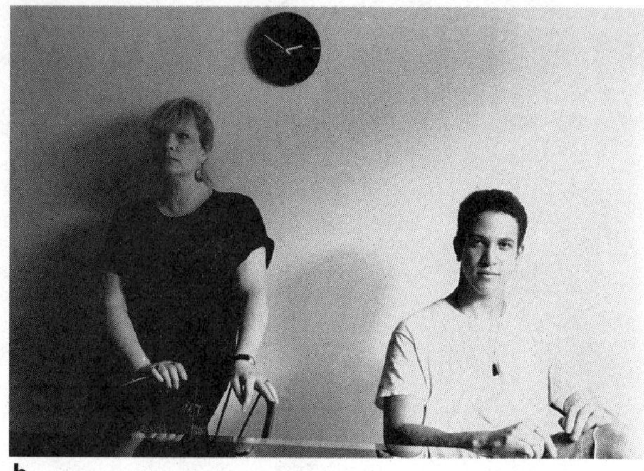
b

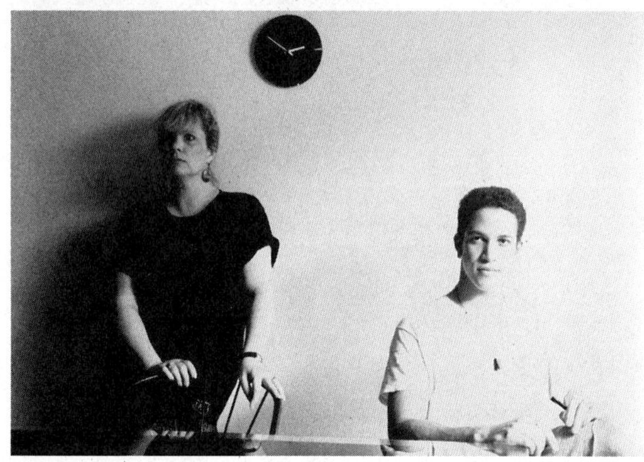
c

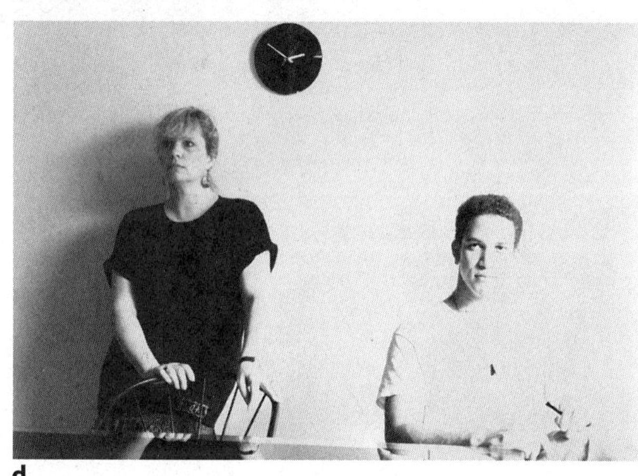
d

Figure 7.1 Exposure Possibilities for a Daylight Interior Window Effect *In the standard day interior, there are three exposure choices: Expose for the person nearer the window (a), use a compromise exposure (b and c), or expose for the person farther from the window (d). Exposure for either person impacts on the rendition of the other.*

about five stops. Again, exposure for somewhere in between may be acceptable if we are unable to boost the lighting on the cat or bring down the outside intensity with neutral density (ND) gels on the window (see Figure 7.2b).

One last example may make this power of the zone system clearer. Suppose we have a shot of a person on a chair and an unlit bed and white pillow in the background. Suppose the exposure reading for the person is T 5.6. The question is how will the white pillow appear if we expose for the person. Normally it would be rendered at zone 8, but that assumes it is in the same lighting as the person. Here it is unlit.

To determine how the pillow would be rendered under these conditions, we first take an incident reading for it. Assume we obtain T 2. This means the pillow is lit three stops under the main subject. Exposure at T 5.6 will underexpose the white pillow by three stops (three zones). The pillow will be rendered as a zone 5 midgray rather than its normal zone 8 white. Other parts of the shot can be previsualized in exactly the same way. For example, if there were a gray cat (normally zone 4) by the pillow, we know it would come out at zone 1, a black cat.

If the lighting on the pillow were at the same level as the main subject, it would be given a normal zone 5 exposure and would reproduce at its standard zone 8. Had the lighting on the pillow been brighter than on the subject, say T 11, then we know the pillow would be reproduced

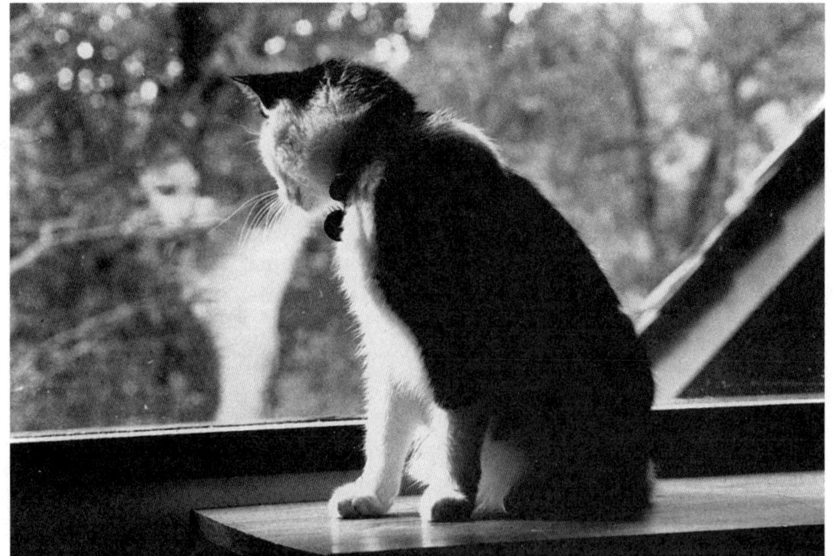

a

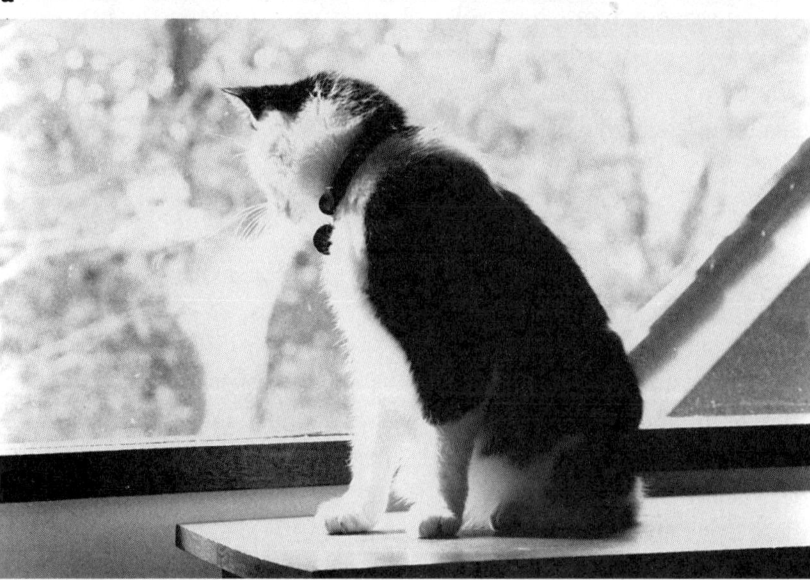

b

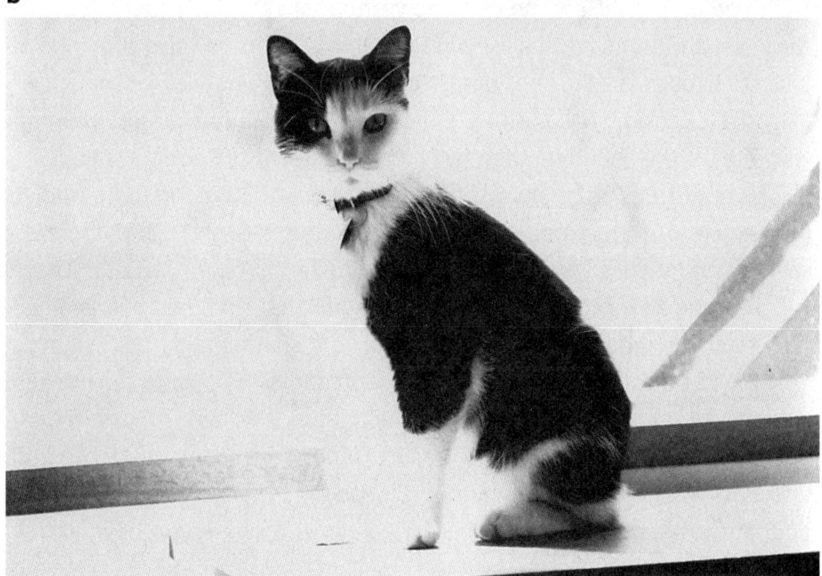

c

Figure 7.2 Exposure Possibilities for a Cat in a Window *There are three choices: Expose for outside the window (a), use a compromise exposure (b), or expose for the shadow side of the cat (c).*

two stops, two zones, above normal, that is, zone 10 maximum white. The cat in this case would be rendered at zone 6 light gray.

We can determine overall subject luminance range using this same method. First, take a reading for the brightest significant luminance and determine its T-stop reading and then zonal rendition relative to the subject exposure as we did with the white pillow above.[1] Then do the same for the darkest significant object. This provides us with our highest and lowest zone values, that is, the subject luminance range expressed in zones. A spot meter can also be used to measure these values.

We typically select the brightest and darkest values by eye, but some cinematographers use a viewing glass to help them see luminances more like the film stock will render them. The viewing glass, also called a pan glass, is normally a Kodak Wratten #90 or equivalent for B & W, and a neutral density filter for color. Viewing glasses are designed to minimize color and facilitate perception of relative brightnesses. They are often used in lighting.[2]

Many cinematographers will not measure subject luminance range but will rely on experience and light by eye, letting dark values fall where they may. These cinematographers would, however, still be careful to balance white highlight values to the key light so that such highlights will not distract from the subject. This balancing is done when lighting.

EXPOSURE FOR OVERLAPPING LUMINANCE RANGES

One common problem is where the subject consists of several overlapping luminance ranges. Even in a very simple subject with a single light source, there are two subject luminance ranges: the light side and the shadow side. Along with the luminance range of the background, these two ranges are the most important ones in cinematography.

Cinematographers must learn to control one luminance range relative to the other. Lighting is the most powerful tool at their disposal to handle these situations, as we shall see in Part III, but exposure also offers possibilities. Exposure for one range of subject luminances automatically excludes exposing for another. Exposure for the bright range automatically means the shadow range will fall lower down the zonal scale.

So, how does a cinematographer, faced with two or more subject ranges, choose an exposure? There is no simple answer, but there are several approaches to a solution. Take for example the portrait in Figure 7.3. Assume an incident measurement shows that six times as much light falls on the bright side of the face as on the shadow side, for example, 100 footcandles to approximately 17 footcandles. Exposure for the light side (placing the face at zone 6) will yield facial shadows $2^1/_2$ zones darker than the light side, a 6:1 ratio as in Figure 7.3b (see also Figure 2.8b and c). This is the normal manner of working: Expose for the light side and let the shadow side fall where it will, or for where you have lit it. In

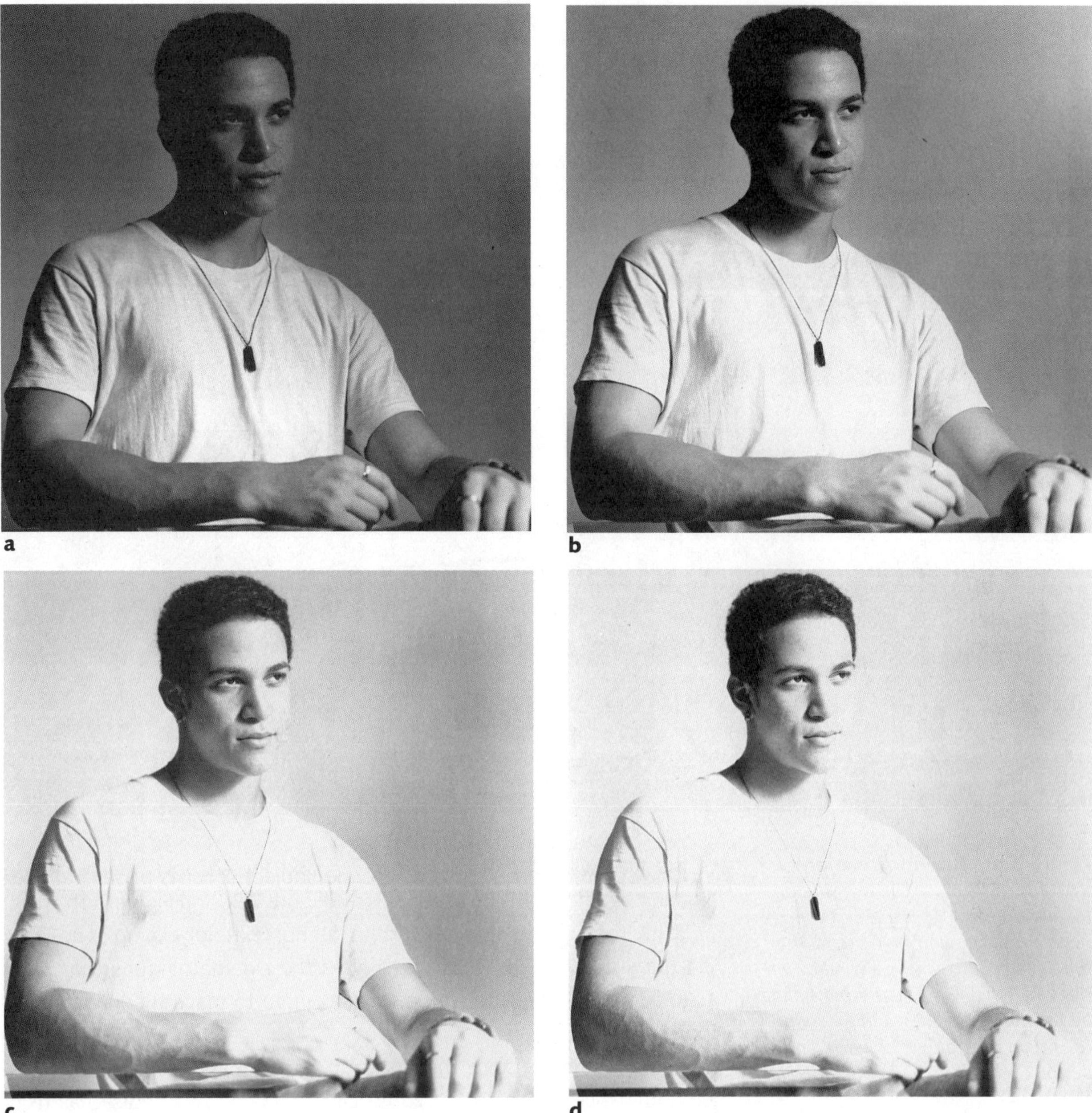

this example, exposure for the bright side puts the face at zone 6 and the shadow side at zone $3^1/_2$.

As we have seen, there are alternatives to this normal, "correct" exposure. For example, the cinematographer might choose to expose for the shadow range and place it at zone 6 ("correct" exposure) on the characteristic curve. Then, values in the shadows will reproduce normally and only an impression of shadows will remain. Values on the light side of the face will automatically reproduce $2^1/_2$ zones lighter than normal at zone $8^1/_2$, which is very white. The result is a lighter version of the first and can be preferable, depending on context (see Figure 7.3d).

The other alternative is to expose in between the two extremes, a **compromise exposure.** If we expose halfway in between, the light side

Figure 7.3 Exposure for Lit and Shadow Sides of a Face *Exposure for the lit side of the face (b) and for the shadow side (d) offers different possibilities. Other possibilities include one-stop underexposure (a) and a compromise placement (c).*

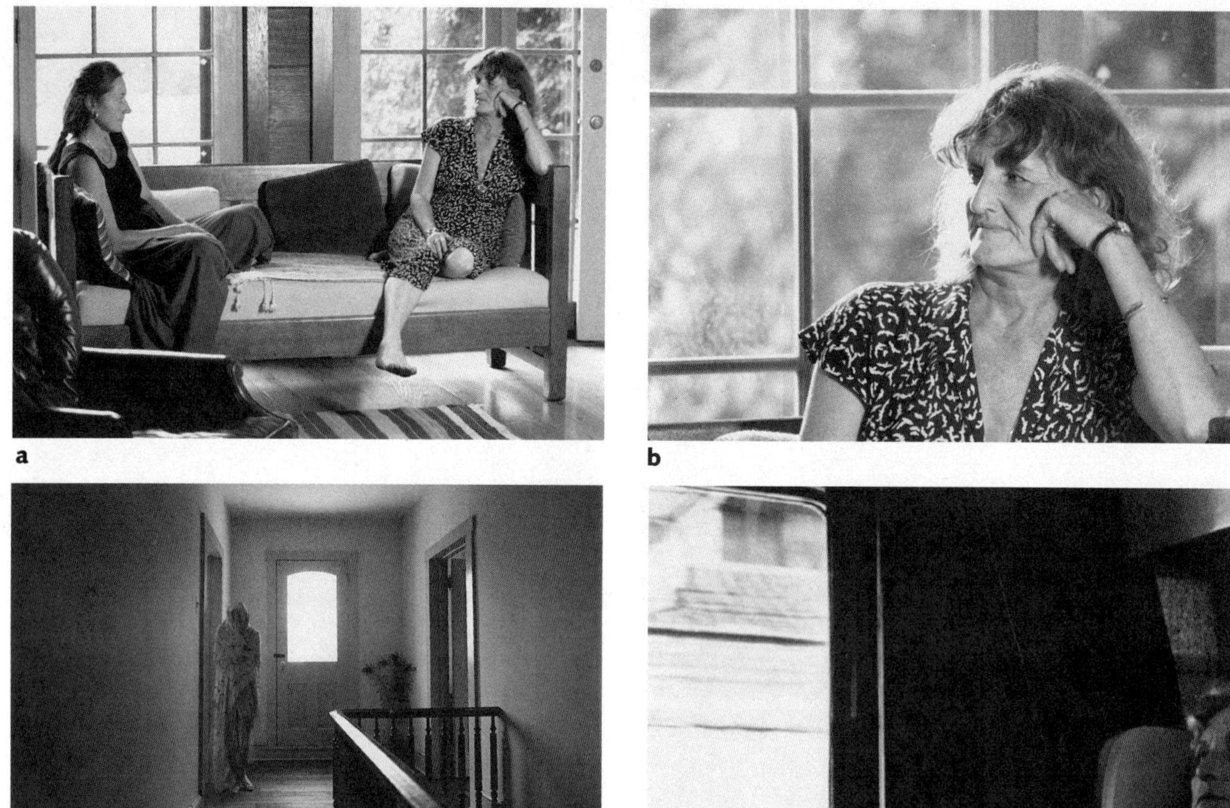

Figure 7.4 Interior/Exterior Window Effects *The two shots in (a) and (b) show typical use of windows as background for persons. The third example (c) shows a window interior with a hallway (detail from a photo by Jennifer A. Tucker), and the fourth (d) a train interior with window and person (detail from a photo by Gerald Lang).*

of the face will fall around zone 7–7½ and the shadows around 4½–5. Nothing significant will be at zone 6 (see Figure 7.3c and Figure 7.1b and c).

Study the lighting analyses for the interior/exterior examples in Figure 7.4 (pages 262–263). Note the choices the cinematographer has made as to how to render the windows and where to place the interior facetones.

It is evident that since the cinematographer can place only one subject luminance range on the zone scale "correctly," a choice has to be made as to which of those ranges to expose for. Other subject ranges will fall higher or lower automatically. Of course, it is just these other ranges overlapping the main range that creates the mood of the image, like overtones in music. As we shall see in Part III, the cinematographer can manipulate these other ranges for effect through lighting.

The point here is that even with just exposure choice, the cinematographer can control and utilize luminance range overlaps through the selection of which range to expose for and where to place it on the zone scale. Visualization in advance is essential since it is only then that the cinematographer can correct the image through lighting, camera-angle change, or movement of the subject.

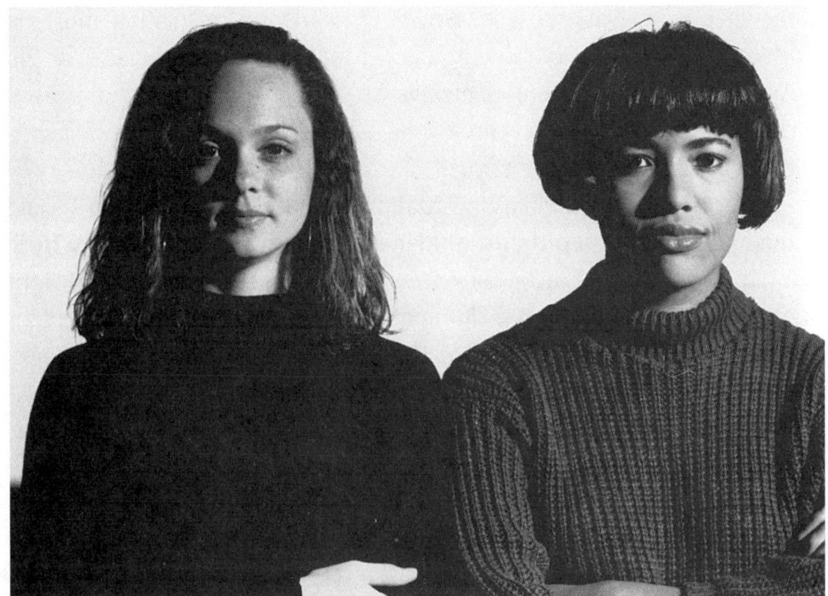

a

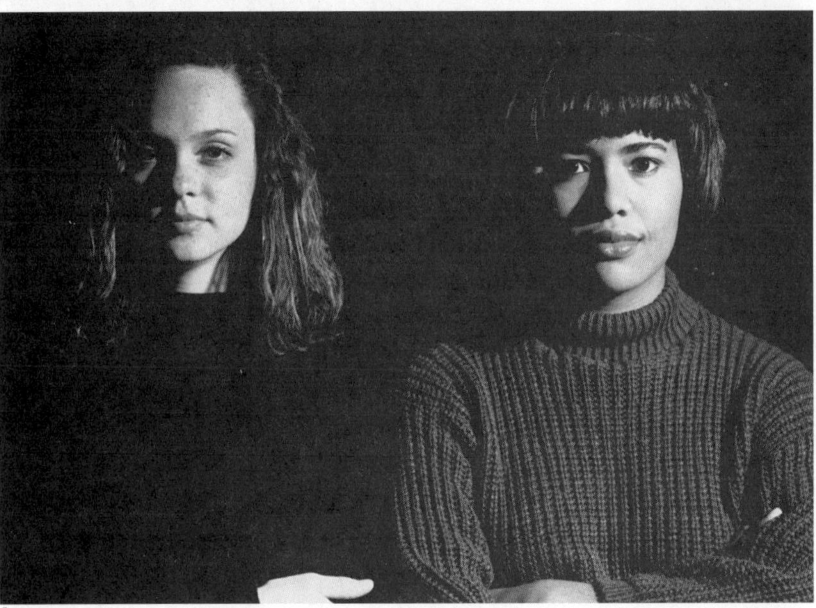

b

Figure 7.5 Actor Facetones Given a Consistent Density by an Incident Meter Even Though the Background Changes from White to Black

EFFECT OF SUBJECT LUMINANCE RANGE ON EXPOSURE

The specific values in the subject luminance range have no influence on an exposure reading determined by an incident light reading. Take for example two actors under fixed illumination in front of a background that changes from white to black. The incident meter will indicate the same T-stop for the faces regardless of the luminance value of the background (see Figure 7.5).

In comparison, an averaging-type, reflected light meter will tend to give reading variations due to the influence of the background on the meter. Spot meters and closeup reading techniques using averaging meters can avoid this changing background problem since they can be directed precisely at the face. However, a mental calculation must be added to the reading to arrive at a consistent placement because, as we have seen, a reflected meter always assumes it's pointed at a zone 5 value. Inbuilt camera meters are of the averaging type and thus susceptible to background reading errors.[3]

Under this fixed illumination situation, it is obvious the T-stop should remain unchanged in order to render the face at the same density from shot to shot. The easiest way to ensure this is with an incident light meter that reacts only to the illumination itself. In fact, with the incident meter, you can vary the level of the illumination as well as the background or foreground and the face will still look the same. This consistency is the reason the incident meter is such a powerful cinematographic tool.

A certain imprecision is built into the keytone method since it ignores actual subject luminances. For example, if a white object is present in the subject, we don't really know whether it will render as zone 8 or 9. We know it will reproduce as white, assuming it's in the same light as the subject, but not its exact zone rendition. Likewise for many of the other objects in the scene. We can measure these values with a spot meter and determine their exact placement, but we normally do this only for very important or troublesome objects at the extremes of luminance range, since this slows down shooting considerably. Mostly we rely on our experience.

With an incident technique, the cinematographer "controls" the reproduction of the subject luminance range by deciding where to place the meter for the reading and then adjusting the lighting accordingly. Normally this is a simple matter, but the lighting of backgrounds and foregrounds with different intensities than the central subject is the starting point for lighting design as we shall see later.

EXPOSURE FOR LUMINOUS OBJECTS

The most common use of reflected readings involves calculating an exposure for a subject not lit by incident light—for example, when filming light sources or other **luminous objects**. These are quite common and include neon signs, sunsets, light bulbs, fires, reflections on water, stained-glass windows, steamed-up windows and shower glass, even sunny street exteriors seen through billowing white curtains. A reflected technique is used whenever it is important to retain the feeling of light, the subtle values of luminosity (see Figure 7.6).

Exposing for luminous objects has many interesting variations, but there are two main situations:

- When the luminous object is the main part of the shot—a light bulb, a sunset over the ocean, a picture of a candle flame.
- When the luminous object is only part of the shot, and not necessarily very important—practicals, such as a lamp in a living room, or a

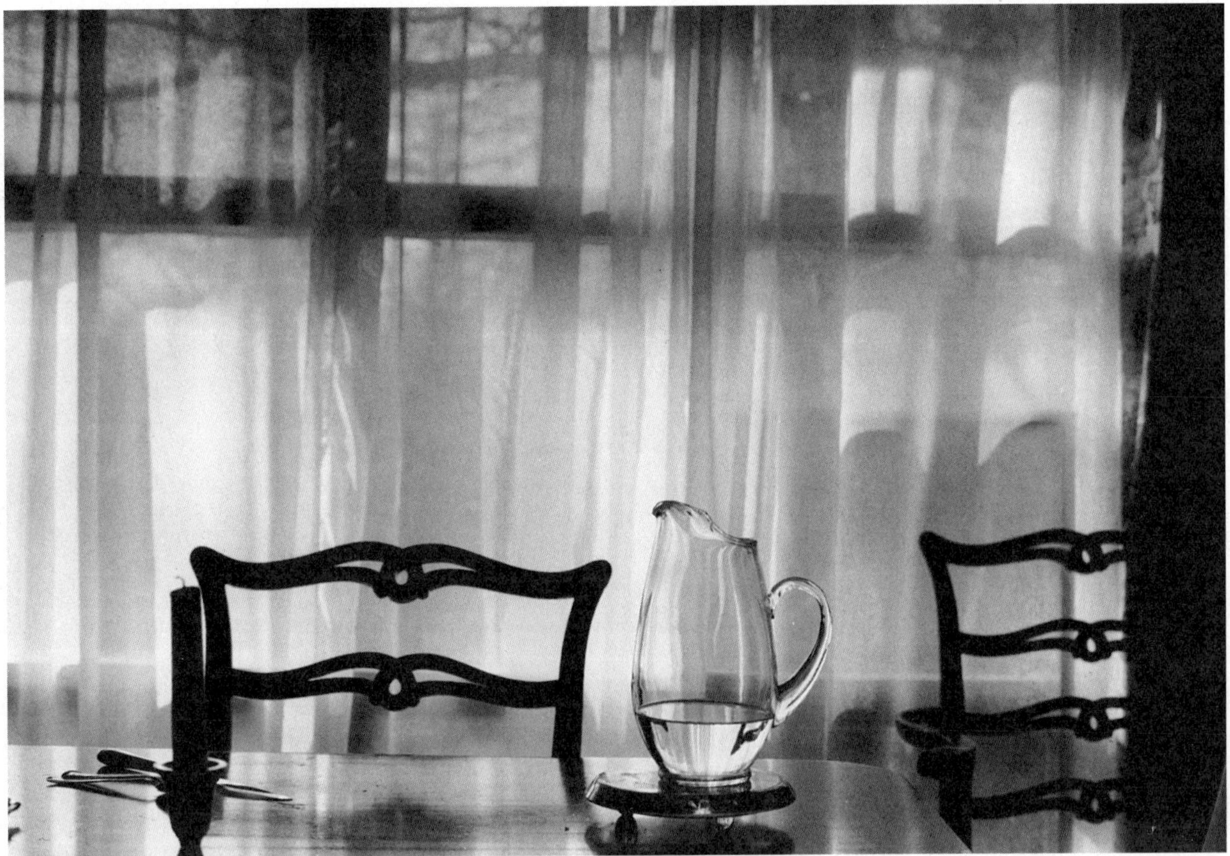

Figure 7.6 Table and Window Still-Life Exposed so as to Retain the Feeling of the Light and the Luminosity *(Photo by Elizabeth Lear Sher)*

stained-glass window in a church, or an exterior closeup framed against the sky.

In the first situation, we use the spot meter (or averaging meter with a closeup technique) to obtain the highest maximum reading possible. With a light bulb or sunset, this is easily obtained by pointing the meter at the bulb or sun. Other subjects, like a candle flame or a lamp, are more difficult to meter and more than one reading may be necessary. The thing to remember is that exposure for the highest reading will render that object as a zone 5 value. Such a placement will be certain to differentiate highlight values and capture the feeling of luminosity, which is often the goal when filming luminous objects (see Figure 7.7).

But such a placement may be too dark as well. It is thus usual to overexpose this maximum reading from one to four stops in order to represent the "glowing feeling" of light. This would give us a zone 6, 7, 8, or 9 value for the object. None of these are "right" or "wrong" exposures; the choice depends on the exact subject and what you wish to do with it (see Figure 7.7). Spot meter readings tend to require more overexposure than averaging-type readings since they are more apt to exclude darker parts of the subject in the reading and thus give higher T-stops than the averaging type give.

Light bulbs, sunsets, the sky, neon signs, and other luminous objects are handled in exactly the same way, obtaining the highest possible meter reading and working from that point. Do not be afraid to ex-

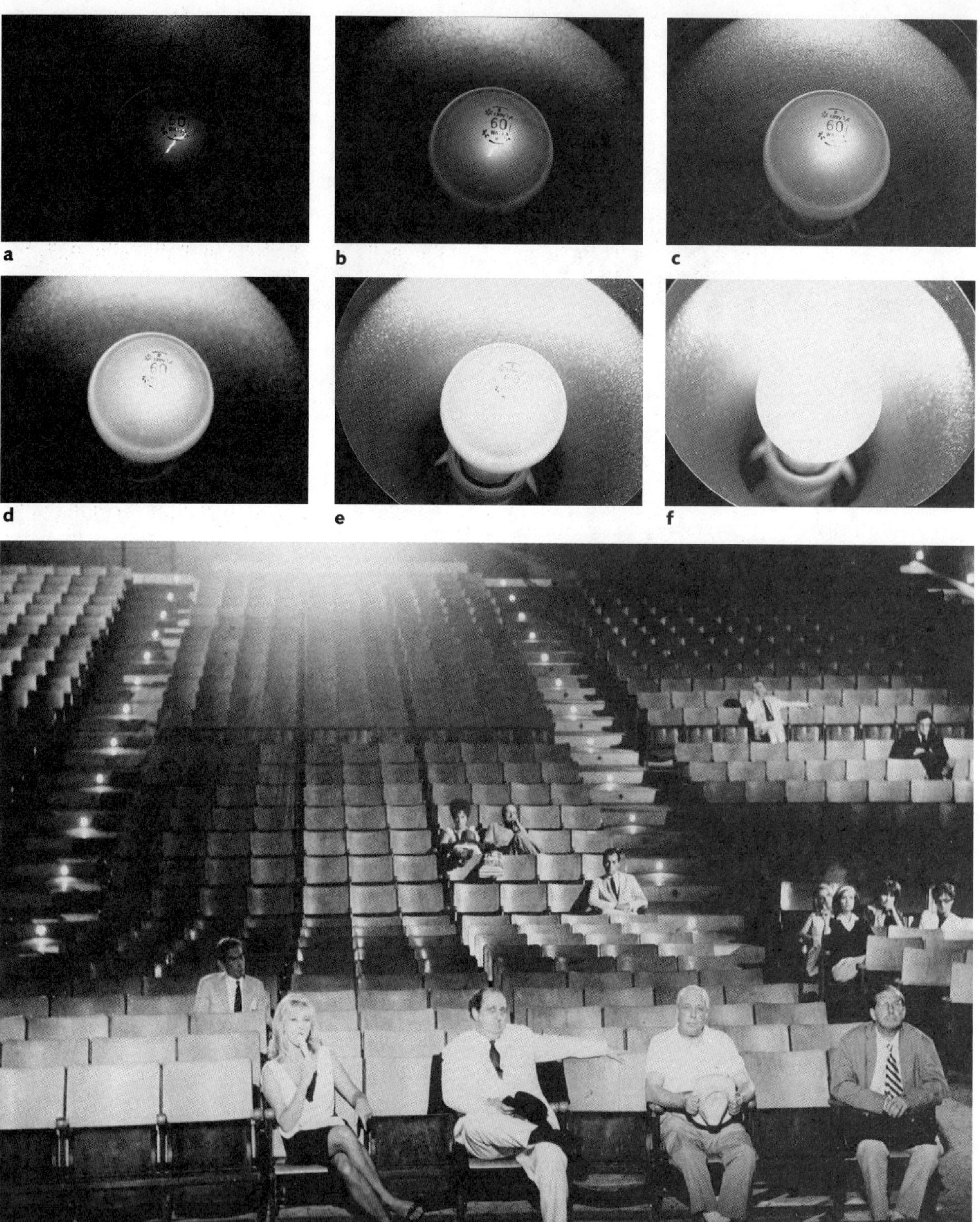

Figure 7.7 Exposure Series with a Light Bulb *In photo (a), the bulb is given a zone 5 exposure. The rest of the series increases the exposure in one-stop increments. The movie theater effect in (g) depends on a correct choice of exposure for the projector light coming from the projection booth (8½, Embassy Pictures, 1963).*

periment. Generally, from one to three stops overexposure is required, but in some situations—say, a sunset in the fog over the ocean—two stops underexposure might be necessary to convey the feeling of the luminosity.

In the second situation, where the luminous object is in view but not the main part of the shot, it's necessary to calculate the exposure as above and then light the rest of the shot referenced to this level. For example, if you decide the luminous background will render best at T 5.6, the rest of the lighting is planned around this T-stop and the shot is exposed at 5.6.

COMPROMISE EXPOSURE

We have mentioned "compromise exposure" several times and have looked at several examples, but this comes up over and over again with mixed interior/exterior situations and needs more explicit investigation.

There are times when the documentary and student cinematographer are unable to light, yet subject luminance range is a problem. Typical examples of this are found in interior/exterior situations—an actor sitting in front of a window with the street outside, a character driving a car with the sunlit street visible through the windows—and face/sky situations—a character with large hat is framed against the sky. The best solution to these situations is found in lighting technique, but there are possible exposure solutions. Let us take as an example, the mixed interior/exterior problem, the case of someone sitting by a window (see Figure 7.8).

Typically an exposure reading outside for EI 100 will be around T 16; we shall assume the light inside measures T 2.8. This is a difference of five stops. Exposure for the person overexposes ("burns out") the street by five stops and moves everything five zones up the zone scale, though this may be the effect the cinematographer wants (see Figure 7.8a). Exposure for the street outside underexposes the person by five stops (zone 6 to zone 1), which means the person is almost a silhouette; again, this may be okay (see Figure 7.8f).

A compromise exposure may be preferable to these two alternatives. Sometimes the compromise is halfway in between the two readings, in this case midway between T 5.6 and T 8 as in Figure 7.8d. At other times, the compromise is closer to one end than the other. In this case, perhaps a half stop over T 4 (T 4/T 5.6) is a better compromise, since facetones will be underexposed only 1½ stops (zone 4½) though, of course, the street background will be 3½ stops overexposed. This is okay if the background is less important (see Figure 7.8c).

With compromise exposures, you are pushing exposure technique into areas best controlled by lighting. Sometimes this works; sometimes not—after all, it is called "compromise" exposure.

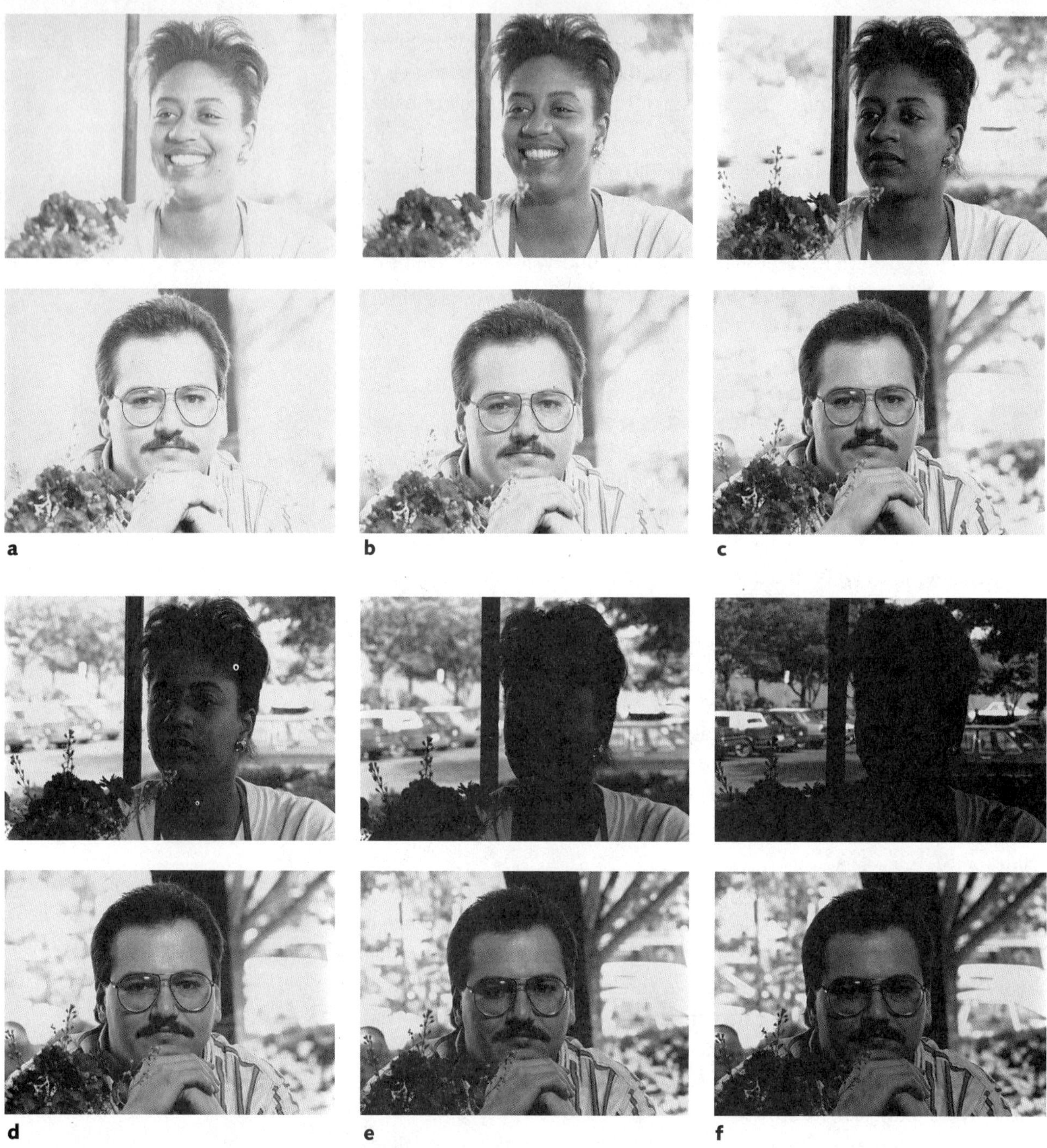

Figure 7.8 Compromise Exposures for Actors in Window
Exposure choices for this situation range from exposure for the faces (a) to exposure for the street outside the window (f). The series illustrates the effect of one-stop increments between these two extremes.

COMBINED INCIDENT AND REFLECTED READINGS

Let us change our example slightly to show how an incident and reflected reading work in tandem. Assume the window is brightly lit but steamed up. We now have a luminous object with which to deal. Taking a spot meter reading of the brightest part of the window gives us T 16 for a zone 5 placement. An incident reading shows T 2.8 for the face. In this example, there is a new variable: Do we wish to overexpose the window to create the feeling of luminosity?

Let's assume we decide to overexpose the window by two stops, that is, give a T 8 exposure to the shot. T 8 is itself a compromise exposure leaving the face three stops underexposed at zone 3. We might decide to try T 5.6 or T 4 instead.

Note that the luminous window determines the initial exposure setting. Lighting the interior face would allow a greater control than would just using compromise exposures.

This same technique may be used for the closeup of our actor with the hat framed against the sky. A reflected reading of the sky is necessary since it functions as a luminous background. A decision must be made as to how much overexposure to give it. A typical sky is about zone 8, so we choose to overexpose it three stops, leaving the person about two stops underexposed (**semisilhouette**). We would either accept this or change it by lighting—using either a reflector or an artificial light such as an HMI.

OVER- AND UNDEREXPOSURE

If exposure is viewed as a creative act, then ultimately "correct exposure" is what the cinematographer wants. But this presumes years of experience—which is why most books define **exposure** in more conventional fashion, something like the following:

> A placement of the subject's luminance range on the characteristic curve of the negative so as to retain a full scale of brightness values, from black to white, with density increases proportional to original subject luminance increases (see Figure 7.9).

This definition sets up a standard for correct exposure, meaning there can be "failures" such as over- and underexposure. **Overexposure** means placing the subject luminance range too high on the characteristic curve. The result is an untrue subject reproduction with the highlights becoming compressed and the lower tones being lightened to gray. The overall feeling of such a picture is "washed-out" (see Figures 7.2c and 7.3d).

In zone system terminology, overexposure for a negative means that zone 5 has been pegged to a higher density than the normal mid-density. Needless to say, unless intentional, only a misreading of the incident meter can lead to this. Overexposure effects can be visualized without difficulty in terms of zones.

Underexposure results when a subject is placed too low on the characteristic curve, with an accompanying lack of separation in the dark tones and a loss of the white end of the scale. The overall impression of underexposure is dark, dreary, and murky (see Figure 7.10a). Underexposure is used for night effects, but usually the cinematographer creates a few bright tones in the shot to prevent any possible "dead" feeling (see Figure 7.10b and c and Figure 2.8d). A normal night setup

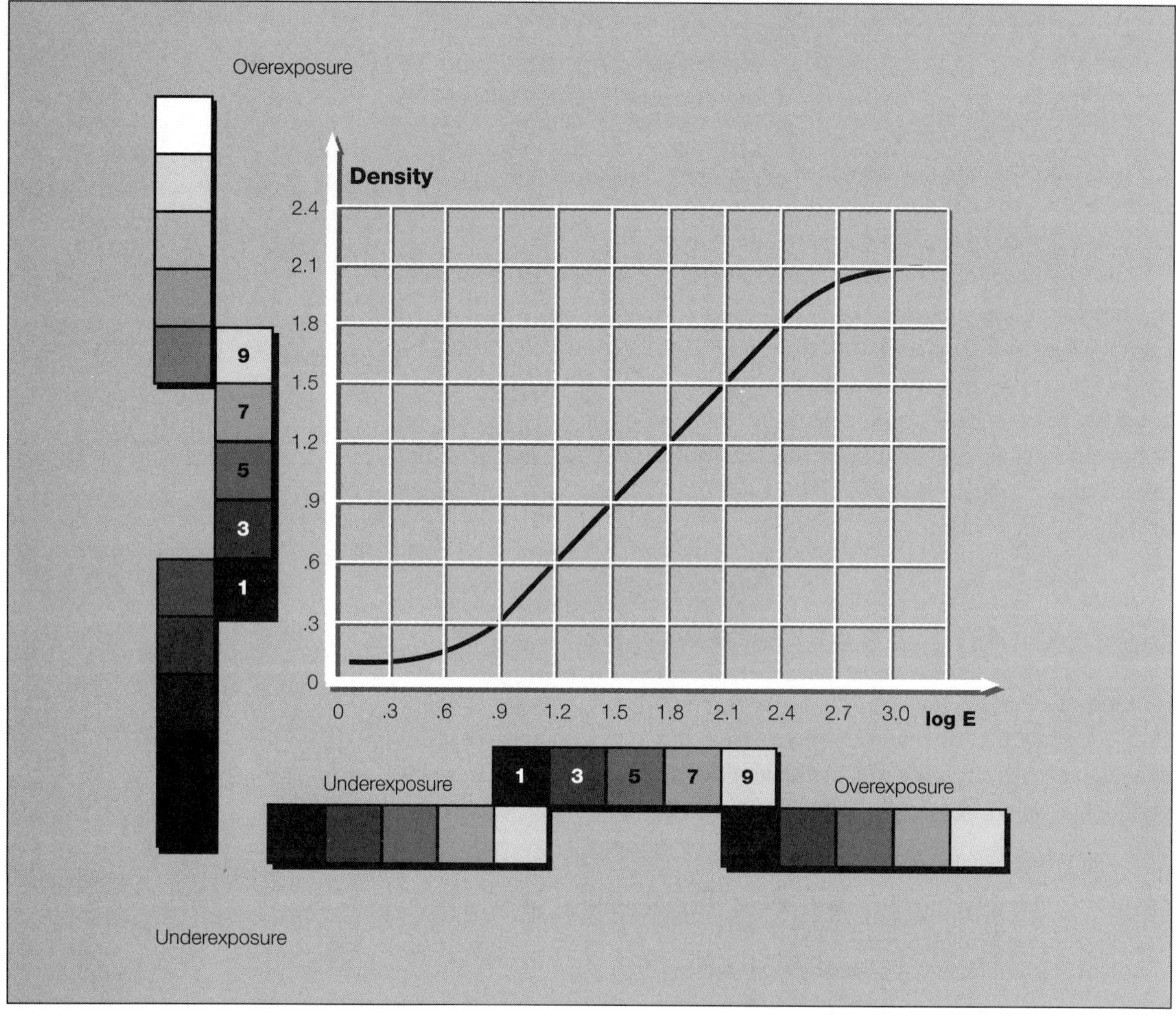

Figure 7.9 Normal Zone 5 Exposure Compared with Over- and Underexposure *This graph illustrates extreme (four-stop) over- and underexposure. The results as portrayed on the density axis are suggestive only and do not portray the true result, which would be mostly white for the overexposure and mostly black for the underexposure.*

has a lot more light than one might imagine and is not at all underexposed (see Figure 7.10d).

Over- and underexposures as "mistakes" are obviously undesirable. But giving over- and underexposures to selected areas of the frame relative to a main subject exposure is important for mood creation. We usually talk about this effect referenced to lighting rather than exposure, however. The topic will be covered in Chapter 8.

ALL-LIGHT/ALL-DARK SUBJECTS

It is common to utilize over- and underexposure with certain extreme subjects—subjects that lack normal tonal distributions—for example, all light-toned subjects such as white dogs playing in snow (see Color Plate 4), all dark-toned subjects like black cats playing in coal, or subjects with low contrast. For example, it is common to underexpose an all-white subject by a stop to ensure highlight separation. It is standard practice to overexpose exceptionally dark subjects for the same reason.

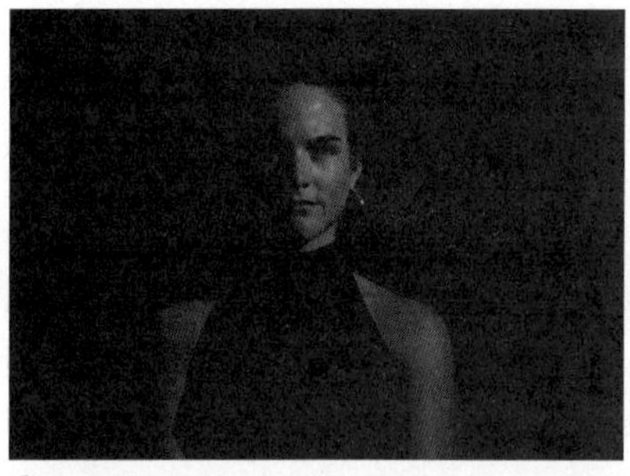

a

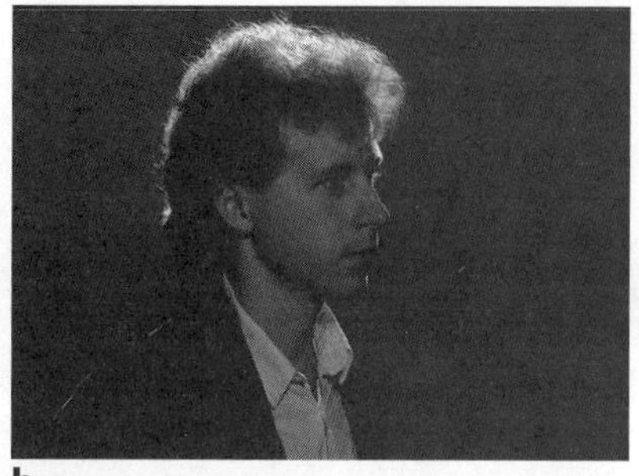

b

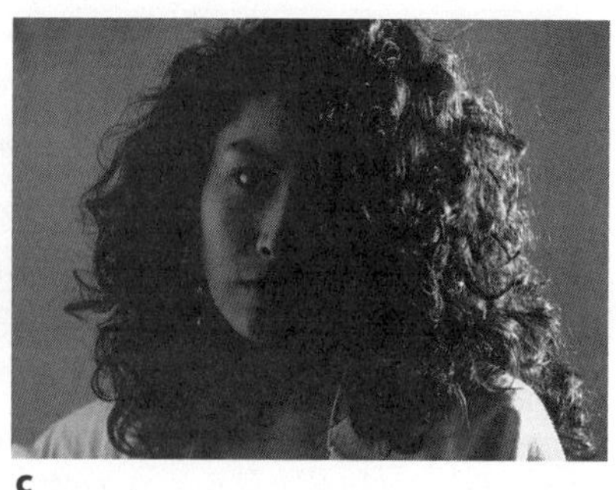

c

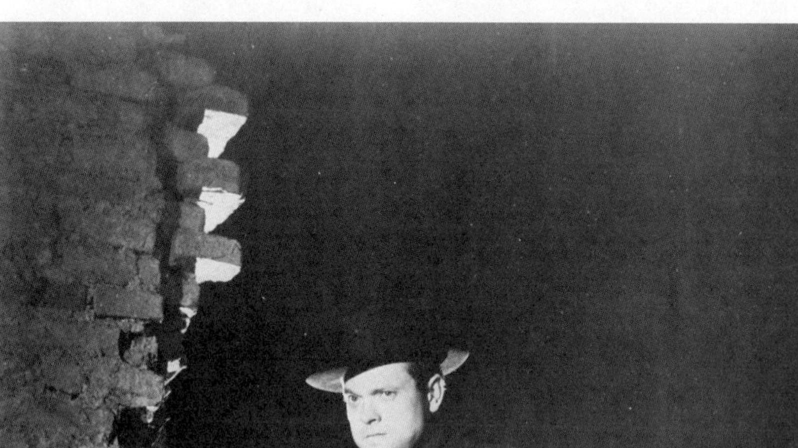

d

Figure 7.10 Underexposure Effects *The almost complete absence of highlight values results in a muddied look (a). Adding a hair light (b) and a slight rim on the hair and shoulder (c) adds visual interest to the shot. The standard night exterior (d) has much more lighting than might be expected (*The Third Man, *Twentieth Century Fox, 1949).*

Another situation where underexposure is used is with panoramic, landscape shots, particularly when there is haze and side or back lighting. Atmospheric haze tends to lighten the shot by rendering dark tones a zone or two brighter than normal. Consequently, one may give a stop or more underexposure on shots of this type.

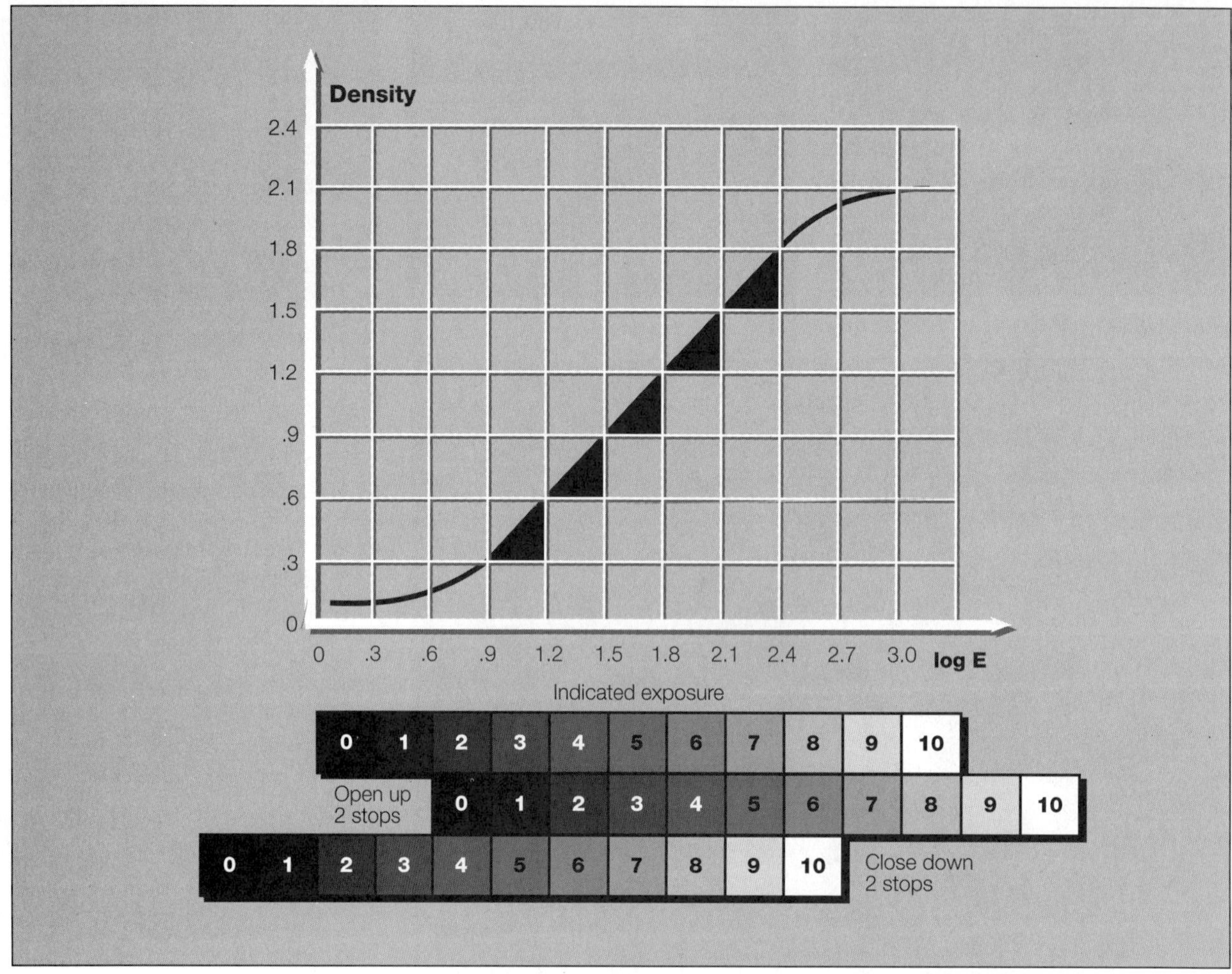

Figure 7.11 Two-Stop Over- and Underexposure

It is possible to use an adjusted incident reading for such shots:

1. Take a standard incident reading for the shot.
2. Take an additional reading by pointing the meter toward the sun.
3. Expose halfway in between. You could also expose for the reading obtained in number 2.

Underexposure by a stop or more is almost always used when the main part of the subject involves atmospheric effects or the feeling of light—for example, sky, reflections in water, and fog. The underexposure is used to retain as much gradation of the highlight values as possible on the negative. Note, underexposure here means relative to a zone 5 incident reading. It would also be possible in some of these examples to apply the reflected light technique for luminous objects described earlier.

Over- and underexposure are accomplished by varying the T-stop setting indicated by the light meter. This moves the range of values up or down on the characteristic curve. Opening up two stops is equivalent to shifting the range of subject luminances up the characteristic curve by two zones; zone 6 becomes zone 8 and so forth (see Figure 7.11).

We have dealt with two common "tricky" exposure problems: (1) exposure for luminous objects such as sunsets and light sources and (2) exposure compensations for all-light/all-dark subjects. The last common exposure technique involves pulling T-stop.

PULLING T-STOP

Similar to situations that require either lighting or a compromise exposure technique are shots where the lighting changes as the shot progresses. This can happen with a panning shot—one part of the room to another—or a tracking or hand-held shot—from outdoors to indoors, or from a bright room to a dark one. The most extreme example involves filming a person walking down the street and following that person into a house or building all in one shot, a common problem in vérité documentary.

The luminance-range problem is not unlike the previous example of the person in the window. The best solution, not usually available in documentary, is to light the interior rooms and balance them to the exterior. Sometimes a compromise exposure is feasible. The other non-lighting possibility is to **pull T-stop**, which involves moving the T-stop ring while filming; it's similar to a focus pull but much harder to hide. Continuing with our earlier example, the T-stop has to go from T 16 outdoors to T 2.8 indoors as the person changes location. Some documentary/news cinematographers learn to do this by eye without thinking. The rest of us need a camera assistant.

It's difficult to hide the T-stop pull. Here, we would pull the stop as we move from exterior to interior. As with a focus pull, the camera assistant can set and mark the lens in advance. In a true vérité documentary situation, you probably would have to guess the exposure for the interior since there will have been no preplanning. One can also try to avoid these situations by choosing alternative locations and shots, or different times of day to shoot. If this were a Steadicam shot in a feature film, the interiors would be lit as necessary.

EXPOSURE WITH THE ZONE SYSTEM: A SUMMARY

As we have seen, there is room for creativity in exposure technique. Also, many looks can be accomplished with exposure techniques as well as lighting since controlling select areas of the frame relative to the principal subject involves both exposure and lighting. The following steps are taken in exposing with the zone system.

1. Through experience the cinematographer imagines normal subject relations and how a shot of the subject will look on the screen. A

Emulsion	Exposure Index	Straight Line		Overall Useful Range	
		log E	zones	log E	zones
Agfa XT100	100	2.0	$6^2/_3$	2.7	9
Agfa XT320	320	2.1	7	2.7	9
Eastman EXR 7245 D	50	1.9	$6^1/_3$	2.6	$8^2/_3$
Eastman EXR 7248	100	2.3	$7^2/_3$	2.8	$9^1/_3$
Eastman 7297 D	250	2.0	$6^2/_3$	2.9	$9^2/_3$
Eastman 7292	320	2.0	$6^2/_3$	3.0	10
Eastman EXR 7296	500	2.1	7	2.8	$9^1/_3$
Fuji F-64 8610	64	1.6	$5^1/_3$	2.3	$7^2/_3$
Fuji F-64 D 8620	64	1.7	$5^2/_3$	2.3	$7^2/_3$
Fuji F-125 8630	125	1.5	5	2.4	8
Fuji F-250 8650	250	1.7	$5^2/_3$	3.1	$10^1/_3$
Fuji F-250 D 8660	250	1.5	5	3.1	$10^1/_3$
Fuji F-500 8670	500	2.0	$6^2/_3$	3.3	11

- ➢ 5 zones = 32:1
- ➢ 6 zones = 64:1
- ➢ 7 zones = 128:1
- ➢ 8 zones = 256:1
- ➢ 9 zones = 512:1
- ➢ 10 zones = 1024:1
- ➢ 11 zones = 2048:1

Table 7.1
Actual Characteristic Curves[4]

face, a white and black cat, an early morning kitchen, a blue sky—all are imagined in terms of zones.

2. The cinematographer knows that exposure for the luminance range from one angle of lighting automatically determines the zone placement of the other luminance ranges present.

3. The cinematographer knows that whatever is exposed for will be faithfully rendered (keytone pegged) if exposure is set as the incident meter indicates for that particular lighting situation.

4. The cinematographer can intentionally change the zonal representation of a subject by changing T-stop. Opening up one stop overexposes by one stop and moves everything up one zone. Conversely, underexposing by one stop automatically moves everything down one zone. What normally would have been zone 6 becomes zone 5. The cinematographer can therefore intentionally create a lighter or darker rendition of the subject through over- or underexposure. Control is possible since the cinematographer visualizes the normal and the over and under renditions before making a choice.

5. The cinematographer knows that areas of the shot under lighting conditions different than the main subject range will be rendered brighter or darker than normal. They will fall into zones higher and lower than normal in proportion to how much their lighting intensity differs from the one exposed for.

We shall cover more of these problems in detail in Part III. For now, Table 7.1 is provided for reference as needed throughout our discussion of lighting and later for our discussion of exposure in electronic cinematography.

NOTES

1. Note that we look for the brightest object, the whitest object in the highest intensity lighting, not specular reflections which are always the brightest luminances. Specular reflections (hot spots) are generally not exposed for per se; instead, they are eliminated or minimized when lighting. Sometimes they are allowed to overexpose and create a feeling of high reflectivity.

2. These viewing filters are available in mounted form and are also found in the swatch books available from filter and gel manufacturers such as Rosco.

3. For a good discussion, see Jack F. Dunn and George L. Wakefield, *Exposure Manual*, 3rd ed. (Kings Langley, England: Fountain Press, 1974), pp. 116–17.

4. As this book goes to press, Kodak has announced a new 16mm color negative: Eastman EXR 200T 7293. Agfa has announced one as well: XTS 400.

III

LIGHTING APPLICATIONS

When it comes to lighting, one of my basic principles is that the light source must be justified. . . . I try to make sure that my light is logical rather than aesthetic. . . . In a studio set I imagine that the sun is shining from a certain point outside, and I decide how the light would come through the windows. The rest is easy.

—*Nestor Almendros*
Light Years

LIGHTING CONTRAST RATIOS

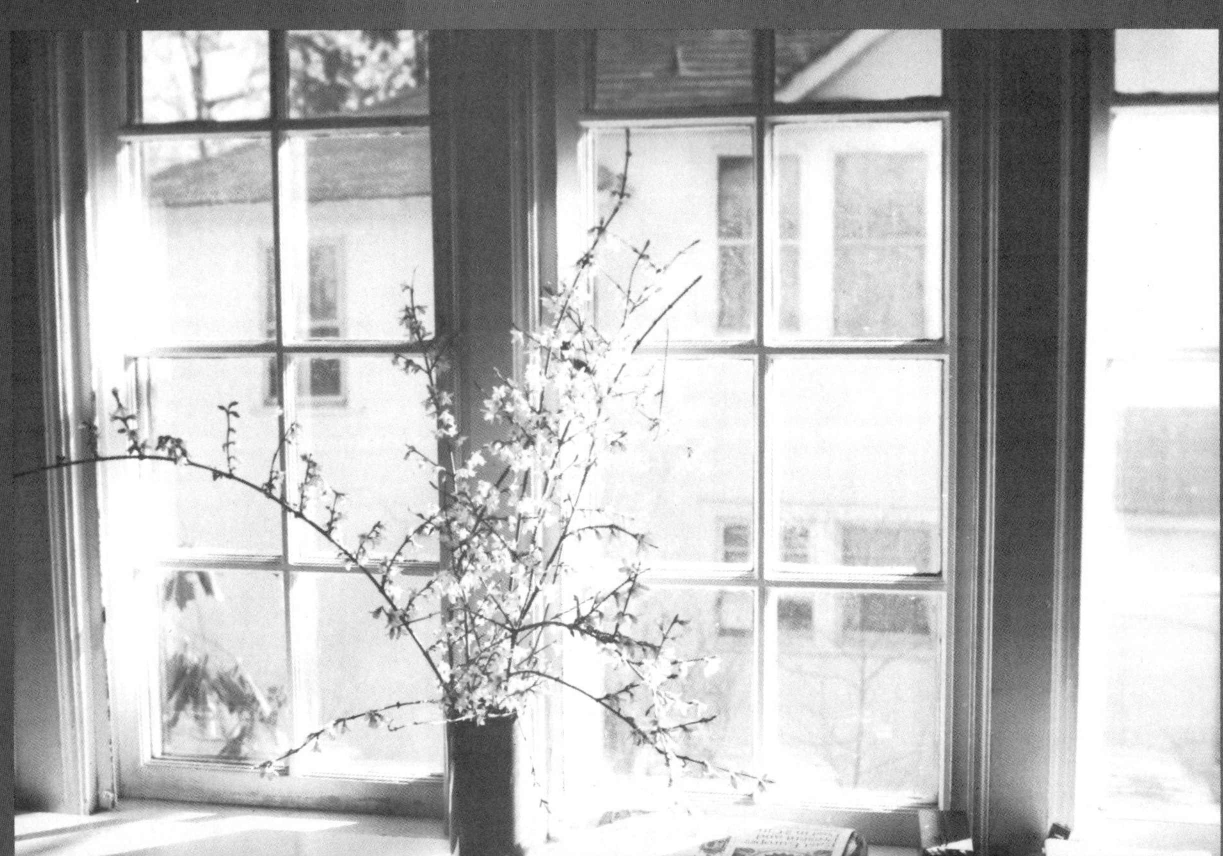

Photo by Elizabeth Lear Sher *"subject lighting ratio"*

8

Lighting in the technical sense is the control of subject luminance range. Subject lighting ratios and subject/background ratios are lighting concepts used to control subject luminance range. Subject lighting ratio is defined as the ratio between the light and shadow sides of a subject. Subject/background ratio is the ratio in lighting intensity between the subject plane and the background or foreground. Both of these ratios are fundamental in mood creation.

IN THIS CHAPTER we commence our study of lighting with a look at two important lighting contrast ratios: the ratio between the light and shadow sides of a subject (*subject lighting ratio*) and the ratio between the lit subject area and the background lighting (*subject/background ratio*).

In Chapter 9 we shall look at various approaches to creating lighting setups and how to tackle certain lighting problems. We shall then turn to the lighting of interiors and exteriors in Chapters 10 and 11. The final chapter of Part Three will describe the duties of a cinematographer and will go through a specific lighting example in detail.

LIGHTING RATIO TERMINOLOGY

There is no standard terminology used to refer to the following three distinctly separate lighting concepts that together form the basis for lighting:

1. The ratio between the light and shadow sides of a subject created by key and fill light.
2. The ratio between the lit subject area, such as the actors, and other parts of the frame, most commonly the background or foreground.
3. The ratio between the brightest significant luminance and the darkest significant luminance.

The following terminology is used throughout the rest of this book:

Lighting contrast ratio refers to all of the above ratios collectively. Contrast, the relation between highest value and darkest, is integral to all three ratios.

Subject lighting ratio (**lighting ratio**) refers to number 1 above, the ratio between the light and shadow sides of a subject. This will sometimes be referred to as the **facial ratio** where the subject in question is an actor or actors and the representation of the face is important. Various other terms exist in the literature. Alan J. Ritsko uses "lighting ratio." Gerald Millerson calls it "contrast ratio," "lighting contrast ratio," and "fill light ratio." Phillip Courter uses "lighting ratio" and "lighting contrast ratio." Anton Wilson uses "lighting ratio." Harry Mathias and Richard Patterson use "contrast ratio" and "lighting ratio." Charles G. Clarke calls it "light ratio."

Subject/background ratio refers to number 2 in the previous list, the difference in lighting intensity expressed as a ratio between the subject plane and other planes, principally the background plane. This is also called "exposure ratio" (Ritsko), "contrast ratio" (Millerson), "face and background contrast" (Millerson), and "subject illumination to background illumination ratio" (Courter).

Subject luminance range refers to number 3 in the list. We used this term extensively in the "Exposure" section of this book. Common alternative designations include "luminance range" (Ritsko); "luminance ratio" (Ritsko, Wilson); "contrast range," "subject brightness range," and "brightness ratio" (Millerson); "scene contrast range" (Courter); and "brightness range," "contrast range," and "contrast ratio" (Mathias and Patterson). Subject luminance range is controllable through lighting and is, ultimately, the range of log E values that have been translated into density values after exposure and development. Subject luminance range is where lighting and exposure intersect. When lighting is complete, the subject luminance range is rendered onto the film emulsion by an exposure setting. This topic was covered in the "Exposure" section.

This chapter deals with subject lighting ratios and subject/background ratios, two lighting concepts used to control subject luminance range. It is common to express these ratios in mathematical terms referenced to footcandle (fc) values, such as 4:1 or 16:1, or to T-stops—the subject was lit two stops, two zones, brighter than the background; the face was lit at T 5.6 on the light side and T 2.8 on the shadow side, a two-stop ratio. We shall use both means for designating ratios.

SUBJECT LIGHTING RATIOS (LIGHTING RATIOS)

Subject lighting ratio refers to the intensity difference between the light and shadow sides of a subject. This difference results from the variety of key and fill light combinations. As mentioned previously, the amount of fill light applied to shadows greatly affects image mood. In the case of lighting ratios, what we are interested in is setting keys and fills to create predetermined moods.

As an aid in learning lighting, we construct subject lighting ratios mathematically. Over time, with enough experience and testing, we learn to visualize how a certain ratio will look on the screen and can instruct the gaffer to set lights accordingly.

Some cinematographers say they like to set lighting ratios "by eye." This means they have sufficient experience to previsualize the effects of a certain fill light intensity; that is, they have attuned their eye to a par-

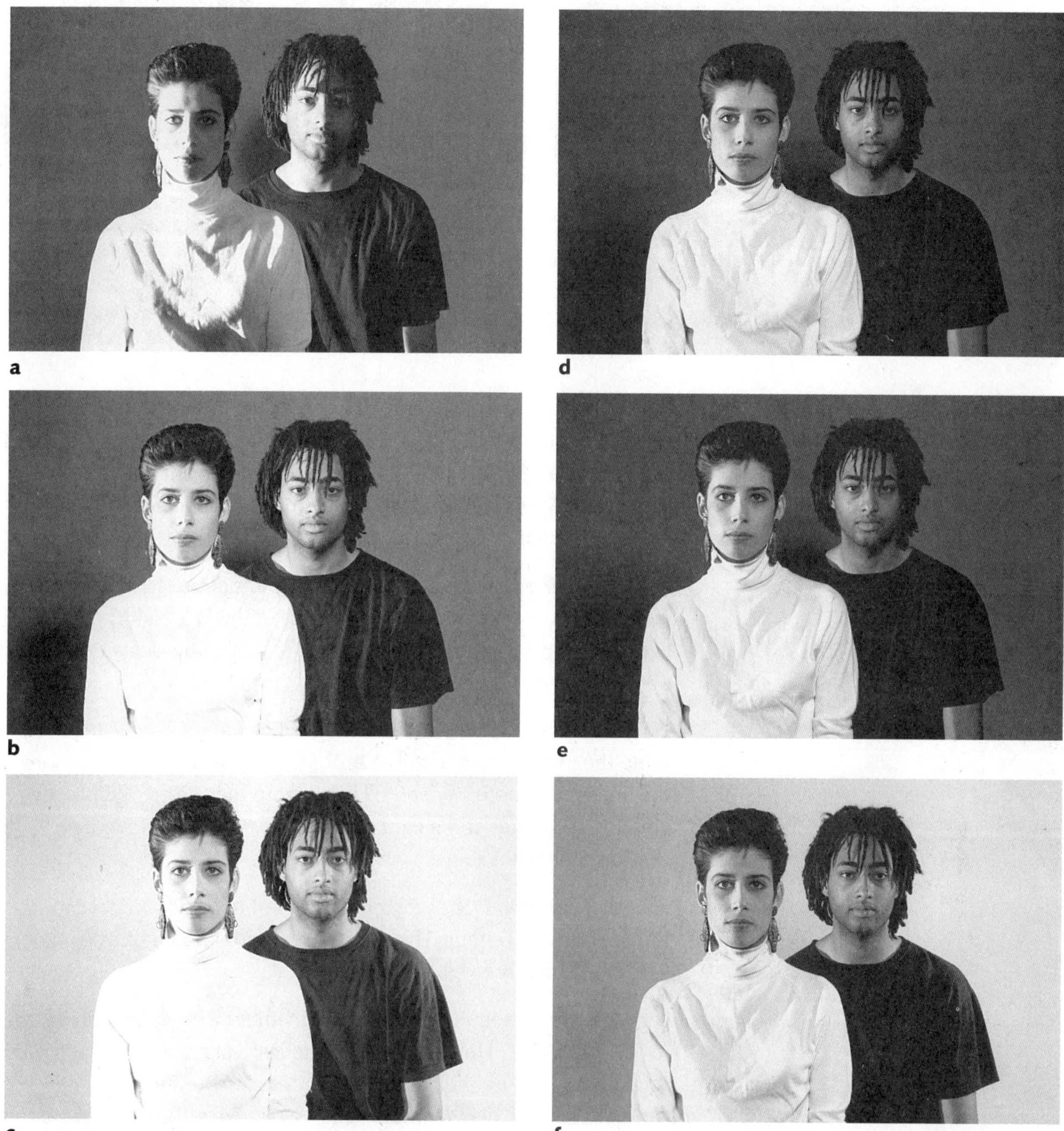

ticular stock's contrast properties. This is fine as long as you know in advance what the image will look like on the screen. In the beginning, the best way to learn how a particular ratio will look is to run lighting ratio tests on the various motion picture stocks.

Subject lighting ratios allow us to recreate select moods by defining the intensity of the fill light relative to the key. Note the different moods available in Figures 8.1, 8.2, 8.6, and in various other examples throughout the book.

We may calculate lighting ratios in a variety of ways. Choice of method does not matter since for a given lighting setup all methods will look the same on the screen, but consistency of method is very impor-

Figure 8.1 Subject Lighting Ratios *Side key with various lighting ratios: (a) 8:1, (b) 2:1, (c) 2:1 with background light raising back wall to light gray; (d), (e), and (f) are the same as (a), (b), and (c) but printed one stop darker.*

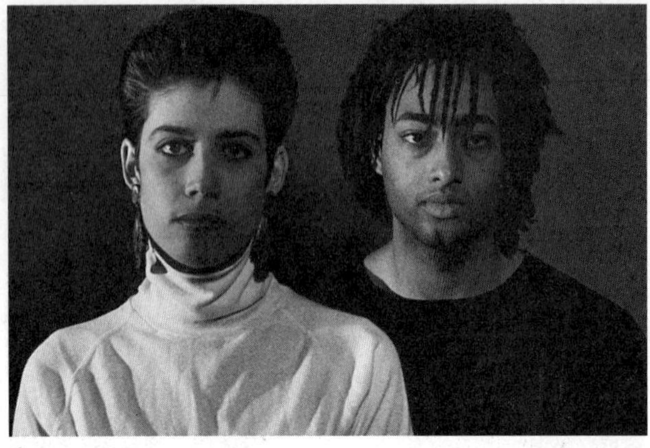
a

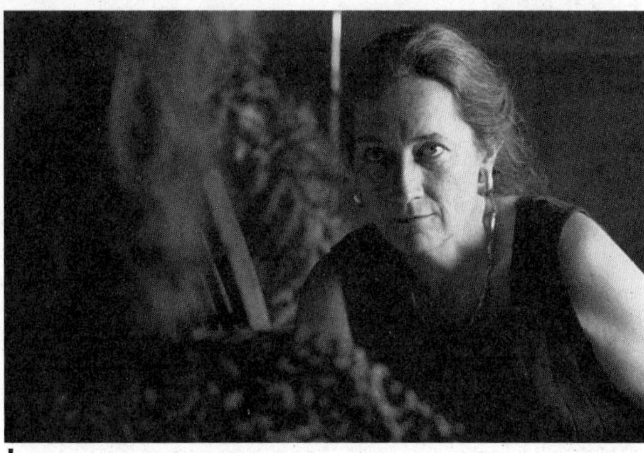
b

Figure 8.2 Side Keys with Frontal Fill

tant. An example should clarify this point. Look at the two shots in Figure 8.2. Both have side keys with some frontal fill. Assume the shots were exposed at T 5.6 calculated from a standard incident reading.

There are a variety of ways you could have calculated the facial ratio in this example when executing your lighting:

- *Incident method.* Incident readings for both sides of face, meter pointed along camera/subject axis, reading the key and fill for the light side of the face and only the fill for the shadow side in footcandles or T-stops (see Figure 8.3).

- *Flat disc method.* Footcandle readings of key and fill lights made by using the incident meter with flat photodisc. The idea is to measure the intensity of both key and fill lights from the subject position by pointing the meter at the light units. The flat disc is used to help exclude other light sources (see Figure 8.4).

- *Spot meter method.* Spot meter readings of both sides of face in footlamberts or T-stops. This is a precise method but not as common as the first two (see Figure 8.5).

Each of these methods yields a mathematical ratio describing the shots in Figure 8.2. However, the numerical values in that ratio vary depending on the method used. Theoretically, the incident and spot meter methods will yield identical ratio values since they are measuring the same surfaces relative to the camera/subject axis. Let's consider this further.

Say that the incident method yields the following values for Figure 8.2b: 120 footcandles for the light side and 20 footcandles for the shadow side of the face. This yields a subject facial ratio of 6:1.

$$\frac{120\text{ footcandles}}{20\text{ footcandles}} = \frac{6}{1}$$

Note that this ratio was calculated by measuring the light side of the face—a mixture of key light and fill (K + F)—and comparing it to the

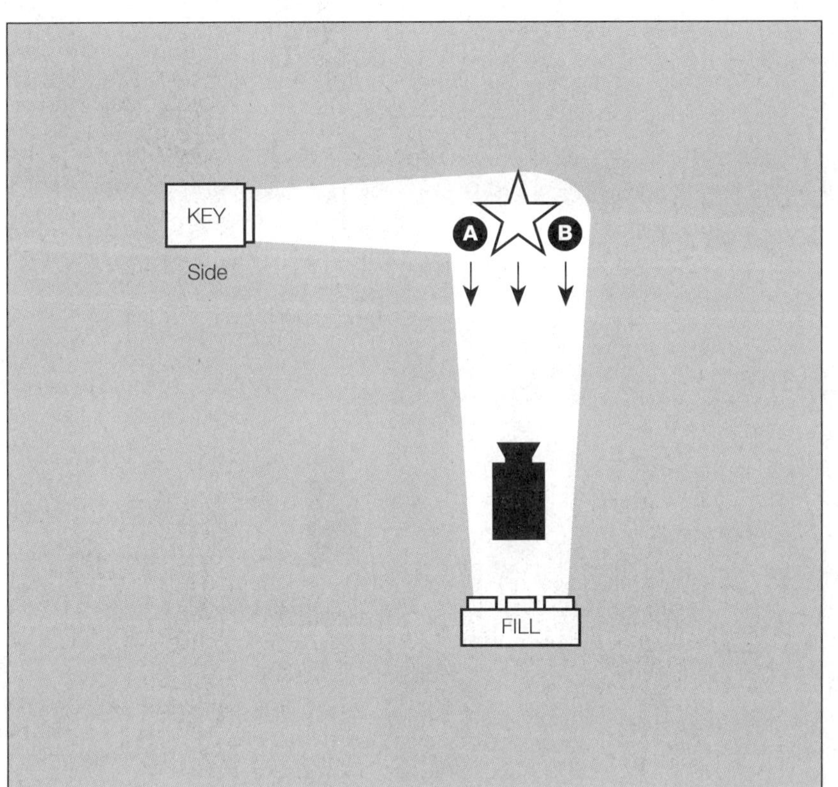

Figure 8.3 Use of Incident Meter with Photosphere to Calculate Subject Lighting Ratio *Readings for the face are taken from positions A—in light side of face, meter pointed toward the camera—and B—in shadow side pointed toward camera.*

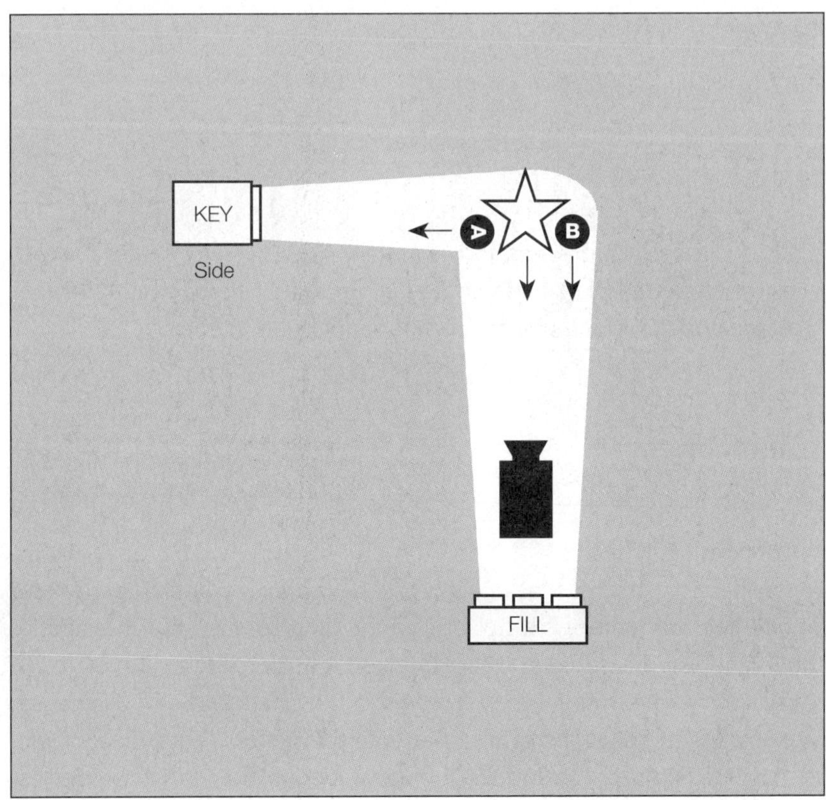

Figure 8.4 Use of Incident Meter with Photodisc to Calculate Subject Lighting Ratio *With the flat disc method, the lights are read directly as in A—meter pointed at the key light—and in B—meter pointed at the fill light.*

Figure 8.5 Spot Meter Readings to Calculate Subject Lighting Ratio *With a spot meter, the readings are read off the lit side of the face (A) and the shadow side of the face (B).*

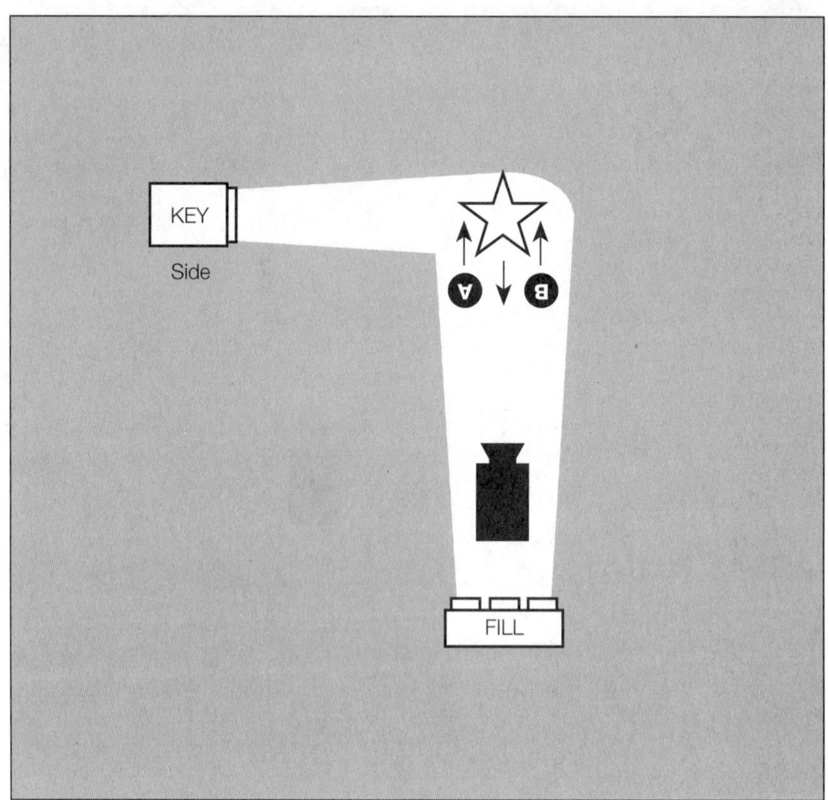

shadow side lit by fill light only. The formula may be generalized to:

$$\frac{K + F}{F} = \frac{120 \text{ fc}}{20 \text{ fc}} = \text{a } 6{:}1 \text{ facial ratio}$$

With the spot meter method, assuming a 36% reflectance for the face (see Figure 8.2b), we obtain a reading of 43.2 footlamberts for the light side and 7.2 footlamberts for the shadow side, that is:

$$\frac{K + F}{F} = \frac{43.2 \text{ footlamberts}}{7.2 \text{ footlamberts}} = \text{a } 6{:}1 \text{ facial ratio}$$

Consider likely readings for the flat disc method, which differs from the incident method in that direct readings of the key and fill are taken by pointing the meter with flat disc at the light source. In our example above, the key measured 100 footcandles (light side = K + F = 100 + 20 = 120 fc). The flat disc method maximizes the side key reading because we point the meter at the light rather than the camera. Thus the key will be at its maximum value and will measure brighter than 100 footcandles (see Figure 8.4).

Continuing our example, assume we obtain a reading of 110 footcandles for the key with the flat disc method. The fill will still be 20 footcandles since it is still read head-on as with the incident method (the slight difference obtained by use of the photodisc instead of the photosphere being ignored). As expected, these readings give us a slightly different ratio than the other two methods do:

$$\frac{K}{F} = \frac{110\text{ fc}}{20\text{ fc}} = 5.5{:}1 \text{ facial ratio}$$

The flat disc method has one simple advantage: You can be very precise with prelighting instructions for the gaffer without specifying camera angle. Example: Give me 110 footcandles on the face from the key. Also, it is simpler to notate on a lighting plot, which means the gaffer can rough in the lighting before the cinematographer arrives on the set. It is also easy to reduplicate the lighting setup later if necessary.

Because the various methods define the subject lighting ratio differently, we obtained different numerical ratios for the exact same lighting setup. Ultimately this does not matter since the image on the screen will be the same, exposed at the same T-stop as determined by a standard incident reading. The crucial thing is consistency. Use the same technique throughout.

METHODS FOR WORKING WITH SUBJECT LIGHTING RATIOS

Many cinematographers work to a predetermined T-stop in order to maintain visual consistency or a particular depth of field. Once the decision is made to expose at a certain T-stop, key lights are set for that level. The fill is added to approximately the right intensity after the keys are placed. Since fills will affect exposure more at 2:1 than at 32:1, once the desired ratio is set up, lights will often have to be readjusted to maintain the selected T-stop, or, alternatively, a different T-stop can be used.

The incident and flat disc methods are the two main ways for establishing a lighting ratio. The overall goal is to be able to previsualize the effect of a certain ratio given your particular method. For example, using the key + fill over fill formula with the meter pointed at the camera (incident method), 2:1, 4:1, 8:1 represent potential visual moods that can be memorized and used when necessary (see Figure 8.6).

Effects of Ratios on White and Black Faces

In zone system terminology, these ratios can be likened to zones or T-stops. For example, with a 4:1 ratio we have a difference of two zones between light and shadow side. If we expose for the light side of a Caucasian face, a nominal zone 6, then we can easily previsualize the shadow side of the face, which in this case will fall at zone 4. If we have

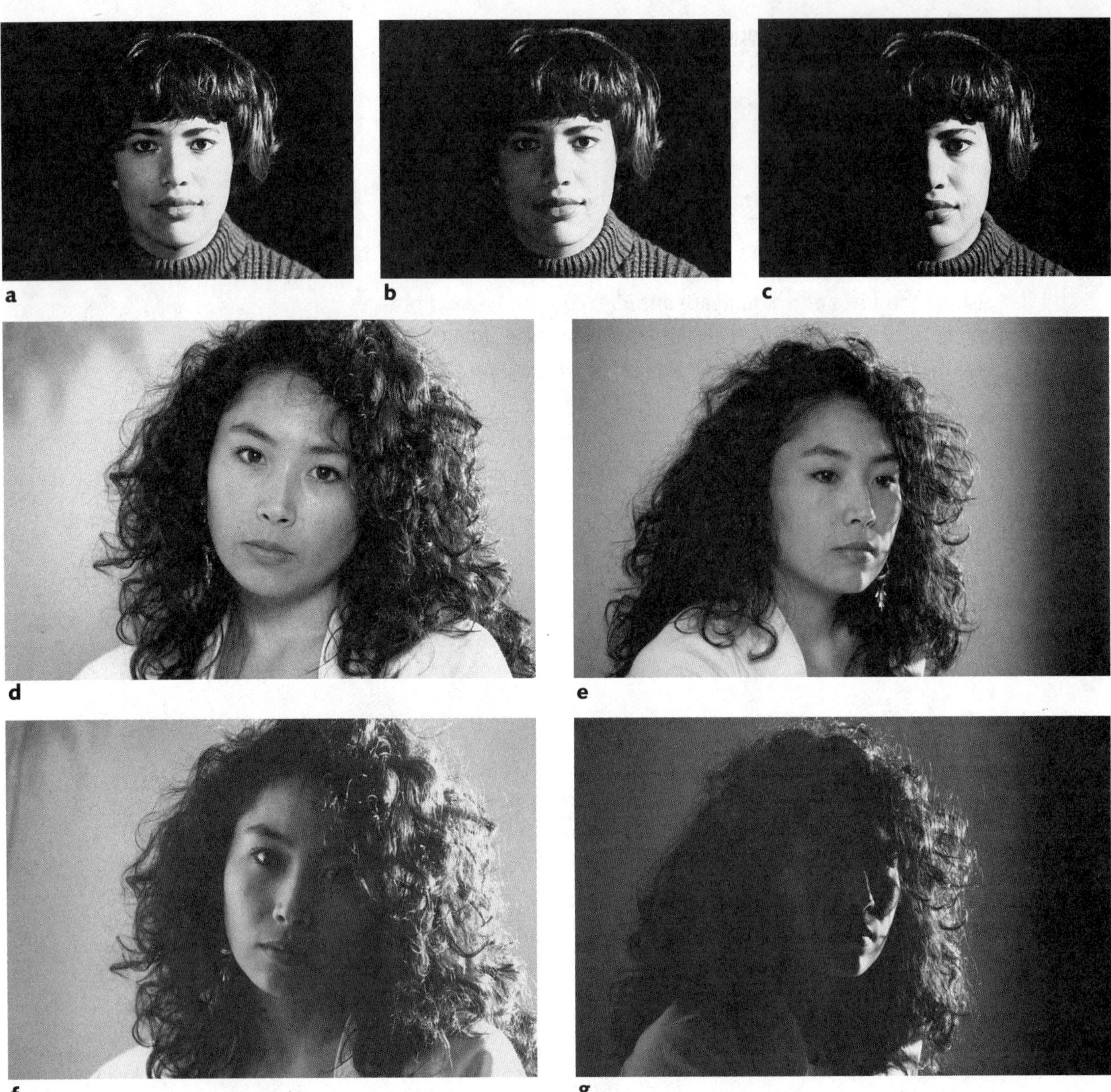

Figure 8.6 Sample Subject Lighting Ratios (Facial Ratios) *(a) 2:1, (b) 4:1, (c) 32:1, (d) 1:1, a frontal key, (e) 4:1, (f) 8:1, (g) 16:1.*

an 8:1 ratio, the shadow side of the face will fall at zone 3. A 16:1 ratio is a four-zone difference and would mean the shadow side falls at zone 2.

Note: This assumes we are exposing for the light side of the face. As we have seen, it is possible, for example with a 16:1 ratio (four zones), to expose halfway in between—a compromise exposure. We then overexpose the bright side of the face by two stops or two zones, rendering it as zone 8. We underexpose the shadow side by two stops or two zones, thus rendering it as zone 4. It is also possible to expose for the shadow side of the face rather than the light side. This helps create the feeling of light falling on the face (see the series of photos in Figures 7.1 and 7.3).

With a darker facetone, if we expose for the light side of the face with a 4:1 ratio, that side will fall on zone 4 and the shadow side on zone 2. With an 8:1 ratio, the shadow side will fall at zone 1. At 16:1 the shadow side will fall at zone 0. One problem with exposure for darker facetones is immediately apparent: The shadow sides of the face tend to render as pure black tones. This is because there is little visual difference on the screen between zones 2, 1, and 0.

One obvious solution is to overexpose the facetone a stop or two compared to the rest of the shot so that the facetone will be placed on zone 5 instead of 4 and shadow values will likewise render lighter (see Figure 7.8). Of course, this works only if there are just dark facetones in the shot (see Figure 11.1).

Where multiple facetones are present—for example, white and black actors—one solution is to light the black facetone a stop "hotter" than other faces in the shot and thus preserve detail in the shadow side. This was done for the shots at the front of Chapters 5 and 7 as well as in Figures 2.27 and 8.7. More fill light can be used in some cases, but this means a 2:1 ratio, which can become overly repetitious with little mood.

Taking Readings for Ratios and Setting Intensities for Rims and Back Lights

When taking readings for ratios, it is usual to shield the meter or turn off other lights. With the flat disc method, other lights are less of a problem. On large production shoots, cinematographers work with gaffers to determine where to position lights. Because light source intensity is measured (flat disc method), the subject need not be present. Lighting can be roughed in while awaiting the actors and director for final camera angle determination. The exposure reading will be taken once the camera setup is finalized.

With either method for establishing the subject lighting ratio of the key and fill, other lights, such as rims and hair lights, are set relative to the intensity of the key. For example, assume we wish to add rim and hair lights to the situations discussed in Figures 8.1, 8.2, and 8.6. Let's assume the hair light is very important and the rim is to be used for subtle modeling effects.

We would start with the hair light. Say we decide to overexpose it two stops. Since the key is 110 footcandles, we would set the hair light initially to 440 footcandles so as to establish the two-stop, 4:1 relationship. Next, we would judge the effect on the actor by eye. We might then lower or raise the hair light's intensity, recording this value in case reshooting is necessary (see Figure 2.10a and b and Figure 7.4b).

Since the rim light is to be subtle, we would set it initially at about the same level as the key, 110 footcandles. While supervising the placement of the rim by eye, we might intensify it slightly to make it more noticeable (see Figure 8.6d–g).

In this example, I have assumed the use of a flat disc technique. With the incident method you would calculate from the 100 footcandles level. You would thus set the hair light at 400 footcandles, as measured

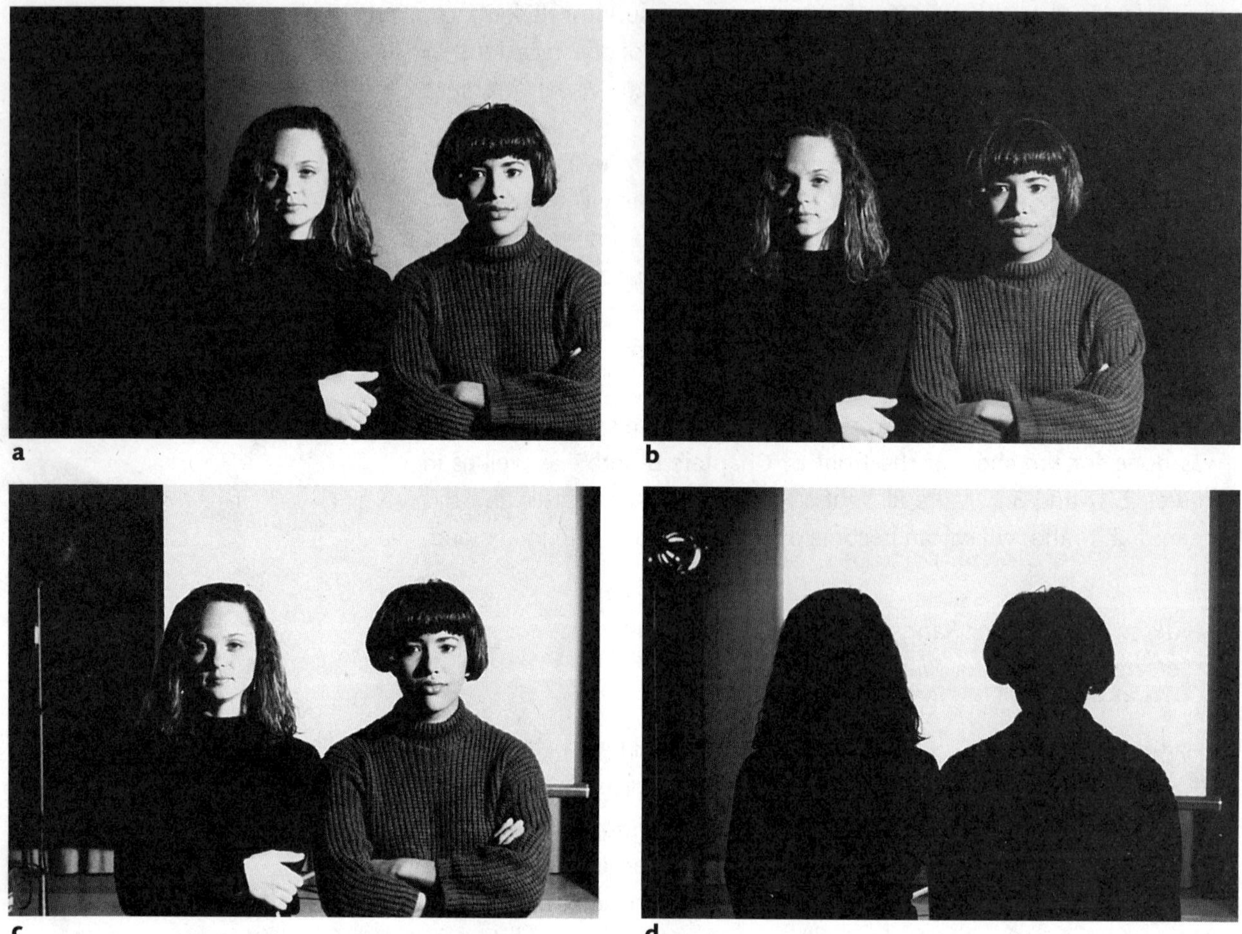

Figure 8.7 Subject/Background Ratios *Starting with a white screen, we can control how it reproduces by changing the intensity of the background light while holding the lighting on the subjects at the same intensity.*

In (a) we have a 16:1 subject/background ratio for the gray part of the screen on the left. This means it was underexposed four stops and renders as a zone 5 instead of its normal zone 9.

In (b) the screen is underexposed eight stops. This renders it as a zone 1 black instead of zone 9. The subject/background ratio would be 256:1.

In (c) the screen is lit to the same intensity as the subjects and thus reproduces at its normal zone 9 value.

In (d) we create a silhouette by lighting the screen and not the subjects. Underexposing the facetones at least five stops while exposing for the white screen in the background ensures that the facetones are rendered at zone 1 instead of the standard zone 6.

from the subject, pointing the meter at the light source with the photosphere on, and the rim at 100 footcandles. You could also use the flat disc to determine these values for the hair light and rim. Consistency is what counts, along with final evaluation by eye.

The next thing we would do for this basic portrait setup is check the eyes. There should be a nice reflection from the fill in this instance. If not, we would add eyelight as necessary.

The last step in building up this lighting setup would be to balance the background, or foreground, to the subject by lighting it to intensity levels based on the **subject plane**, generally the most important plane for lighting purposes. Alternatively we could light the background first and then set our actor's key levels (see Figure 8.7).

SUBJECT/BACKGROUND RATIOS

When we first looked at background/set lighting in Chapter 2, we discussed the relationship between the subject and background. Here we shall examine ways to control background relative to subject plane. We should start by emphasizing the gestalt principle that light tonal values tend to advance and dark values to recede. By creating bright backgrounds we de-emphasize depth because light values advance toward the subject plane. With dark backgrounds we enhance the depth effect because dark values recede from the subject.

These advancing and receding effects also operate in color. Not only is the luminance value (brightness or darkness) of the color important, but the degree of saturation also affects depth. Tinted, pastel colors (white plus hue) tend to advance whereas richer tones (black plus hue) tend to recede. In addition, warm hues tend to advance and cool hues to recede.

The relationship between subject and background may be conceptualized exactly as we did with subject lighting ratios. The subject—equivalent to the light side of the face—is placed in a background context—equivalent to the shadow side of the face—within a known ratio. This subject/background ratio also applies to subject/foreground. We meter the **background** and **foreground planes** by putting the incident meter in the lighting on the background or foreground and pointing it at the camera in the standard manner. This reading is then compared to the reading for the subject.

The first step in lighting a background is to determine whether the subject plane or the background is to be the basis for the exposure of the particular shot. For example, if the subject is lit to T 8, we might then light the background to a T 5.6 level, thus underexposing it one stop. The T-stop for exposure is determined with the initial lighting setup, be it the subject or background. Alternatively, we could light and plan exposure around the background level of, say, T 2. We would then light the actors to the desired level relative to the background. The rule of thumb is to underlight backgrounds one stop.

The zone system allows for an accurate previsualization of subject/background relationships. For example, take the simplest case, a person foregrounded against a white wall. Let's assume we want to duplicate what we see. That means we need to light the person and the wall to the same T-stop so that the wall will render white (see Figures 8.7c and 2.20a).

But suppose the director desires a midgray background. This means the white wall must be rendered at zone 5 rather than at its standard zone 9 value. In this instance, it must be underlit by four stops (four zones) relative to the subject. For example, if the subject is lit to a T 8 level, we make sure the light on the wall is at T 2. Exposure at T 8 will then render the subject as normal in front of a midgray background (see Figures 8.7a and 2.20b).

In the same manner, by underlighting the background eight stops, we can make the white wall black, a zone 1 value (see Figures 8.7b and 2.20c). To do this we must light the subject eight stops brighter than the background. If we light the subject to T 16, then the wall can be held to T 1.0 and rendered as a zone 1 black value.

Treating the subject/background as a ratio problem allows for a precise previsualization in zones which, in turn, tells us how much relative light intensity to give each plane. We work from subject to background or from background to subject depending on which plane is more important for exposure determination.

As an example of working from the background plane, take a person against a light gray, zone 7 wall, and assume we desire to create a silhouette against a white wall. A **silhouette** by definition means we light the background and not the subject. The question is, How much do we light the background relative to the subject? For a pure black silhouette, the Caucasian facetone (zone 6) must be rendered at zone 2 and preferably zone 1. We shall underexpose it five stops (five zones).

To create a white background, we must overexpose the light gray in order to render it as zone 9. In this case, we will need a two-stop overexposure. Starting with the background, we provide overall flat illumination so that we obtain a T-stop of 16 intending to expose at T 8. We then meter the subject and find the person measures around T 1.4 or lower, since no light is allowed to fall on her. This means that with an exposure at T 8, the back wall will go from zone 7 to zone 9 and the face will go from zone 6 to zone 1—from T 8 to T 1.4 is five stops. We thus obtain our silhouette effect (see the similar example in Figure 8.7d).

We have used the zone system here to determine relative intensities for subject and background planes in exactly the same manner as we did for subject lighting ratios. The silhouette is an extreme example, but more subtle effects, such as **semisilhouettes**, work on the same principles. We will explore these ideas further in Chapters 9 and 10 where we will see that for a variety of different lighting effects, the relationship between subject and background can be analogized to this basic silhouette technique. Though we have used a black, gray, and white example, the same principles apply to colors, the difference being that colors under- or overexposed become more or less mixed with black (underexposure) or white (overexposure).

SUMMARY

In this chapter we looked at how lighting contrast ratios are used to establish lighting setups. The central concepts examined were:

- *Subject lighting ratio*—the ratio between the light and shadow sides of a subject created by key and fill light.
- *Subject/background ratio*—the ratio in lighting intensity between the subject and the background (foreground).

We saw there are two principal methods for establishing subject lighting ratios:

- The *incident method*, which compares readings for the light and shadow sides of the subject.

➢ The *flat disc method*, which measures the intensity of the light unit directly and compares readings for the key and fill.

It was emphasized that consistency of method is very important in learning to control the moods that derive from subject lighting ratios. We saw that ratios impact differently on white and black faces and that rim and back light intensities are set relative to the key light.

In the section on subject/background ratio, we saw that the cinematographer can control the rendition of backgrounds by manipulating the intensity of the background lighting and that the various effects may be previsualized in terms of zones. We also saw that a lighting setup can start with either the subject plane or the background plane. In either case, a variety of subject/background relationships are obtainable including silhouettes and semisilhouettes.

LIGHTING SETUPS

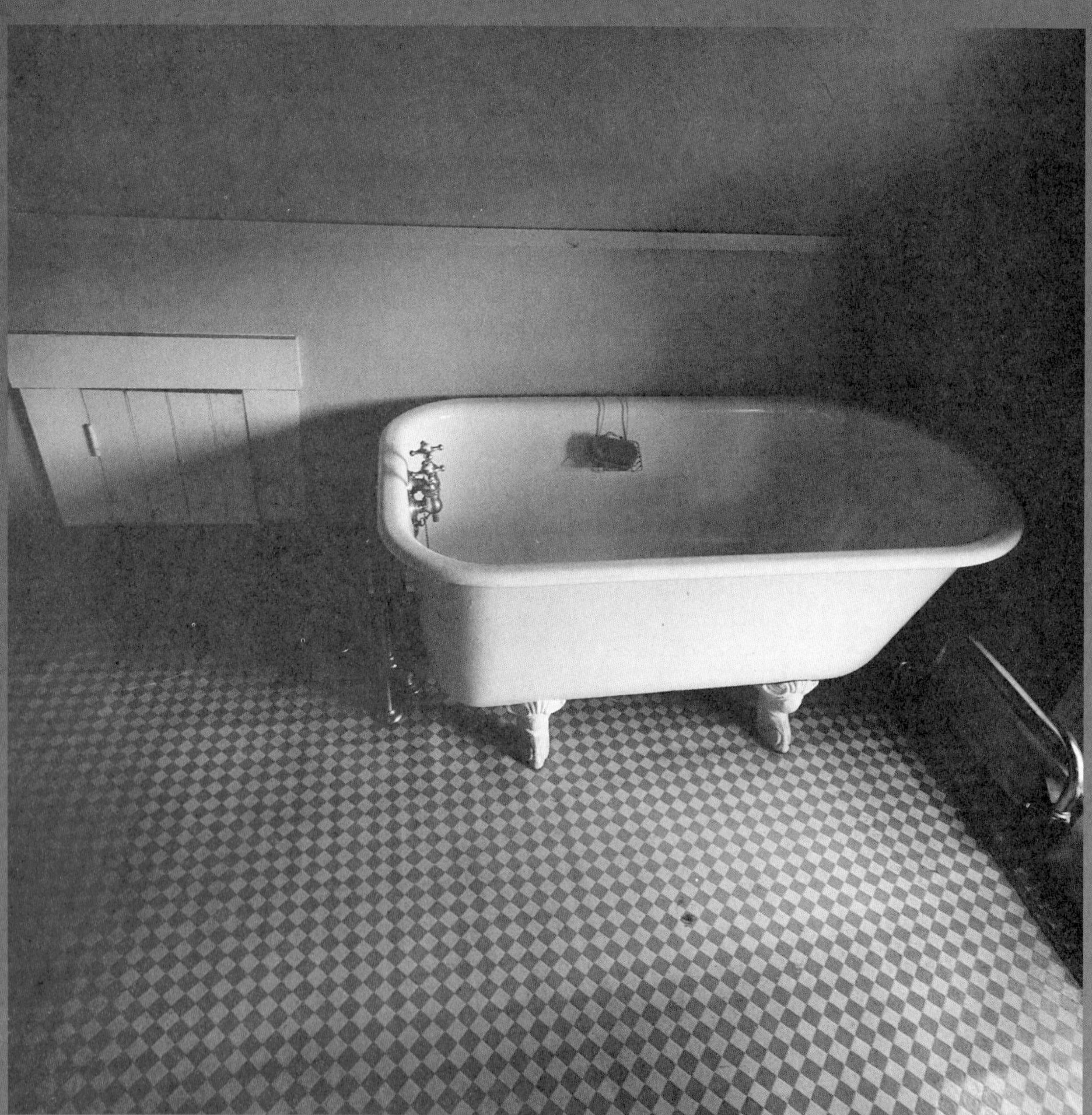

Photo by Jennifer A. Tucker

"natural light"

Lighting is an art, therefore, the cinematographer must be able to react to a variety of unique situations. There can be no fixed rules. In this chapter, we'll deal with planning the lighting for a film. We'll assume an overall style has been determined (see Appendix F, "Lighting Style"). Our goal here is to explain the factors a cinematographer must consider in order to achieve a specific look.

A SET OF lighting considerations can be formulated to guide the cinematographer in conceptualizing and executing a lighting setup. First, the cinematographer must select an overall look for the film and determine the impacts of lighting on the theme and mood. Once such base determinations are made, the cinematographer has a variety of options available to execute his ideas. These potential options are discussed in this chapter.

OVERALL LOOK

A key consideration is the determination of an overall look for the film. This look derives from consultation with the director and her visual interpretation of the script. Input also comes from interactions with the production designer, as well as set and costume designers. Once the overall look is agreed on, the cinematographer will be left to execute and interpret the requirements of that look from scene to scene.

A film's look derives from a variety of visual sources external to film itself and, of course, from film conventions and fads then in effect. For example, a film like *Dick Tracy* clearly derives its look from comic books. Painting is used a lot for look ideas. For example, consider the use of Edward Hopper's painting style in *Pennies from Heaven* or Caravaggio's chiaroscuro painting style in the biographical film *Caravaggio* or the van Gogh look in Robert Altman's *Vincent and Theo*.

As for film style conventions, the use of film noir techniques and looks in *Blade Runner* derives from the older B & W noir films; but the use of lots of backlit smoke in *Blade Runner* was part of a "smoke" fad during the late 1970s and 1980s evident in films as diverse as *A Man Called Horse* and *Flashdance* as well as a host of music videos.

MOOD AND THEMATIC CONCERNS

Mood is created through the patterning of light and shadow and is controlled by manipulating facial and subject/background ratios. The cinematographer works to establish mood and emotional responses to his or her images. This is possible on an overall level as well as on a scene-to-scene basis depending on the specific needs of the production.

Lighting has strong impacts on the meaning levels of a film. Consider the scene in *Close Encounters of the Third Kind* where the spaceship descends and the alien appears. The scene is bathed in an aura of light and "otherworldliness" which is, of course, a principal thematic element. Through selective lighting, cinematographers can emphasize characters, objects, and other details which in turn contribute to the meaning of the film.

APPROACHES TO LIGHTING SETUPS

An interior may be in a studio or on location. In the studio situation, we light everything and have lots of control. At a location, either we block off available light so that we can treat the location as a studio interior or we use the available light along with supplemental lighting as necessary.

Lighting is generally roughed in on a setwide basis. We move to closeups and medium shots from that basic scheme. It is the long shot that takes the most time to light. Asking yourself who and what is important makes the execution of the lighting setup more efficient. These questions force you to concentrate on the framing of the shot through the camera viewfinder. This is where lighting should be perfected, not outside the framelines.

Natural Light Approach

When filming on location, many cinematographers work with **available light**—ambient daylight, light bulbs, and lighting fixtures present at the location—in an attempt to preserve the natural look, which is one of the reasons the location was selected in the first place (see the shot opening this chapter). Available light is seldom totally acceptable and is commonly supplemented with artificial units. For example, we often use a large HMI from outside a window to simulate daylight or sunlight.

The **natural light** approach was in vogue during the 1960s and 1970s and was made possible by the introduction of high speed lenses and faster film emulsions. Prime examples would be cinematographer Raoul Coutard's work on the *nouvelle vague* films and Nestor Almendros's use of twilight in *Days of Heaven*.[1] Philosophically, the natural light approach was a reaction against the glossy, overly fine-tuned studio lighting of the time with its large amount of "artificial" back light and "perfected" closeups.

Consider the following quote discussing the lighting of Claude Chabrol's film *Madame Bovary* by cinematographer Jean Rabier. "Prior to production, Rabier and Chabrol discussed lighting in great detail. 'Again, we wanted to be very true to the soft local light, and wherever possible, we've shot in natural daylight with a minimum of lights,' says Rabier."[2]

With the natural light approach, lighting setup time is generally minimized and the overall look for that scene is more open to spontaneous change. With this style, your lighting plan springs out of the natural location. The use of actual candlelight for key lighting by John Alcott in *Barry Lyndon* provides a good example of natural light pushed to the extreme. The photographs in Figure 9.1 illustrate the range from natural light to artificial studio lighting.

As an example of how the natural light method works, suppose the location is a poolroom in the back of a tavern. The determination has been made to use what's already available—lights over the pool tables, neon signs provided by the various beer companies, small lights on a couple of tables. This means we will be working at very low levels, around T 2, and will need to use small units for supplementing so that they fit in with the feel of the place. After scouting the location, you plan your lighting setup on paper, elaborating which, if any, supplemental units to use, where to place them, where to use filtration, diffusion, and so forth. Available light, supplemented with key lighting on the two people, was used on the shot in Figure 10.4. Much the same effect can be created with artificial light (see Figure 9.1b and c). Figure 9.2 shows an artificially lit day interior which may be compared to the available light chapter opening image.

Studio Approach

The alternative to a natural light approach is to light everything from scratch, the normal procedure in a studio situation. This approach to lighting generally indicates a large production unit with lots of equipment, a commercial or feature film shoot. This tradition encourages large-scale interactions—if done well, the subtlety of natural light is replaced with the subtlety of artificial light. The lighting in *The Color Purple*, *Superman*, and *GoodFellas*, as well as in numerous, stylized music videos, such as Michael Jackson's *Black or White*, illustrates the studio approach and the many possibilities for using artificial light (see Figure 9.1c–h).

If our poolroom example were in a music video, available lights would be used or switched off to the degree they fit in with the imposed style. A heavily smoked, back lighting would likely be applied to the pool room. Localized setups would highlight singers and other select subject areas. Background lights and neon signs would be hung as props. With lighting-from-scratch styles, the lighting in effect "creates" the location.

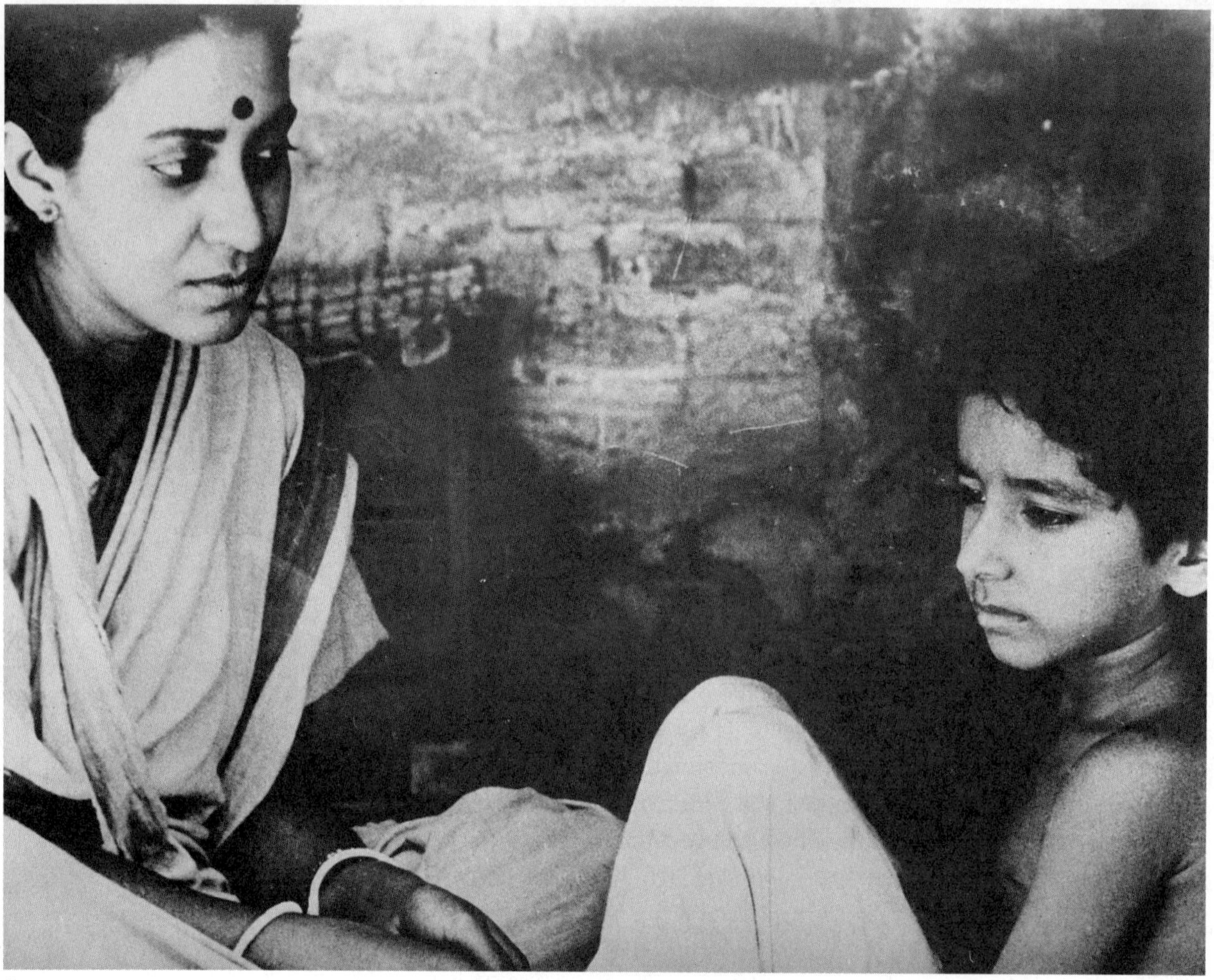

a

Figure 9.1 Lighting Styles: From Natural Light to Artificial Studio Looks *This series of photos is arranged so as to illustrate a natural light style (a) and the evolution of that style—moving more and more away from the natural—to end with the highly artificial studio style of the Hollywood musical as in (h). The publicity still in (a) is from* Pather Panchali, *1955; (b)* Fat City, *Columbia Pictures, 1972; (c)* Raggedy Man, *Universal City Studios, 1981; (d)* $8^1/_2$, *Embassy Pictures, 1963; (e)* Ashes and Diamonds, *1958; (f)* Touch of Evil, *Universal-International, 1958; (g, h)* Top Hat, *RKO Radio Pictures, 1935.*

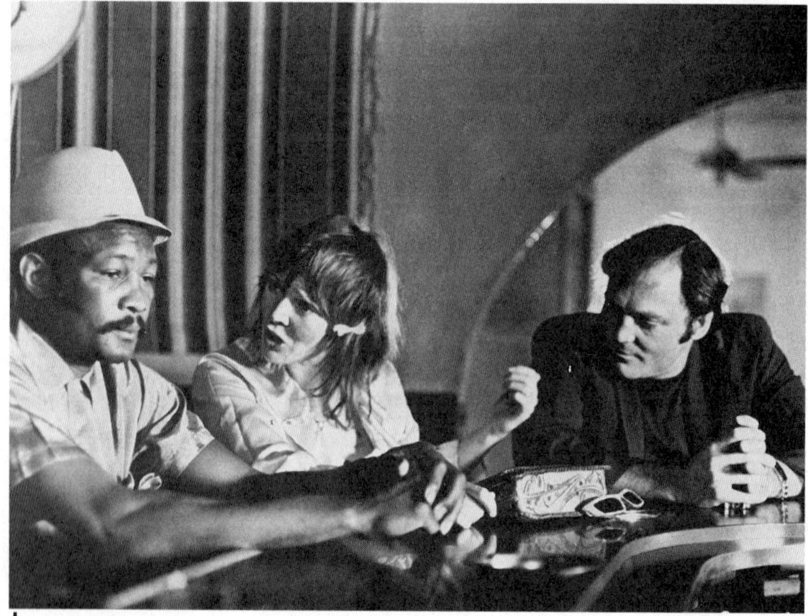

b

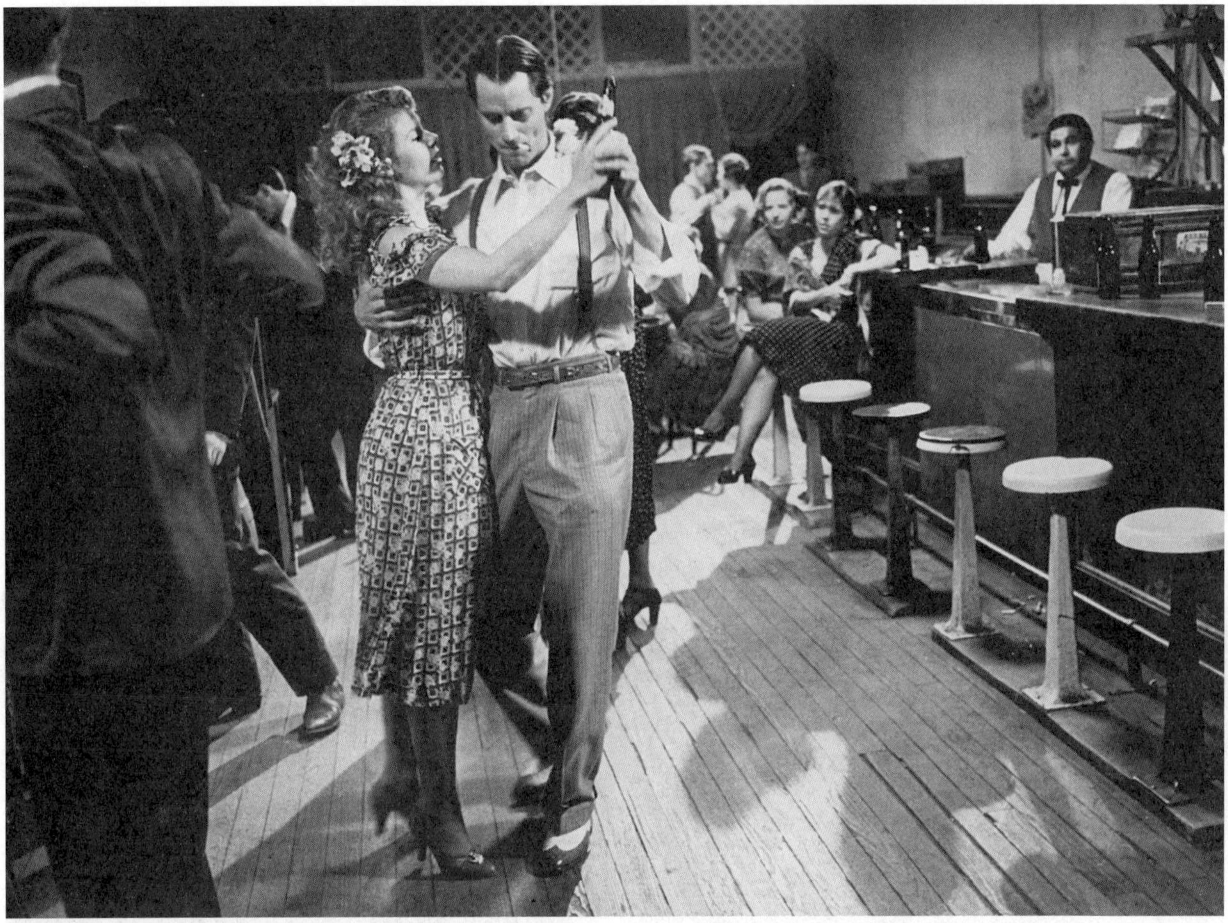

c

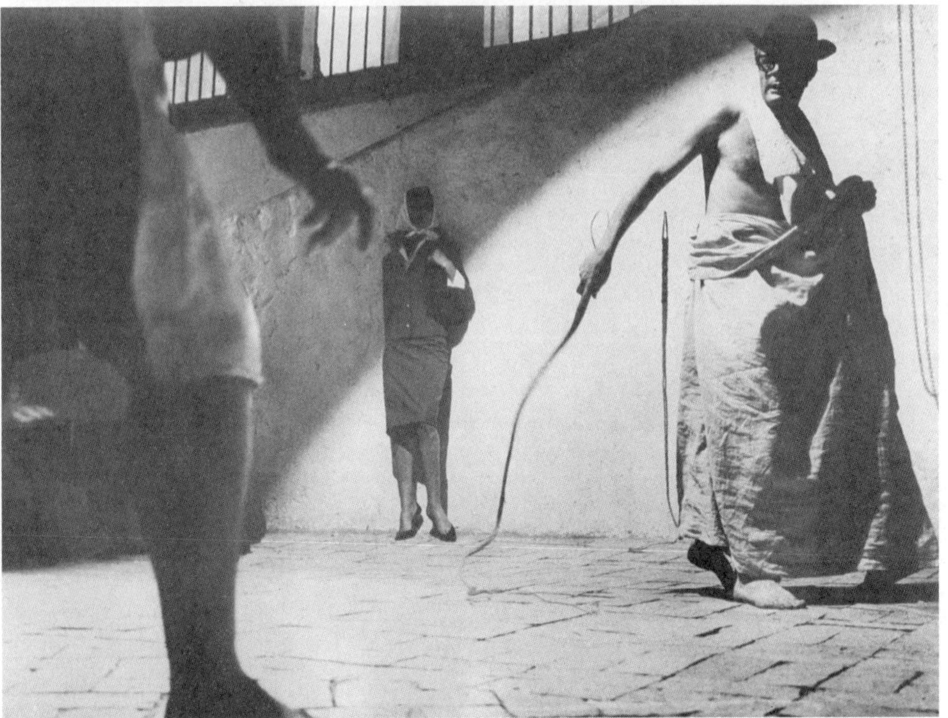

d

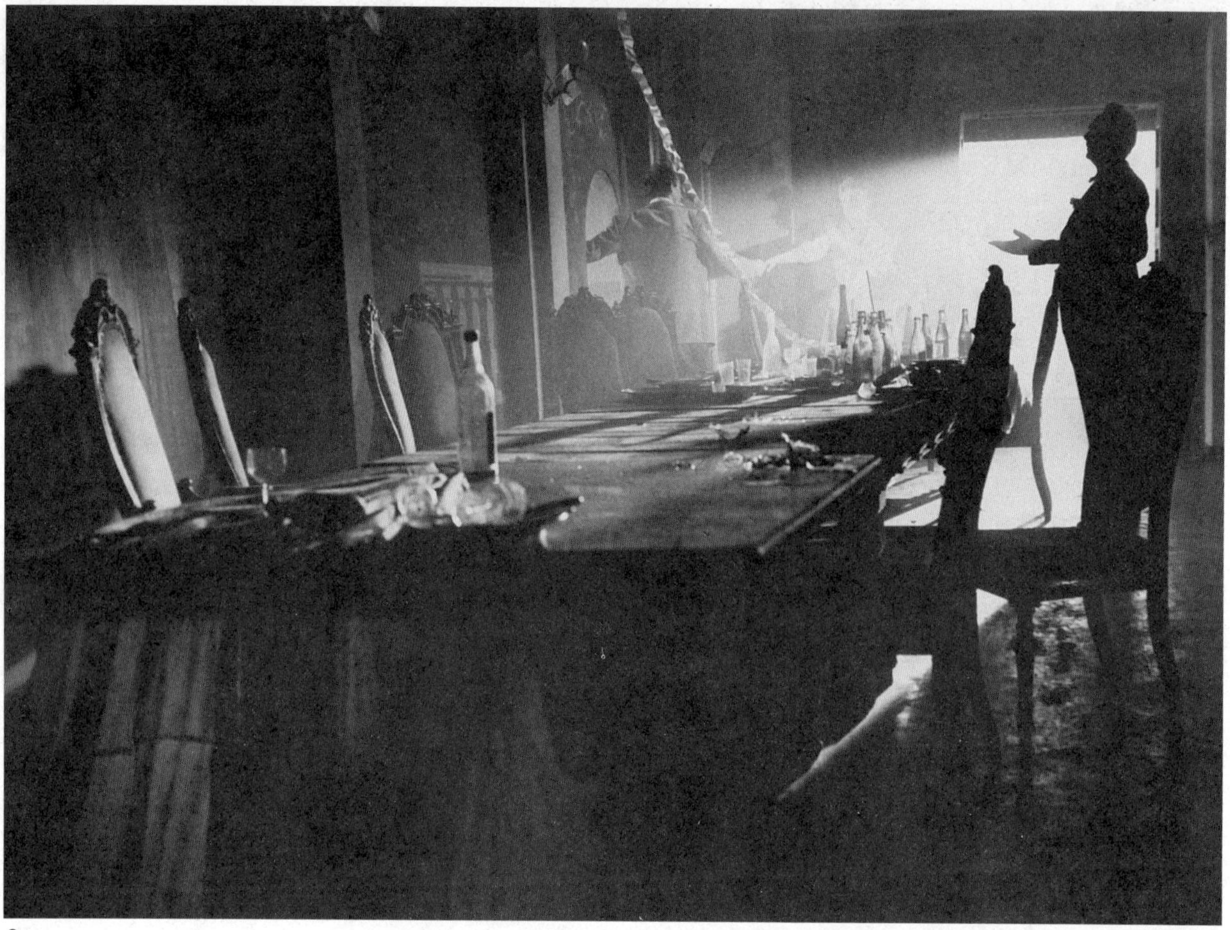

e

Figure 9.1 (continued)

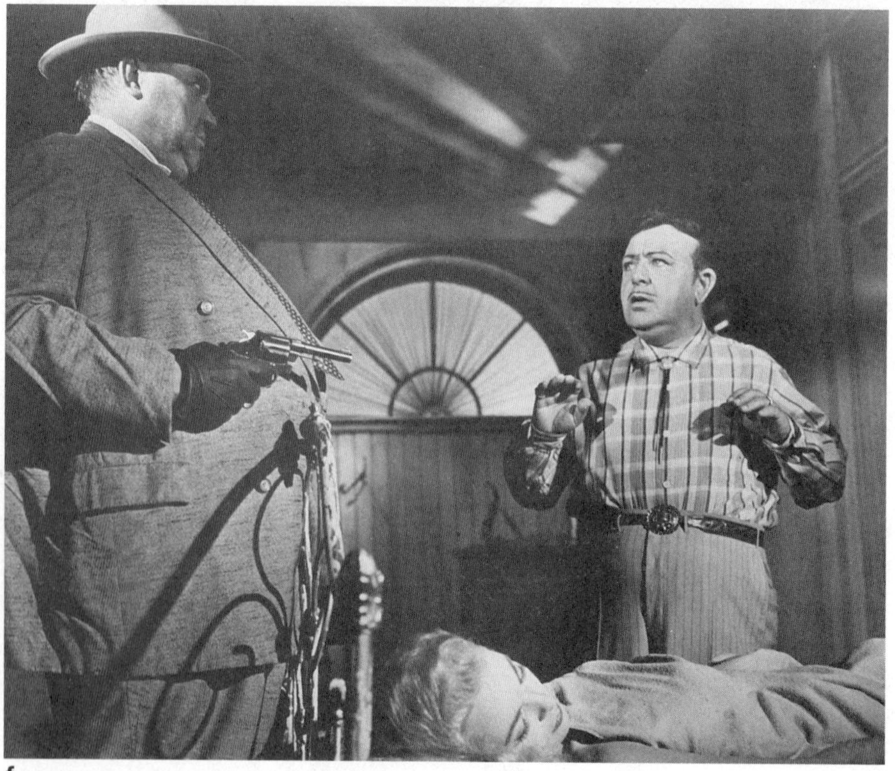

f

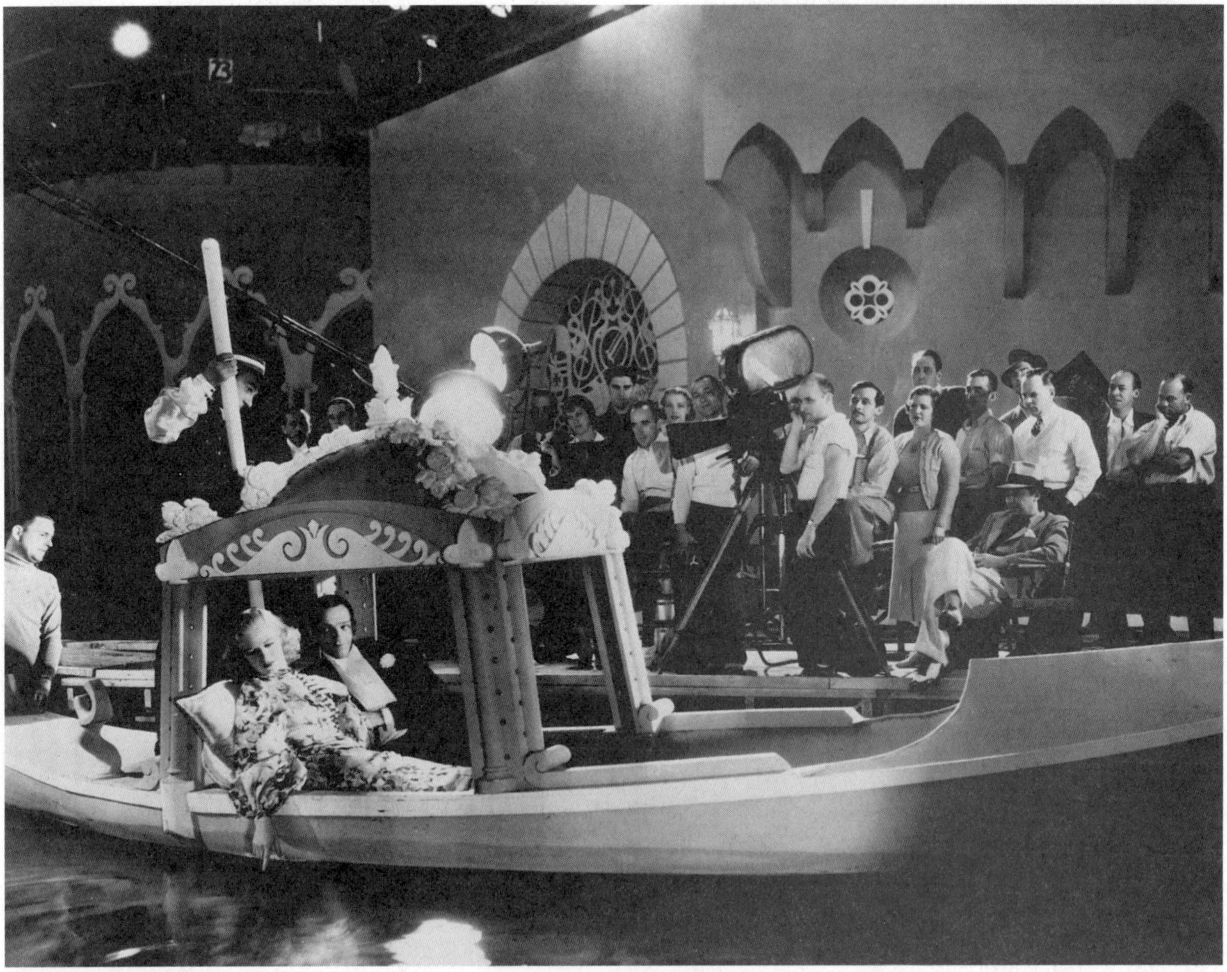

g

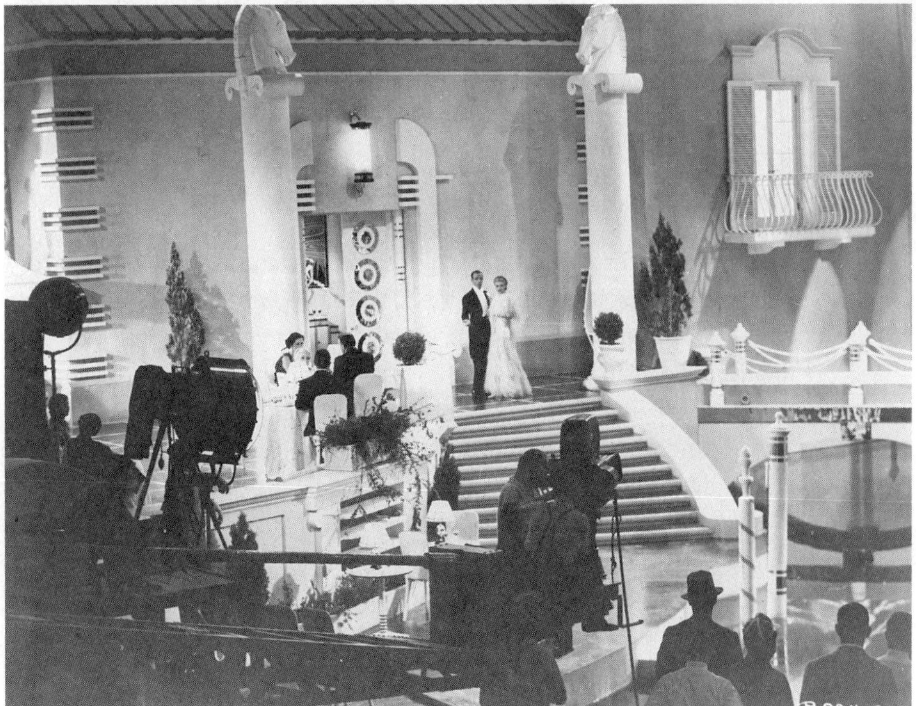

h

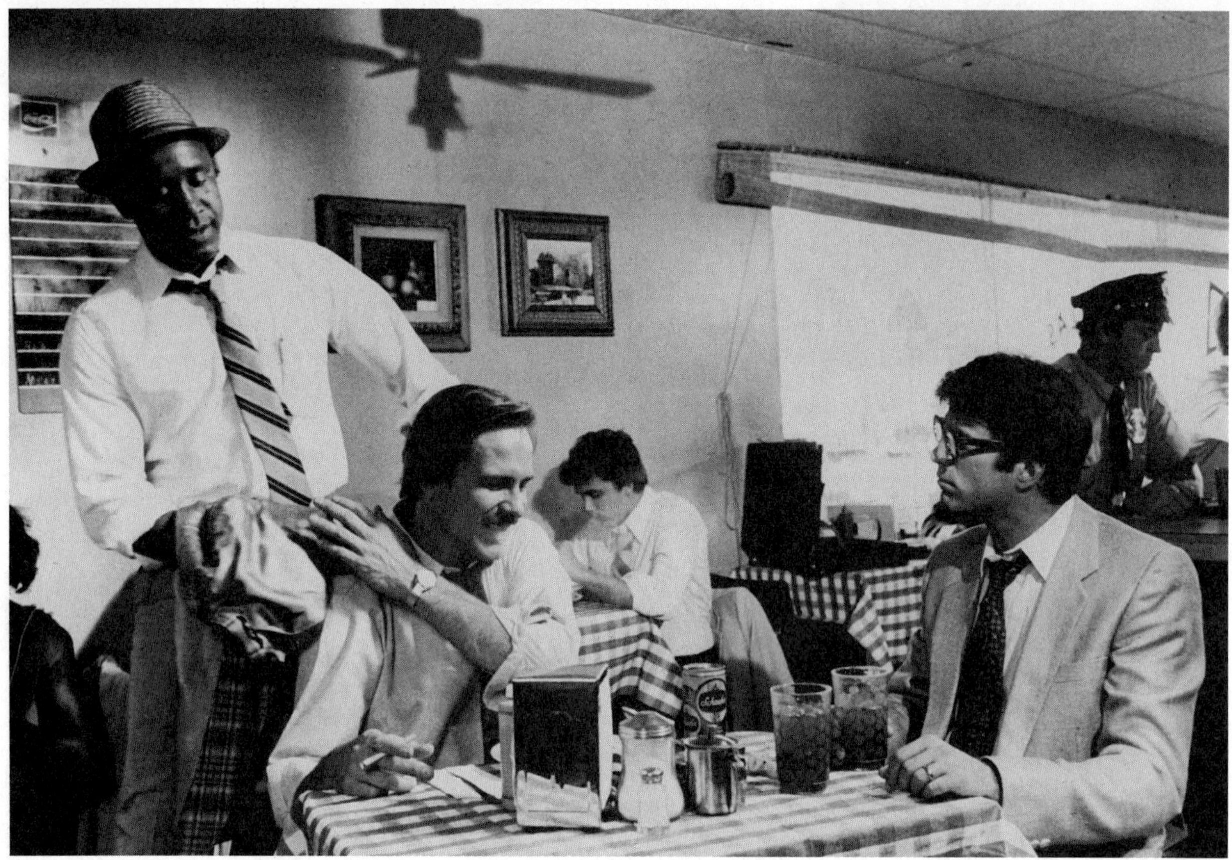

Figure 9.2 Artificial Light Used in a Realistic Fashion *(Cafe interior from* Body Heat, *The Ladd Company, 1981)*

A cinematographer must be able to work with both natural light and studio methods since in any given film both approaches are almost always utilized. Interesting images can result from either method though certain looks require a particular working method. In general, commercials and television programming result from an interventionist, large-unit studio style. Documentary styles use more natural light approaches.

Use of Lighting Plans or Plots

Lighting proceeds through a series of trials and errors. While setting lights, new problems and new ideas will arise and be dealt with. Initial lighting execution (roughing in) is a very creative act as well as a very empirical one. You continually ask yourself: Is this what I want? A variety of devices are used to help establish the setup: Polaroids, viewing glasses, or if time permits, stills and film tests. Fine-tuning perfects the setup and is judged through the camera viewfinder.

Though lighting plots are not common in film, for student work a lighting plot should be made of the final setup, as shown in Figure 9.7a. The plot schematizes the lighting setup and maps the types of lighting units used along with the position, angle, intensity level, and degree of diffusion or color filtration for each. This written record will facilitate lighting during reshooting should that be necessary. A photo of the lighting setup can also be useful.

Overlighting: A Danger to Avoid

Overlighting means the tendency to use too much light, particularly fill and rim on actors and overly high intensities on backgrounds. The result is actors who always look lit and backgrounds that are overly bright and intrusive. Overlighting destroys the moods inherent in an actual location and inhibits the creation of mood in a studio situation.

Overlighting derives from insecurity and leads to unnecessary lighting in beginning work. Inexperienced cinematographers light background actors not within the frame, or perfect the lighting on lead actors regardless of their movements or insignificance in a particular shot. In the worst case, lighting is set for the long shot, which generally takes a lot of time, when only closeups and medium shots are asked for.

SPECIFIC PROBLEMS

There are a number of recurring lighting problems that need addressing in every film. Some involve the lighting for the film as a whole, and some are more scene-specific. The basic considerations that must be addressed include: where to place facetones, whether to use stylized partial lighting, whether to shoot everything with the same T-stop, where to set the source motivation, whether to prelight sets, whether to light backgrounds first, how to accommodate actor movement, how to check the balance of the lighting intensities for the setup, which gear to use, and how to position that gear. We will now look at these recurring problems in more detail.

Facetone Placements

One subtle technique is to **place (peg) facetones** higher or lower than the normal **zone 5 exposure** placement, which renders black facetones at zone 4, brown facetones at zone 5, and Caucasian facetones at zone 6. In Chapter 7 we discussed exposing for the shadow side of a face. This results in a zone 7, or higher, placement of facetones. The result is a light, "up" mood (see Figures 7.1d and 7.3d).

Higher-than-normal facetones can also be flattering to actors. Where the facial ratio is 2:1–4:1, exposure for the shadow side overexposes the light side a stop or two. This technique was utilized in the Swedish film *Elvira Madigan* as part of its overall romantic, Impressionistic lighting style.

Another possibility is to peg facetones at levels lower than normal, imbuing them with a heaviness and gray sobriety. Many beautiful effects result from this use of semisilhouettes. With semisilhouettes, exposure is usually pegged to the background, which, for best effect, is lighter than the actors. The result can be romantic or morose depending on specifics.

With a semisilhouette technique, facetones are around zone 4, two stops under the standard zone 6 (see Figure 9.3a–e).

In the series of shots in Figures 7.1, 7.3, and 7.8, we discussed the effects obtainable with a compromise exposure. For a given facial ratio, it is possible to split the exposure between the light and shadow sides of

Figure 9.3 Facetone Placements: Semisilhouettes and Compromise Exposure Effects *Darker-than-normal placement of facetones (semisilhouettes) can have very interesting effects on mood. In (a) the face is just slightly darker than normal. In (b) and (c) we see a more typical semisilhouette effect, with the face about two to three stops darker than normal (photo b is by Maria Viera; c is a detail from a photo by Jennifer A. Tucker).*

In (d) and (e) we see that the semisilhouette (d) is created by underexposing the foreground actors about two stops relative to the background, which is held constant for both normal (e) and semisilhouette (d) effects. See in this regard the discussion of silhouettes in Figure 8.7(d).

Another interesting facetone placement is illustrated in (f), (g), and (h). Hard light and a high subject lighting ratio, 128:1 or more, are used. A compromise exposure is then given so that the lit side of the face is three or more stops overexposed and the shadow side underexposed a similar amount. The result can be very dramatic.

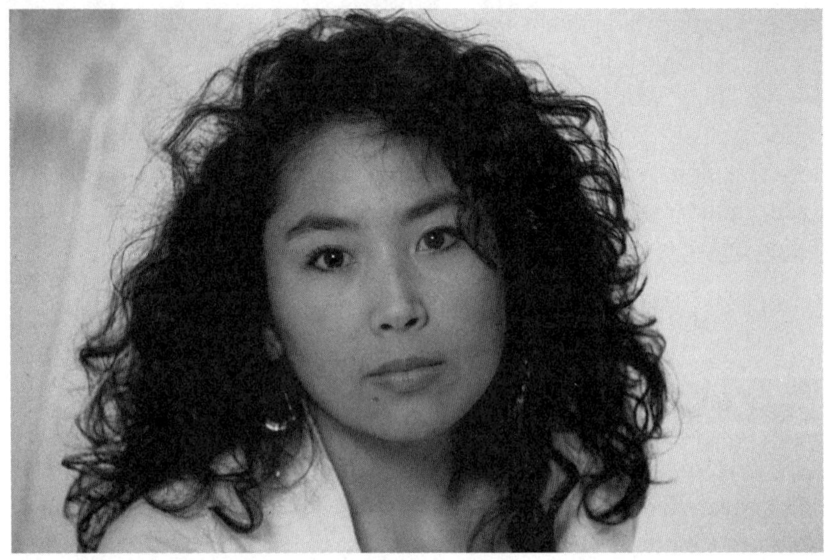

a

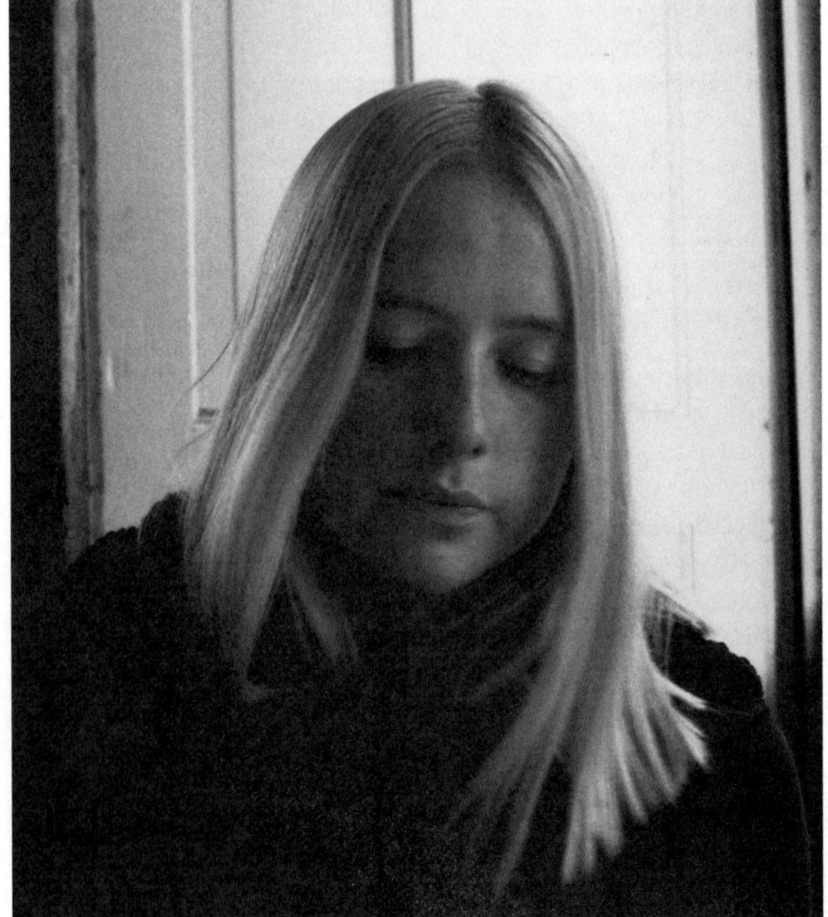

b

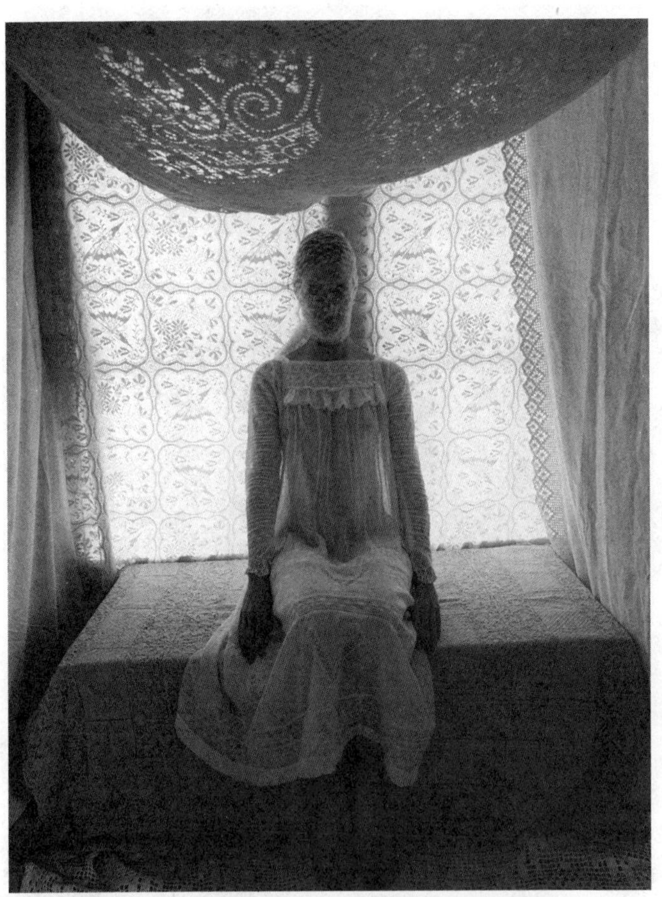
c

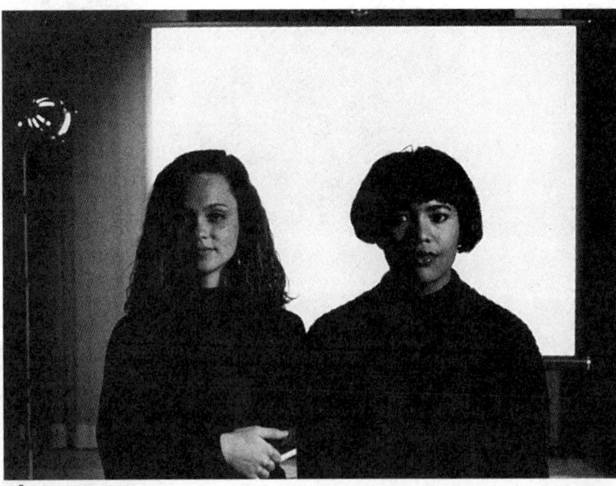
d

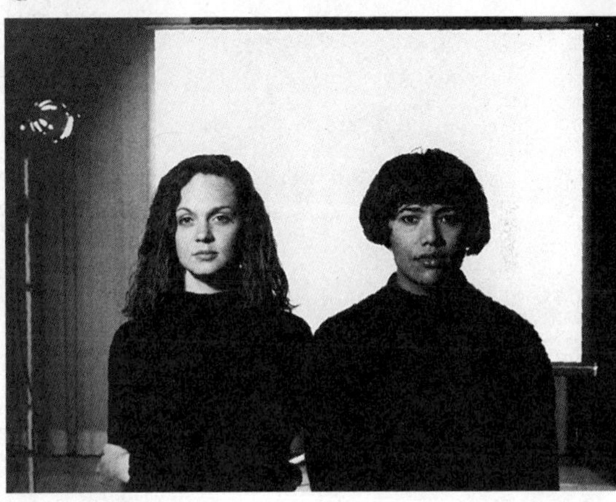
e

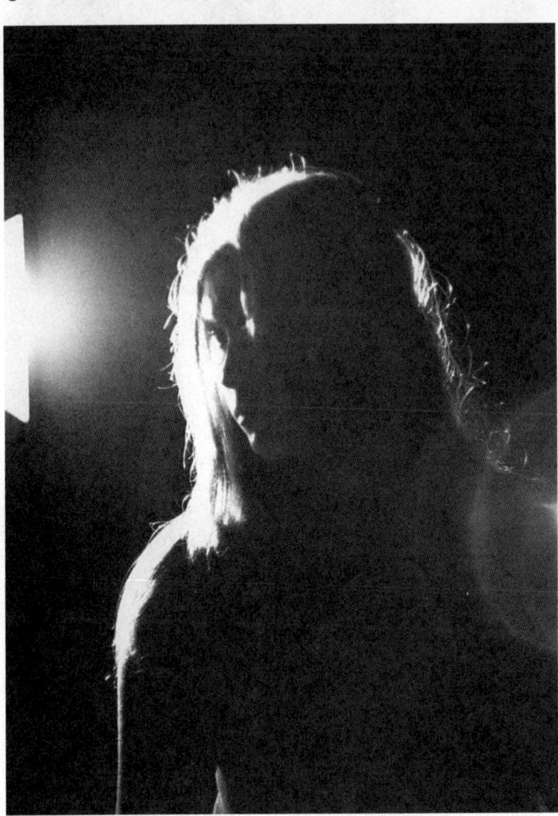
f

Figure 9.3 (continued)

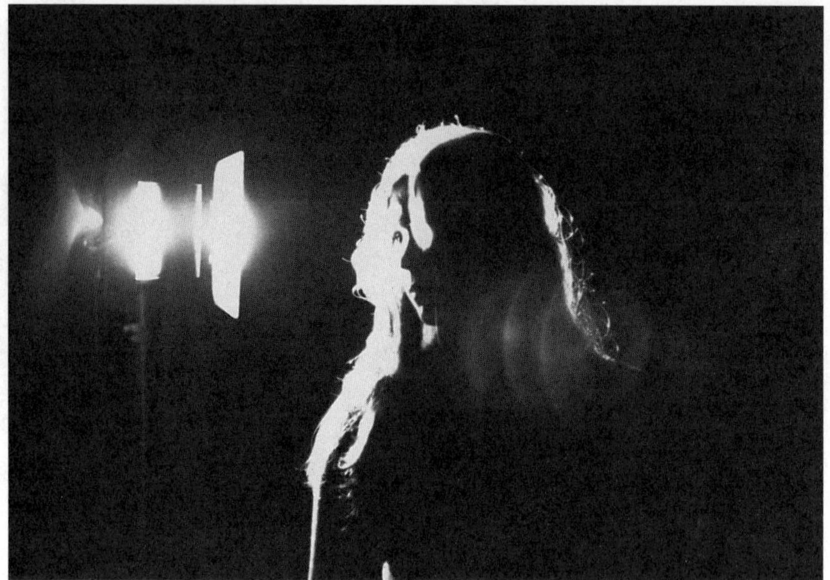

g

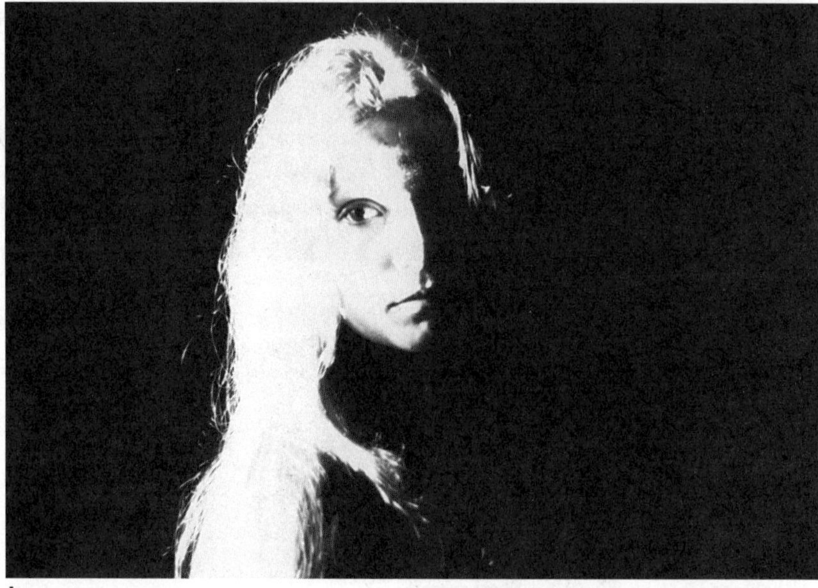

h

the face. With high facial ratios, say, 16:1, you overexpose the light side two stops and underexpose the shadow side two stops. Little importance is attached to zone 6. This technique was used in Jean-Gabriel Albiccoco's *Girl With the Golden Eyes* to create an abstract pattern of light and dark within a moody, low-key context. Such an effect derives from the use of high facial ratios, rear keys, and minimal fill (see Figures 9.3f–h and 1.3c).

Variations in facetone placement may be utilized throughout a scene or an entire film. The cinematographer should remain alert to their potentials, even though 90% of facetones are at a standard zone 5 exposure placement.

Partial Lighting

There is a facial lighting technique, popular in the 1930s through the 1950s, we should mention here. In noir, melodrama, and other dramatic films, cinematographers shaded light from the forehead and body so that it would not draw attention away from the face and eyes (see Figure 9.4). This technique is still used in music video and color noir films, though often as a form of intentional artificiality, a deliberate visual quoting of older film forms.

Another standard practice derived from the 1940s and 1950s is the emphasizing of one actor in a two-shot by keeping the foreground actor silhouette or semisilhouette. This often results from **cheating**—the slight repositioning of actors, props, and lights for better effect—and is done to focus the audience's attention on a particular character (see Figure 9.5).

T-Stop Consistency

Feature-film cinematographers often work to a predetermined T-stop, a stop used, for example, for all the interiors in a film. The theory is that such consistency will give uniformity to the various shots in a scene and enhance the illusion of reality. Sometimes a particular T-stop is fundamental for the lighting setup, such as when depth of field is required. In low-budget productions, T-stop consistency is not always possible, though consistency within a given scene is possible and should be maintained.

Lighting Motivation

As stated in Chapter 1, most cinematographers approach lighting a scene by using existing light sources—a window, doorway, or table lamp—as motivation for the direction, quality, and color of the illumination. Selection of the main motivating light source determines the direction and angle of the key light and the corresponding lighting logic for the entire scene (see Figure 9.6).

Where there is no motivating in-shot light source, we usually invent one off-screen. For example, in a night bedroom scene, the lighting can be motivated by an imaginary streetlight outside the window. In the case of nonrealistic lighting styles, a lighting setup with a logical spatial continuity is less important and sometimes unimportant.

Prelighting of Sets

Prelighting is common in feature films. It refers to a gaffing crew's lighting the next set or location while filming is going on at the current

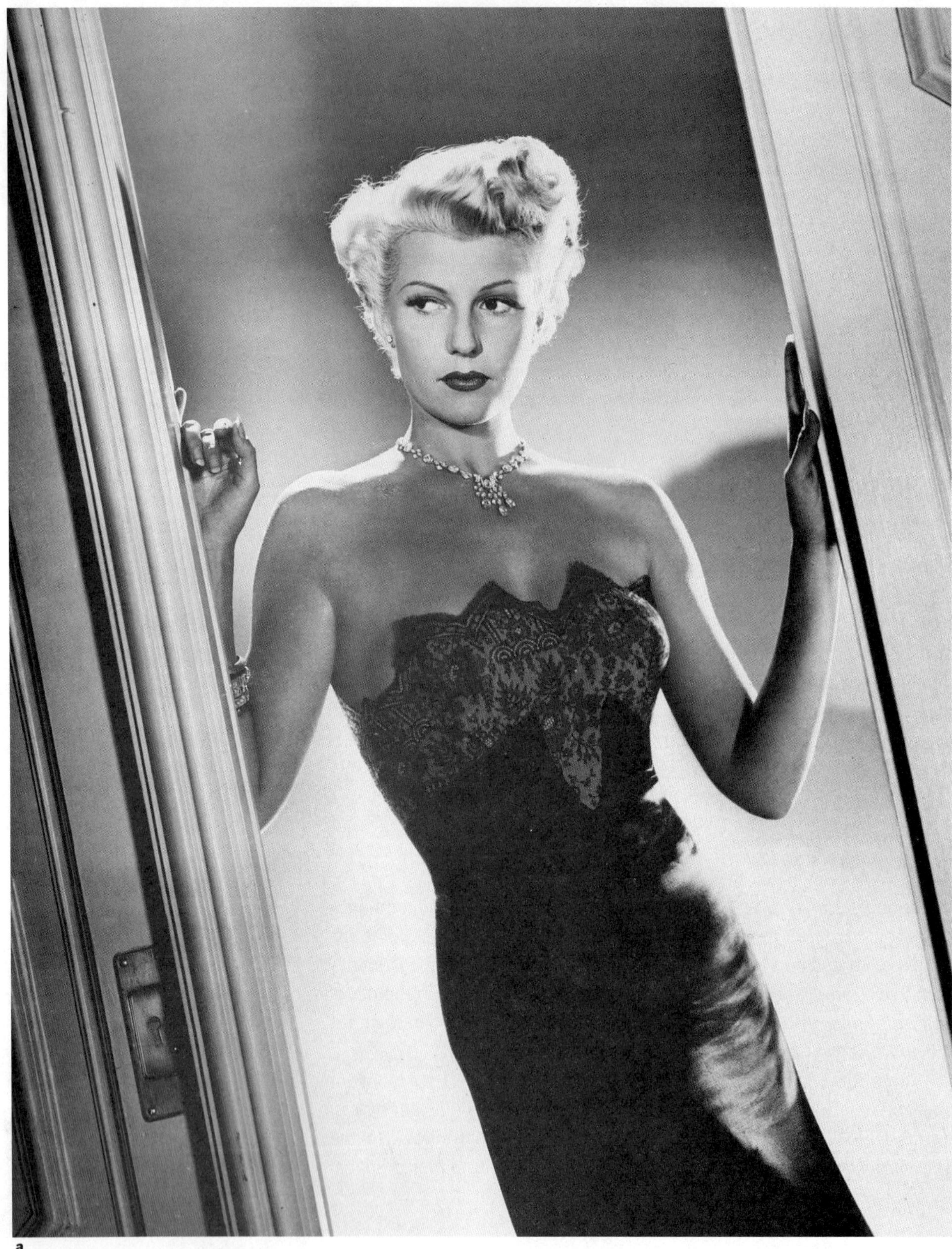

a

Figure 9.4 Partial Lighting *A common technique during the 1930s and 1940s was to selectively light the star. Usually this meant lighting the face and shading off the light on the body as in (a) and (b) here. Sometimes this was extended to include shading off parts of the face and emphasizing others as in Figure 1.7. The photo in (a) is a Columbia Pictures publicity still of Rita Hayworth. The publicity still in (b) is from* The Devil is a Woman, *Paramount Pictures, 1935.*

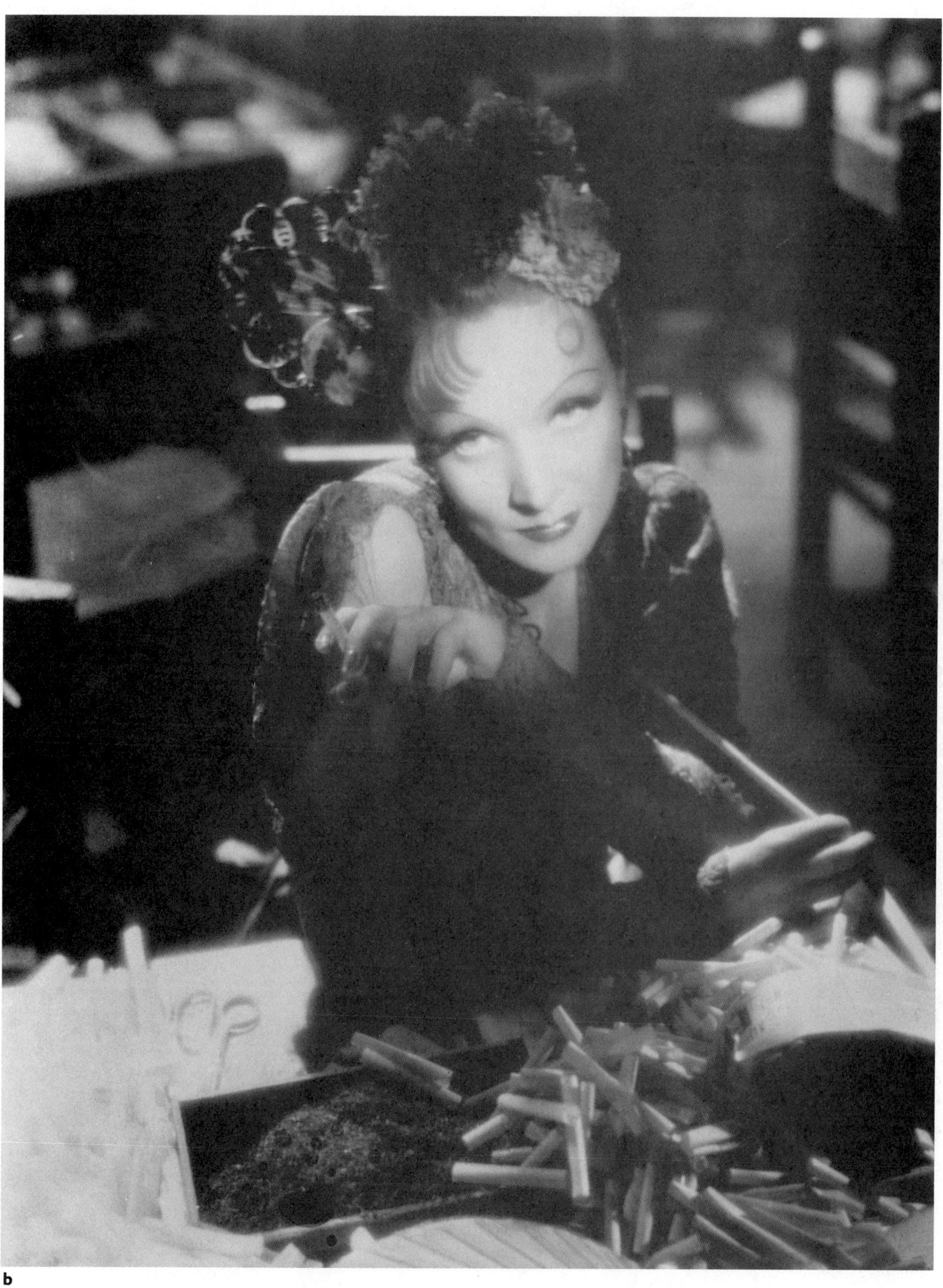

b

Figure 9.5 Keeping the Foreground Actor Semisilhouette in Two-Shots

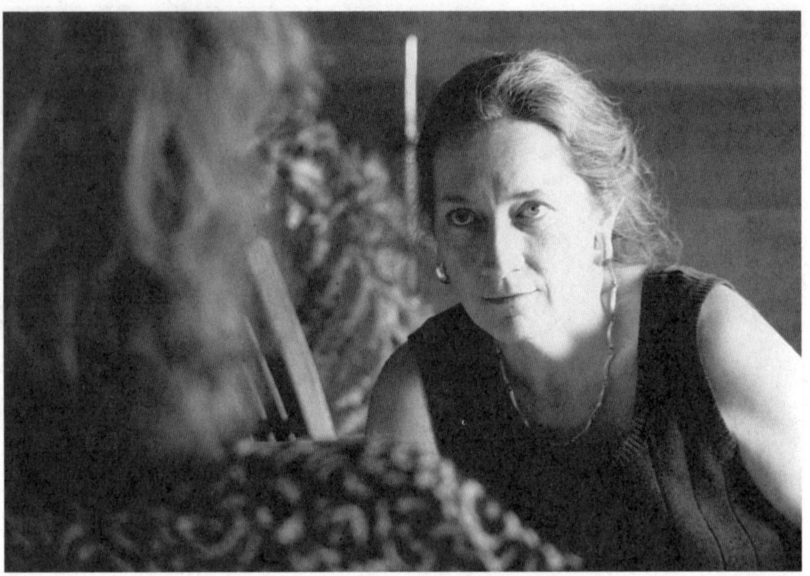

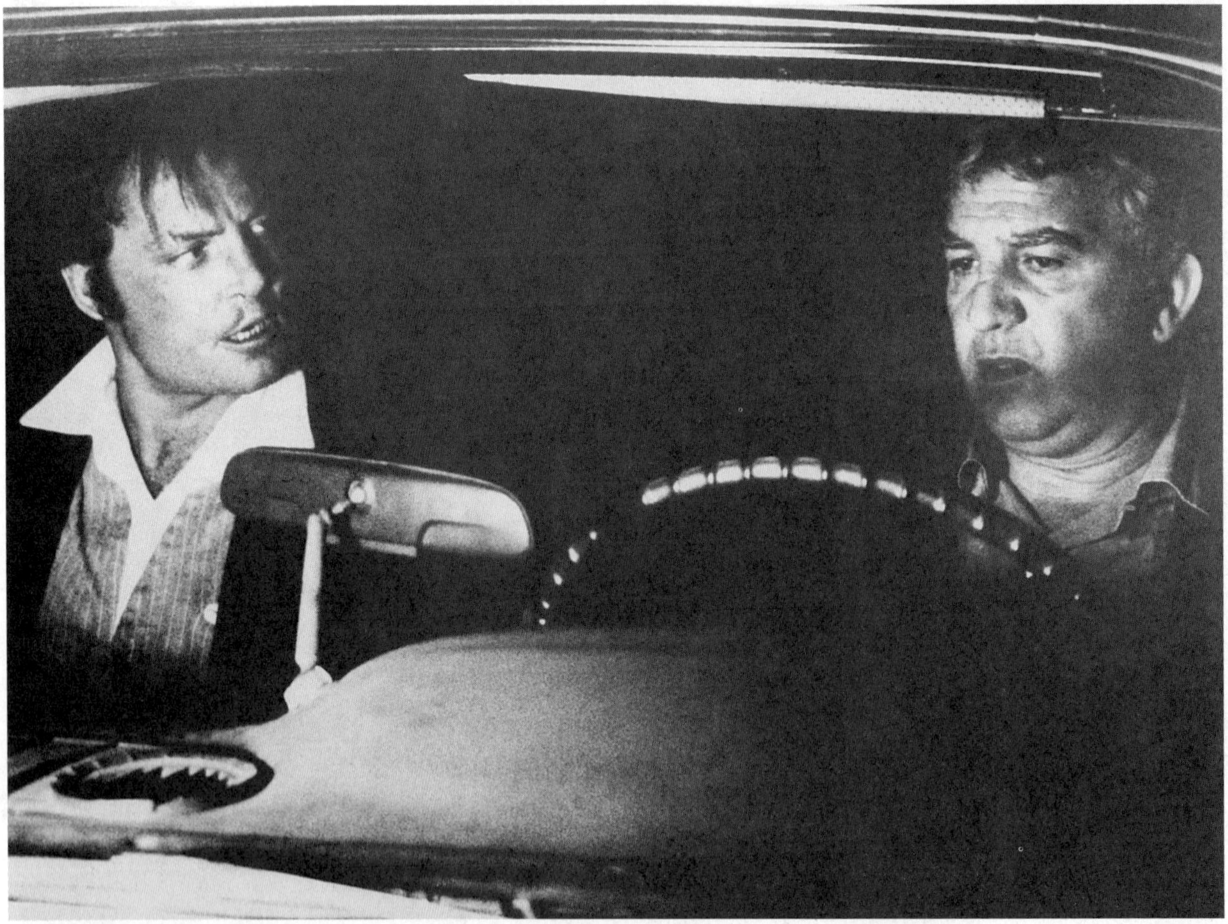

Figure 9.6 Motivated Lighting: Night Car Interior *(Fat City, Columbia Pictures, 1972)*

set. With prelighting we can usually perfect the background lighting but only rough-in subject areas, fine-tuning those when the principals are on the set. In low-budget films, prelighting of sets is uncommon.

Lighting Subject or Background First

Whether to light the subject or background first is often a matter of personal preference. As we saw in Chapter 8, theoretically, there should be no visible difference since both involve the establishing of the same subject/background ratio. However, where prelighting is being used, usually the backgrounds are perfected first. On low-budget films, we generally light the subject first—although in the poolroom example discussed earlier, where the background was already lit with beer signs and other lights, we would blend in our subject lighting accordingly.

Actor Movement

When lighting for movement, key areas of action are identified and each given its own lighting setup. For example, suppose we track an actor as she enters a door at frame left, walks screen right to sit at a table, gets up to dance, returns to the table, then leaves. Each of these specific action areas will have its own setup. The overall plan might require the door to be darker than the table and the table brighter than the dance floor. Exposure might be referenced to the table at T 2.8 with the dance floor and doorway lit to T 2 levels.

Generally, it is a good idea to let actors enter and exit localized lighting setups rather than illuminating them uniformly throughout the shot space. In this example we would not light the area between the doorway and table or between the table and dance floor. We might, however, accentuate the actor with rims when she is in those areas. The complete setup might look like the plot in Figure 9.7a.

The human eye and mind like variety. The moving actor is inherently interesting. Varying the lighting intensity throughout a shot adds to the visual interest.

Checking the Shot with a Meter

Usually after all fine-tuning is completed, the cinematographer will walk through the shot pointing an incident meter at the camera to check for lighting variety and to measure the main areas for proper intensity. In our example, the cinematographer would enter through the door, go to the table, and proceed to the dance floor. This would ensure levels are set as planned.

Figure 9.7 Lighting for Actor Movement *In (a) we plot our lighting for the scene described in the text. In (b) we can see the complicated grid of lights actually used to create localized setups and a complete lighting scheme for a dance-floor scene (*Top Hat*, RKO Radio Pictures, 1935).*

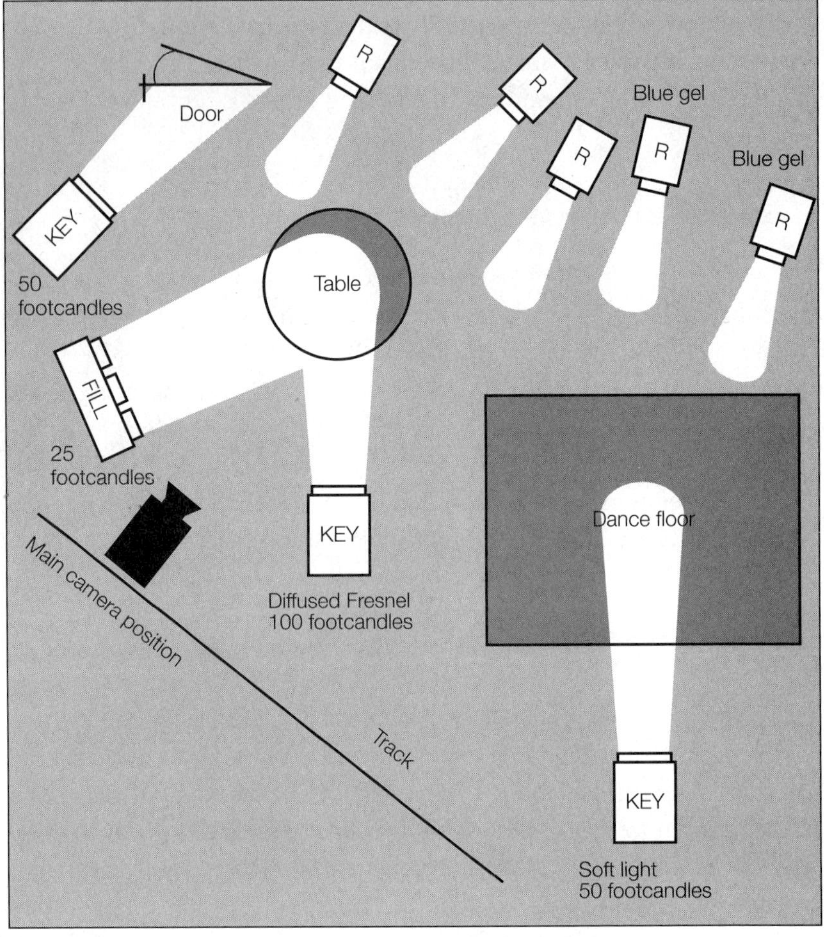

a

Light Selection and Placement

Normally, you have planned your lighting and know whether you need 10Ks or Midgets (see Appendix A, "Lighting and Grip Gear"). Sometimes, particularly on independent and student productions, only limited lighting equipment is available. Given this situation, you work with the gear you have, accepting the fact that this may limit your approach and look possibilities.

Light placement requires creative solutions. It is one thing to say you want 100 footcandles from position X and another to hide and mount the lights to accomplish this. Somehow, through the use of scaffolding, polecats, gaffer tape, wall mounts, and imagination, the lights do get there (again, see Appendix A). On large crew shoots, many more options and workers to help are available. In any event, care must be taken not to damage walls, paint, and the like.

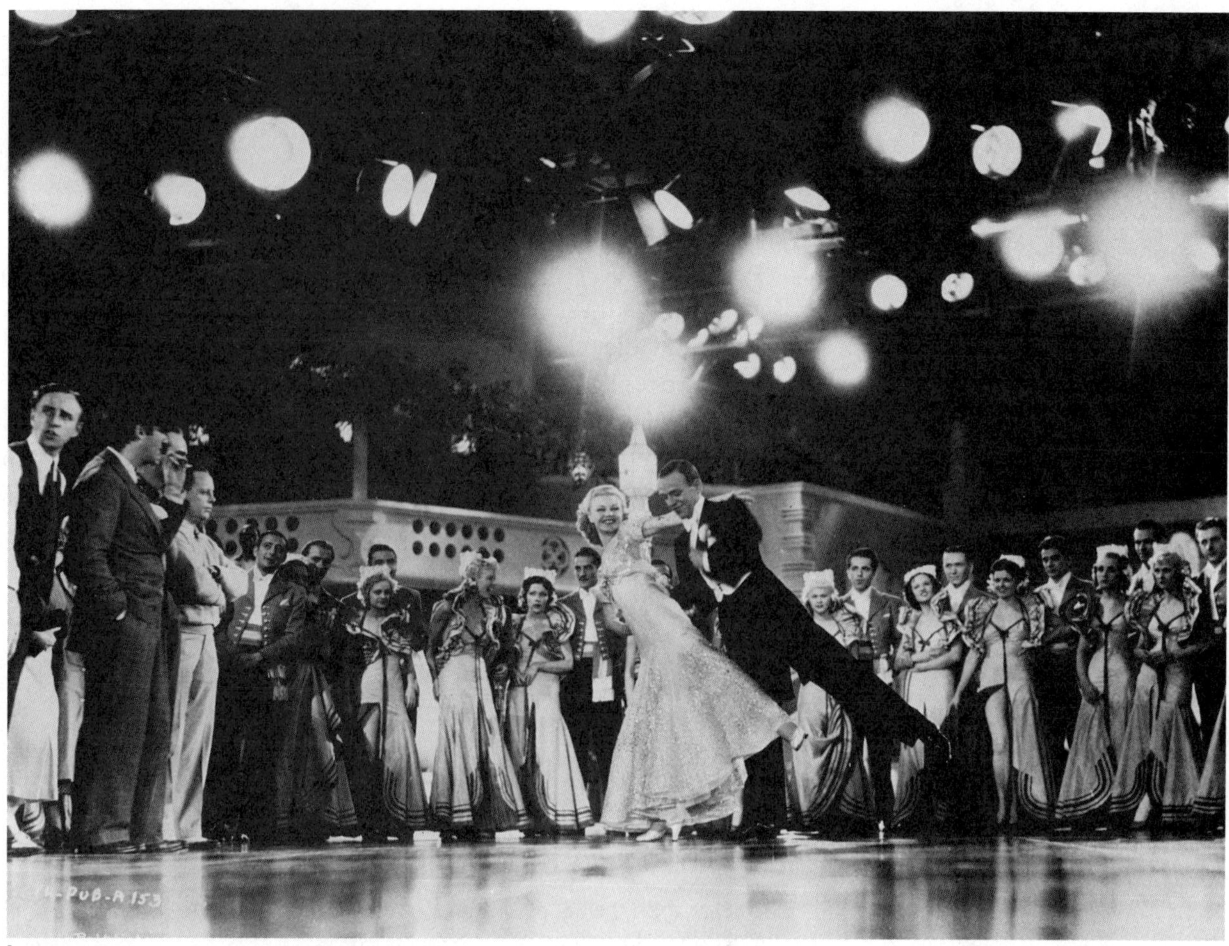

b

SUMMARY: LIGHTING AS EXPLORATION

A formulaic application of such concepts as key, fill, and subject lighting ratio seldom leads to interesting images, which is why cinematographers are continually reminding us that they light by eye, that they never measure lighting ratios, and so forth. Techniques like lighting in planes, cheating lighting in closeups, using under- and overexposure to create lighting changes are just that—techniques. The important thing is *vision*.

In an interesting discussion of his approach to lighting, Nestor Almendros says:

> More and more I tend to use only one light source, which is what usually happens in nature. I reject the typical lighting of the forties and fifties, which consisted of a main or "key" light, supplemented by a "fill" light, with another light behind to show off the stars' hair-dos and make them stand out against the background, yet another for the background itself, another to show off the wardrobe, and so on *ad infinitum*. The result had nothing to do with reality, where a window or a lamp, or at most both of them, normally provide the only sources of light. Since I lack imagination, I seek inspiration in

> nature, which offers me an infinite variety of forms. Once the key light has been decided, the space around it and the areas that might be left in total darkness are reinforced with a very soft gentle light, until what is reproduced on film is close to what the eye would really see.[3]

Almendros obviously takes a natural light position in this passage, but to be underlined for our purposes is that he emphasizes the observational, "seeing" element as an approach to lighting. Almendros is noted for his interesting images.

Try to conceive of a lighting setup as the creation and lighting of a filmic space. Let the ideas flow from the initial conceptual breakthrough. Evaluate them by eye, always searching for a freshness to the lighting. Concepts such as key and fill will then function as reminders to aid you in fleshing out your ideas. This approach will help to keep your lighting from being overly mechanical. Ultimately, no book can teach lighting; it can only point out avenues to explore.

NOTES

1. See the discussion of natural light in Gerald Millerson, *The Technique of Lighting for Television and Film*, 3rd ed. (Oxford, England: Focal Press, 1991), pp. 244–46.
2. Ian Blair, "On the Set of *Madame Bovary*," *Film and Video: the Production Magazine* (November 1991): 6–8, 76–78.
3. Nestor Almendros, *A Man with a Camera* (New York: Farrar, Straus and Giroux, 1986), pp. 8–9.

LIGHTING INTERIORS

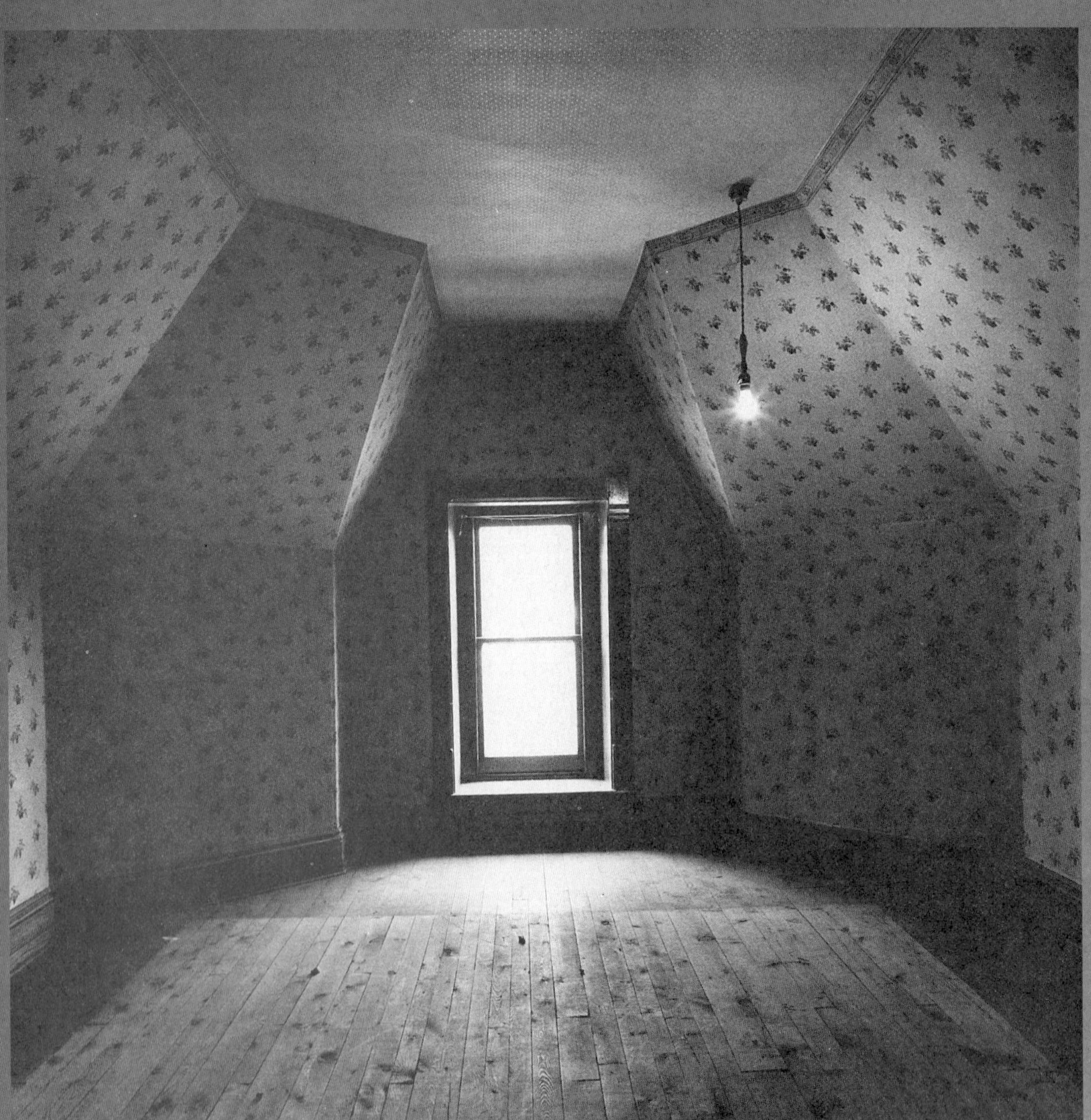

Photo by Jennifer A. Tucker

"window and luminous objects"

10

In this chapter we address the considerations that arise in lighting interiors. We discuss lighting for long shots and the techniques for matching closeups to those long shots. We look at a variety of other problem areas, including establishing and maintaining a lighting logic with time and spatial continuity. In addition, three common situations are examined in detail: mixed interior/exterior situations, shots containing luminous objects, and night interiors.

In Chapter 11 we shall look at lighting for exteriors. In Chapter 12 we shall go over a detailed example of interior/exterior lighting. That chapter will also deal with the cinematographer's duties in setting up an actual production.

LIGHTING INTERIORS entails creating interesting long shots and matching closeups to those long shots. The cinematographer must establish and maintain a lighting logic with time and spatial continuity while providing visual variety and interesting facetone placements. Ideas for solving problems in lighting interiors are often found by going to the real place and observing the natural lighting. For example, visiting a bowling alley and studying the lighting aids the cinematographer in creating a "bowling alley" on film. Three situations occur so often they should be mastered as a matter of course: mixed interior/exterior situations, shots containing luminous objects, and night interiors. All three are controllable through techniques elaborated in this chapter.

LIGHTING LONG SHOTS

Because of the numerous variables and large areas involved, the long shot is usually the most difficult to light. It is also usually the most important shot within a lighting scheme because it sets the mood possibilities for the other shots in the scene. Most of the lighting principles we've looked at so far concern lighting persons. Lighting for a long shot centers around lighting a place. The following elaborates basic considerations.

Establishing a Logic for the Illumination

The long shot provides the audience with most of its geographic and spatial cues. The location of motivating light sources is established. A basic logic for the illumination is constructed by answering such questions as these: Is the interior lit by the large window? Does the fireplace light the den for the night interior? Are the card players lit by the table lamp? From the cinematographer's point of view, it is preferable to shoot a scene's long shots first; once that's accomplished, the lighting may be perfected for closeups and other shots without the cinematographer having to worry about recreating the long-shot lighting setup.

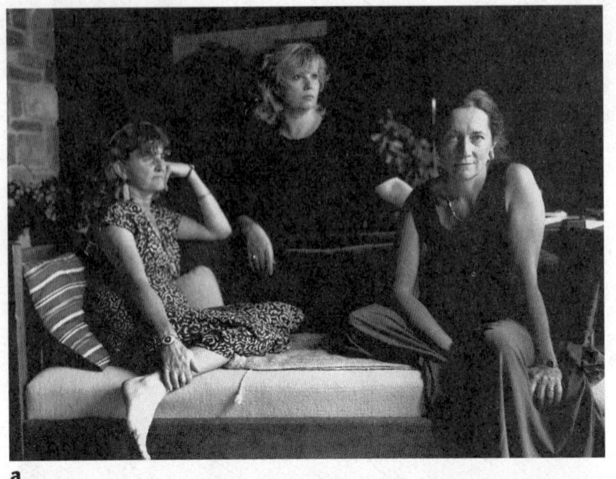

a

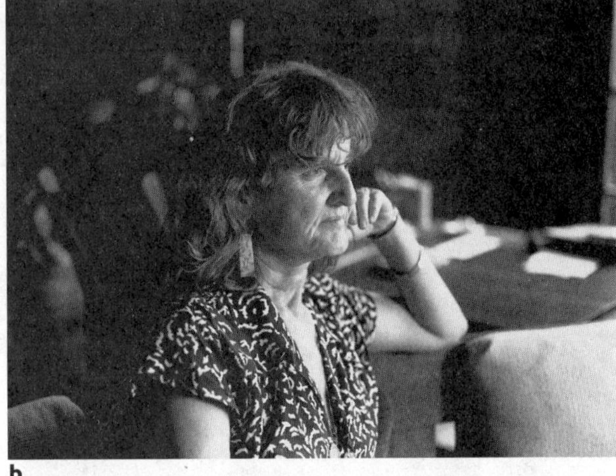

b

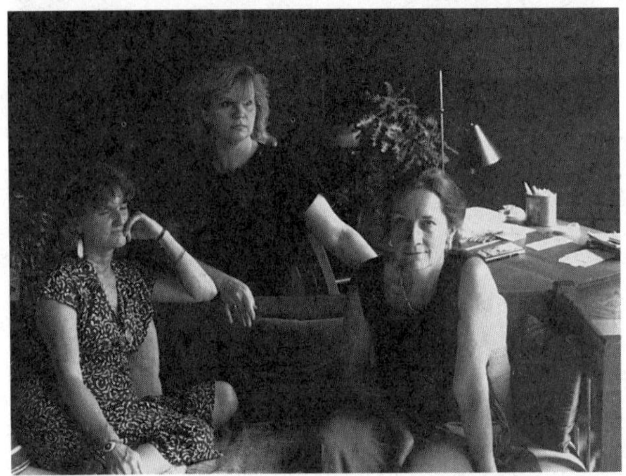

c

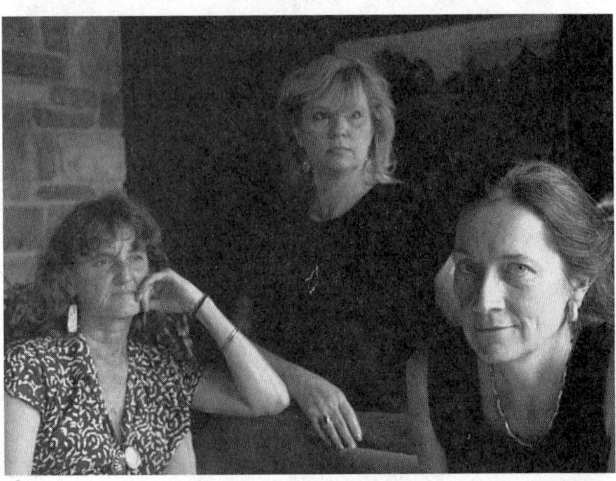

d

Figure 10.1 Establishing a Lighting Logic for a Long Shot
The lighting in the long shot (a and c) establishes a window effect coming from frame right with no fill and a subject/background ratio of about 8:1, two to three stops underexposed on the back wall. Note how the background light comes from the same direction as the foreground lighting. In fact, both windows are faked with lights placed outside the actual window and directed onto the subjects and the background. The background light is particularly effective in establishing the window effect on the table (c) as it falls off naturally to the darker back wall.

In the medium shots (b and d) and the closeup (e), this lighting logic is maintained. This means the shots would intercut and the illusion of a continuous space/time would be maintained. The increased facial ratio in (e) would intercut with (c) or (d) since the logic of the actor's head turn would allow for a change in the facial shadows, even though that change might have been a lighting "mistake."

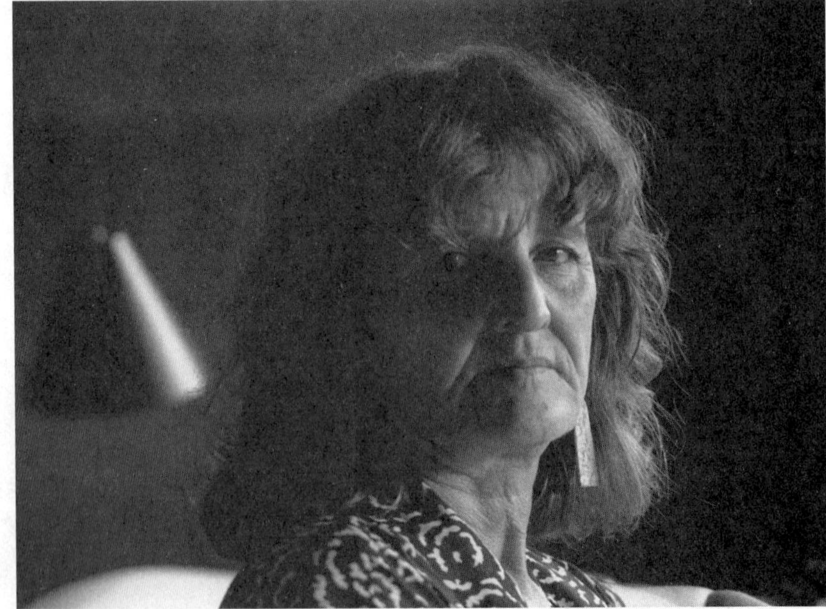

e

Lighting for a long shot involves establishing a lighting logic and maintaining a consistent balance between the relative intensities within the frame. For example, if the scene is a day interior as in Figure 10.1, the window area frame right may be lit two stops brighter than the couch area. The background wall may be two stops darker than the couch area.

In this example, we generally expose for the actors on the couch, but even then we have to pick which actor since the window effect provides more intensity on the actor frame right than on the other two. The logic of a window effect means that as actors move between couch and window, or couch and back wall, they will become lighter or darker depending on their distance from the window. This is generally desirable since it duplicates the real-life situation. Exposure could be based on the window area, in which case the actors on the couch would be two stops underexposed and four stops underexposed by the back wall. This technique could be used to create a gloomier, moodier rendition than the one basing exposure on the couch area.

From our discussion in Chapter 9, it should be clear that there is no one "correct" facetone placement within the changing lighting dynamics common to most films.

Day and Night Effects

For a given location or set, the lighting, in conjunction with the narrative's logic, will create the time frame for the scene. The lighting for a long shot establishes whether a scene is day or night. The differences between the two are easily summarized. With day interiors, subject/background ratios are lower than with night interiors. Day interiors use motivated sources such as windows and doorways. Night interiors rely on **practicals**—fireplaces, table lamps, and the like—to provide motivated sources. Actors in night interiors are lit with more rim lights and higher facial ratios than in day interiors (see Figure 10.6).

Lighting Setups and Shooting Order

Lighting is a slow, expensive process, so it is standard practice to shoot all the scenes with a given lighting setup before moving to the next setup. In our example, the director will likely want to shoot toward the window as well as the back wall. There may be lighting complications resulting from tracks, pans, and crane shots. We may divide the physical space in Figure 10.1 into three main shooting positions. Changing from one position to another will require lighting adjustments, which should have already been planned into the overall lighting scheme for the scene.

To elaborate, assume three camera positions are used to shoot the scene in Figure 10.1: 16 camera setups from A (the basic long shot), 8 camera setups for closeups from position B (toward the window), 10 closeup setups from C (toward the back wall). It would be desirable to shoot all the A setups, then move to the other two positions. Only a long shot from position A would require all lighting to be in place. From position B, the back wall lighting is irrelevant and may be turned off. Likewise, from position C the window is essentially a frontal key and can be cheated as necessary.

The cinematographer must have a clear grasp of the lighting's spatial logic and mood in order to maintain an overall lighting continuity in the mind of the spectator—which, after all, is the only place the illusory film space is perceptually intact.

MATCHING CLOSEUPS TO LONG SHOTS

Because the lighting in a long shot concentrates on establishing a sense of place, the lighting on actors' faces is rough and in need of improvement for closeups. In the long shot, this rough lighting generally does not matter since actors are usually on the move and small enough in frame so that unflattering facial shadows and the lack of eyelights are not visible on the screen.

We perfect the lighting setup on the actors as necessary when we film the closeups for a scene. Fill light is added that was not present in the long shot. Key lights are diffused and repositioned for better effect. Backgrounds and actor positions are cheated to improve lighting and composition. The result is that closeups maintain the illusion of the source motivation in the long shot, in this case the window effect.

As you will recall from Chapter 9, cheating means a slight repositioning of actors, props, and lights for better effect. For example, we might turn an actor so as to obtain a more pleasing facial shadow, or we might seat the actor on a pillow to gain height, or add an eyelight to bring life to the face. None of this cheating will be noticeable on the screen if certain elements of the long-shot lighting setup are maintained:

- *The basic spatial logic* For example, in Figure 10.2, the window should be preserved as an overexposed back/rim light on the actors in closeup or two-shot.
- *The consistency of facial and subject/background ratios* In composing closeups and two-shots, facial ratios are best kept the same as in the long shot, though slight alterations are permissible. The same goes for subject/background levels (see Figure 10.2).

Matching closeups to long shots requires care. Too much change will be noticeable as, for example, interjecting heavily diffused lighting for closeups into nondiffused long shots—a common technique in the 1930s (see Figure 9.4b).

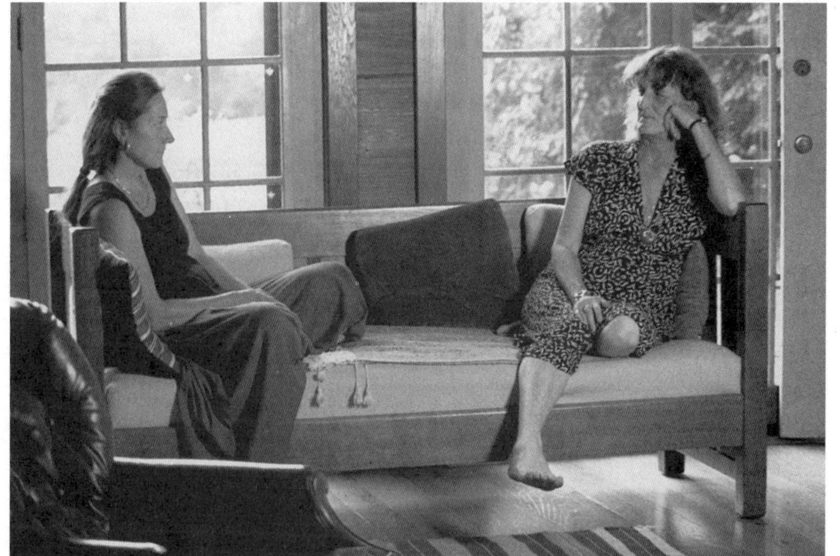

a

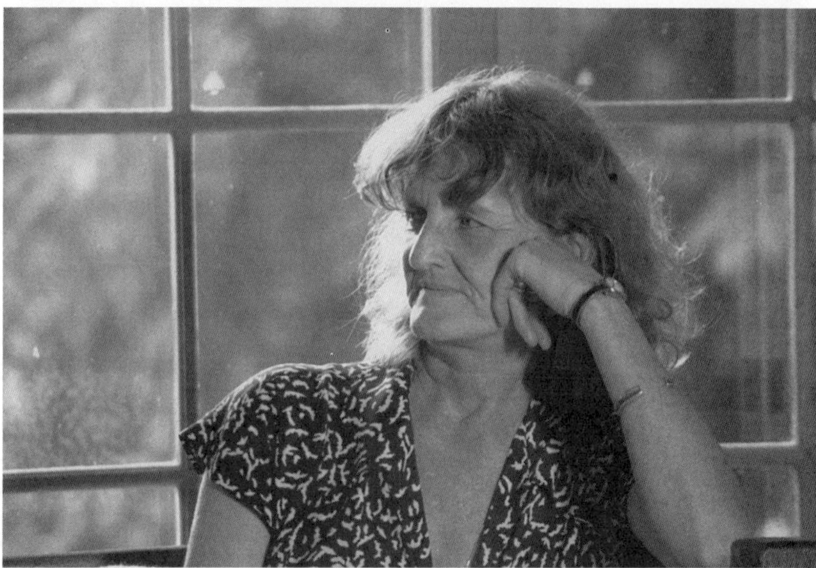

b

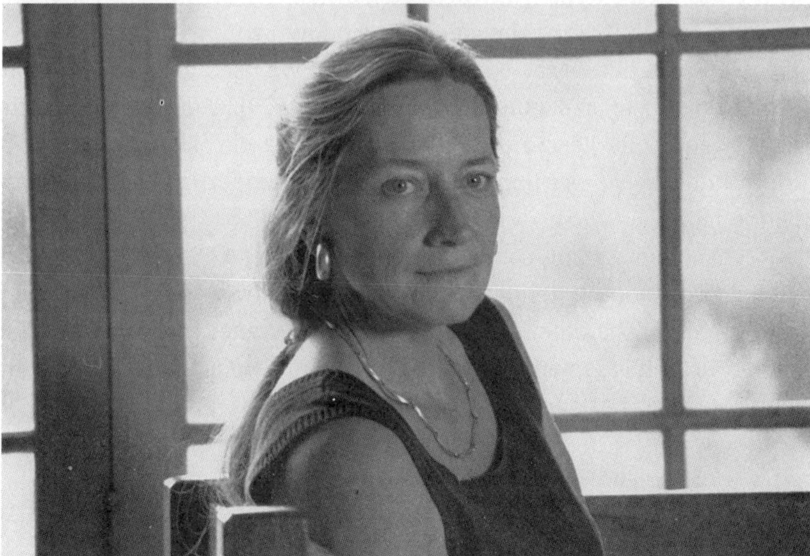

c

Figure 10.2 Matching Closeups to Long Shots *These photos result from fill light and rim lights placed outside the windows to illuminate the subject's hair. This lighting setup is analyzed in Part V, "Lighting Analyses," Figure 7.4a and b.*

CONTROLLING BACKGROUNDS AND FOREGROUNDS: INTERIOR/EXTERIOR SITUATIONS

Mixed interior/exterior situations are common since windows, doorways, and other external light sources are often an unavoidable component of the shot. This exterior source may be an important factor in framing the shot or merely part of the background. There are three aspects to consider with mixed interior/exterior situations: (1) the maintenance of a consistent exposure level for the window, or any other exterior source, over time, (2) the balancing of interior and exterior intensity levels, and (3) the manipulation of indoor/outdoor color temperatures for effect.

Maintaining Exposure Level Consistency

The central problem when shooting on location is the changing light conditions caused by the sun's movement and weather variations. One day is sunny, the next gray. The cinematographer cannot rely on natural light outside the window for shooting any scene that requires more than a few hours. That's because one script interior may be shot at 9:00 A.M. and the next script setup at 3:00 P.M. The two shots will not cut together to create an illusion of reality since the lighting conditions will have changed dramatically.

In these situations, the cinematographer has to control the window effect over time with either total or partial simulation. Total simulation involves blacking out the natural exterior light and using HMIs or other artificial lights to replace it. Partial simulation means supplementing outside available light with artifical light to maintain a consistent window exposure level over time.

The choice of method depends on whether or not the window is part of the shot. If it's not in view, we can blacken out any available light and position our lighting to simulate the window light (see Figure 10.1). If the window is part of the composition, then we need to treat it as an in-shot element, as in Figure 10.3 (pages 152–53). We can use neutral density and color gels to control the intensity and color temperature of the window while positioning HMIs out-of-frame to simulate the daylight effect.

To maintain lighting consistency it is essential to first shoot all setups where the window exterior is visible. This will allow you to fake the window effect for the other shots as needed. For scenes that can be shot in a short time, it is sometimes possible to treat the window as a consistent light source and balance interior lighting to it.

Balancing Interior and Exterior Levels

Our first decision in an interior/exterior situation is what to expose for, since, as we saw in Figure 7.8, the difference between indoor actor and outdoors is likely to exceed five or six T-stops. To select an exposure setting requires being able to answer the following questions: What is the "feeling" we want to convey for this window effect? What kind of mood(s) can be achieved given our specific situation, and what kinds of moods are sought for this particular film? Answering these three questions allows us to decide whether the actor should be intentionally underexposed a stop or two or the exterior overexposed a stop or two in order to convey the feeling of outside light penetrating a darker interior (see Figure 10.3).

Likewise, time of day outside the window is very important. Is it early morning, a gray day, twilight? Is the light soft, hard, diffused, from high or low in the sky? Asking these questions brings to the foreground the elements necessary for solving the lighting problems inherent in an interior/exterior situation.

As a working example, assume that the natural interior reads T 2 and the exterior T 16. Suppose we want to see detail in both actor and exterior. This means that exposure for one or the other will be inadequate. Let's assume we decide to overexpose the exterior 1½ stops to convey a sense of outside brilliance—we could overexpose up to 3 stops for effect. Likewise we decide to underexpose the actor 1½ stops, a slight semisilhouette effect, though we could underexpose another stop or so depending on our desired mood.

Having made these determinations, we still must decide whether to light the actor, use neutral density (ND) gels on the window to bring down the exterior, or combine both techniques.

Since the window establishes a strong directionality for the illumination, lighting the actor will essentially amount to simulating the daylight that would naturally reflect off the walls of the room with a soft fill. This situation presents two technical problems: balancing interior/exterior light intensities and color temperatures. Let's deal with each of these separately.

The first thing to determine is our working T-stop. In this case, we desire to overexpose the outside by 1½ stops. There are two ways to determine the outside T-stop: (1) Go outside in the light falling on objects visible in the shot and take an incident reading, or (2) treat the window as a luminous object and utilize a reflected light technique. Here we shall use method 1; the second method will be dealt with in the next section.

Our incident reading gives us a T 16. Overexposing that 1½ stops means we will expose for halfway between T 8 and T 11 (T 8/11). As an aside, when referring to a particular T-stop, we need be accurate only within ¼–⅓ of a stop. The human eye cannot perceive variations less than a ¼ stop.

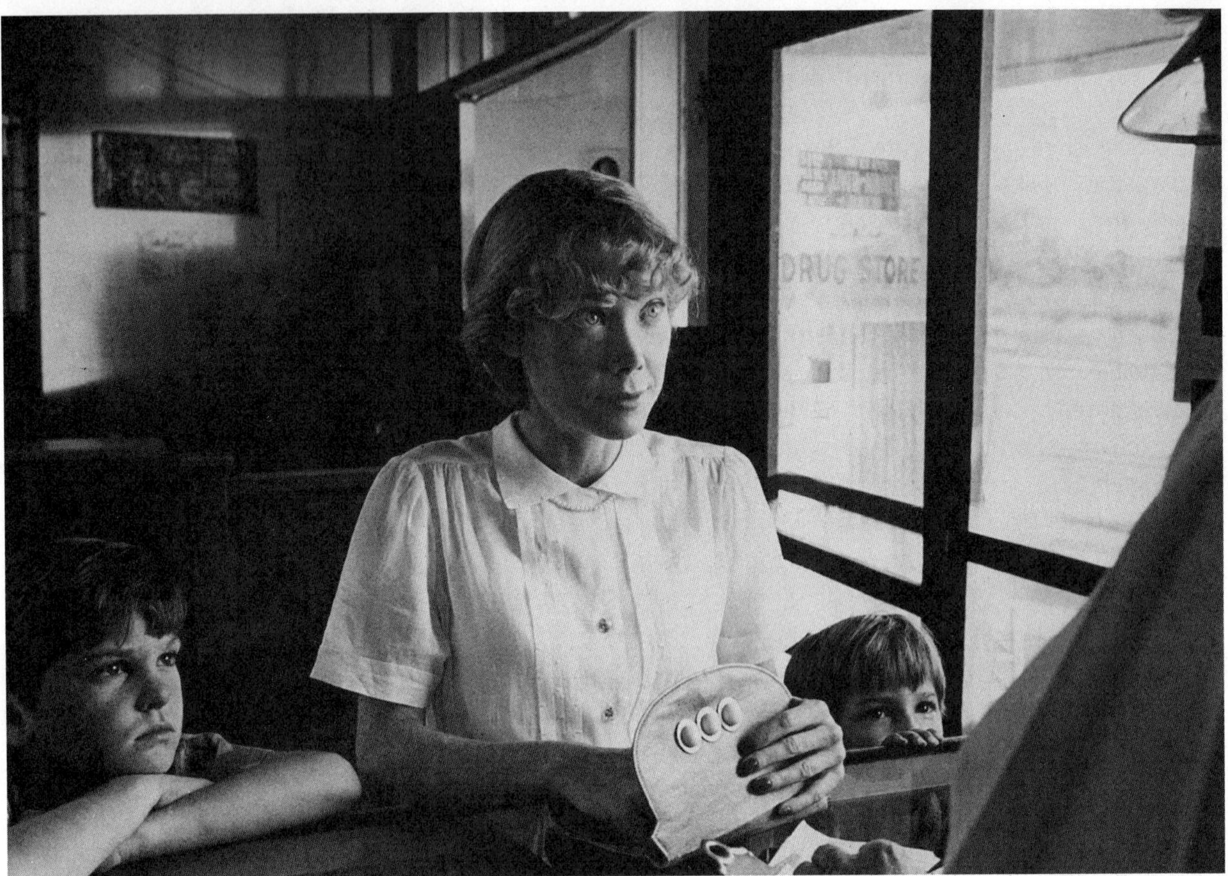

a

Figure 10.3 Day Interior/Exterior Window Effects *Working with in-shot windows and doorways involves balancing exterior and interior levels. For example, in (a), (b), and (c), the cinematographer most likely determined the exposure for the outside window and then coordinated the interior lighting accordingly. Where complete control of the exterior is available—such as in a studio—the cinematographer may work first with the interior and then set the exterior level (as in c). Either method should have similar results. Three different situations are illustrated in the photographs.*

*In (a) the actors are lit with soft light simulating the window frame right. Fill is used to create a 4:1 facial lighting ratio. The exterior visible through the window is overexposed about four stops, but occupies only a portion of the frame and is not bothersome. Note the light from frame right shadowing across the back wall. The bright patch is at about the same intensity as the key, but mostly the background is subdued, 8:1 or 16:1, three or four stops underexposed. A good interior/exterior effect is the result (*Raggedy Man, *Universal, 1981).*

*In (b) we have a high-key treatment with very soft interior lighting. The exterior is overexposed about three stops relative to the soft, frontal key light on the subjects. Rim light on the two actors background left preserves the daylight window/open door effect. The actor foreground right also has a very slight rim. The interior is lit overall to minimize shadows (*Dangerous Liaisons, *Warner Bros., 1988).*

*In (c) the window effect is downplayed by using the venetian blinds. The actors are lit by lights coming from angles that are not quite in line with the window direction. For example, see the shadows on the hat and on the booth behind the man. The intensity of the fill is also quite high relative to the window "key" light. The result is a more artificial look in comparison to (a) (*The Last Picture Show, *Columbia Pictures, 1971).*

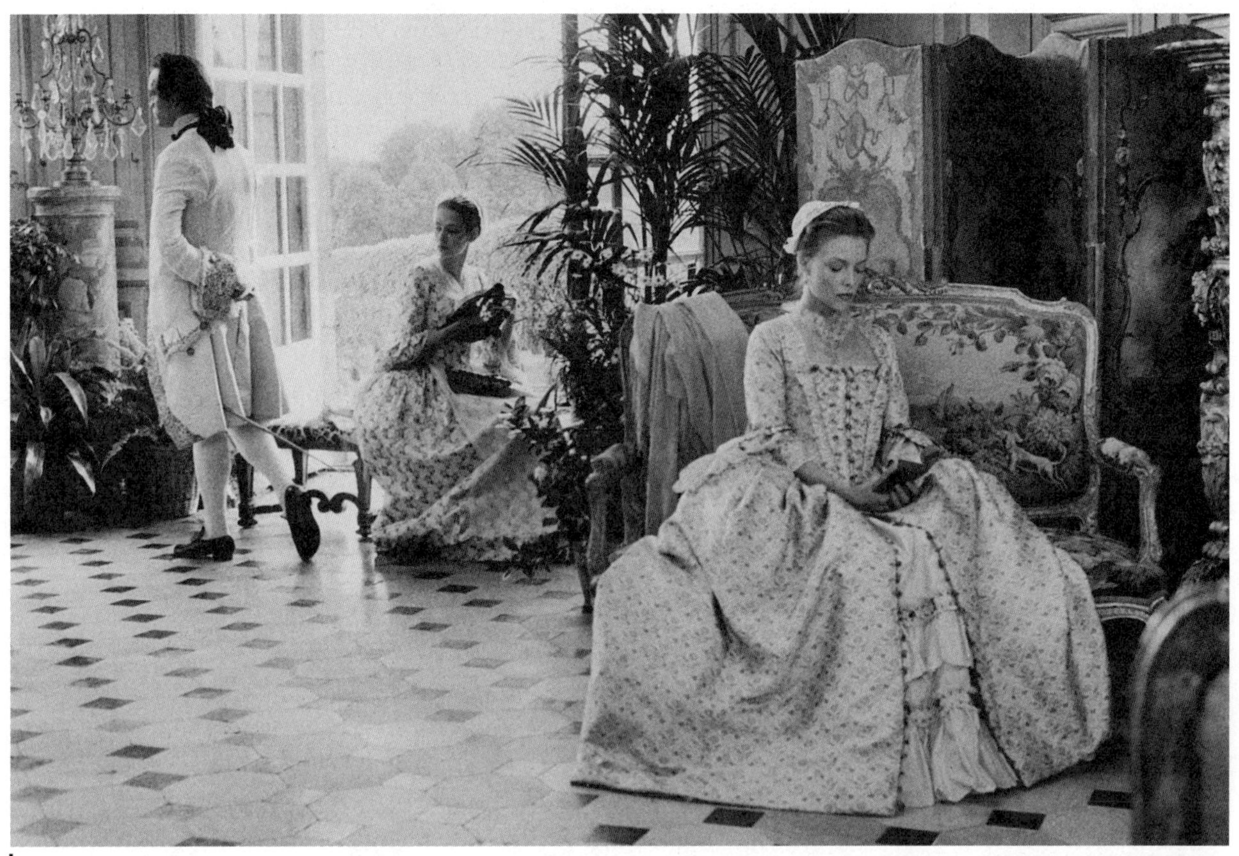
b

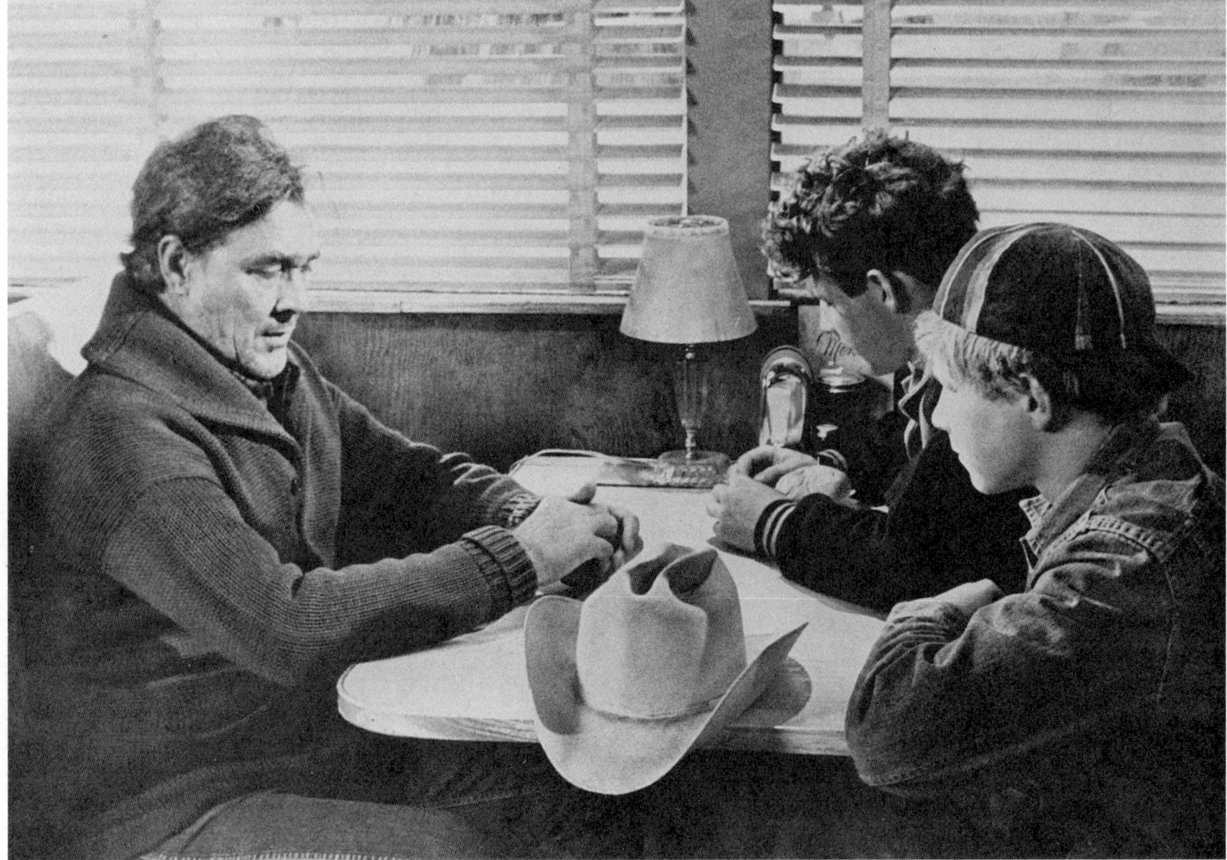
c

The next step is to determine how much lighting intensity to put on the actor. Because we previsualize underexposing her by 1½ stops, we need to light the actor to a T 5.6 level, 3 stops over the initial T 2 level and 1½ stops under the T 8/11 exposure level for the shot.

An alternative method is to reference exposure to the light level on the actor, which in this case is T 2. This means we would expose the shot at T 2.8/4, halfway between 2.8 and 4.0, in order to underexpose her the desired 1½ stops. Having determined the outside level to be T 16, we would then gel down the windows to the desired level. In this example, we wish to overexpose the exterior 1½ stops. Referenced to T 2.8/4, we would need to bring the window down 3 stops, from T 16 to T 5.6. A .9ND window gel will do just that for us (see Appendix A, "Lighting and Grip Gear").

These two examples reference exposure to the outdoors and the actor respectively. The two methods will look identical on the screen except for the depth of field variations caused by the use of different T-stops. We could also use a combination of these two approaches to control the shot's final look.

Let's assume we go with the ungelled windows and base our exposure around the exterior level at T 8/11 as described. We will add a soft or diffused light as fill at a T 5.6 level on the actor. But we still must deal with the uncorrected color temperature (see Appendix G, "Color and Texture Controls").

Indoor/Outdoor Color Temperature Balance

There are various ways to handle indoor/outdoor color temperature balance. If we are shooting with a tungsten balance film stock, we can use quartz lamps inside (3200 K) and place RoscoSun 85 window gels over the window to convert the daylight to 3200 K. In this case, we would have to recalculate our neutral densities since the #85 gel will cause a ⅔ stop reduction. For example, we might use a .6ND with the #85 gel to achieve a 2⅔ stop reduction. However, we have decided not to gel the windows. This leaves us with two choices. We can leave the windows uncorrected and let the outside go bluish on the assumption that contemporary audiences are used to the convention that outside is "blue" and inside is "warm." Alternatively, we can shoot with a daylight-balanced stock and either blue-gel the interior lighting to bring it up to a daylight balance or use daylight-balanced HMIs. We could also use ungelled quartz lights and let the actor go warmish, but this is rather unflattering on facetones and is not very common.

We have worked through the permutations in this example because interior/exterior situations are so common. The cinematographer has a choice of methods to use to solve intensity-level differences and balance color temperatures. What we decide to do is a matter of style and the moods we wish to create on the screen. Ultimately, interior/exterior situations invoke the same concepts and considerations as the subject/background and silhouette range of choices described in Chapter 8.

Warm and Cool Color Effects

There are two ways to control warm and cool color effects: (1) by use of colored gels on the lights—ambers, blues, greens and so forth—or (2) through an intentional mismatch of color temperatures. Many cinematographers leave keys and fills at a standard color temperature while gelling rims and background lights. For example, your keys may be 3200K and your rims warmed to convey a candlelight effect. Other cinematographers gel both keys and fills. Good examples of these effects may be viewed in *The Two Jakes*, *Love at Large*, and *The Fabulous Baker Boys*.

We sometimes shoot outdoors on tungsten balance stock without using the color correcting #85 filter. This causes the image to go bluish and can be used for a "cool" effect. We can let part of the frame go blue while maintaining correct color temperature on the main subject as in the window example just discussed.

Working with color requires a developed artistic sensibility and sensitivity to color nuance. In many cases, color effects are best left to the set and costume designer (see Appendix G).

LUMINOUS OBJECTS: LAMPS, CANDLES, AND OTHER PRACTICALS

We dealt with exposure for luminous objects in Chapter 7; here, we deal with how to incorporate them into the lighting scheme. The chief factors in dealing with luminous objects are:

- Their presence will usually determine T-stop possibilities unless the cinematographer can control their intensity by using dimmers or altering their wattage, for example, by replacing 100-watt bulbs with 25-watt ones.
- The T-stop must be determined with a spot meter or averaging reflected reading instead of an incident meter. Such T-stops are surprisingly high, a T 5.6–T 64 range.
- As a rule of thumb, if luminous objects are in the shot but not overexposed, and it appears the actor is lit by them, then, in fact, the actor is lit by auxiliary lighting from outside the frame simulating the luminous object.

Let us look at each of these factors in detail.

Presence of a Luminous Object Determines T-Stop

A luminous object sets the parameters for the T-stop setting because T-stop values for luminous objects are relatively high, T 5.6–T 64, compared with normal ambient light values, T 1.4–T 2.8. As with the window in our preceding example, the presence of a luminous object of significant size results in a subject luminance range greater than a film stock can handle. This means we either light the rest of the shot around the luminous object's T-stop value—the general solution with large or uncontrollable luminous objects—or reduce the value of the luminous object to fit in with our lighting setup. This can be done by decreasing the source voltage, changing the bulb wattage, or applying neutral density filtration.

In Figure 10.4, the neon signs and mirrored bar area were metered and overexposed about two stops. Key light was added based on that calculation (see Figure 10.4b). Overexposure and underexposure effects for the same subject/background ratio are also shown.

T-Stop Must Be Determined with a Spot Meter or Averaging Reflected Reading

As we saw in Chapter 7, where there is a significant in-shot luminous object it is necessary to first meter the luminous object and determine a zone placement for it, usually from zones 7–9. The T-stop required for the desired zone placement establishes the T-stop for the shot. These levels are surprisingly high, usually T 5.6 and up. Once this T-stop is established, lighting the shot may proceed as usual.

In our example in Figure 10.4, we assumed we cannot control the intensity of the luminous object. On feature-scale shoots, another method of working is available. The cinematographer first decides which T-stop to use. Luminous objects are then reduced in intensity so as to fit in with that T-stop. The principles used to balance luminous objects and incident illumination are identical to our example. They are just used from the opposite direction.

A Rule of Thumb for Luminous Objects

In-shot light sources (practicals) or other luminous objects may be used to light actors or serve only as props. A luminous object greatly overexposed, four stops and up, is most likely being used for lighting. A luminous object not greatly overexposed is functioning as a prop and not being used for lighting unless another kind of cheating is going on. Methods for cheating include painting the side of the bulb toward the camera, cutting holes in the lamp shade away from the camera, hiding small light units ("peanuts") on the fixture, and gelling the side of the bulb toward the camera.

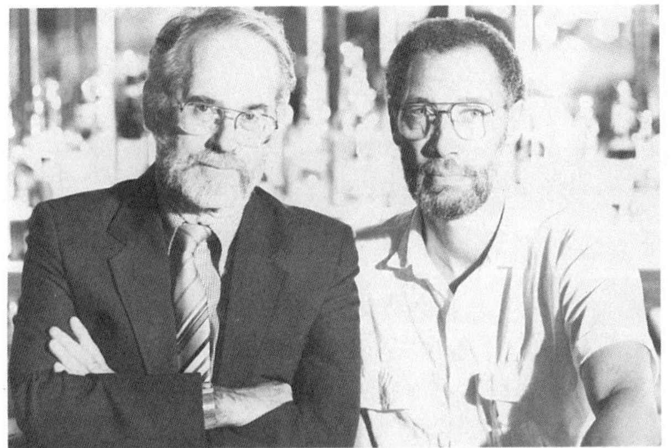

a

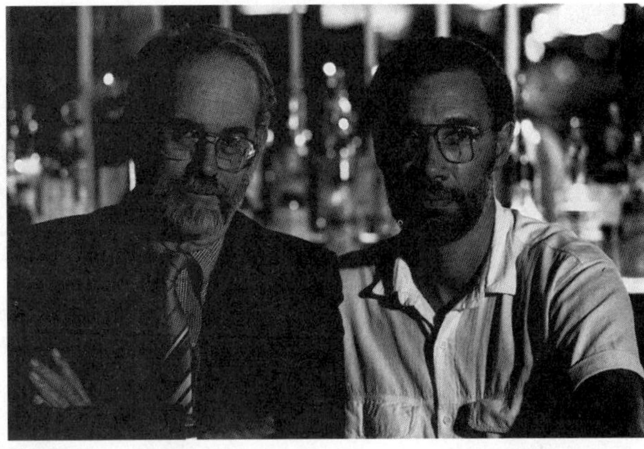

c

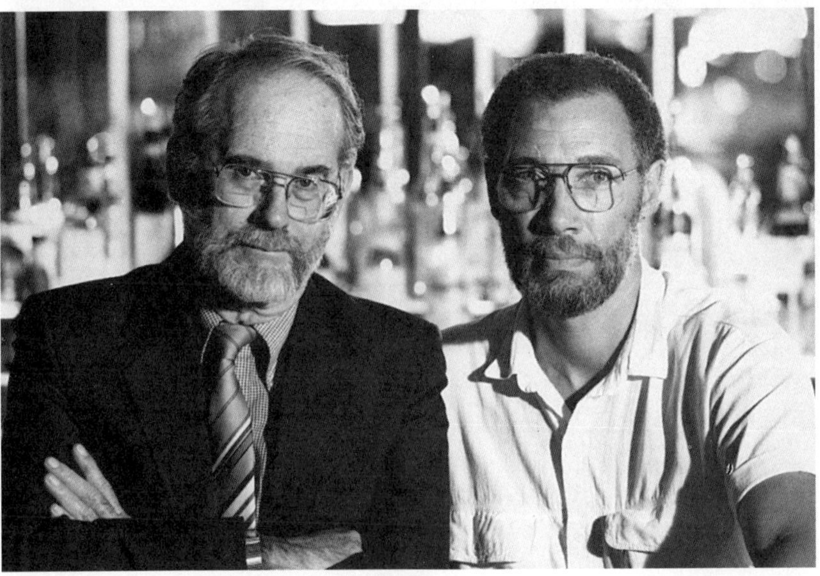

b

Figure 10.4 Working with Actors and Luminous Objects—Bar Interior *In this example, the neon lights in the bar mirror were overexposed intentionally two stops (b) after taking an averaging reflected reading. The reflected meter indicated a T 11 setting, and the shot in (b) was exposed at T 5.6 after a key light was added to the actors to bring them up to the appropriate T 5.6 level. In (b) the actors are given a zone 5 exposure, that is, exposure for their faces. In (a) they are overexposed two stops and in (c) underexposed two stops to show the range of possibilities in this simple, one-light setup based on available bar lighting.*

The rule of thumb, then, is this: An in-shot light source is only lighting parts of the shot if it is greatly overexposed. Where it is not greatly overexposed, its effect is being simulated by other lights outside the frame. Though there are ways to avoid this rule—for example, by gelling, painting, or dulling the camera side of the practical with spray paint—in general the rule holds.

A good example of our rule of thumb is found in the banquet scenes in Stanley Kubrick's *Barry Lyndon*, which were lit by candlelight. Whenever the candles are not in shot, the lighting has a certain soft feel and beautiful quality; but whenever the candles are in shot, they are greatly overexposed, so overexposed they appear as jets of light. Because of this extreme overexposure, the standard practice is to simulate the practical with auxiliary lighting (see Figure 10.5a).

Consider the example of an actor standing by a table with a shadeless lamp apparently lighting him (see Figure 10.5c). The cinematographer has four choices:

- Light the actor with the bulb, expose for the actor, and overexpose the bulb.

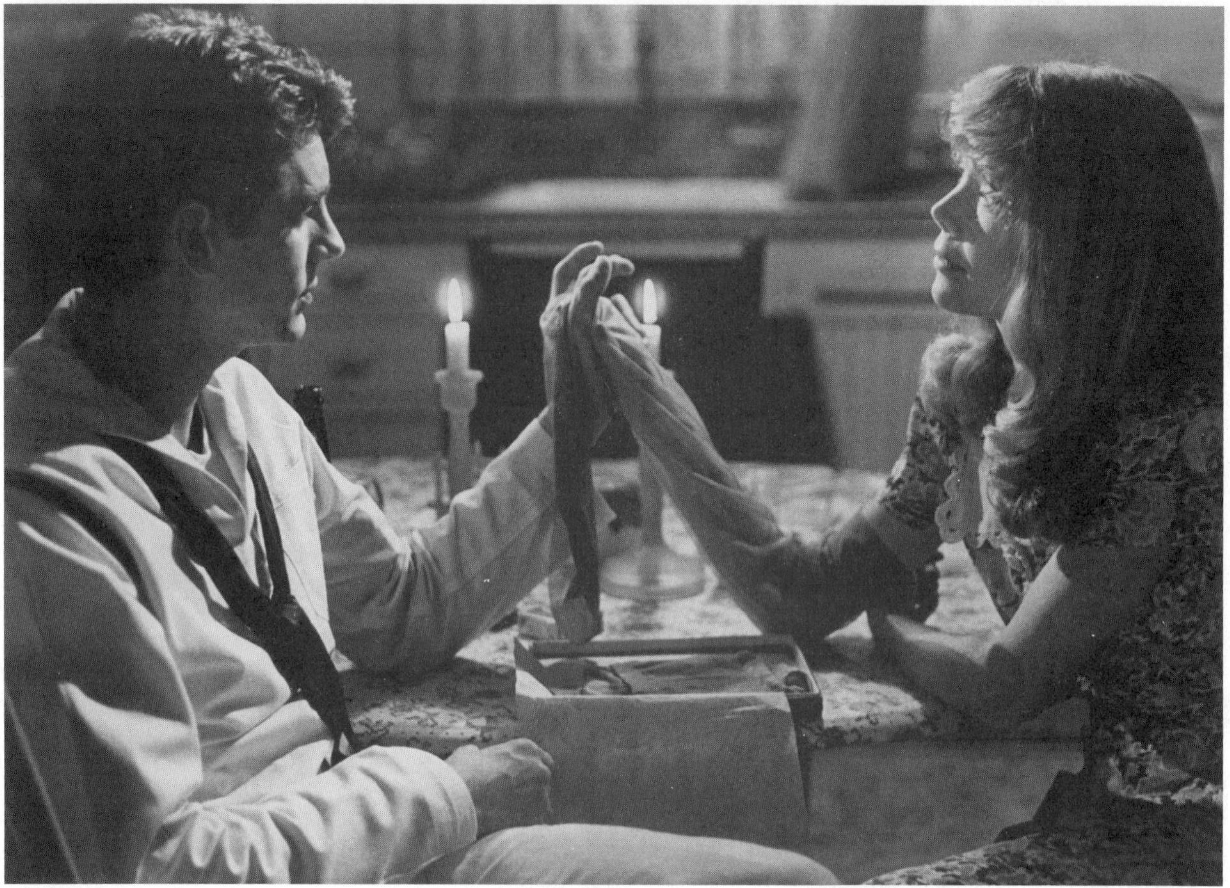

a

Figure 10.5 Simulating Practicals *The candles are used as a prop in (a). The lighting is from the three-quarter rear position and is positioned a bit too high to duplicate the exact direction of the candles. This is thus a loose simulation (*Raggedy Man*, Universal, 1981).*

In (b) the actor is lit by a key from the front left. This leaves the lamp on the wall frame left as a prop. In both (a) and (b) there is a suggestion of motivated light. In (c) the actor looks as if he is lit by the naked light bulb, which is overexposed about two stops. Exposure for the bulb was determined with a reflected reading. Once that T-stop was determined, a 650-watt Fresnel quartz light was situated just outside of frame left. It is that Fresnel which lights the actor as a three-quarter front key. The illusion is more convincing in (c) because of the duplication of the direction of the in-shot source and because of the overexposure of the source.

- Light the actor with the bulb, expose for the actor, and tone down the side of the bulb toward the camera (using gel or spray paint).
- Light the actor with the bulb and expose for the bulb. This leaves the actor severely underexposed.
- Light the actor with a "Midget" outside of frame balanced to a zone 6 placement for the actor. Overexpose the bulb a couple stops. This was done in Figure 10.5c.

As with the window example, there are color temperature considerations here since the light bulb (c. 2600 K) will yield warm facetones if used to light the actor, whereas the out-of-frame "Midget" will not. Depending on context some cinematographers might put a filter over the "Midget" to warm the image on the theory that we all know household bulbs produce a warmish light.

If a shade is on the lamp, then our rule doesn't hold. By cutting out the lamp shade away from the audience, we can light the actor with the bulb and use the lamp shade as a neutral density filter to contain the lamp's exposure value. Alternatively, we can use a small auxiliary light hidden behind the lamp shade to simulate the lamp effect.

Lamps are a common practical. The lamp shade itself can be treated as a luminous object since it is generally translucent. To convey the feeling of a lamp with shade requires overexposing the base and sometimes the top of the lamp to create the feeling of light. You might also have to

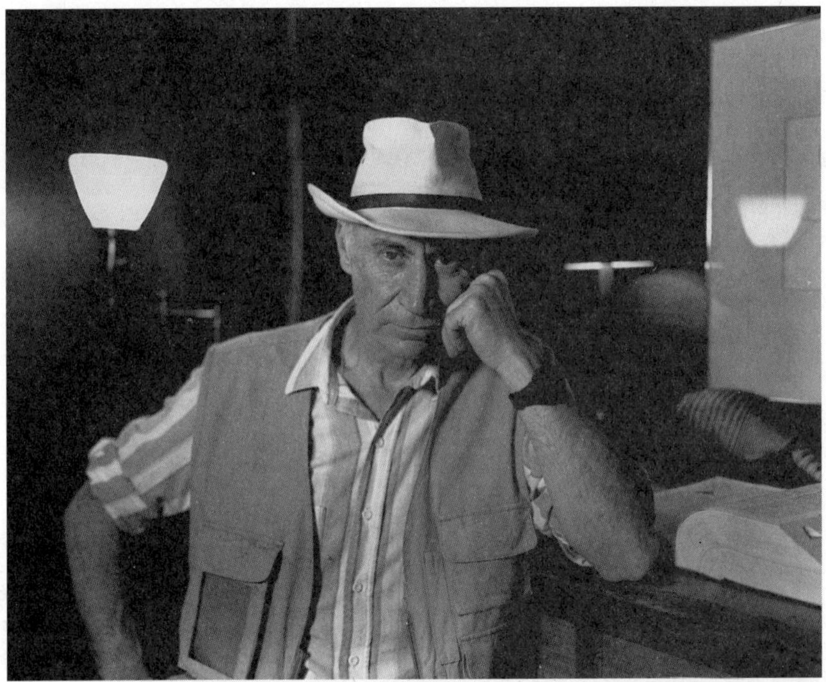
b

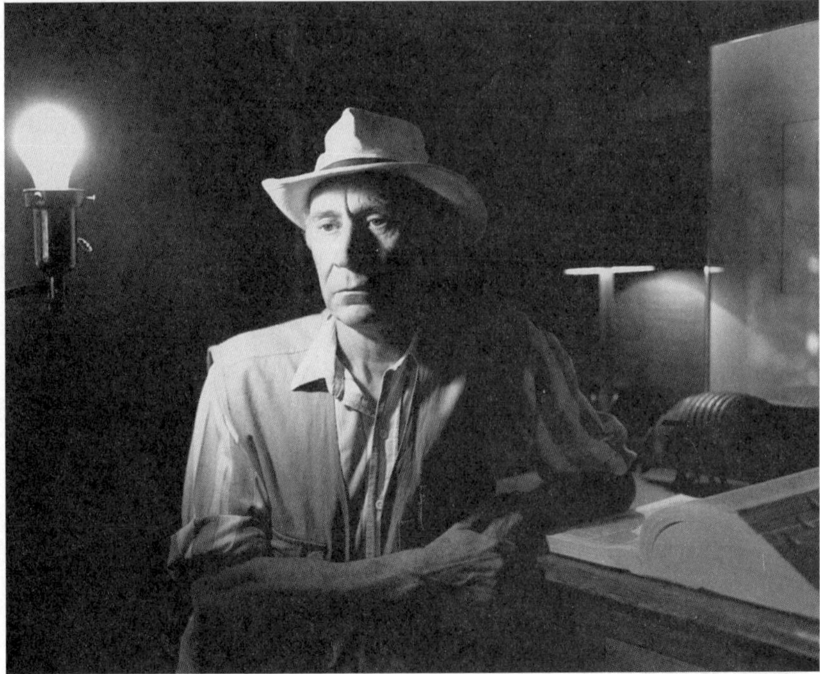
c

shine a small spot on the background to simulate spill-off from the lamp. An incident meter can be used to control this situation.

Lamps are also likely to be turned on and off during a shot. This involves a two-stage lighting design—with and without the lamp. A good working parameter is to establish a two- or three-stop difference between when the lamp is off and on, including the simulating auxiliary light if present. A "correct" exposure level with standard facetone placement is usually set for when the lamp is on. When the lamp goes off, we have a darker, gloomier lighting setup. Sometimes a bluish color balance is used to simulate night or moonlight effects.

NIGHT INTERIORS

A study of night interiors reveals several things:

- Windows, doorways, and the like are dark because it is night outside.
- Lamps, overheads, and other practicals are on, but ambient light is much less intensive and more localized than with a day interior.
- Facial ratios are higher, from 6:1 to 32:1.
- Rim and back lights are used more as keys to create large shadow areas on the face.
- Subject/background ratios are higher, in the order of 8:1 to 32:1 (see Figure 10.6).

With these differences in mind, night interiors may be approached along the general lines of day interiors (see Figure 10.7, pages 162–63). Interior/exterior balance considerations are the same as for day exteriors except that with night exteriors you have much more control because you are usually lighting the exterior. For example, to establish "reality" and pictorial depth outside the window, we put rim light on trees and bushes to simulate streetlight. Even when using available night lighting, such as on a night street, the exterior level and lighting directionality do not change over time as during the day. This gives us from dusk to dawn to shoot without lighting continuity problems.

Color Temperature Effects at Night

Conventional color codings utilize a bluish gelled lighting for night/moonlight effects and a light coral or amber gel for "warm" interior effects. These two are generally coupled with a white light since their effect is relative to context. For example, in night indoor/outdoor effects, bluish rim light can be applied to a figure in a doorway, in conjunction with a warmed key and a "white" fill. It is best not to overuse these color effects as they tend to draw attention to themselves.

SUMMARY

The general rule of lighting is this: When you have something to light—a night club, filling station, kitchen, whatever—go to the actual location and observe its lighting. In a studio situation, this is very important as the danger of looking too artificial is always present. On location, you often have available light to work with. As long as you can define for yourself the essentials of a location in terms of lighting ratios, you will be able to duplicate the feeling of any particular place—a bar, living room, restaurant, or bowling alley. Using the natural as a source for ideas solves the key visualization problem. The rest is execution.

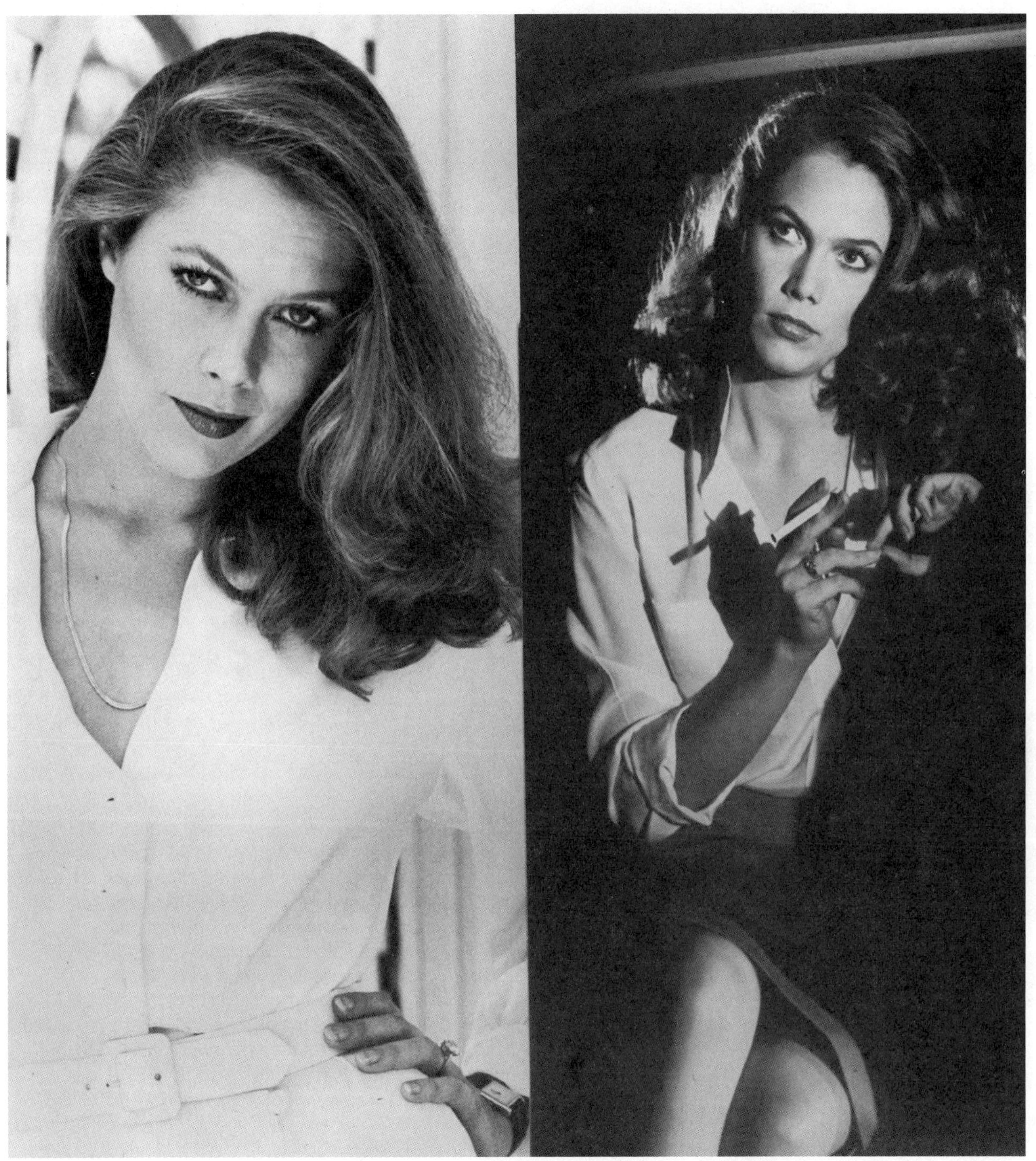

Figure 10.6
Comparing Day and Night Interiors
(Publicity photo of Kathleen Turner for Body Heat, *The Ladd Company, 1981)*

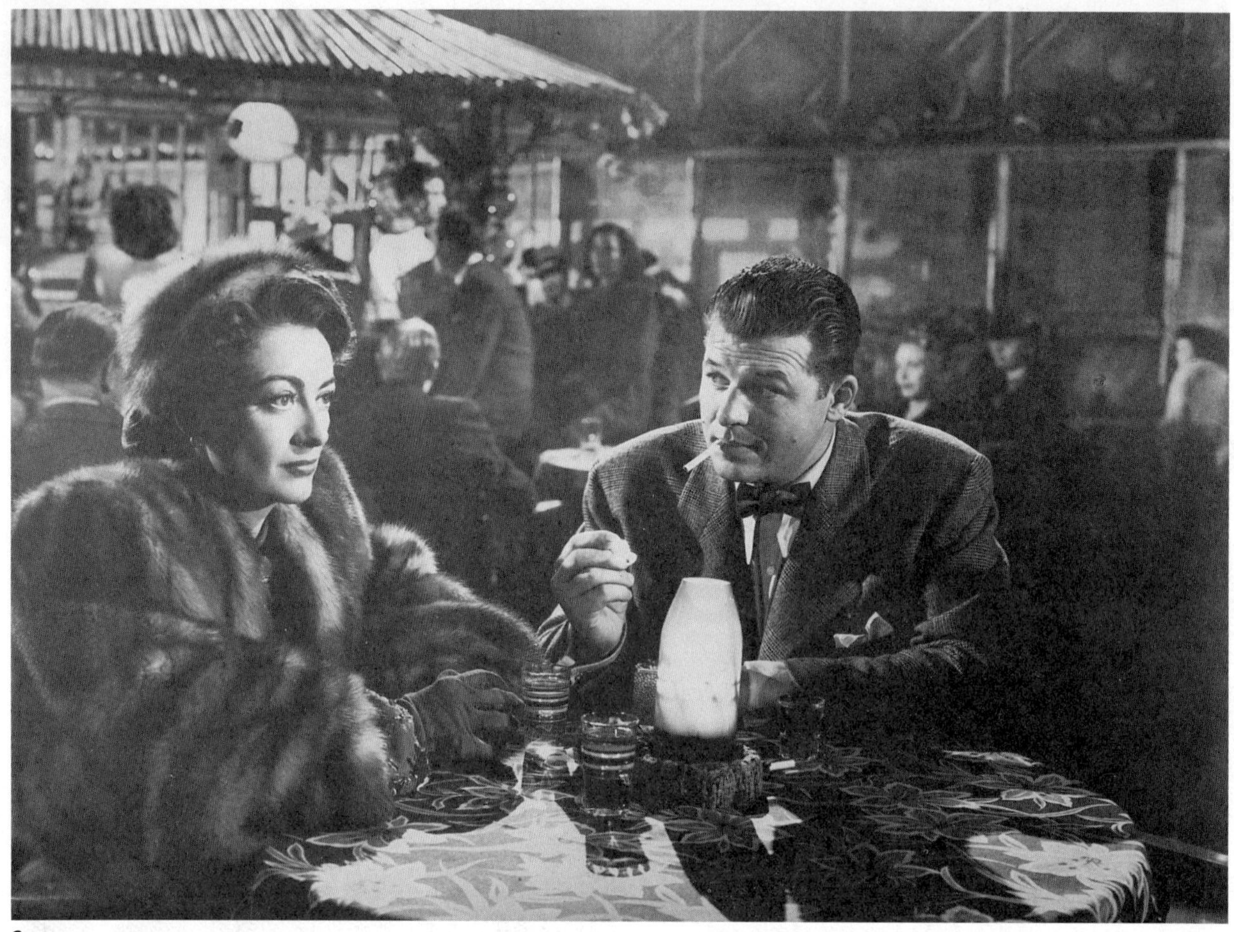

a

Figure 10.7 Examples of Night Interiors *Studio-style set lighting for large-scale night interiors is represented by the nightclub scenes in (a) and (b). Note the intricate control over the lighting for various parts of the set allowed by the lack of a ceiling and thus the possibility for a variety of pools of light. Both examples maintain high subject lighting ratios, 6:1 or more, and dark backgrounds. In (a) there is also quite a bit of back light on the foreground actors (*Mildred Pierce*, Warner Bros., 1945). The still in (b) is from* Ikiru*, Brandon Films, 1952.*

*In (c) the cinematographer has used a soft rim and key effect with a partial lighting technique on the face, shading off the top of the actor's head and her arm area. The patch of light on the window ledge quickly transitions to shadow. The result is a soft, mysterious nighttime bedroom lighting effect (*The Third Man*, Twentieth Century Fox, 1949). Comparing this photograph to Figure 2.21a illustrates the differences between the handling and balancing of the background in day and night interiors. The lighting setup here might also be planned for her to turn on or off a bedside lamp.*

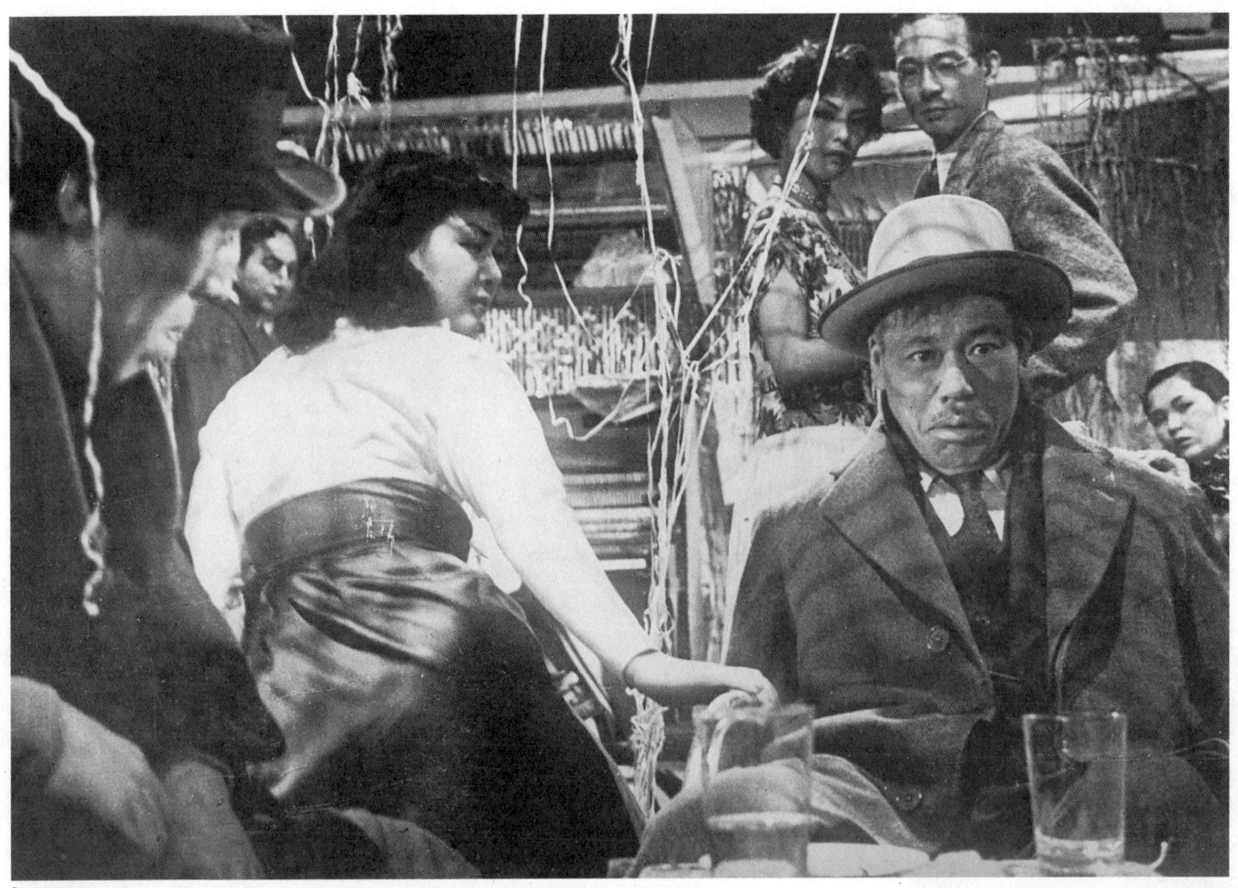
b

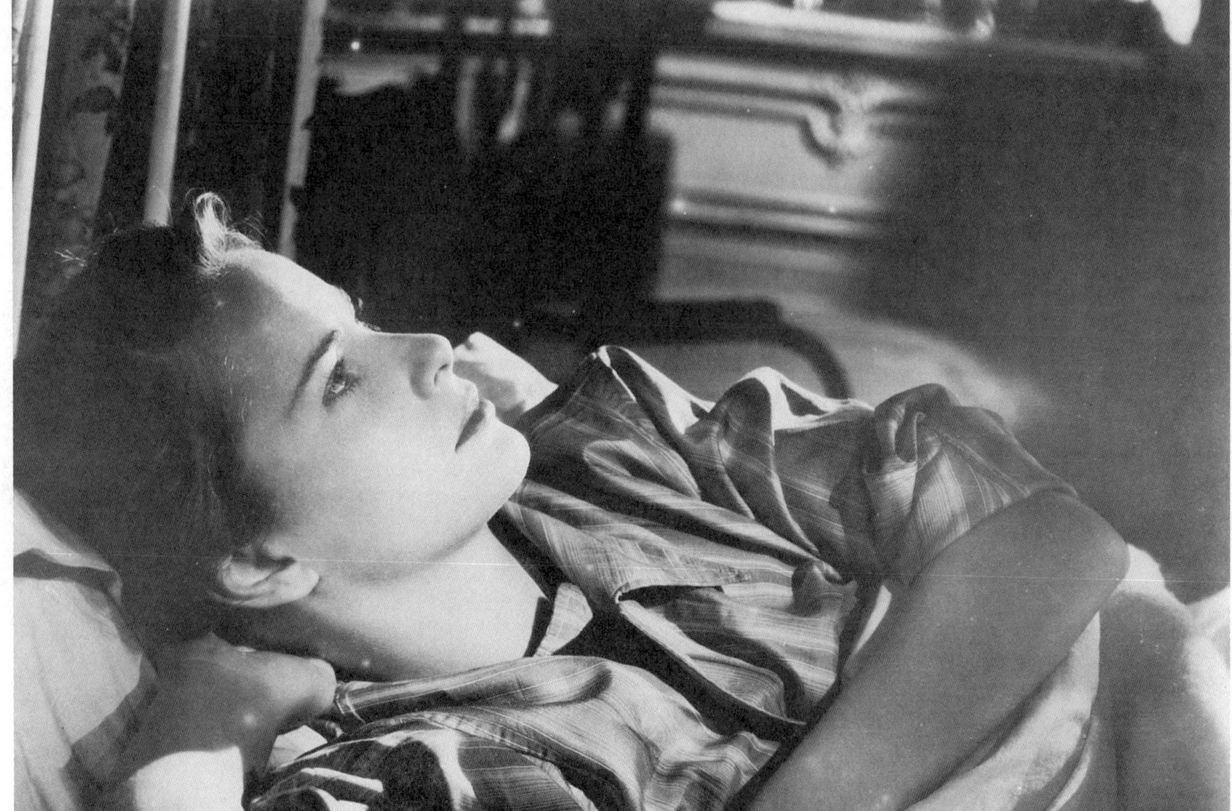
c

LIGHTING EXTERIORS

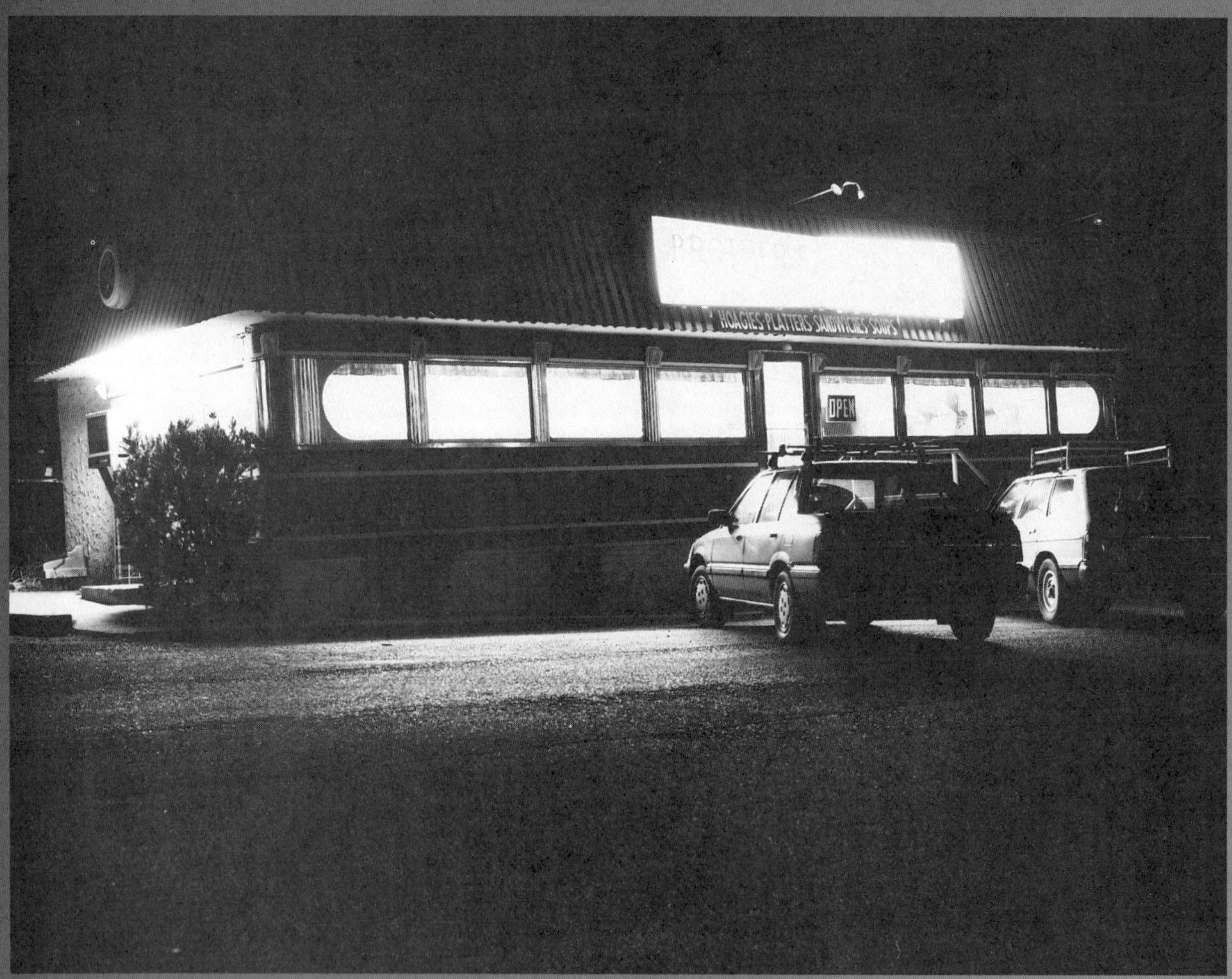

Photo by Steven Rosenberg

"night exterior"

In this chapter, we look at ways to work with and control sunlight—from bright daylight and gray skylight to twilight and sunsets. We discuss ways for controlling contrast outdoors and ways for dealing with a number of recurring day exterior situations. We then proceed to examine magic hour and how to control it, and end with a discussion of lighting for night exteriors. In Chapter 12, we shall go over in some detail how to handle an actual location lighting situation.

EXTERIORS INVOLVE the same lighting principles as interiors except the cinematographer has less control over the natural elements, sunlight, skylight, and weather. We shall see that the principles we have developed for interior lighting—concepts such as subject lighting ratio, subject/background ratio, color temperature balance, key, fill, and rim light, the zone system, and motivated lighting setups—work equally well for exterior situations.

TIME OF DAY

The angle of the sun affects color saturation and subject/background balance. Much contemporary lighting avoids direct sunlight on faces because of the resulting full-color saturations and dark facial shadows. Using the sun as a back light or shooting under a light gray sky is often preferred since colors are less saturated.

The sun's position in the sky relative to our camera setup determines whether we can use it for key or rim purposes. As a key the sun causes high facial ratios, so exterior fill light is often needed. HMIs are standard for exterior fills. They may be softened by bouncing them onto the subject or by shining them through diffusion, which converts them into soft lights. Reflectors are also used to fill shadow areas (see Figure 11.1).

High facial ratios can sometimes be avoided by diffusing the sun with butterflies and overheads, or by placing actors in the shade or shadows. Diffusing harsh, direct sunlight is a standard technique that gives a soft light effect. The diffusion lowers the sunlight's intensity, however, so that care with the subject/background ratio is required. The alternative is to stage the shot so that actors are lit by overall shade. Shade gives a nice-quality soft light on the faces but can present color temperature problems since it is bluer than standard daylight. Again, there may be subject/background ratio problems due to the lowered intensity on the actors.

From about 10:00 A.M. or 11:00 A.M. to 2:00 P.M. or 3:00 P.M. de-

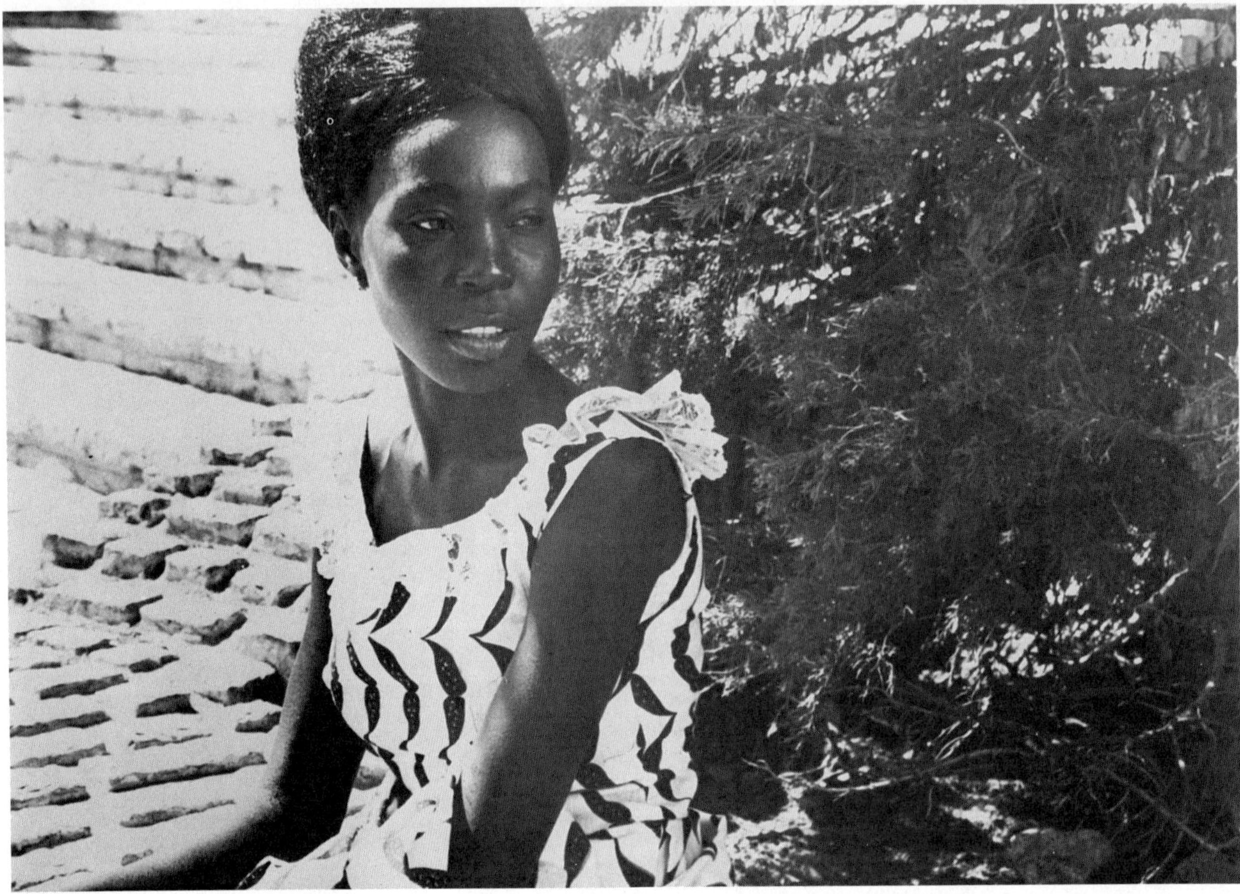

a

Figure 11.1 Exterior Sunlight Requires Fill *Fill light is evident on the faces in (a), (b), (c), and (e). Lack of a fill leaves the subject too dark as in (d). Publicity still (a) is from* Black Girl, *New Yorker Films, 1965; (b) is from* Mildred Pierce, *Warner Bros., 1945; and (c) is from* Dangerous Liaisons, *Warner Bros., 1988.*

pending on the geographic latitude and time of year, the high sun causes particularly ugly facial shadows and dark eye sockets. Many cinematographers either avoid shooting during this time frame or diffuse the sunlight. This effect is similar to the effects of frontal keys from the high position that we looked at in Figure 2.2c and f.

Using the sun as a rim has two consequences: an overall desaturation of the colors (see Color Plates 1, 2, and 3) and usually the need for facial fill lighting (see Figure 11.1).

Shooting outdoors requires care with lighting continuity and the matching of closeups to long shots. The cinematographer must be aware of sun positions throughout the day. Shots destined to cut together are often filmed hours apart, in which case the sun's continuity must be maintained with artificial lighting. It might even be necessary to shade actors from the actual sunlight and simulate the sun with HMIs. One old-time solution was to film the closeups against a rear screen, which solves the control problem but is considered too artificial for today's image looks.

On gray days, using HMIs and arcs allows the cinematographer to simulate sunlight. In this case, the natural daylight functions as a soft overall fill. Shooting early morning and late afternoon gives warm sun effects with interesting angularity to the sunlight. These warm effects are often enhanced with graduated filters.

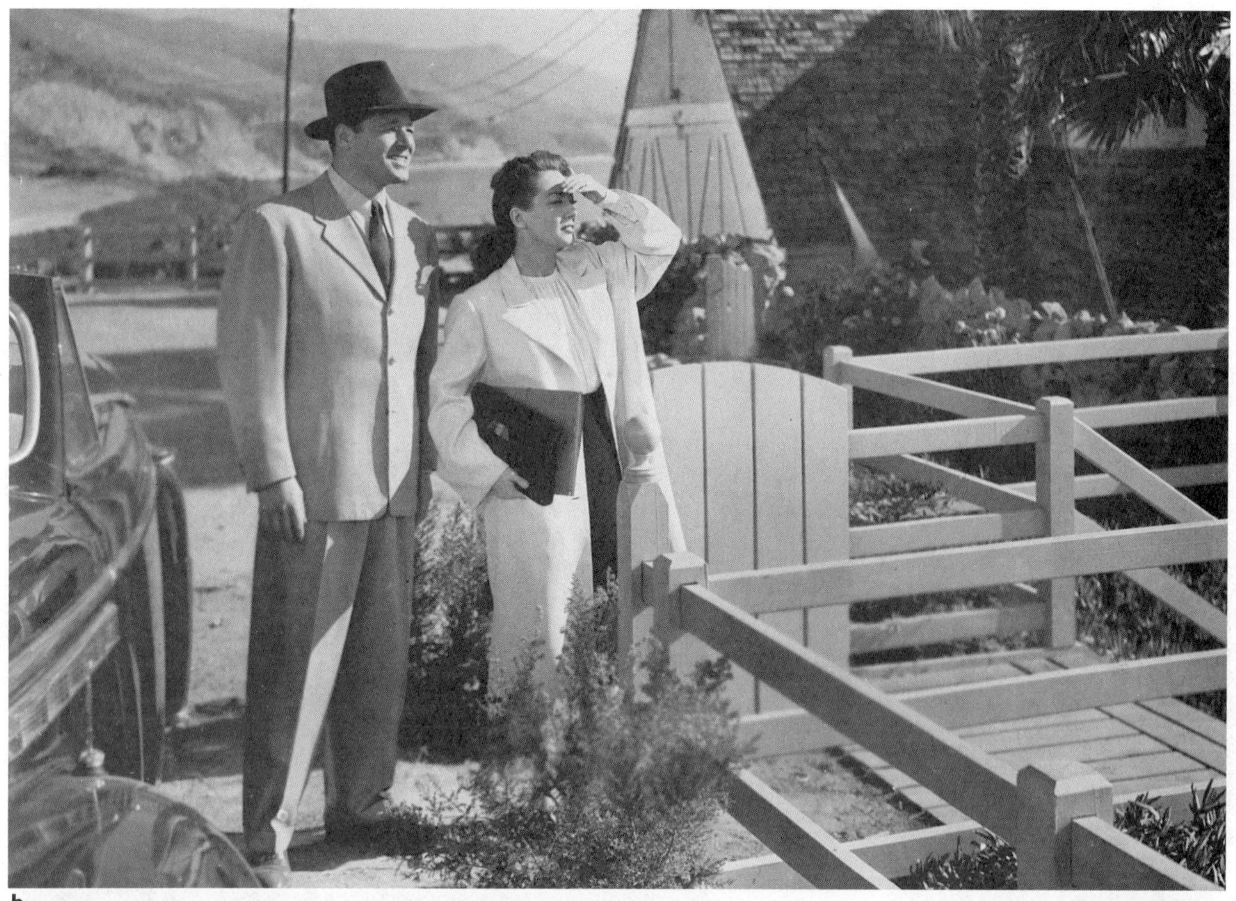
b

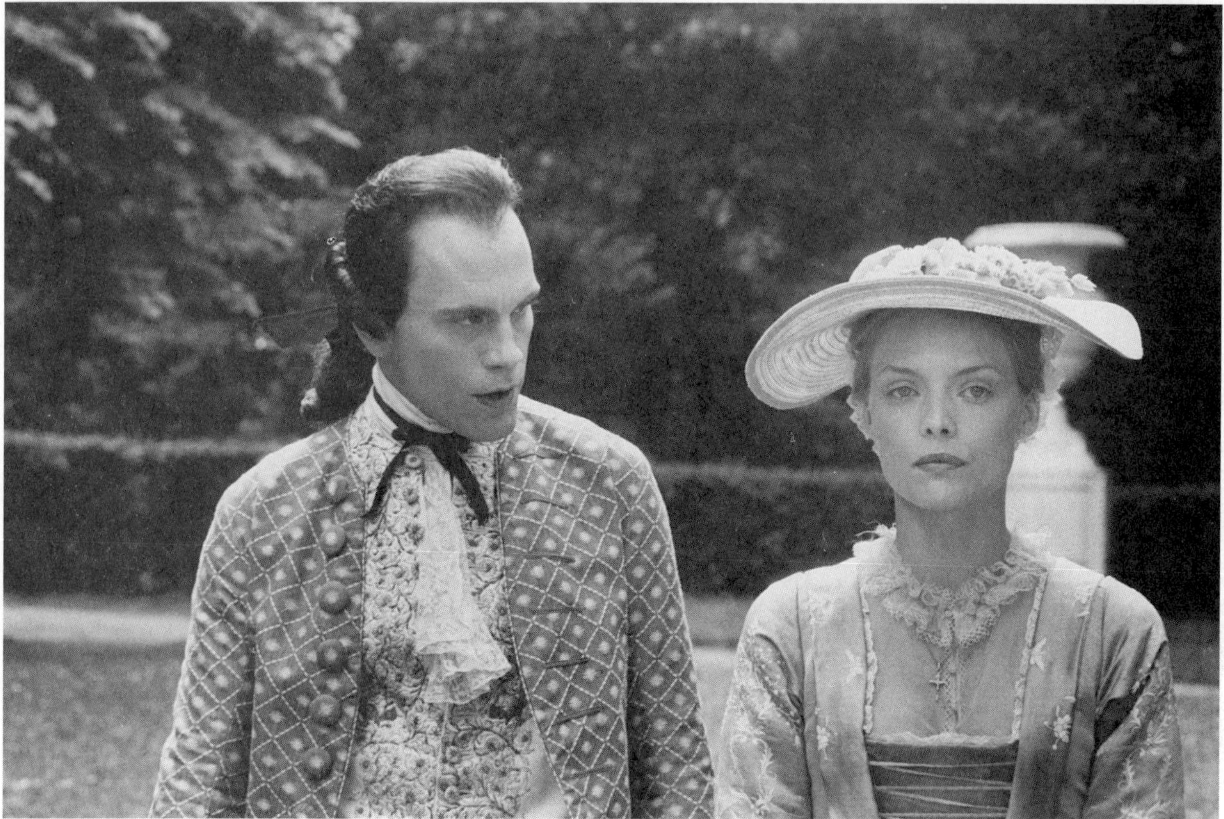
c

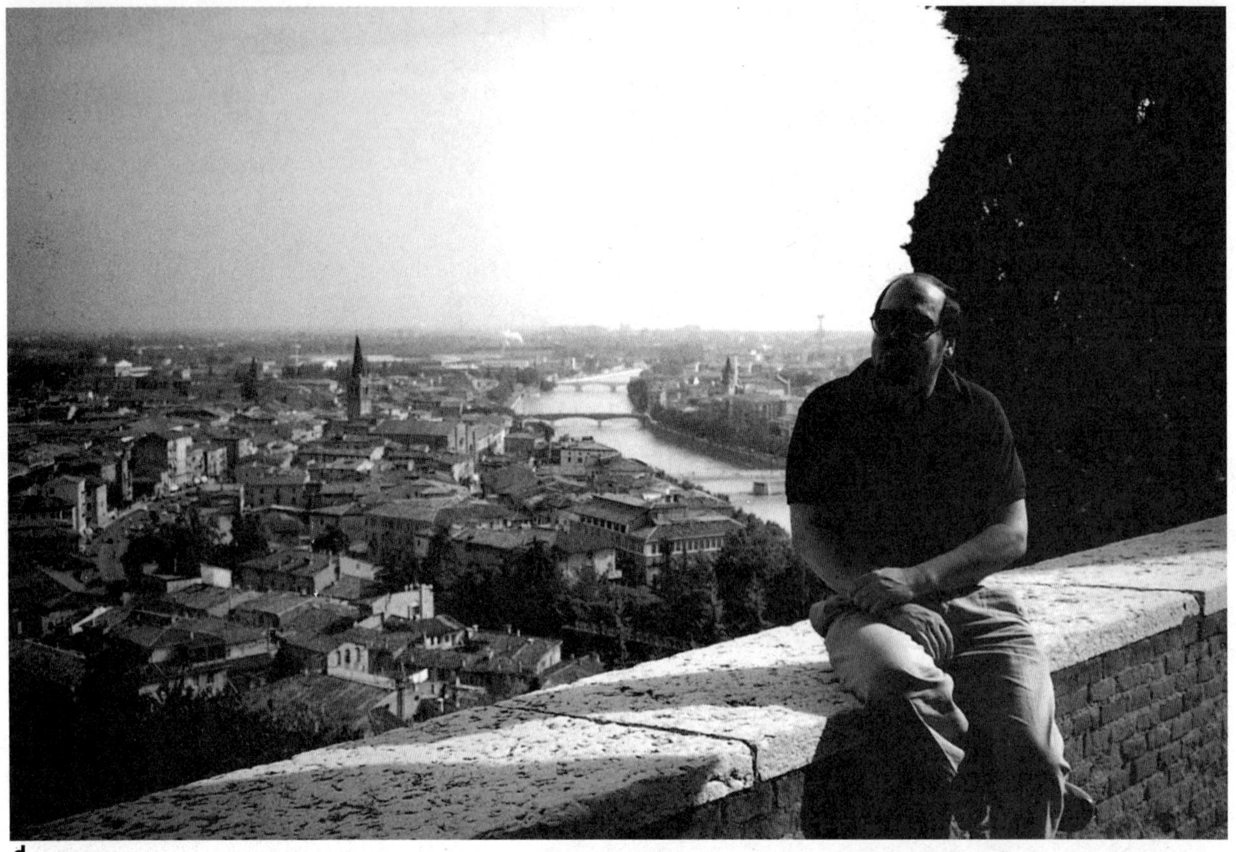

d

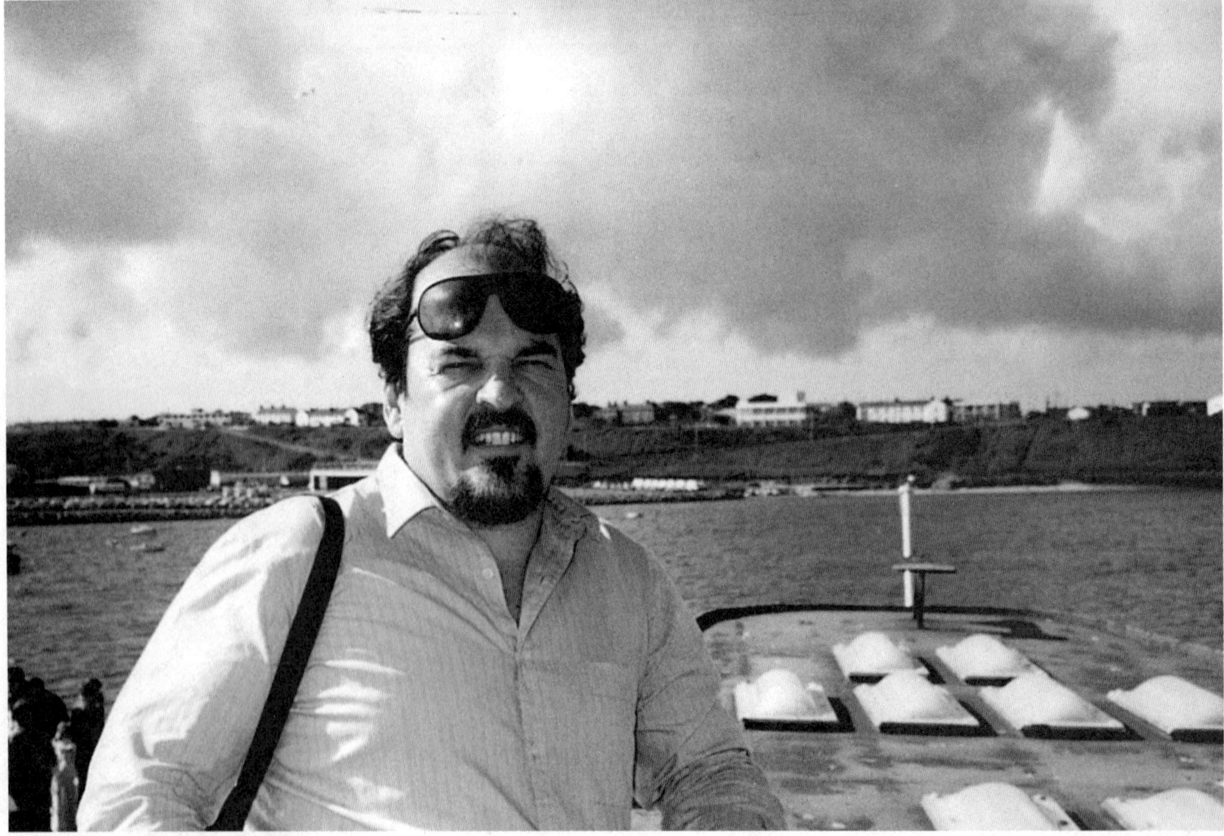

e

Figure 11.1 (continued)

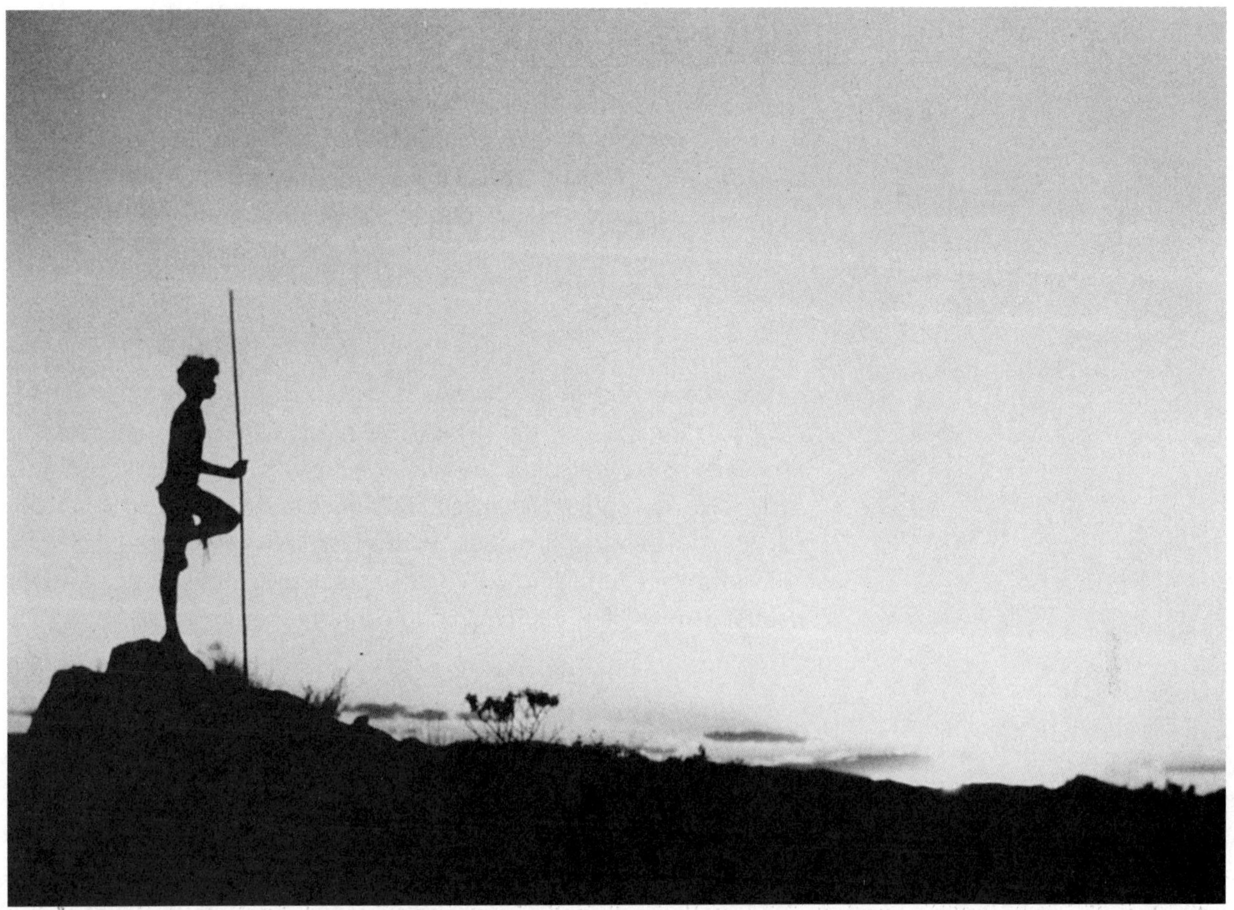

Figure 11.2
Sunset Silhouette Effect
(Walkabout, *Twentieth Century Fox, 1971)*

Twilight, or *magic hour*—the time from just before sunset until dark—is a favorite time to shoot. A similar magical quality light is obtained at dawn. (Magic hour will be discussed shortly.) Sunrise and sunset offer semisilhouette and silhouette possibilities (see Figure 11.2). Colored filters may be used to enhance and control the color effects.

TIME OF YEAR

Choice of time of year to shoot, coupled with choice of location, has a decisive impact on overall look. First, there is the difference in light based on geography. The summer light in North Africa has a different feel than the summer light in Denver. Time of year also influences feel because the difference in the sun's height in the sky alters the directionality of the illumination. Sun position can give very different looks to big city exteriors and urban landscapes. There are also obvious differences in the seasonal character of a location—winter versus summer; barren landscape versus verdant foliage; fog, rain, and snow.

The cinematographer may be able to state only a preference for shooting dates since economic considerations, director or star availability, and studio deadlines are apt to be more determinative than lighting considerations.

CONTROLLING CONTRAST

One important difference between exteriors and interiors is that much of exterior lighting is concerned with limiting image contrast, particularly on faces. Contrast impacts on the choice of film stock, the use of fill light outdoors, and whether flashing techniques are required.

Choice of Film Stock

With contemporary practices a stock's exposure index (EI) does not always determine how the stock is used. Just as slower stocks may be used indoors for effect, an outdoor scene may look best on a fast stock such as Eastman Color Negative EXR 7296. Choice of film stock is determined by the desired final look. When fast stocks are used outdoors to take advantage of their lower contrast and less-saturated color palettes, neutral density filters are required to control exposure levels.

Controlling Contrast Range

One way to cut contrast is to add fill light to the scene. This is possible with closeup and midshots of actors but is impractical for larger areas within the frame such as the shadow side of a building. To bring up detail in large shadow areas we must utilize lab or on-camera flashing techniques.

LABORATORY FLASHING **Flashing** involves subjecting the emulsion to a low-intensity light in order to lower its contrast. Flashing may occur before normal exposure (preflashing) or after normal exposure (postflashing). There is no on-screen difference between the two. Postflashing is more flexible since it allows for flashing individual rolls differing amounts (percentages) depending on the actual lighting situation. Postflashing also allows for the possibility of running end tests before entire rolls are flashed and processed. Flashing affects only the dark areas of the characteristic curve and reduces overall contrast by raising the density values of the dark areas as in Figure 11.3.

It's possible to flash a negative with a colored light, thus affecting the overall color rendition as well as the contrast property. Flashing was in vogue during the 1970s, when cinematographers like Vilmos Zsigmond explored its possibilities and wrote about the results in the *American Cinematographer*.[1] Today, on-camera devices such as Arriflex's "VariCon" (formerly "Lightflex") and Panavision's "Panaflasher" offer a precise, shot-by-shot alternative to flashing in the lab.[2]

ON-CAMERA FLASHING DEVICES: VARICON AND PANAFLASHER Like laboratory flashing, on-camera devices result in a lowering of effective

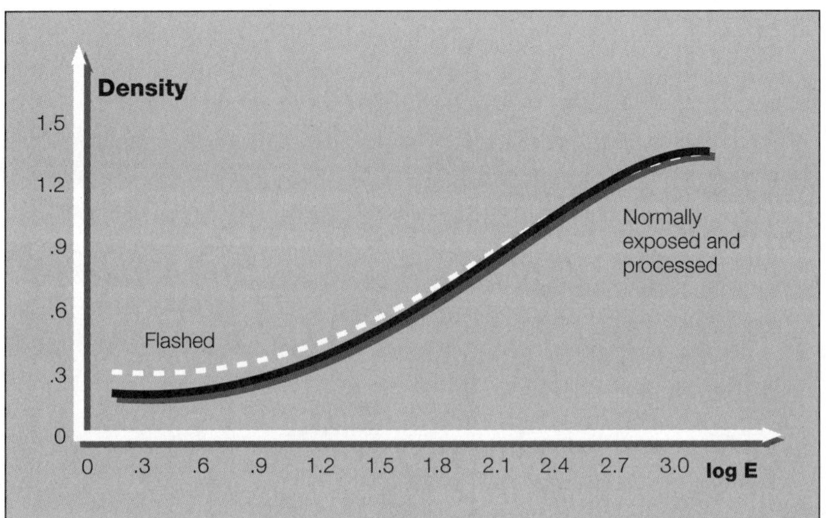

Figure 11.3 Effects of Flashing on Film Negative

emulsion gamma by spreading small amounts of light into dark areas of the curve. These devices are mounted in front of the lens (VariCon) or between magazine and camera body (Panaflasher) and flash the image during shooting.

As with laboratory flashing, various degrees of enhancement and color effects are available. With VariCon the effect may be evaluated through the viewfinder to some extent. The advantage of VariCon and Panaflasher over laboratory flashing is that they may be used on a shot-by-shot basis. An additional benefit from on-camera flashing is that less fill light is necessary for actors. This would be true of laboratory flashing as well, but the on-camera flashing device allows for analysis in the field rather than later on at the lab.

VariCon can be used with video as well as film cameras. Since this device expands the effective log E range of the original, it's particularly useful when originating on limited straight-line media such as videotape.

TYPICAL DAY EXTERIOR SITUATIONS

Dealing with common exterior problems involves access to many specialized types of equipment, most likely unavailable to the student cinematographer. As mentioned earlier, patience and diligence will have to substitute for such equipment.

Car Shots

Whether shooting from inside or outside a car, the lighting problem is how to bring car interior levels up to avoid silhouetted actors or overexposed backgrounds. The problem is identical to the actor in-front-of-the-window, interior/exterior situation we discussed earlier in detail,

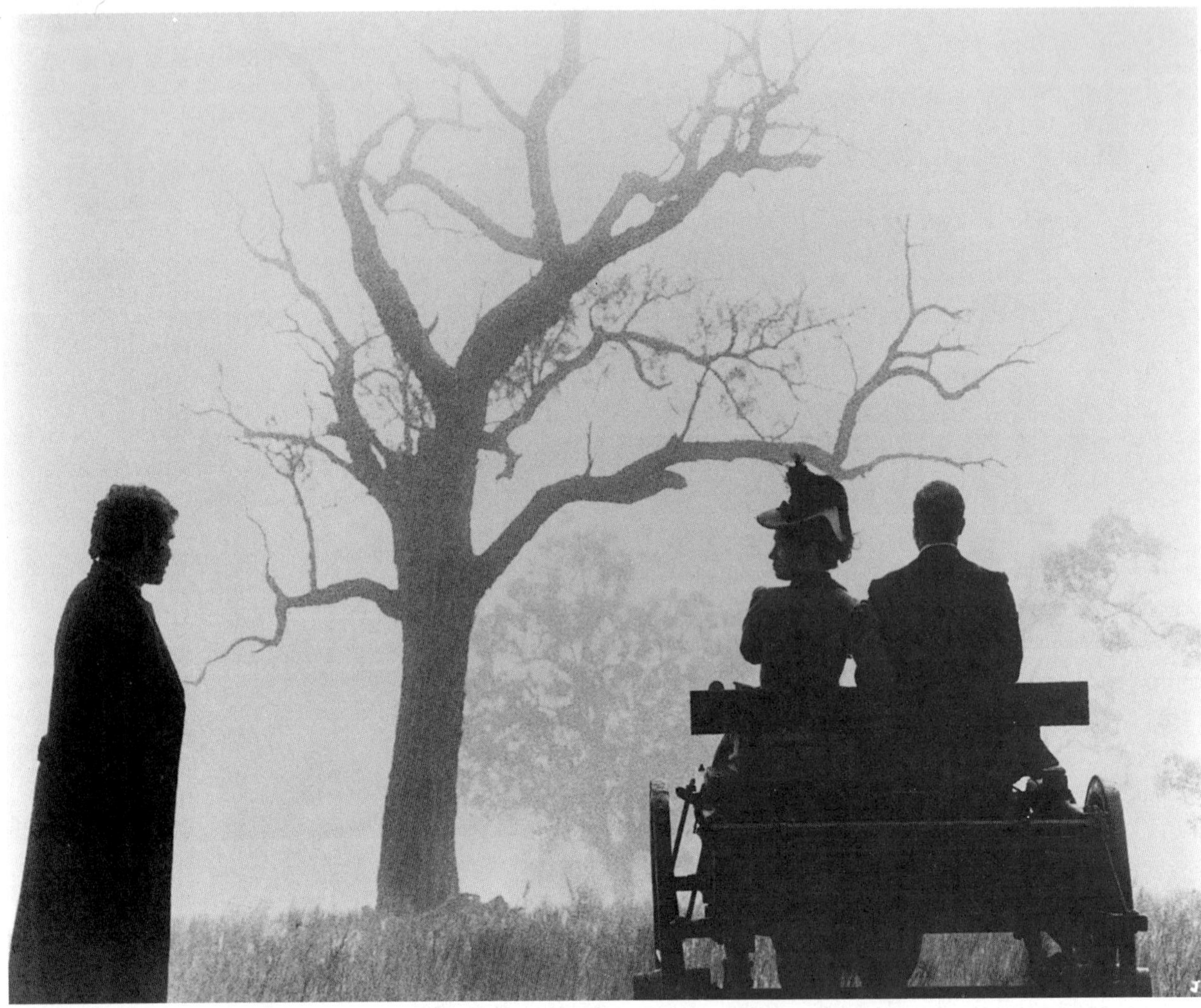

Figure 11.4 Atmospheric Effect Enhanced by Back Light
(The Chant of Jimmy Blacksmith, 1978)

and the solutions are the same (see Figure 10.3 and accompanying text). We light the car interior, or gel down the windows, or combine both techniques.

Rain, Fog, and Other Atmospheric Effects

Atmospheric effects such as rain and fog (smoke) are used a lot in contemporary cinematography. These may be natural or artificially created, the latter being preferred for control purposes. Smoke in particular enhances the look of films, from *Indiana Jones* and *Robin Hood* forest scenes to stylized music video images. Atmospheres like smoke are used for interiors as well as exteriors.

Back lighting is mandatory for making such atmospheric effects visible on the screen. We must either use the sun as back light or add HMIs from rear positions (see Figures 11.4 and 11.6). Without adequate back light, atmospheric effects will lose their "bounce" and look drab and dull, if perceptible at all.

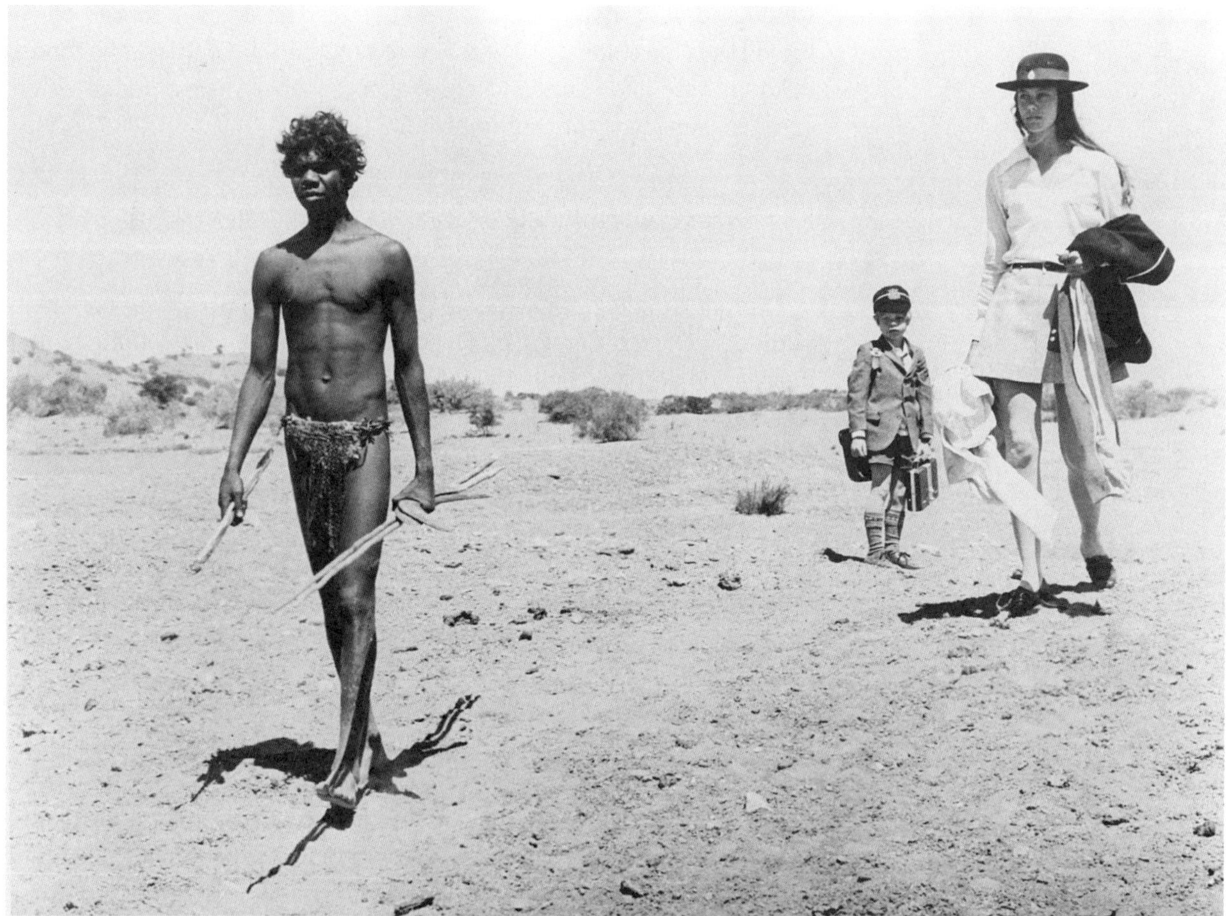

Figure 11.5 Desert Scene with Hard Sunlight *The shadows on the actor frame left are very black in comparison to the shadows on the two actors frame right. The latter are presumably not filled with an additional light but are receiving bounced light from the ground. This photograph illustrates the problems in lighting for mixed-facetone situations, a topic discussed in Chapter 9 (*Walkabout*, Twentieth Century Fox, 1971).*

Forest, Jungle, and Other Extreme Luminance Range Situations

These situations involve gloomy shadow areas with pools of light penetrating the darkness. Some films have exploited this forest darkness by intentionally placing actors in the shade and overexposing the sunlit backgrounds. This results in a light, desaturated background reminiscent of some Impressionist paintings. As a general rule, we expose for the shadow areas and allow the sunlit areas to overexpose. If available, we can use a VariCon to bring up detail as well.

John Alcott, the noted British cinematographer, was famous for shooting in the jungle without a #85 filter, for example, in *Greystoke*. He claimed this provided a certain green effect hard to obtain otherwise.[3]

Desert and Beach

The feeling of bright sunlight is necessary here (see Figure 11.5). The problem is to create a fill light that blends in without looking artificial, unless artificiality is desired. Large overheads and butterflies are used to soften and bring down the intensity over certain areas. Bounced or diffused HMIs make ideal fill lights. TV commercials are particularly good at utilizing these and other backgrounds to enhance their products—from designer jeans to luxury automobiles.

Weather Continuity: Faking Sun and Faking Clouds

One of the most aggravating tasks is maintaining lighting continuity outdoors. The economics of filmmaking are such that shooting often must go on despite changes in weather conditions. The cinematographer must be able to match shots filmed at various times of day. This includes adding HMI or arc "sunlight" to make a cloudy day look sunny or diffusing sunshine to simulate a gray day.

Backup devices are held ready to fake weather conditions such as rain or snow. For example, garden hoses and even fire trucks can be used to simulate rain (see Figure 11.6). Small independent and student productions generally wait until the weather is right to shoot.

Cheating Two-Shots

A routine technique outdoors is to cheat the background and lighting directionality of two-shots. Actor A is shot with the sun as a rim and actor B, who would logically be in frontal lighting, is also filmed with the sun as a rim. To do otherwise is to create shots that appear to lack lighting continuity when cut together.[4]

MAGIC HOUR

One of nature's gifts to the cinematographer is the lighting available at **magic hour**, that time of day around twilight or dawn when colors seem iridescent and the world of objects magical. Cinematographers have long exploited this lighting condition, from the opening title sequence of the television series *L.A. Law* to the exteriors in *Days of Heaven*, an Academy Award winner for cinematography. Magic hour is also routinely used to represent night exteriors, the sky being dark enough for a night effect but with sufficient light intensity for filming (see Color Plates 5–12).

There are two separate definitions of magic hour. The narrow definition is the time frame from just after sunset until the sky loses its luminosity, a period of about 20 to 30 minutes varying with the latitude and time of year. "Just after sunset" is usually taken to mean when car headlights and the lights in office buildings and houses start coming on. The effect peaks when they are as bright as the sky. As in the *L.A. Law* title sequence, it's common to use glass skyscrapers, city skylines, and bodies

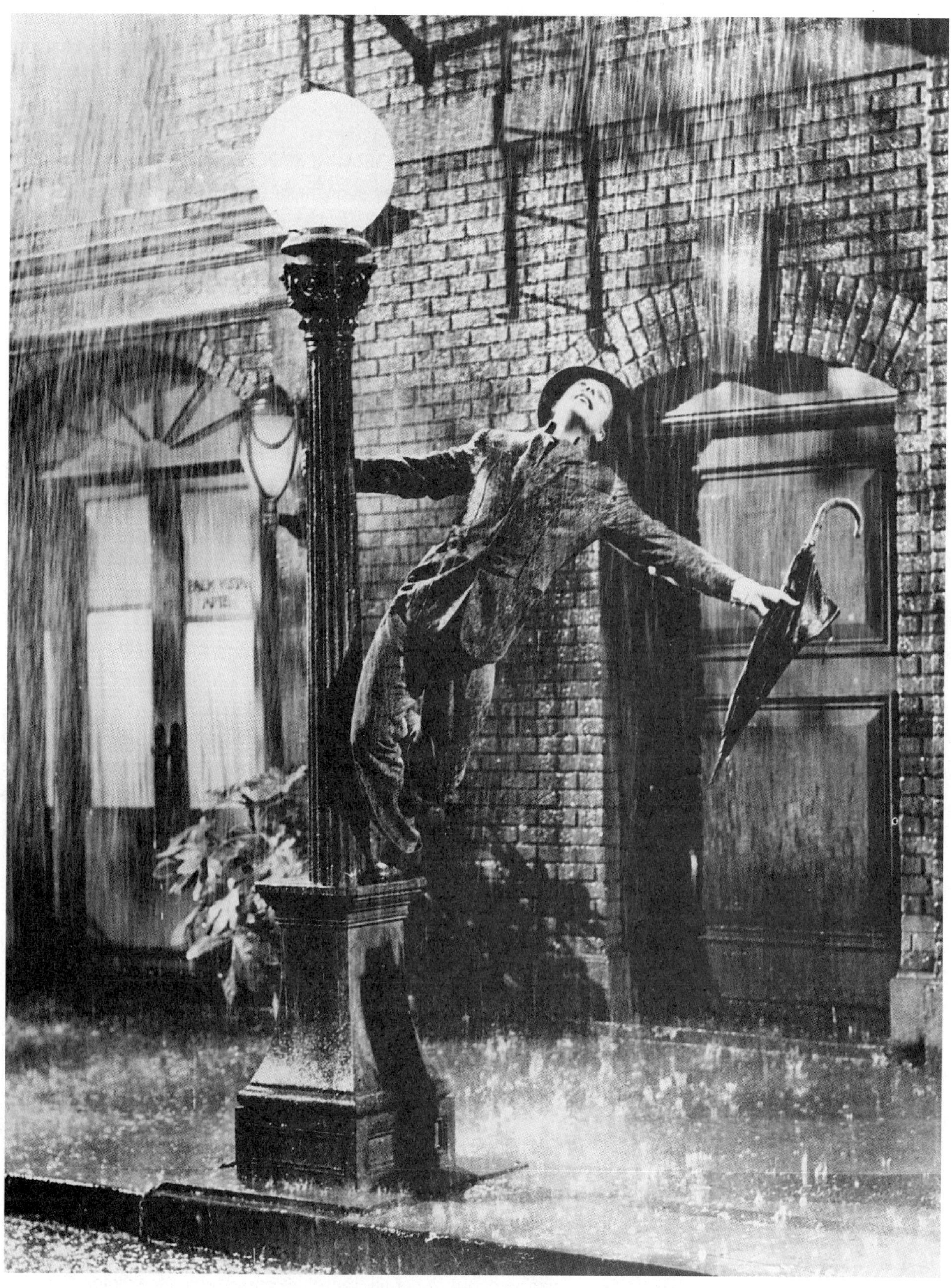

Figure 11.6 Back Light Is Essential for Making Rain Visible
(Singing in the Rain, *MGM, 1952)*

of water to enhance the effect (see Color Plates 9 and 11). This discussion of magic hour is referenced to the typical twilight situation. Cinematographers using a dawn magic hour would have to define the effect from the opposite direction because at dawn the sky becomes gradually lighter rather than darker.

In the looser, more expansive definition of magic hour, the time frame starts during the warm sunlight of late afternoon, about an hour before sunset, and runs until dark. This definition provides a longer time frame for shooting but a greater range of lighting changes to deal with. This longer magic hour was used in *Days of Heaven* to great effect.[5]

The problems involved in shooting a magic hour sequence are enormous since from moment to moment, the overall color and brightness of the sky and light changes. A further complication is that the magic hours from one day to the next exhibit great variations in color. It isn't easy to shoot a magic hour sequence over a period of days, but with filtration and careful additions of supplemental lighting, usually rim or fill, a cinematographer can work with this effect.

The key to magic hour is in understanding that it is the light itself that is being filmed. Since the effect involves luminosity, a reflected reading is essential to control the sky. To maintain facetone consistency requires an incident reading. Monitoring these two readings over time is necessary to capture the effect.

The two photographs in Color Plates 5 and 6 reveal the passage of time from just before sunset to about 15 minutes later. In Color Plate 5, an incident reading was used. Color Plate 6 required a reflected reading for the sky as it was too dark for an incident reading. Color Plates 7 and 8 trace the passage of time from about 5 minutes after sunset to dark. Note that exposure may be based on either the sky or the lamp. Note also that the lamp's exposure value is the same in each photograph.

Control of magic hour derives from reflected readings of the sky. Generally, we determine our T-stop by opening up two stops from the averaging-type meter reading, just as we would with a sunset. Any supplemental lighting on actors is balanced to the T-stop determined from the sky as in Color Plate 16.

NIGHT EXTERIORS

Lighting night exteriors ranges from using huge Musco lights, crane-mounted banks of HMIs capable of providing enough intensity to film from a quarter mile away, to filming with available light and adding small amounts of supplemental illumination. There are aberrant color temperature problems with sodium vapor and other lamps popular with urban planners, but generally these are correctable (see Color Plate 13). With high-speed lenses and fast emulsions we can film with only a few footcandles of illumination. Ironically, there is the danger of overexpos-

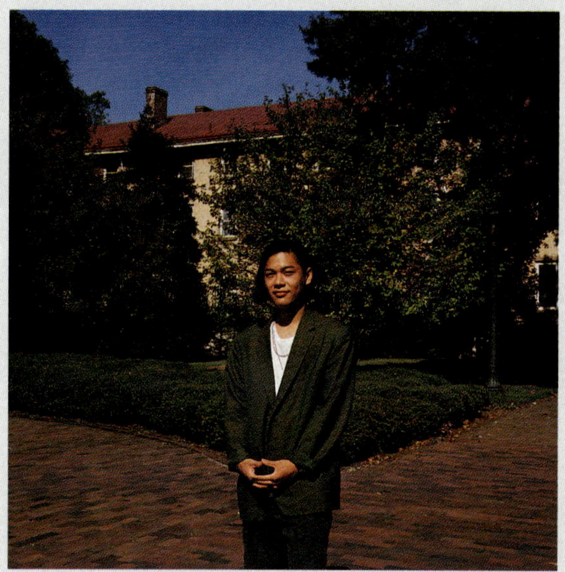

COLOR PLATE 1 *Frontal lighting results in the fullest color saturation.*

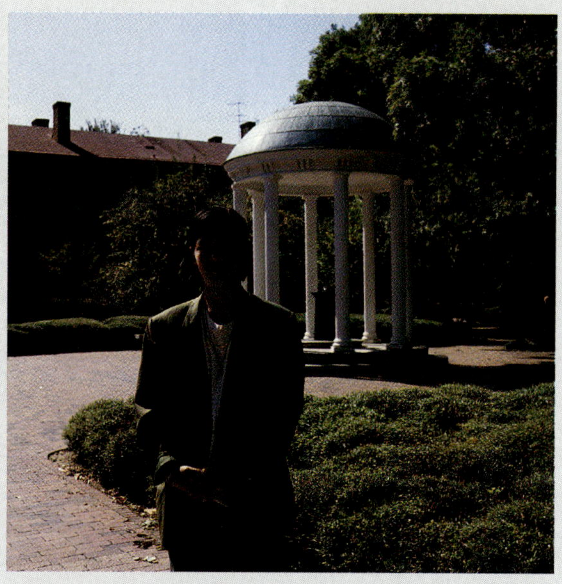

COLOR PLATE 2 *Saturation decreases as the light source moves to the side and rear positions.*

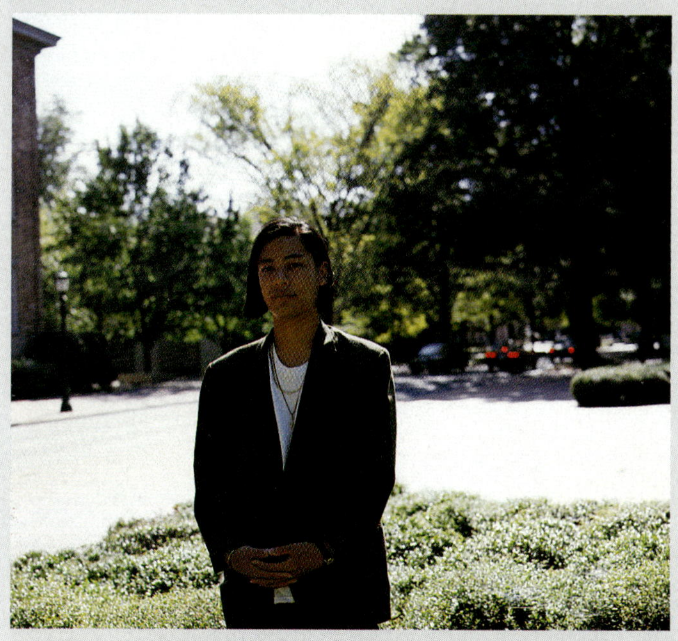

COLOR PLATE 3 *Desaturation is most evident with backlighting.*

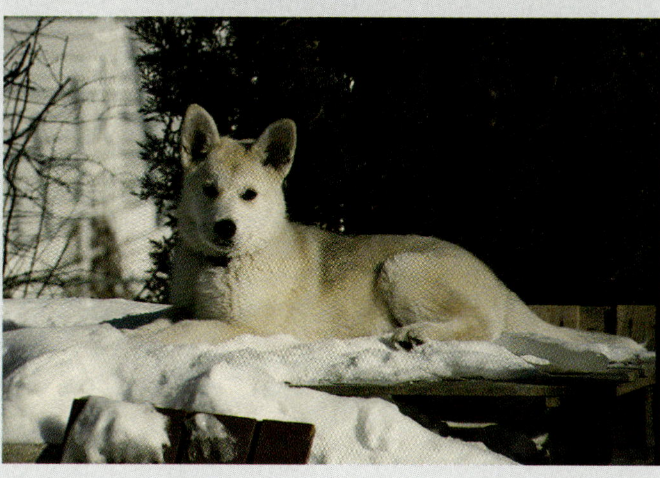

COLOR PLATE 4 *All-white or light-toned subjects, such as a white Siberian husky on snow, often require underexposure to retain separation between the various highlight values.*

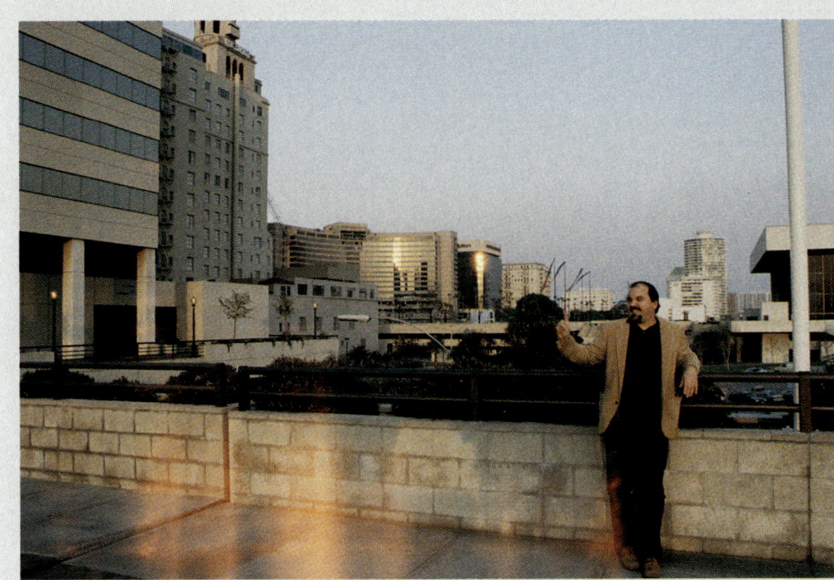

COLOR PLATE 5 *Early magic hour, before sunset, incident reading.*

COLOR PLATE 6 *The same as Color Plate 5 but 45 minutes later. Late magic hour is often used for night effects.*

COLOR PLATE 7 *A street light against the sky at magic hour. The exposure was calculated with a reflected reading of the lamp opened up two stops.*

COLOR PLATE 8 *The same as Color Plate 7 but about 15 minutes later. Again, exposure was given for the lamp.*

COLOR PLATE 9 *Magic hour effect enhanced by glass buildings (photo by Nikola Stanjevich).*

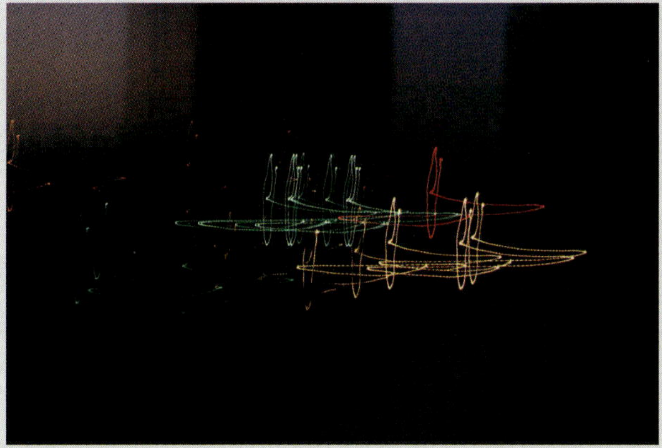

COLOR PLATE 10 *Late magic hour effect with buildings and neon lights (photo by Mike Rubin).*

COLOR PLATE 12 *Very late magic hour effect with timed exposure to create light streaks (photo by Mike Rubin).*

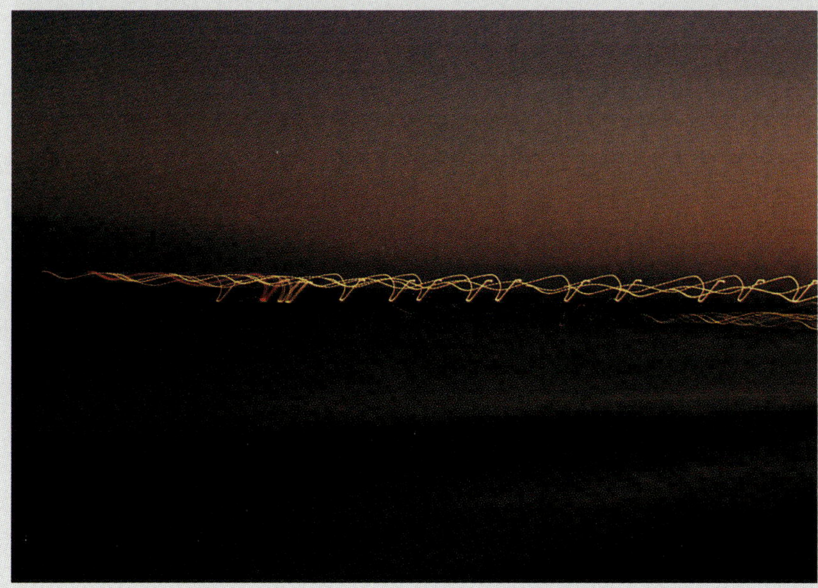

COLOR PLATE 11 *Late magic hour effect over water (photo by Nikola Stanjevich).*

COLOR PLATE 13 *Night exteriors with luminous objects pose special problems. The odd color temperature is due to the sodium vapor lamps that illuminate the parking garage.*

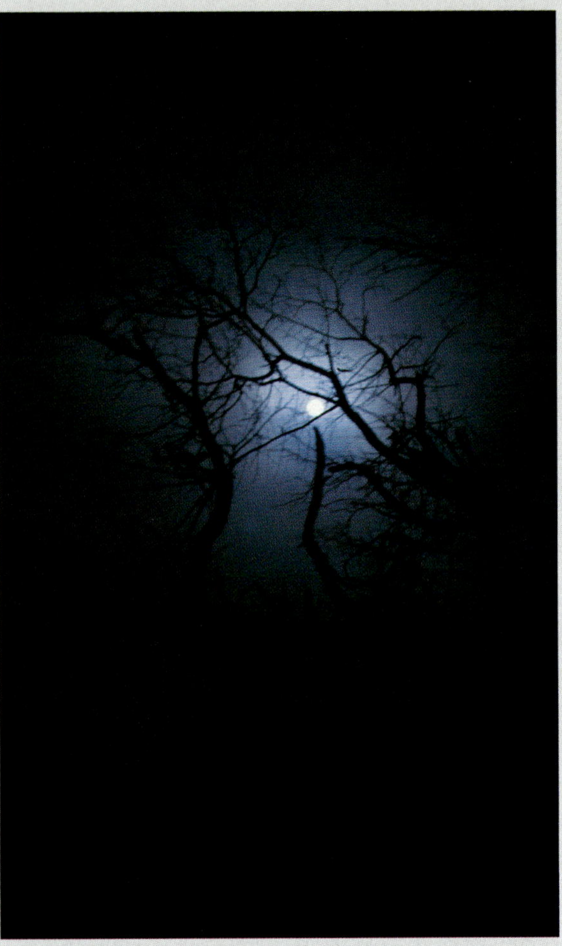

COLOR PLATE 15 *The mood of the foggy night would have been lost if the moon had been overexposed.*

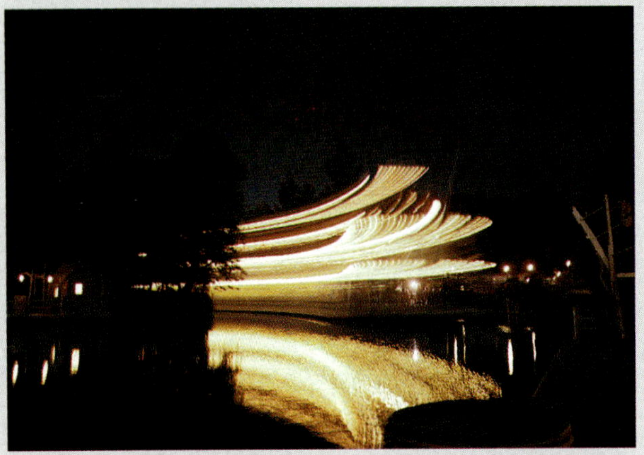

COLOR PLATE 14 *The luminous effect is enhanced by overexposure and the reflection of lights in the water (photo by Lee Scott).*

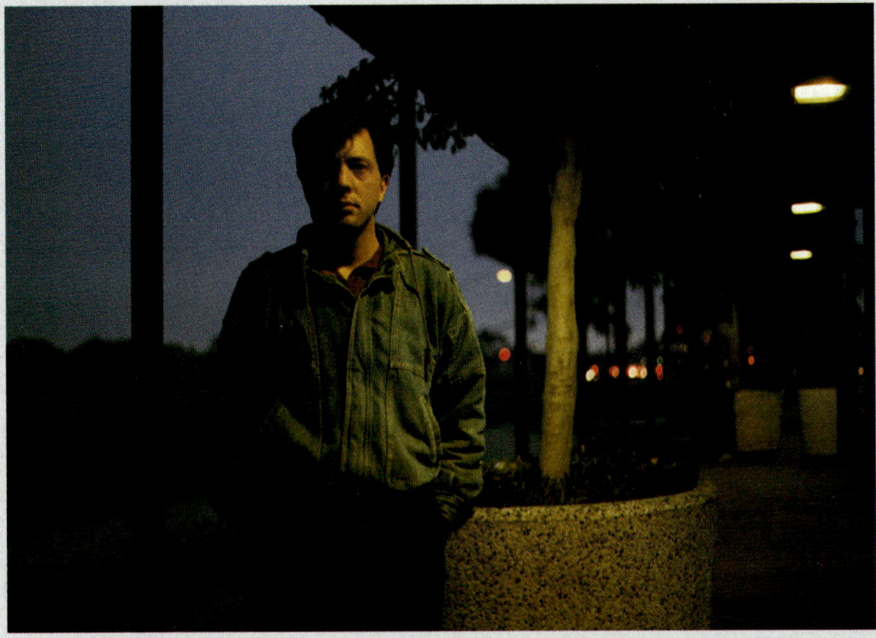

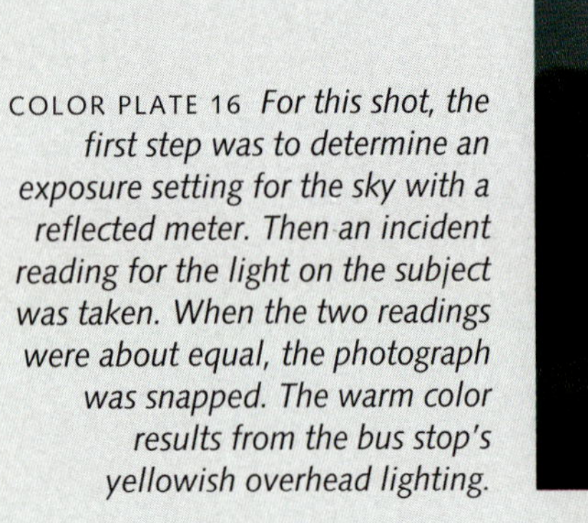

COLOR PLATE 16 *For this shot, the first step was to determine an exposure setting for the sky with a reflected meter. Then an incident reading for the light on the subject was taken. When the two readings were about equal, the photograph was snapped. The warm color results from the bus stop's yellowish overhead lighting.*

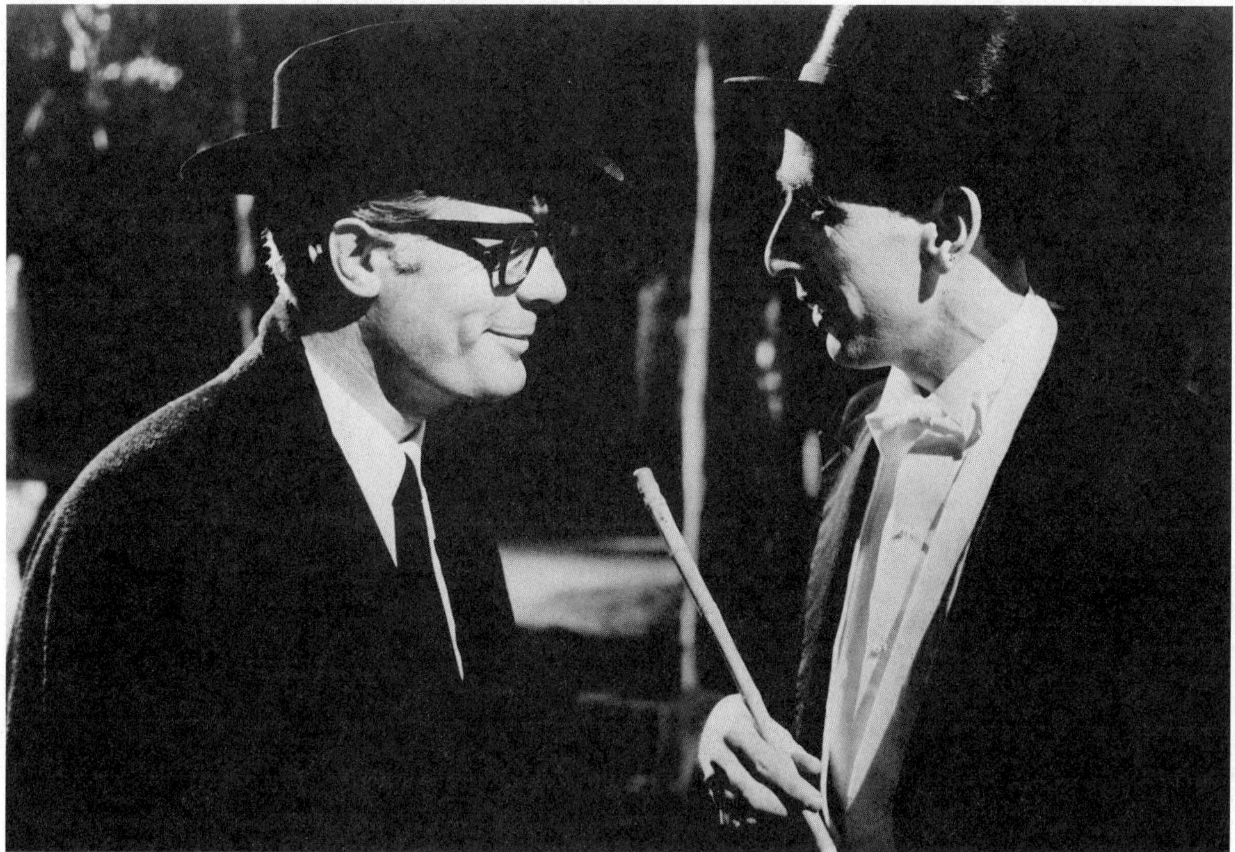

a

ing neons and other luminous objects when filming night exteriors with available light (see Color Plates 14 and 15).

Night exteriors involve the same problems as large interiors. We have to decide whether to use available light, where to place the lighting units, and what look to go for. Like our examples in Chapters 9 and 10, lighting the night exterior consists of implementing an overall plan, establishing motivated sources and a logic for the illumination, and providing localized key and fill setups wherever necessary. The illustrations in Figure 11.7 and throughout this book attest to the variety of possible night exterior looks.

Trickier night situations involve campfire scenes and moonlit forests, but again there are no new principles involved beyond our standard set of basic considerations and our all-important previsualization of "what is a night exterior."

Figure 11.7 Examples of Night Exteriors *Night exteriors are usually a delight to light since the cinematographer starts with a dark frame, which allows for a true painting-with-light. A lot of back light is used along with high subject lighting ratios. Sometimes streets are wetted down to create a surface the back light can glisten off of (b). Often neons and other signs are used as part of the background (c). Night exteriors use the same lighting principles we applied to night interiors in Chapter 10. Publicity still (a) is from* 8 1/2*, Embassy Pictures, 1963; (b) is from* The Third Man*, Twentieth Century Fox, 1949; and (c) is from* Blade Runner*, The Ladd Company, 1982.*

Cars and Streets

Car interiors at night are like car interiors in daylight except there is no window problem. Having determined a T-stop for the street exterior and gelled down overbright luminous objects, lighting from inside the car consists of hiding small units so as to light the actors (see Figure 9.6). One possibility is to use optical fiber lights, which can be positioned

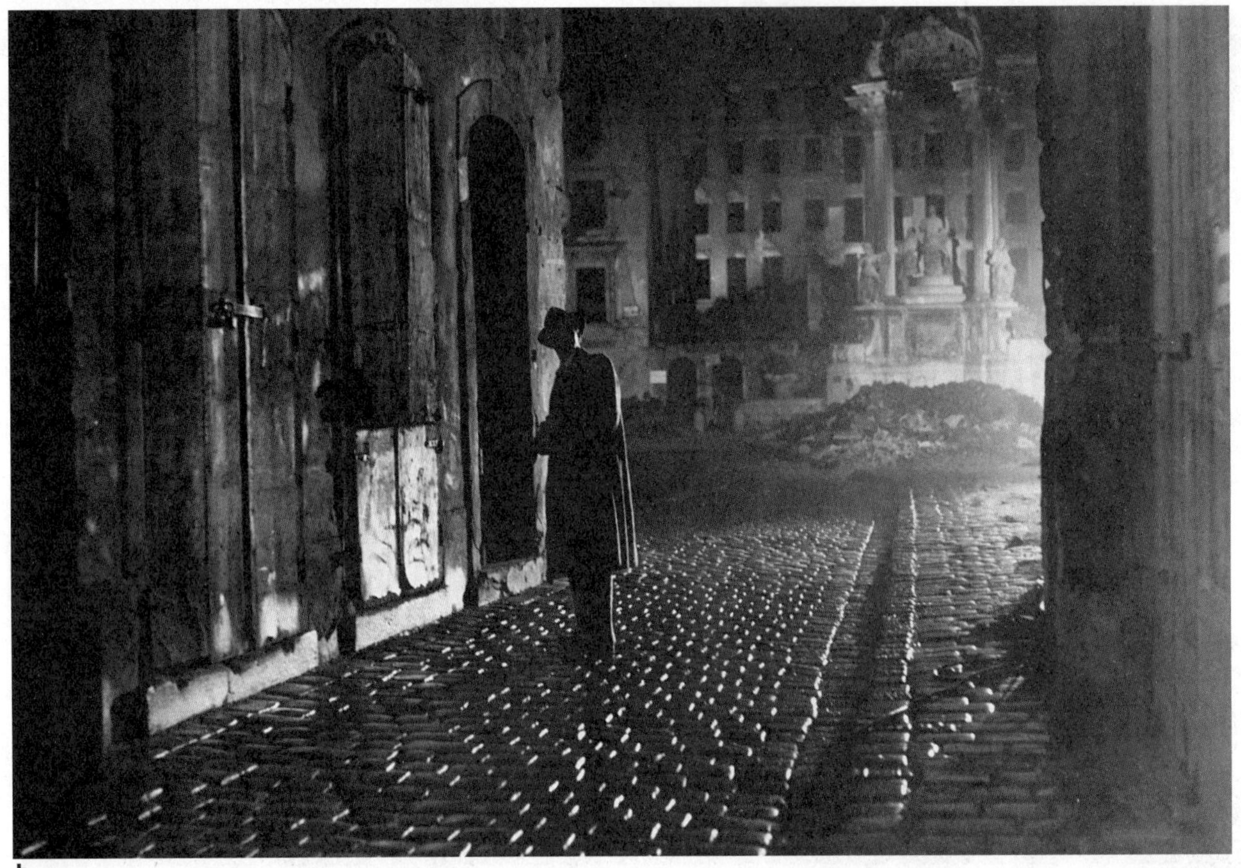

b

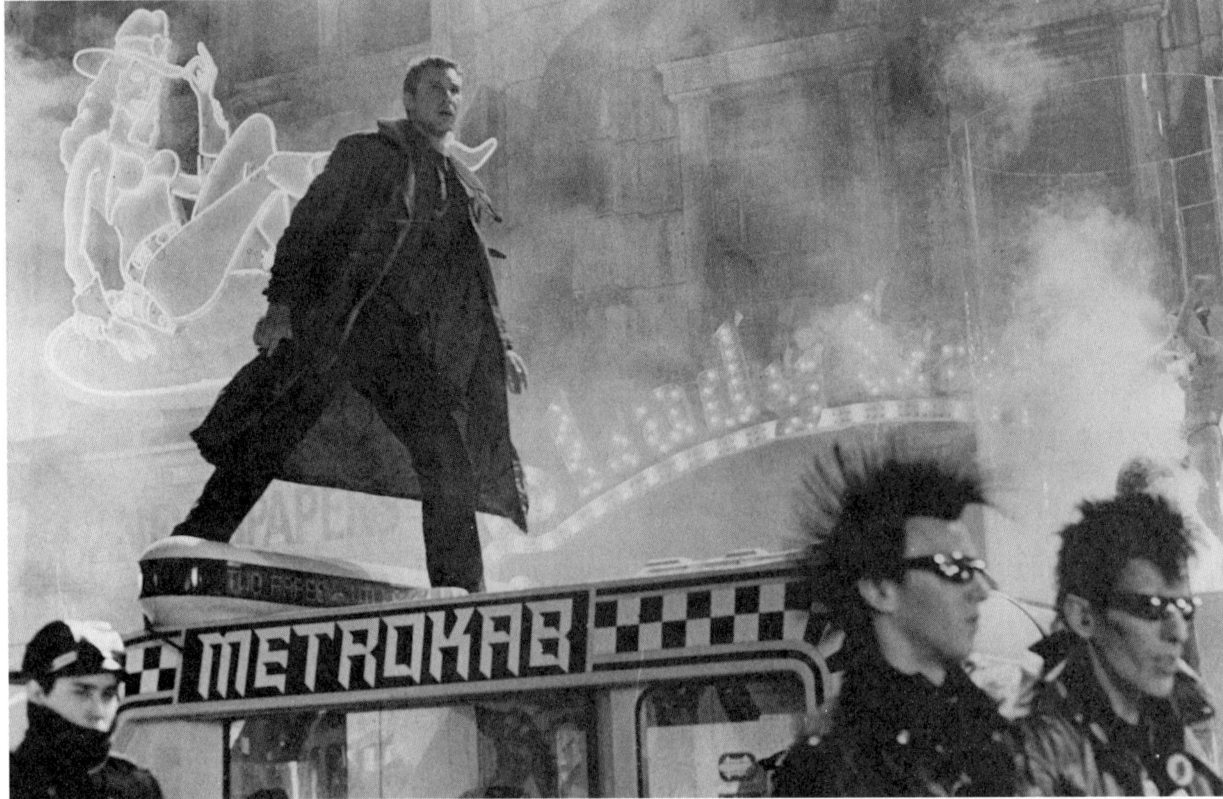

c

Figure 11.7 (continued)

wherever desired and powered from a unit hidden in the trunk. Such flexibility is marvelous for the cinematographer.

Where available levels are inadequate, streets may be lit with Musco lights, HMIs, or arcs using the same basic principles as for interior lighting: key, fill, rim, subject/background ratio, and the like. When lighting a street, the convention is to use high-intensity back lighting with perhaps smoke added for effect (see Figure 11.7c). Another convention is to wet the street, which causes the high overhead back lighting to glisten and reflect nicely off the pavement (see Figure 11.7b).

SUMMARY

Because we have so little control over lighting conditions, the most important considerations affecting exteriors are: choice of location, time of day, and time of year. The cinematographer must be aware of natural light and atmospheric change in order to deal with the many contrast problems inherent in exterior filming. There's little the cinematographer can do to change the basic nature of the location. Besides the many difficulties in controlling daylight, there are the problems in working with magic hour, nighttime, and weather continuity. Ultimately, the secret to imaginative exteriors is patience and diligence—patience to wait for the necessary time of day or even weather conditions, diligence in finding the best location for the desired effect.

NOTES

1. Vilmos Zsigmond, "Behind the Cameras for *Heaven's Gate*," *American Cinematographer* (November 1980): 1110–13, 1164–65. Herb A. Lightman, "On Location with *Deliverance*," *American Cinematographer* (August 1971): 796–801. See also: Anton Wilson, "Cinema Workshop—Flashing," *American Cinematographer* (August 1974): 892; and "Cinema Workshop—Flashing II," (September 1974): 1016, 1099.

2. See Isidore Mankofsky, "Contrast Control Made Easier," *American Cinematographer* (July 1990): 81-86; and Arri Product Information "UPDATE," 1990.

3. Joss Marsh and Nora Lee, "Greystoke—the Legend of Tarzan and the Apes," *American Cinematographer* (May 1984): 58–68.

4. See discussion of this technique by Vilmos Zsigmond in Kris Malkiewicz, assisted by Barbara J. Gryboski, *Film Lighting* (New York: Prentice-Hall, 1986), p. 153.

5. Nestor Almendros, "Photographing *Days of Heaven*," *American Cinematographer* (May 1979): 562–65, 592–94, 626–32.

SETTING UP A PRODUCTION: THE CINEMATOGRAPHER'S DUTIES

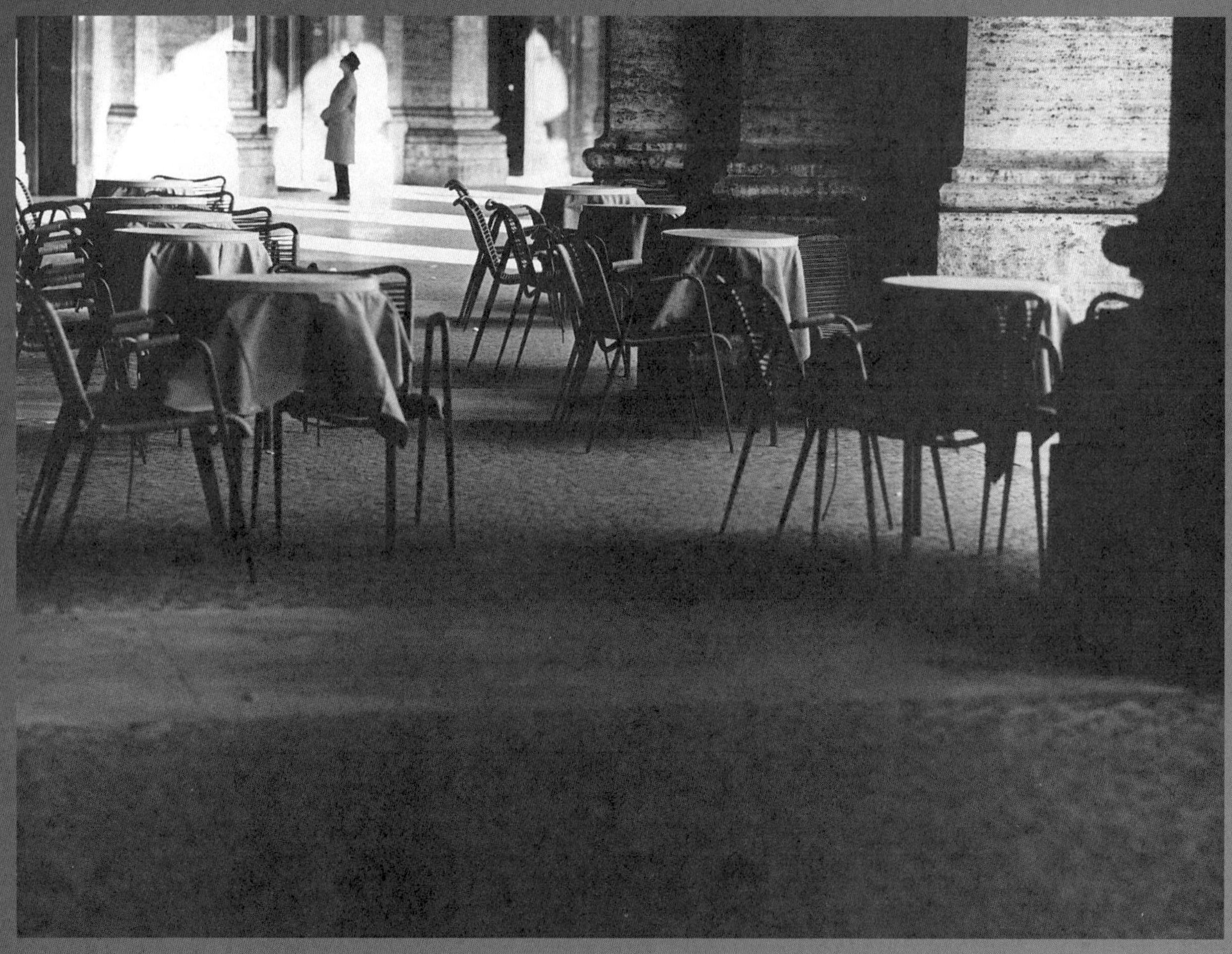

Photo by Gerald Lang *"day exterior"*

12

The cinematographer is responsible for the overall look of the film. From generalized aesthetic style decisions to detailed lighting plots, the cinematographer creates a lighting design for the film. This chapter describes the cinematographer's basic duties and discusses lighting a typical situation in detail.

FOR THE cinematographer, setting up a production requires activity in three basic areas: (1) aesthetic decisions and research, (2) testing, and (3) planning the execution of the lighting.

AESTHETIC DECISIONS AND RESEARCH

Eastman Color, Fujicolor, and Agfa all yield different looks on the screen. Emulsion choice is thus critical. Since each emulsion provides a palette of color and mood possibilities, a cinematographer must be aware of all available emulsions and their look parameters. Testing and actual experience with each emulsion yields comparisons, as does studying the work of other cinematographers.

To select a look for a film requires consultation with the director and the production designer and determination of the ultimate meaning of the film. That determination will affect the final lighting style—for example, whether it's to be realistic or stylized (see Appendix F, "Lighting Style").

The cinematographer must determine the nature and quality of the light to be used: whether to use soft or hard light or a mixture, whether to utilize direct or indirect illumination, whether to use available or artificial sources or both, whether to create an overall low- or high-key mood. All of these factors come into play in determining a film's lighting approach.

The cinematographer can do research for the director to determine overall style by locating ideas in paintings, photographs, illustrations, and other films and videos. If a director is able to tell a cinematographer, "I want this scene to look like X in such and such film," it is the cinematographer's professional responsibility to be able to duplicate that look.

TESTING

Although several types of tests are common, the most typical are lighting tests of the various locations. These are used to try out various lighting ideas and to determine what illumination is available to work with. Different lighting styles might be applied to the same scene as a means for helping the director choose between them. Emulsion and equipment check tests are often coupled with the lighting tests.

Exposure tests on the emulsion include **push and pull development** (over- and underdevelopment), overexposing and underprinting, and other manipulations. The goal is to determine the developing and printing parameters to achieve the desired look on the screen. These emulsion and exposure tests will be used to determine lab printer-light settings for night and day interiors and exteriors (see Appendix H, "Lab Printers").

The equipment check or shakedown test is another important preproduction procedure. With the actual camera and lenses to be used on the shoot, scenes are filmed to make sure that everything is working—in particular, that the various prime lenses are compatible for intercutting and that the zoom is sharp enough to match the primes.

Testing is also desirable where one is using diffusion, filtration, or flashing devices. Other common tests center on the actors—their make-up and their clothes—and on the sets and props. On feature films it's standard practice to test all variables affecting overall look.

PLANNING THE EXECUTION OF THE LIGHTING

Before shooting begins the cinematographer should have visited the sets and locations and determined equipment needs as well as an overall approach to the lighting and its execution. Although the execution of the lighting occurs at the production stage, preproduction planning is essential, preferably in conjunction with the gaffer who will aid in carrying out the lighting plan.

As we have discussed, there are two overall approaches to lighting a set or location. One is to light the background first and then build up the subject lighting areas. The second is to light the subject and then balance in the background accordingly. Sometimes the choice of approach is more a function of economics than of aesthetics or technique.[1]

Some setups involve large-scale lighting problems: for example, city night exteriors involving lighting three city blocks, a large circus interior, or the Vienna opera house. Some setups are small: a liquor store doorway on the city street, the circus band, or a dressing room in the opera house. As the scale changes, the equipment used to execute the setup varies, but the basic principles remain the same.

It makes a difference whether we're shooting in a studio or on location, mainly because on location we have less control over mounting lights and no way to remove walls and ceilings. From the audience's point of view there should be no perceptible difference. Viewers don't care whether the lighting is a 10K 40 feet away or a Lowell Quartz D stuck up in the corner of a room.

As mentioned earlier, it's the cinematographer's responsibility to be able to duplicate looks from real life, photos, films, videos, paintings, any source whatsoever. To be able to do so, he or she must first be able to read the screen image, working backward to decipher how the image was lit or textured. This requires an extensive knowledge of lighting principles and concepts and the ability to control lighting.

Some cinematographers use Polaroids on the set to aid in judging lighting. After setting the basic lighting with the gaffer, they take a series of stills to help judge how the film will render the setup. As mentioned, it's useful to plot the actual lighting setup in case it is necessary to reshoot and match parts of scenes months later. Polaroids of the setup are also helpful for reshooting.

DETAILED LIGHTING EXAMPLE

Let's go step by step through a lighting setup, using a cafe for our set. Assume we have the following working parameters: day interior in an elegant cafe, two walls have floor-to-ceiling windows looking out onto street exteriors, two days to shoot, large actions such as people entering and exiting the cafe although the main emphasis is on a couple sitting at one of the tables, and the director may want a tracking shot from exterior to interior. All of that will become the opening scene of what is to be a Hitchcock-like spy film (see Figure 12.1).

Aesthetic Considerations for Cafe Scene

There are a number of aesthetic considerations to address. The following discussion represents only one approach to this hypothetical situation. Other cinematographers would approach this lighting setup in their own way. Also, the problems and working parameters described here change from film to film—which is why cinematography is so interesting and challenging.

OVERALL LOOK The main look of the film has been imposed by the producer—a *James Bond* film, high-gloss look as in fashion photography. The director would prefer the contemporary equivalent of film noir, a color noir style like that of *Blade Runner*, rather than the high-glamour look. Guess who wins this one?

For the visual style, then, we will use a sharp, high-key glossy look with good color saturation and a lot of depth of field. Some scenes, par-

Figure 12.1 Cafe Scene Example—Day Interior/Exterior *This schematic shows the general layout of the cafe location described in the text. The central action areas are labeled and camera setups 1 and 2 indicated.*

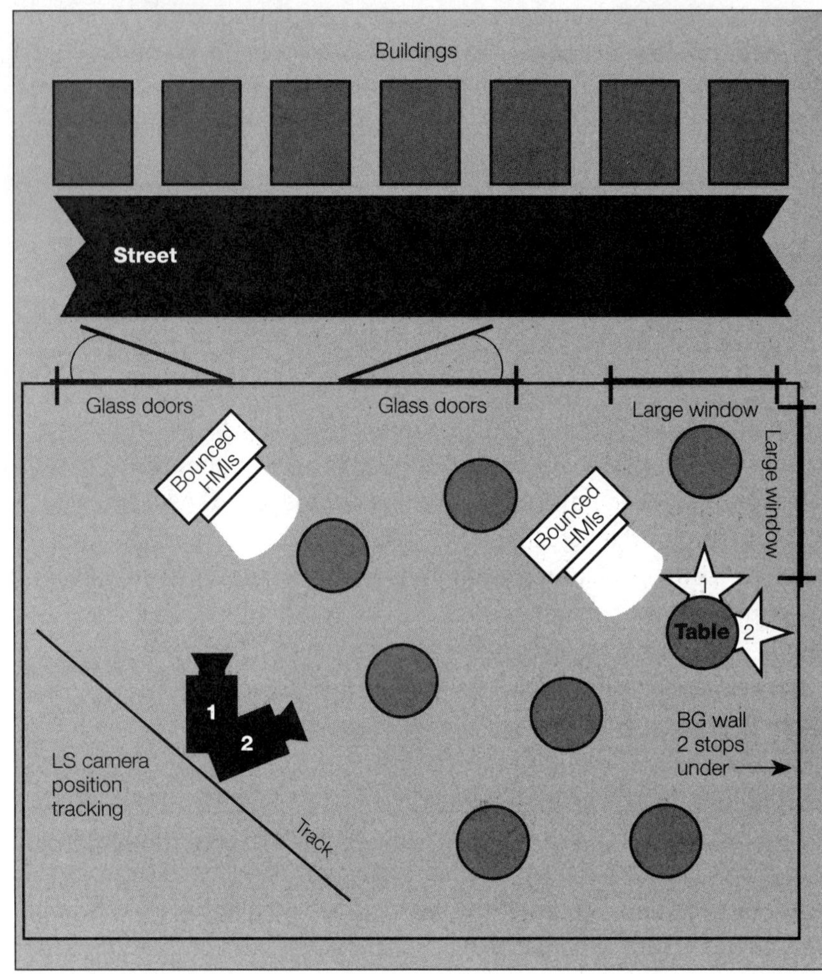

ticularly at night, will deviate from this overall style, but basically we'll shoot with high-quality, matched prime lenses and go for a fine-grained look. Talks with the designer have emphasized how important the sets and colors will be in setting the overall mood.

LIGHT QUALITY The director desires hardish lighting, but not too hard. Tests show she prefers the look of diffused HMIs and spots with selective pools of light. For this opening scene we can use a softer application to establish the romantic theme.

SUBJECT LIGHTING RATIOS These will vary from scene to scene, but 2:1 and 4:1 will be standard range because "high gloss" means fashion photography, a sharp, see-everything, richly colored image style. As part of this look, a study of fashion photography reveals a high, bright placement of facetones is useful, between zones $6^1/_2$ and 7.

SUBJECT/BACKGROUND RATIOS The range will vary from scene to scene for effect, but a low ratio will be used quite a bit to obtain that high-key, glossy look.

COLOR EFFECTS The director and designer agree to put color effects into the sets and costumes, so few color lighting effects are anticipated except for a fantasy scene that will be shot in a jungle without a #85 filter and in several moonlit exteriors in the Alps where we'll blue the light.

FILM STOCK Several stocks were tested with the camera and lenses to be used. Everyone seems happiest with a daylight stock (EI 250), even for most interiors, because of the colors. Enough of one emulsion batch is ordered to cover a 10:1 shooting ratio for the film. A faster film (EI 500) will be used as needed, keeping in mind that the director doesn't like its greens. As part of these tests, a set of printer lights has been established at the lab for workprinting. There are four separate combinations for day and night exteriors and interiors.

TYPES OF LIGHTS A new 18K HMI has been marketed, and we'll be trying those out as well as using a number of 12K HMIs. We'll need a lot of footcandles for our sharp images; they tested great at T 5.6. We will rely on large units with moderate diffusion for our standard quality. A Musco light will be needed for two large-scale, night exteriors. A variety of small HMIs and quartz units will be available, as well as a selection of grip gear and a range of gels, silks, and frosts for diffusion and color temperature control.

The preceding aesthetic considerations and their technical solutions have resulted from the interplay among producer, director, cinematographer, and designer. We've all worked together before and have come to agree that films like *Flash Dance* and *Top Gun* have the look we're after.

For the opening scene, we'll use bounced HMI lights to create a soft interior lighting balanced to the outside. Several visits to the location have revealed that we can shoot from about 1:00 P.M. until 6:00 P.M. because the street outside the restaurant will be in shadow then as a number of large buildings block the sun. After 5:00 P.M., we enter early twilight conditions that we can use to shoot the last few shots of the scene. We can't shoot earlier than 1:00 P.M. because the sunlight creates a high-contrast background that we don't want. We will use mornings to rig lights, rehearse shots, and cheat closeups that have other parts of the cafe for background.

Technical Considerations for Cafe Scene

Listed below are the considerations and decisions relevant to establishing our lighting scheme. The gaffing crew will rough in everything from our descriptions and working sketches while we are still shooting at a hotel set a mile away.

INTERIOR/EXTERIOR PROBLEM As mentioned, we can depend on a fairly consistent window effect from 1:00 P.M. until 5:00 P.M. This effect measures T 8 using an incident meter out in the street. During shooting we'll monitor this T-stop to ensure a consistent subject/background ratio. The street should be in full shade all afternoon, and little change in intensity is anticipated. Should the exterior darken because of clouds, we will either wait for them to pass or alter the intensity of the interior accordingly. For example, we could scrim the HMIs to lower their intensity.

We have selected an ideal working stop of T 5.6, letting the background overexpose one stop. This gives us a 1:2 subject/background ratio that will ensure a light, bright image look. The background will go bluish because of the color temperature (CT) of the shade. We could use window gels to warm that up, but tests have shown that the bluish look with properly balanced facetones is pleasing.

Were it necessary, we could have gelled the cafe windows for either intensity or color temperature, but by shooting when the street is in shade we have solved this problem in a simpler fashion. For this scene we'll shoot daylight balance with the HMIs and use the daylight-balanced stock (EI 250).

There are four main long shots. The most difficult is a dolly from the exterior into the cafe. The assistant cameraperson suggests we pull T-stop, from T 8 to 5.6 for the interior, but this might be too overt. Instead, we'll shoot with a roving fill that will hold the actors between T 5.6 and T 8 (T 5.6/8). We will let them go to T 5.6 at the table, which will not have the exterior as background so we don't have to worry about its effects there. We'll expose the entire dolly shot at T 5.6/8.

LIGHTING DIRECTIONALITY This is fairly simple since, ostensibly, the windows in the cafe are lighting everything for this afternoon interior. We've talked the director into shooting away from the windows at the back of the cafe. This means we can control the interior background at will. Only the street exterior is beyond our control. However, the director says she can shoot all the long shots at the same time. This should minimize any street continuity problems.

For our interior lighting, we'll establish our directionality by bouncing HMIs off white foam core placed on the window side of the cafe high on the walls or ceiling. We will also light the parts of the cafe away from the windows by bouncing light from the ceiling or self-standing foam core as necessary, being careful to maintain the window directionality. The basic bounced light amounts to a window-motivated side key. We will balance its intensity for T 5.6 throughout the cafe, letting it slowly fall off to T 4 and T 2.8 in the darker parts of the interior, particularly the background wall (see Figure 12.1).

Our lighting is soft and the walls are light enough to fill in facial shadows with scattered light to a natural 4:1 ratio. We decide to add some very soft, bounced fill to bring the faces at the table to 3:1; we make sure there's enough reflection from these to function as eyelight. We add a slight rim light for the closeups, again prompted by the window (see Figure 12.2).

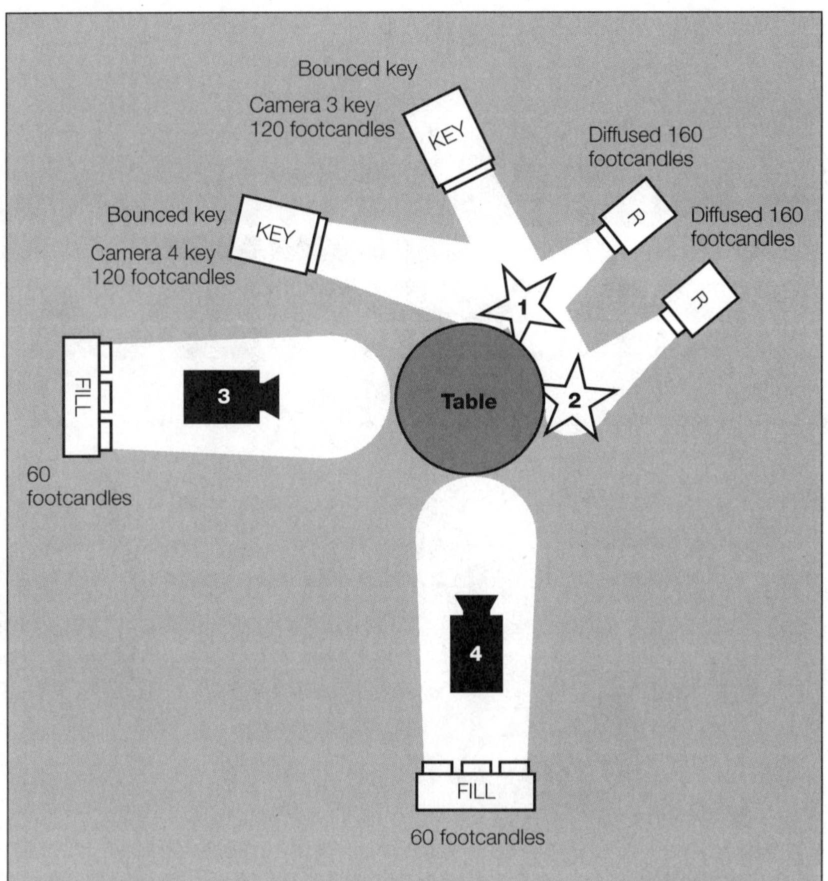

Figure 12.2 Detail of Table Lighting Setup for Day Interior
This schematic indicates how the table area is lit for two-shots and closeups as described in the text.

CAMERA ANGLES We are lighting two camera positions for long shots as shown in Figure 12.1. Closeups will be shot from camera positions 3 and 4 as shown in Figure 12.2. We're going to cheat the backgrounds in the closeups from camera position 3 to eliminate the window in the background. As mentioned, we are planning to shoot all four long shots first. Once the above lighting is set up we will notate it on a lighting plot.

A Possible Occurrence: Changing the Cafe to a Night Interior

The above was shot and screened as described. When the lead actor saw the dailies he objected to his makeup and demanded a reshoot. The director was happy to reshoot since she felt the scene lacked "punch" and wanted to rewrite the dialogue one more time. She also wanted to change the scene to a night interior. The producer relented because of his relationship with the actor. A reshoot was ordered.

On a night visit to the cafe, the cinematographer noticed the following: The place was beautifully lit with subtle, intimate lighting—but only to a T 1.4 level. This wouldn't yield enough depth of field, so the decision was made to establish a higher level at T 4 and switch to a faster stock (EI 500) and shoot tungsten balance.

The street outside the window was empty except for an occasional passing car. It would render at zone 1, below the threshold of the stock.

Figure 12.3 Cafe Scene Example—Night Interior/Exterior
This schematic shows the general lighting setup for converting the cafe scene into a night interior/exterior. Details of the lighting for the tables is shown in Figure 12.4.

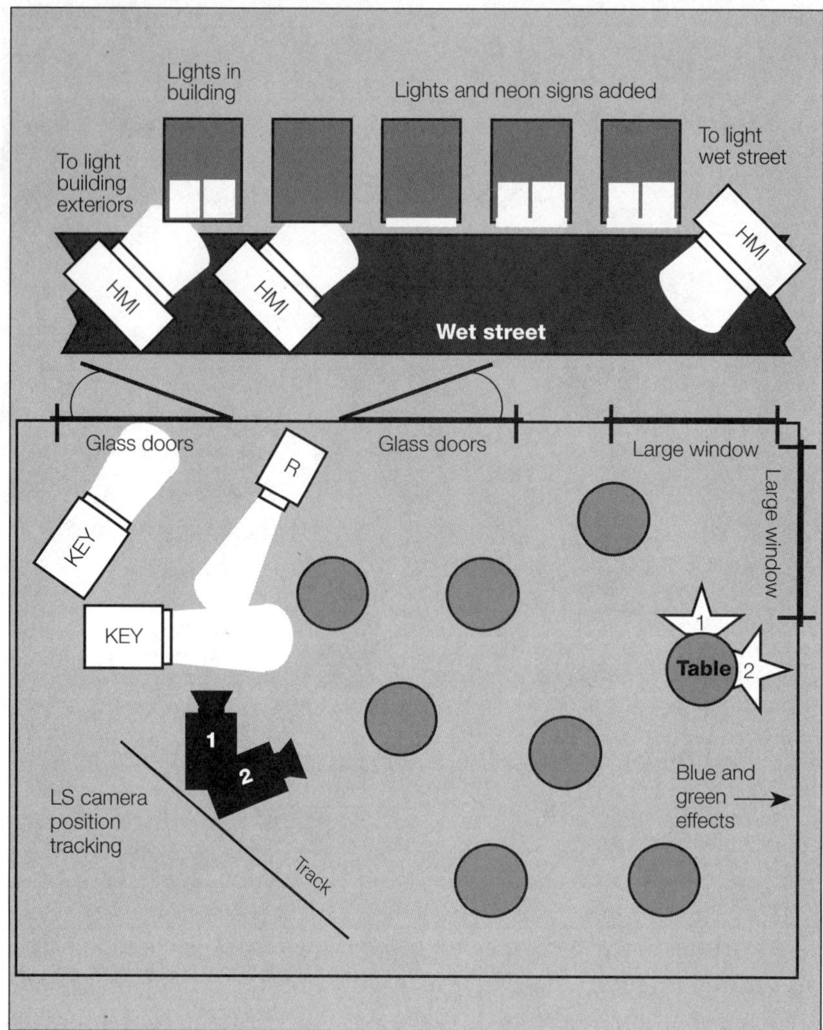

Lighting the street was in order. Cars could be hired to drive by, and colored neons and fake street lighting could be ordered. A basic illumination was applied to bring the buildings across the street to around T 2. Two banks of daylight-balanced 12K HMIs were adequate for this purpose. Neons were added to the buildings, and a large number of lights were arranged inside some of the windows. These were balanced by eye (see Figure 12.3).

Once the street was at a basic T 2 level with neons and other luminous objects around T 5.6, the interior lighting setup was tackled. Basically, each table had an artificial lamp shaped like a candle and a white tablecloth. Small spots were used to fake the candle effect and the candle bulbs were changed to a lower intensity so that they wouldn't burn out. Soft, fill light was added to the actors and the ratio set at 4:1 (see Figure 12.4). The back wall of the cafe was lit with colored lighting, mostly greens and blues. A piano bar was installed in the background for visual variety. Strings of lights were added to various interior walls for effect. Finally, after two days, the night lighting setup was ready for shooting.

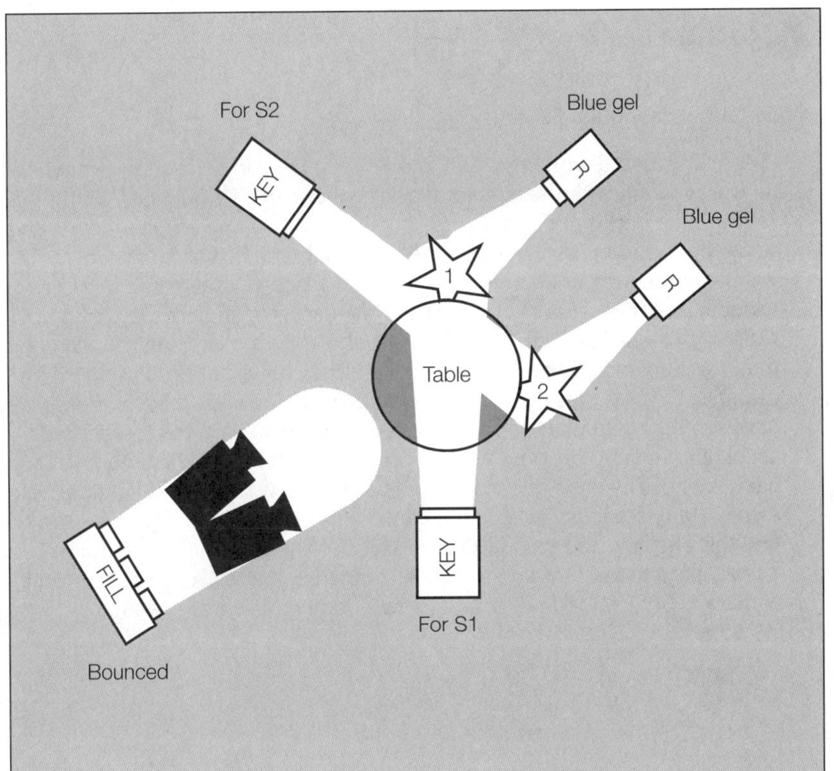

Figure 12.4 Detail of Table Lighting Setup for Night Interior
This schematic indicates the lighting setup for two-shots and closeups for the night interior described in the text.

The overall feel was more dramatic than the day interior. The tracking shot from exterior to interior was particularly effective. Water was added to the street so that lights reflecting off it created a wet-pavement, "big city" look. A slight rain effect was needed to justify the wet pavement. The director liked the effect so much that she decided to make the rain an integral part of the scene. Backlight was added so that the rain would be visible.

Instead of the roving fill, a series of spotlights were used to illuminate the actors as they entered and went to the table. Inside the cafe, quartz lights were bounced off foam core to provide fill light for dark areas of the frame. Altogether about 20 lights were used outdoors and about 40 indoors, mostly because of the large size of the cafe. The tungsten-balanced stock (EI 500) was used, with the bluish night exterior deemed appropriate.

SUMMARY

The art of lighting consists of working with the location, adding lights step by step, then reacting to the setup. Our example is intended to provide a question/answer framework for the beginning cinematographer, a position from which to start lighting. Faced with the assignment presented in this chapter, different cinematographers would arrive at different solutions; this is why cinematography is so creative.

NOTE

1. Gaffer Richmond Aguilar says:

> When I started working with Laslo Kovacs, I would be roughing-in when he was working with the director blocking the scene. I would be lighting the set from the background, or maybe outside, working toward the foreground, to the principals in front of the camera. By that time he will know where they will be on their marks and whether he will want to key the scene from the window or not. . . . I start lighting from the background because we do not really know what the actors will do in front. When the director is working on that, I will go and do the windows outside and we will talk and establish, for example, that perhaps the sun comes through the window back there, so we have something to work from. The other school is to light the foreground action and to cut it off from where you don't want it, and then work your background. The basic question is: where the hell will you start lighting the scene? Every scene has a key to it, something that will work for you. . . . You find this one key, and if you like it you work from there. Many times it is awfully hard to get that one thing. (As quoted in Kris Malkiewicz, assisted by Barbara J. Gryboski, *Film Lighting* [New York: Prentice Hall, 1986], pp. 94–95.)

IV

ELECTRONIC CINEMATOGRAPHY

Electronic cinematography combines the most sophisticated techniques of film production with state-of-the-art video equipment. The object is to give video production the same potential for creativity and aesthetic refinement that exists in film and to take full advantage of the creative possibilities of the electronic medium that do not exist in film.

—Harry Mathias and Richard Patterson
Electronic Cinematography: Achieving Photographic Control over the Video Image

ELECTRONIC CINEMATOGRAPHY: VIDEO THE FILM WAY

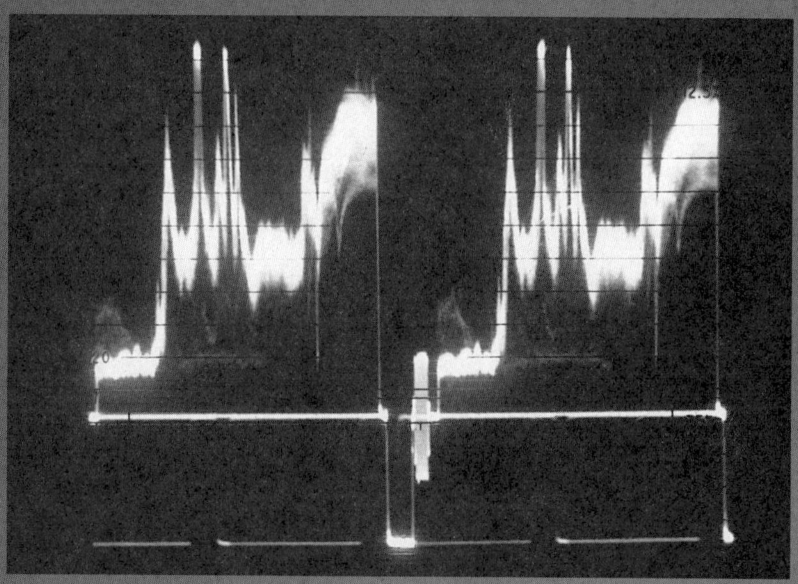

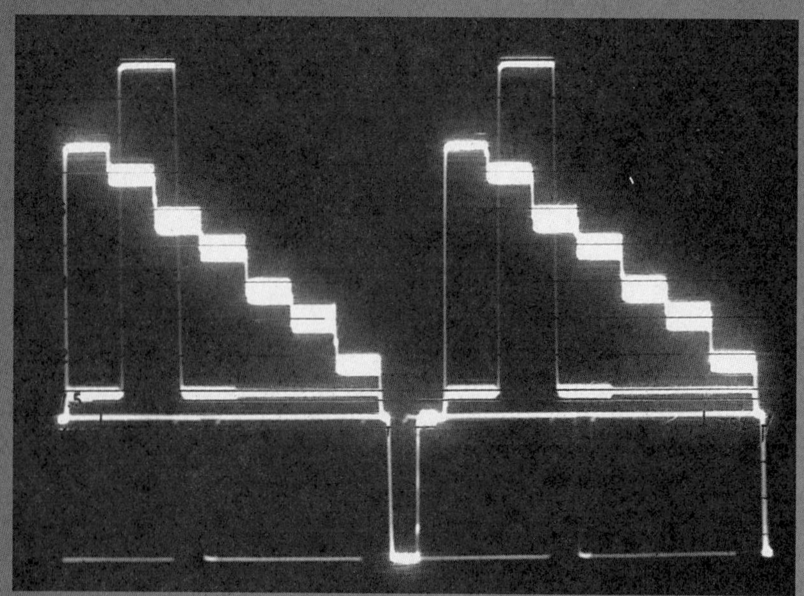

"waveform displays"

13

Both the zone system and film exposure theory can be applied to video although there are substantial differences between the two media. The application of film techniques and attitudes to video production introduces a new concept, "electronic cinematography."

THE WIDESCALE use of film negatives, with Rank Cintel **flying spot scanner** transfer to 1" video master and release on video, has forced cinematographers to understand video technology and processes. Confronted with a finished product on a television monitor instead of a screen, many a cinematographer has concluded video is inherently inferior as an imaging technology. Yet video's relentless thrust must be analyzed and experimented with, not just rejected, since for the moment taking advantage of the merits of both technologies is the order of the day. Much research and development has gone into video technology including digital imaging, high definition, and the development of video cameras with increased light sensitivity.

Film manufacturers have responded to the video challenge by developing faster emulsions with improved image quality. The availability of stocks with exposure indices of 500 has led to the development of lighting styles and techniques virtually impossible with current video technology. Likewise, improvements in emulsion grain characteristics have forced the video industry to pursue newer technological breakthroughs such as **high definition television (HDTV)** in an attempt to compete with the film image. A look at changes in film emulsions over the past 20 years reveals that from the point of view of lighting, current video is similar to film stocks of the 1970s.

Current 16mm and 35mm stocks are superior to their 1970s equivalents. For example, with 16mm the standard stock of the 1970s was Ektachrome Commercial (ECO), a low-contrast color reversal designed for printing, not for projecting as with most other reversals. ECO 7255 had an exposure index (EI) of 25 tungsten/16 daylight. This was later improved with the introduction of ECO 7252, which had an exposure index of 50 tungsten/32 daylight. Faster stocks were available, such as Ektachrome EF 7242, 125 tungsten/80 daylight, but these were difficult to print because they had projection contrast gammas. Fast color reversals were mostly used for television news and sports where the original could be projected.

Neither ECO nor the faster color reversal stocks led to quality screen or television images since the prints generated were overly contrasty and subject to aberrant flesh-tone renditions. Though quality lighting and interesting images were possible, particularly in experimental areas, most of the time the color reversal technology inhibited creative lighting because of its excessive contrast. Image looks were severely restricted because only soft frontal light with low facial and subject/background ratios yielded acceptable facetones and overall image contrast. There was a tendency for all color reversal films to look alike.

Color negatives, 7254 and 7247, were available in 16mm but were seldom used in the United States because most labs outside of Los Angeles and New York were not set up to process and print 16mm negatives. Currently, there are 13 16mm color negatives available from Kodak, Fuji, and Agfa with speeds up to EI 500 (see Table 7.1). Color negatives are superior to reversals because they have longer straight lines and greater overall useful ranges. The key point for our purposes is that current video technology offers the cinematographer straight line lengths similar to color reversals.

FILM QUALITY VERSUS VIDEO QUALITY

Producers of quality television programming, TV series, TV commercials, and music videos are likely to shoot on film negative, transfer to video, and edit off-line video. These producers shoot on film because they desire a high-quality, feature look—the fabled "film look." Part of the film look comes from greater concern for production values than in television production—in particular, by allowing time for lighting and, more important, by using film-style, single-camera shooting procedures. The lighting resulting from single-camera production is greatly improved over multicamera techniques, which invariably involve lighting compromise.

Other factors in making the film look the quality standard are film's superior technical properties such as resolution and longer straight lines, which can translate a greater subject luminance range than current video cameras. The "video look" has thus resulted from a number of causes, both economic and technological, all of which foreground video's inability to translate visual values as successfully as film.[1]

Some argue it's possible to improve the general look of video by applying film exposure and lighting techniques to video images. This is the essence of electronic cinematography—the application of film values and practices to the video image, pioneered by Harry Mathias and Richard Patterson in their book, *Electronic Cinematography: Achieving Photographic Control over the Video Image*. This book is the most important contribution to exposure theory since J. F. Dunn's work in the 1950s and Ansel Adams's formulation of the zone system back in the 1940s. Mathias and Patterson argue that the contemporary cinematographer working in video should apply film's long-established exposure and lighting techniques exactly as would be done were video a new film emulsion.

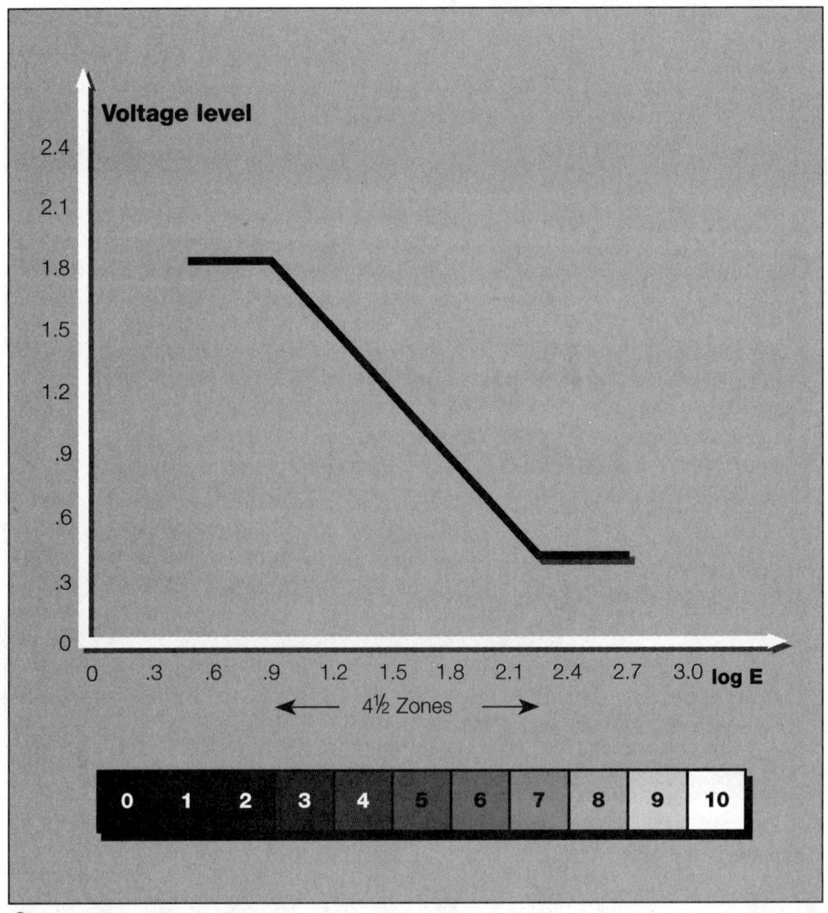

a

Figure 13.1 Comparing Film and Video Imaging Systems
(a) Transfer characteristic curve for a typical video signal graphed as a positive image. Note the sharp cutoff on the toe and shoulder areas. For a transfer characteristic, the log E is plotted against the log of the voltage level of the signal. This is very similar to the film characteristic curve. (b) Transfer characteristic curve for a video camera graphed as a negative for comparison with film negatives. Video cameras have log E ranges greater than the 25:1 range of the broadcast signal, but these are clipped back when broadcast. (c) Typical color-reversal film curve provided for comparison purposes.

DIFFERENCES BETWEEN FILM AND VIDEO

For our purposes, there are two key differences between film and video systems:

- Film negatives have straight lines of about 6 zones and useful ranges of from 8 to 10 zones, 512:1 as a rough average, whereas the broadcast video signal offers only a 4½ zone range, about 25:1. Even though pickup tubes can handle 40:1 and CCD cameras up to 50 or 60:1, the overall range is clipped back to 25:1 when broadcast. This means video as televised offers the rendition possibilities of the old 16mm color reversal stocks (see Figure 13.1).
- Film curves exhibit sloping toes and shoulders. That means they gradually approach and depart from nominal straight-line proportional responses, whereas the transfer characteristics for most video cameras exhibit sharp cutoffs of values. Video lacks the curved toes and shoulders that film has.

Cameras with **gamma compression circuitry**, such as the Panasonic AJ-D310, Ikegami HK-343 S, or Panavision's "Panacam," can

Figure 13.1 (continued)

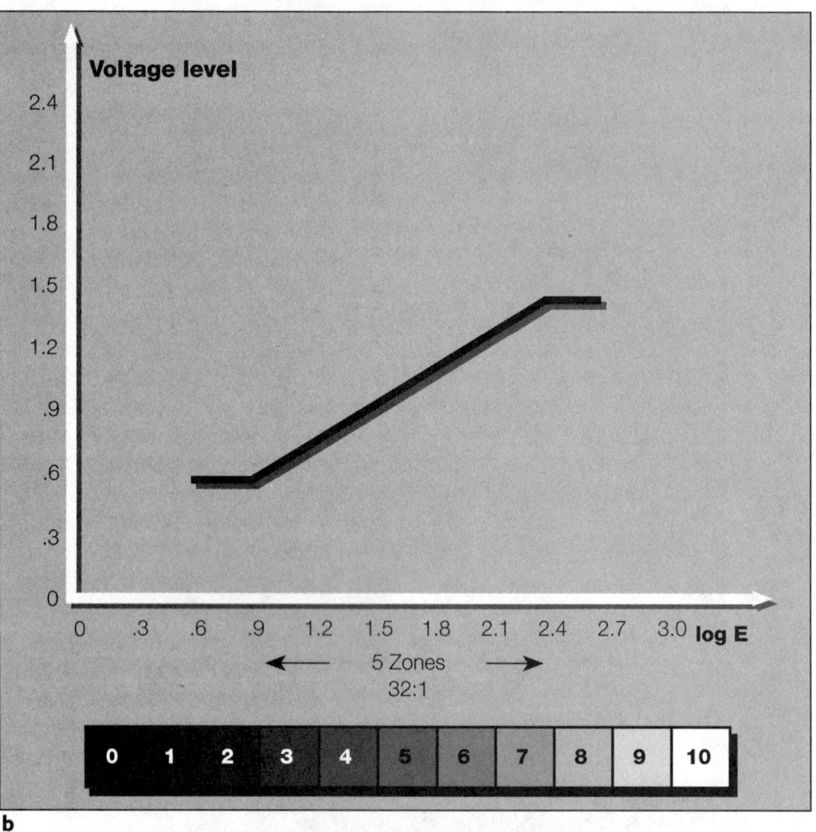

b

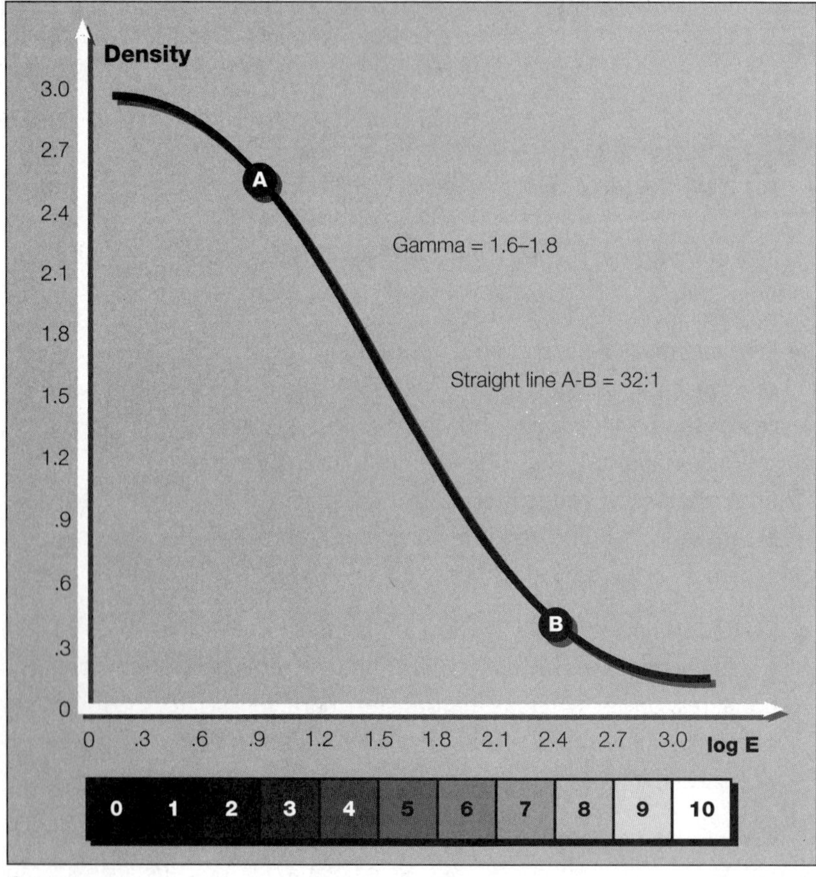

c

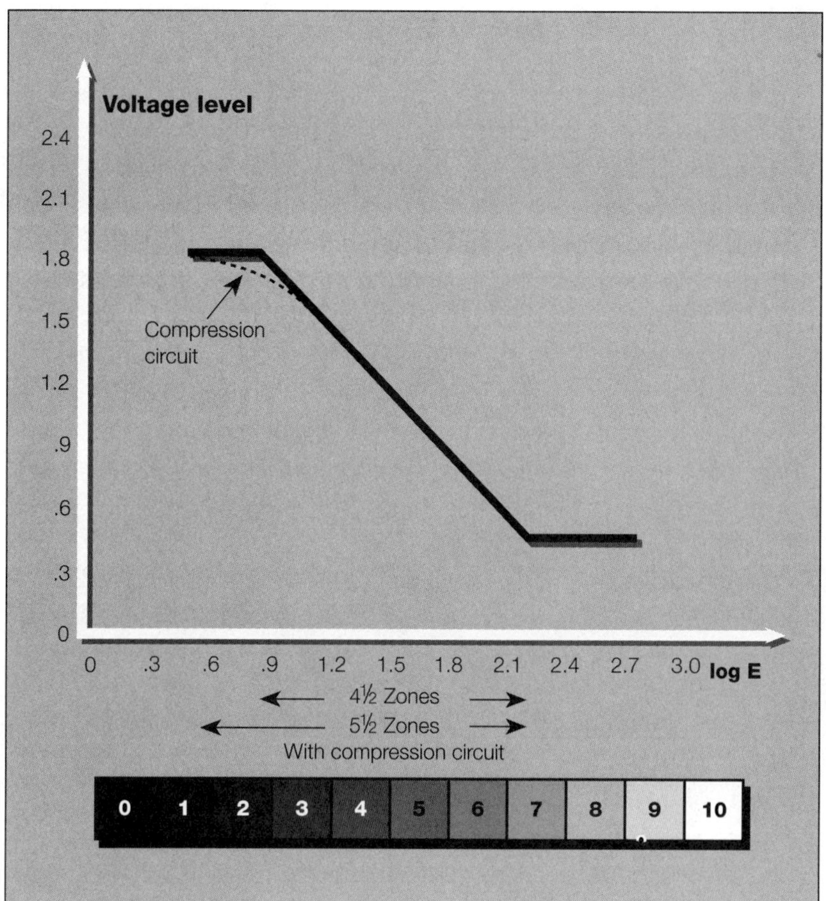

Figure 13.2 Gamma Compression Circuits *To obtain a film look, it's necessary to alter standard video curves by electronically creating a shoulder. This takes away some of the sharp changes present in the video look at the highlight end. These shoulders are created by gamma compression circuits and function much like a limiter on a Nagra tape recorder.*

This graph shows a transfer characteristic curve for a video system using a camera with a hypothetical gamma compression circuit. The gamma compression circuit expands the straight line response about a zone to 5½ zones. Even though that signal is compressed on broadcast to 25:1, the extra information still provides luminance value differentiations greater than from the standard camera.

extend the log E reproduction range by 1 to 5½ zones. They do this by compressing, though still differentiating, two upper zones into one. This flattening of values approximates a film stock's shoulder and gives some of that film look to the video signal (see Figure 13.2).

The film straight line provides an immense advantage in translating visual values. According to Mathias and Patterson, a film negative can represent over 100 shades of gray whereas a video camera is limited to about 72.[2] The film negative thus offers a greater amount of visual information to the video system when compared to a video camera. This information is represented by a range of densities sufficiently low in contrast so as to be preserved even when transferred to video and broadcast.

Nevertheless, a cinematographer, knowing video's useful range is from 4½ to 5½ zones depending on whether the camera has a compression circuit, should be able to light in such a way as to create images of sufficient quality. The key thing to control is overall subject luminance range, the ratio of maximum significant brightness to significant shadow value. With a video system, subject luminance range can be measured precisely and easily with a waveform monitor.

WAVEFORM MONITORS

The waveform monitor is an electronic means for measuring the video signal. In essence, it provides an accurate series of spot meter readings for the entire video signal. Where there is a highlight value, the waveform monitor gives a high reading, vice versa for a low value. Study carefully the display of black and whites in the examples in Figure 13.3.

The scaling on waveform monitors is in **IRE units** (Institute of Radio Engineers) and, except for 7.5 IRE units, is incremented in units of 10. The zero part of the scale is used to adjust the monitor when setting up. This is explained in Appendix I, "Setting Up a Video Monitor and a Waveform Monitor." Standardized video signals run from black values of 7.5 IRE to white values at 100 IRE units (see Figure 13.4). Luminance values falling lower or higher than these figures are clipped when broadcast.[3]

The broadcast video signal then can range from 7.5 to 100 IRE units. Each 20 units on the scale is equivalent to 1 T-stop, 1 zone, assuming the gray gamma is at the standard .45 setting. This results in the following zone-placement possibilities:

100–80	*= 1 zone*	
80–60	*= 1 zone*	
60–40	*= 1 zone*	**Total: 4.6 zones = 25:1***
40–20	*= 1 zone*	
20–7.5	*= .6 zone*	

Figure 13.4 provides additional examples of waveform monitor displays. Some of these displays are from photographs in this book. The reader may thus compare the image with its corresponding waveform monitor display.

CHARACTERISTIC CURVES AND GAMMA IN VIDEO

Overall gamma for video is defined as the sum of the individual gammas in the imaging chain. Most variables are at a nominal gamma of 1.0, but a receiver picture tube is around 2.2, and thus standard camera gamma is .45 to ensure an overall of 1.0. One key difference between film and video is that video systems utilize a three-gamma concept whereby it is possible to electronically manipulate white, gray, and black gammas independently. In fact, gamma in video refers to the middle gamma, the gray gamma value. When we say the gamma is at .45, this is the one we mean.

* With a gamma compression circuit in the camera, this is effectively extended to 5 1/2 zones, 50:1, through the compression of luminances from 80–120 IRE into 80–100 IRE on the scale. These subject luminances, though differentiated, are still broadcast with a 25:1 range. It is also possible with some video cameras to gain a zone by recording signals up to 120 IRE and then compressing in postproduction.

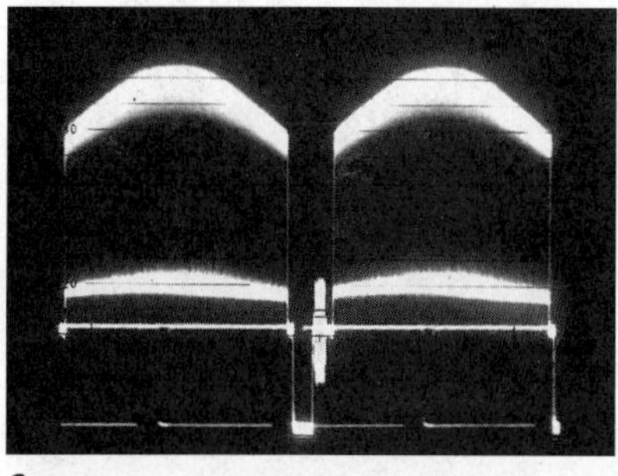

a

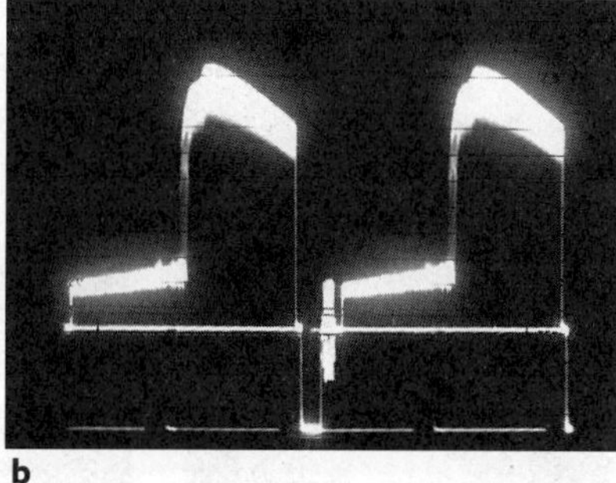

b

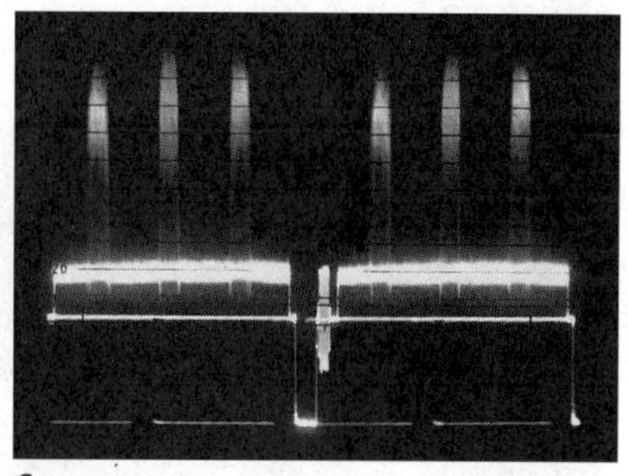

c

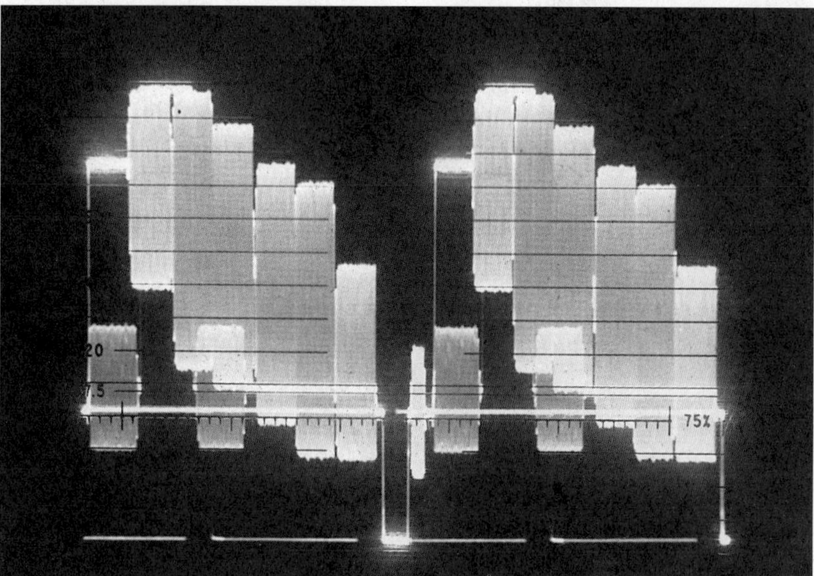

d

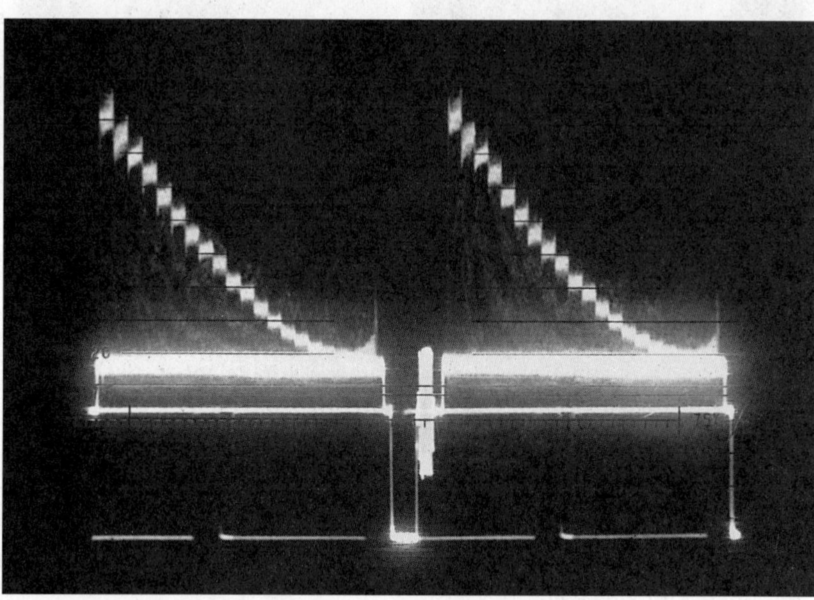

e

Figure 13.3 Waveform Monitor Displays *(a) Waveform display for half-black/half-white frame—created by placing a black card in the bottom half of frame and a white card in the top half of frame. (b) Same as (a) but with the black card left half of frame and the white card right half of frame. (c) Black cloth with light gray, rectangular-shaped decorative patterns. (d) Waveform display for standard color bars. (e) Waveform display for multistep gray scale.*

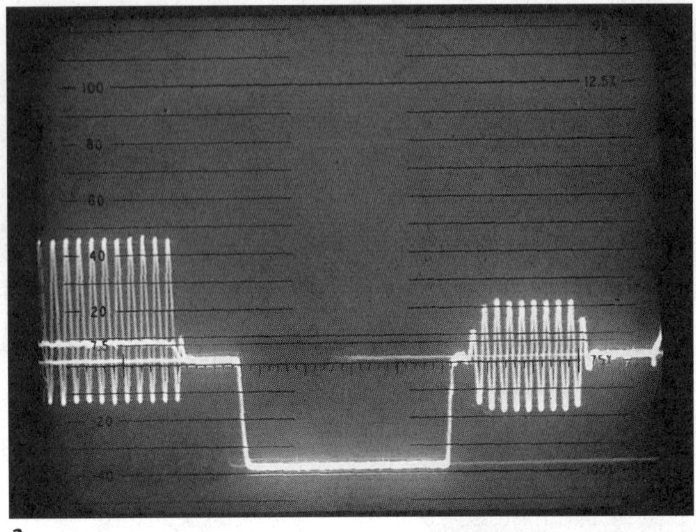

a

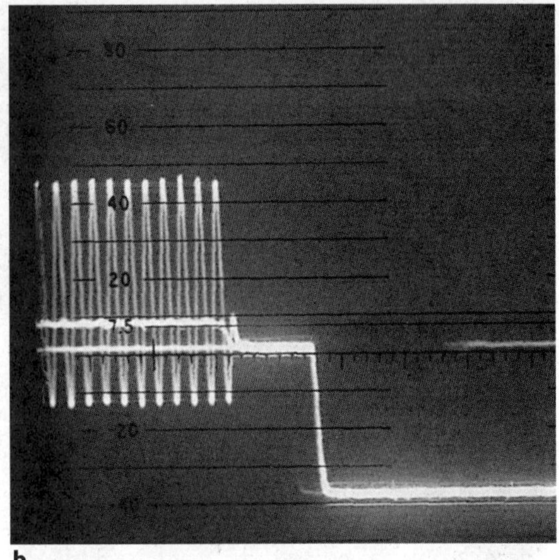

b

Figure 13.4 Waveform Monitor Scaling and Displays of Photographs in Book
(a) Waveform display. The waveform monitor displays technical information concerning sync, color, and blanking. We are concerned only with the video portions of the display. (b) Closeup detail of (a) showing IRE scaling on waveform monitor. (c) Waveform display for high-key photograph as in Figure 2.14a. (d) Waveform display for photograph opening Chapter 1. (e) Waveform display for dark, low-key photograph as in Figure 7.10a. (f) Waveform display for photograph opening Chapter 3.

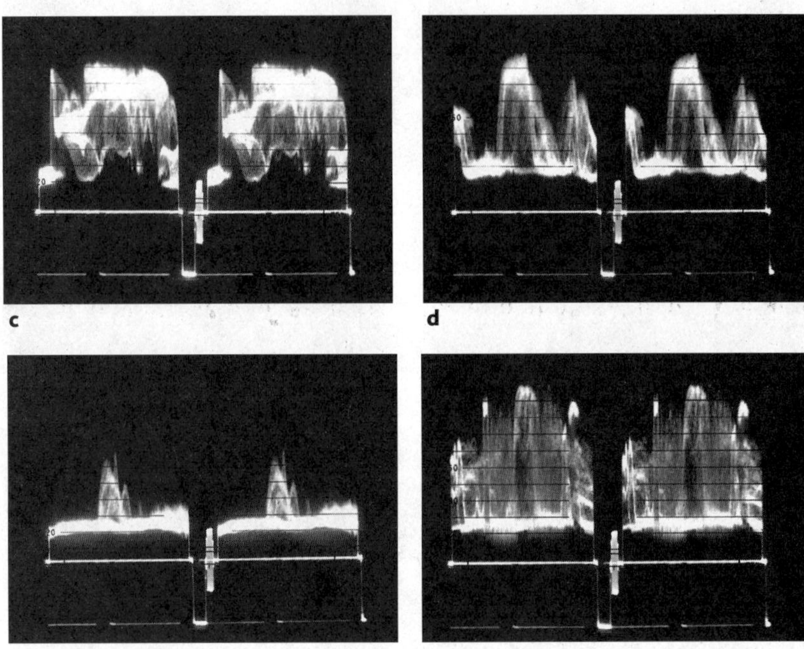

c d e f

Alteration of **black value gamma** is termed adjusting **pedestal** or black level.[4] Adjusting black level gamma is equivalent to flashing film; that is, the IRE value for blacks is raised, effectively reducing the original subject contrast. Besides high-end cameras such as Panacam and Betacam SP camcorders, industrial-quality cameras, like the Sony DXC-327, allow for pedestal/black value adjustment electronically. Some of these cameras also provide overall sensitivity adjustments that can affect final image look (see Figure 13.5).

Alteration of **white value gamma** is called adjusting white level or gamma compression. White value or highlight gamma is adjusted automatically by circuits built into the camera—for example, the gamma compression circuits in a Panacam—but where those circuits start to take effect is adjustable (see Figure 13.2). Utilizing the gain circuitry to boost

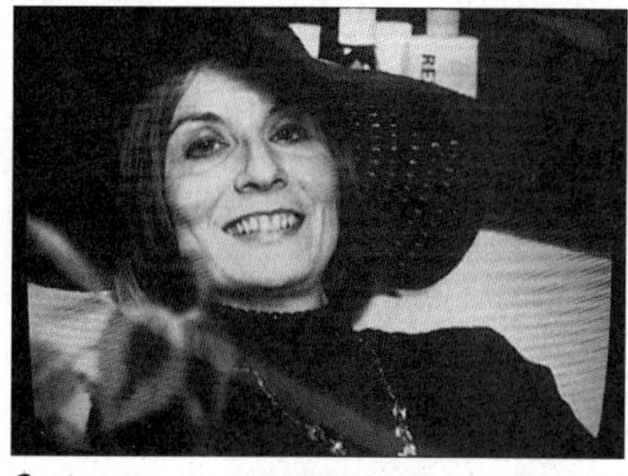
a

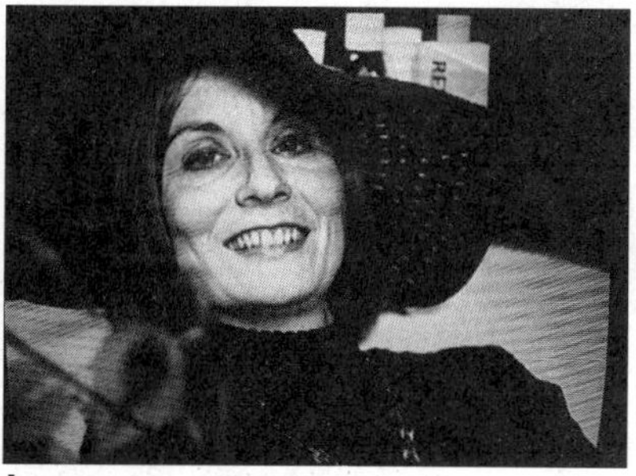
b

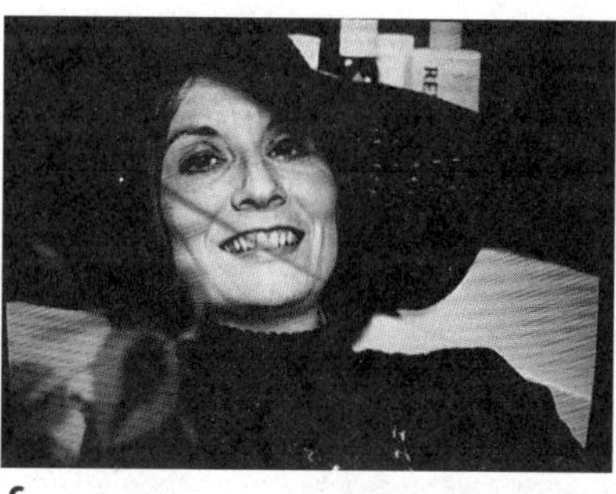
c

Figure 13.5 Pedestal (Black Gamma) Effects *The three photographs were taken off a video monitor while the black gamma was adjusted: (a) minimum black gamma setting—note the flashing effect derived from lightening the blacks electronically; (b) standard black gamma midsetting; (c) darkest possible setting for black gamma.*

exposure index also affects white value gamma by giving it a higher value. This results in increased contrast in highlight areas. This is accompanied by an increase in video signal noise and is generally not a good way to vary white value gamma.

Adjusting the **gray gamma** does not affect black and white extremes, but it does affect how lower and upper zones are represented. Raising gray gamma from the standard .45 compresses black values slightly and provides more room for highlight values. Lowering gray gamma has the opposite effect (see Figure 13.6).

ZONE THEORY APPLIED TO VIDEO

The fundamental assumption of exposure is that an 18% reflectance, the average value of reflectances commonly present, placed at a mid-density point on the negative yields prints of acceptable quality with good facetones, consistent middle grays, and controlled highlights. Let us elaborate this for video, taking as an example the simplest possible lighting scheme: full frontal lighting where no shadow range is created. In this situation, a normal zone 5 exposure places an 18% reflectance at zone 5, a 36% at zone 6, a 72% at zone 7, and, were there such a thing, a 144% reflectance at zone 8. A maximum reflectance of 96% would fall at about zone 7 1/2.

From 18% to 96% represents 2 1/2 zones of change (5 to 6, 6 to 7, 7 to 7 1/2). With video, a 96% white reflectance, zone 7 1/2 value, should be very near 100 IRE units on the waveform monitor to avoid the clipping effect. This placement would retain separation between important highlight values. A zone 5 value (18%) would then fall around 50 IRE (see Figure 13.7). The simplest way to accomplish this placement would be to use a waveform monitor to set an 18% gray card to the desired setting. Note that placing zone 5 at 50 IRE units means zone 6 will be at 70 IRE and zone 7 at 90 IRE. Likewise, zone 4 will fall at 30 IRE and zone 3 at 10 IRE, giving us our total range of about 4 1/2 zones.[5]

The video exposure technique proposed here parallels film exposure; however, we're using a waveform monitor in place of a spot meter. We have assumed the simplest possible lighting scheme. Any increase in subject luminance range will create contrast reproduction problems for the video system.

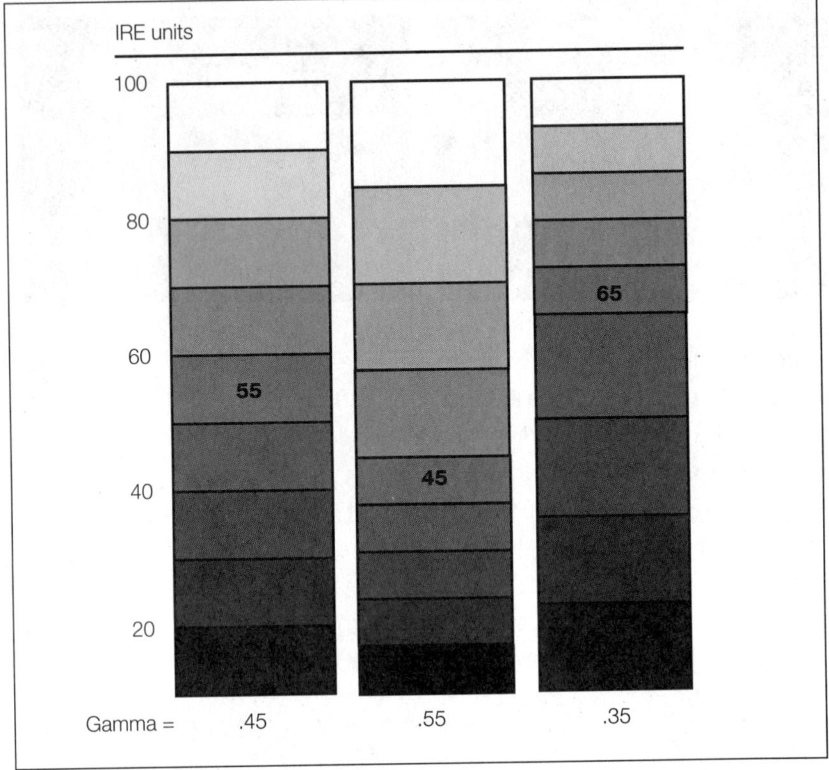

Figure 13.6 Effects Obtained by Adjusting Gray Gamma *Standard gray gamma (.45) evenly spaces gray values. The midgray is at 55 IRE units. Raising the gray gamma to .55 lowers the placement of the midgray to about 45 IRE units. This effectively stretches the higher values as illustrated in the middle column. Lowering the gray gamma to .35 raises the midgray to 65 IRE units and stretches the black values as shown in the right column.*

Exposing video would be simpler if we could work out an "exposure index" for the video system and use the incident meter to peg the 18% midgray. If desired, we could still use the waveform monitor to check luminance range placement on the video curve.

HOW TO CALCULATE AN EXPOSURE INDEX EQUIVALENT FOR A VIDEO SYSTEM

This is so simple, it's hard to believe that video has relied on waveform monitors and a reflected technique to determine exposure for so long. Basically what you do is set up the video camera for tungsten balance and hook it to a waveform monitor. Light a gray card or a Kodak gray scale, and put the gray value or middle chip on the Kodak scale at 50 IRE units. This is done by adjusting the T-stop on the video camera until the chip is at 50 units. This will give the zone 5 pegging illustrated in Figure 13.7.

Next take your incident meter, put it in the light falling on the gray card, point it at the camera, and take a reading. Normally for film the meter is set for a particular exposure index, a reading is taken, and we arrive at a T-stop. Here, we know the T-stop and meter reading and have to work backward to determine the exposure index. The type of meter determines how you do this. On the Sekonic, you line up the meter reading on the Hi or Lo scale mark and adjust the ASA/ISO ring

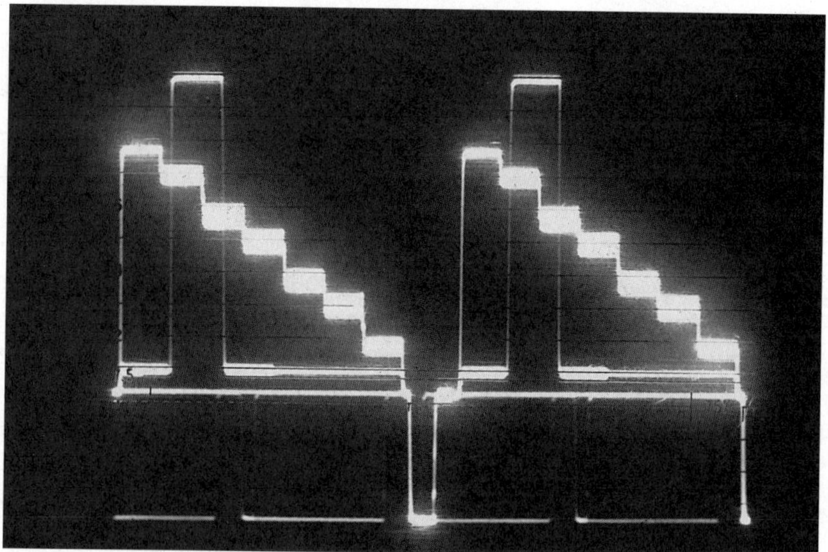

Figure 13.7 Placement of Midgray Chip at 50 IRE Units
This display reveals how the standard IRE gray scale reproduces when the midgray chip is placed at 50 IRE units. This is a lower placement than normal (midgray chip at 55 IRE units) for the reasons specified in the text. Note the white value is placed at 100 IRE units and the black value at 7.5 IRE units.

IRE UNITS

IRE	Zone
100	
	zone 7 (90 IRE)
80	
	zone 6 (70 IRE)
60	
	zone 5 (50 IRE)
40	
	zone 4 (30 IRE)
20	
	zone 3 (10 IRE)
7.5	

until the T-stop on the video camera is lined up across from the 1/60th shutter speed.[6] The exposure index thus indicated is the speed setting for that video camera. Thereafter, readings may be taken in the standard film way with an incident meter.

A quick test would be to increase or decrease the light on the gray card, take a reading, and set the indicated T-stop on the video camera. If all goes well, the chip is once again at 50 on the waveform monitor. We can now expose with this video system as we would with film, that is, set our lighting with the incident meter and "expose" the video image by setting the T-stop on the lens as indicated by a standard incident reading.

The typical video camera will have an EI of around 100 though newer, high-end cameras will rate higher. If we need more speed we can increase the gain setting on the video camera. This can yield video speeds of 400 or better. Increasing gain is equivalent to pushing film emulsions and has similar drawbacks and image deterioration. Reflected metering techniques will be used as in film, except that with video you can use the waveform monitor to expose luminous objects more precisely.

FILM ATTITUDES IN VIDEO PRODUCTION

Though we desire consistent facetone densities in film and video, those densities are placed within a wide variety of background contexts. Control and variation of the ratio between face and background is an essential facet of the cinematographer's artistry and one of the central techniques in creating mood with lighting. The cinematographer essentially pegs his or her exposure and then lights around that initial zone placement to configure the images, a painting with light.

Approaching video with these attitudes, the cinematographer would think nothing of pegging Caucasian facetones to zone 6 and having that represent the brightest value in the subject. But this "film" attitude would immediately collide with standard television engineering procedures that routinely place the brightest value in the scene at 100 IRE units without regard to the nature of the desired lighting style or even as to what that brightest value actually is.

In this case, a placement at 100 IRE would destroy the mood of the face and image by brightening two stops overall—equivalent to pegging midgray at zone 7 by intentionally overexposing two stops. We would never accept this from a film lab nor should we from a video engineer.

Of course, cinematographers long ago learned to "trick" the video system by incorporating **reference whites** into dark-toned, low-contrast film shots destined for television. In the preceding example, a shaft of light on an off-white object would be incorporated into the composition for no other reason than to provide something other than the face to put at the 100 IRE level. In like manner, a **reference black** can be included to protect light-toned, low-contrast images. High-contrast images will peak at both ends in any event and do not require such references.

Mathias and Patterson say the director of photography should retain all of film's visual repertoire of ideas and techniques when approaching video. They cry out for experimentation and exploration of the manifold possibilities inherent in the electronic image. From this point of view, the zone 5 placement described in the previous section should be regarded only as a starting point. Experimentation with the zone 5 placement is equivalent to determining the best exposure index rating for a film stock. This is standard practice in feature work where EI is varied to create particular effects or looks. For example, color negatives are sometimes rated at 640 rather than 320, not because of the gain in speed but because of the resulting differences in look—contrast, color saturation, and overall feel. For like reason, it is not uncommon to shoot high-speed negatives outdoors in bright sunshine even though you need neutral density filters to control exposure. The texture and look of your images are all-important.

Obviously, tests are needed to determine standards and individual value preferences. It could be that for a particular purpose facetones render better at 40 or 45 IRE units. Mathias and Patterson point this out with reference to *Raiders of the Lost Ark*, which they estimate has facetone placements around 30 IREs in its video release.[7] Video offers sophisticated signal-processing possibilities in postproduction, so your careful work can be undone if you are not alert.

Be aware, though, of the standard video rule: Caucasian facetones should be between 60 and 80, around 70 IRE units. Darker brown and black facetones will fall on zones 5 and 4, at 50 and 30 IRE units respectively. Also remember that engineers are apt to ignore facetone consistency altogether and place any maximum brightness at 100 IRE and darks at 7.5, letting facetones vary from lighting setup to lighting setup.[8]

With these considerations in mind, use of the zone system in video is simple. As with film, it allows for previsualization of the image, though previsualization is easier in video than in film. For one thing, a waveform monitor aids in previsualization. For another, a TV monitor can be hooked up for direct viewing of the image.

Mathias and Patterson argue against the use of on-set monitors.[9] Their arguments are persuasive, yet to leave out the eye seems intuitively disadvantageous, particularly where we are asked to substitute the technical artificiality of a waveform monitor. This is a complicated issue that takes us beyond exposure into lighting matters. This issue will be discussed in the next chapter.

SUMMARY

In this chapter we have examined several basic differences between film and video in terms of exposure and zone theory. In general we have seen that the video image can be approached from a film point of view and that the exposure concepts we developed in Part II can be applied to video. We can thus compare a video system's straight line and overall useful range with those of a film stock.

We have looked at the important role the waveform monitor plays in video and have shown how to determine an exposure index (EI) equivalent for a video system. With these technical basics understood, we can now turn to lighting and image looks for video–electronic cinematography.

NOTES

1. The 35mm film image remains our standard for quality because 35mm offers a longer straight line with finer resolution than do the rival production media. On the other hand, video postproduction offers powerful advantages—the central one being computerized controls. Computerized video systems utilizing time code, coupled with switchers, digital video, and other black-box special effects, have challenged film as far as postproduction goes. Though beyond the scope of this text, it is important to recognize video's superiority in this area when compared to film editing and lab procedures.

   The advantages of both film and video editing procedures may possibly be derived through use of the relatively new random-access video-disk editing systems, such as the CMX 6000, which are essentially computerized memory systems using neither videotape nor film technologies. These random-access systems are capable of generating edit decision lists (EDLs) for video on-line sessions or key number lists for neg cutting and subsequent film answer prints. These systems, along with digital audio workstations for posting audio tracks, will revolutionize film and video postproduction procedures because they offer all the aesthetic advantages of film with the technological advantages of digital storage and computerized controls. Of course, cost is a determining factor, so control-track video systems and film flatbeds probably will be around a while.

2. Harry Mathias and Richard Patterson, *Electronic Cinematography: Achieving Photographic Control over the Video Image* (Belmont, Calif.: Wadsworth, 1985), p. 84.

3. IRE units have no particular relationship with percentage reflectance. For example, an 18% reflectance is not equivalent to 18 IRE units.

   Clipping is done to ensure noninterference with the sound track on the highlight end and noninterference with syncing information on the black value end. Clipping is a feature of the broadcast system and may be avoided with cable transmission and other video signal modes.

4. See Mathias and Patterson, op. cit., pp. 104–5.

5. Video cameras are generally set up using the EIA (Electronics Industries Association) nine-step gray scale. The middle chip, a 13.4% reflectance, is rendered close to 55 IRE units. The next step up in the EIA scale is a 19.5% reflectance. At a gamma of .45, this reproduces at 68 IRE units. This makes 18% equivalent to 65 IRE units. Zone 6 (36%) is at 85 IRE units, and zone 7 would fall at 105 IRE units. This means we lose most zone 7 renditions because of clipping.

EIA Chip Chart (reflectances)	**IRE Units (approximate)**
60.0%	100
41.3%	90
28.4%	78
19.5%	68
13.4%	55
9.2%	45
6.3%	35
4.4%	25
3.0%	20

   The standard EIA placement sacrifices highlight values to less important shadow values. By placing the cross-over chip (13.4%) at 55 IRE units, we risk losing important highlight value differences. On a scale where only $4^1/_2$ zones are available to work with, it makes more sense, as a practical matter, to peg zone 5 to a lower value (50 IRE). This placement results in extra space for highlights at the expense of shadow values by lowering the midgray placement three-quarters of a zone. A 96% reflectance now falls at 100 IRE units. This placement is similar to changing the gamma to .55, which also results in a "stretching" of the curve for white values (see Mathias and Patterson, p. 98). A placement of 18% at 50 IRE units does not modify gamma, though; thus it would still be possible to increase the gray gamma to .55 for even more differentiation of highlight values (See Figure 13.6). Gamma compression would expand highlight detail possibilities even further. With gamma compression, a higher placement of zone 5 would be much less disadvantageous.

   If this sounds too pedantic, remember that video's handling of subject luminance range is one of its disadvantages when compared to film. Since our theory postulates less importance for shadow values and zones 1–3, gains in the highlight area are of major importance.

6. It doesn't matter which shutter speed you use as long as you use that same setting when shooting with the video camera later. However, 1/60th (the nominal time for one field in NTSC) is close to film camera shutter speeds

and thus allows for direct comparison of EIs between film and video. The 1/60th shutter speed will also be useful with cameras having electronic shutters calibrated in 1/60th increments.

7. Mathias and Patterson, op. cit., pp. 11–12, 104.

8. Mathias and Patterson, op. cit., pp. 100–104.

9. Mathias and Patterson, op. cit., pp. 180–82.

LIGHTING TECHNIQUES FOR ELECTRONIC CINEMATOGRAPHY

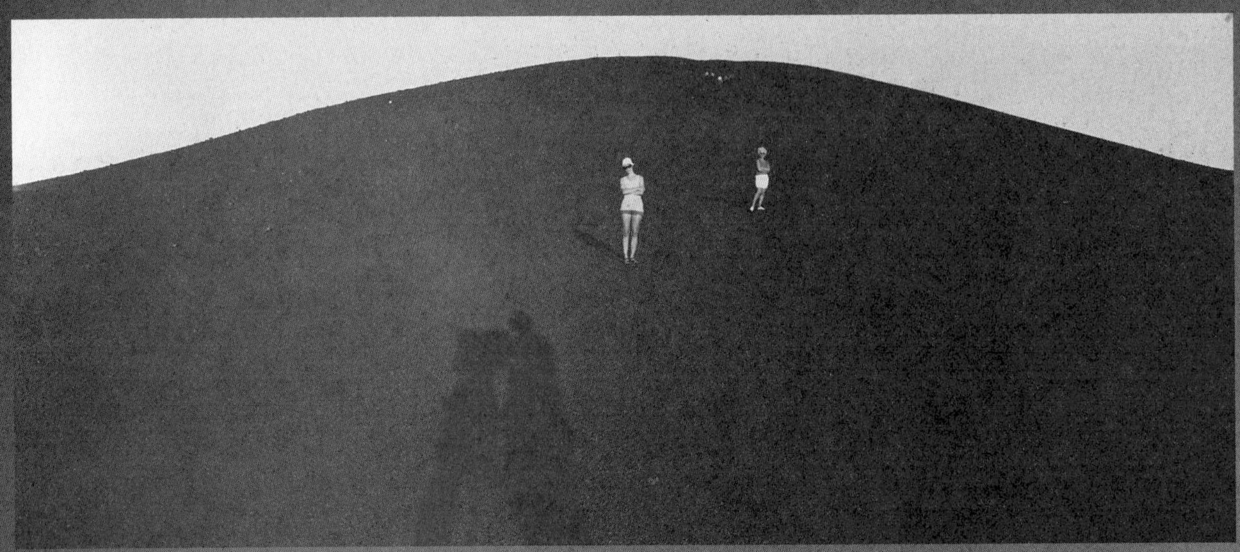

Photo by Gerald Lang

"alternative looks"

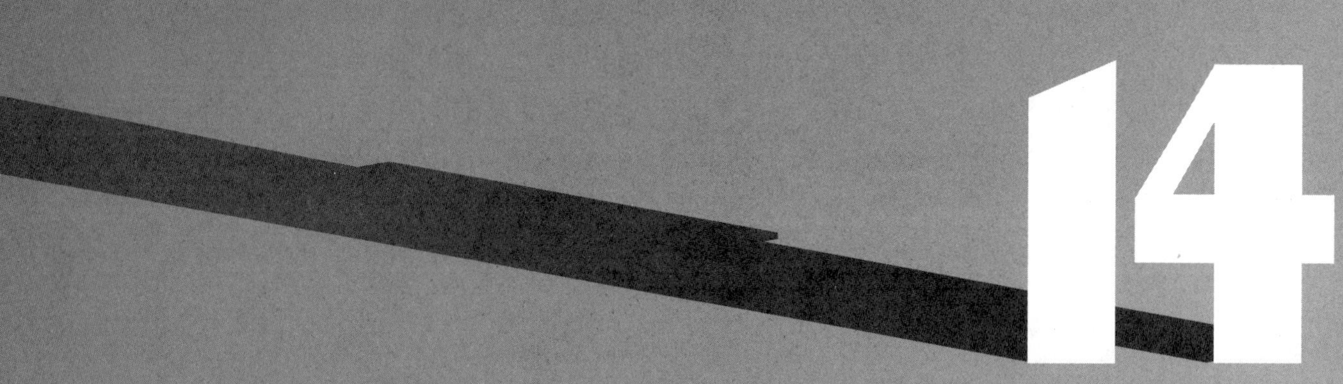

Film lighting practices can be used to create more varied and interesting images on video, moving it away from television conventions. There are alternative looks available to video through experimentation. Video offers one advantage over film in that, if care is taken with the visual monitor, it's possible to evaluate the lighting and image look while at the set.

AS ARGUED in Chapter 13, much of the uninteresting look of work originating on video results from unimaginative applications of technical rules without variation. An example is the familiar "put the whites at 100 IRE and the blacks at 7.5." The result: Most of the interesting lighting on television originates on film, from series such as *thirtysomething* or *L.A. Law* to alternative programming like *Twin Peaks* or music videos. Experimentation with video image surfaces, textures, and lighting is primarily relegated to video art and its outlet in museum screenings. But with the increasing use of video by filmmakers, it's necessary to develop new video concepts like electronic cinematography. The key technical differences between film and video from the standpoint of lighting are as follows:

- Film has a longer useful straight line, 256:1 versus 25:1 in video.
- Film emulsions exhibit curved toes and shoulders, not sharp cutoffs as with video.
- Film emulsions are generally faster (EI 500 versus EI 100) and thus allow for more low-light techniques though newer video cameras are rapidly gaining in sensitivity. Unfortunately, high definition TV (HDTV), which promises new look possibilities, is for the moment inherently very slow, in the range of EI 50.

With these limitations in mind, let's look at some video lighting possibilities.

THE STANDARD VIDEO LOOK

The key to lighting for video is holding the subject luminance range to the $4^1/_2$ zones allowed by the standard system or $5^1/_2$ zones when working with a camera with a gamma compression circuit. All the rules concerning video in the literature—subject lighting ratios no greater than 3:1, facetones at 70 IRE, subject/background ratios no greater than 4:1—are an attempt to deal with this limited straight line.

Lighting from any angle other than frontal creates problems for the video system, problems well known to those familiar with color reversal film stocks: (1) contrasty, unpleasant facetones, (2) an inability to convey dark value detail, and (3) the lack of a subtle discrimination of visual values. The standard video look, like its color reversal predecessor, relies on low facial and subject/background ratios with rim light for accent.

The use of footcandle levels on the order of 100–150 fc in studio situations yields a routine set of color saturations as well. The result is that conventional, bright, happy television lighting found on innumerable game shows, sitcoms, and news shows.

AN ALTERNATIVE LOOK

One way to open up the video look is to use low-intensity, softish, overall frontal illumination—the kind of light naturally available in day interiors. This light may be created by bounced light, heavy diffusion, and softlights. With this type of lighting, there are no significant shadow areas.

As an experiment, take three desk lights with 60-watt bulbs. Find a day interior with enough ambient light to reach T 2 at EI 100. Hook up a monitor to the video camera. Look at the variety of low-light possibilities. Ignoring the warm color temperature, use the desk lamps to illuminate and fill as necessary. Note that what is gloomy to the eye—for example, dark areas of a naturally lit room—looks interesting on the video monitor. This natural lighting is soft, indistinct, and fuzzy. Colors are muted in comparison to the standard over-the-air look. The point is that it's possible to light video in ways that are not considered broadcast quality but that make interesting video images. Except for video artists, few of us know the possibilities and limits of video. Not enough exploration has yet occurred.

In the following discussion it's assumed you are lighting with an incident meter and checking luminance range with a spot meter or waveform monitor *or* you are exposing and lighting the video image by eye with a monitor as guide. The choice between these two methods of working will be discussed later. For now, note that neither method of working utilizes built-in camera meters (autoexposure). It's also assumed you are working with a CCD camera so that you may, as with a film camera, point it at light sources without danger of tube burn-in, lag, and the like.

INTERIOR/EXTERIOR SITUATIONS

In the actor-in-the-window example discussed extensively in Chapters 7 and 10, we saw that exposure determination for the window involved choices about how much to overexpose the window or to underexpose the actor, choices that were crucial to the final feel of the image. The immediate problem with video is that such a film technique, possible because of film's ability to translate long subject luminance ranges, is beyond the video system's capabilities. With video, you are forced to reframe in order to exclude the window or to light the actor so bright relative to the window that you lose the window effect altogether. Use of gamma compression circuits improves the final result. Likewise, subject/background ratios are restricted to such a small range of possibilities in video that you are in constant danger of having each scene look like the next. The result is that the same mood is created over and over again.

The difficulty here is to retain detail, create visual variety and mood, and avoid a repetitive lighting style. Use of colors, rather than luminance variety, suggests a solution and a way to open up the video look. By use of color is meant, as with the Impressionists, a painting with color, rather than, as with Vermeer, a painting with light. The electronic cinematographer will have to work much more closely and creatively with the set designer, since lighting concepts such as subject/background ratio are helpful only within a very narrow range of possibilities.

LUMINOUS OBJECTS

As with mixed interior/exterior situations, luminous objects present problems for video. It's difficult to retain the feeling of their luminosity. Eliminating such objects won't work either since you then risk unrealistic image looks. Large luminous areas, such as steamed window panes or a sunset, will work in video if you are able to utilize a silhouette/semisilhouette effect on the actor. Unfortunately, standard film uses of practicals, lamps, candles, and the like are precarious. It's necessary to reduce luminance values on practicals or accept overbright, "burned out" effects. Such situations are best evaluated with a video monitor.

NIGHT INTERIORS

With video it's difficult to obtain the kinds of black values available in film. Dark grays predominate. Contrasty lighting styles such as noir are hard to achieve. Night interiors lose much of their feel. It's difficult to establish high subject lighting and subject/background ratios to convey "night" without creating too much contrast for the system to handle. For the reasons given in Chapter 13, better night effects are obtained by going via a film negative and video transfer to the final broadcast signal.

COLOR TEMPERATURE EFFECTS

Color temperature effects work very well in video and in ways not available to the cinematographer. For example, video cameras require white balancing. This is equivalent to matching the color temperature of a film emulsion with that of the illumination, for example, putting on a #85 to shoot outdoors. But white balancing is more exact than the film equivalent. It fine-tunes the color balance similarly to a lab timing of the film negative.

It's possible to white-balance to nonwhite hues: off-whites, grays, creams, even yellows, oranges, or blues. This technique can be used to "warm" or "cool" the video image in very subtle ways. The effect has to be evaluated over a monitor and can be enhanced or toned down in postproduction.

VIDEO COLORS

To avoid that richly colored, sharp image built into current video systems requires working with low-intensity light levels and small amounts of supplemental soft light. This represents an alternative look. Such a look results from the change from a richly saturated, brightly lit color palette to a muted, subdued range of hues. VariCon on-camera flashing and filtration with nets are other ways to work with video colors. Color can also be controlled electronically in postproduction where paintboxes and other electronic color controls allow for subtle effects.

A more serious problem is encountered when shooting video for day exteriors since bright, saturated video hues are even more predominant. As with color negative film stock, it helps to avoid direct sunlight and shoot in shady situations or under gray sky conditions. Videographers have come to realize that a good rule for sunny days is to shoot early morning or late afternoon and avoid shooting from roughly 11:00 A.M. to 3:00 P.M.. This minimizes the impact of those bright, saturated video hues.

There is a great danger your video images will all look alike. Shooting on rainy days, in the winter, and at dusk are all techniques that will help defeat the built-in color palette. As with film, night exteriors are best shot at twilight or in places with a lot of ambient street light, neon signs, and so forth. No new principles are involved with electronic cinematography, just an awareness of the limitations of video listed at the beginning of this chapter.

USE OF VISUAL MONITORS ON THE SET

In *Electronic Cinematography*, Mathias and Patterson argue that the central problem in video production is the lack of a director of photography (DP) who is in charge of the look of the image. They contend that, from the cinematographer's point of view, video lighting requires no new principles. They further argue that, if film techniques and practices are followed and control over the image look is given to a DP rather than an engineer, video lighting effects comparable to film's will result.

Video, however, offers an intriguing prospect that film doesn't. By using a monitor it's possible to evaluate the lighting as it is executed. Let's explore this idea in more detail.

There are three principal approaches to lighting for video:

1. *Traditional way*. Use a spot meter and incident meter to set lights, follow the traditional ratio rules with three-point, key, fill and rim lighting, 2:1 subject lighting ratio, 2:1 subject/background ratio, everything at 100 fc, and, without looking, allow the engineers to "expose" the image using waveform monitors. The central problem is that exposure is divorced from lighting and is used noncreatively. This method is too mechanical, standardized, and conventionalized.

2. *Mathias and Patterson way*. Establish an exposure index equivalent for the video system, and use an incident meter to set lights and determine T-stops. Use a waveform monitor to check subject luminance range, and light with ratios suitable for a film emulsion with a 32:1 overall straight line. This method relies heavily on the waveform monitor for image evaluation. The problem is that you still have to imagine how the image will look. Experience is necessary to evaluate the data from the waveform monitor. Mathias and Patterson do not recommend use of a visual monitor at the set because of potential inaccuracies and the danger that producers, directors, and actors will attempt to make lighting decisions based on the monitor's inaccurate visuals.[1]

3. *Use of on-set monitors*. This amounts to lighting and even exposing by eye. The lighting is built up with reference to a monitor. No meter is used. You use your eye to evaluate ratios and special effects and to create an overall mood. You still may use a waveform monitor if desired to monitor exposure and to check overall luminance range.

The central advantage of method 3 is that it makes possible a painting with light and color by eye. Using the monitor, we see as the video system "sees." This has always been the dream of the cinematographer: to see as the film stock "sees" without having to wait for processing and workprinting.

Why throw away this immense advantage? The answers are many for Mathias and Patterson, but mostly involve concerns in large production situations—too many cooks spoil the image, so to speak. By using method 2 and not having monitors on the set, the DP retains control over image look as in film, at least until the postproduction sessions. On smaller shoots and particularly in student situations, Mathias and Patterson's arguments have less force. It's more feasible to evaluate the look on the monitor while lighting rather than waiting for a later screening session.

There are technical problems associated with using a monitor as in method 3: Monitors vary and light hitting them can give false indications of the actual image look. All the cinematographer can do to avoid these pitfalls when working in video is to accept them and try to minimize their effect, knowing inconsistencies can be corrected in video postproduction.

The advantage of lighting by monitor is that you can see as you work, like a painter. The disadvantage is that you are trying to achieve a final timed look without waveform data. Judging the look off a monitor can be misleading, given the perceptual adaptability and relativity of the human eye.

Color bars are one means to achieve standardization when using a monitor. The cinematographer can adjust the color bars on the reference monitor before lighting and refer back to the bars as needed throughout the shooting day, to readjust the eye so to speak. It's essential not to change or readjust monitor settings until a particular scene is completed since that will tend to yield inconsistent images. With this technique, it's possible to light and expose referenced to the monitor. Method 3 is at least worth experimenting with since it holds much promise for lighting artistry. Multiple shadows, hot spots, uneven intensities, ugly facial shadows, and the like can all be avoided via the monitor without having to learn through years of experience to see as the video system "sees."

SUMMARY

Electronic cinematography liberates video from television standardizations and invites the infusion of film practices and attitudes. The key advantage of video is that it offers what cinematographers can only dream about: the ability to visually analyze the final image with a monitor at the shoot itself. The eye and the medium can thus collaborate in lighting and exposure without the necessity for a mechanical, metered interface. The system's limitations and possibilities are instantly visible. Used with care, the on-set monitor allows for a true painting with light and color.

NOTE

1. See discussion in Harry Mathias and Richard Patterson, *Electronic Cinematography: Achieving Photographic Control over the Video Image* (Belmont, Calif.: Wadsworth, 1985), pp. 161, 180–82.

V

LIGHTING ANALYSES OF SELECTED SHOTS

TO ANALYZE a lighting setup and determine the number and direction of lights, we have to be like Sherlock Holmes and work backward from the lighting evidence. We look for significant shadows so as to determine light angles. We look for significant highlights and reflections so as to determine the presence of fill light, eyelight, hair light, and so forth.

The following analyses from Chapters 1, 2, 7, and 9 show the technique one has to use to learn lighting from the screen. In many ways, this is the most important part of the book, since once the analytic ability is developed, the cinematographer may learn directly from film, video, and photographic examples. In the examples provided here, the lighting has been frozen with a still frame, which does not allow for an analysis of the film's lighting as it accommodates actor movement. Only analysis of a video clip can illustrate lighting's handling of movement.

Sometimes it is very difficult, even impossible, to figure out a lighting setup with certainty. Alternate explanations are equally possible (see the analysis of Figure 1.5c). But that's all right. What we are interested in is an accurate observation of the visual data and the construction of a plausible hypothesis as to how the effect was created. It doesn't matter how the shot was "really lit"—that's often very difficult to know since light is such a complicated phenomenon. Besides, from the point of view of re-creation, it doesn't really matter which of two analyses is right, as long as both account for those visual elements you would need to duplicate if asked to re-create the effect. Suggested exercises for practicing analysis and diagramming are provided at the end of Appendix J, "Suggested Exposure and Lighting Exercises."

It's the cinematographer's duty, if asked, to provide a reasonable imitation of a given lighting effect, even if it's done with a different lighting setup. Whether you use one light or three just doesn't matter. Of course, if actually asked to duplicate a specific effect by a director, you would put the actor in a similar set or location and observe the various effects created by different lighting arrangements as you work with the lights. You would observe your own lighting, previsualize the final on-screen results, and try to duplicate the desired effect. Awareness of the effect is what a lighting book can teach. The rest is up to the cinematographer and his or her creative awareness.

Key Used for Lighting Diagrams

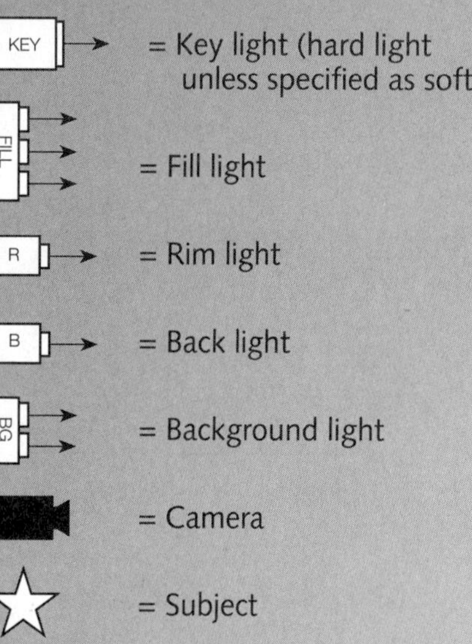

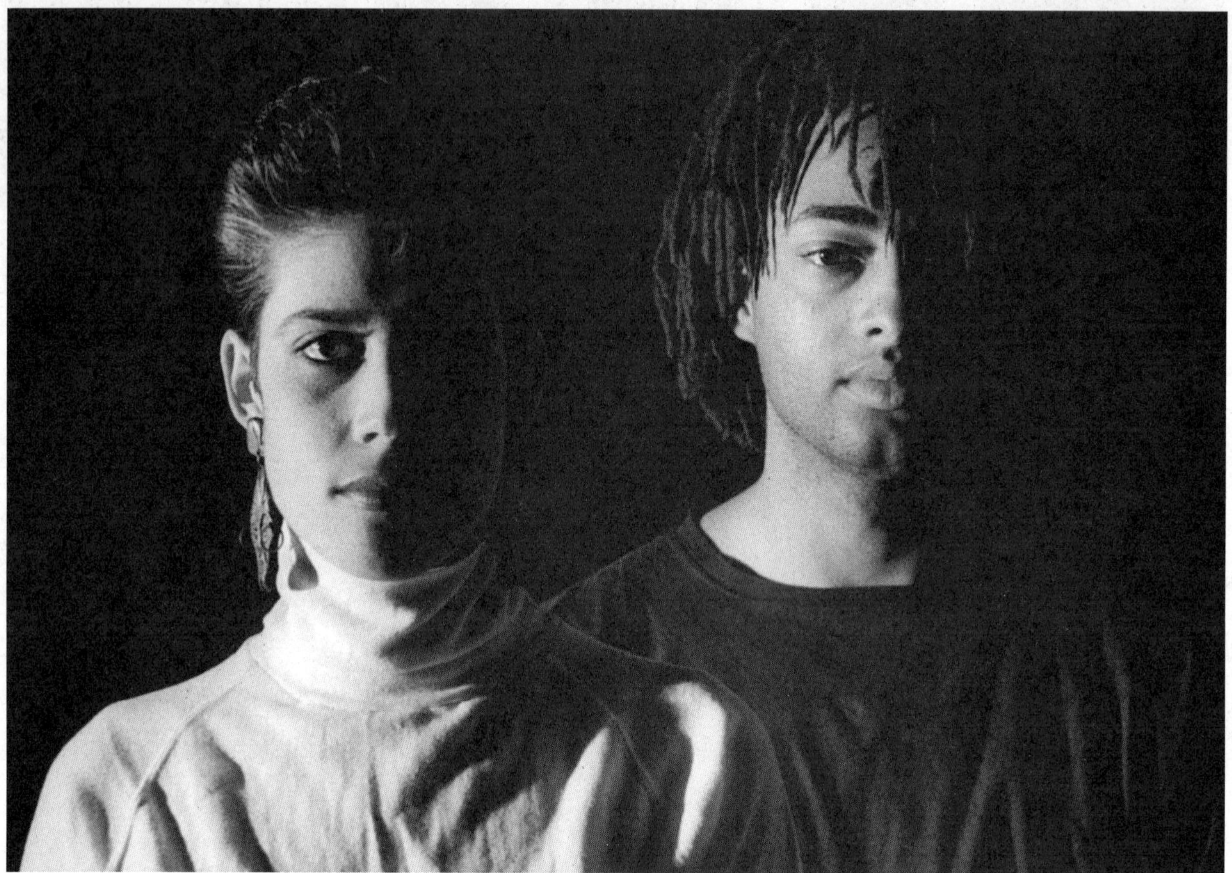

Figure 1.1a (page 4) Side key.

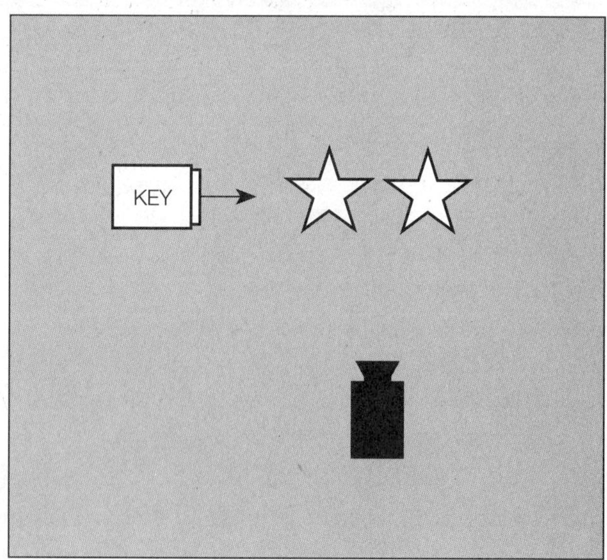

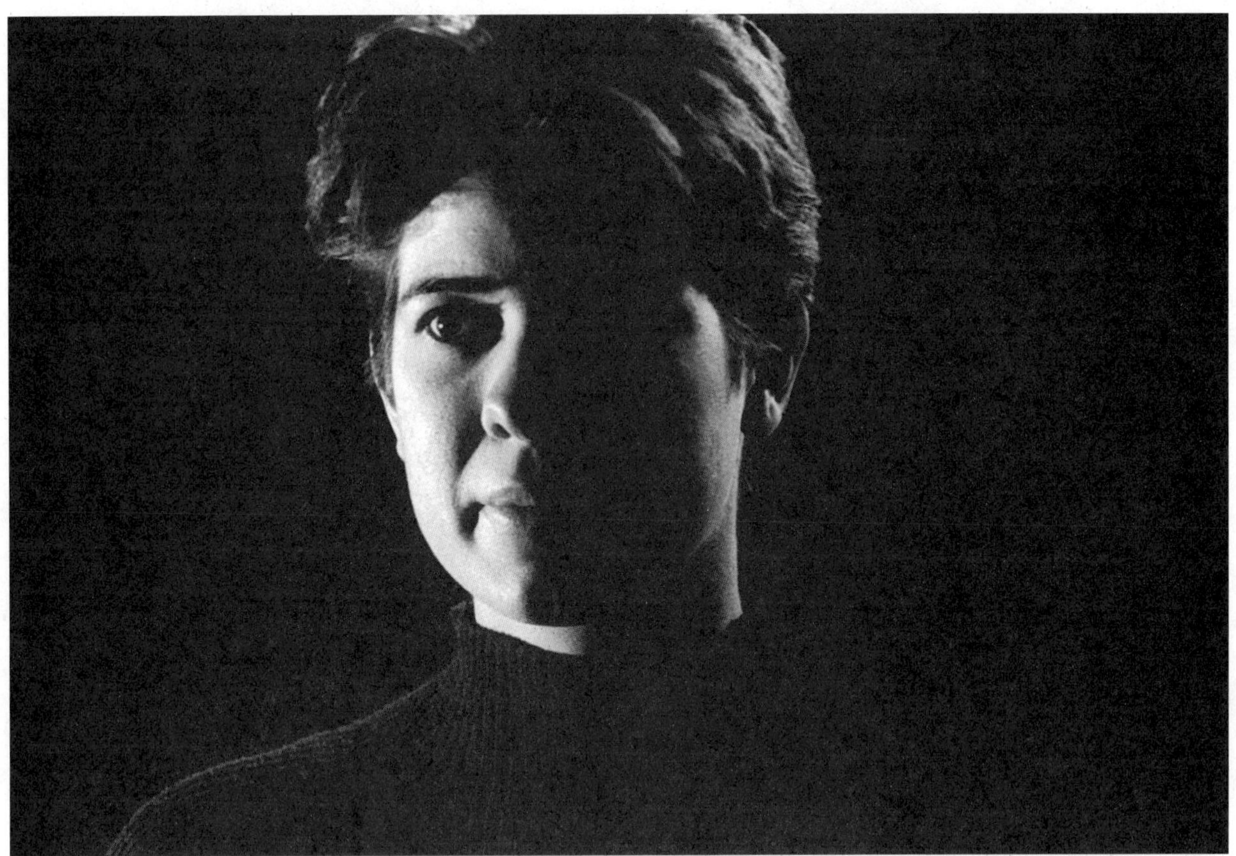

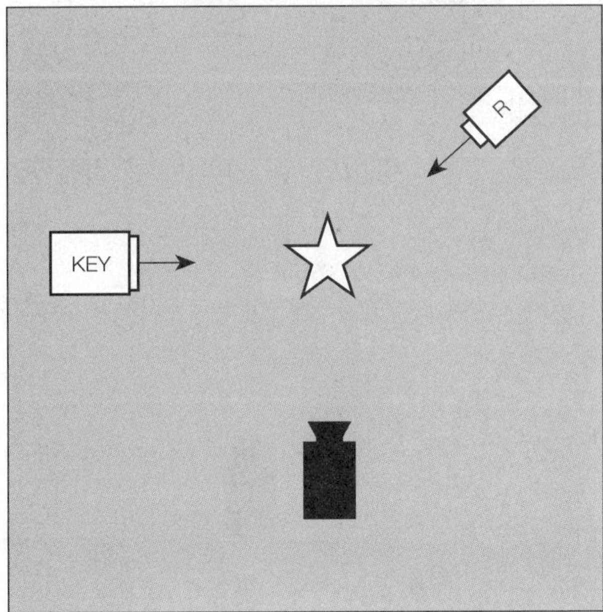

Figure 1.1b (page 4) Here a modeling light has been added to the side key effect in Figure 1.1a. This supplemental light rims the person's hair and neck and is about one stop darker than the key light, which comes from the left side.

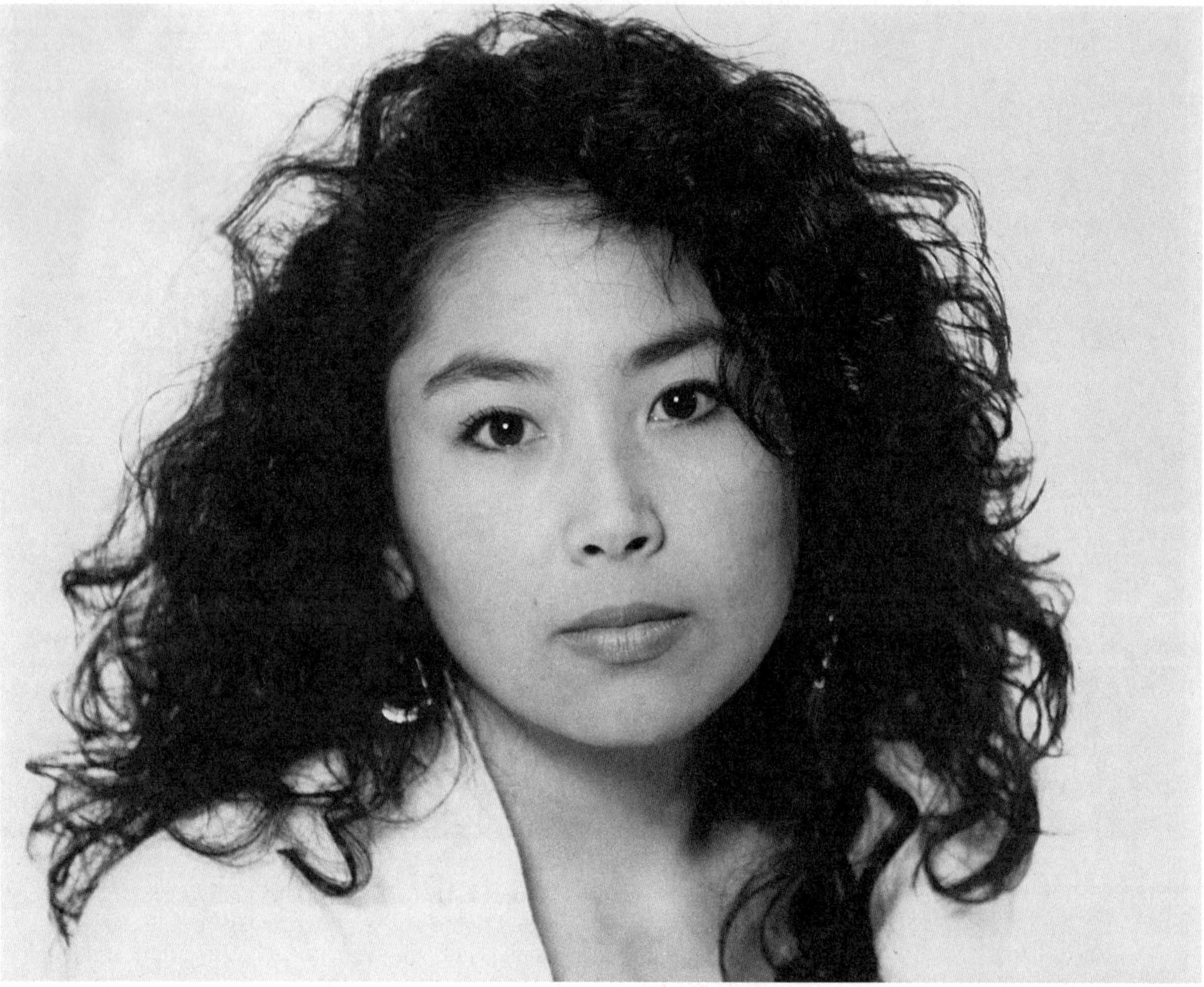

Figure 1.1c (page 4) The white background in this shot gives it a high-key, bright feeling.

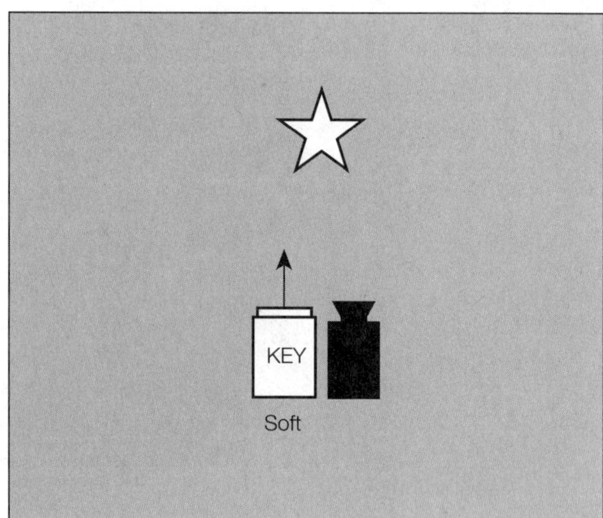

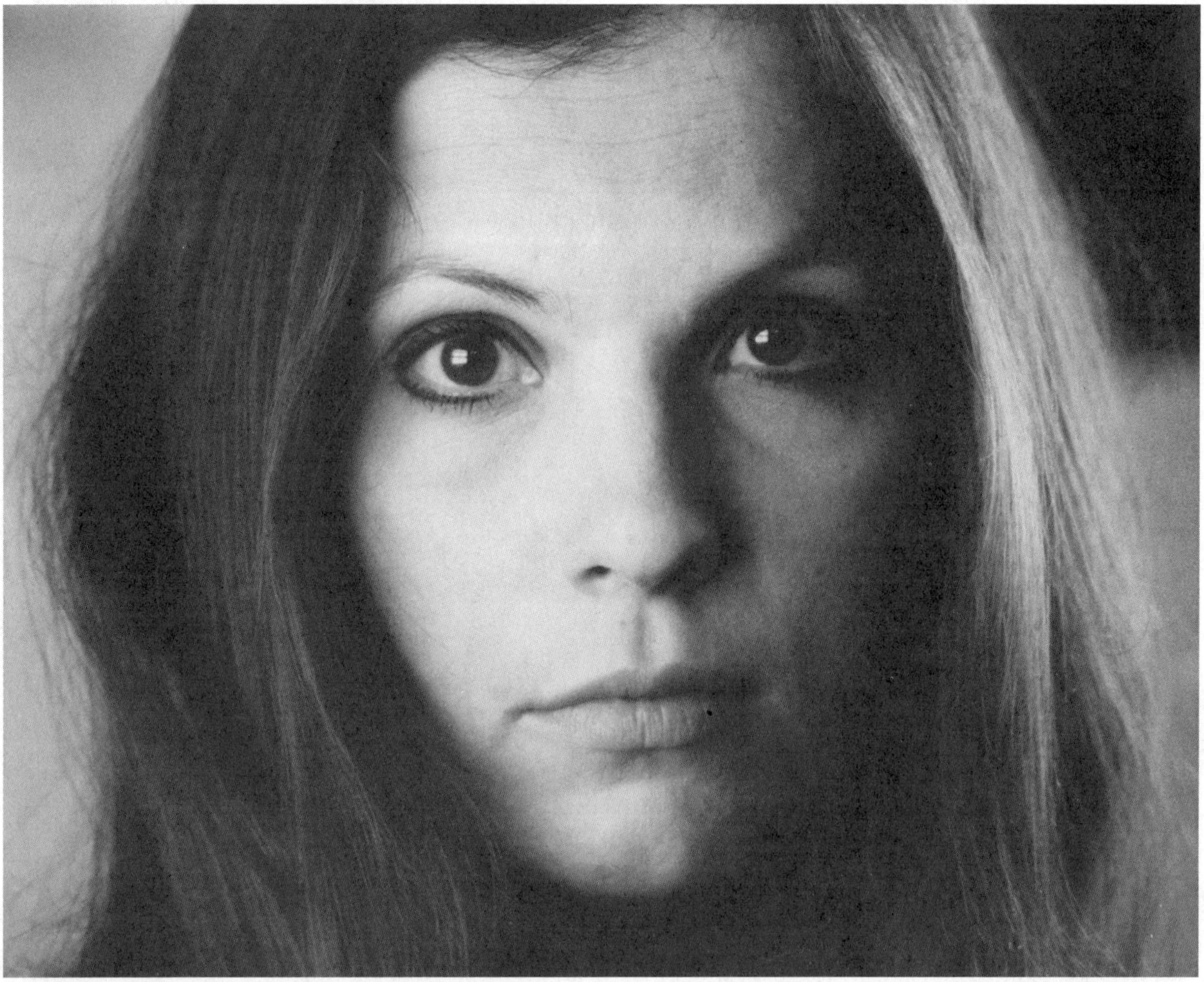

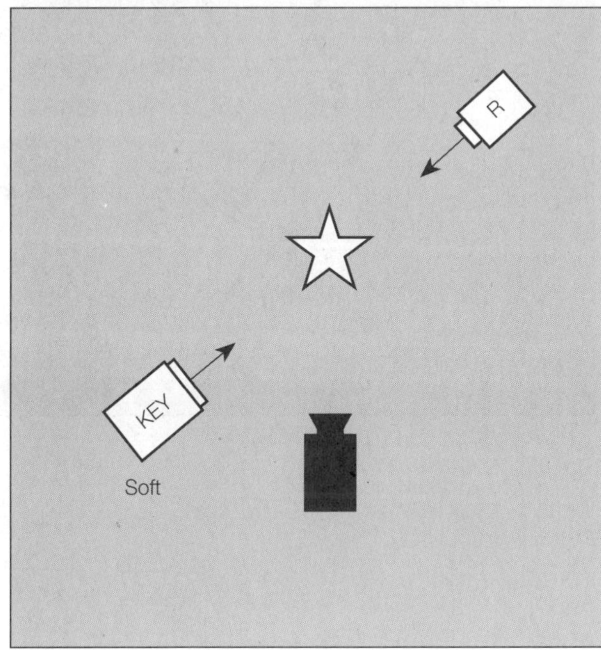

Figure 1.1d (page 4) In this example, the key light is very soft, hence the gradual transition to the shadow areas. The rim light from the right side is also soft and has about the same intensity as the key. This rim light accents the hair. Note the large light source reflected in the eyes, indicating the key is large in size, such as from a softlight or a window. Compare how the darker background in this shot changes the mood from that of the example in Figure 1.1c.

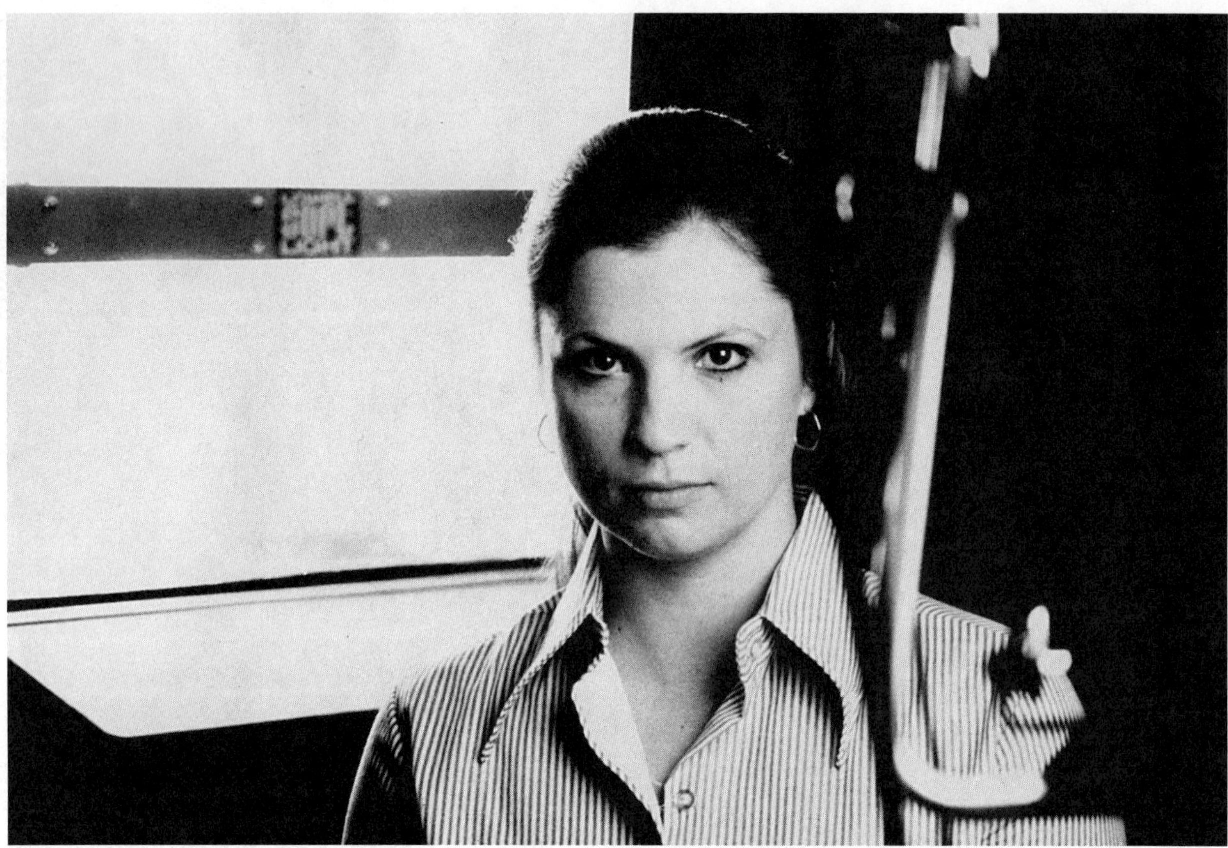

Figure 1.3a (page 6) Both key and rim are Lowell softlights. They can be partially seen in the shot. The key comes from slightly off-center right. The back light is in the kicker position, across the circle from the key. Both lights are about the same intensity. Note how the kicker softlight is completely burned out, a luminous object problem.

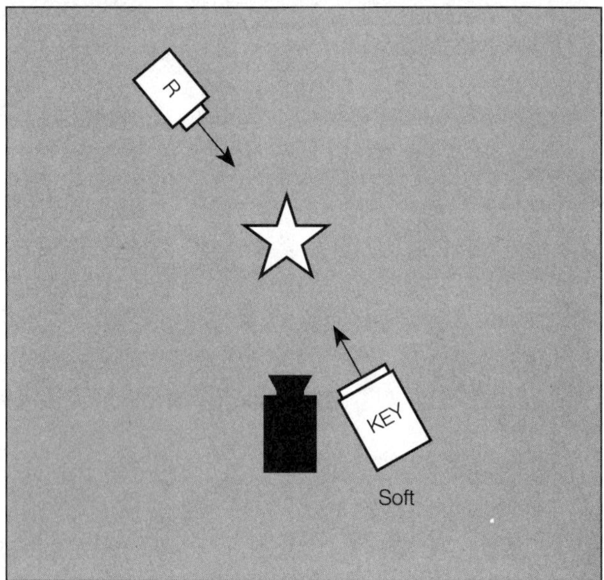

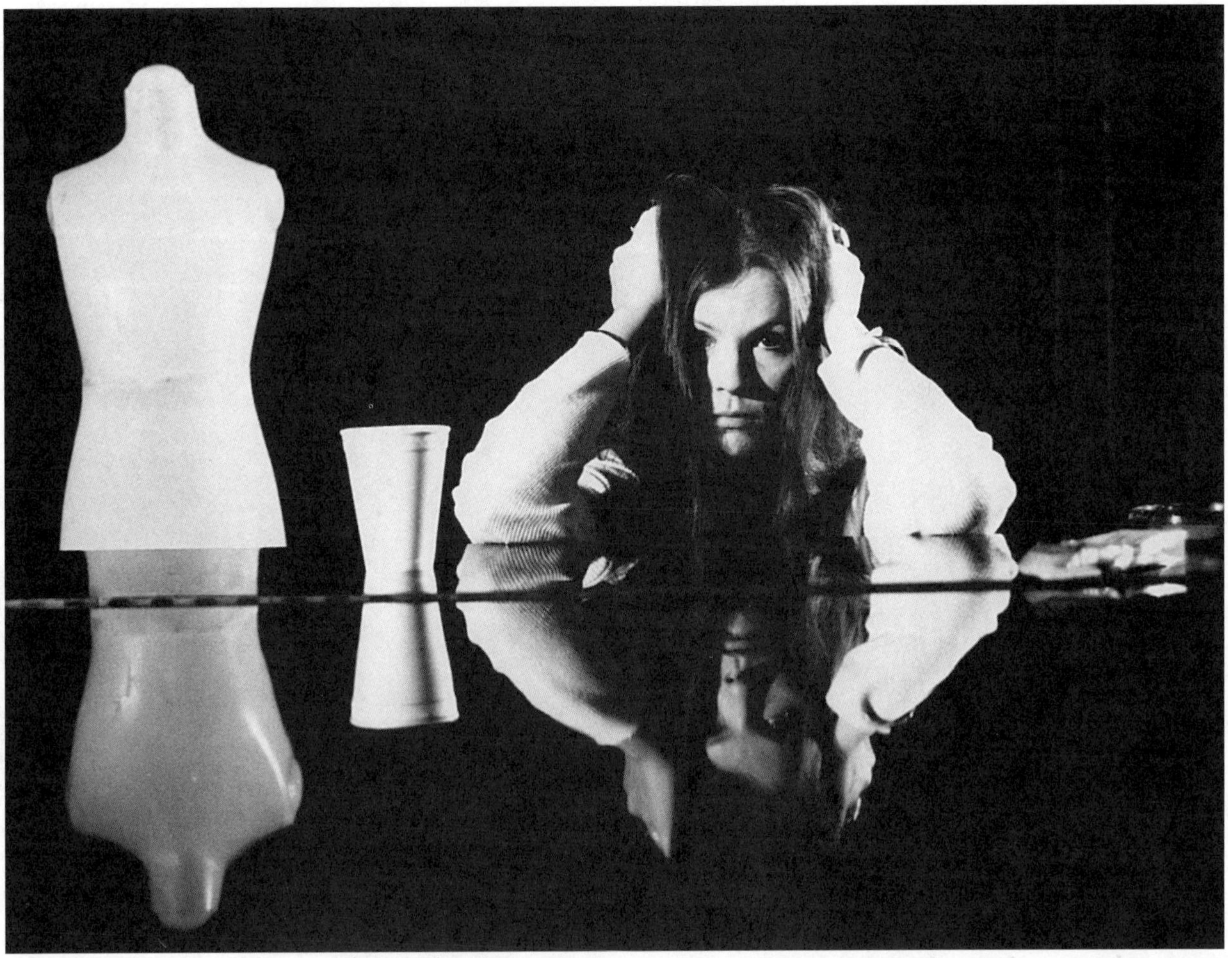

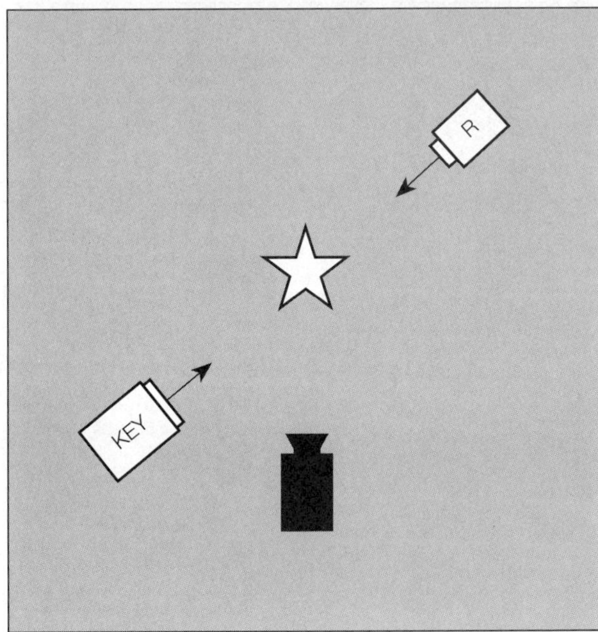

Figure 1.3b (page 6) This is a more complicated setup than we've had so far. The first light we look for is the key on the face. We immediately notice the shadow-side triangle patch of light, which means the key is coming from the left three-quarter front position. We can tell the key light is fairly hard by noticing how sharply defined the facial shadows are on the subject. Light from the three-quarter front left cannot illuminate the hair on the right side of the model; therefore, we conclude there is a rim light from frame right creating these effects.

Both of these lights are confirmed by observing their effects on the mannequin as well as the Styrofoam cup. Note that both of these objects are more easily analyzed by viewing their reflections in the piano top. The key light has caused a hot spot reflection on the mannequin as has the rim light from frame right. The light coming from frame right is far enough behind the subject so as not to light her face, only her hair. Its presence is particularly evident on the neck and shoulder of the mannequin.

The Styrofoam cup is lit from the left and right in approximately equal intensities—note the shadow line on the front of the cup; therefore, we may conclude the key and rim light are roughly of similar intensity. The shadows on the face are black, which indicates there is no fill light being used.

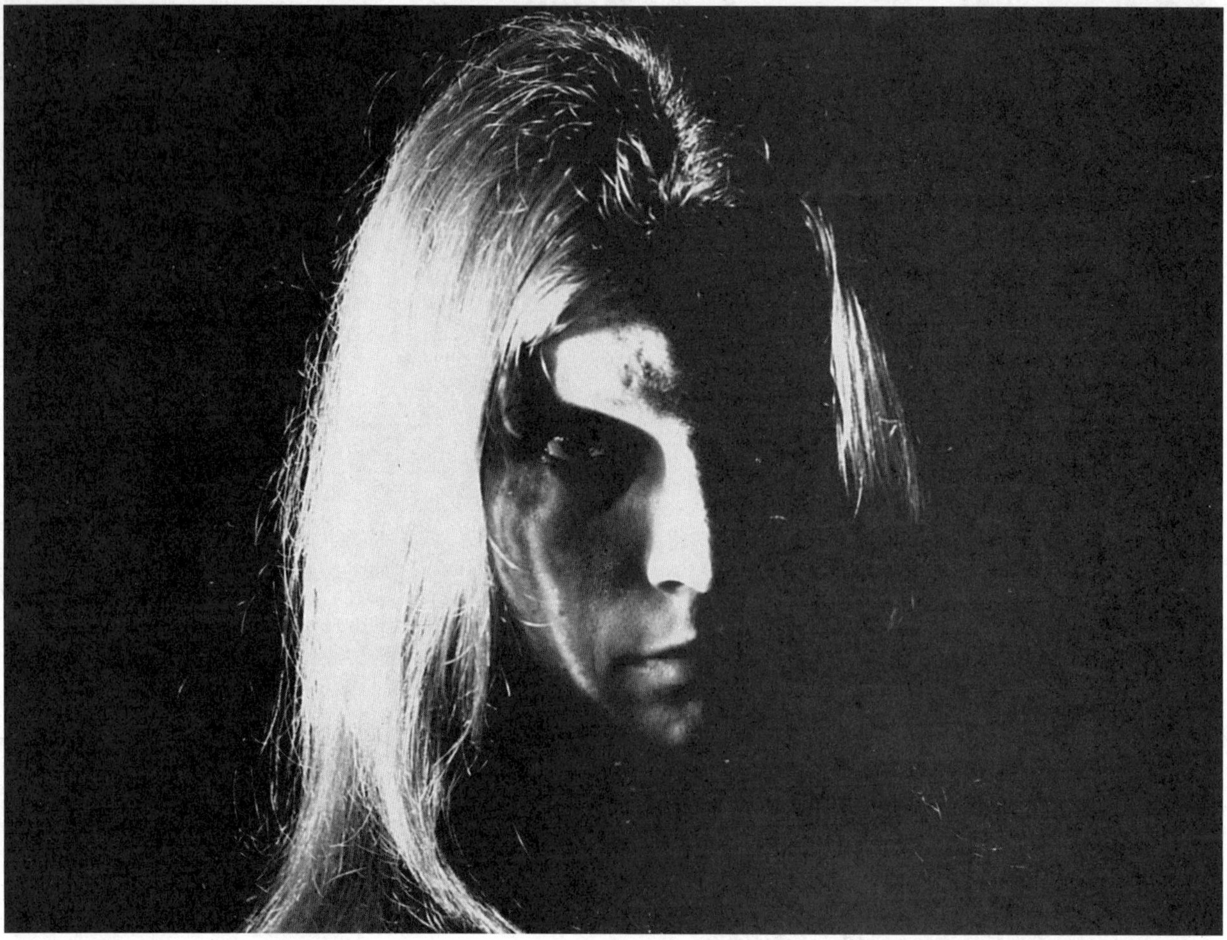

Figure 1.3c (page 6) Note how the hair is used to create interesting facial shadows in this hard light example. The strong side key from the left is three or four stops overexposed. But even so, the shadow side of the face is left black since there is no fill light. The side key also emphasizes the texture on the hair.

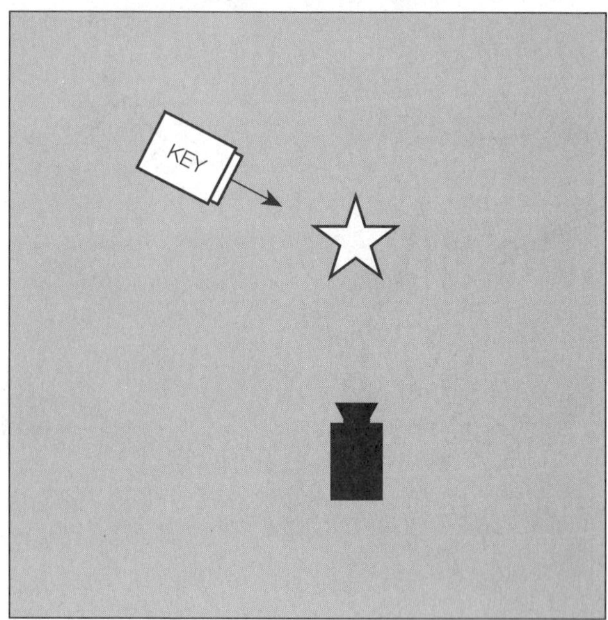

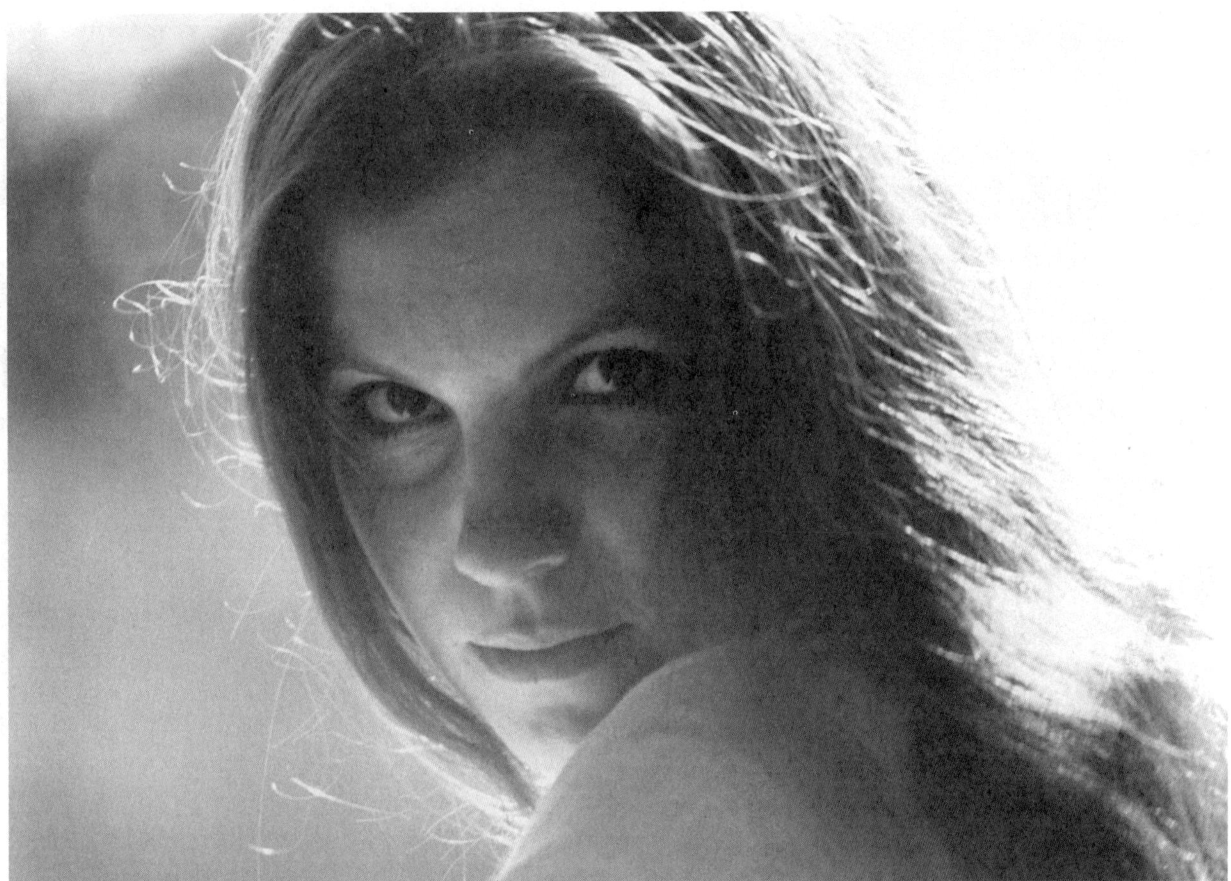

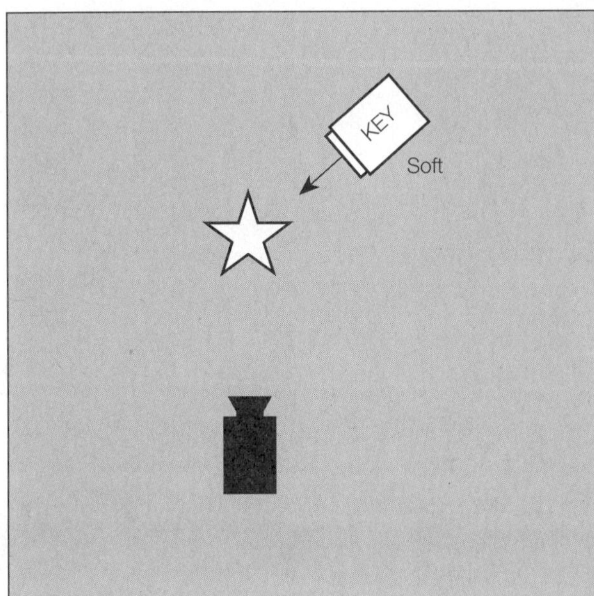

Figure 1.3d (page 6) The soft light in this example contrasts with the hard light in Figure 1.3c. The key light comes from the back right direction and does not strike the face. Presumably it is diffused sunlight, like on a light gray day. We can see the front of the subject because of the light bounced off her white blouse. Note how the chin is hotter than the rest of the face and that the reflection of the blouse is visible in the bottom of the subject's eyes. No evidence exists for arguing there is any additional fill.

The background is out of focus and is presumably lit by ambient light like the face. Probably this is an available light shot. Note how the cinematographer uses grays to convey mood in comparison to the blacks and whites in Figure 1.3c.

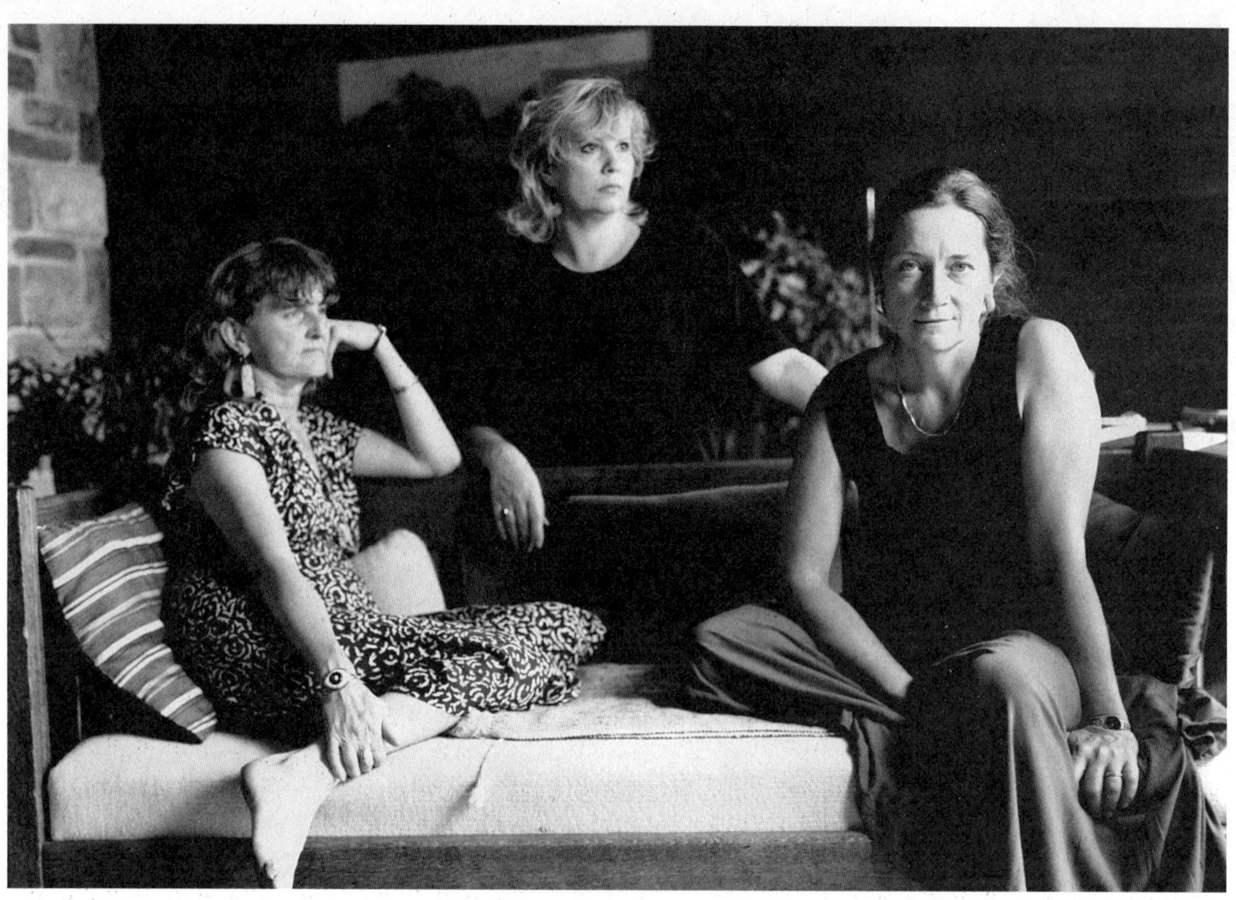

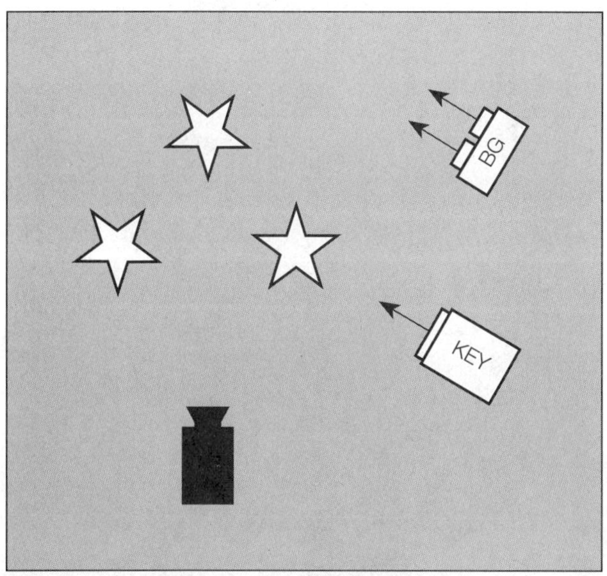

Figure 1.5b (page 8) This shot conveys the feeling of a window frame right. The directionality of the light establishes the effect. The shadows are fairly soft. In fact, this shot was lit with two open-face quartz lights diffused with Tough Frost. One light was used for the women, from a three-quarter front right position. The other was placed on the background from the same angle. It was of lesser intensity and serves only to bring up the table and plants frame right and the picture on the back wall. No fill light was used as light scattered about the couch area was sufficient to lighten shadow areas.

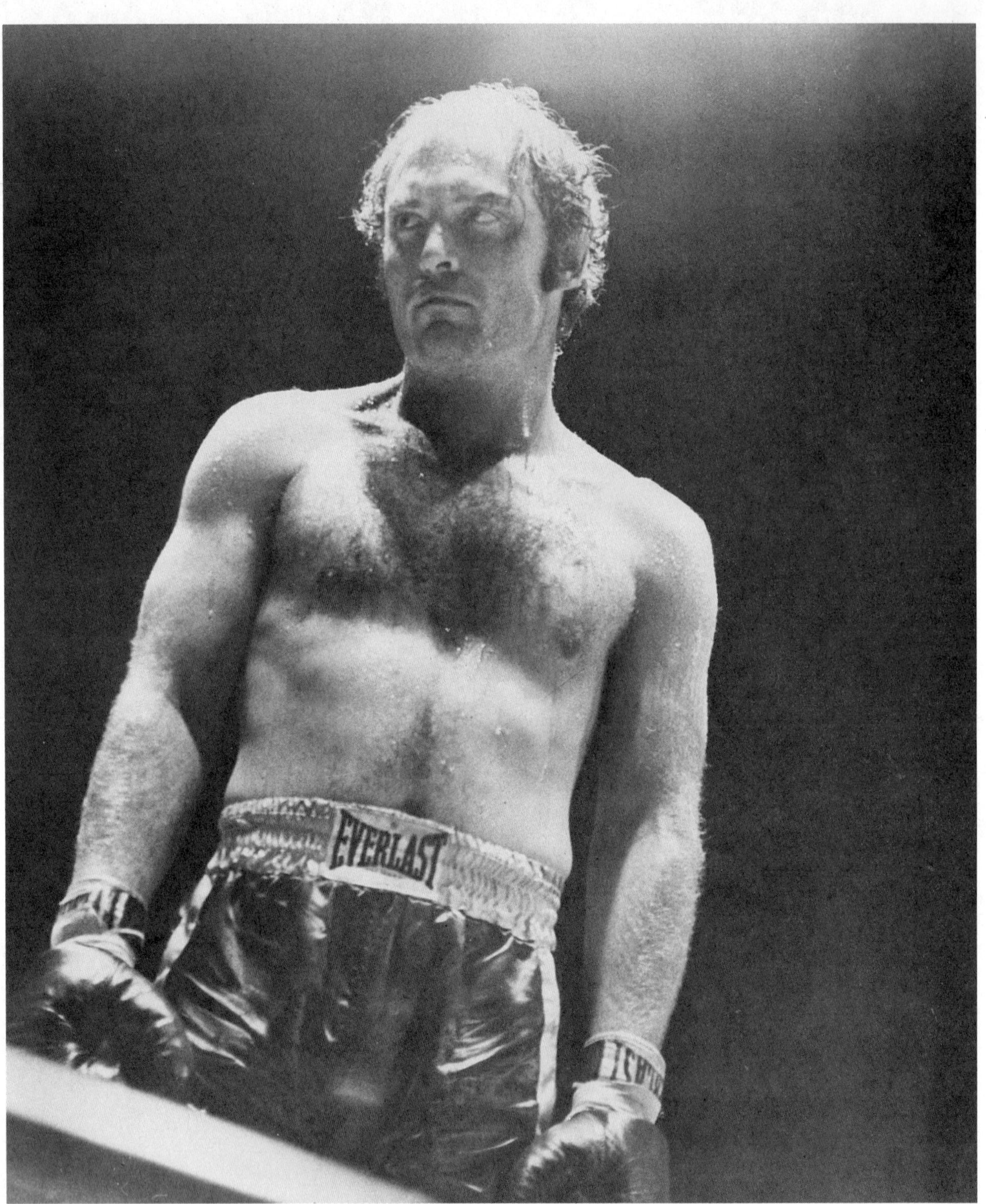
EVERLAST

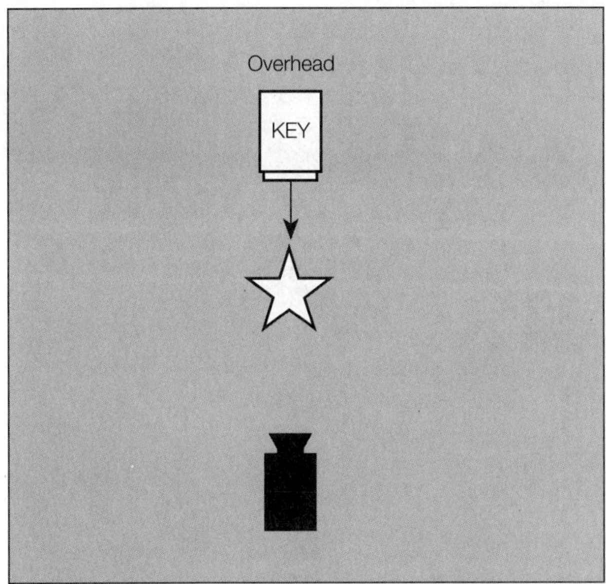

Figure 1.5c (page 8) (*Fat City,* Columbia Pictures, 1972) This is a good example of top lighting. The strong source directionality derives from our knowledge that boxing rings have a lot of lights above the boxers. In this instance, the top light is from the back of the subject—note the shadow of the head on the chest. The overexposed top of the head indicates exposure was for the chest and arm area, which was at a lower intensity than the light on the head. Probably the front of the boxer is illuminated with light bounced off the white canvas of the ring. It fills in the facial shadow somewhat, and the lack of an eyelight reflection indicates there was no fill.

This example could be given a different interpretation. Top back lighting is still used, but it is supplemented with top frontal lighting. This would still leave the facial shadow but would account for the lighting on the arms and chest differently than the first interpretation would. This seems plausible, because as we know, boxing rings have more than one light above the ring.

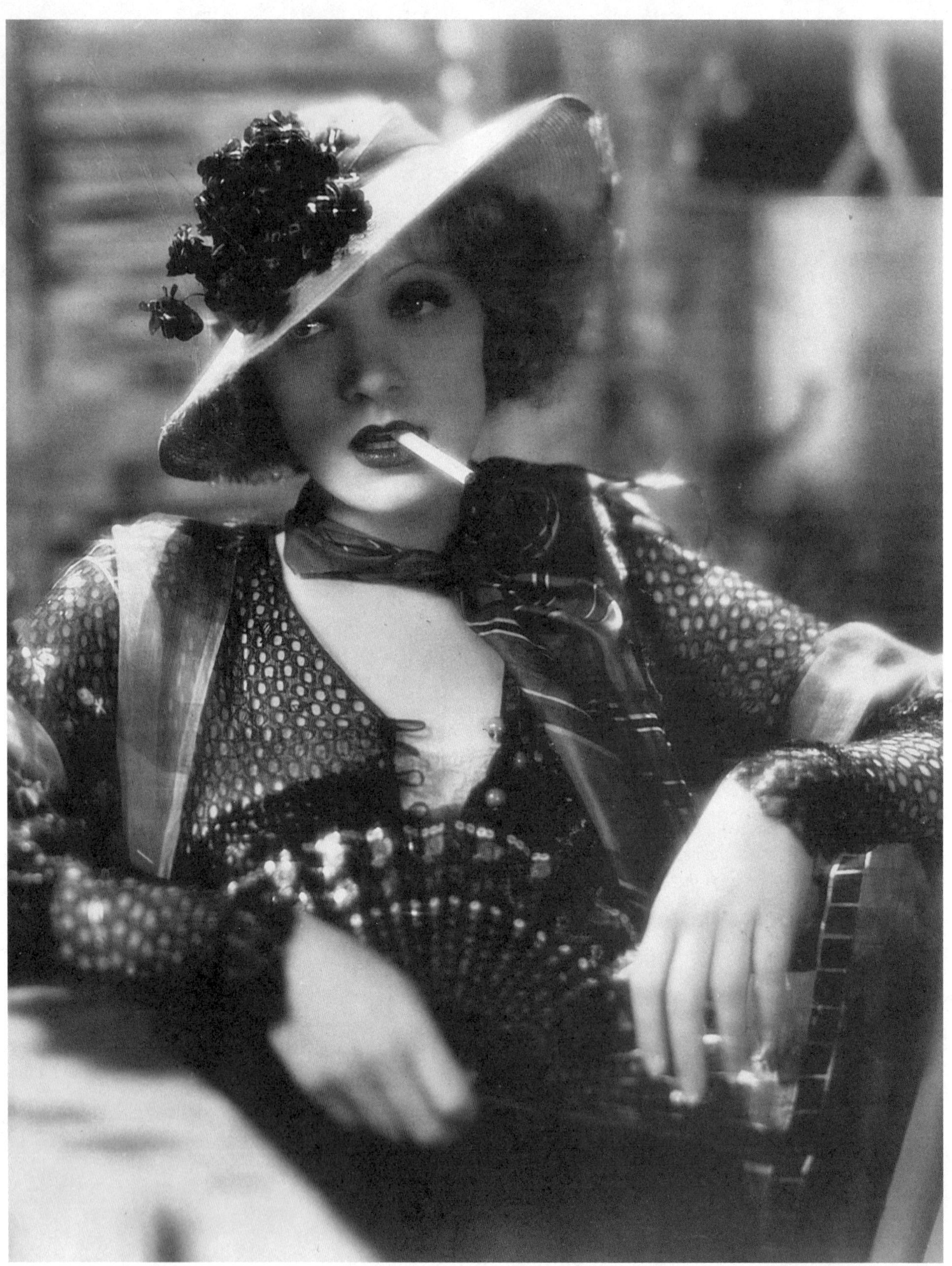

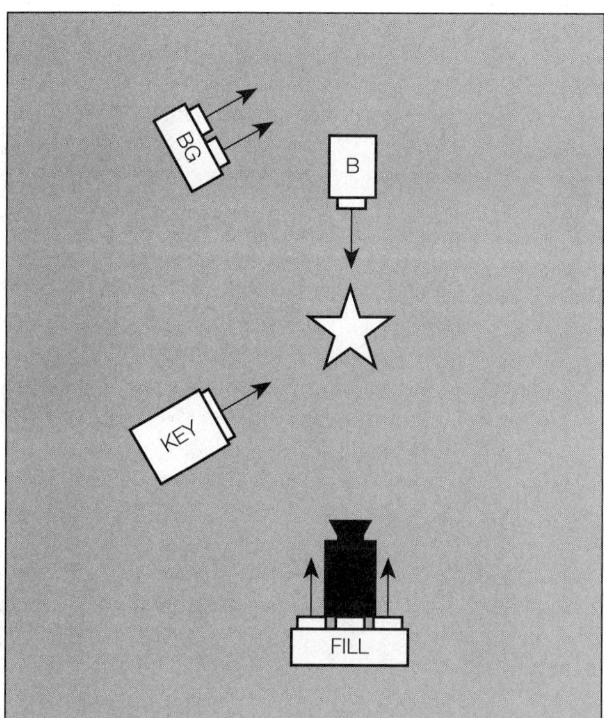

Figure 1.7 (page 10) (*Blonde Venus*, Paramount, 1932) This shot is relatively complicated. A back light from the top highlights the hat, shoulder frame left, and arm frame right. There is a fill light since we can see the reflection in the subject's eyes. The question is whether there are two lights on her face or just one. It could be the fill light is actually a frontal key used with a partial lighting technique (patches of light and shadow) so that it lights her chin, the cigarette, the tip of her nose, and her blouse area while filling in the rest of her face and body. Such an effect can be created by using a translucent "cookie" or even Tough Frost with holes patterned on it.

Or, it could be there are two lights: a fill light (see reflection in the eye frame right) and a key coming from above frame left that illuminates only her chin, cigarette, tip of nose, and blouse area. The best argument for this two-light setup is the small blouse-eyelet shadows on her chest and the shadow her upper lip projects onto the cigarette. I prefer this latter explanation, but it's very difficult to tell.

One interesting thing, there are two differently shaped reflections in her eyes. One is a simple circle shape, the other looks like a bank of footlights in a theater. The brightness of the latter gives quite a spark of life to the face. These lights indicate that a separate eyelight might have been used for one of the eyes or that the angle of the eyes caused an uneven reflection pattern.

The background light is set about a stop darker than the key area so that it doesn't distract from the star. There is so much diffusion that the shadows are softened to almost nonexistence. On analysis, the lighting setup is very complicated. After all, the film, *Blonde Venus*, was directed by Josef von Sternberg, famous for his lighting of Marlene Dietrich.

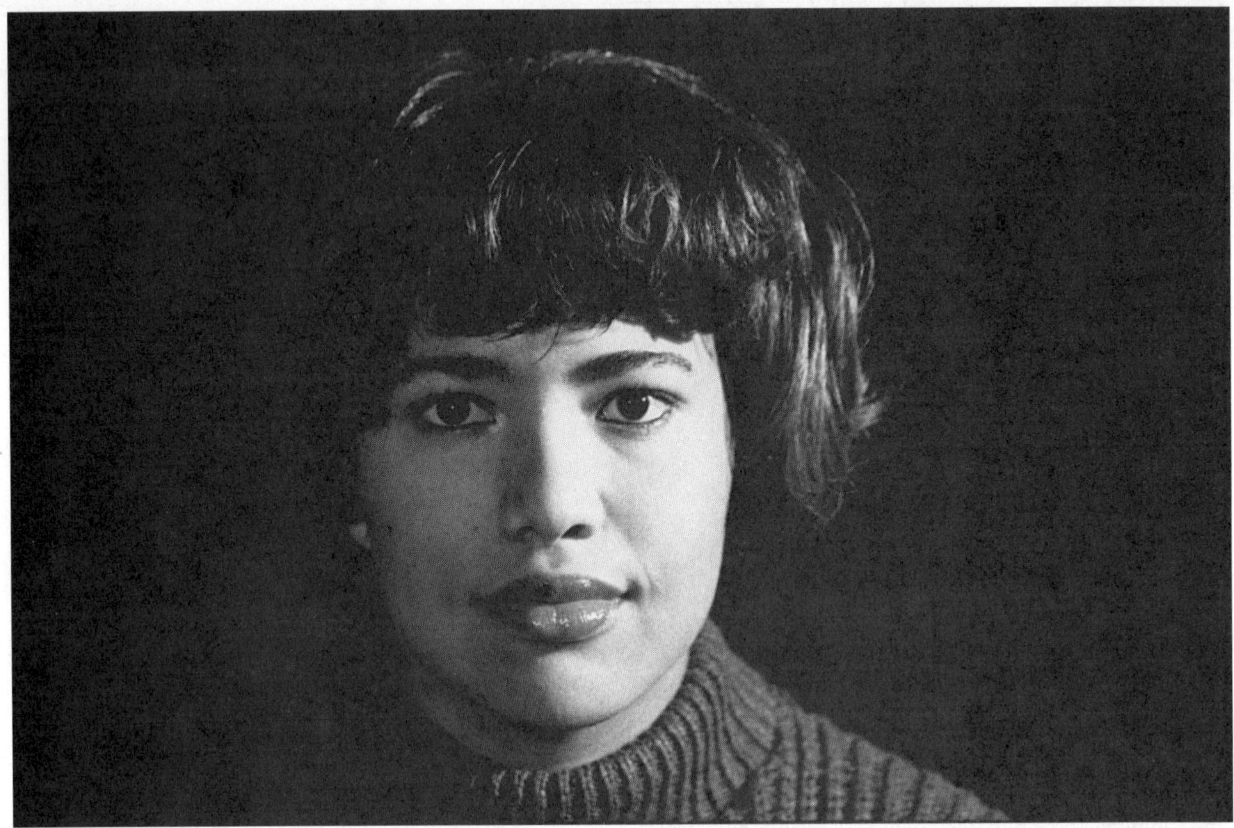

Figure 2.6a (page 20) A side key from the right splits the face in half and provides texture on the sweater and the hair. There is a fill light at about a 3:1 ratio; its reflection is visible in the shadow side eye. The eye frame right has two reflections, from the fill and a larger one from the key.

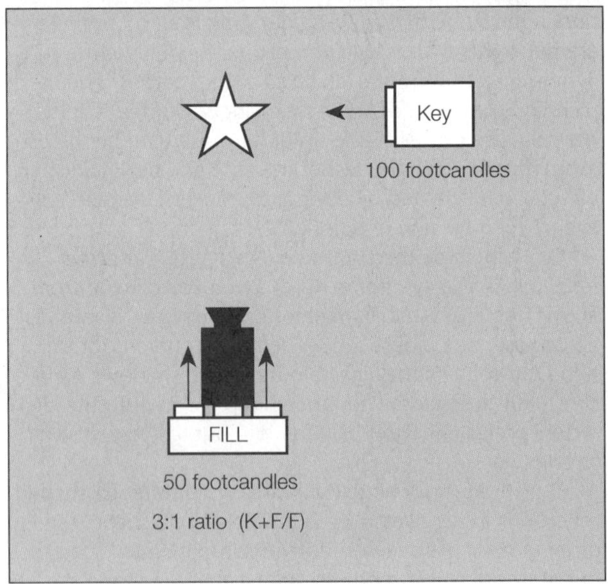

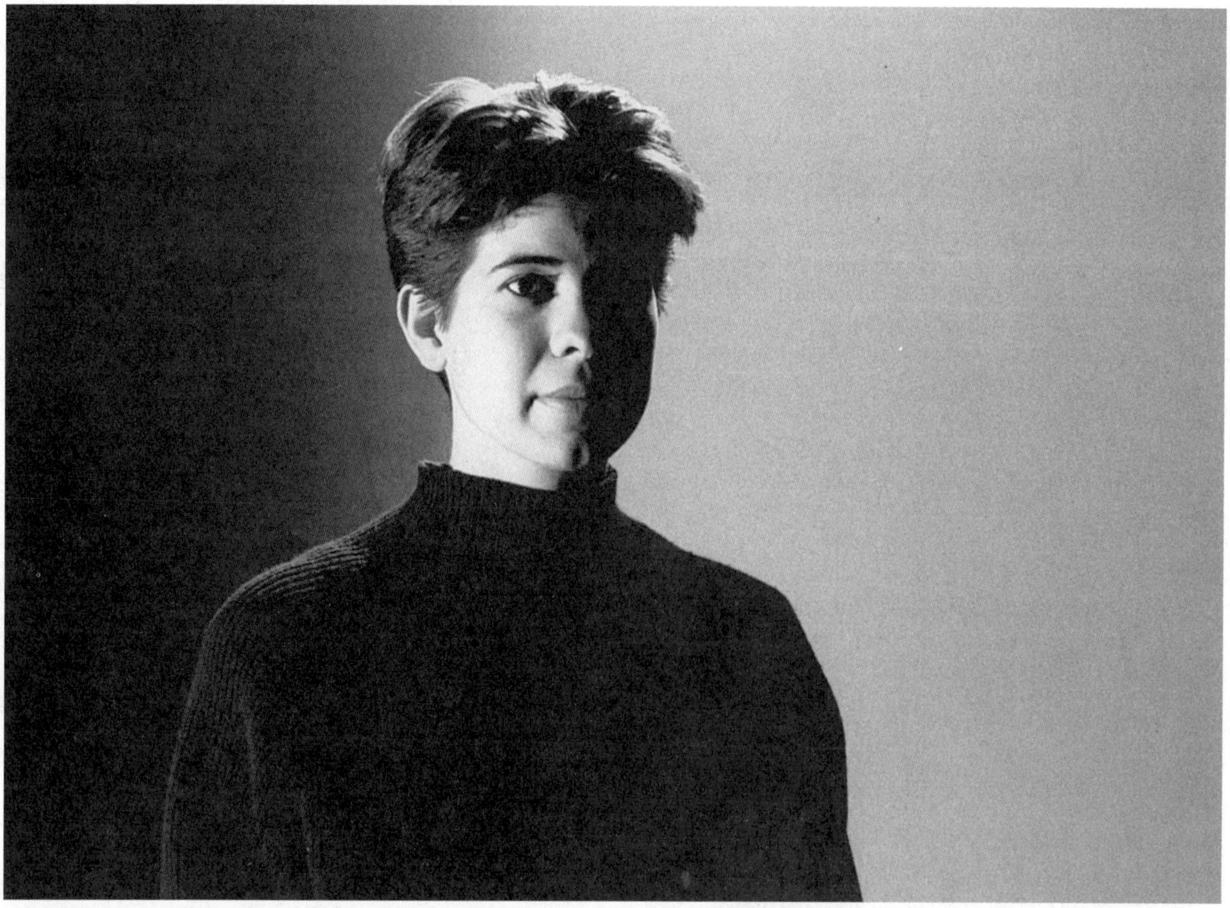

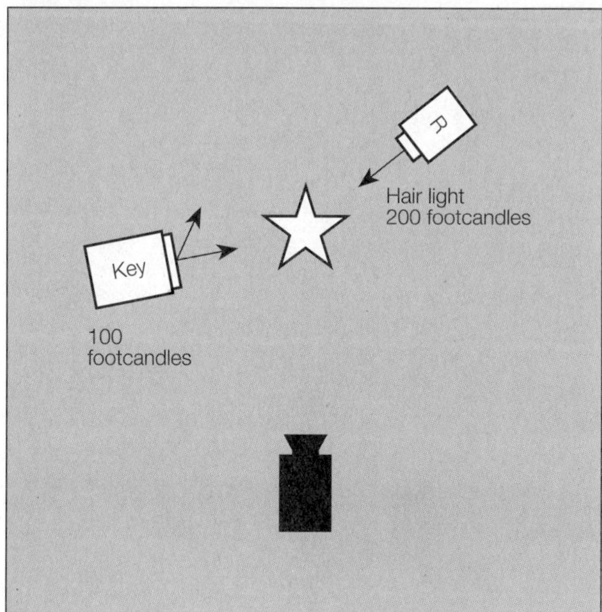

Figure 2.6b (page 20) Note how the key from the left illuminates part of the background and falls off gradually to frame left. There is no fill light; thus the facial shadow is very black, about a 32:1 ratio. The hair light is about a stop brighter than the key and accents the shoulder frame left and the subject's cheek frame right besides providing a strong emphasis for the hair.

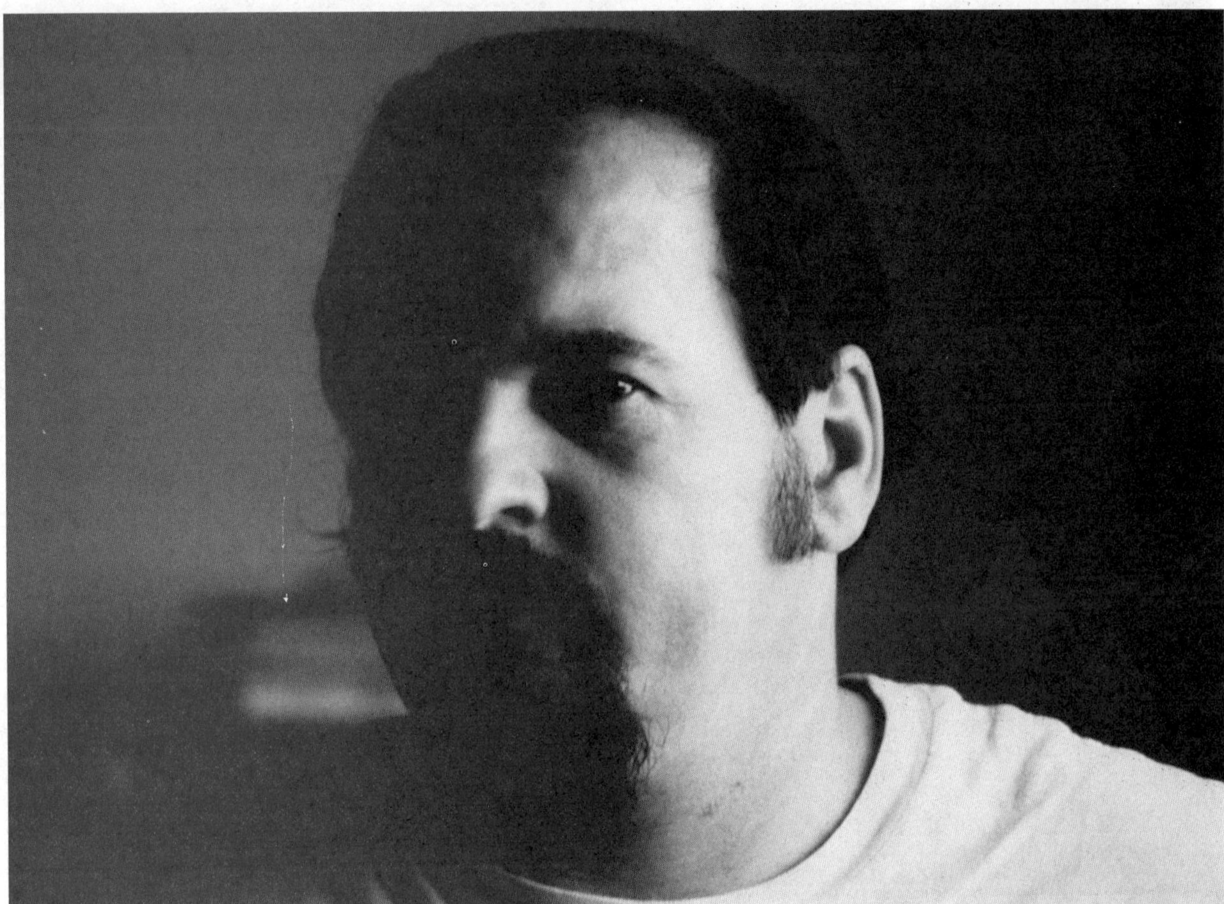

Figure 2.6c (page 20) This shot employs an available light side-key effect. There is no fill; hence the shadow side eye is lost in darkness. Available light on the wall behind the subject is about four stops darker than the key on the face, which amounts to a 16:1 subject/background ratio.

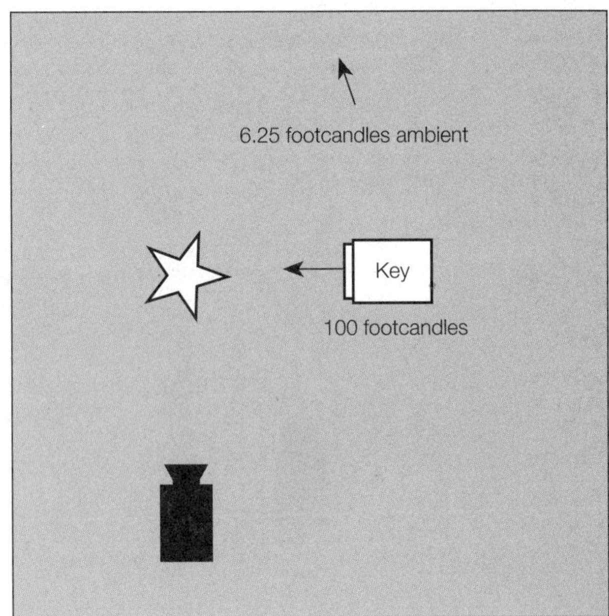

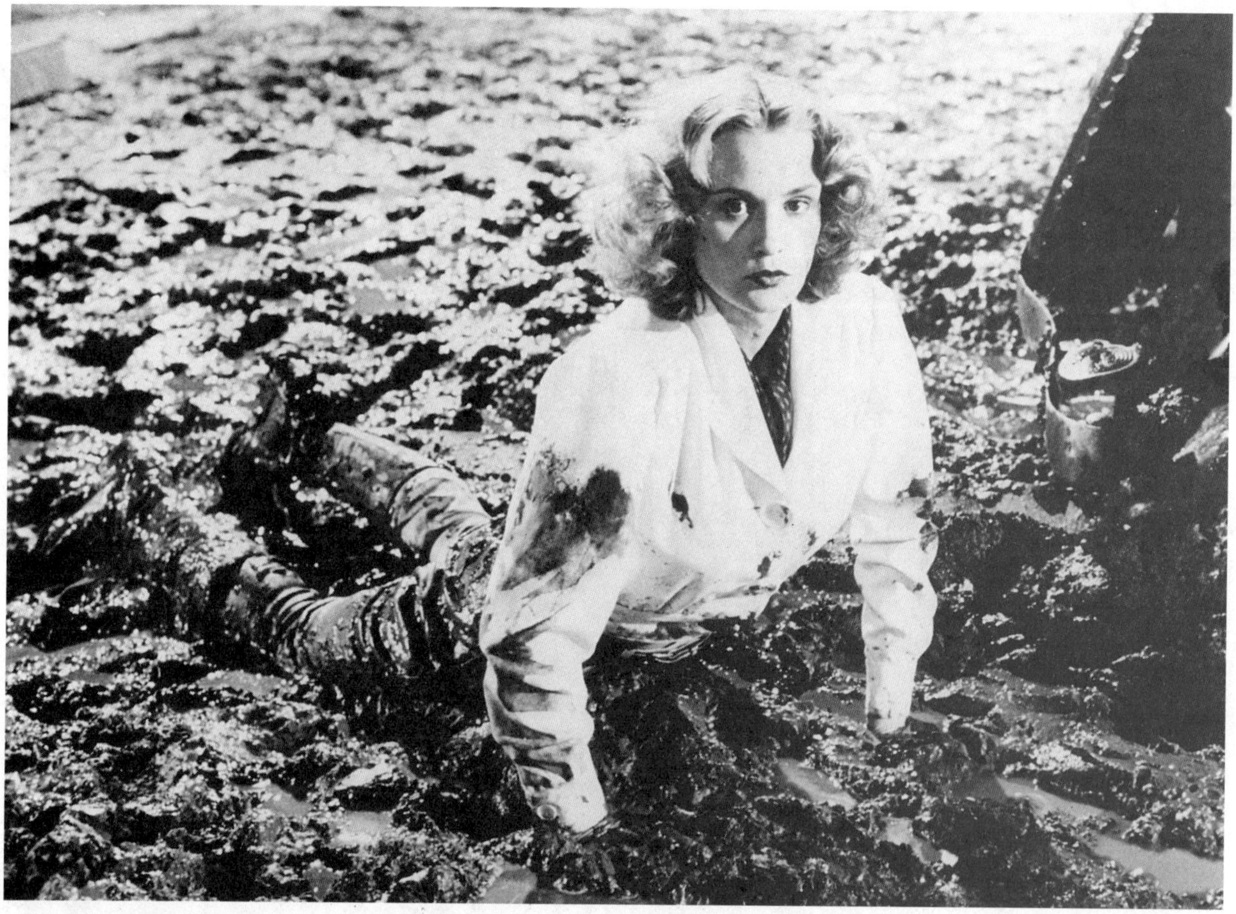

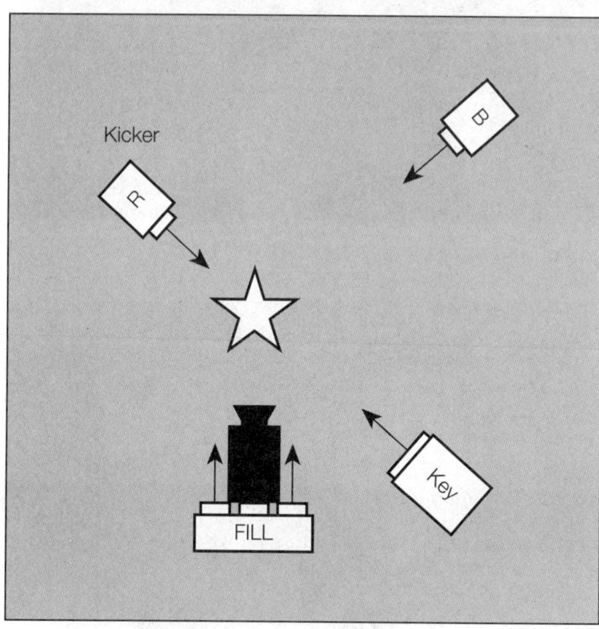

Figure 2.15a (page 29) (*Frances*, Universal City Studios, 1982) This image features a strong back light effect on the mud and subject's hair. Back light on the mud makes it glisten and is a couple of stops hotter than the three-quarter front key light on the actor. The back light is from a fairly low angle so as to emphasize the texture of the mud. The actor is lit in Rembrandt style (see Figure 2.18) with about a 6:1 lighting ratio. Note how her key from the three-quarter front position has little effect on source directionality compared to the back light on the mud. Also note that the kicker on her hair coming from frame left, though motivated by the back lighting, may not result from the back lights themselves.

The back light appears to come from top frame right. This leaves a highlight on the top and frame right side of her legs and pants. Also the mud top frame right is overexposed, which indicates that that part of the background is closer to the light source than is top frame left. The kicker on her comes from frame left and creates a rim on her arm frame left as well as her hair, which indicates that it comes from a lighting unit separate from the back light.

To be emphasized is that the lighting on the subject is independent of the lighting on the mud (background) for the most part. This tends to give an artificial feel to the setup. Also, the back light is rather hard, probably an arc or a large HMI, while the lighting on her face is softened slightly.

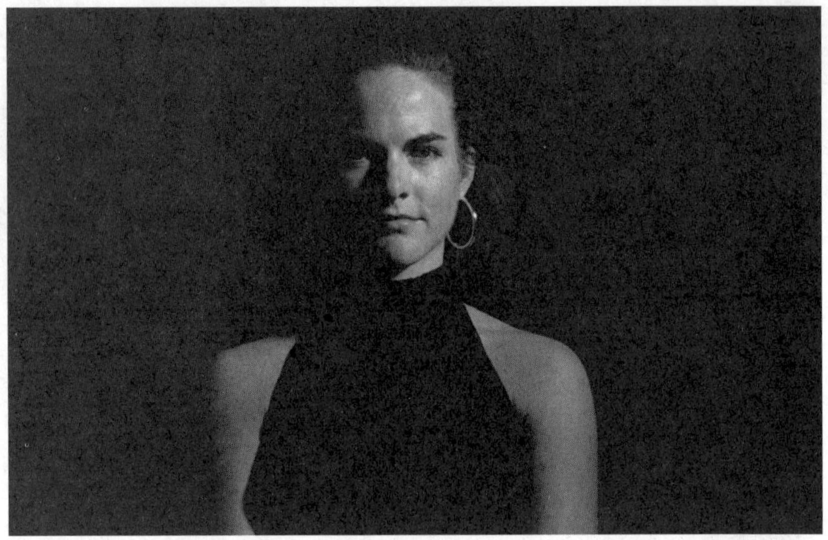
a

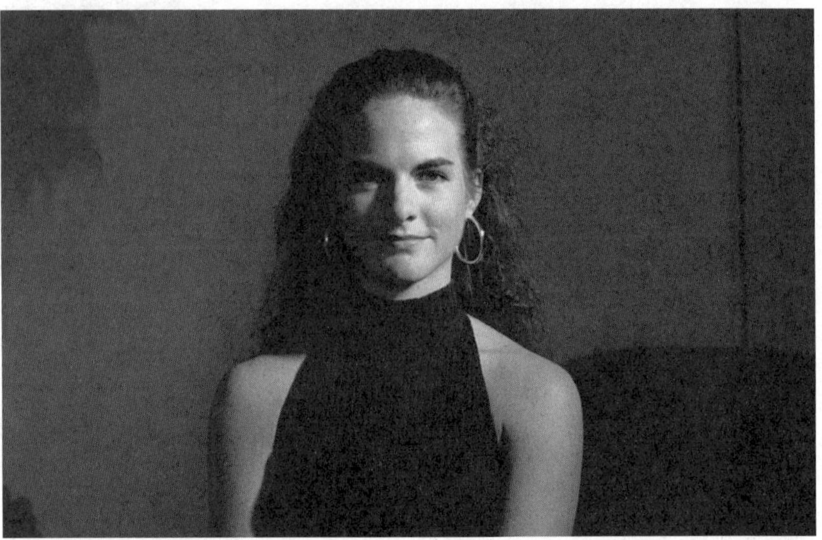
b

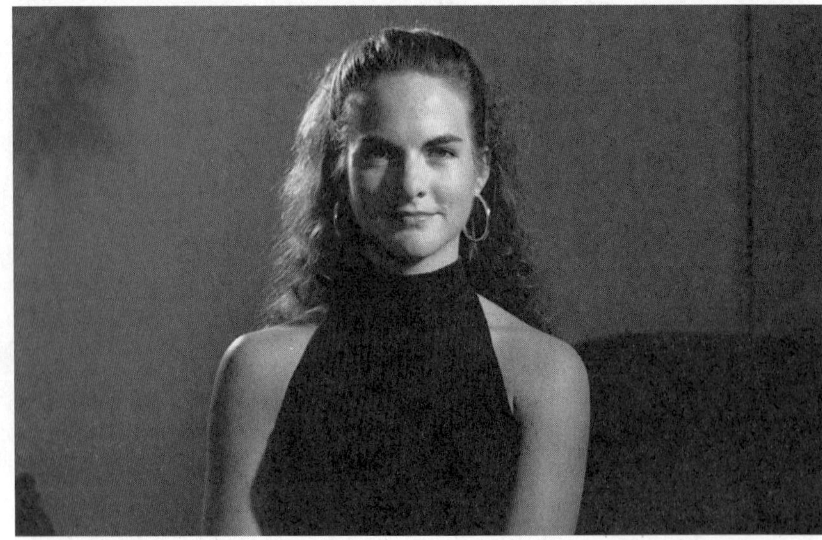
c

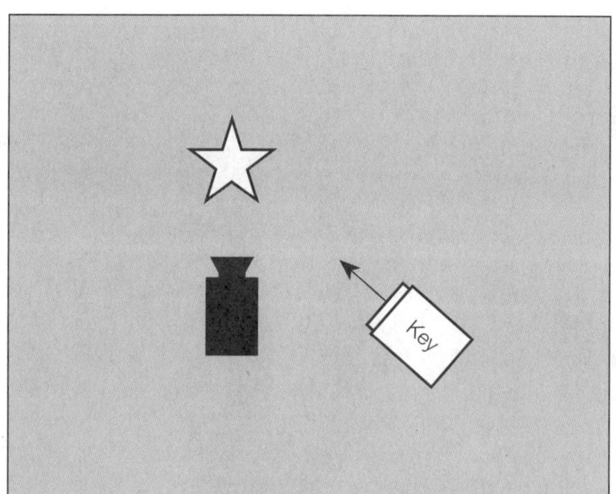

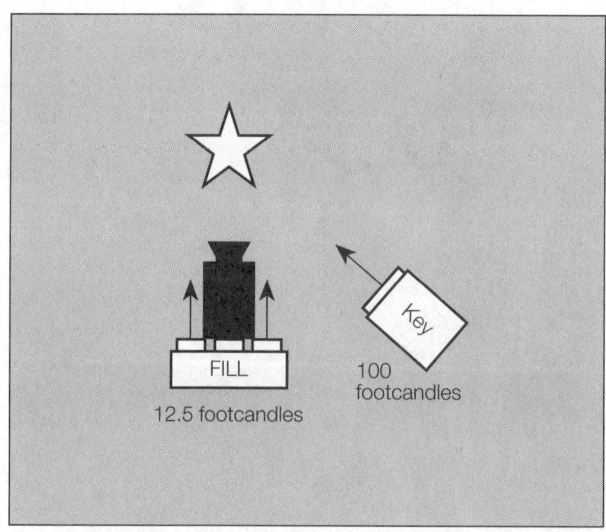

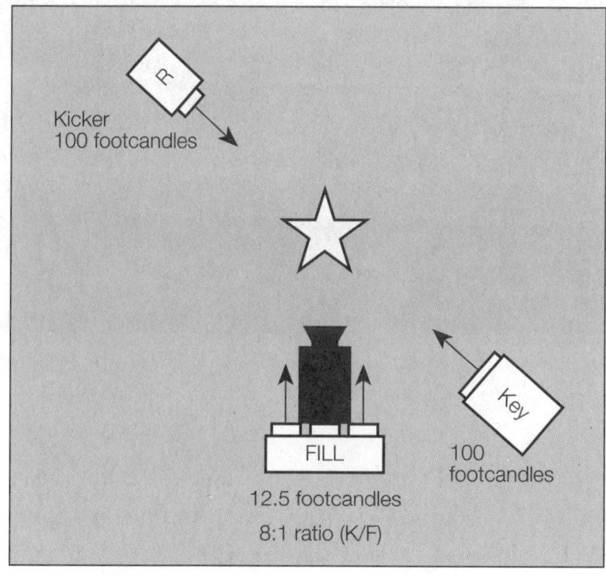

Figure 2.18 (page 34) Classic, Rembrandt lighting effect with three-quarter front key only (a), the addition of a slight fill at about an 8:1 lighting ratio (b), and the addition of the kicker in (c). The kicker comes from across the imaginary circle from the key, provides a rim effect on the hair and shoulder, and is set to about the same intensity as the key. The slight amount of background light in (b) and (c) comes from the fill itself. In reality the wall was white.

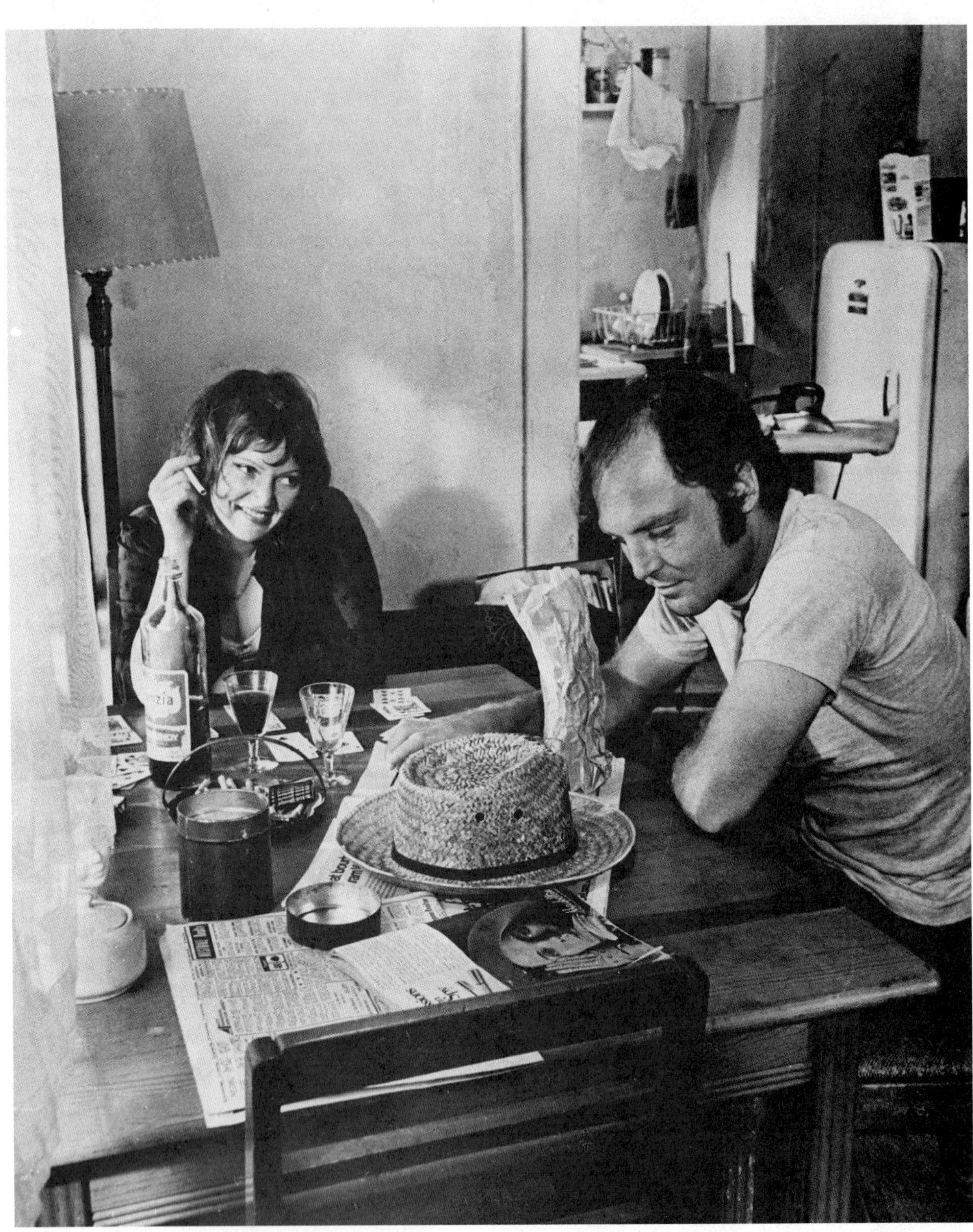

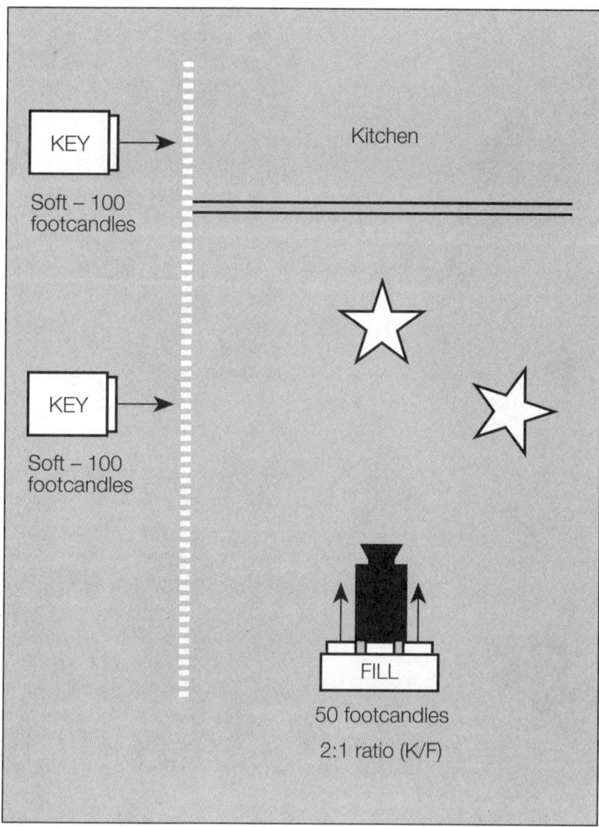

Figure 2.19b (page 35) (*Fat City*, Columbia Pictures, 1972) This day interior effect is established by the motivated lighting from the window frame left. As with an available light interior, the light is mostly soft. Even the key light through the window is softened by the curtain and perhaps additional diffusion. Note how the key light has been patterned in with patches of light and shadow. We can determine the angle of the key light by observing the shadow of the woman's head on the wall behind her along with the window/curtain highlight. There is also a window highlight on the man's face and arm frame left. This is very subtle and could be created by spill from the light on the woman or result from another light coming through the window.

There is a lot of very soft, bounced fill hitting the table foreground and man frame right, which illuminates the wall behind the woman. Her head shadow on the wall and the man's facial shadows are very light indicating a 2:1 lighting ratio—window as key to fill light intensity. Reflections from this fill can be seen on the table foreground right and the man's chair. This fill also creates a highlight on the man's head frame right. The nose shadow on the woman is very dark indicating she has been flagged off from this fill light. Because of the high amount of fill, the window effect is not as strong as it would be in reality. For example, with available light, the falloff to the man would underexpose him several stops, but here the fill level, though suggesting natural falloff, prevents him from being more than a stop darker than the woman (see Figure 7.1 and its analysis). Also, since this scene is exposed for his face, objects near the window would be more overexposed. Here they are about a stop overexposed. The effectiveness of the realistic illusion is hard to judge since the original is in color.

There are two approaches to establishing this setup; both will result in the same effect. One approach is to create the window effects and then add fill as necessary. The other approach is to light the two rooms with the overall illumination and then add the window highlight effects.

The motivated window effect is repeated in the small kitchen seen through the doorway background right. The window is patterned in gently. The dishes and refrigerator get highlights (note the plate's shadow on the wall), and the rest of the kitchen has an overall fill at about a 2:1 ratio. The source directionality in the background thus duplicates that of the main subject area in the foreground. Since the lighting ratio is 2:1, we can see everything in the photo.

This is the standard way to establish a realistic illusion—single source motivation coming from the window frame left with high interior fill levels and a lot of bounced, ambient light to duplicate the natural daylight interior. The emphasis on natural light in this photo represents the lighting of a place rather than the actors. The actors are inserted into the lighting scheme along with the chairs and table and kitchen background and are not given a star treatment in any way. The effect here is so well done that we are not sure whether they are in a set or real-life location. This represents the ideal for the natural-light school of thought.

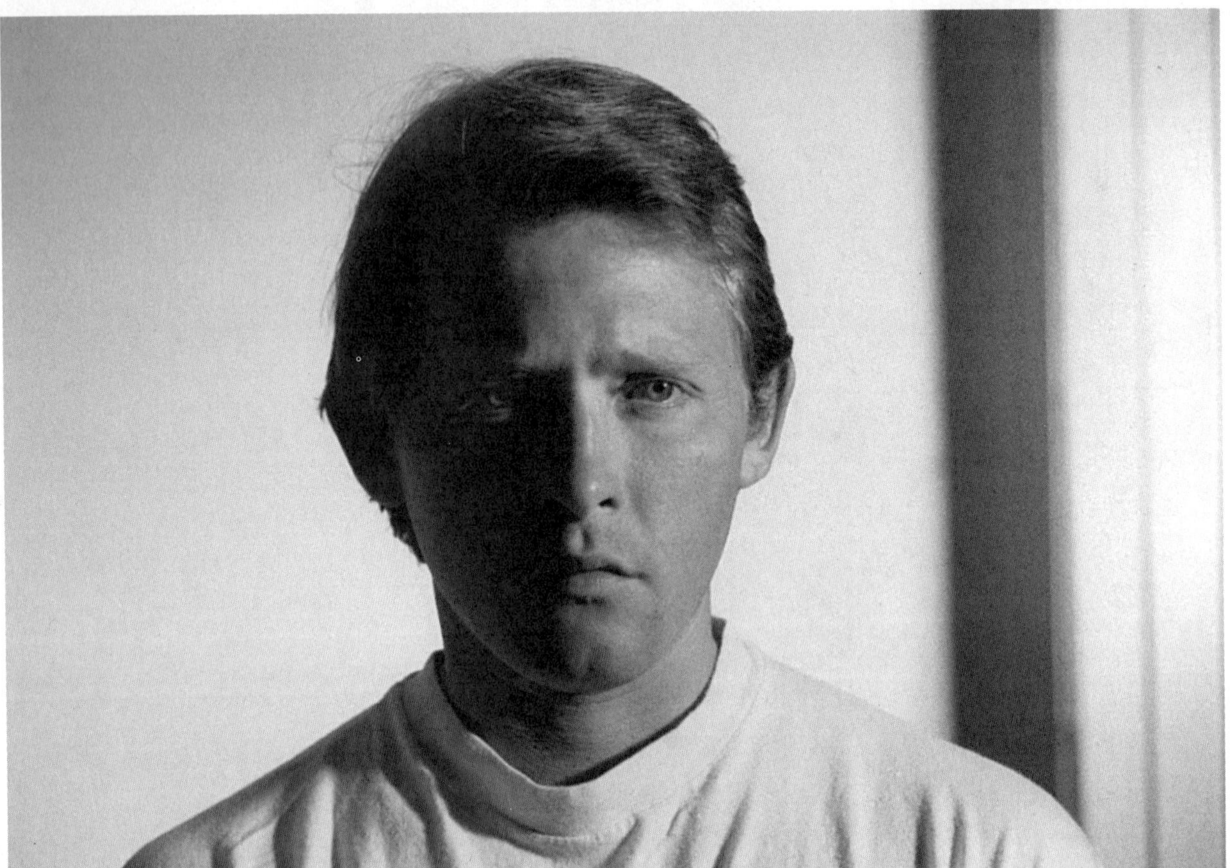

a

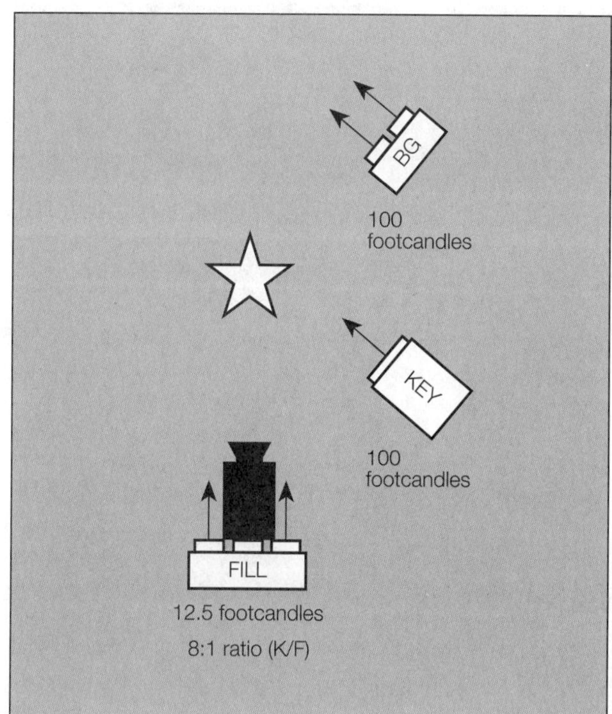

Figure 2.20 (page 36) (a) Three-quarter front key, 8:1 facial ratio; (b) three-quarter front key, 2:1 facial ratio; (c) three-quarter front key, 6:1 facial ratio. The point of these three shots is to show how the background lighting can be controlled so as to render the background white (a), midgray (b), and black (c). In fact, the wall was white. This means the wall was lit to approximately the same level as the key light in (a) so that it rendered as its true white zone 9 value. In (b) the zone 9 value was reduced by four stops to a zone 5 level, and in (c) by eight stops to a zone 1 value. The lighting diagrams indicate how this is done.

b

BG
6.25 footcandles
4 stops under
KEY
100
footcandles
FILL
50 footcandles
2:1 ratio (K/F)

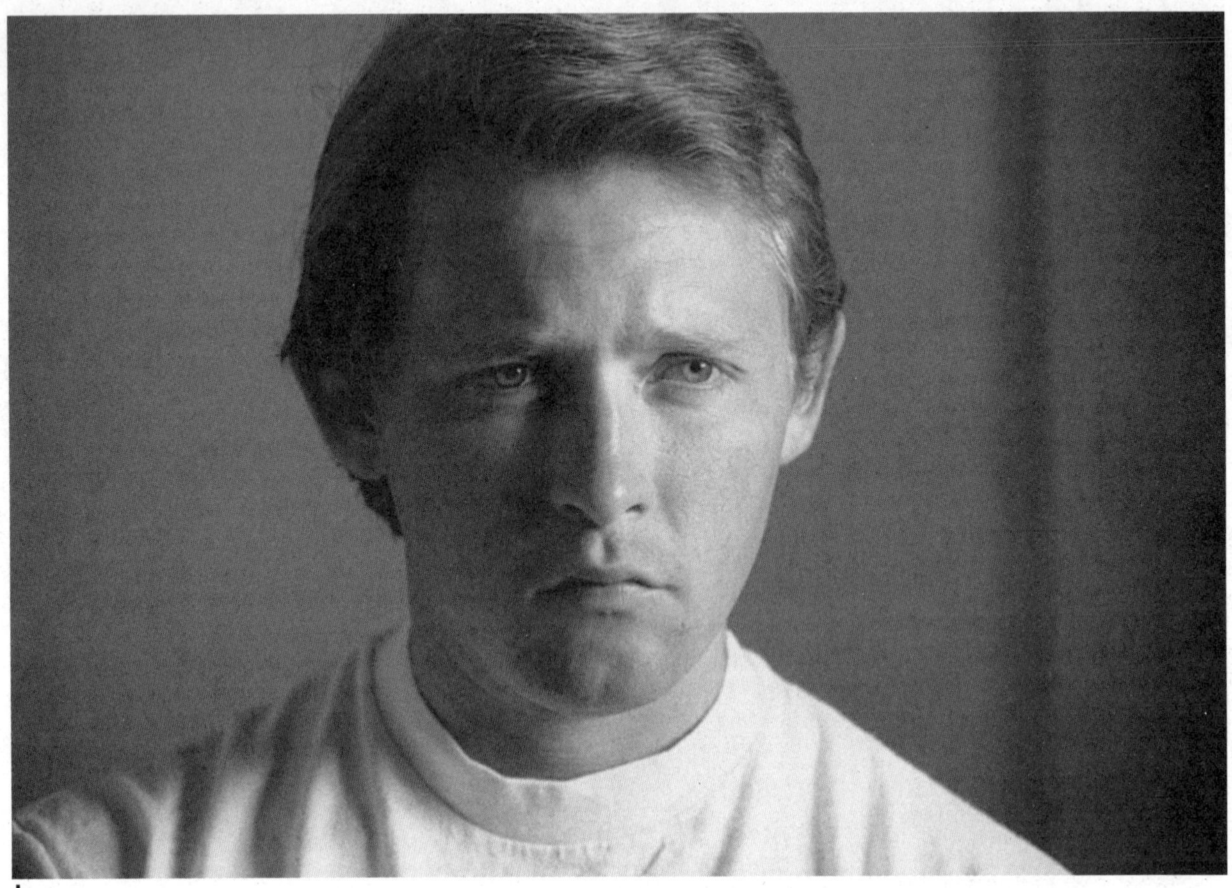

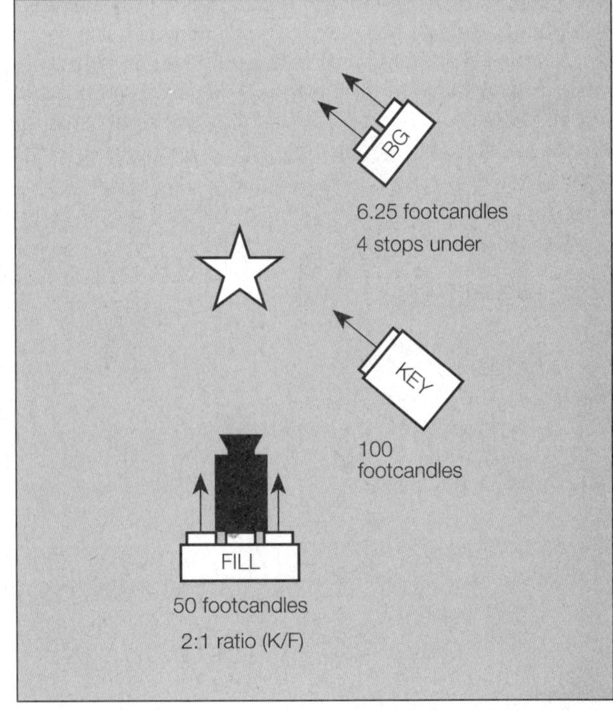

c

BG
.4 footcandles
8 stops under
KEY
100
footcandles
FILL
18.75 footcandles
6:1 ratio (K/F)

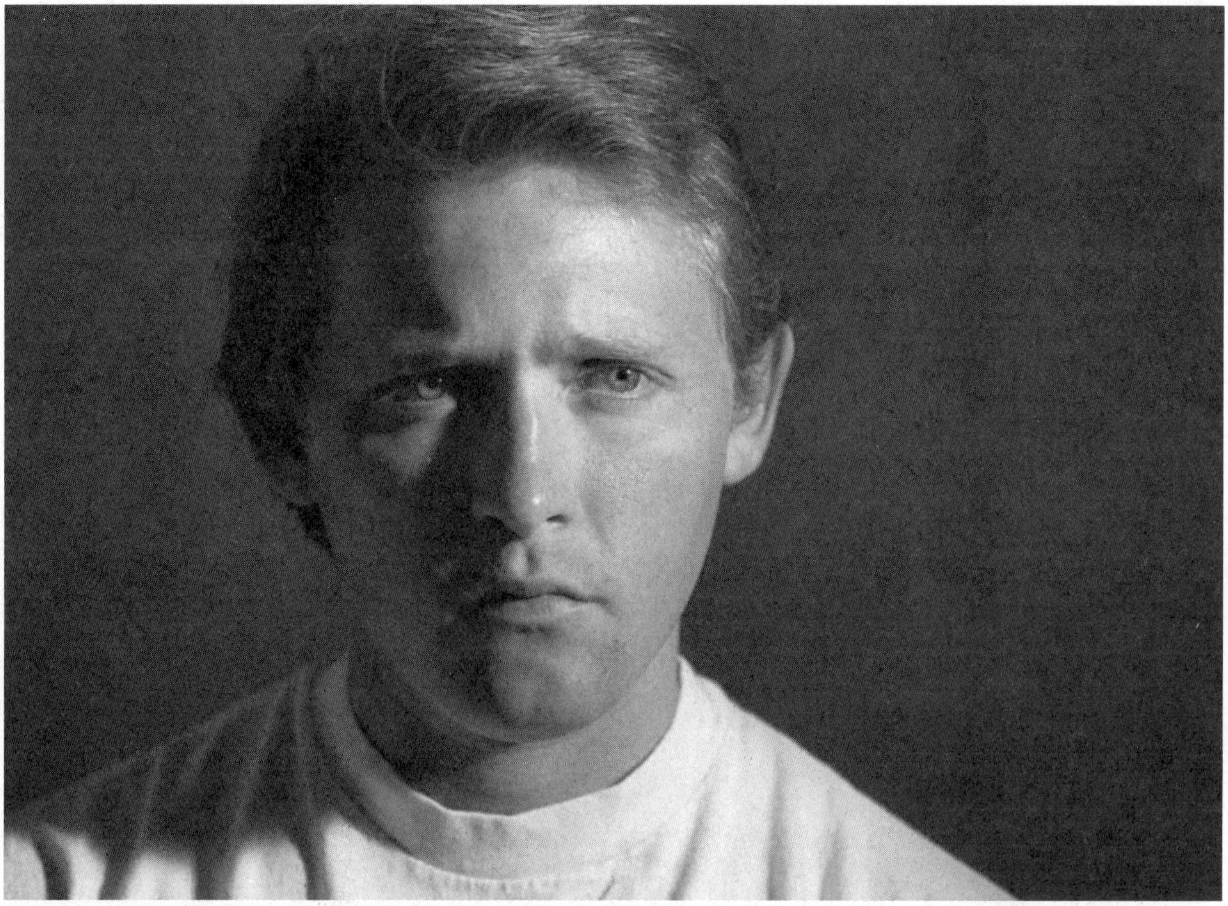

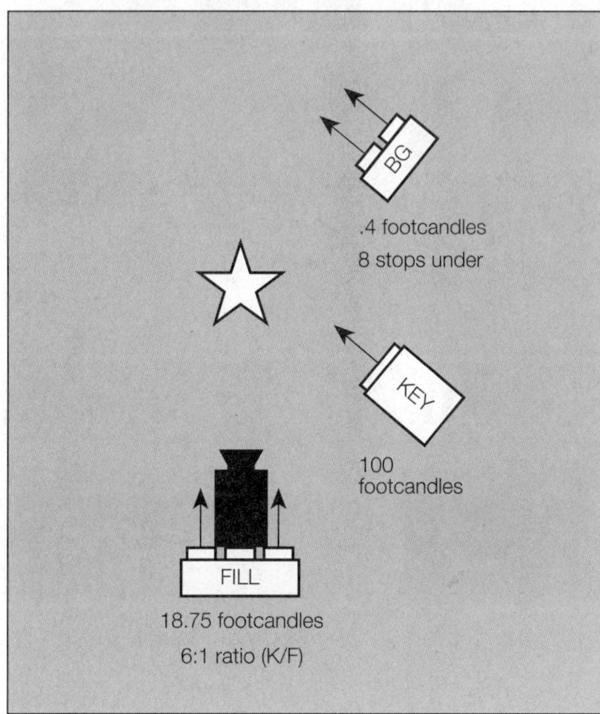

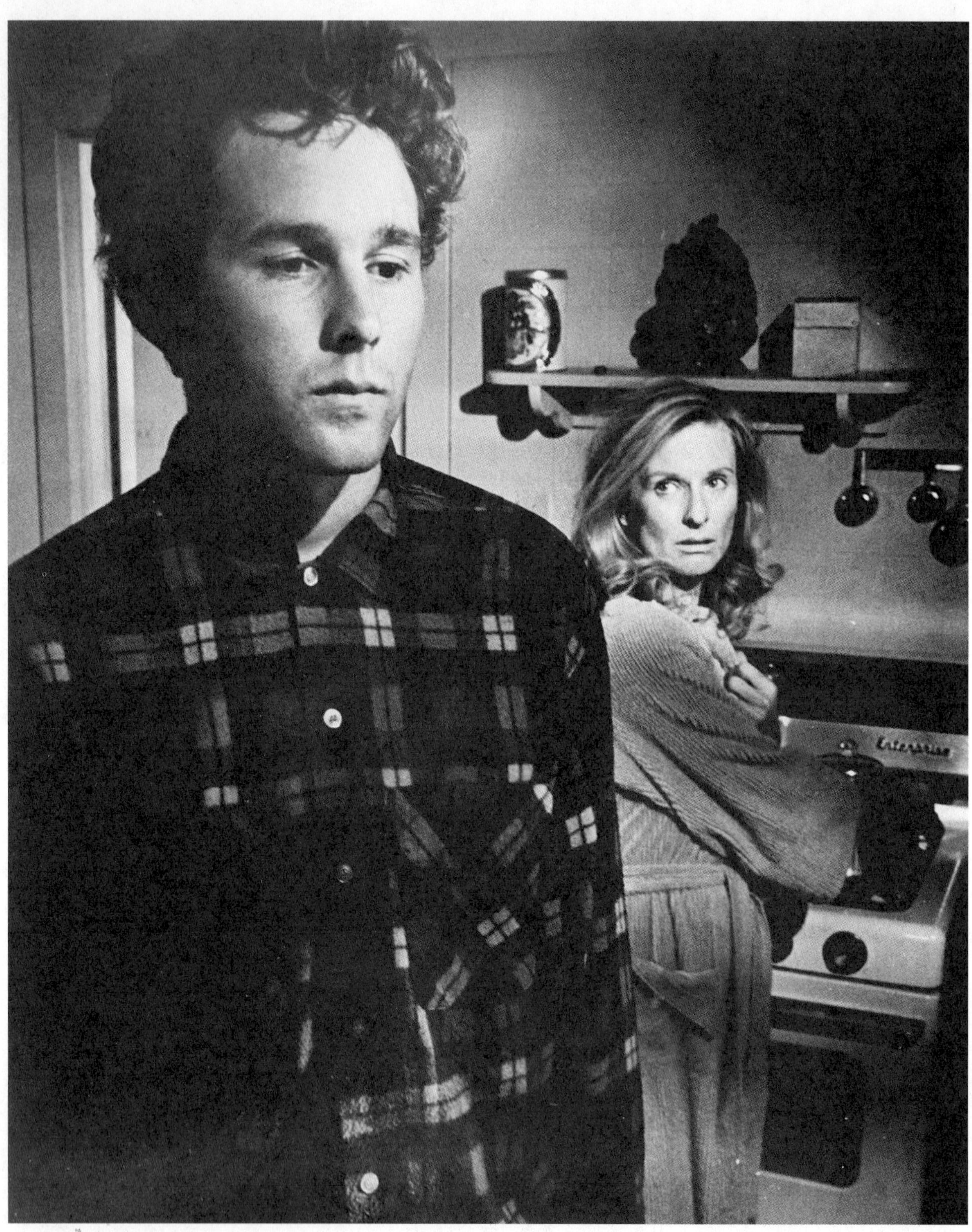

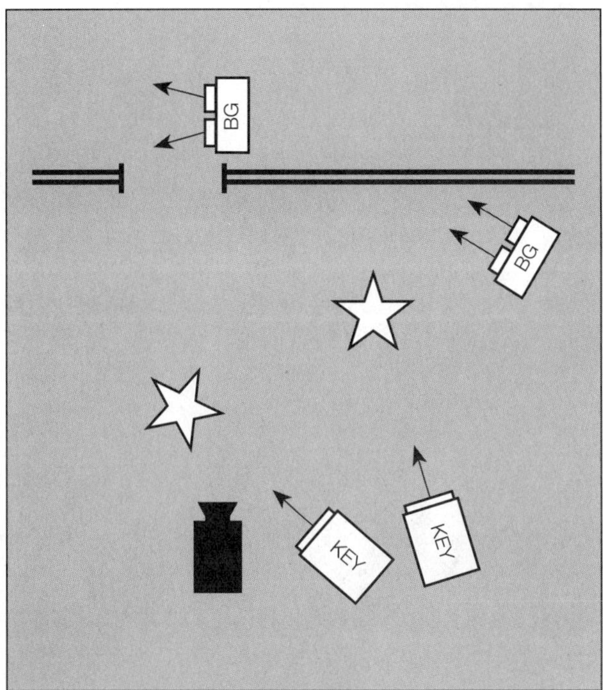

Figure 2.20d (page 36) (*The Last Picture Show*, Columbia Pictures, 1973) This shot illustrates how backgrounds may be handled and controlled. The first thing to notice in this night interior is that the key lighting for both actors appears to come from an overhanging kitchen light and is partially shaded off their bodies so that only their faces are lit. The lighting is fairly hard as can be seen from the sharp, black shadows on their necks and the background wall.

Both actors are lit frontally, but since they are fairly far apart spatially, we can surmise that two lights are being used to simulate the single, overhead source. This seems to be reinforced by the fact that there are two reflections on the pans hanging on the wall frame right. Note the different angles the shadows make on the actors' necks. As in Figure 2.19b, the key light is patterned on their bodies leaving the faces emphasized. There is no fill light evident; the shadows are very black.

Since it is a night interior, the background is kept dark. It is lit from the same angle as the woman (see the shelf shadow on the wall), so it is lit by either her key light or another light from the same direction. Again, the two reflections on the pans frame right might be emanating from her key and a separate background light. Either way, the background lighting has been flagged off severely top frame right. The top of the stove has also been shaded off to keep our interest on the two characters. Behind the actor foreground left we can see a doorway. The cinematographer has lit the wall outside the door and placed a bright rim of light on the door frame, again suggesting an overhead light in the hall or other room. It is possible the lighting outside the doorway comes from the same light source as the one lighting the background wall and shelf—her key or a separate fixture. In any event, the hallway light is at about the same intensity as the key. There is a lot of texture on his shirt and her bathrobe. This could result from small clothes lights or could just be a result of the angle of the key and its patterning on their bodies.

The lighting used here, controlled pools of light, is best accomplished with Fresneled light units, a painting with light effect. The overall result is a realistic, kitchen interior at night, but the patterning of light and shadow also creates a moody low-key effect. Comparing this example with the one in Figure 2.19b reveals much about the differences between day and night interiors. Contrast the use of large amounts of overall fill in the daylight interior with the absence of fill in the night interior. Compare the use of soft ubiquitous daylight in the day interior with the selective, precisely controlled pools of hard light in the night interior. Both photographs are examples of motivated, realistic styles. Both imitate the real-life equivalent and utilize our knowledge of natural and artificially lit locations to maintain their illusion of reality.

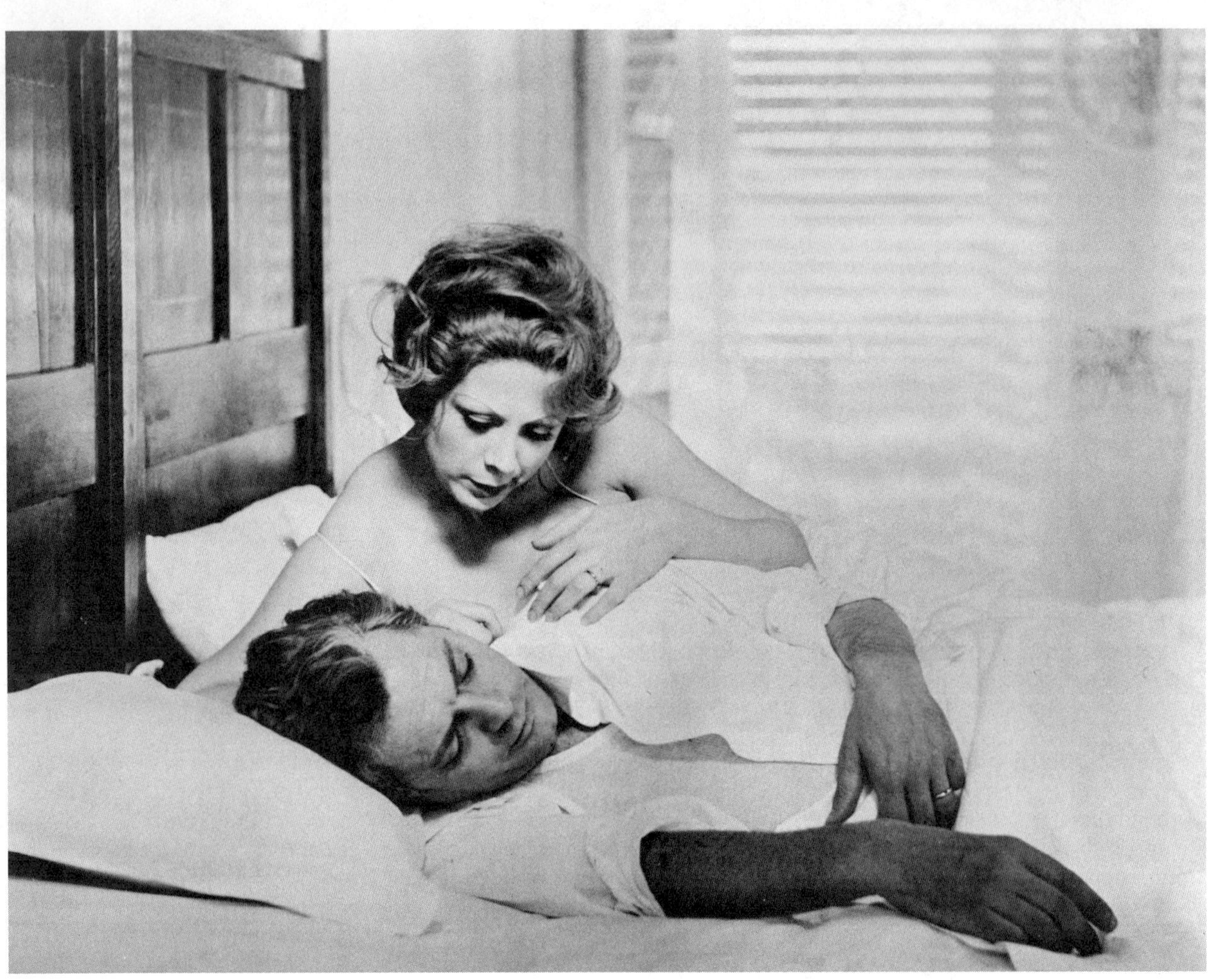

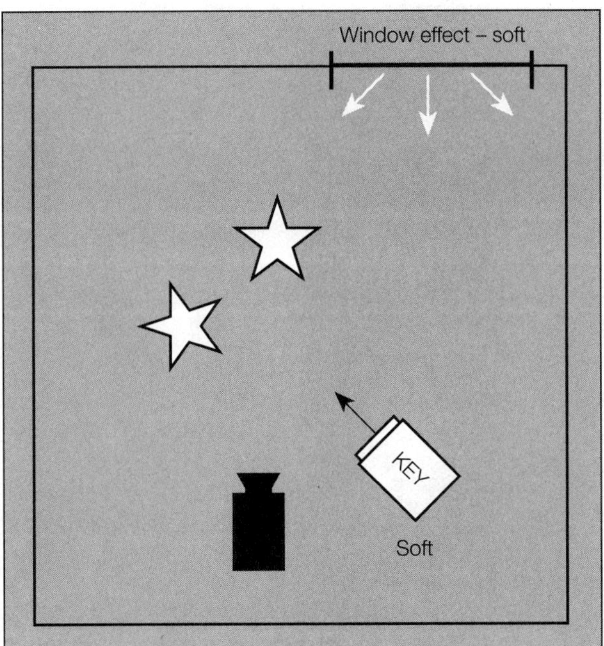

Figure 2.21a (page 37) (*8 1/2*, Embassy Pictures, 1963) This shot uses a high-key background, a window effect with much gauze. There is a lot of softish window light pouring into the back half of the frame through the window and onto the bedstead area. Note how the venetian blind pattern is visible on both the curtains and bedstead. The feeling is bright, early morning. The level of realism is low in this photo since the actors are obviously not lit by the window, which functions more as an interesting background. If we assume the window was exposed at T 5.6, then they are lit to about T 5.6 as well. They stand out too brightly relative to the window for a natural light effect. This is more a star-style lighting treatment.

The woman has an overhead frontal key on her face. There is no attempt to simulate the window's directionality. The neck shadow indicates the direction of the key light. The man's key appears to be a softened version of hers—note the nose shadow on his face—and could be either a spilloff from hers or a separate light. His nose shadow is lighter than hers, which would normally indicate a separate fill light, but here there is so much white sheet to reflect light that the nose shadow may be lighter than her neck shadow only because it is closer to the sheet.

The key light effect comes from above, frame right, and has been shaded off along his foreground arm and the pillow area bottom frame right. It is fairly softish, particularly on him. She is given a harder, glossier look in comparison to the more natural light on him. This may result from her makeup as much as the lighting. The final result is a high key effect: It's all white sheets, white pillows, white curtains, and white shirts. The background is more for mood than realism.

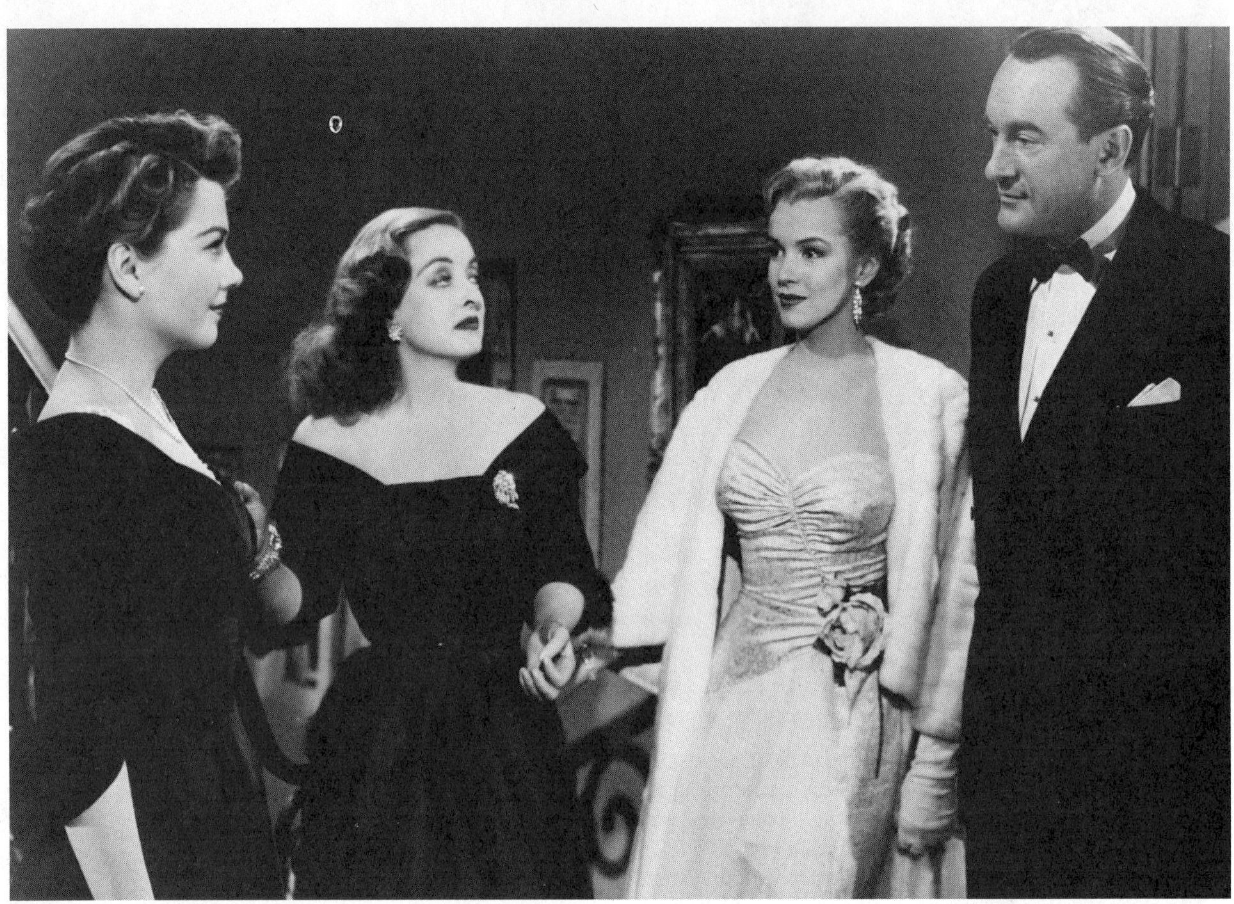

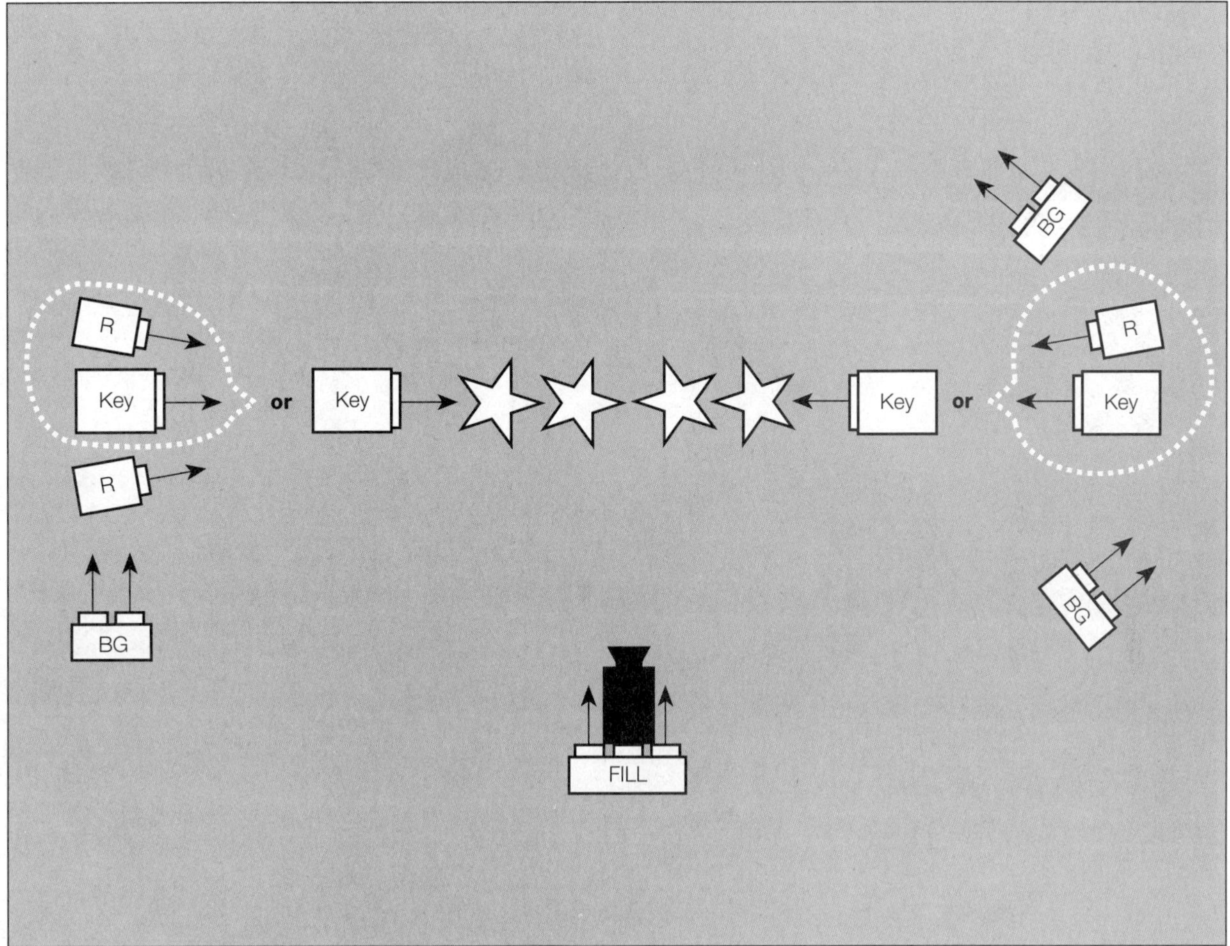

Figure 2.21b (page 37) (*All About Eve*, Twentieth Century Fox, 1950) In contrast to Figure 2.21a, here the background walls are kept dark, about three or four stops underexposed relative to the key light. This is a standard night interior that relies on back light to separate the actors from the background. Like the shot in Figure 2.20d, the four actors are lit as though from a single source above them. In this case, however, the key lights appear to do double duty as back lights. The key lighting the couple frame right functions as a hair light for the actors frame left, and vice versa. It could be that the hair lights are kept separate from the keys, in which case it would be easier to control their intensities relative to the key. In either event, the hair light is quite dominant and about three stops overexposed relative to the key for the actors frame right.

Fill light has been added to the faces as well, as evidenced by the neck shadow on the woman frame right. The fill is about 4:1 but has little effect since most of the key lighting is frontal relative to the actors' faces and facial shadows are minimized. The only other light on the actors is a light from frame left that creates a rim on the arm of the actress frame left. It could be this is spill from the hair light on her, though it seems to come from too low an angle for the hair light.

The background is lit to a dark level and is flagged off top of frame to keep our attention on the actors. The background is at about a 16:1 ratio relative to the subject plane. A separate light appears to be lighting the staircase frame left. Its effect is most visible on the railing, and in fact, it is flaring slightly in the top and bottom frame left of this publicity still. This light is probably the one responsible for the bannister shadow on the back wall bottom center frame. The bannister shadow is very sharply defined; hence hard light is being used. The background frame right also has some light, which balances the bannister highlight frame left. By separating the lighting on the actors from the background, the cinematographer can use the background for compositional and mood effects while still maintining an interesting visual variety.

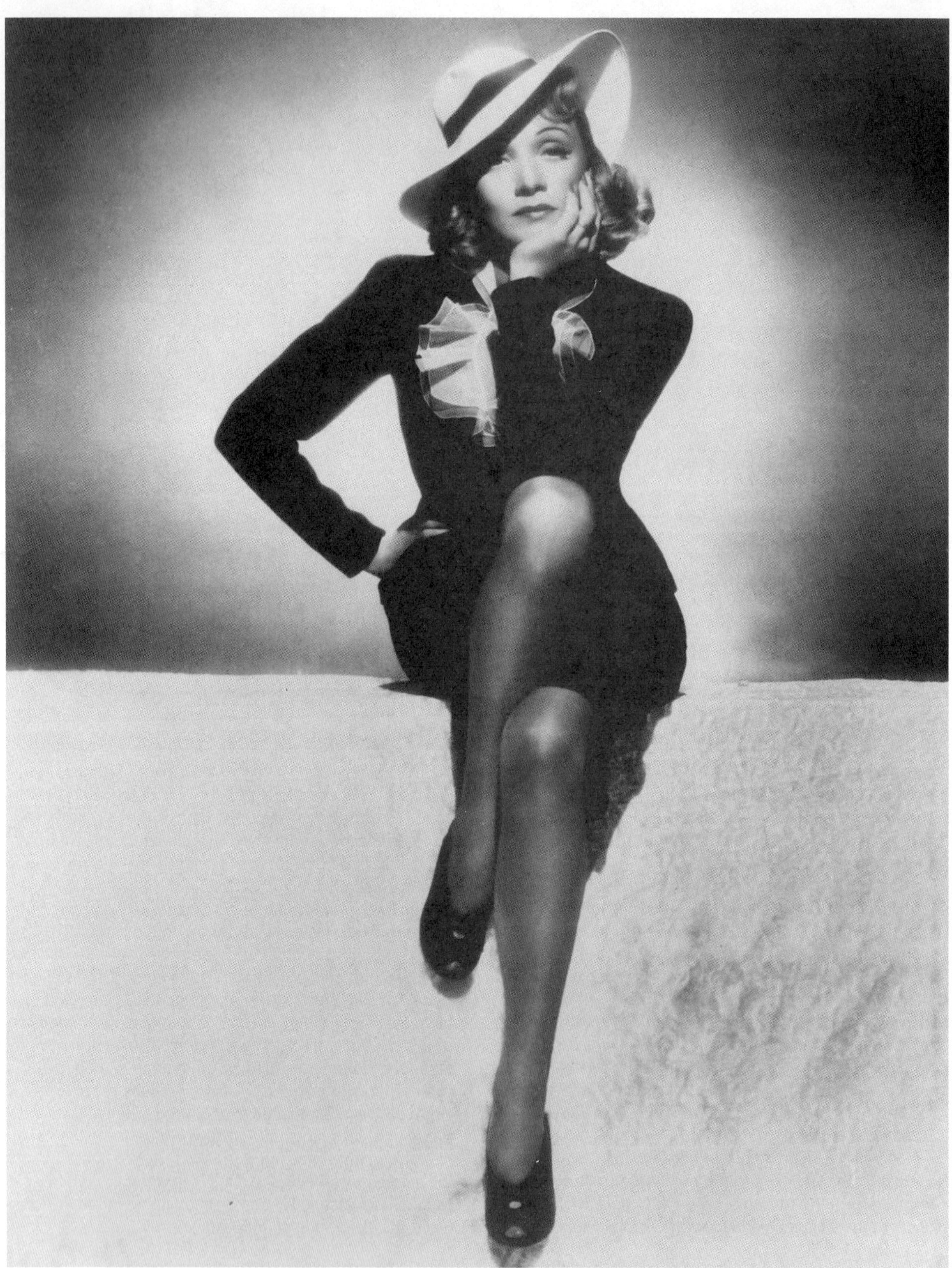

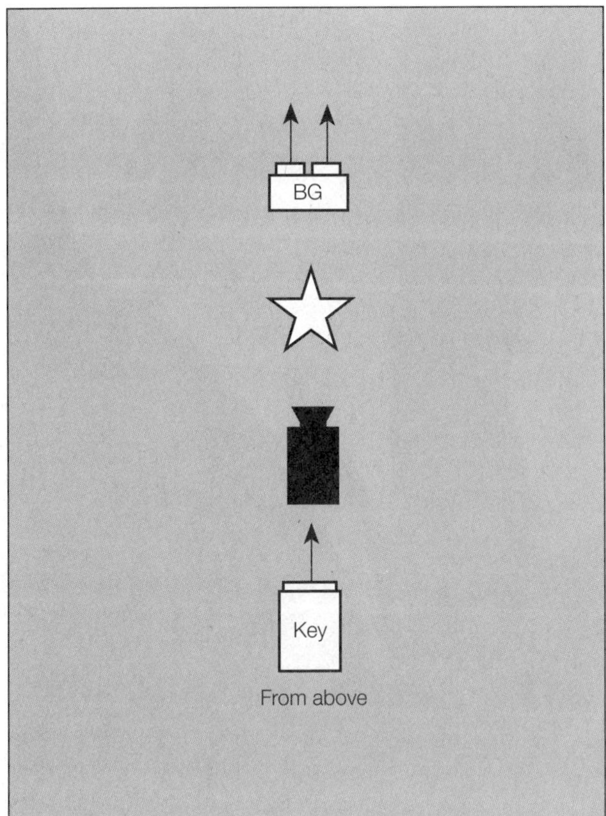

Figure 2.22a (page 38) (Paramount Pictures publicity photo of Marlene Dietrich) The subject is lit by an overhead, frontal key. The shadow thrown by the brim of her hat indicates a fairly hard light source. The overhead key lights her full body as can be seen from the foot shadows on the white fabric. Both knees reflect the light as well. The fabric exhibits some texture frame right; this appears to result from the key itself, not an additional light.

A light has been positioned behind the subject to illuminate the background. It has been given a jagged-edge effect and falls off rapidly to dark gray. By lighting the background behind the actor to about a stop brighter than the key, the cinematographer obtains a cameo setup, which separates the black dress from the background effectively and creates a kind of "glowing" effect. Note how the cinematographer has patterned the white part of the background to match her shape so that where her elbow sticks out she is still in front of white wall. The wall behind her is probably off-white in reality.

The top of her hat is overexposed and has the same glowing effect as the background. It is presumably overexposed because of the angle it presents to the key light and the fact that it is closer to the key than her face is. The scattering, glowing effect results from diffusion on the camera lens.

This is an interesting lighting setup and is similar to a silhouette effect—black against white—except that here the background is lit only to about a stop brighter than the foreground. Separation is done by placing black against a white field. There is thus no need for back light separation.

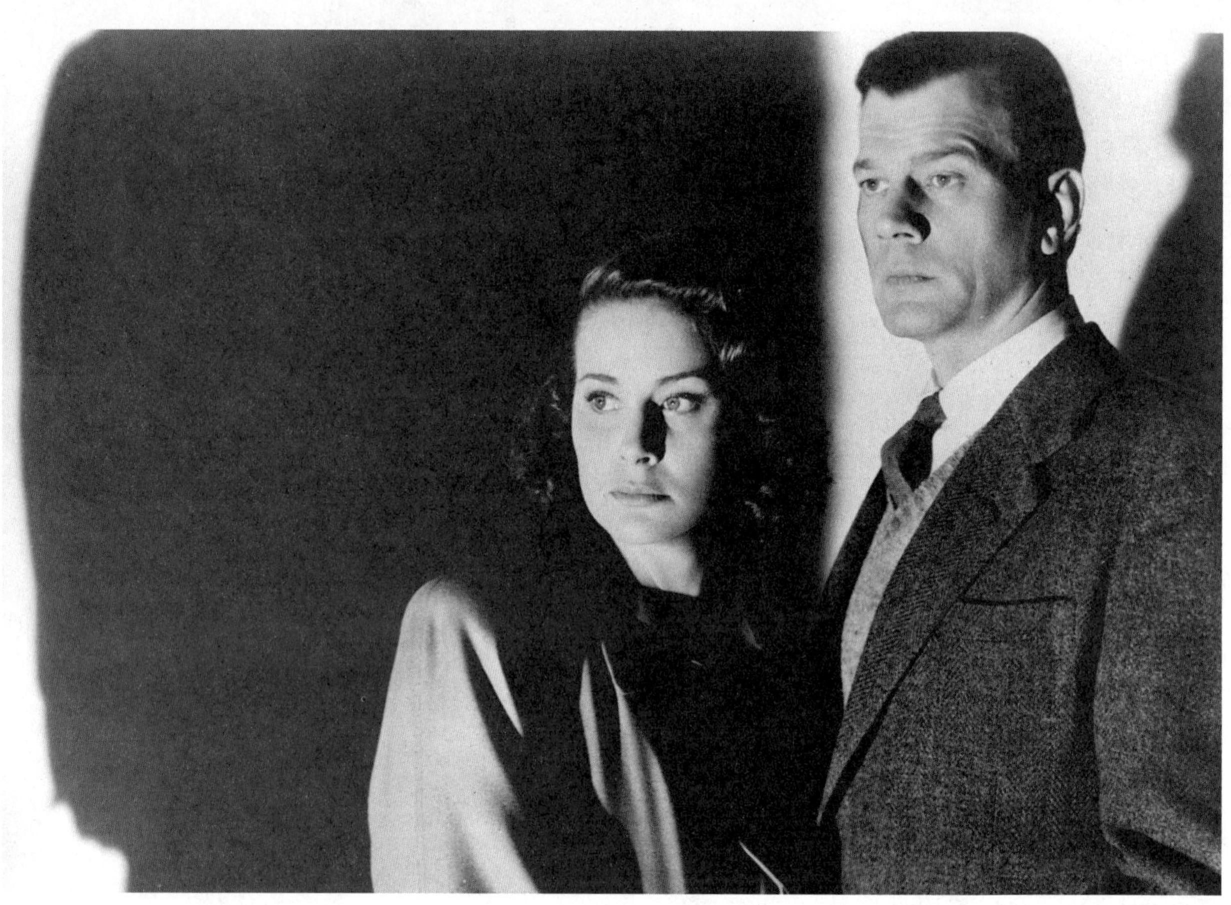

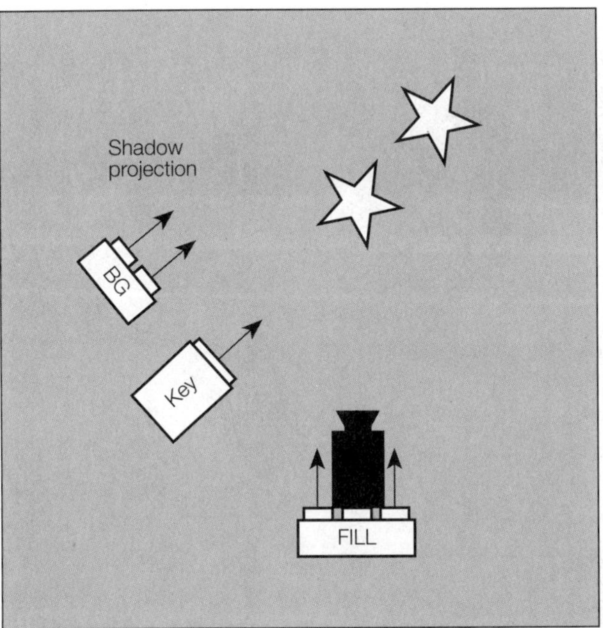

Figure 2.22b (page 38) (*The Third Man*, Twentieth Century Fox, 1949) Another example of a subject/background effect. Here the door outside frame left has been opened, lighting the two actors and creating a pattern of black and white on the background. The key light comes from a frame left position and throws a shadow on the wall behind the actor frame right. The key comes from about a three-quarter front position and throws strong nose and coat shadows. The key is hard and comes from a camera-level position as evidenced by the nose shadows. The edge of the shadow between the black and white portions of the wall, presumably created by the door itself, has been carefully positioned so as to fall between the two actors. There is no evidence of fill light though the key provides an eyelight for both actors.

There appears to be a figure standing in the doorway. Presumably, this is "Harry Lime, the Third Man." The evidence for this is that there is a shadow of a large man frame left. If this is so, then the lighting on the background may be more contrived than it appears since it would be necessary to project the figure and doorframe shadows precisely to maintain the compositional balance as visible in this shot. In this case, the background and key would come from different sources.

This shot is a good example of the use of black and white patterning on the background, to create not only mood but meaning as well—the implication is that she is "evil," or untrustworthy, in comparison to him. This results from her being placed against a black shadow and him against white. This patterning also creates visual variety and a strong nighttime effect in a world of intrigue and mystery.

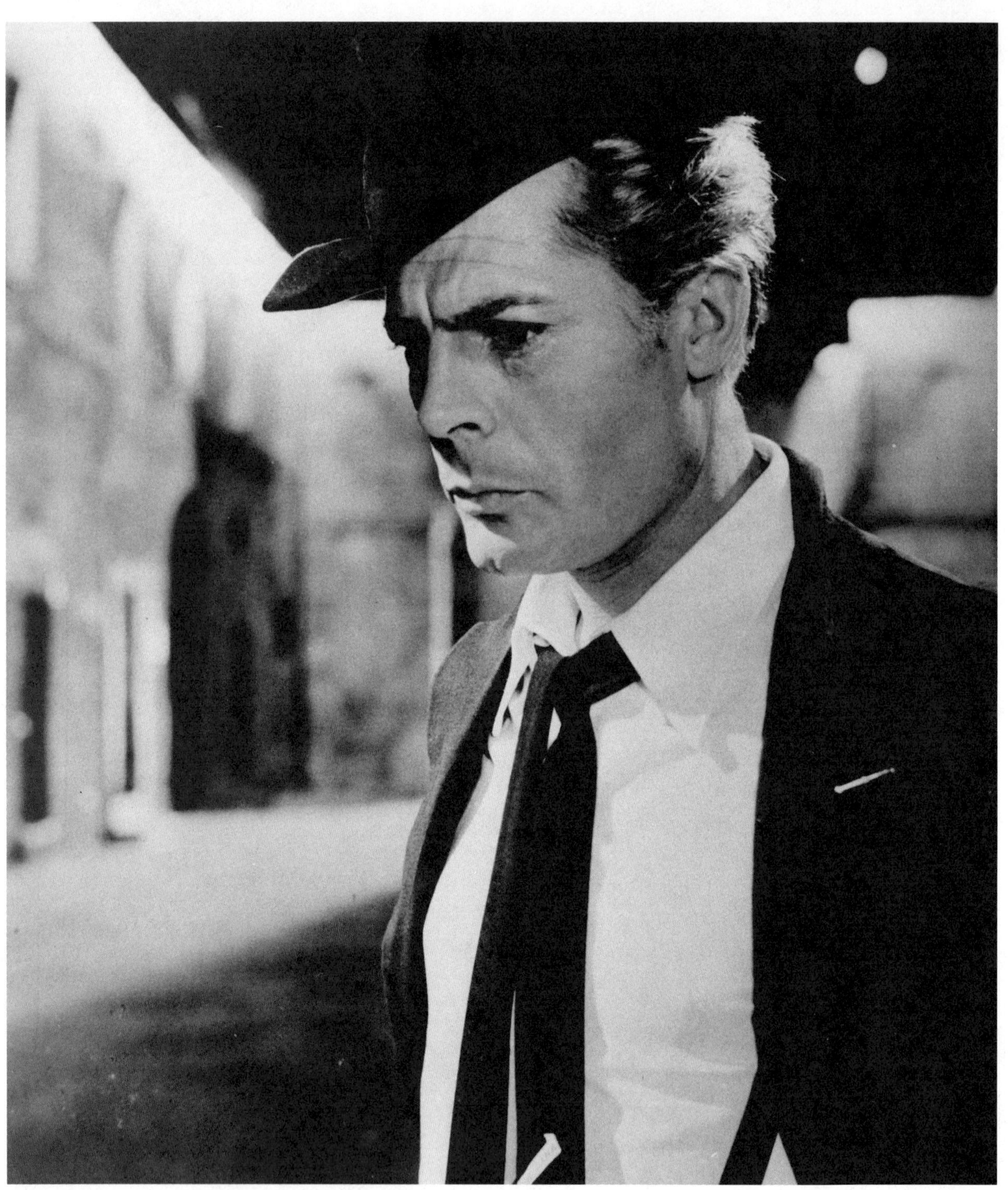

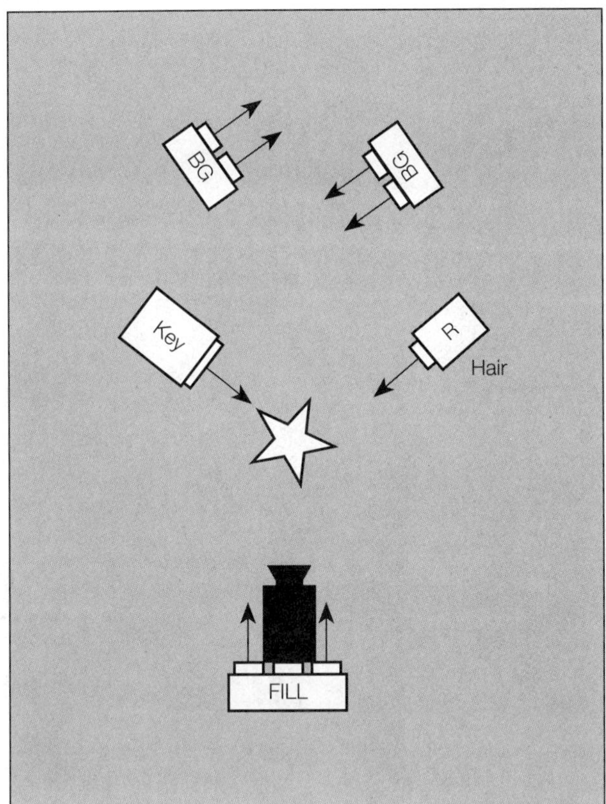

Figure 2.23a (page 39) (*8½*, Embassy Pictures, 1963) This shot reveals how lighting can be used to create a balanced composition. The lighting on the actor is independent of the background lighting. The actor has a three-quarter rear key striking his hat, chin, and body from frame left. The fill is set to about a 4:1 ratio. A back light rims his shoulder, neck, and hair frame right.

The background lighting is arranged so that the buildings and part of the pavement frame left are highlighted. The top of the building frame left and the edge of the shadow frame left create two vectors that lead our eyes to the character's face. Note how the bright vector from the top of the building is continued by the key light on the actor's chin. The actor's bright white shirt is balanced against the dark pavement frame left. His face holds our attention because of the two graphic vectors and also because the blackness at the top of frame holds our eye "down" onto his face. Obviously, the first function of the background lighting is to establish the night exterior, but having accomplished that, the cinematographer may utilize background lighting for compositional purposes.

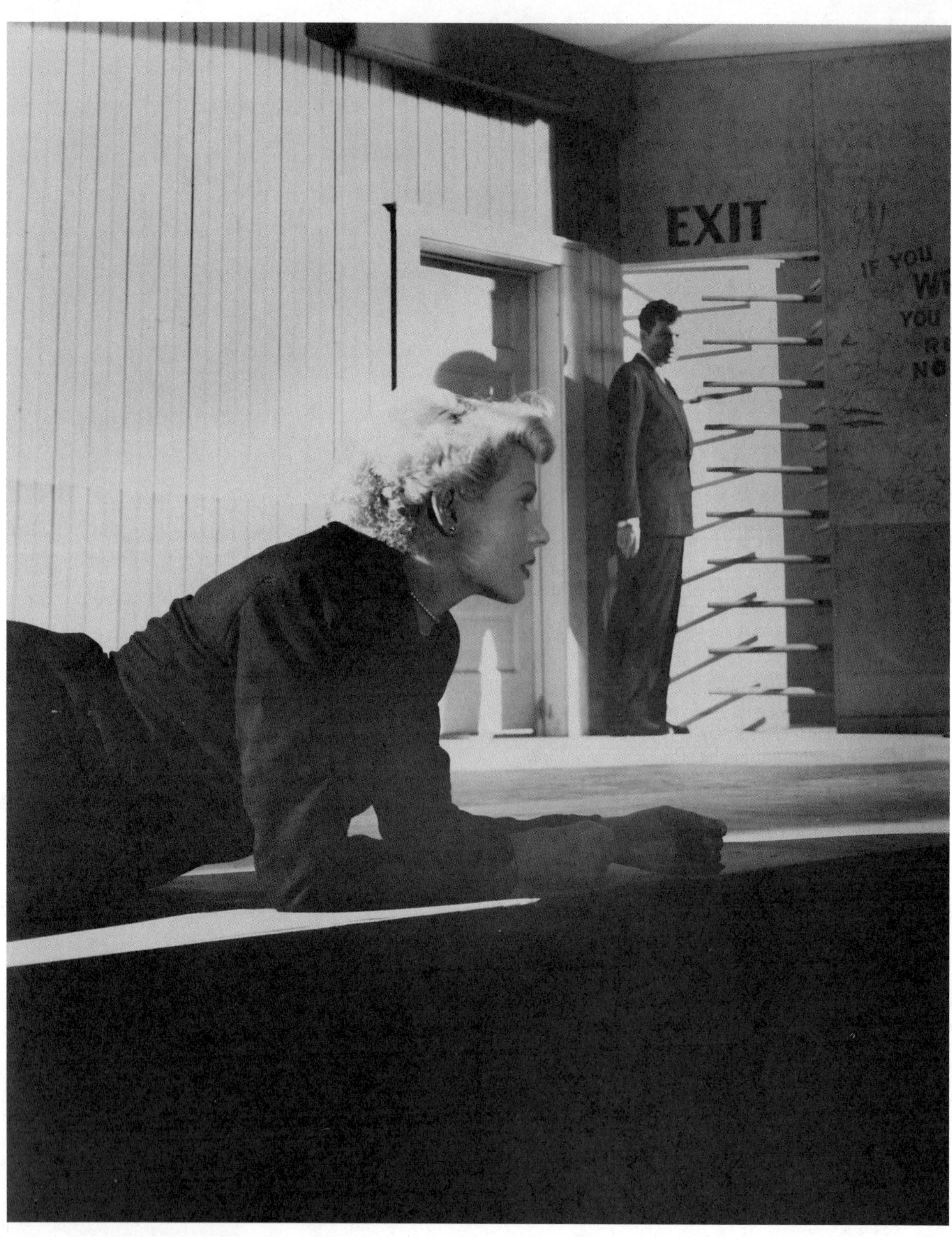
EXIT
IF YOU

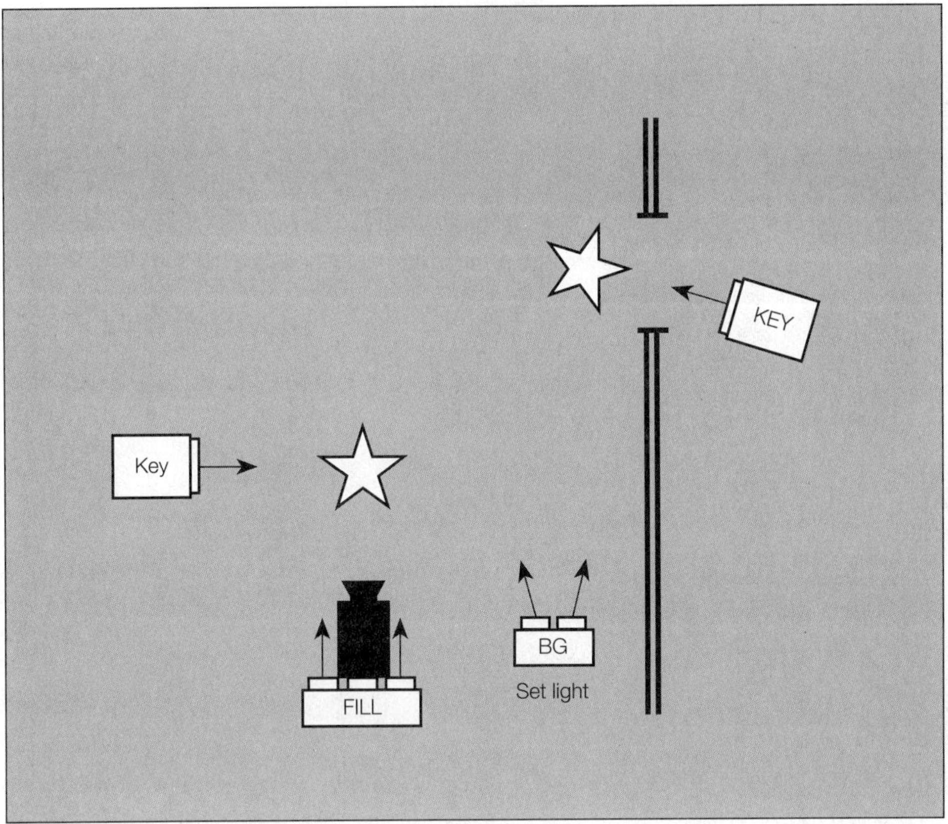

Figure 2.23b (page 39) (*The Lady from Shanghai*, Columbia Pictures, 1947) This shot illustrates the complexities of the Hollywood-studio style of the 1940s and 1950s and the reliance on shadow projections to create interesting patterns of light and shadow. As in Figure 2.23a, the black floor area and the white wall in the background are used to provide compositional balance. The woman frame center is lit from the back and above. Note the strong hair light. The man in the background is lit with a spotlight coming through the exit doorway. The key on the background subject is shaded off so that the wall immediately behind the figure is in shadow. The bar gate is arranged so that its shadows on the wall fill the rectangular doorway.

A shadow area is maintained on the floor between the two figures and their respective key lights. Fill light is used to lighten the woman's face, but it is shaded off her hands. Another light puts the white wall behind her at a zone 8 level. It also brings the "exit" wall frame right up to about zone 5. The combination of the light coming through the doorway and the background light results in the hotter rectangle on the wall top frame left.

This is a complicated lighting setup. Since we are in a studio, a large number of lights can be used—and controlled—to create a frame full of mood and mystery, with a lot of visual variety and an interesting composition.

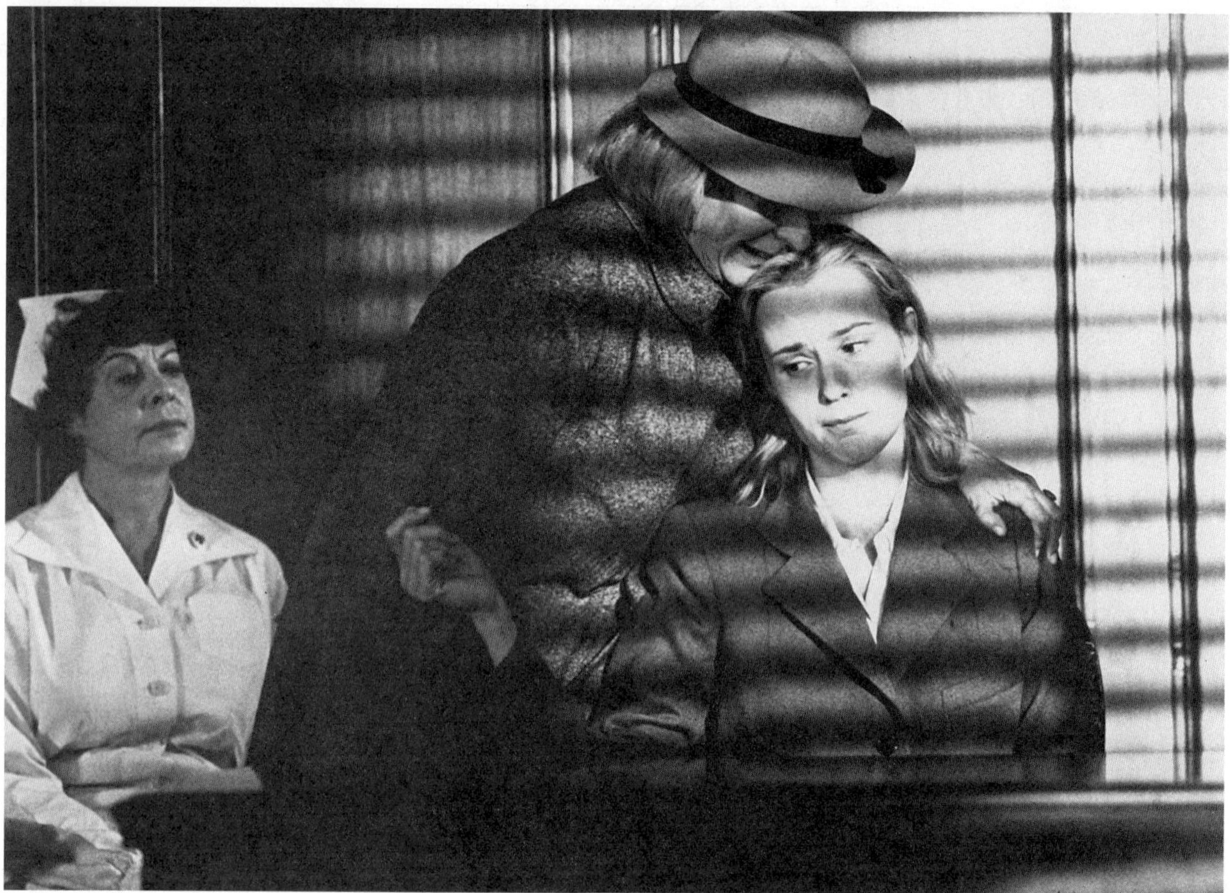

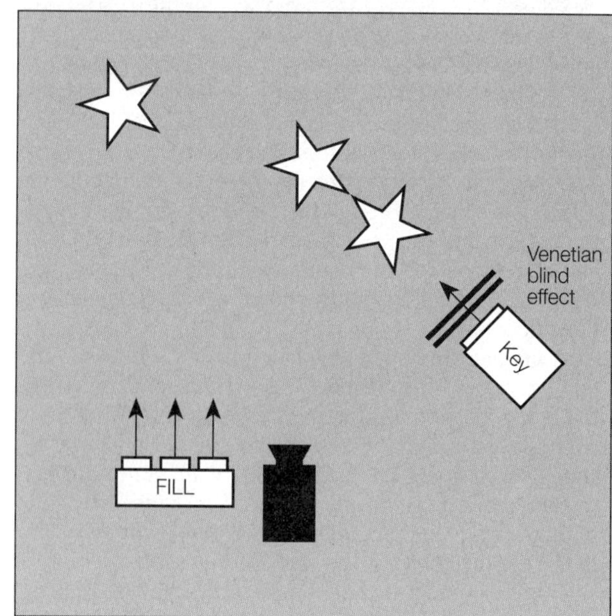

Figure 2.24 (page 40) (*Frances*, Universal City Studios, 1982) The two actors frame right are lit by a key light patterned with a venetian blind. This key is positioned so that the wall frame right is hotter than the actors. At the same time, it is flagged off so as to create the darkness on the left side of frame. Fill light has been added to keep the nurse at frame left and the hand center frame about two to three stops underexposed. Note how the right side of the nurse's face is lit from the glare of the key light off the wall. The nurse could be lit with a separate light as well, as there is quite a bit of light and shadow on her blouse frame left.

The result is an interestingly controlled use of a venetian blind effect—very natural and realistic. It is also common to project the venetian blind by itself onto the background wall, lighting the actors in front of the wall separately and without the venetian blind shadows.

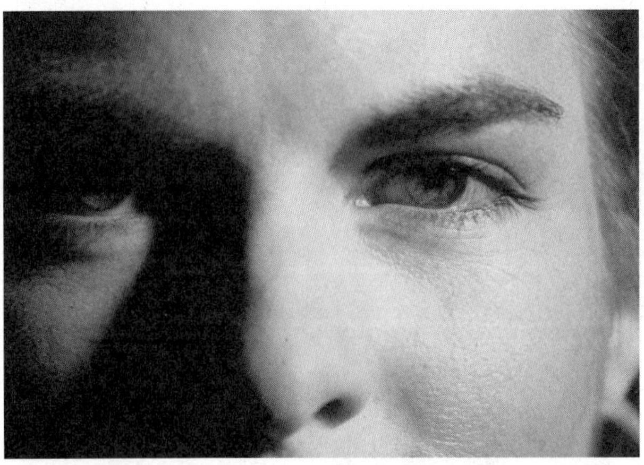

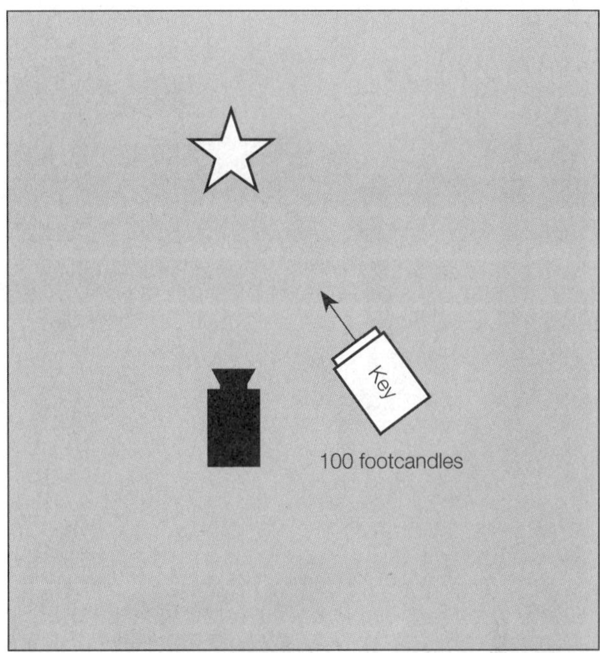

Figure 2.25a (page 41) This view uses only a three-quarter front key from the right. The shadow-side eye is mostly out of the triangular patch of light. There is a certain deadness to the eyes, particularly on the shadow side.

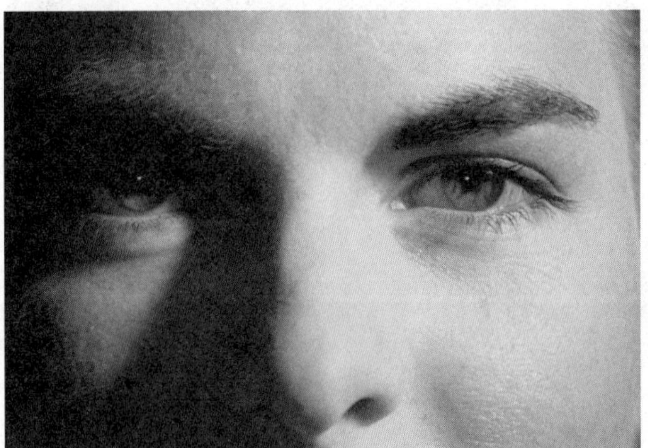

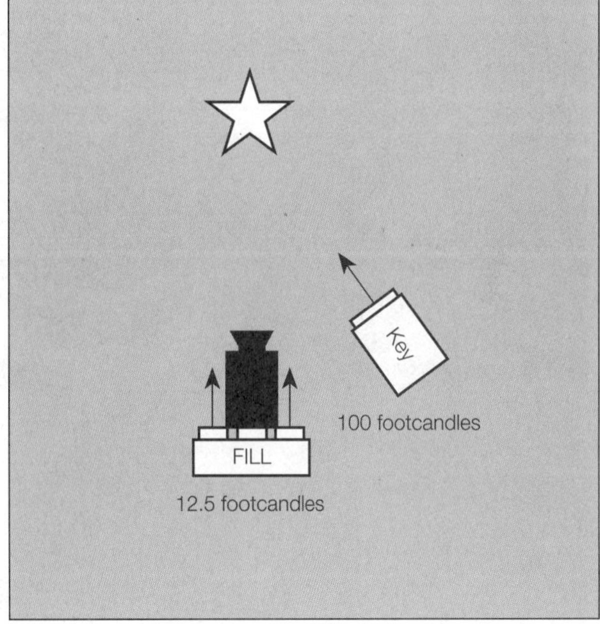

Figure 2.25b (page 41) A fill light has been added to the setup in Figure 2.25a. The lighting ratio is at about 8:1. The fill light also reflects as a tiny dot from each eye. It thus functions as an eyelight, bringing life to the eyes of the subject.

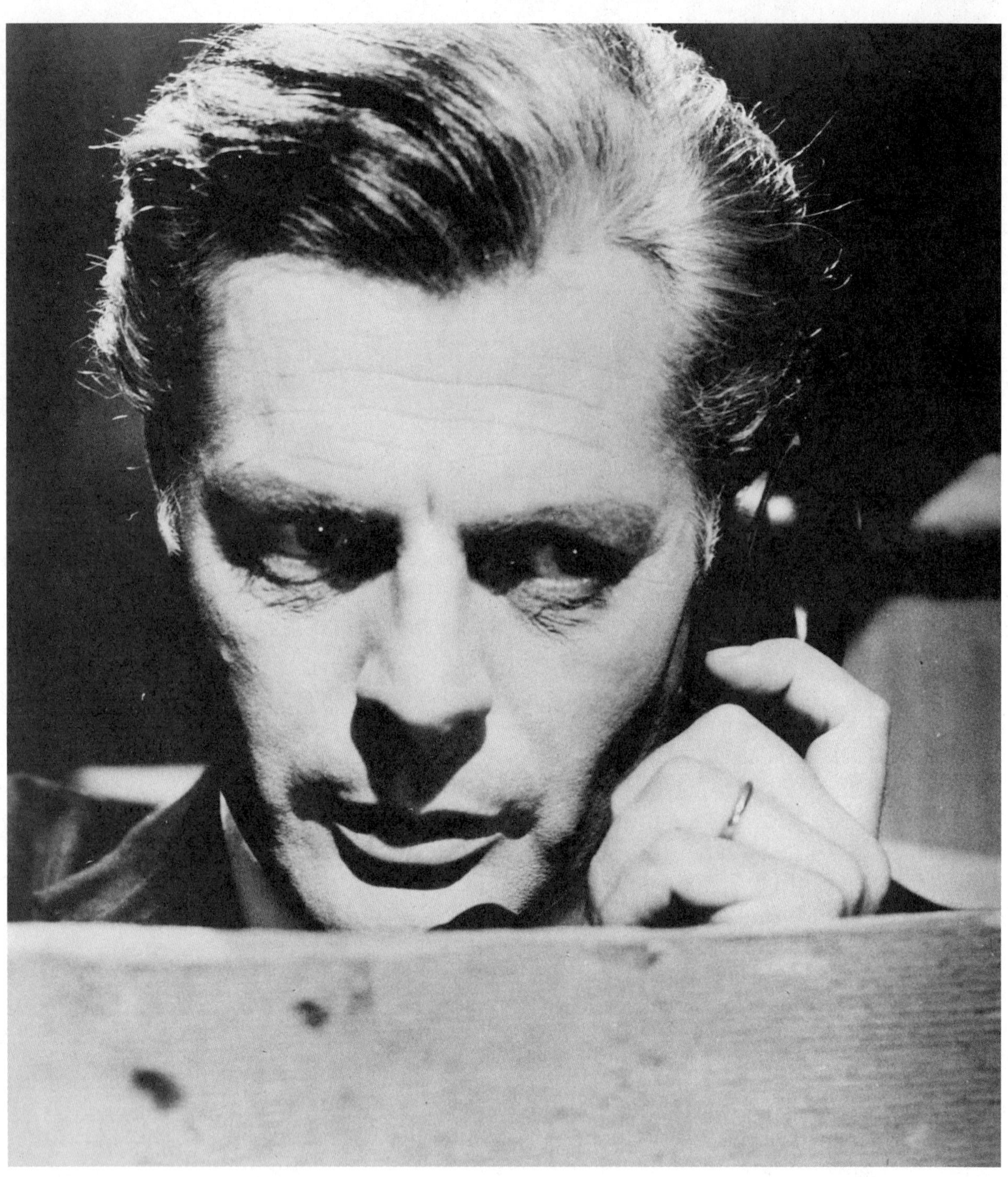

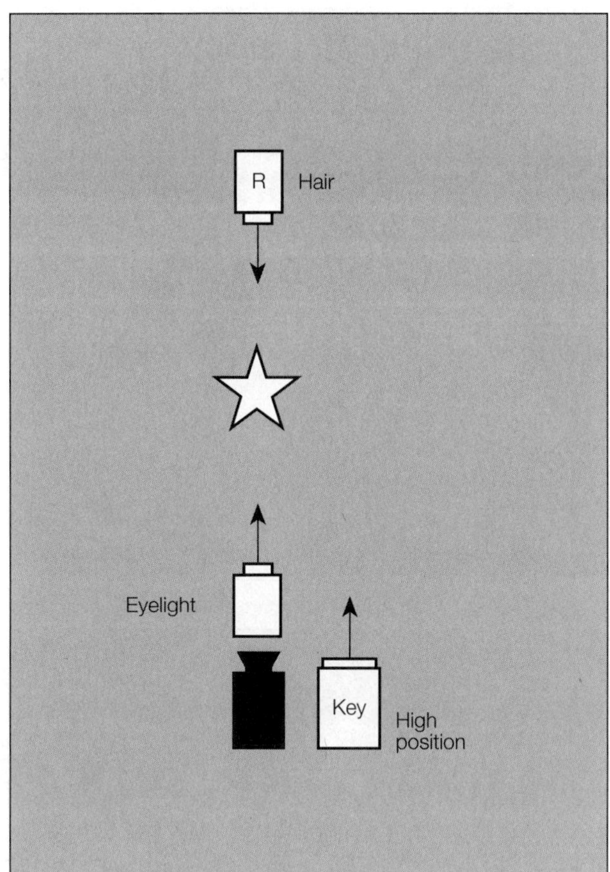

Figure 2.25c (page 42) (*8 1/2*, Embassy Pictures, 1963) This shot shows the same tiny eyelight reflection in the actor's eyes, which serves to bring them alive. Here there is a fairly hard, overhead frontal key. Note the blackness and hard edges of the nose shadow. There is a strong hair light from the back as well. A very weak fill functions mostly as an eyelight. It could be there is no fill, but that the cinematographer used a flashlight or other tiny light to create the eyelight reflections. In any event, the light was so weak in comparison to the key, it had little effect on the shadows; yet without that eyelight, the actor's eyes would have been pools of blackness.

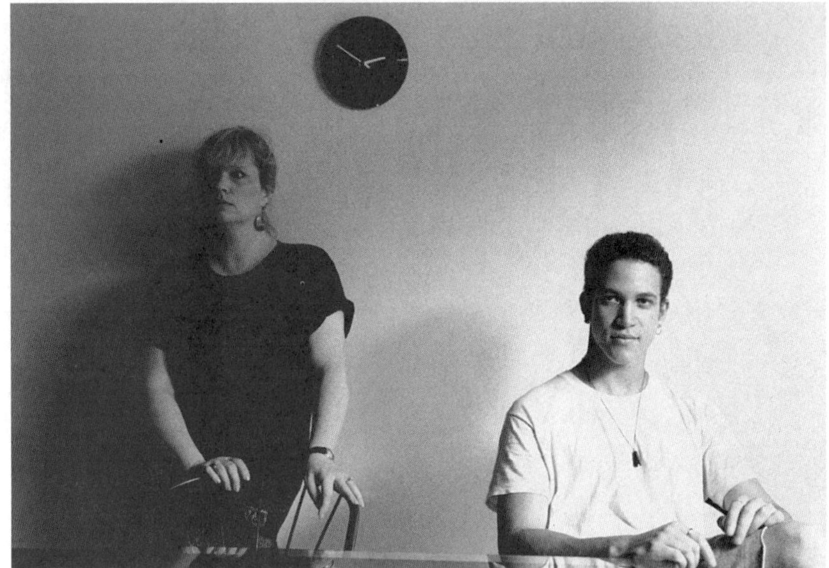

a

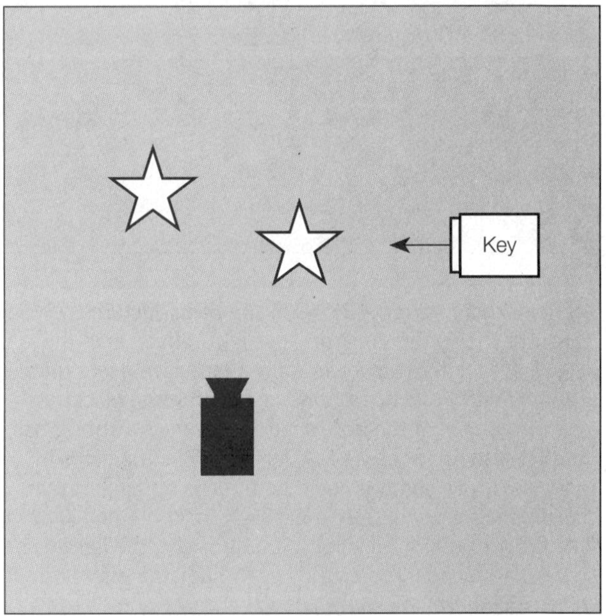

Figure 7.1 (page 88) *In this series of shots, a window effect was created by placing a softlight outside the house and shining it back through the glass door onto the actors. Available light was also coming into the room, but the artificial light was necessary to obtain a T 2 on the subject at frame left. The softlight was arranged so that it had an interesting falloff on the back wall with about a two-stop difference in intensity between the two actors. In (a), exposure was for the man foreground right and the woman was about two stops heavy. In (d), exposure was for the woman, which left the man about two stops overexposed. (b) and (c) represent compromise exposures. The main point here is that you can't really tell how the shot was lit, whether natural or artificial light was used, or a mixture of both, as in this case.*

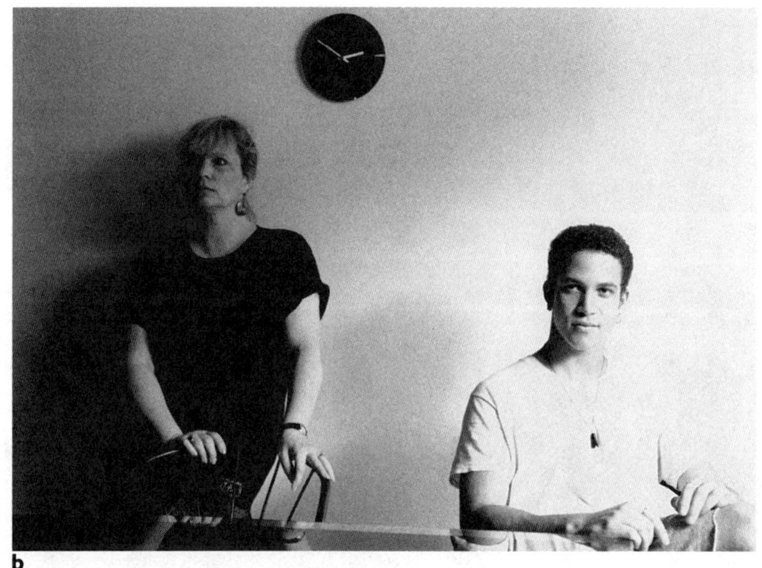
b

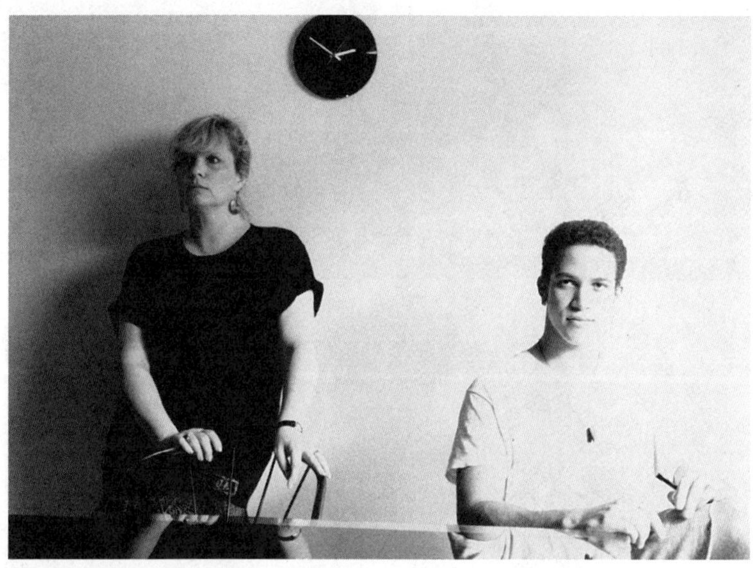
c

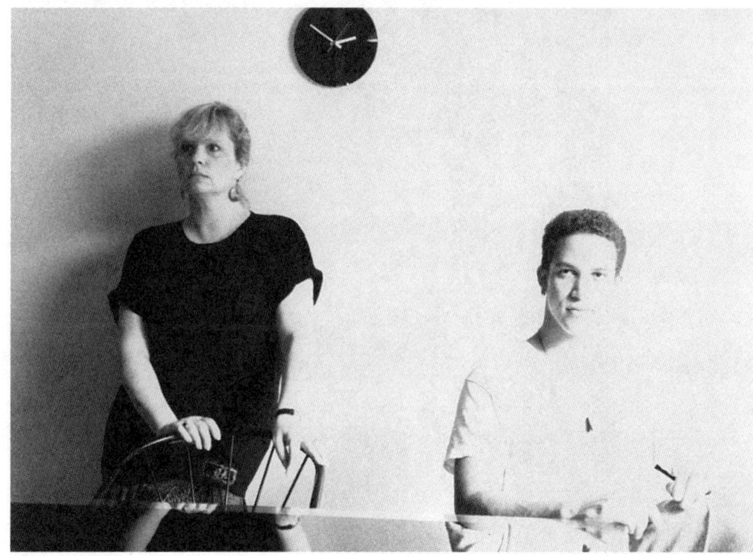
d

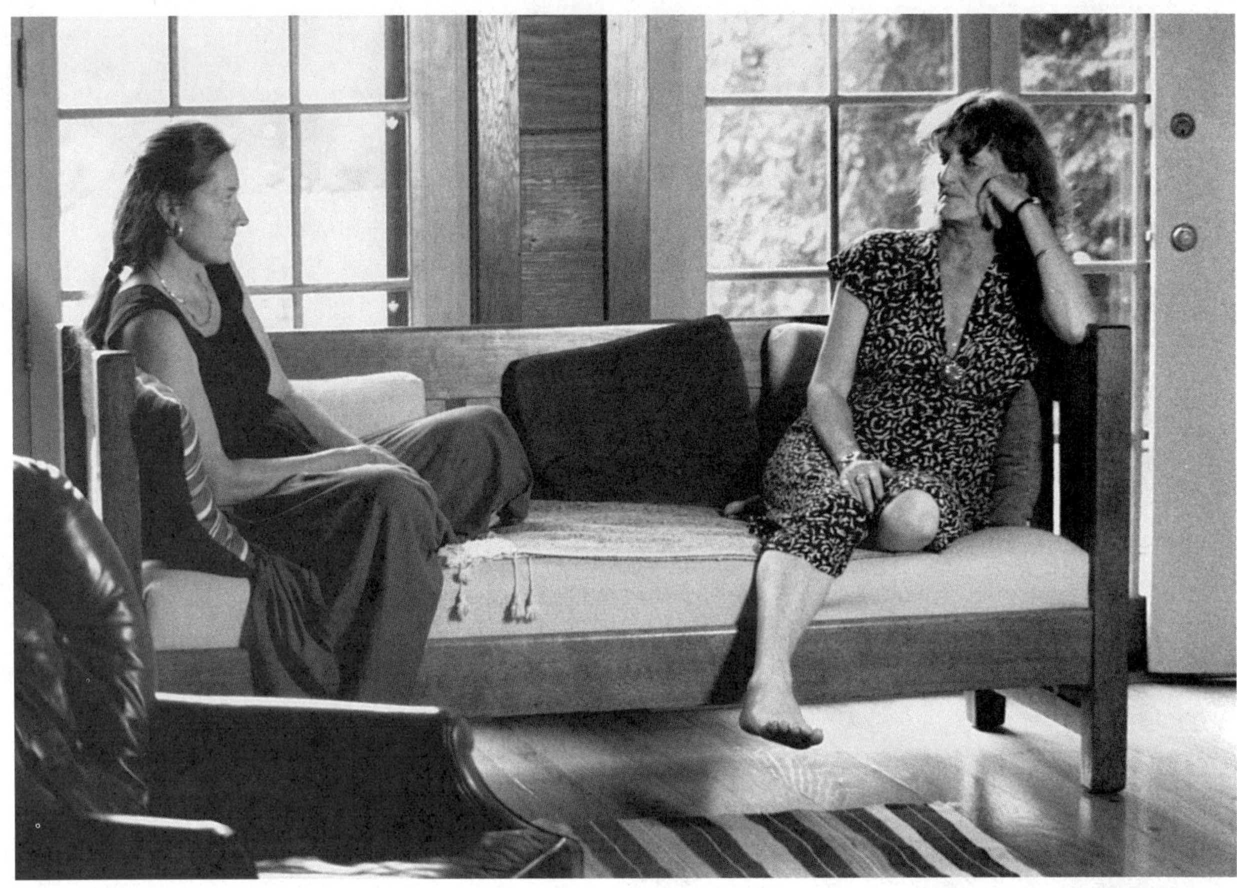
a

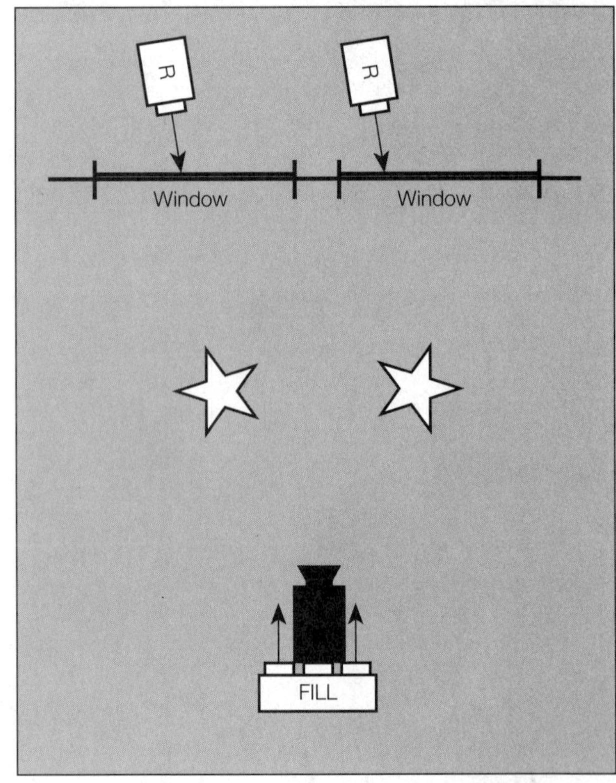

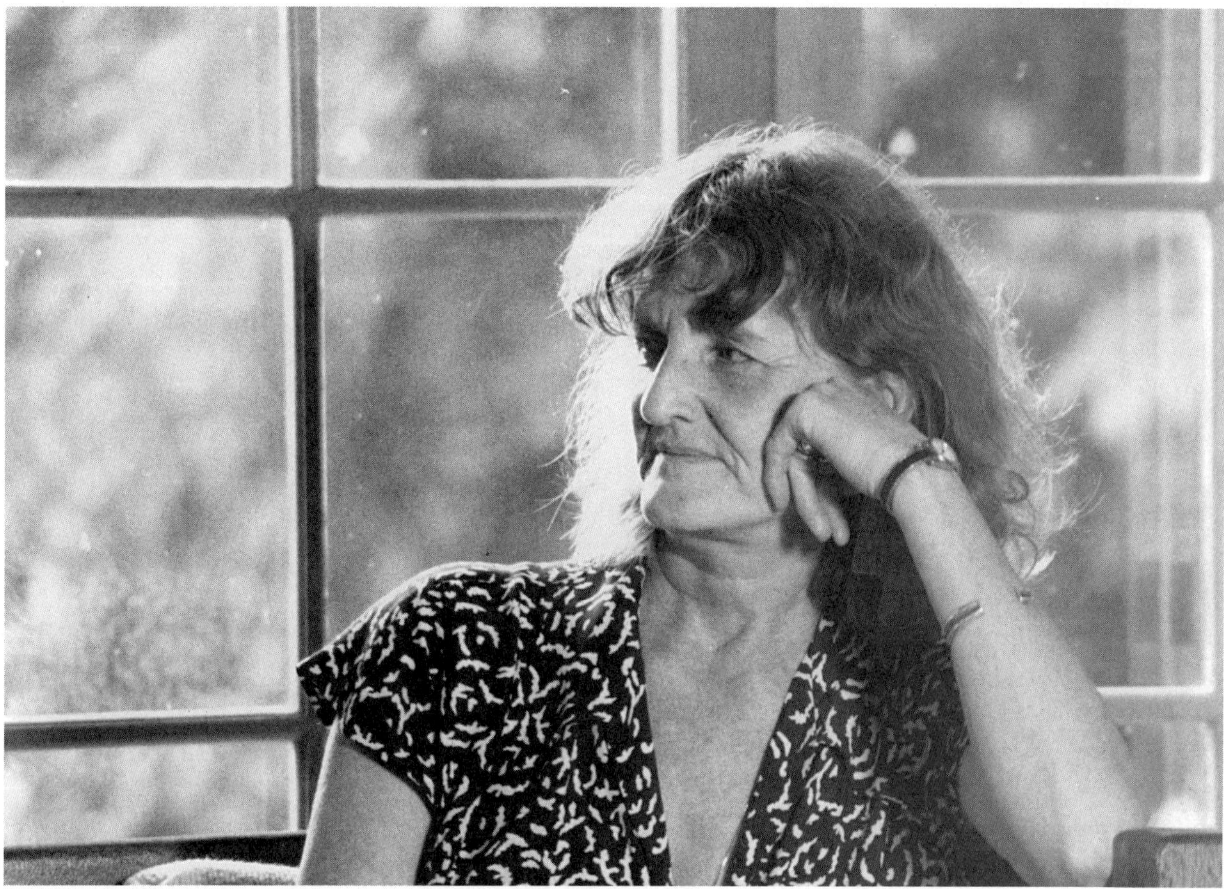

b

Figure 7.4 (page 92) For this window effect, the exposure was based on the level obtained by filling in the subjects with frontal fill light and exposing for their faces. This fill is a little too overt as it creates a glistening reflection on the small wall area between the two actors in the long shot (a). Inside levels were around T 2.8. The outside was at T 32 in the sunlit areas and about T 5.6 in the tree shadow areas. Outside the window was overexposed about seven stops for the left side window and about two stops for the frame right window, which consisted of tree shadows.

For both long shot (a) and closeup (b), a rim light was placed on both actors from outside each window. These rims were overexposed about three stops and are very important in creating the feeling of light outside the window, particularly in the closeup (b). Note how effective the reflections on the leather chair foreground left and the floor bottom right are in creating the feeling of a daylight interior/exterior. These reflections result naturally from available light (skylight) coming through the window and are strong visually because they are overexposed.

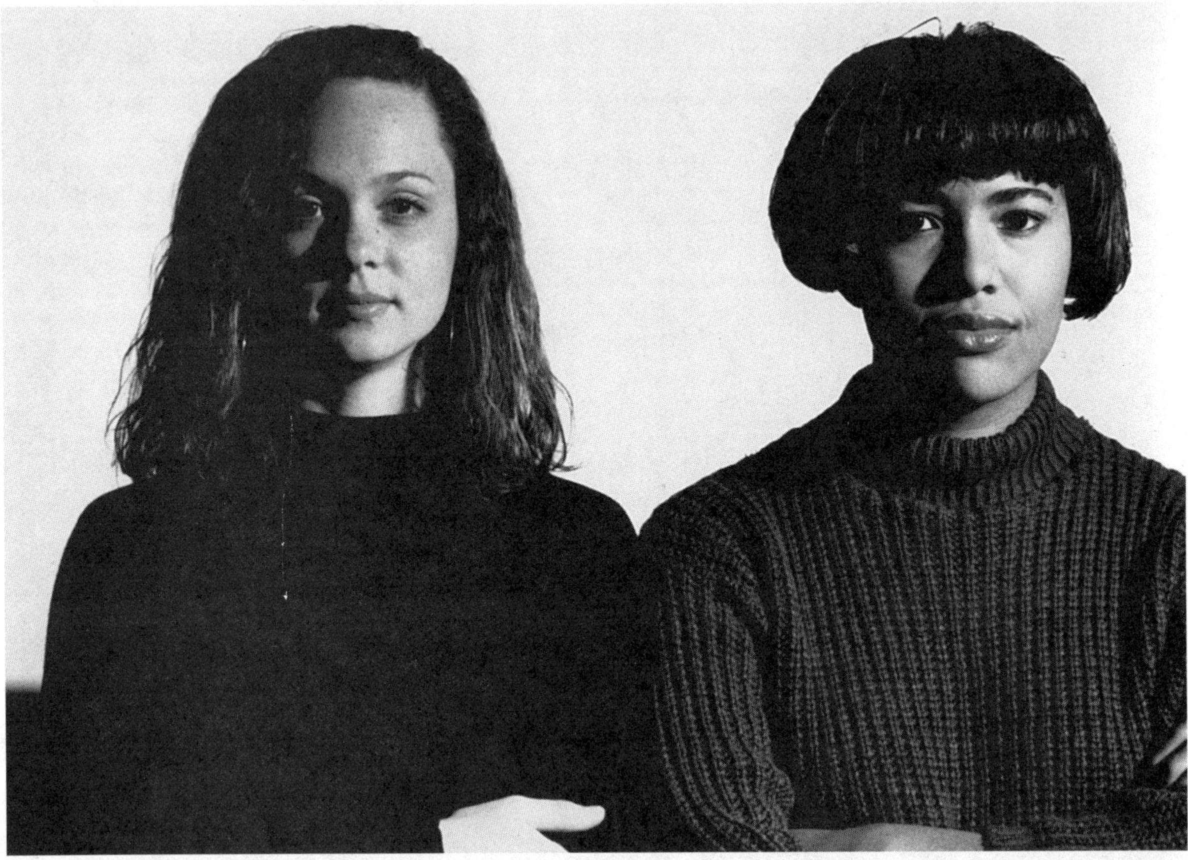

a

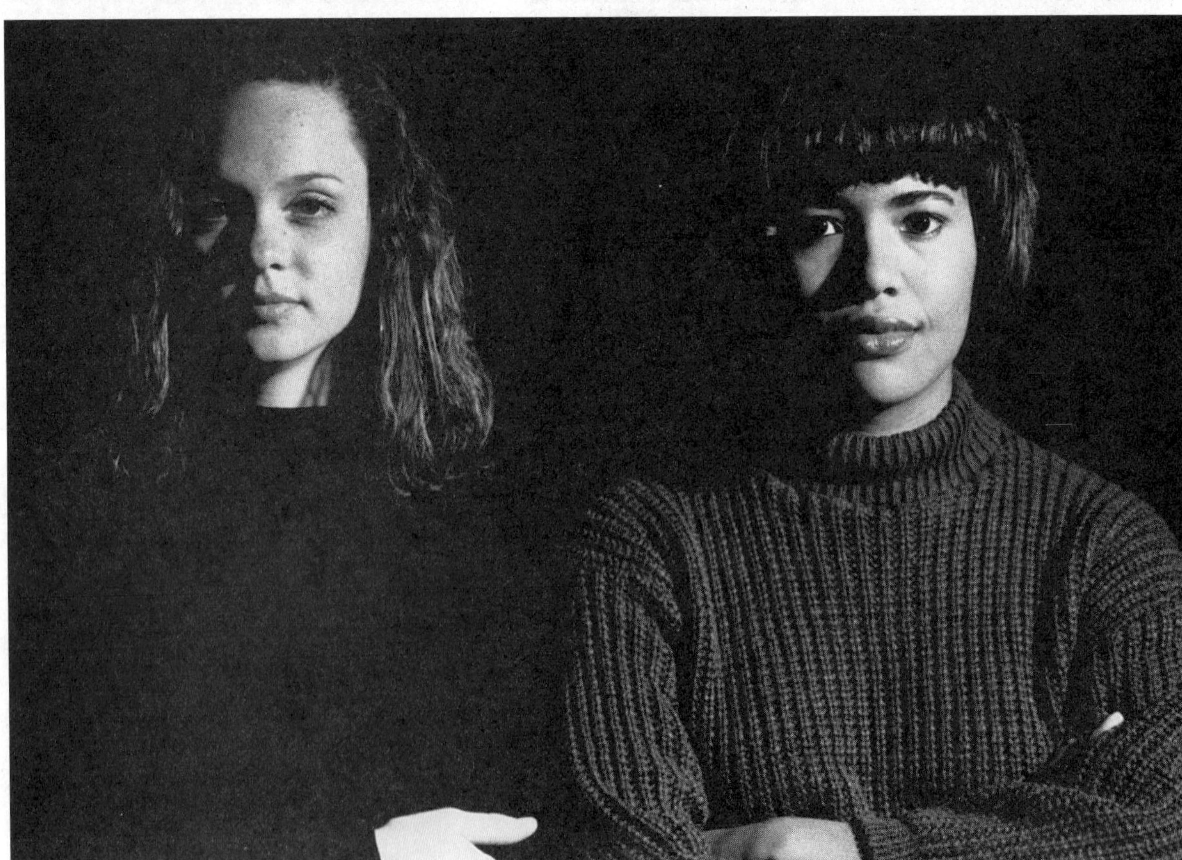

b

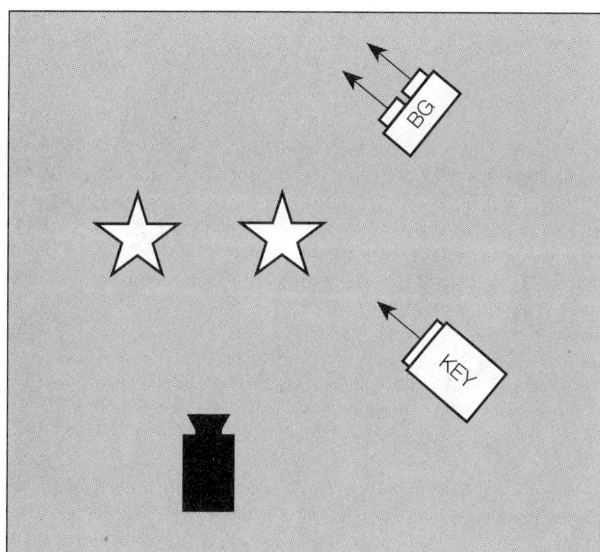

Figure 7.5 (page 93) Background levels are controllable through selection of an appropriate subject/background ratio. For example, in (a), the background is lit to the same intensity as the key and is rendered at its normal zone 9 white value. In (b), the level of the white screen in the background is 8 zones (8 stops) less intense than the subject key level. The result is the background is rendered as a zone 1 value. White becomes black.

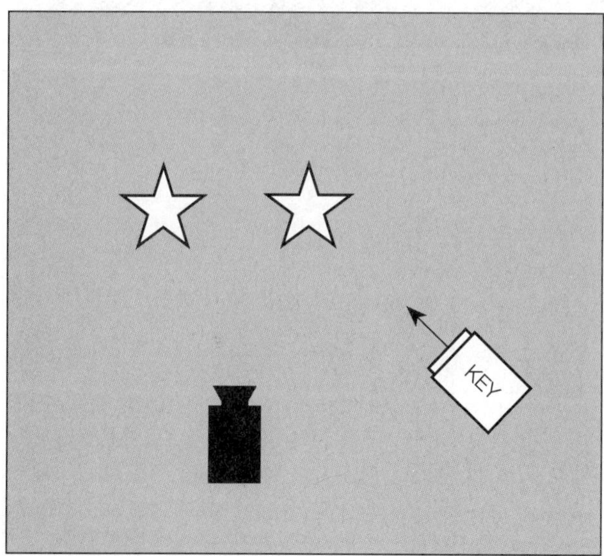

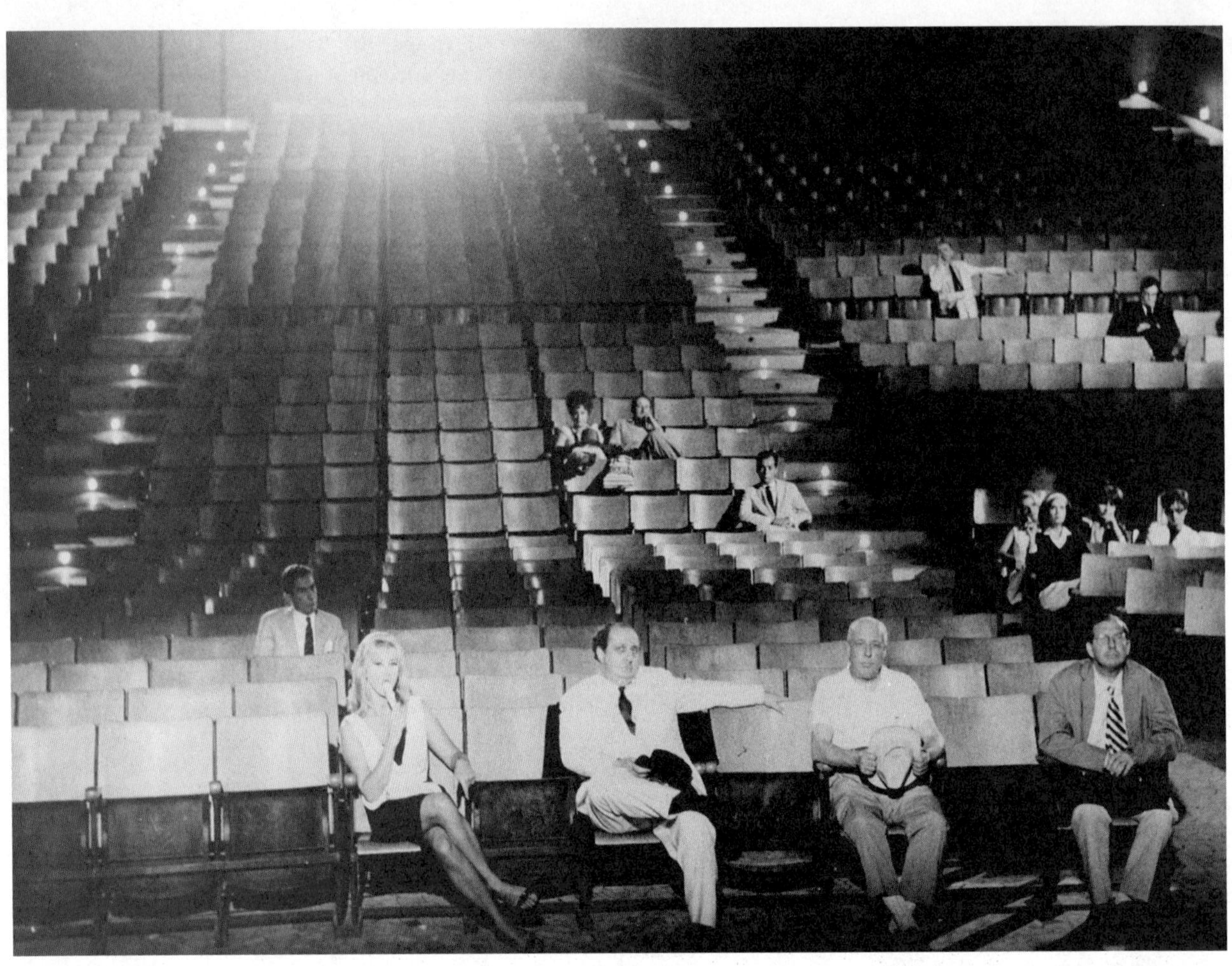

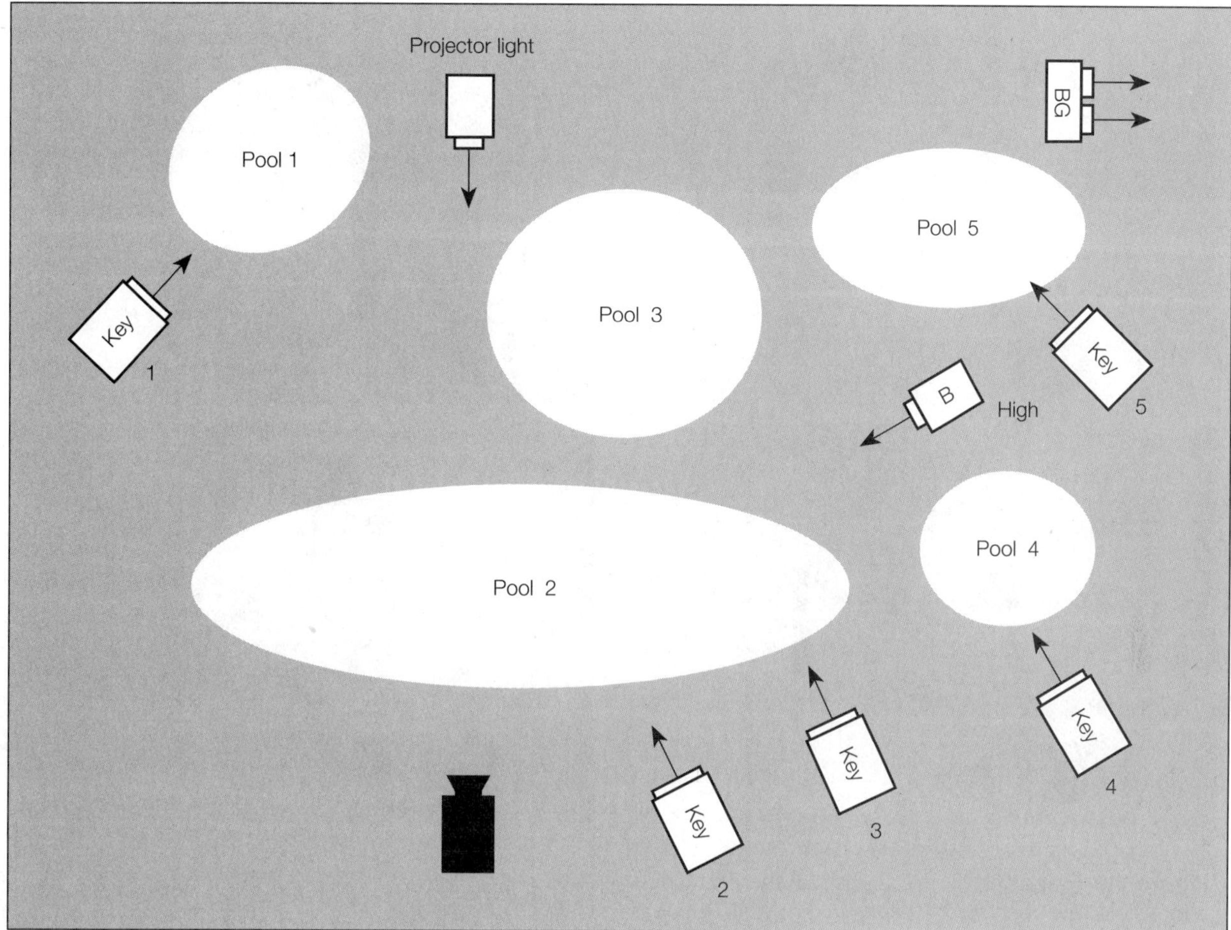

Figure 7.7g (page 96) (*8 1/2*, Embassy Pictures, 1963) In this night interior long shot, the cinematographer has selectively lit various parts of the theater. There are five principal pools of light. They are all at the same intensity except for the first row foreground, which is about a stop brighter than the rest. This is to suggest that because the front-row actors are closer to the (unseen) movie screen, they are brighter. Four of these keys come from frame right, but the one lighting the top left of frame comes from frame left. All five pools of light are unmotivated and thus subject to being noticed if we are not hooked by the plot at that particular moment. In fact, within the context of the film, this lighting setup works because shots from this angle are intercut with shots of the screened images.

A projector light effect emanates from the projection booth in the background. This is fairly easy to simulate with a 35mm xenon projector. Note the beam is highly overexposed relative to the actors, but this overexposure is held to a small total part of the frame and is accepted as realistic rather than aggravating. Smoke could have been used to enhance the back light effect even more. The aisle lights are just visible indicating they are of low intensity as luminous objects. Back light is visible on the hair of the five foreground actors and probably derives from the projector light effect itself, though it could easily be rigged separately from high above the top of frame. Another back light hits the seats and back of the actor foreground right. The shadows under the seats show this light comes from the rear and frame right, not from the projector effect. There is also a theater-aisle lighting effect in top frame right.

Three points are to be emphasized here. First, lighting a large area involves breaking it down into meaningful units and selectively lighting those smaller areas. Second, the overall lighting logic, source motivation, and so on are generally maintained, but not perfectly. Cheating and unmotivated effects are often necessary. And third, this lighting is so complicated, a director would have to shoot all the setups, at least the long shots, from this angle before shooting other angles, such as toward the screen. Lighting a setup of this size might take 6 to 8 hours. It would be very difficult as well as expensive to tear it down and redo it a day later.

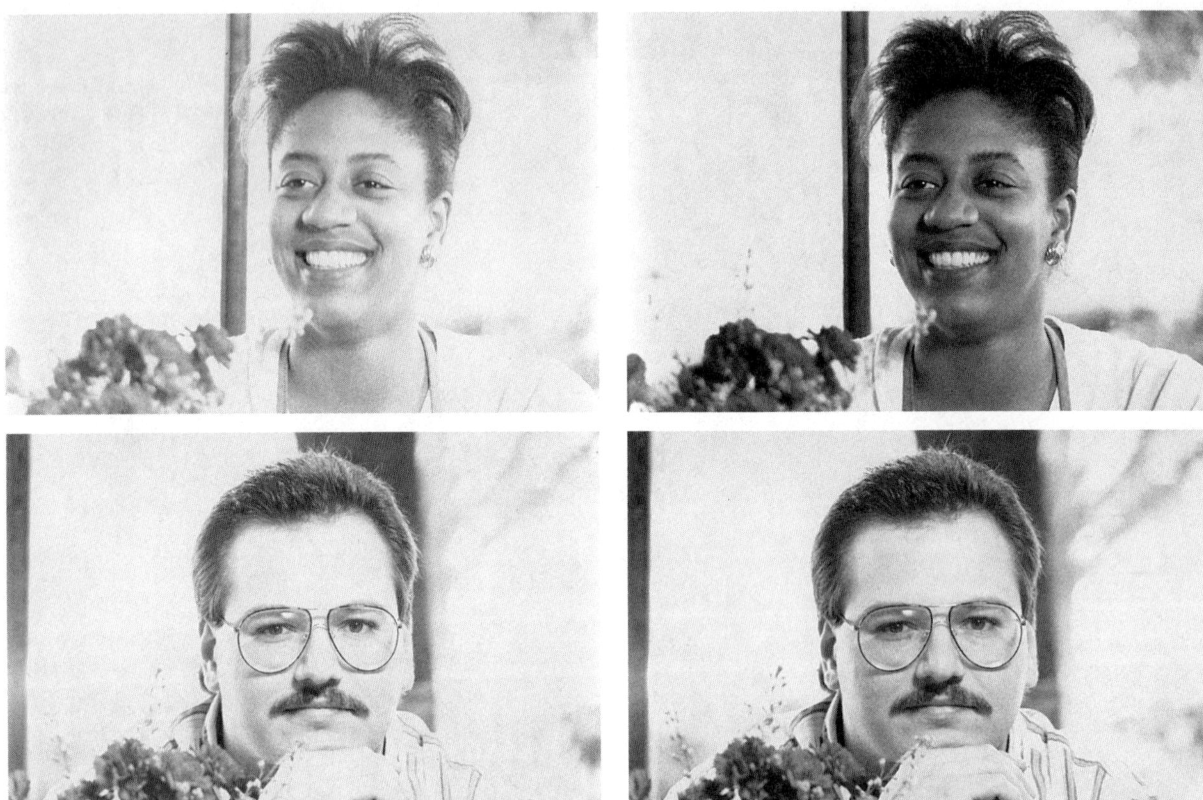

Figure 7.8 (page 98) The long shot for these CU shots is located at the opening to Chapter 7. A soft fill light was added to the two subjects sitting in the window to bring them up to about T 4. The outside level was around T 22, a difference of five stops. A series of exposures were given, from exposure for the face (a) to exposure for the outside (f). Each shot in the series represents about a one-stop difference in exposure. Note that the black facetone reacts differently to underexposure (e) than does the white facetone. Consequently, it might be best to give the woman an extra stop worth of fill intensity if both faces are to be in the same shot (as in the long shot).

This series was shot to illustrate exposure possibilities. Were it necessary to preserve detail in both subject and background, the cinematographer would have two choices. The first would be to place window gels on the cafe windows to bring down the outside intensity. For example, a .9 neutral density gel would leave the outside two stops hotter than the inside fill level. This would be appropriate for a day interior/exterior effect such as here and would leave the background approximately as in (d) with facetones as in (a). The second choice would be to bump up the fill level inside to T 11. Again, this would leave the outside two stops overexposed assuming you expose for the faces.

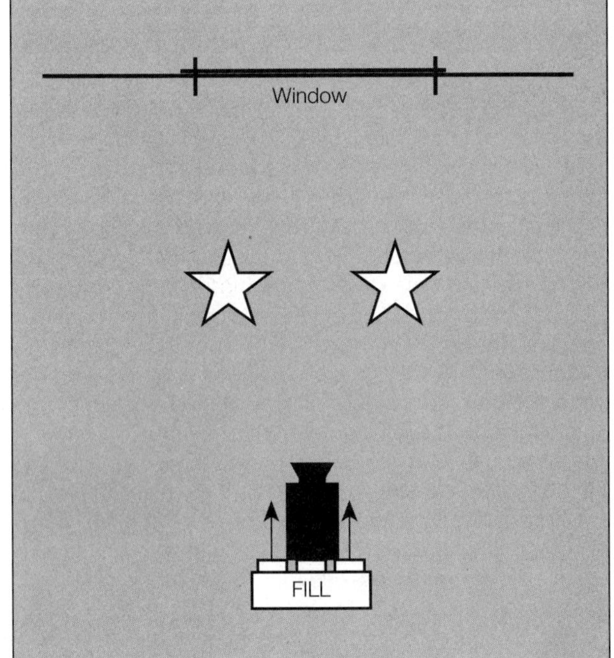

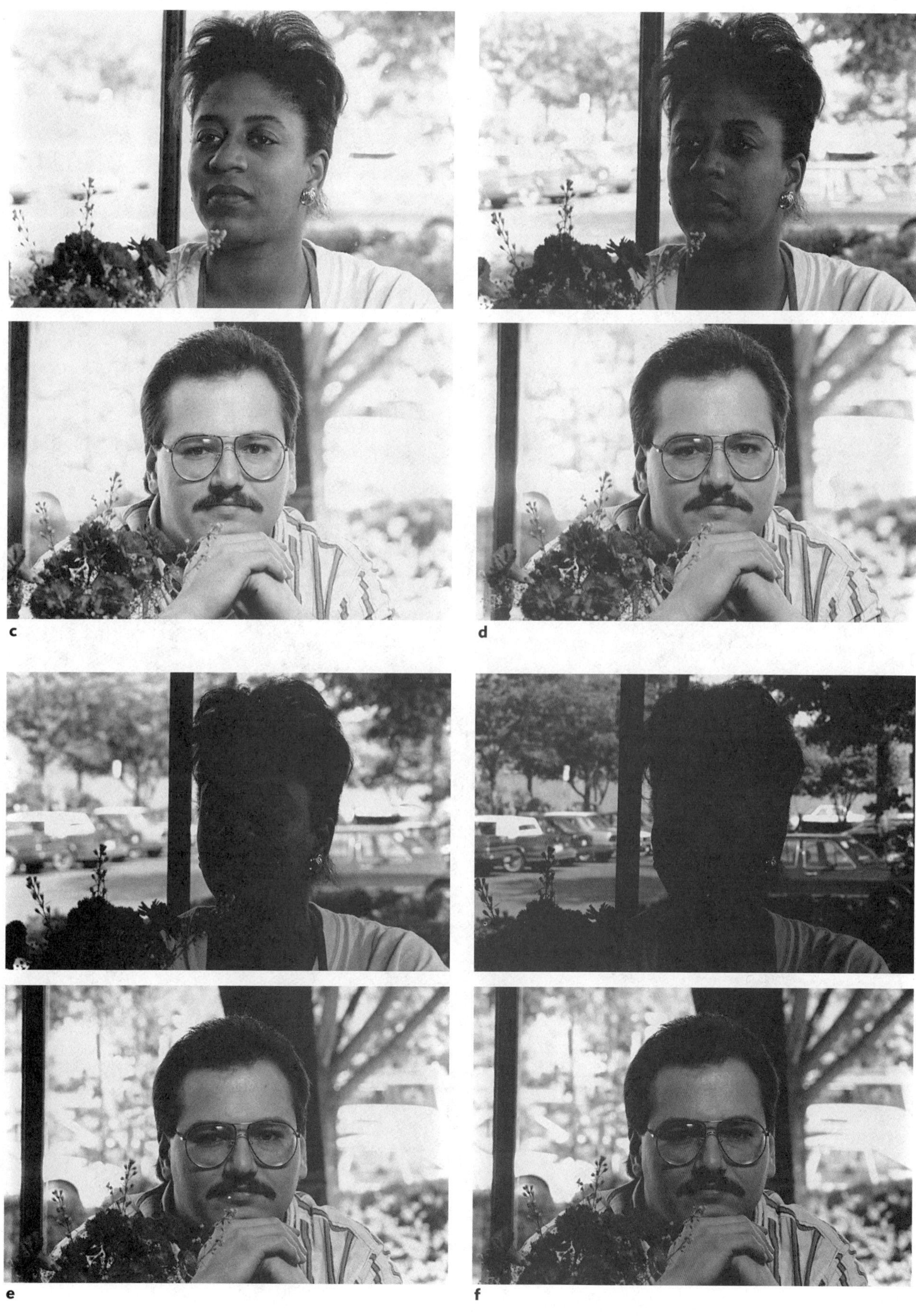
c
d
e
f

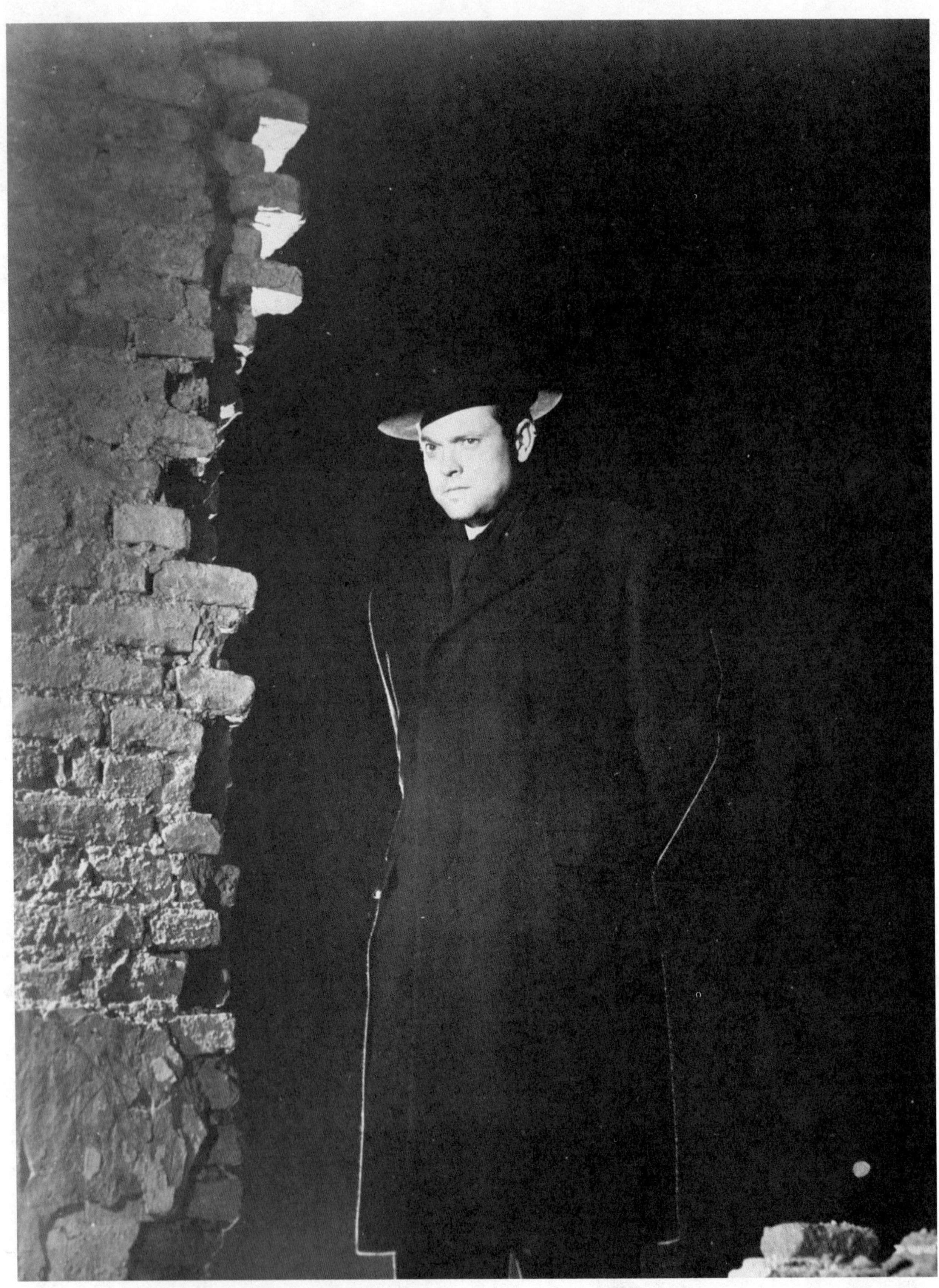

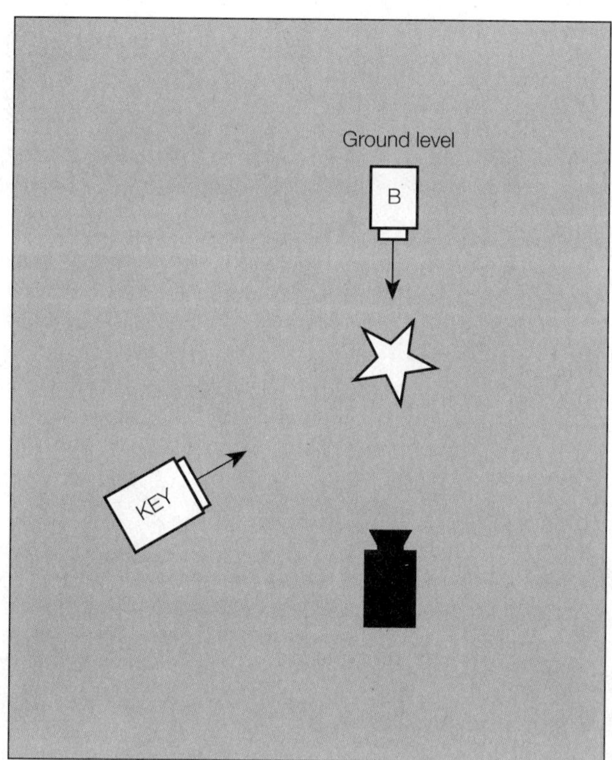

Figure 7.10d (page 101) (*The Third Man*, Twentieth Century Fox, 1949) Night exteriors exhibit the same lighting principles as day exteriors, but cinematographers use a lot more light than you might imagine. In this shot, a frontal key rakes the brick wall and lights the actor's face. A back light, probably an arc from ground level behind the actor, rims both sides of the body and the underside of his hat, accents the brick wall at top left frame, and puts some light on the ground at frame right, though this latter could come from a separate light unit or even the key. Nighttime exterior lighting allows for many painting-with-light possibilities. There may or may not be sources to motivate the setup.

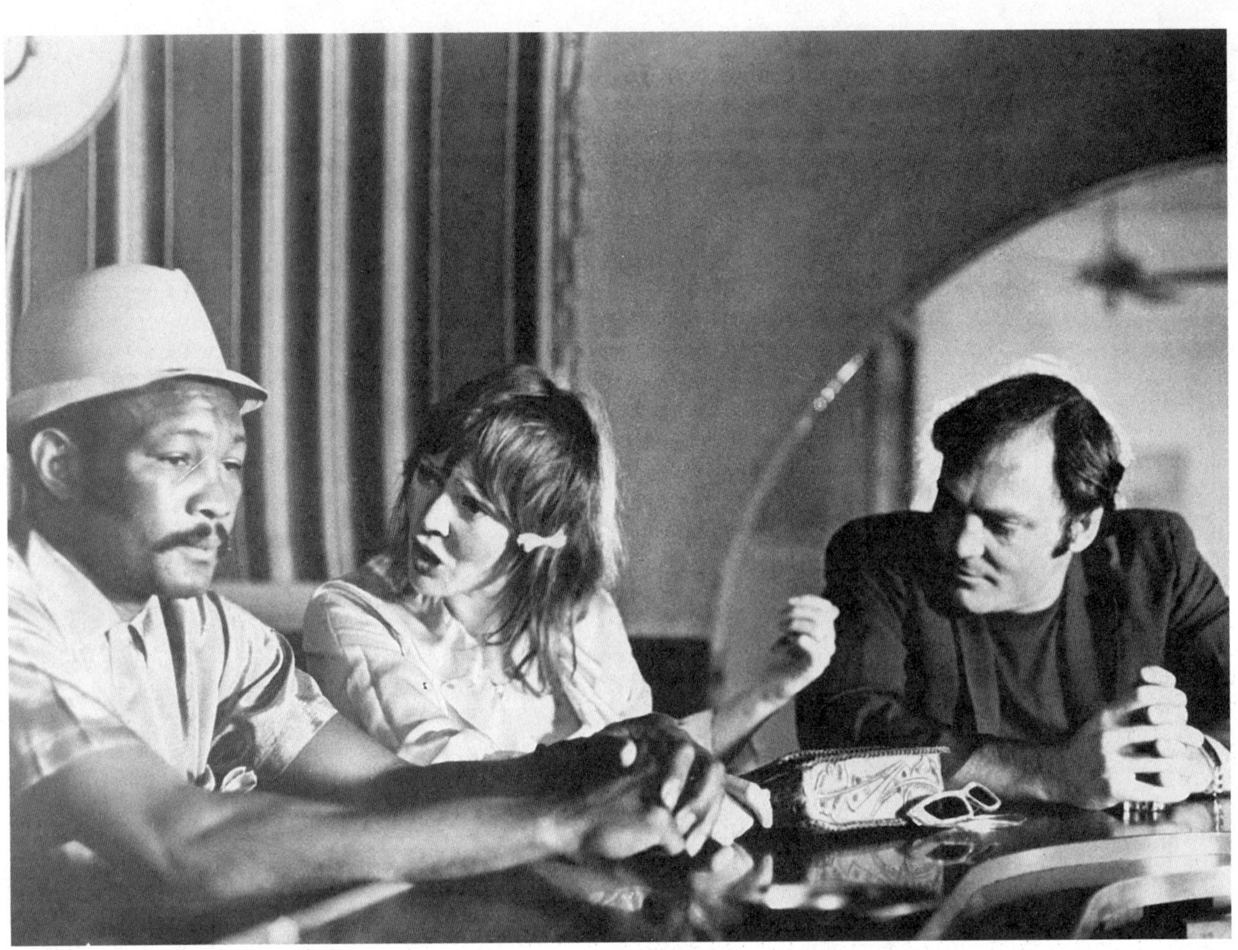

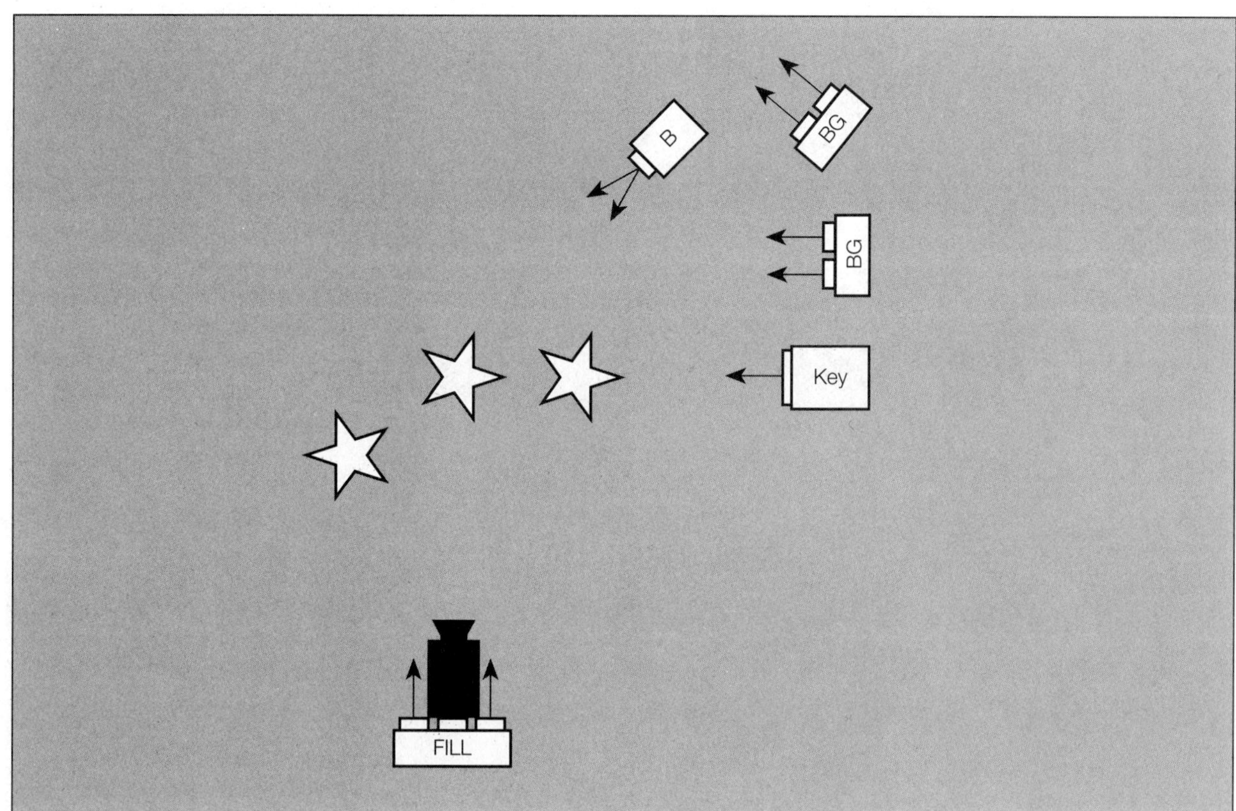

Figure 9.1b (page 126) (*Fat City*, Columbia Pictures, 1972) In this realistic bar interior, the key light comes from frame right and creates a side key effect on the two actors frame right and a frontal key on the actor frame left. Though we do not know the source of this key, it feels realistic. The fill is at about a 6:1 ratio on the center actor but more like 16:1 on the actor frame right. The wall behind them at frame left is lit from the side and held to about a four-stop, 16:1 subject/background ratio. Strong back light comes from the room in the background frame right. It is very bright on the actor frame right and rims the center actor. The back room also has light on its wall, about two stops darker than the key lighting.

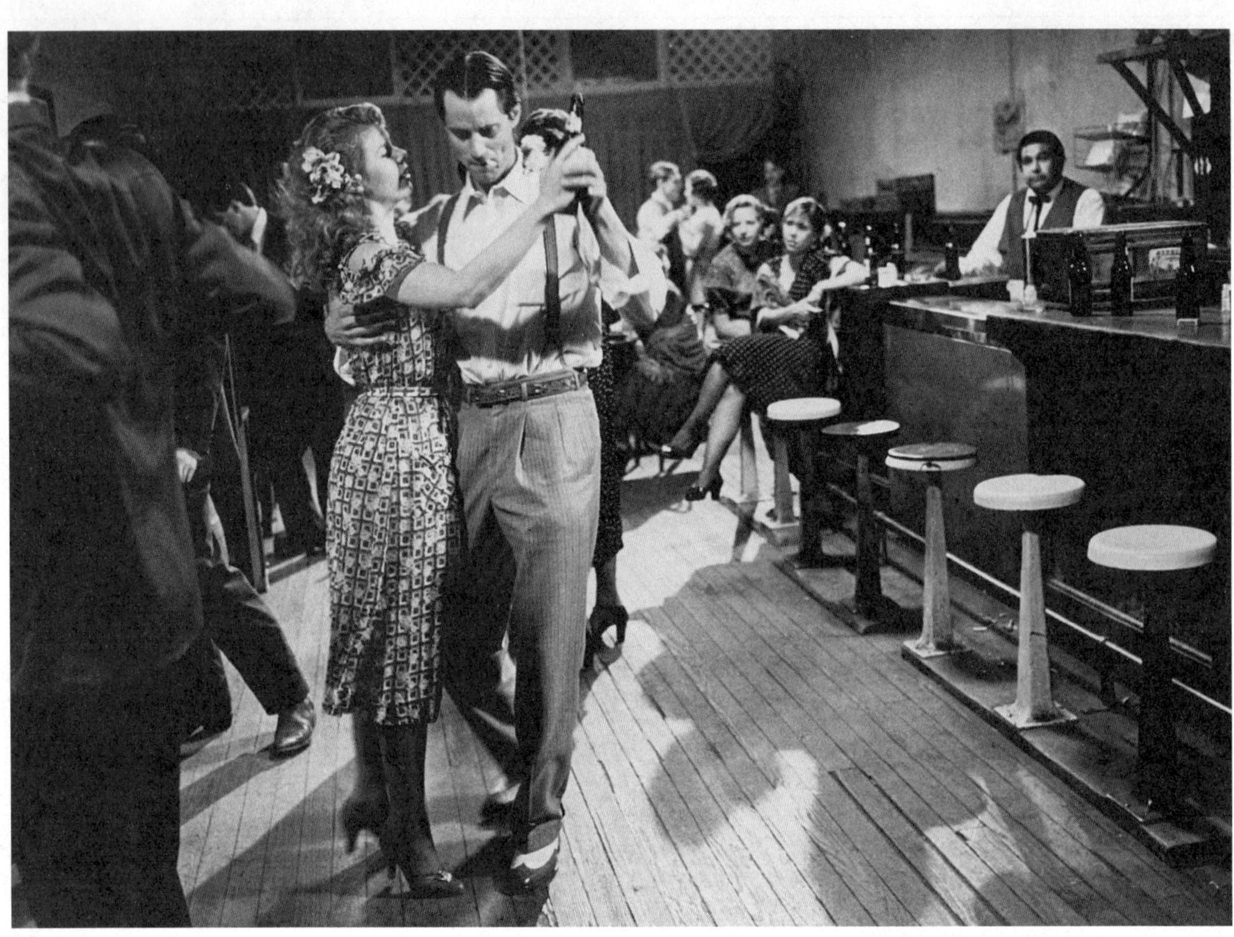

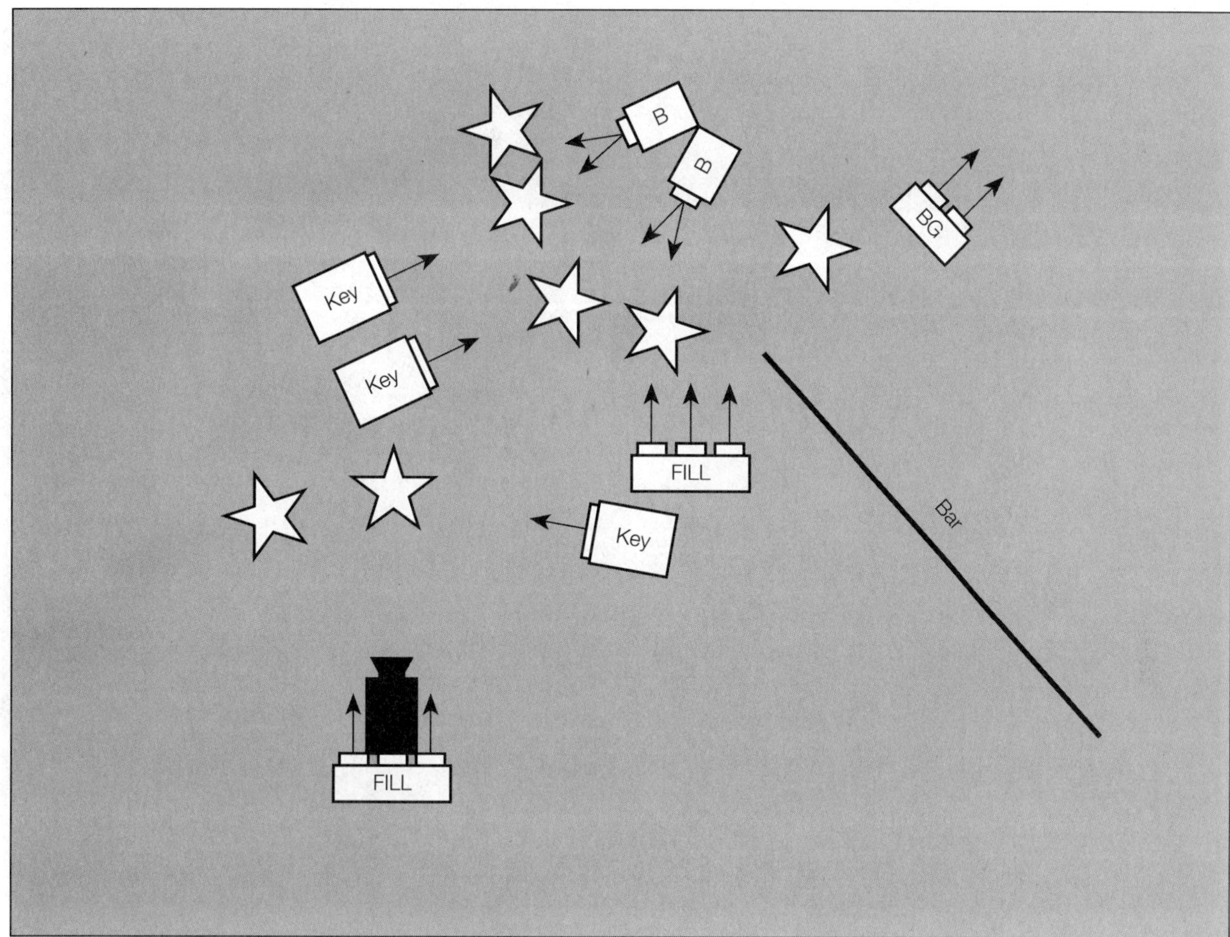

Figure 9.1c (page 127) (*Raggedy Man*, Universal City Studios, 1981) Strong back light causes bright hair and rim effects on the actors as well as throws large shadows on the floor foreground center and right. The key light for the foreground actors center frame comes from the right side (note his head shadow on her face) and is flagged from their lower bodies. Key lighting for the background actors and the bartender and bar area comes from the frontal left side of frame.

The fill light on the foreground actors is about 2:1. The fill on the background actors and bartender is around 4:1. The background is patterned with shadows and held about three stops dark. The actors frame left are only partially lit by the fill and back light. It's hard to know how many lights are being used here—note the large number of reflections on the beer bottles on the bar—but the basic effect is realistic and dominated by the back light emanating from the ceiling area in the background.

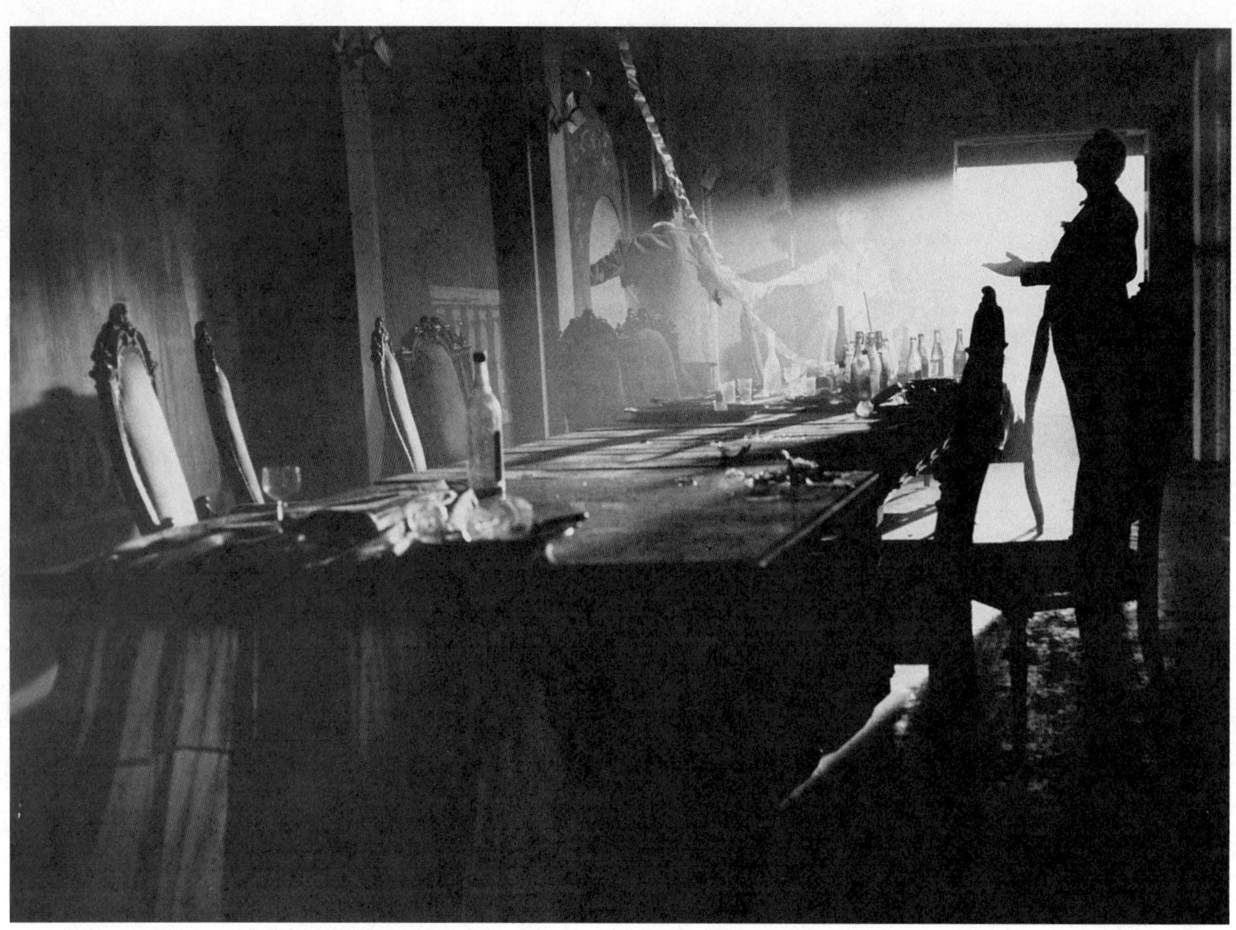

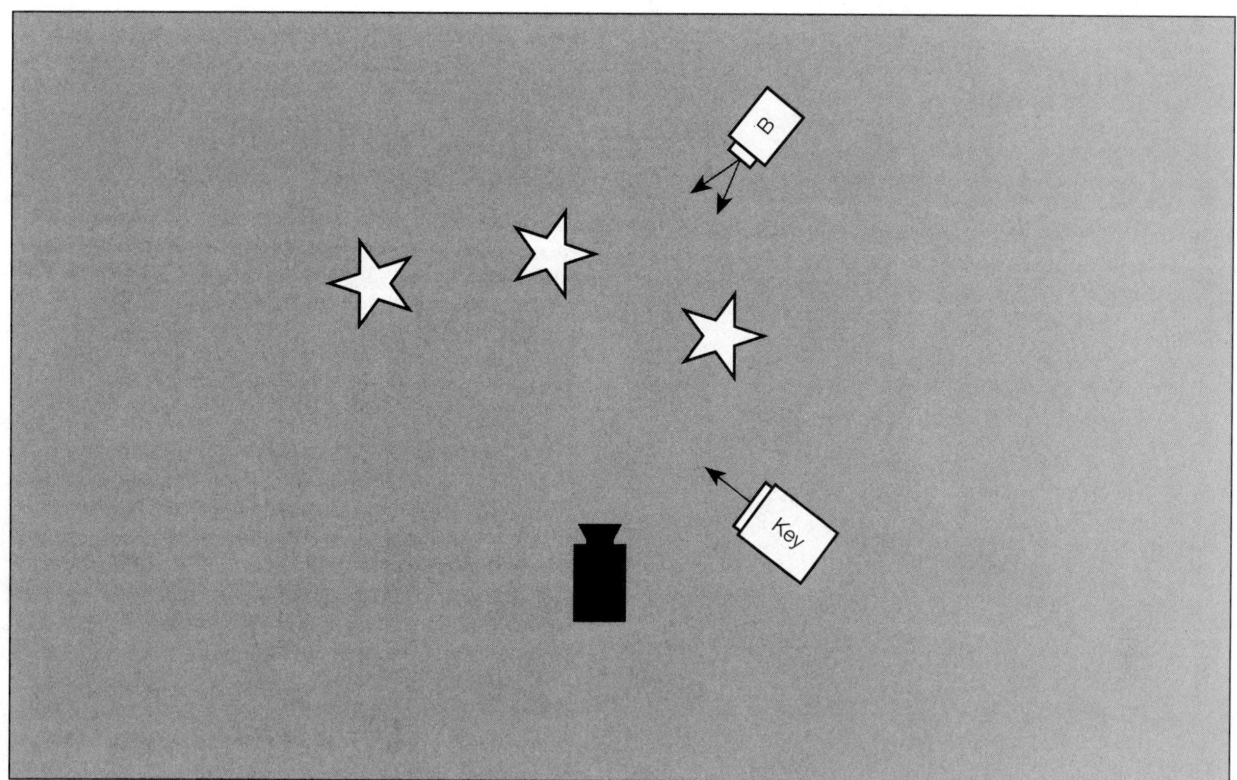

Figure 9.1e (page 128) (*Ashes and Diamonds*, 1958) This effective lighting setup relies on a very strong, hard, back light coming from the room background right. The light is overexposed, and artificial smoke is used to accentuate the effect and make it more like a light beam. The silhouette of the actor frame right also emphasizes the light beam.

There is a key light on the two actors background left, but the flare of the back light source disguises it for all practical purposes. This second key comes from three-quarter front, frame right. It throws a shadow on the wall to the left of the woman and illuminates her and the man in the doorway. The cinematographer has done a good job here, in controlling the light beam, the amount of smoke used, and the exposure setting. The result is a beautiful composition in black and white.

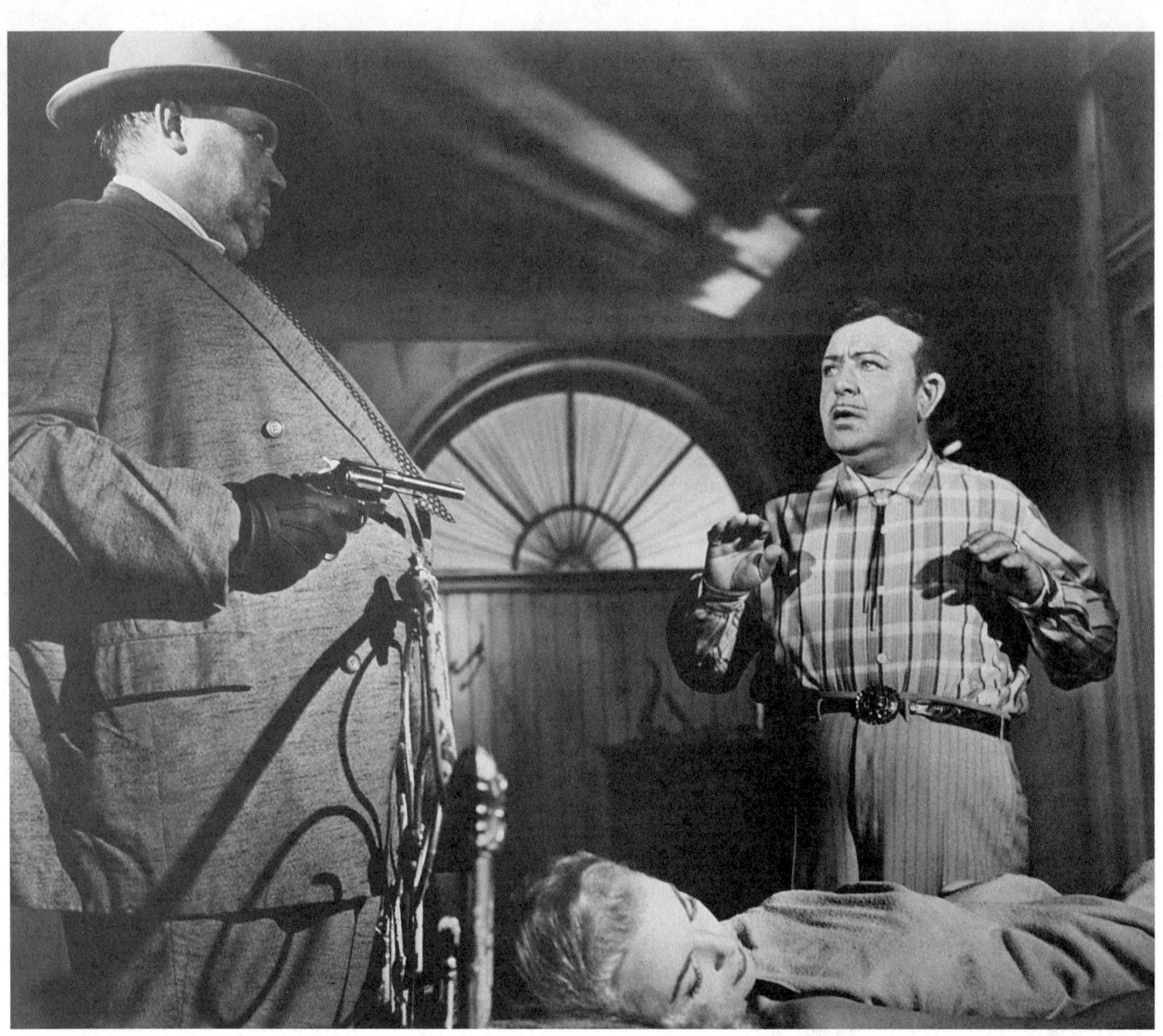

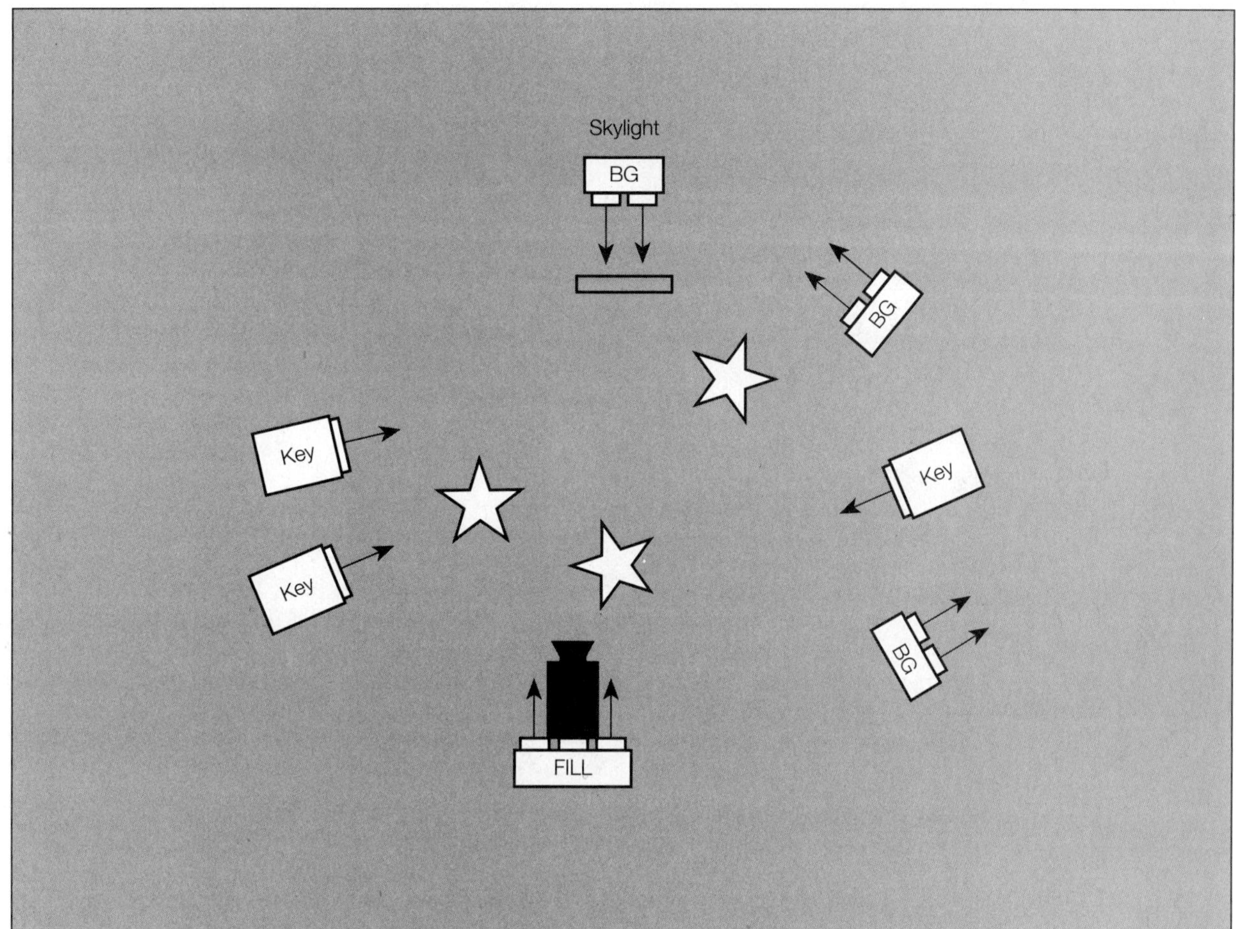

Figure 9.1f (page 128) (*Touch of Evil*, Universal-International, 1958) An "eccentric" lighting style is employed throughout this film. A lot of the lighting comes from below camera height. This allows for shadow effects on walls and ceilings as in this photograph.

Three fairly hard keys are used: One strikes the actor frame right frontally and lights his face and arm frame left. Another comes from frame left and illuminates the back of the head and hat of the sheriff. It's possible that both of these effects result from a single key frame left. The third comes from frame right and lights the woman on the bed, the gun, and bedstead so as to throw the wonderful, baroque shadow on the large gut of the sheriff. The third key also illuminates the arm frame right of the man on the right. Note the differing angles of his two arm shadows.

There is some fill at about a 6:1 ratio, but it is used very selectively, for example, on the face of the sheriff and the hair of the woman on the bed. This is obviously a painting-with-light style that relies on a number of small Fresneled spotlights for controlled and selective lighting. Note, for example, the projection of the shadow of the odd-shaped object on the dresser onto the background wall center frame; and, of course, the wonderful shadow projected onto the ceiling through the curtained skylight in the background. The only other background light is seen on the right side of frame. This could be the result of spill from one of the keys frame left, or caused by a separate unit. This shot provides a good example of the baroque, heavily shadowed, painting-with-light style of B & W cinematography developed and refined during the 1940s and 1950s by a number of cinematographers.

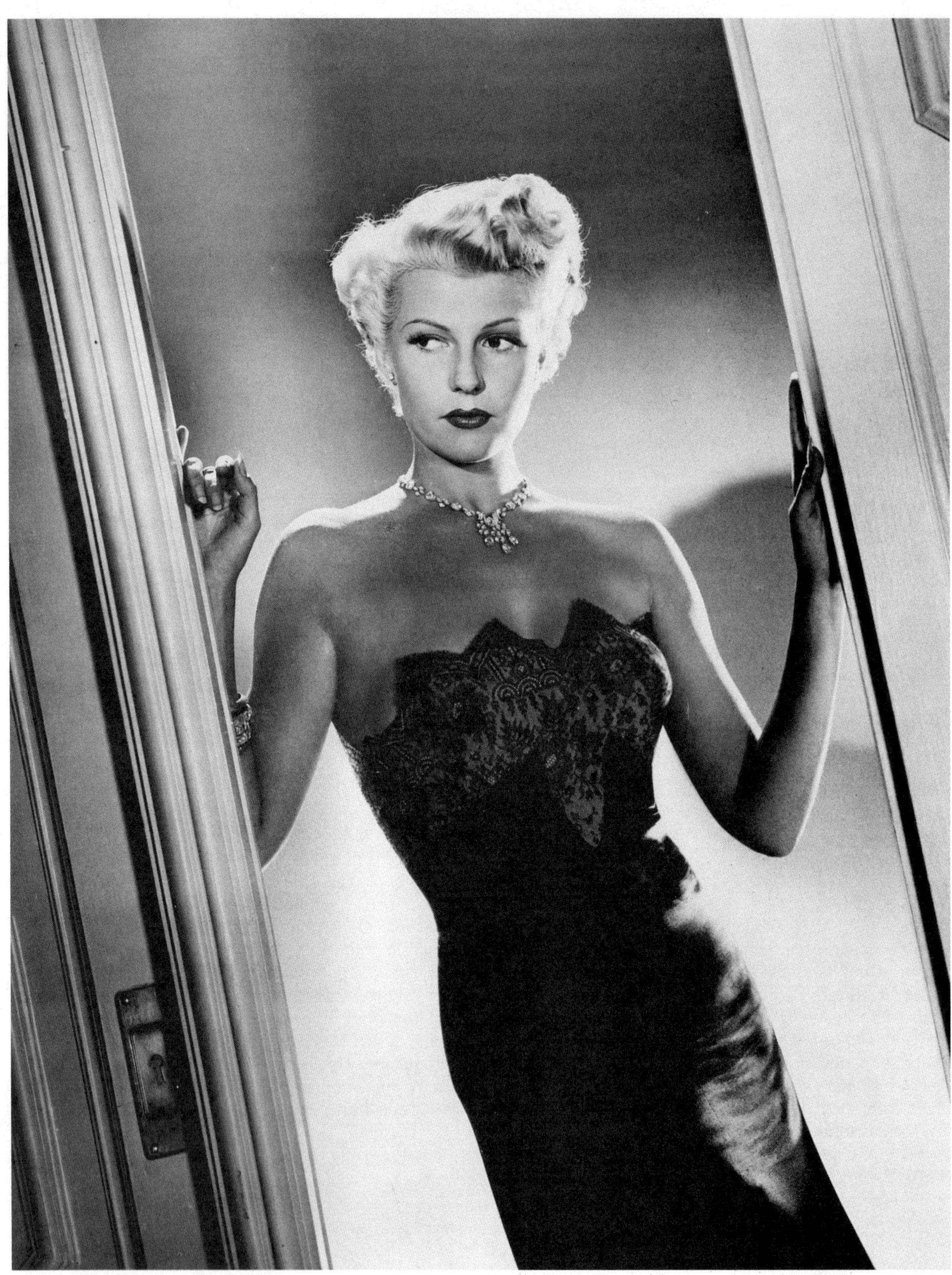

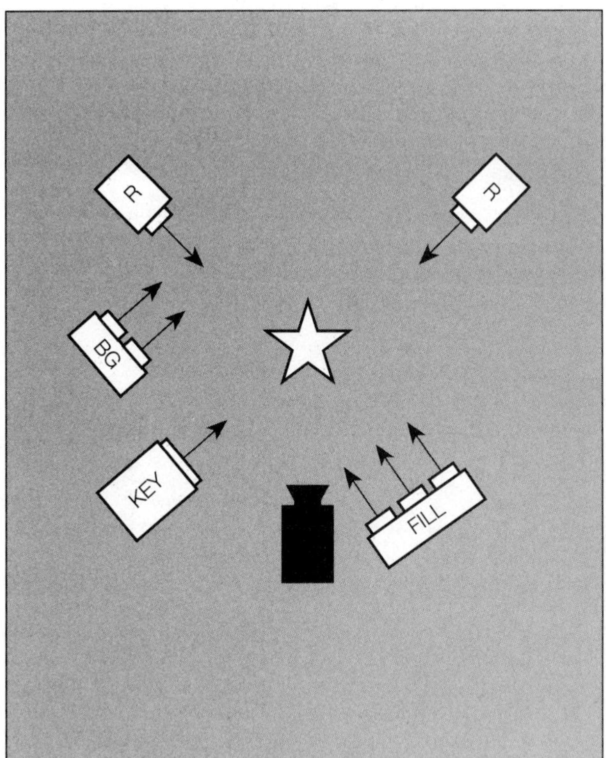

Figure 9.4a (page 136) (Publicity photo of Rita Hayworth for *The Lady from Shanghai*, Columbia Pictures, 1947) In this interesting, skewed composition, the cinematographer has used partial lighting on the face and figure. The key on the star's face is in the frontal position just left of and slightly above the camera. We can see this from her slight nose and neck shadows and her head shadow on the wall frame right. The body is about two stops darker than the face and appears to be lit by the fill coming from camera right. This light also illuminates the door frame.

Note how the background light has been flagged to preserve the top half of her shadow on the wall while the background light bottom frame whitens the wall so as to create a cameo effect—her black dress and dark body against the white wall. See Figure 2.22a for another example of cameo-style lighting. The background light on the top of frame has been patterned to create the interesting shadows top frame.

Two striking rim lights, about three stops overexposed, create an interesting double rim effect. One comes from the right and rims the star's hair and proceeds down to her hips where it puts an interesting sheen on her dress. This light is from a camera-level height as can be seen from her head shadow just visible on the door frame left. The other rim comes from high above frame left and highlights her hair, shoulder, and fingers frame left.

The result of this low-key setup is a beautiful, slightly mysterious portrait of a femme fatale/anima image composed of a wide range of midgrays. This is a complicated and very controlled lighting setup.

APPENDIXES

LIGHTING AND GRIP GEAR

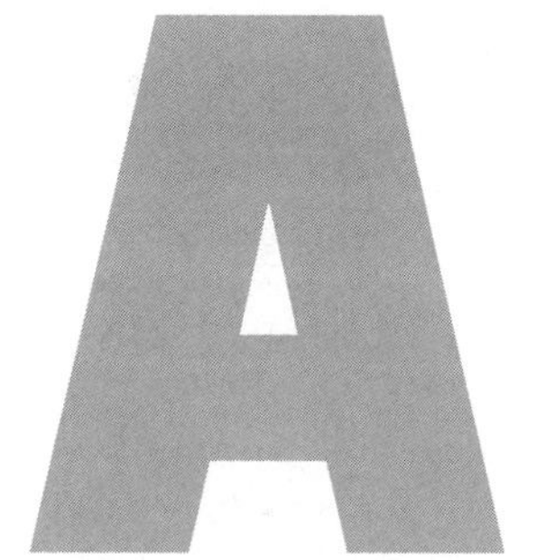

There are a variety of books available that go into lighting and grip gear in great detail. Recommended are Verne and Sylvia Carlson's *Professional Lighting Cameraman's Handbook*, Kris Malkiewicz's *Film Lighting*, Gerald Millerson's *Lighting for Television and Film*, Michael and Sabrina Uva's *The Grip Book*, and the equipment catalogs of the various manufacturers, which feature illustrations of virtually every item available.

Bulbs and Lamps

Bulbs and lamps range in quality from hard (carbon arcs) to soft (frosted household bulbs). Intensities vary from 12K (12,000-watt) HMIs (halogen metal iodide) and 350-amp (D.C.) Titan arc lamps to quartz bulbs less than 100 watts and 25-watt household bulbs.

Filament-Type Bulbs	**Arc-Type Lamps**
Quartz (tungsten halogen)	AC types—gas discharge metal halides (HMIs)
PAR (parabolic aluminized reflector—sealed beams)	DC types—carbon arcs (Brutes)
Photofloods	
Tungsten filament bulbs including household bulbs	

Though usually AC powered, the filament-type bulbs may be DC powered as well.

Quartz Fixtures

Quartz housings are designed for both hard and soft light effects. Hard light is obtained by focusing the beam with a Fresnel lens or by designing the housing to concentrate the beam as with an ellipsoidal spotlight. Softer effects are obtained by using an open-face housing or internal reflected design as with a softlight. The commonly used Fresnels allow for focusing or spreading the beam by moving the bulb and reflector relative to the lens. The following charts the salient features of Fresneled quartz lights.

Fresnels

Features

- ➢ shape of beam varies from wide to narrow
- ➢ controls how large an area is covered
- ➢ has a hard quality with sharp shadows, contrasty
- ➢ light intensity falls off slowly along beam
- ➢ edge of beam falls off quickly to shadow values
- ➢ beam is made more narrow (more focused) by moving bulb away from lens and vice versa

Fresnels are used as key lights and as back lights to accentuate objects and actors. They are also used to create distinct light and shadow patterns—to "paint" with light.

Fresnel housings are designed for a wide range of intensities and beam sizes. A typical series follows. Only a sampling of the many names given to these lamps is provided.

Inky Dink	20–250	watts
Midget	200–600	watts
Baby	1000	watts
Junior	2000	watts
Senior	5000	watts
Tener	10,000	watts

Removing the Fresnel lens converts the lamp into an open-face type. This produces more light intensity, but the beam is broader and less focused.

Open-Face Lights

Open-face units are not as controllable as Fresnels, though some, such as the Lowell DP, allow for beam-size change by movement of the bulb relative to the housing. The advantage of the open-face design is more light output relative to size. This makes the unit effective for filling in large areas with overall illumination and for bouncing light off foam core. Open-face units can be diffused to obtain a softer light quality. The more specialized designs, such as softlights, are usually designed for specific applications such as a soft fill.

Features

- ➢ broad overall illumination, though parabolic housings narrow beam somewhat
- ➢ beam falloff obeys inverse square rule as compared to slower falloff with Fresnels
- ➢ edge of beam falls off gradually to shadow values, thus half tones are more prominent than with Fresnels

Like Fresnels, open-face units come in a variety of types designed for specific purposes, from nooklights to softlights. Here is a sample:

Typical Open-Housing Types

Lowell DP	1000 watts
Mighty Mole	2000 watts
Broads + Scoops	500–2000 watts
Set + Nook	250–1000 watts
Softlights	1000–8000 watts

Other Light Types

Besides Fresnels and the variety of open-face lights, cinematographers utilize sealed beam PAR-type bulbs, fluorescents, photofloods, photographic enlarger bulbs, highly specialized lights such as LTM's fiber optic system (small HMIs connected to heads with optical fibers), homemade "coffin" softlights, and practicals such as candles, kerosene lamps, and firelight sources.

HMI/Arc Types

Large-scale lighting requires large HMIs or carbon arcs, which are generally powered by generators. HMIs are arc-type sources that are very efficient, about three times more efficient than quartz bulbs. Large HMIs are designed to replace arcs and Nine- and Twelve-Lights (FAY and PAR types). HMIs offer substantial advantages over arcs: less heat, no smoke when operating, no need for an operator to adjust carbons, and more efficient luminous output.

HMIs range from 10Ks and 12Ks to small units that compete with quartz lighting. The smaller HMIs—from 200 to 2500 watts—are available in both Fresnel or open-face (with safety glass) designs. HMIs require ballasts to eliminate flicker and strobing effects. Newer designs automatically remove flicker from the lights electronically and thus allow for shooting with a variety of shutter angles and camera speeds.

The Brute arc draws 225 amps at 215 volts DC and puts out the hardest (most like the sun) light beam. Brutes and other arcs and HMIs require glass, either a Fresnel lens or a Pyrex safety glass, to protect the crew and actors from their ultraviolet radiation.

Both HMIs and arcs require color correction to establish and maintain a consistent daylight balance as their operating color temperature varies from the standard 5500K and changes over time. The HMIs in particular vary greatly in their color temperature because the color temperature of each bulb varies with its age, about 1 degree Kelvin per hour of use. Some HMI systems record the amount of time a bulb is used, and you can calculate an approximate color temperature from that information. The better practice is to use a three-color color temperature meter to measure actual color temperature and the amount of correction required.

Lighting Unit Selection

Equipment selection is a reflection of lighting philosophy as well as budgetary constraints. The following charts the types of lights most frequently used in contemporary cinematography.

Table A.1 Lights Used Most Frequently in Contemporary Cinematography

Feature/TV Commercial	Small Scale—Student and Independent
Day Exteriors	
HMIs	Quartz with Tough Blue gel
Carbon arcs	Reflectors
Fay Nine- or Twelve-Lights	Sunguns (battery-powered quartz lights)
Quartz with Tough Blue gel	
Reflectors	
Night Exteriors	
HMIs	Available light
Carbon arcs	Quartz
PAR lights	Anything that will illuminate
Neons and other signs	
Day/Night Interiors	
HMIs/quartz of all types	Quartz
Softlights	Softlights
Bounced light	Bounced light
Available	Available
Photofloods	Photofloods
Household bulbs	Household bulbs
For Outside Window to Create Daylight Effect	
Large HMIs	Available
Nine- or Twelve-Lights	Quartz with Tough Blue gel
Arc	

Grip Gear for Lighting

Lighting units have accessories that are designed to control or change the lamp's intensity, beam pattern, color, and light quality. These accessories also have other special applications. Accessory devices either mount on the light unit or are held by a C-stand placed between the light source and the subject. Most of these devices were developed in the studio era to make studio light controllable. Those shooting in natural light styles use these devices less than do those working in studio situations. To mount these devices, gaffers need asbestos gloves, gaffer's tape (heat resistant), alligator clamps, black tinfoil, and a host of tools to avoid cutting and burning their hands.

Accessories That Mount on the Lighting Fixture

- *Barndoor*. The familiar attachment with adjustable leaves (two or four) that allows for restricting the light beam's path. Fits onto the lamp housing in a variety of ways.
- *Scrim*. Stainless wire net that mounts in the holder behind the barndoor and reduces light intensity. Available in single (one-half stop), double (one stop), and half single and half double (used to reduce the intensity of part of the beam). Scrims may be stacked for greater effect.
- *Gel holder*. Frame for mounting gels and diffusion materials on light units. Smaller productions often use clothespins to hold gels to the barndoor leaves.
- *Snoot*. Conelike metal device that mounts on lamp housing and converts the beam to a very narrow pattern.
- *Pattern projection*. A snootlike device designed to hold and project shadow patterns. Metal cutouts can be shaped to duplicate familiar shadows such as venetian blinds, jail windows, tree branches, and the like.
- *French flag*. A flexarm that mounts on the light and positions a small black flag to help control the beam spread. French flags are also used on cameras to prevent lens flare from stray light.

Self-Standing Accessories

- *Flags/cutters*. Opaque fabrics stretched over rectangular-shaped frames. Designed to cut out light from selective areas of the shot. Usually mounted on C-stands.
- *Cucaloris*. Opaque patterns placed in front of lights to throw shadow patterns into the shot, for example, to make it look like the light is coming through tree branches. Commercial "cookies" come in a variety of patterns. They may also be made of translucent celo plas-

tic. The plastic yields a lighter shadow pattern as light passes through parts of the cookie. Cookies may also be homemade using posterboard or cardboard.

- *C-Stands and sandbags*. C-stands (Century stands) are all-purpose stands designed to hold flags, cookies, gels, nets, scrims, and even lighting units. The C-stand utilizes grip and gobo heads with extension arms to allow for placement in a variety of positions. Sandbags are used to secure the C-stands.
- *Nets*. Metal or cloth screens that come in a variety of meshes. Like scrims, they are used to cut light intensity. Nets come in a variety of framed sizes for a number of applications. Some are framed open ended so as to hide the scrim holder. Nets are also colored to assist in subtle color effects and reductions of intensity.
- *Dots and fingers*. Small scrims or flags for selective use on small areas within the shot.
- *Silks and screens*. Diffusion materials for large areas. When large and secured by several stands these are referred to as overheads, though the overhead frame might also contain scrims, reflection materials, or opaque materials.
- *Overheads*. Large frames for mounting silks and other materials. Typically 9′ x 12′ up to 30′ x 30′.
- *Butterflies*. Small overheads, usually held by one stand.

Two Basic Electrical Considerations

Calculating the amount of wattage allowed by a given circuit is something easily done and allows the cinematographer to work out how many light units can be used with a particular circuit. Handling electricity requires professional training since the dangers are so great. Ultimately, safety is the key word to remember concerning electricity.

W = V x A One of the first things a cinematographer does, or has the gaffer do, is work out power requirements and check the capacity and location of circuit breakers/fuses and outlets. Large loads require specific size cables, extension cables, switches, and so on (consult Malkiewicz, Ritsko, and Carlson for details).

To calculate the size of generator needed or to determine how many watts one can draw from a household circuit, use the formula $W = V \times A$ (watts equal volts times amps—easily remembered as the "West VirginiA" rule). For example, a house circuit has a 20-amp circuit breaker. At 110 volts, we can draw 20 x 110 = 2200 watts maximum—two 1K Fresnels, for example, or one 2K softlight. A 250-amp generator could power 27,500 watts (250 x 110)—ten 2 K softlights plus seven 1 K Fresnels.

SAFETY AC lights are deadly around water and humidity. DC power is safer. Most quartz lights can be powered AC or DC by changing the bulb. Feature films typically utilize DC/AC generators for their power. Independents typically utilize available circuits.

One important safety consideration concerns the use of tie-in boxes. A tie-in taps into the main power supply to a house or building, bypassing the building's mains and circuit boxes. Only qualified electricians should attempt this tie-in (see Ritsko, *Lighting for Location Motion Pictures,* pp. 208–13, for details). Likewise, a proper grounding of all electrical connections is very important.

One other thing to be careful of, particularly on location, is to make sure that cables are taped down so that people won't trip and fall or pull lights over. A gaffing crew (even of 1 person) is very handy here.

Summary

The size and budget of your production generally determine the type and quantity of lighting units you have access to. With a feature film, you must be prepared for all situations. The cinematographer must fit into the scheduling needs of actors as well as deal with a large variety of weather conditions. Rare is the director who has the power to wait for a lighting condition to develop. If the sun goes in—fake it with a Brute! The result is obvious: trucks full of lights, gels, grip gear, ready for anything.

At the opposite end we find natural light and documentary approaches. Take your light as you find it, and carry as little gear as possible. Documentary crews often show up with a basic portable kit (say, three 650-watt quartz lights with Tough Frost and maybe some foam core) and "go with the flow." On features, you control all the lighting. On documentaries, you utilize available light and supplement it as necessary. In between is where most of us operate.

B

LIGHT METERS

Incident and reflected meters are calibrated to the same basic assumption concerning midgray: that it should reproduce at a mid-density point on the characteristic curve. For example, if 100 footcandles of light are incident upon an 18% surface, by definition 18 footlamberts are reflected toward the camera. The incident meter measures the 100 footcandles, the reflected meter the 18 footlamberts. Both arrive at the same T-stop.

What fouls everything up for a reflected meter is when the surface is not 18%. For example, assume 100 footcandles are shown onto a white surface that reflects 90 footlamberts. The incident meter measures the 100 footcandles and gives the same exposure setting as before. This is correct since it allows the white surface to be brighter, hence whiter, than the midgray.

But the reflected meter will give a different exposure setting for the second example. It assumes the white surface is really a midgray one lit brighter than previously. This is obviously erroneous, and thus the user must apply a correction to the meter's indicated reading. This "correction" is itself subject to error, and thus cinematographers utilize incident meters rather than reflected meters for calculating exposure.

The most precise reflected light meter is the spot meter, which is used by cinematographers to measure specific luminance values and overall subject luminance range. Spot meters are also used to calculate exposure for luminous objects—such as neon signs or the sky at magic hour.

To summarize, both kinds of meters are calibrated to the same basic consideration: that an 18% reflectance is best reproduced at roughly the mid-density point on the characteristic curve. The meters differ in how they arrive at that calculation, however, and that difference has led to the incident and reflected exposure techniques discussed in Chapter 6.

Taking Incident Readings

We should quickly review techniques for taking incident readings. The rule is simple: If you want what you see (nominal "correct" exposure), you expose for the indicated meter reading. This will peg zone 5 in the subject to a midgray rendition on the screen. The reading itself is obtained by placing the meter in the light falling on the subject and pointing the meter at the camera lens. The hemispheric disk on the meter takes into account the angle of incidence of the light (the lighting directionality) by substituting its own three-dimensionality for that of the object. Remember, wherever the meter is placed is given a "correct" zone 5 exposure. This rule operates over a wide range of angles of incidence.

Exposure for backlight situations is trickier because the meter tends to overexpose the shadow areas. Some cinematographers take a reading in the normal way and then close down somewhat to preserve the shadow values. This is done by shutting down a half stop or more. A similar technique is to expose halfway between the normal toward-the-camera reading and the reading obtained by pointing the meter toward the light source. Some cinematographers expose for the latter value only (see Figure 2.11).

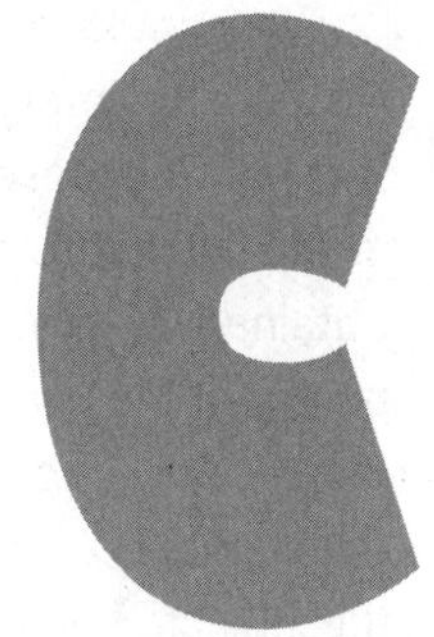

FILM STOCKS AND CHARACTERISTIC CURVES

The sensitometric pioneers, Hurter and Driffield, graphed the ways emulsions react to light with the now familiar H & D characteristic curve, also known as the D log E curve (D log H curve under international standards). This curve plots the density changes for a given emulsion as it is subjected to incremental increases in lighting intensity. The curve is referenced to standardized processing procedures.

The characteristic curve tells us that negative film stocks yield density increases in direct proportion to exposure increases within certain limits and distort that relationship outside those limits. The more exposure you give the negative, the more it reacts chemically to the light and the greater the density obtained after processing (see Figure C.1).

The following definitions are basic to the classic H & D curve as in Figure C.1.

- *Minimum density*, usually called fog level, is a very small amount (.1) and is a property of the film stock (emulsion fog level plus base density).
- *Toe* is the lower curved part of the characteristic curve that corresponds to the initial reactions of the film to exposure.
- *Shoulder* is the gently curved upper portion of the curve illustrating the falloff of the film's reaction after a certain point. On the shoulder, the negative is at maximum density.
- *Straight line portion* (AB) is where increases in exposure yield increases in density in roughly direct proportion. A specified increment of exposure (X_E) on the straight line will yield a corresponding incremental increase in density (X_D). It does not matter if these increments of exposure and density are the same, only that they are consistent—directly proportional (see Figure C.1c).

  Sensitometric science would remind us that, in fact, the term "straight line" is not accurate since the line is not straight. For our purposes the term will suffice, remembering that "straight" is a

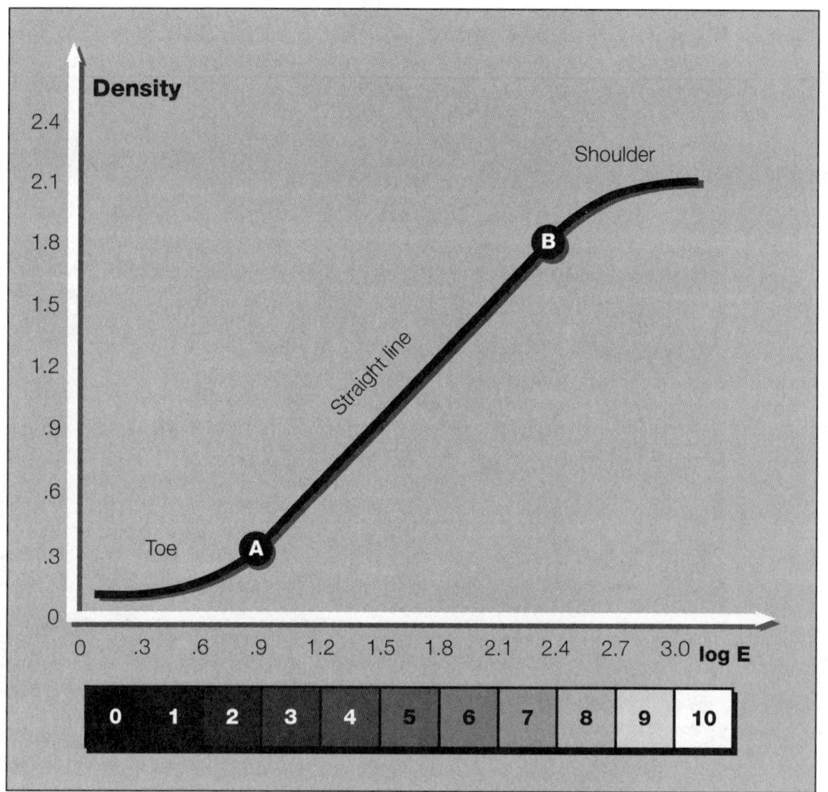

a

Figure C.1a H & D Characteristic Curve *Idealized Negative with Gamma = 1.0 The characteristic curve for a negative shows how an emulsion gets more dense with increases in exposure. Using a sensitometer, we subject an emulsion to light in increments of increasing intensity. After processing, we measure the densities of the negative and plot those density changes as a function of exposure increases.*

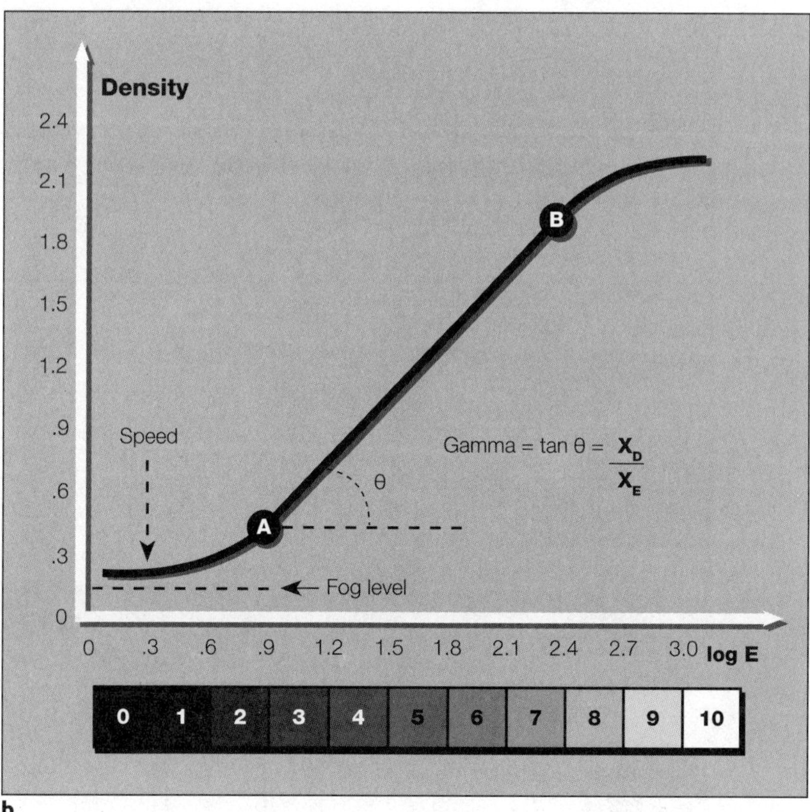

b

Figure C.1b Basic Definitions for a Characteristic Curve *Speed = the distance from the density axis to the beginning of an emulsion's reaction to light. The closer to the density axis, the faster the emulsion. Fog level = the innate density of the emulsion and base as measured by processing with no exposure to light. Gamma = the tangent of θ. By definition, this is equivalent to the change in density (X_D) divided by a given increase in exposure (X_E). See Chapter 5 for a more thorough discussion.*

Figure C.1c Relation Between Exposure and Density Response *For low exposure levels, the density increases slowly (the toe). Then the emulsion reacts linearly: Equal increments of exposure in log E units yield equal increments of density increase. On the shoulder, the exposure/density relationship again becomes nonproportional. Increasing the exposure just barely increases density. In short, an emulsion requires a certain amount of exposure just to react to light, then it responds in linear fashion along a certain range of log E values, then its reaction ceases since it is completed.*

Gamma is defined as X_D over X_E and is referenced to the straight line portion of the curve. In this example, gamma = 1.0 since $X_D = X_E$.

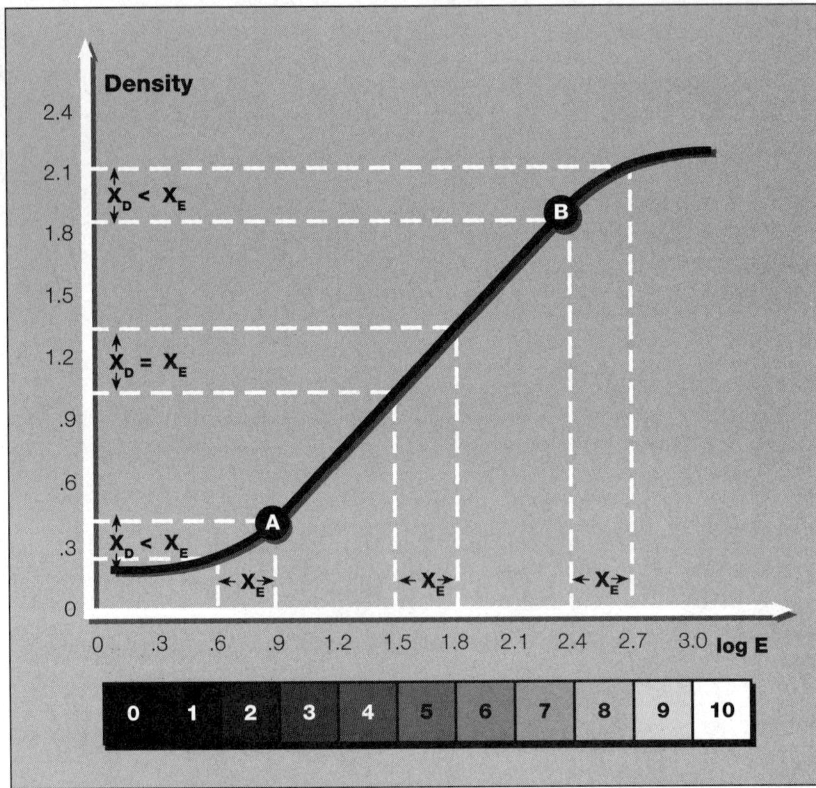

c

Figure C.2 Typical Release Print *The combination of a negative (gamma = .65) and print stock (gamma = 2.6) results in a release print with a gamma of approximately 1.7 (.65 x 2.6 = 1.7). See Chapter 5 for further discussion.*

Characteristic curves for positives (prints from a negative) and reversal originals slope from top left to bottom right in contrast to the curve for a negative, which slopes up to the right as in Figure C.1.

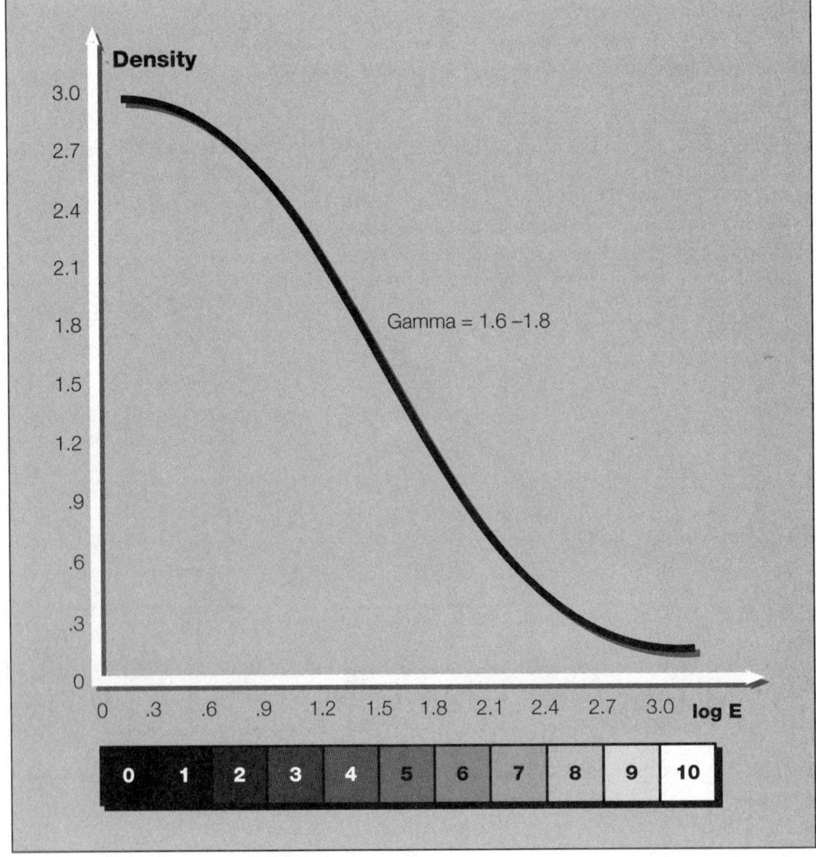

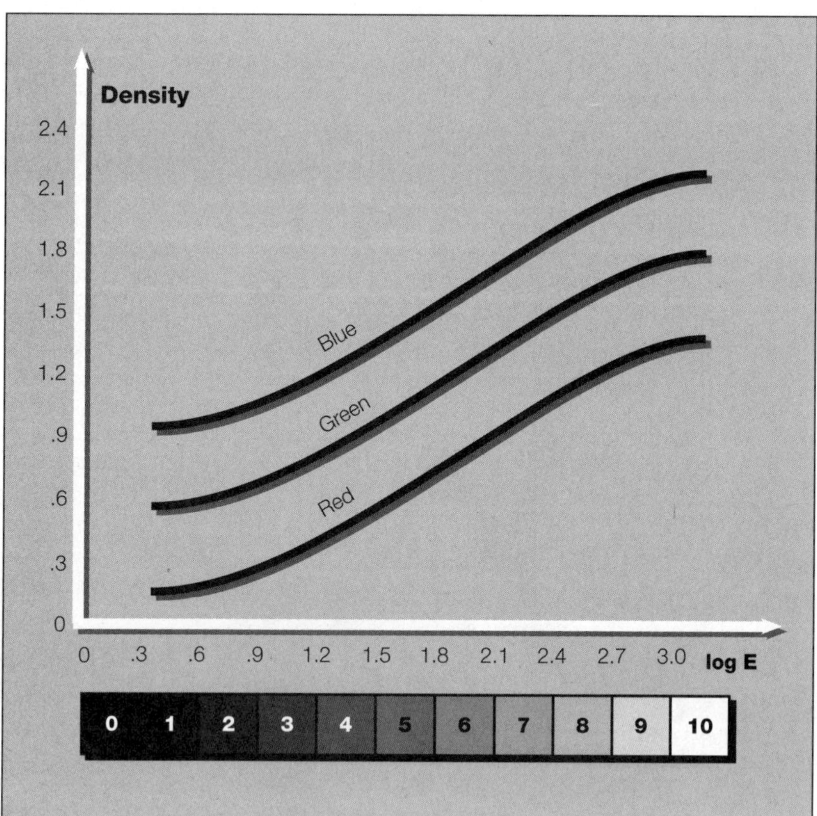

Figure C.3 Typical Color Negative: Gamma = .65–.70

gross simplification. Likewise, "direct proportion" and "consistent" relationship are simplifications to the actual situation in sensitometric science.

Prints from negatives are made with negative print stocks. The print stock reverses the densities on the camera negative so that whites in the print have lower densities than blacks and thus appear lighter on the screen than blacks (see Figure C.2). For color negatives, characteristic curves are graphed with three separate curves, one for each primary color: red, green, and blue. These three curves tend to be parallel and thus possess similar gammas though they cover different density ranges. Essential for color control and processing consistency, the three curves are usually symbolized by the red one for purposes of discussion (see Figure C.3).

The Axes of the Graph: Log E and Density

With a negative emulsion, as log E values increase, the negative gets darker and darker, and the corresponding density values increase. From the point of view of luminance range, original luminance values are represented on the negative by various density values. High luminances are given high density values and low luminances are given low density values (see Figure C.4).

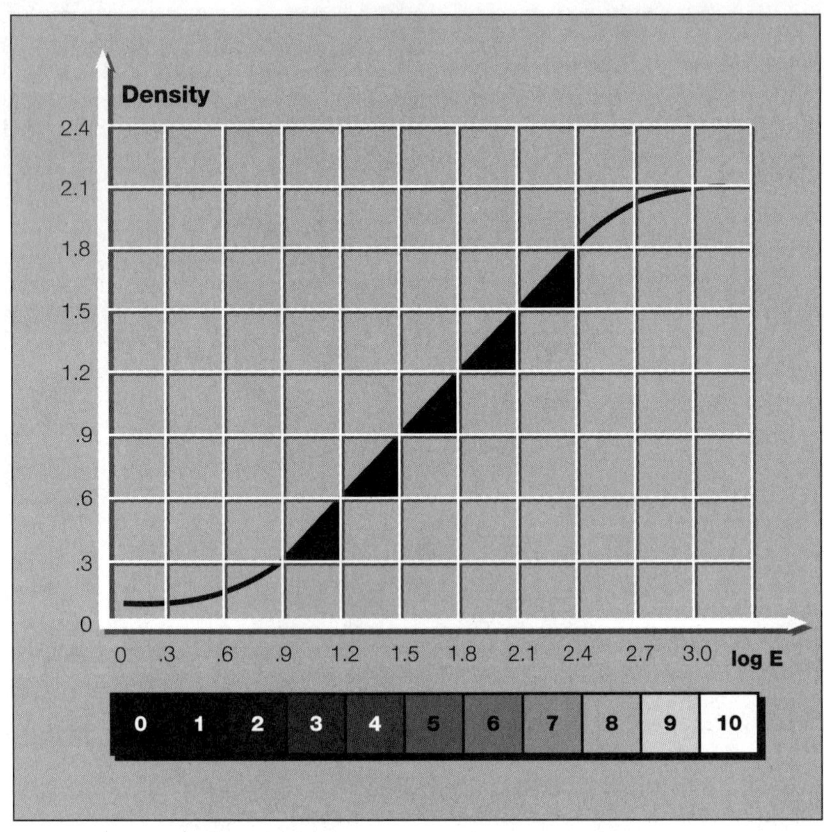

Figure C.4 Placement of Subject Luminance Range with Exposure *A film stock is able to reproduce a given subject luminance range by translating high subject values into maximum densities on the negative. This means they reproduce as whites in the print. Darker values are given correspondingly lower density values, which makes them darker in the final print.*

Table C.1 Comparison of Geometric and Arithmetic Progressions

2x (doubling) Geometric Progression [each number is twice the previous]	Arithmetic (logarithmic) Equivalent [each number is .3 plus the previous]
1	.3
2	.6
4	.9
8	1.2
16	1.5
32	1.8
64	2.1
128	2.4
256	2.7
512	3.0
1024	3.3

For convenience both the exposure and the density axes are graphed logarithmically. This converts a geometric progression, in which units are *multiples* of a fixed constant, into an arithmetic one, in which units are formed by *adding* a certain constant. Utilizing logarithms cuts down drastically on the space required for an accurate graph. An explanation of basic logarithms applicable to film is contained in Appendix D. The relationship between a 2x geometric scale and a .3 arithmetic scale (.3 = the log of 2) is very important in film and should be memorized.

Time should be taken to understand these graphs. Log E and density are terms from sensitometric science and, though hard to grasp at first, provide the factual basis for the zone system which provides us with a more visual language somewhat easier to use and understand than the terms from sensitometry.

LOGARITHMS

D

Logarithms convert geometric progressions (units are multiples of a fixed constant) into arithmetic ones (units are formed by adding a certain constant). Utilizing logarithms cuts down drastically on the space required for an accurate graph. All logs here are to base 10.

DEFINITION OF LOG To what power 10 would have to be raised to obtain the number in question.

If $N = 10^x$ then $\log N = x$.

For example:

$$100 = 10^2 \quad \text{the log of } 100 = 2$$
$$10 = 10^1 \quad \text{the log of } 10 = 1$$
$$1 = 10^0 \quad \text{the log of } 1 = 0$$
$$2 = 10^{.3} \quad \text{the log of } 2 = .3$$

LOGS OF FRACTIONS AND DECIMALS The log of a fraction or decimal is expressed as a negative number with an overbar above the characteristic (number to the left of the decimal). The mantissa (number to the right of the decimal) is always positive.

For example: The log of .0005 is $\bar{4}.6990$
$\bar{4}$ = the characteristic .6990 = the mantissa

number	.125	.25	.5	1.0	2	4	8	etc.
log	$\bar{1}.097$	$\bar{1}.398$	$\bar{1}.699$	0	.3	.6	.9	etc.

A LOG TABLE FOR NUMBERS INVOLVING A MULTIPLE OF TWO The most important series for film involves the multiple of 2:

number	1	2	4	8	16	32	64	128	256	512	etc.
log	0	.3	.6	.9	1.2	1.5	1.8	2.1	2.4	2.7	etc.

Note that the log of 2 is .3 and as the numbers increase geometrically (1 x 2 = 2 x 2 = 4 x 2 = 8 etc.), the logs increase arithmetically by adding .3 to the preceding number: .3, .6, .9, and so on.

WHEN TWO NUMBERS ARE MULTIPLIED,
IT IS EQUIVALENT TO ADDING THEIR LOGS

Example: 2 x 2 = 4 .3 + .3 = .6 (log 2 = .3, log 4 = .6)
2 x 4 = 8 .3 + .6 = .9 (log 8 = .9)

SCALE OF NUMBERS CORRESPONDING TO WHOLE NUMBER LOGS

This is the scaling typically used by film manufacturers.

log	$\bar{3}.0$	$\bar{2}.0$	$\bar{1}.0$	0	1.0	2.0	3.0
number	.001	.01	.1	1	10	100	1000

As each log increases by 1.0, each number is multiplied by a factor of 10.

Another example: using the number 4 (with log of .6):

log	$\bar{2}.6$	$\bar{1}.6$	.6	1.6	2.6
number	.04	.4	4	40	400

SOME BASIC UNITS OF ILLUMINATION

There are a variety of terms you will run into concerning illumination. Most originate in the science of photometry. Some are very odd terms indeed. The following is intended only as a reference for when you run into a term you don't understand. The *Encyclopedia of Film and Television* and Webster's should be consulted as needed.

➢ *The basic unit* from photometry is the *lumen*. A lumen is a unit of radiated light energy or "luminous flux." The power of a lighting unit can be ranked in terms of its output specifying the lumens available measured at a specific distance from the unit. The power of a light source is also discussed in units called *candelas*. One candela = 12.56 lumens (4 x pi lumens) by definition. (Note: pi = 3.14.)

➢ *Efficiency of a light source*. Some bulbs are more efficient than others; that is, they generate more lumens of light for a given amount of electrical energy. Thus, we can compare the efficiency of bulbs in terms of *lumens per watt*.

➢ *The measurement of incident light*. If a light source illuminates a surface of 1 square foot with 1 lumen we say it has a lighting intensity of 1 *footcandle*. This is, of course, the standard unit for scaling incident meters. When lighting we say, for example, that the key light is 100 footcandles and so forth.

➢ *The measurement of reflected light*. Incident light is reflected by objects back toward the camera. This is expressed in terms of luminance value (brightness) using units called *footlamberts*. One footlambert is reflected by a perfectly diffusing source when illuminated by 1 footcandle. Real-world objects reflect only a part of the light illuminating them so that the relationship is better expressed as

footlamberts = footcandles x % reflectance

Chapter 3 contains a more detailed explanation of this relationship.

➢ *Metric equivalents*. In the metric system, incident light is measured in *lux*. One lux is the incident light that lights 1 square meter with 1 lumen. One footcandle = 10.76 lux. One lux = .093 footcandles. Reflected light is measured in *nits*. One footlambert = 3.42 nits. One nit = .292 footlambert.

F

LIGHTING STYLE

The concept of style can refer to several different ideas: (1) the style of a film overall—whether it is high- or low-key, soft or hard, naturalistic, realistic, or stylized; (2) the style of a certain cinematographer throughout a series of films or a particular film—Nykvist's soft light style, Almendros's magic hour style, Hall's hard light style, Wexler's documentary style; or (3) the type of lighting applied to a certain genre—film noir style, musical comedy style, TV commercial style. Choice of style varies with the approach of the cinematographer, the meaning of the film, and the views of the director.

Elements of Style

The following elements may be combined to form lighting styles.

- *Light quality*. Derives from the type of lighting applied, whether it is hard or soft, direct or indirect, overall or selective in scope.
- *Light source directionality*. This refers to the angle of incidence of the illumination applied to the subject (see Chapter 1). The directionality of the key light defines mood and the relative proportions of light and shadow in the frame.
- *The ratio of light to shadow areas in the image*. This refers to whether we light everything in the shot or not. Large shadow areas and areas of obscurity can be very important stylistic devices. The proportion of light to shadow is related to high- and low-key effects as well as to subject luminance range.
- *Overall key of lighting*. You can have high-key lighting, which is bright and cheery, or low-key lighting, which is dark and brooding. Most scenes strike a mood somewhere in between.
- *Subject luminance range*. This refers to the range between the brightest significant luminance value and the darkest, that is, the overall contrast in the subject measured in footlamberts and usually expressed as a ratio.

- *Lighting ratios*. Subject lighting ratios are thoroughly discussed in Chapter 8. Lighting ratios are tied in with the overall key of the lighting. Low lighting ratios tend to create a brighter, happier feeling—and are thus used in musicals and comedies—whereas higher lighting ratios create a darker, dreary, or even frightening mood—and are thus often found in horror films, thrillers, or mysteries.
- *Placement of subject relative to background/foreground*. We light in planes with the subject usually in the middle plane. We then relate the background and foreground to that subject placement—the subject usually being an actor's face. We then determine whether the background is to be lit lighter, darker, or at the same level as the actor's face; that is, we place the subject in a tonal context. This choice becomes a matter of style.
- *Choice of film stock*. In choosing an overall palette or color key, the cinematographer influences the overall style.
- *Processing and printing*. Techniques such as using a Vari-Con device, flashing, overdeveloping, blowing up and other optical printer manipulations, choice of printer lights and print stocks, all affect image renditions and textures.
- *Degree of sharpness of the image*. Both light and subject may be "smoked," diffused, or left unmediated; that is, rendered with the sharpness built into the lens and emulsion grain.
- *Placement of facetones*. This refers to whether the overall placement of facetones in the film is "normal" (a zone 5 exposure) or whether they are placed darker or lighter for mood. Generally, black facetones are placed around zone 4, and Caucasian facetones at zone 6, but certain styles might place them at other zones; for example, with Caucasian faces, zone 7 or zone 5 might be used, depending on the mood of the film.
- *Degree of transparency* (hidden versus overt). In most films, the fact that many scenes have been artificially lit is hidden. This situation masks the facts of production behind a realistic illusion as in the classic Hollywood seven-light technique. In such films, lighting plays a functional, thematic-support role. The alternative is to make lighting a central aesthetic dimension, as important as the narrative. This approach results in a pictorialist, foregrounded, stylized lighting, for example, the color effects in *Dick Tracy* or *One From the Heart*. Whether lighting is realistic or stylized is generally a directorial decision made after consultation with the cinematographer.

In *Sight/Sound/Motion*, Herbert Zettl states that lighting has two main functions: (1) the realistic, which is to articulate a filmic space/time and establish a filmic illusion, and (2) the symbolic, which is to articulate an inner emotional environment, to create moods and objectify our inner lives. We may reference these categories to realistic and pictorialist, painting-with-light styles. As described, both types of lighting styles represent extremes. Often in any one film, we can find a combination of both.

G

COLOR AND TEXTURE CONTROLS

Lighting and color are powerful features of cinematography. With their almost direct access to the viewer's unconscious, lighting and color create image moods and make a substantial contribution to the overall feeling and significance of the film. Anyone who has viewed Bergman's *Cries and Whispers* or Visconti's *Death in Venice* knows the power of light and color.

Generally, cinematographers can control the light element (indeed, this is their main function) but have less control over the color factor, which is heavily influenced and controlled by the design/art direction side of filmmaking (set, costumes, props) and the director's aesthetic goals.

Most film/video is in color. Color is an aesthetic and artistic possibility linked to lighting and must be controlled. Whereas the masters of light (as pertains to emulsions) have been photographers, the masters of color have been painters. Only in animation can we control color as a painter can. But in our cinematography we must be as sensitive to color and its moods as a painter since our lighting influences color and determines saturation and overall color effect.

A thorough study of color is of vast importance for the cinematographer. Such an investigation is beyond the scope of this book. The interested reader should consult books like *The Perception of Color* by Ralph M. Evans, *Art and Visual Perception* by Rudolph Arnheim, and *Color in Your World* by Faber Birren.

Visual look as we will use the term incorporates overall image feel, that is, the interplay of light and color. The importance of lighting technique on color rendition and subsequent image mood cannot be overemphasized. Besides color, texture techniques—diffusion, grain, contrast—are just as important in creating a particular look. The following discussion of color and texture should be considered as a guide for future tests and investigations.

Color Controls

A cinematographer has many methods for controlling color and creating color effects. Among these are:

1. light source gels
2. lens filtration
3. color temperature effects
4. lighting angle and time of day or year
5. quality of lighting
6. emulsion choice
7. exposure and processing effects
8. lab printing controls
9. art design—sets and costumes

Normally, a cinematographer incorporates effects from all but method 8 in the negative, reserving the lab controls for fine, subtle corrections and changes. Many labs will go to much effort to please the cinematographer in timing and printing the original; in fact, many special color effects are possible only through close, joint cooperation. Electronic color controls also provide a variety of computer-controlled, very subtle color possibilities for working with video, including the transferring of negative to video.

LIGHT SOURCE GELS Light source gels allow for color temperature corrections and intentional color effects. Gelling light sources enables the cinematographer to create color effects in select areas of the shot, whereas camera filtration and printing controls operate nonselectively over the entire frame.

There are four basic types of light source color gels.

- The blue series (for converting tungsten to daylight balance and for "cool" light effects)
- The amber/orange series (for converting daylight and HMIs to 3200K and for warm color effects) and the accompanying amber/straw correctors for arcs
- The green and magenta series (for correcting fluorescents and discharge lamps including HMIs)
- The color range for colored lighting effects.

Sample pads of available gels may be obtained from the various manufacturers: GamColor, Rosco, Lee, and so on. Also consult the ads in *American Cinematographer* magazine.

Most of these light gels are available in heat-resistant, polyester "Tough" form for mounting on light units and cheaper, acetate forms for mounting over windows, doorways, and the like. For a realistic lighting scheme, the basic goal is to balance all illumination to a known color temperature (usually daylight, tungsten, or fluorescent) and make final overall corrections in the lab or during video post. For stylized effects, the lab fine-tunes and perfects the color effect.

Working with selected color lighting effects ("painting with color") is easily overdone and gives the best results when kept subtle. As Sergei Eisenstein pointed out in the early 1930s (see *The Film Sense*), there is no language of color. Yellow, for example, does not always signify sun and vitality (cf. malaria and van Gogh's *Night Cafe*); simply put, the meaning of yellow is relative to its context. The cinematographer then must create the appropriate context in his or her lighting in order for these colors to establish and maintain their traditional psychological significances, such as blue is "cool" or red is "warm."

Overuse of color effects destroys the authenticity of the image. As with light, the cinematographer must study natural colors to understand their complexities.

LENS FILTRATION Lens filters are used to control the color temperature (CT) balance between the illumination and the film emulsion. Normally, they correct the balance so that the film will reproduce colors in the subject as nearly as possible as the eye sees them: blue as blue, light green as light green. There is an almost unlimited choice of color filters available, and color off-balances are often used for effect. For example, we sometimes shoot a tungsten-balanced negative outdoors without a #85 filter so as to gain a coldish, bluish image. The manufacturers' brochures and ads should be consulted to learn about filters (Tiffen, Harrison and Harrison, Cokin, etc.).

COLOR TEMPERATURE EFFECTS The color temperature of the various light sources can be manipulated for a variety of effects and mood control. For example, we may leave the color temperature of select areas of the frame out of balance. To create the feeling of a winter night with warm interior, we could blue the outside lighting to 4500K, amber the inside lighting to 2800K, and expose the film at 3200K even though nothing in the shot is at this color temperature. In this example, we might leave some 3200K light in the shot (say, as keys on actors' faces) to establish the neutral context for both warm and cool effects. Besides gelling, dimmers can be used to warm selected lights.

LIGHTING ANGLE AND TIME OF DAY OR YEAR Frontal lighting maximizes color saturation, and back lighting desaturates. This effect is particularly evident outdoors (See Color Plate 1).

Time of day determines both the angle of the sun and the color temperature of the daylight. These features are most evident with sunrise/sunset effects and early morning/late afternoon warm effects.

Time of year is important because it determines the height of the sun in the sky, likely weather conditions (snow, rain, or overcast), and, of course, whether the earth is barren or verdant. These factors obviously affect the rendition of the subject's colors.

QUALITY OF LIGHTING Coupled with the effects of lighting angle, hard light yields more saturated hues than does soft, diffuse light because hard light creates greater contrast.

EMULSION CHOICE Each emulsion offers a slightly different color palette. Not only does Fujicolor look different from Agfa or Eastman Color, but fast Fuji looks different from slow Fuji. Awareness of the potential palettes inherent in each emulsion is an important factor in the lighting and color design of the overall film.

EXPOSURE AND PROCESSING EFFECTS Cinematographers manipulate exposure and processing to aid in color control. For example, underexposure with overprinting (or overdevelopment), or overexposure with pull development (underdevelopment) affects grain structure and yields different colors than does standard exposure and printing. Flashing can also vary color rendition.

LAB PRINTING CONTROLS Printing controls allow for color effects in conjunction with exposure and processing. For example, use of B & W mattes with color negs can be used to mute colors. Various effects can be obtained through the manipulation of printing intermediates and the use of low-contrast print stocks.

ART DESIGN: SETS AND COSTUMES In the earlier days of B & W, art directors asked cinematographers which "colors" they wanted the walls painted, that is, what tonal values they wanted to render on film. Later, directors like Visconti elevated color into the aesthetic fabric of their works through careful control of set and costume design as well as lighting. The problem is to ensure that the cinematographer is involved with set design and location selection in the preproduction stage since lighting can only bring out what is inherent in the production designer's color scheme.

Not only does this mean the cinematographer and the production designer should work together early on, but, ideally, the designer would have the ability to see as the film stock "sees." Of course, then the cinematographer must also understand basic design principles as they apply to color. No lighting plan can cure a bad color scheme—this is why color control is as important to the final image look as the lighting.

Texture Controls

The major manufacturers of light-quality control media (Rosco, Lee, GamColor) offer a variety of diffusion gels in both acetate (theater type) and polyester (for high-heat situations). The filter manufacturers also provide a wide range of diffusion filters. We may conveniently divide these materials affecting light quality into diffusion gels and filters and reflection media.

DIFFUSION GELS AND FILTERS Diffusion gels are used extensively for selective diffusion effects, as compared with camera lens diffusion, which affects the entire image. Diffusion comes in a variety of grades or densities in three principle forms: Frosts, Silks, and Spuns.

Gels may be mounted on lamp housings or in overheads/flags/butterflies and inserted between the illumination and the subject. Cinematographers also test and use such materials as tracing paper, Velveteen, and Vinalite for diffusion effects.

It is necessary to experiment with these materials in order to become acquainted with their often subtle effects on light source quality. It is also possible to combine diffusion materials with other gels (e.g., blues for tungsten-to-daylight conversion) so that you can, for instance, add a Tough Blue Frost gel to a light source.

It is also common to create diffusion through use of a lens filter. Filters designed to lower contrast also tend to have a softening effect on the image. Principal filter manufacturers are Tiffen and Harrison and Harrison. These filters come in a series and start with slight effects (e.g., #1/2 or #1/4) and progress to heavier effects (e.g., #5). Typical lens diffusion possibilities include:

- *Diffusion* #1/2–#5. A series of manufactured diffusers, from slight to heavy.
- *Softnet filters* #1–#5. Designed to replace the use of nylons and other nets stretched over the lens, these are essentially nets mounted in glass. Available with black, white, red, or skintone tints.
- *Dutto filters (black dot texture screens)* #1–#5. Another means for diffusing that tries to minimize the blooming of hot spots which oftens accompanies diffusion filters.
- *Regular fog* #1/8–#5. Originally designed for fog simulation effects. Now used to cut, or lower, contrast. Softens image.
- *Double fogs* #1/8–#5. Similar to regular fogs but more effective for reducing contrast.
- *Soft contrast filters* #1–#5. Designed to soften contrast and mute color.
- *Low-contrast screens* #1/8–#7. Designed to replace the fogs for lowering contrast, but many cinematographers prefer fogs. Low-contrast screens give some desaturation of color. Again, they tend to soften the image.

- *Supafrosts* #1–#7. Contrast reducer much like the low-contrast screens. Available in a range of intensities.

Most of the preceding lens diffusers are available in graduated (partial) forms so that they impact only on select areas of the image. These diffusers affect color saturation and are often used to alter the color palette provided by the film emulsion. Obviously, a large variety of effects are possible. Tests and experiments must be conducted in order to control results. For example, on some of the net effects, the viewfinder is unable to reveal the true amount of diffusion recorded on the image.

The degree of diffusion obtained with a particular filter varies with the focal length and T-stop you are using. The same diffusion on a telephoto has a greater impact than on a wide-angle lens. Likewise, the diffusion effect is greater at T 2.8 than at T 11. This means to match a CU with a long shot you have to use differing degrees of diffusion. If the CU is shot with a higher focal length lens, then it will require less diffusion than the LS. If the same focal length lens is used for both CU and LS, then the CU will require more diffusion in order to match the LS. Also, 16mm requires much less diffusion in general than 35mm since it is already a softer image. Again, effects should be tested prior to actual shooting.

Some cinematographers use diffusion regularly; others prefer the sharpness provided by current lenses. Obviously, this is a matter of style and an area subject to fads. A good discussion of the use of these lens filters, along with tips and guidelines, is found in Malkiewicz, *Film Lighting*, pp. 62–67.

REFLECTION MEDIA Reflection materials are used to bounce light, as with a sun reflector, or to create a very soft light source for a scene ("bounced" light). Reflection materials vary from specular, mirrorized types to diffuse, matte surfaces. Reflection media come in a variety of silver, gold, white, and color choices as well as in scrim form.

H

LAB PRINTERS

Instead of T-stops, the lab timer works with printer points (printer lights). Most labs use automatic printers such as the Bell and Howell additive printer, which has 50 printer light settings with increments of .025 log E each. The nominal middle setting is usually around light 25 (termed point 25). This is not a universal standard, however, and varies slightly from lab to lab; some labs may be at a 30, for example.

With additive printers approximately 12 points are equivalent to one T-stop (this varies with the lab as well; some have eight lights to a stop). It is thus possible to change an original 25 points (about two stops) with subtle minute increments. The rule of thumb is that a negative is correctable for density up to two stops in either direction with the proviso that at the ends of the scale, print quality falls off since the negative itself may be deficient.

To vary the colors in a film image, additive printers utilize light valves for the three primaries (red, green, and blue). Each color may be varied by the 50 points so that a color setting is usually expressed as follows: R25 G30 B18. Point settings determine the color balance and density of the print being struck.

Lights are usually in the 20s and 30s, but small variations are normal: for example, 36-34-25 is quite acceptable. The higher the light number, the greater the amount of light being used to print the negative. The use of higher printer lights indicates the negative is "heavy" and overexposed. Most negatives print in the 30–35 light range. Some cinematographers intentionally overexpose their negatives from 1/2 to 2/3 of a stop on the theory that heavier negatives produce more satisfactory colors and release prints.

To aid in timing, a video color analyzer is usually employed. This allows the timer to see in advance the effect of various color and density changes on the original. Such subtle controls enable a high precision fine-tuning of the image.

The relationship between the lab and a cinematographer can be a frustrating one. Spoken language invariably fails to convey the necessary information about the visual image. We are left to communicate with the timer in words that only hint at the visual possibilities in printing (e.g., a touch darker, too bluish). How the timer is supposed to translate this verbal imprecision into printer lights is a major barrier to overcome in arriving at the final, timed answer print.

Many feature cinematographers work out a specific light valve combination with the lab prior to principal photography and have the lab print all negatives with that combination. Different combinations are often used for night and day exteriors and interiors, which provides a fixed reference point for subsequent lighting. It also ensures that a timer's visual preferences do not enter in, but then one can lose the timer's experience and possible input.

SETTING UP A VIDEO MONITOR AND A WAVEFORM MONITOR

Setting Up Color Video Monitors

As argued in Chapter 14, color monitors have a variety of uses on the set: evaluating lighting, exposure, color, diffusion effects, and overall look. Setting up the monitor involves standardizing to color bars. Most cinematographers rely on the yellow and magenta bars to properly adjust for color. Brightness, contrast, and saturations are usually set by eye using the bars as reference. The central thing to remember when using the monitor to evaluate is that it is essential not to change the monitor settings until a particular setup is finished. To change on-screen looks, you should adjust T-stop on the camera or the lighting but not the monitor adjustments. This ensures your look will be captured on tape and be consistent with the rest of the scene. To do otherwise is to risk inconsistencies in the image's colors and contrast (see Chapter 14).

Mathias and Patterson elaborate a more thorough method for monitor adjustment. They delineate how to set brightness (blacks), contrast (whites), hue (colors adjusted to yellow and magenta), and saturations (chroma). For more details, see *Electronic Cinematography*, pp. 158–61.

Waveform Monitors

Since the waveform monitor represents a series of spot meter readings across the image, it is a highly accurate representation of relative subject luminance values. It also suffers from the limitations of all reflected readings and presents the problem of ensuring consistent facetones for a variety of lighting conditions. With this in mind, the waveform monitor will be useful to some cinematographers and little used by others.

Setting up a waveform monitor is relatively easy. The scope is manufactured so that the blanking level (voltage level for scanning beam when shut off and preparing for next line or field) is at 0.0. To avoid the interference of this blanking level with the black values in the visual signal, we adjust black level on the waveform monitor to 7.5. This means that the darkest subject value will reproduce at 7.5 rather than at 0.0.

The next step is to determine exposure for the scene. In Chapter 13, we discuss setting an 18% gray card at 50 IRE units. This is done by setting T-stop on the camera, either with a gray card technique or by use of an incident meter based on a prior calculation of the particular camera's exposure index equivalent (see Chapter 13), and by ensuring an illumination intensity level suitable for that video camera.

This gives us a black level of 7.5 and a T-stop for the scene. Since 100 IREs represents maximum white, we have a range of approximately 4½ zones to work with in our lighting (from 7.5 to 100 IRE units). The waveform monitor should be used to monitor highlight values over 100.

What this boils down to practically speaking is that we should set black level (pedestal) and then expose so that midgray is at 50 IRE. We then light so that our most significant highlight value falls at about 100 IRE on the monitor. The alternative to this very technical approach is to utilize a visual monitor as discussed in Chapter 14. See Chapter 5 in Mathias and Patterson, *Electronic Cinematography*, for further information on setting up waveform monitors.

SUGGESTED EXPOSURE AND LIGHTING EXERCISES

J

The following exercises are designed to test many of the concepts discussed in this book. They may be performed individually or in groups. The exercises may be shot on film stock, videotape, or slide film. It is possible to obtain some of the Fuji and Eastman Kodak motion picture negative stocks in 35mm cartridges, which are processed, printed, and then mounted as slides.

EXPOSURE EXERCISES

Light Meter Exercises

1. *Incident meters*. Shine a variety of keys on a face and full figure, practice exposing for back, rim, and three-quarter rear positionings. Try readings taken with the meter pointed at the camera, at the light source, and halfway in between. Take notes and study the relative effects of exposure technique on facetone and shadow area renditions. Shooting 24 of these will alleviate fears of how to take readings for backlit situations.

2. *Incident meters*. Go outside and take a series of slides with the sun positioned as frontal key, three-quarter front key, side key, three-quarter rear, and back key. Note the effect on color saturation as the sun moves from frontal to rear. As with exercise 1, a variety of exposure readings are possible for the three-quarter rear and back positionings.

3. *Spot meters and averaging reflected meters*. Take a high luminance range subject and measure the various luminances. Expose for each luminance, and see how the meter puts it at midgray on the characteristic curve. Notate the range of luminances, and expose for an 18% reflectance (use a gray card or an incident meter). Analyze the slides and the resulting luminance range placements. Intentionally underexpose and overexpose the subject, and analyze those effects.

Zone System Exercises

4. On the slides from exercise 3, correlate the notated luminance values in footlamberts with their resulting zone values.

5. Find a series of photographs, and label zone values. Do this for color as well as B & W.

6. Take a black object and through one-stop exposure increments place it on zones 1 through 9. Do the same for a white object and a midgray object.

7. Expose a face lit with a side or three-quarter front key and no fill. Expose for the light side, shadow side, and halfway in between. Compare the feel of the resulting images.

Film Stock Tests

8. Set up a series of gray scales so as to create a very long luminance range (e.g., light three gray scales seven stops apart so that the middle chip on scale B is seven stops brighter than the one on scale A, and the middle chip on scale C is seven stops brighter than the one on B). Measure the actual luminances with a spot meter and notate them. Expose several film emulsions (expose for the middle scale "B"), and compare the resulting prints. Note the feel of the different emulsions that results from their differing straight lines and overall useful ranges (see Table 7.1 in Chapter 7).

9. Take a number of color negatives, and shoot the same scene with each. The scene can be interior or exterior, night or day, or all of these. With each stock, overexpose 1 and 2 stops, underexpose 1 and 2 stops. Have the lab time these to the correct exposure so that you can see the effects of printing down and printing up on each negative as well as the differences between the individual film stocks and how they respond.

10. As in exercise 9, take a selection of negatives (e.g., an Eclair with eight different magazines loaded with a different stock), and film the exact same scenes. Pick a variety of scenes, from day exterior to night exteriors with a range of backlit and cross-lit situations. Compare the stocks. For this test it is best to film a gray scale and color chip chart at the head of each roll so the lab can time to that and provide a one-lite workprint for evaluation. These two series of tests will give a working knowledge of the look possibilities of each emulsion. Don't forget that Fuji, Kodak, and Afga also have their own print stocks. Generally, labs will print on the brand of your choice. Print stock will also affect final image look.

Exposure Experiments

11. Perform the face/background test described in Figure 8.7. Use an incident meter and change the backgrounds, then repeat the series using a spot meter and averaging meter.

12. Using a spot meter, expose a variety of luminous objects with intentional under- and overexposure. Do the same with an averaging meter. Compare the results. Tackle a large variety of luminous objects: light bulbs, sunsets, water reflections, neon signs, stained-glass windows, and so on. (see Figure 7.7).

13. Overexpose a selected exterior and interior in one-stop increments (see exercise 8). Study the feel of these overexposed shots.

14. Find all-light and all-dark situations, shoot using a range of over- and underexposures, and evaluate the results. Do the same for a panoramic longshot with haze or fog.

15. Perform the person-in-the-window series as described in the text (see Figure 7.8 and "Balancing Interior and Exterior Levels" in Chapter 10). Study the various exposure choices and their resulting look on the screen.

16. As in exercise 15, but experiment with the various color temperature choices (see "Indoor/Outdoor Color Temperature Balance" in Chapter 10).

17. Perform the person and lamp series as described in the text (see Figure 10.5 and accompanying text). Get comfortable with integrating and combining reflected and incident readings, by mixing luminous objects with incident lighting setups.

18. Perform the magic hour series as described in the text (see "Magic Hour" in Chapter 11 and Color Plates 5–12). Note the variety of color effects possible, from late, golden afternoon to night looks. Study the differences between shooting away from the setting sun and toward it. Take time to sit one night and observe the magic hour and the changing sky.

Exposure for Electronic Cinematography

19. Redo exercises 2, 8, and 15–18 as described above. Note how video differs from the film responses. (It would have been possible to use video at the same time as conducting the film tests.)

20. Perform the waveform monitor series of displays described in Figures 13.3 and 13.4.

21. Conduct pedestal (black gamma) tests in a variety of situations. Change the gamma and notate the results for reference.

22. Practice setting midgray at a variety of IRE positions on the waveform monitor, and note the resulting differences in look.

23. Work out the exposure index equivalent for your video camera (see Chapter 13).

LIGHTING EXERCISES

Almost all the examples and photographs discussed in the book may be used for lighting exercises. These will supplement the more intense experience resulting from working on actual films.

24. Find examples of films on video that exhibit a variety of lighting styles. Analyze a scene or two from those films in detail. Lay out lighting plots, identify ratios, and so on.

25. As in exercise 24, but analyze a particular cinematographer's style throughout a series of films (e.g., Sven Nykvist's work in the Bergman films or Conrad Hall's work in the 1970s).

26. As in exercise 24, but analyze the entire film's use of lighting ratios, luminance range, and so on. Make a scene outline of the film and try to account for the variety of lighting setups in terms of the script/film's meaning.

27. Take a number of short poetic phrases (Haiku, imagist poems, lines from rock songs) and translate those words into visual images. The goal is to create images that convey moods similar to the words.

28. Take a scene from a feature and recreate that lighting setup and look paying attention to the composition, lighting, and colors. You can do this with film or video or even slides. This is a very difficult exercise, particularly if you are incorporating movement and filming it.

29. Shoot slides of night exteriors with available light. Add to those street scenes an actor whom you light (see Color Plates 13 and 16).

30. Take an actor in a night interior and experiment lighting him or her with a variety of sources: flashlights, kerosene lanterns, car headlights, candles, and so on. Become aware of the lighting and color effects possible with such sources.

31. As exercise 30, but strive to change and experiment with light quality (e.g., use diffusion, bounce, silks, Fresnels, etc.). Become aware of the range of light-quality possibilities and the resulting differences in feel on the screen (see Chapter 1).

32. Practice with the various keys from a variety of angles (see Figures 2.1–2.11).

33. As in exercise 32, but add a variety of fill lights at the various ratios (see Figures 2.12–2.14 and 8.1–8.6).

34. Practice with the various rim and back light positionings (Figures 2.15–2.17).

35. Photograph a mathematical series of facial ratios—2:1, 4:1, 8:1, 16:1, and 32:1—on a variety of different facetones. Compare the results (see Figures 8.1–8.6).

36. Create silhouettes and semisilhouettes (see Figures 8.7 and 9.3).

37. Practice with interior/exterior color temperature effects as in Chapter 10, "Warm and Cool Color Effects."

Here are several more advanced examples (Exercises 38–41) suggested by a reviewer whom I thank.

38. Choose an interior location that gets no natural light, or build a set in a studio. Light this location for early morning, afternoon, and night. Pay careful attention to lighting angle, shadows, and color. Then light the same scene for a very unrealistic, highly stylized look.

39. Choose a large interior location. Block out areas of actor movement as in Chapter 12, and light for these various areas.

40. Shoot a night interior with all lighting provided by natural sources (e.g., a fireplace, table lamp, or television). Hold these intensity levels to around 5–10 footcandles, and push the film to obtain sufficient exposure.

41. Supplement the sources in exercise 40 with artificial light to raise the exposure level by two stops. Maintain the natural quality, direction, and color of the luminous sources.

Lighting for Electronic Cinematography

All the preceding lighting exercises may, of course, be conducted on video as well as on film.

42. White-balance the camera to various colors, and note the different, subtle color effects possible (see Chapter 14, "Color Temperature Effects").

43. Conduct the luminous object experiments described in Figures 7.7, 10.4, 10.5, and accompanying text.

44. Take your video camera and actors outdoors, and shoot in bright-sunshine. Videotape the same location during late afternoon and magic hour. Compare the differences in color.

Practice Lighting Analyses and Diagrams

In Part V, we analyzed in detail a number of lighting setups. There are a number of other examples in the book that would prove valuable to analyze.

45. *Day interior/exterior window effects*. Analyze and diagram the window lighting effects in Figures 10.2 and 10.3. Compare your analyses with the one for Figure 2.21a in Part V. Then reshoot one of these examples on film or video.

46. *Luminous object simulation*. Analyze and diagram the luminous object effects in Figure 10.5a (candlelight) and in Figure10.5b and c (light bulbs). Reshoot these examples both by using the actual light source to illuminate the actor(s) and by simulating the effects of the practical with an out-of-frame light unit.

47. *Day and night effects*. Analyze and diagram the day and night effects in Figure 10.6. Identify the differences between day and night as pertains to the lighting. Take a single location and plan the lighting for rendering it as a day interior and for a night interior.

48. *Night interiors*. Analyze and diagram the lighting setups in Figure 10.7. Compare and contrast these with the daylight interior setups in Figure 10.3 and the night interiors in Figures 2.20d, 10.5a, and 10.6.

49. *Night Exteriors*. Analyze and diagram the lighting setups in Figure 11.7. Identify the ways these exteriors are the same as the night interiors in Figure 10.7. Identify the ways they are different.

GLOSSARY

Angle of light-incidence *Refers to the direction the lighting comes from in a particular setup as referenced to the camera/subject axis. Also called* **light source directionality.**

Available light *Light naturally present at the location. May be ambient daylight or artificial light; for example, the daylight coming into a room from a window, or the neon signs and street lights on a big city street at night.*

Back light *In most general terms, light from the rear of the subject is called back light or back lighting. Back light supplements key and fill lights and models, accentuates, and separates actors and objects from backgrounds. Back light may be further differentiated, depending on the angle it comes from and its effect on the subject (see Figures 2.15 and 2.16).*

We use three terms to describe the different types of back light: "back light," "rim light," and "kicker light." "Back light" is light coming from directly behind the subject, usually from above. It is used to highlight hair and separate the subject from the background. See **rim light** *and* **kicker light**.

Background light *Illuminates backgrounds relative to key light intensities. Sometimes called* **set light**.

Background plane *The important part of the shot behind the subject. Lighting is controlled by dividing the shot into different planes. The most common are the* **subject plane**, *the background plane, and the* **foreground plane**. *Levels for the background are set by putting the incident meter in the lighting on the background, pointing it at the camera and comparing that reading to the one for the subject.*

Black value gamma/black gamma *The gamma for the black values in the video signal as compared to the gray and white gammas. Black gamma is controlled by adjusting pedestal or black level. Adjusting black level gamma upward is equivalent to flashing film; that is, the IRE value for blacks is raised, effectively reducing the original subject contrast. Besides high-end cameras such as Panacam and Betacam SP camcorders, industrial-quality cameras, like the Sony DXC-327, allow for pedestal/black value adjustment electronically.*

Bogus shadow *An area where light has not reached; therefore, not truly a shadow (caused by an object obstructing light), but a dark area in the subject where there is no light. Photographically equivalent to a shadow area, the bogus shadow is really a matter of tonal gradation.*

Brightness range *Older term for the range of luminances in the subject, the overall luminance range. We use the term* **subject luminance range** *in its stead.*

Cast shadow *The standard shadow type that an object or person forms by shutting out light from an area of the shot.*

Characteristic curve *A graph depicting the reaction of an emulsion to light. The cinematographer places the subject luminance range onto the emulsion's characteristic curve when exposing. This recreates the luminances as a corresponding range of density values, first in the negative and subsequently in the print (see Appendix C, Figure C.1).*

Cheating *Means a slight repositioning of actors, props, and lights for better effect. For example, we might turn an actor so as to obtain a more pleasing facial shadow, or we might move an object slightly for a closeup. Cheating implies the change is not noticeable to the viewer.*

Compromise exposure *Exposing between two readings so as to retain values from both ends of a long subject luminance range. A typical example would be a person sitting in a window. We take a* *reading for the outdoors (T 16) and for the actor (T 2) and expose about halfway in between, say, T 5.6. Instead of compromise exposures, wherever possible we light the subject so as to reduce the subject luminance range to a manageable amount.*

Cucaloris ("cookie") *The name for a flat, patterned object placed between a wall and the set light so as to create a shadow on the wall.*

Diffuse reflectance *or* **reflection factor** *Most objects reflect a percentage of the light falling onto them. This property of the object is termed its diffuse reflectance.*

Exposure *The placing of the subject's luminance range onto the characteristic curve of the negative in a controlled manner. In more technical terms, exposure is the scientific way to relate* **subject luminance range (log E values)** *to negative density values and, ultimately, print values.*

Exposure index (EI) *Measures the relative speed by which an emulsion reacts to light. For example, a film with an EI of 200 is twice as fast as one with an EI of 100. By setting the ASA/ISO scale on the light meter, we calibrate the meter to that particular film stock's "speed."*

Eyelight *The light used to create a reflection and give a sense of aliveness to the eyes (see Figure 2.25). The eyelight does not have to illuminate the subject in the exposure sense, just reflect off the eyes. Eyelights are generally of low intensity. Any open-filament bulb will suffice. The eyes are often illuminated by key and fill lights so that a separate eyelight is unnecessary.*

Facetone placement *Refers to where the faces are placed on the characteristic curve in the zone system. A normal placement—called a zone 5 exposure placement—renders black facetones at zone 4, brown facetones at zone 5, and Caucasian facetones at zone 6. Some cinematographers place facetones a zone higher or lower for effect.*

Facial ratio *A synonym for* **subject lighting ratio (lighting ratio)**. *Used where the subject in question is an actor or actors and the representation of the face is of prime importance.*

Feel *Refers to the emotional, subjective nuances of a shot—the rhythms, textures, colors, and tonal values that cause a viewer to say that the shot has the feel of emptiness, boredom, nostalgia, and the like. Feel goes to the depth of the image, its meaning level.*

Fill light *The light used to control the degree of blackness in shadow areas particularly of faces (see Figures 1.7 and 8.1–8.6). The key light determines shadow placement. The fill light is used to lighten (fill in) those shadows while avoiding the formation of new shadows. Fill lights are almost always soft, even when keys are hard. This is because the slow fall-off of soft light provides a more natural fill, almost invisible in its effects.*

Flashing *Involves subjecting the emulsion to a low-intensity light in order to lower its contrast. Flashing may occur before normal exposure (preflashing) or after normal exposure (postflashing). There is no on-screen difference. An alternative to lab flashing is the use of a lense-mounted device such as a VariCon.*

Flying spot scanner *A device, such as the Rank Cintel or the Bosch, which provides high-quality transfers of film negatives to videotape. Flying spot scanners transfer the film image line by line to videotape and are superior to film chains. Flying spot scanners are used to release feature films on video and to post music videos shot on film negative.*

Footcandle *Unit of measurement for incident light used by incident meters. Technically the light arriving on a 1-foot square surface as lit by a standard candle at a distance of 1 foot.*

Footlambert *Unit of measurement for reflected light used by spot meters and averaging-type, reflected meters. Technically, the light reflected by an ideal surface (100% diffuse reflectance) lit by 1 footcandle. Reflected and incident light are related as follows: footlamberts = footcandles x reflectance (%).*

Foreground plane *The important part of the shot that lies in front of the subject and is lit separately from the subject (see the discussion under* **background plane**). *The foreground plane is balanced to the subject by taking an incident reading and then comparing that reading to the one for the subject.*

Gamma *The slope of the straight line on an emulsion's characteristic curve. Mathematically, gamma = difference in density (X_D) divided by difference in log E (X_E). Theoretically, a gamma of 1.0 means the film stock faithfully reproduces the subject's luminance range, or at least the important part of it, by providing a corresponding density range such that increments of X_D and increments of X_E are equal.*

Gamma compression circuit *Device for electronically creating a "shoulder" for a video camera. Effectively extends the log E reproduction range of* the video camera by 1 zone to $5^1/_2$ zones. The circuit compresses two upper zones into one. This flattening of values approximates a film stock's shoulder and gives some of that "film look" to the video signal (see Figure 13.2). Currently, only high-end cameras have this feature.

Gray card Refers to the 18%, midgray card used for calibrating light meters so that they yield **zone 5 exposure** readings—that is, the meter places 18% subject reflectances at the mid-density point on the characteristic curve for that emulsion.

Gray gamma Gamma setting for gray values in a video camera. Adjusting the gray gamma does not affect black and white extremes but does affect how lower and upper zones are represented. Raising gray gamma from the standard .45 compresses black values slightly and provides more room for highlight values. Lowering gray gamma has the opposite effect. (See Figure 13.6.)

Hair light Back and rim light directed at the hair so as to emphasize it. Used often in shampoo commercials and glamour cinematography. There are several types of hair lights (see Figure 2.26).

Hard light Descriptive term for direct, high-contrast light from small, intense light sources such as the sun. Hard light is inherently high in contrast and thus gives us very black, sharply defined shadows. Hard light is highly directional and focused as with a spotlight. Direct sunlight, arc lights, and ellipsoidal and Fresneled spots are good hard light sources (see Figure 1.1 and Appendix A, "Lighting and Grip Gear").

High definition television (HDTV) Emerging video technology with greater definition than current systems which attempts to provide a higher-quality video image, one more able to compete with film images. The system will utilize a widescreen aspect ratio on its television sets.

High-key Descriptive term for a lighting setup that conveys an overall light, bright, cheery mood. The term is used very subjectively (loosely) to stand for an image with mostly gray and white values that does not have a lot of moody shadow areas.

Highlight method Exposure method that concentrates on the placement of highlight values. Essentially the same as the **incident method**.

Incident light The light that illuminates objects. It may come directly from a light source: the sun, the sky, or a light bulb, or it may be reflected onto an object from other objects. For example, the moon reflects light to the earth; a white wall reflects light around a room. Incident light meters measure the intensity of incident light in units called **footcandles**.

Incident (highlight or **keytone) method** The exposure method that arrives at an exposure reading by measuring the light incident upon the subject with an incident meter. The incident meter is designed to reproduce zone 5, midgray, 18% reflectances at the **mid-density point** on the characteristic curve. The incident method ensures constant densities for certain "keytones" (zones 3–7) independent of their context. For this reason, the incident method is also referred to as the **keytone method** since we concentrate on placing certain keytones—faces and 18% midgrays—on the characteristic curve and ignore other subject luminance values, though we take these into account in our lighting. After facetones, we worry about highlight values in film work. The theory of the incident exposure method attempts to ensure safe placements for highlight values, if need be, at the expense of shadow values.

IRE units The scaling on waveform monitors is in IRE (Institute of Radio Engineers) units and, except for 7.5 IRE, is incremented in units of 10. The zero part of the scale is used to adjust the monitor when setting up. This is explained in Appendix I, "Setting Up a Video Monitor and a Waveform Monitor." Standardized video signals run from black values of 7.5 IRE to white values at 100 IRE units (see Figure 13.4). Luminance values falling lower or higher than those two figures are clipped from the video signal when broadcast.

Key light or **key** The key light is the main subject light that sets the tone for the rest of the lighting and establishes how the subject will be represented. As its name implies, the key light, or key, is the most important light source affecting the shot. It establishes the spatial logic and motivation of the lighting and determines the placement of facial shadows and shapes and thus overall image mood. A number of lights may be used to simulate the effects of one key light source.

Keytone method The exposure method that emphasizes certain "key" tones for exposure purposes. In cinematography, facetones are of primary importance. The middle zones contain most facetones and are thus pegged or placed on the characteristic curve so as to ensure their optimum reproduction and differentiation. The keytone method thus pegs zones 4, 5, and 6 onto the middle of the characteristic curve. In theory, the keytone method is identical to the **incident method,** which emphasizes a zone 5 placement as discussed above. To summarize: Through exposure we place (peg) the *keytone (zone 5) at a predetermined point on the characteristic curve (mid-density point); the remaining zones then fall into place automatically.*

Keytones *The most important zones (keytones) for cinematography. The middle zones (4, 5, and 6) and the highlight zones (7 and 8) are of central importance because they represent most facetones and highlight values.*

Kicker *or* **kick light** *Used in this book to stand for a particular type of rim light, light from a three-quarter rear position used in conjunction with a three-quarter front key (see Figure 2.18). The term is also commonly used in the United States to stand for* **rim light***, the latter being the more common term in England.*

Kicker is also used to mean a light that selectively highlights a certain portion of the shot, say, a bottle of perfume in a commercial. This type of kicker would not necessarily come from the back positions.

Latitude *The traditional term for the length of the straight line of the characteristic curve as projected onto the log E axis and measured in log E units. Latitude is the same as* **log E range of the straight line** *and is discussed more thoroughly there. Latitude is an unfortunate term since it implies there is room for error in exposure, which there isn't except with very low contrast subjects. Latitude has little to do with "permissible error," but rather with the range of log E values translated into density values by the straight line portion of the curve. We shall avoid the term and use "length of the straight line" and "log E range of the straight line" in its place.*

Length of the Straight Line *The length of the straight line of the characteristic curve as projected onto the log E axis and measured in log E units. Same as* **log E range of the straight line** *discussed more thoroughly under that heading.*

Light source directionality *Refers to the direction the lighting in a particular setup comes from as referenced to the camera/subject axis. This is usually determined by the placement of the key light. Light source directionality is also called the* **angle of light-incidence***. Light source directionality has an important influence on the amount of shadow area in the frame.*

Lighting *Technically, lighting is the creation or control of* **subject luminance range***. Exposure is the relating of that subject luminance range to the emulsion. Aesthetically, lighting is the use of light on the subject so as to create the desired image mood and meaning. These are simple definitions, but it takes the entire book to flesh out their ramifications.*

Lighting contrast ratio *is a collective term for the various lighting ratios used in film: subject lighting ratio, subject/background ratio, and subject luminance range. Contrast, the relation between highest value and darkest, is integral to all three ratios. Lighting ratio is often used to stand for what we call subject lighting ratio. This is explained in the text.*

Log E value *The logarithmic value of exposure (E) and the scaling used on the horizontal, exposure axis of the characteristic curve. Both zones and T-stops relate simply to the log E axis of the characteristic curve where an increment of .3, the log of 2, is equivalent to a doubling of the exposure given, a doubling of the subject luminance value. Moving from zone 6 to 7 represents an increase of .3 on the log E scale. Table 4.1 makes this clear.*

Log E range of the straight line (latitude) *By projecting the straight line portion of the characteristic curve onto the log E axis we can calculate the amount of luminance range in log E values that the emulsion can handle accurately. This we will refer to as the log E range of the straight line. A typical negative might have a log E range of 2.4, that is, eight increments of .3 log E where each increment amounts to a doubling of the previous value. We use log E range to plan our lighting since the log E range represents the amount of subject luminance range the emulsion can translate into screen densities.*

Look *Refers to the image's surface properties, its particular style. From the look of Almendros's work in* Days of Heaven *to the look of contemporary music videos and commercials, the look of an image—which is instantaneously accessible and confrontable—is fundamental for lighting style.*

Low-key *The opposite of* **high-key***. Low-key effects involve shadows and a lot of dark tones with their accompanying mysterious, morose, dark moods. Like high-key, low-key is a subjective term identifying a lighting setup that emphasizes middle and dark tones with only small areas of bright light.*

Luminance *Refers to the actual quantitative measurement a particular subject reflectance gives off under a given amount of illumination as measured in footlamberts. For example, a subject reflectance of 90% will give off 90 footlamberts of light if illuminated by 100 footcandles. Ultimately, the subject to be photographed constitutes a series of luminance values that we must reproduce on the emulsion.*

Luminous object *An object with a photographic luminance value independent of incident light. These are mainly light sources such as fires, light bulbs, neons, fluorescents, candles, and "glowing* *objects" such as television sets, backlit photographic slides, stained-glass windows, computer terminals, sunsets, sun in fog, and so on. Large areas of brightness within a shot may also be treated as if they were luminous objects. This category includes large windows, stained-glass windows, shower stalls, mirrors, and water reflections. The presence of a luminous object has important consequences for exposure as discussed in the text.*

Magic hour *One of nature's gifts to the cinematographer is the lighting available at magic hour, that time of day around twilight or dawn when colors seem iridescent and the world of objects magical. Cinematographers have long exploited this lighting condition, from the opening title sequence of the television series* L.A. Law *to the exteriors in* Days of Heaven, *an Academy Award winner for cinematography. Magic hour is also routinely used to represent night exteriors, the sky being dark enough for a night effect but with sufficient light intensity for filming.*

There are two separate definitions for magic hour. The narrow definition is the time frame from just after sunset until the sky loses its luminosity, a period of about 20–30 minutes varying with the latitude and time of year. The effect is at its peak when car headlights and the lights in office buildings and houses become as bright as the sky. As in the L.A. Law *title sequence, it's common to use glass skyscrapers and large city skylines to enhance the effect (see Color Plates 9 and 10). This definition of magic hour is referenced to the more typical twilight magic hour. Cinematographers using a dawn magic hour would have to define the effect from the opposite direction because at dawn the sky becomes gradually lighter rather than darker.*

In the looser, more expansive definition of magic hour, the time frame starts during the warm sunlight of late afternoon, about an hour before sunset, and runs until dark. This definition provides a longer time frame for shooting but a greater range of lighting changes to deal with. This longer magic hour was used in Days of Heaven *to great effect and is discussed in the* American Cinematographer, *May 1979 issue.*

Mid-density point *If we project the toe and shoulder of the characteristic curve horizontally to the density axis, we obtain two density points for that emulsion. The mid-density point is halfway in between. The incident meter is designed to reproduce zone 5, midgray, 18% reflectances at the mid-density point on the characteristic curve.*

Midgray *The average for all naturally found diffuse reflectances was calculated to be an 18% reflectance by Hurter and Driffield. This is called midgray and is the basis for a zone 5 exposure.*

Motivated lighting *Means that the illumination appears to come from a particular light source such as a window, table lamp, or ceiling light. This light source is either in-shot or has been previously identified as present. In some cases, the cinematographer invents a plausible imaginary source based on our shared experience of lighting. Lighting that is not motivated may come from anywhere and tends to be more symbolic as compared to the realism of motivated lighting.*

Natural light *The lighting philosophy that believes we should light shots as they would be found in nature and everyday life. The natural light approach was in vogue during the 1960s and 1970s and was made possible by the introduction of high-speed lenses and faster film emulsions. Philosophically, the natural light approach was a reaction against the glossy, overly fine-tuned studio lighting of the 1940s and 1950s.*

Normal exposure *A zone 5 exposure is the normal exposure in film and results in a faithful reproduction of key middle zones by placing the zone 5 subject luminance at the mid-density point on the characteristic curve. The rest of the zones then progress outward from that key point. Zones that fall onto the toe or shoulder are, of course, distorted.*

Overall gamma *A camera original is but one link in a complete system involving print stock, internegative, processing method, and so on. Overall gamma is the term for linking these disparate elements together. Overall gamma equals the product of the gammas of the individual components in the imaging system.*

Overall luminance range *The same as* **subject luminance range**—*the ratio of highest significant luminance to the lowest. The overall luminance range of the subject commonly extends to 500:1 or more (see Figure 3.4).*

Overall useful range *The combination of straight line plus toe and shoulder as projected onto the log E axis. The longer the straight line and overall useful range, the larger the subject luminance range that can be translated and the more subtle the visual rendition possible (see Figure 5.3).*

Overexposure *A placing of the subject luminance range too high on the characteristic curve. The result is an untrue subject reproduction with the highlights becoming compressed and the lower tones being lightened to gray. The overall feeling of such a picture is washed-out (see Figures 7.2c and 7.9).*

Overlighting *The tendency to use too much light, particularly fill and rim on actors and overly high intensities on backgrounds, which causes low subject/background ratios. Overlighting destroys the moods inherent in an actual location and inhibits the creation of mood in a studio situation.*

Partial lighting *This is a lighting technique popular in the 1940s and 1950s in noir, melodrama, and other dramatic films. The cinematographer shades light from the body to emphasize the face or shades light from the forehead so that it will not draw attention away from the eyes (see Figure 9.4).*

Pedestal/black value gamma *The gamma for the black values in the video signal. Black gamma should be distinguished from gray gamma and white gamma. Black gamma is controlled by adjusting pedestal or black level. Adjusting black level gamma upward is equivalent to flashing film; that is, the IRE value for blacks is raised, effectively reducing the original subject contrast. Besides high-end cameras such as Panacam and Betacam SP camcorders, industrial-quality cameras, like the Sony DXC-327, allow for pedestal/black value gamma adjustment electronically.*

Placing (pegging) facetones *Refers to the* **incident method** *for exposure and its emphasis on placement of the middle zones. The normal facetone placement in film results from a* **zone 5 exposure**, *which renders black facetones at zone 4, brown facetones at zone 5, and Caucasian facetones at zone 6.*

Practicals *Refers to in-shot light sources such as a table lamp, a candle, or a light bulb. Practicals are used to establish motivation for the lighting setup and as props but generally are not used to light actors.*

Prelighting *A common technique in feature films. It refers to a gaffing crew's lighting an upcoming location or set while filming is going on at a previously lit location.*

Printing contrast *The best prints are obtainable when the negative gamma is around .6–.7. An emulsion with a gamma in this range is said to have printing contrast since that emulsion is designed for printing rather than projecting. These stocks are low contrast since their density increments X_D are less than their plotted X_E values.*

Projection contrast *The most acceptable on-screen images come from prints with gammas in the range of 1.6 to 1.8. This is known as projection contrast. This gamma range is reduced by projector flare, screen reflectance, and ambient light to near the ideal 1.4 by the time it's on the screen.*

Proportional density differences *On the negative, the straight line assigns a density difference to a given log E increment. These need not be equal but do have to be proportional for the film to provide a replica of reality on the screen.*

Pulling T-stop *Involves moving the T-stop ring while filming. It is similar to a focus pull but much harder to hide.*

Push and pull development *Push development extends the development time relative to the specified standard, and pull development decreases development time. These techniques are used to change overall image look or to compensate for exposure conditions. Push and pull development is one kind of emulsion test used to determine "look" possibilities. Other techniques include such manipulations as overexposing and underprinting or underexposing and overprinting, both with standard development.*

Reference black *A black subject value inserted into light-toned, low-contrast film images to prevent their being automatically darkened when broadcast over television.*

Reference white *A white subject tone inserted into dark-toned, low-contrast film shots destined for television. Without a reference white the television system will boost the brightest subject luminance to a white level and alter the mood of the film image.*

Reflectance (reflection factor) *The same as* **diffuse reflectance** *Most objects reflect only a percentage of the light falling onto them. This property of the object is termed its diffuse reflectance or reflection factor. We say a white object has a reflectance of 90%, a black object a reflectance of 4%, and so forth.*

Reflected light *Light is reflected to the eye from objects. Reflected light is the light we see and the light we use to expose film with. The light reflected by an object is measured by a reflected light meter in units called* **footlamberts**.

Reflected method *The exposure method that uses the light reflected from the subject to determine an exposure setting. This is in contrast to the* **incident method**. *The reflected light meter, like the incident meter, is designed to reproduce an 18% reflectance at a mid-density point on the characteristic curve. The difference is, the reflected meter assumes that what it is measuring is always a zone 5 value even when it isn't. This means the user has to make an adjustment to the indicated reading to arrive at a "correct" exposure.*

Rembrandt effect *A standard film lighting technique derived from some of Rembrandt's paintings. A three-quarter front key is used to create the familiar triangle-shaped patch of light on the shadow side of the face. Fill and a kicker are added to arrive at the standard three-point lighting effect, which also utilizes a chiaroscuro, light and shadow, patterning (see Figure 2.18).*

Rim light *Angled light from the rear that rims or outlines all or part of the subject. Rims are used to create on hair and edges of cheeks the highlights to which we have become accustomed. Rims supplement key and fill lights and, like back light, model, accentuate, and separate actors and objects from backgrounds.*

Some authors use the term kicker for this light. Still others call it a back light, but we shall use the term rim, which emphasizes the effect and allows for more than one of these lights in a particular setup (see Figures 2.15 and 2.16).

Roughing in *The establishment of a tentative, initial lighting setup that will be perfected when the actor positions are finalized and the camera position determined.*

Roving fill *Used with tracking and dollying shots. The light is mounted on the camera or dolly or carried by a grip. The idea is that wherever the camera goes, the fill will follow. Referred to as a basher or Obie when mounted on the camera and used as a general fill for any shot.*

Semisilhouette *A person about two stops underexposed usually foregrounded against a light-toned background. Similar to a silhouette except the actor is not completely black.*

Set light *A light used to illuminate parts of the set, usually a background. Same as a* **background light**.

Shadow projection device *A special spotlight designed to project a variety of shadow patterns onto walls, for example, venetian blind shadows familiar in the noir style.*

Shoulder *The part of the characteristic curve where the straight line ends and where subsequent exposure yields a nonproportional response that distorts luminance values.*

Side key *A key light that comes from the side of the camera/subject axis. A camera-level side key on a frontal face is a classic lighting setup. The lighting divides the face in half with a vertical shadow (see Figure 2.6).*

Silhouette *Lighting a white background five or more stops brighter than the subject and exposing for the background results in the familiar black outline against a white background.*

Soft light *Light is soft when its shadows have indistinct edges and result from a gradual fall-off of light. Soft light is lower in contrast than hard light and consequently has lighter, more gray shadows. Soft light is less directional than hard light and is often called omnidirectional, or "directionless." Large light sources that are heavily diffused, bounced, reflected, or filtered yield light which is soft in quality. Examples are: the painter's north light—reflected sky light such as in a Vermeer interior—the shadows under a tree, a gray overcast sky, floodlights, and bounced lights (see Figure 1.1).*

Specialized lights *General term for lights having specialized functions such as eyelights and hair lights. Generally used to fine-tune the lighting setup.*

Straight line *The part of the characteristic curve where log E differences are given proportional differences on the density axis. Luminances placed on (pegged to) the straight line will be accurately represented on the screen.*

Subject/background ratio *Subject/background ratio refers to the difference in lighting intensity expressed as a ratio between the subject plane and other planes, principally the background plane.*

Subject lighting ratio (lighting ratio) *The ratio between the light and shadow sides of a subject created by the key and fill light. Two technical definitions are used: (1) key + fill/fill, (2) key/fill. The subject lighting ratio impacts on the overall mood of the image. Subject lighting ratio will sometimes be referred to as the* **facial ratio** *where the subject in question is an actor or actors and the representation of the face is important.*

Subject luminance range *The range of luminances in the subject, from the highest significant luminance to the lowest. This is also called overall luminance range, or sometimes, brightness range (see Figure 3.4).*

Subject plane *Since we light in planes, the main subject area, the subject plane, is usually the most important plane for lighting purposes since actors are generally the most important part of the shot. Other key planes are the* **background plane** *and the* **foreground plane**.

Three-point lighting *The triple combination of three-quarter front key, fill, and kicker (three-quarter rim) applied to an actor forms a lighting triangle called three-point lighting (see Figure 2.18). The term is also used to refer to any combination of key, fill, and back light.*

Three-quarter front key *The favored position for the key in classic Hollywood-style lighting. It comes from above at a 45-degree angle and creates the familiar triangle-shaped patch of light on the shadow side of the face (see Figure 2.5).*

Three-quarter rear key *The back side version of the three-quarter front key. The three-quarter rear key is a very dramatic, moody key often used for night exteriors. It works best using a hard light source with a film noir or melodrama lighting scheme (see Figure 2.8).*

Toe *The lower part of the characteristic curve where dark values fall. Like the shoulder, the toe distorts subject luminance relationships but is nevertheless useful in translating those luminances into on-screen differentiations.*

Underexposure *Represents a placement of the subject too low on the characteristic curve with an accompanying lack of separation in the dark tones and a loss of the white end of the scale. The overall impression of underexposure is dark, dreary, and murky (see Figure 7.10a).*

VariCon *Lense-mounted device for flashing when shooting. The effect reduces contrast by lightening black subject values and may be monitored through the viewfinder.*

Waveform monitor *The waveform monitor is an electronic means for measuring the video signal. In essence, it provides an accurate series of spot meter readings for the entire video signal. Where there is a highlight value, the waveform monitor gives a high reading, vice versa for a low value (see Figure 13.3). The scaling on waveform monitors is in* **IRE** *(Institute of Radio Engineers)* **units** *and, except for 7.5 IRE, is incremented in units of 10.*

White value gamma *The gamma in the video signal applied to highlight values. Controlled by adjusting white level or through gamma compression. White value or highlight gamma is adjusted automatically by circuits built into the camera, for example, the gamma compression circuits in a Panacam, but where those circuits start to take effect is adjustable (see Figure 13.2). Utilizing the gain circuitry to boost exposure index also affects white value gamma by giving it a higher value. This causes other image deteriorations, however.*

Zone 5 exposure *The incident meter is designed to reproduce zone 5, midgray, 18% reflectances at the mid-density point on the characteristic curve. This is called a zone 5 exposure. Exposing for (pegging) zone 5 places the other two middle zones, 4 and 6, highlight zones 7 and 8, and lower values 2 and 3, at their respective density points (see Figure 6.1). A zone 5 exposure renders black facetones at zone 4, brown facetones at zone 5, and Caucasian facetones at zone 6. Also see* **mid-density point**, **midgray**, **reflectance**, *and* **zone system**.

Zone range of the straight line *The number of zones the straight line of the negative can accommodate. To calculate this, divide the log E range of the straight line by .3. For example, if a color negative has a straight line of 1.5 log E, it has a five-zone range (1.5 divided by .3 = 5). If a color negative has an overall range of 2.4 log E, this is equivalent to an eight-zone overall range.*

Zone system *The 11 steps or zones of the gray scale form the basis for the zone system as devised by photographer Ansel Adams. The gray scale, which can be applied to both subject luminances and density values on the negative, is ultimately viewed as screen values. Figure 4.1 describes the typical contents of each zone. Since each zone of the gray scale represents a .3 log E, it is simple to correlate zones to the characteristic curve. The 11 zones are represented on the negative as indicated in Figures 5.1 to 5.4.*

SELECTED BIBLIOGRAPHY

Adams, Ansel. *The Negative*. Boston: Little, Brown, 1981.

Almendros, Nestor. *A Man with a Camera*. New York: Farrar Straus Giroux, 1986.

Alton, John. *Painting with Light*. New York: Macmillan, 1949.

American Society of Cinematographers. *American Cinematographer* Magazine. Hollywood: ASC Holding Corp. Current.

Arnheim, Rudolf. *Art and Visual Perception: A Psychology of the Creative Eye*. Berkeley: University of California Press, 1974.

Campbell, Russell, ed. *Photographic Theory for the Motion Picture Cameraman*. New York: A. S. Barnes, 1981.

———. *Practical Motion Picture Photography*. New York: A. S. Barnes, 1979.

Carlson, Verne, and Carlson, Sylvia. *Professional Lighting Cameraman's Handbook*. 2nd ed. London and Boston: Focal Press, 1992.

Clarke, Charles G. *Professional Cinematography*. 2nd ed. Hollywood: American Society of Cinematographers, 1968.

Courter, Philip R. *The Filmmaker's Craft: 16mm Cinematography*. New York: Van Nostrand Reinhold, 1982.

Davis, Phil. *Photography*. 6th ed. Dubuque, Iowa: Wm. C. Brown, 1990.

Dunn, J. F., and Wakefield, G. L. *Exposure Manual*. 3rd ed. Kings Langley, England: Fountain Press, 1974.

Eisenstein, Sergei. *Film Form: Essays in Film Theory*. New York: Harcourt Brace Jovanovich, 1969.

———. *The Film Sense*. Rev. ed. New York: Harcourt Brace Jovanovich, 1969.

Gillette, J. Michael. *Designing with Light: An Introduction to Stage Lighting*. 2nd ed. Mountain View, Calif.: Mayfield, 1989.

Happé, L. Bernard. *Your Film and the Lab*. 2nd ed. London and Boston: Focal Press, 1983.

Malkiewicz, Kris. *Cinematography*. 2nd ed. New York: Prentice-Hall, 1989.

Malkiewicz, Kris, assisted by Gryboski, Barbara J. *Film Lighting: Talks with Hollywood's Cinematographers and Gaffers*. New York: Prentice-Hall, 1986.

Mathias, Harry, and Patterson, Richard. *Electronic Cinematography: Achieving Photographic Control over the Video Image*. Belmont, Calif.: Wadsworth, 1985.

McDonough, Tom. *Light Years*. New York: Grove Press, 1987.

Millerson, Gerald. *The Technique of Lighting for Television and Film*. 3rd ed. London and Boston: Focal Press, 1991.

Nurnberg, Walter. *Lighting for Photography: Means and Methods*. 16th ed. Philadelphia: Chilton Book Company, 1968.

———. *Lighting for Portraiture: Technique and Application*. 7th ed. Philadelphia: Chilton Book Company, 1969.

Palmer, Richard H. *The Lighting Art: The Aesthetics of Stage Lighting Design*. Englewood Cliffs, N.J.: Prentice-Hall,1985.

Ritsko, Alan J. *Lighting for Location Motion Pictures*. New York: Van Nostrand Reinhold, 1979.

Salt, Barry. *Film Style and Technology: History and Analysis*. London: Starword, 1983.

Samuelson, David W. *Motion Picture Camera & Lighting Equipment*. London and Boston: Focal Press, 1986.

———. *Motion Picture Camera Techniques*. London and Boston: Focal Press, 1984.

Schaefer, Dennis, and Salvato, Larry. *Masters of Light: Conversations with Contemporary Cinematographers*. Berkeley: University of California Press, 1984.

Spottiswoode, Raymond, ed. *Focal Encyclopedia of Film & Television Techniques*. London and Boston: Focal Press, 1969.

Uva, Michael, and Uva, Sabrina. *The Grip Book or How to Become a Motion Picture Film Technician* (i.e., *Grip*). Valencia, Calif.: Independent Cinema Technology and Videos, 1988.

von Sternberg, Josef. *Fun in a Chinese Laundry: An Autobiography*. New York: Macmillan, 1973.

Wheeler, Leslie. *Principles of Cinematography.* London: Fountain Press, 1965.

Young, Freddie and Petzold, Paul. *The Work of the Motion Picture Cameraman*. New York: Hastings House, 1972.

Zettl, Herbert. *Sight/Sound/Motion: Applied Media Aesthetics*. 2nd ed. Belmont, Calif.: Wadsworth, 1990.

INDEX